# THE GRAND SURPRISE

# THE
# GRAND
# SURPRISE

## The Journals of
# LEO LERMAN

Edited by Stephen Pascal

Alfred A. Knopf • New York • 2007

THIS IS A BORZOI BOOK PUBLISHED BY ALFRED A. KNOPF

Copyright © 2007 by Stephen Pascal

All quotation from the letters, journals, Vogue articles, and other papers of Leo Lerman is made with the permission of his estate, for whose cooperation the author is most grateful.

Grateful acknowledgment is made to the following for permission to reprint previously published and unpublished material:
The Truman Capote Literary Trust: Excerpts from letters from Truman Capote to Leo Lerman (February 1948, January 1951, and July 1952) and excerpt from "Call It New York" by Truman Capote (Vogue, February 1, 1948). Reprinted by permission of The Truman Capote Literary Trust, administered by Alan U. Schwartz, Trustee.
Tavia Ito: Excerpt from a letter from Maya Deren to Leo Lerman (September 7, 1956). Reprinted by permission of Tavia Ito.
La MaMa E.T.C.: Excerpt by Leo Lerman from a 1967 La MaMa E.T.C. program. Reprinted by permission of La MaMa E.T.C.
Parapsychology Foundation: Excerpt from Leo Lerman's review of Wars I Have Seen by Gertrude Stein (Tomorrow Magazine, Creative Age Press, May 1945). Reprinted by permission of Parapsychology Foundation.
Playbill Incorporated: Excerpts from "The Playbill Diarist" columns by Leo Lerman, September 1957 and January 1958. Reprinted by permission of Playbill Incorporated, Arthur T. Birsh, Chairman.
The Glenway Wescott Estate: Excerpt from a letter from Glenway Wescott to Bernard Perlin, January 21, 1948. Reprinted by permission of Anatole Pohorilenko, literary executor to the Glenway Wescott Estate.

Library of Congress Cataloging-in-Publication Data
Lerman, Leo, 1914–1994.
The grand surprise : the journals of Leo Lerman / by Leo Lerman ; edited by Stephen Pascal.—1st ed.
p. cm.
Includes index.
ISBN-13: 978-1-4000-4439-9 (alk. paper)
ISBN-10: 1-4000-4439-1 (alk. paper)
1. Lerman, Leo, 1914–1994—Diaries. 2. Lerman, Leo, 1914–1994—Correspondence. 3. Periodical editors—United States—Diaries. 4. Periodical editors—United States—Correspondence. I. Pascal, Stephen. II. Title.
PN4874.L376A3 2007
070.5′1—dc22
[B]    2006048735

Manufactured in the United States of America

FIRST EDITION

*To Gray Foy*
*For letting Leo tell his story*

am reminded that for a long time, in my childhood, in my adolescence, I
made up histories about myself, my family, my "friends." I still believe some
of these stories and even find myself telling them, and those who hear them
also believe them, for the fantastic world of the "smart" magazines and social
columns of the rotogravures of my childhood—what is left of them—are now as
open to me as those ruins that one finds everywhere in Rome. Like those ruins,
some of it has disappeared—forever; some of it has been used to erect other
structures or for ornament; some of it is lived in.

—JOURNAL • FEBRUARY 8, 1953

# CONTENTS

# ACKNOWLEDGMENTS

Transforming the materials left by Leo Lerman into this volume required the encouragement, guidance, and contributions of many—archivists and editors, freelancers and friends. I cannot list all of them here, but my gratitude to each is nonetheless genuine.

First among the work's supporters stand S. I. Newhouse, Jr., and Victoria Newhouse, whose enthusiasm helped launch this project and whose aid and cooperation never ceased. Also crucial to accomplishing the task was Columbia University's Rare Book and Manuscript Library, to which Leo bequeathed his papers. Jean Ashton and Bernard Crystal there showed remarkable adaptability by leaving this archive in my custody until the job could be finished.

Leo's files held a great deal, but many of his letters, photographs, articles, and unfinished projects required searching. In these quests, I relied on the guidance—and often the toil—of archivists. Exemplary were those at the Beinecke Rare Book and Manuscript Library, both the Condé Nast Archive and Library, the Deutsche Kinemathek–Marlene Dietrich Collection Berlin, the Fairchild Archive, the Getty Research Institute, the Howard Gotlieb Archival Research Center, the New York Public Library's Manuscripts and Archives Division, the New York Public Library for the Performing Arts, the University of Wyoming American Heritage Center, and, again, Columbia University. Working with each of these institutions was rewarding, whatever we finally found.

Ultimately, I drew a large share of this collection from letters written by Leo, and most of them came through the generosity of his friends or their descendants and trustees. My sincere thanks go to Forest Hunter (for Richard Hunter's letters from Leo), Kenward Elmslie (Ruth Landshoff-Yorck's), Peter Riva and Silke Ronneburg (Marlene Dietrich's), Amy Gross (hers), and Alan Schwartz and Gerald Clarke (Truman Capote's). For providing rarely seen photographs from family collections, I am indebted to Emily Harding, Alexandra Plaut Hekking, Nancy Lerman, and Jane Imbs Trimble.

Dozens of Leo's friends and family members told me stories and answered questions. Among the most generous were Robert Davison, Eugenia Halbmeier, Joel Kaye, Leo's cousin Allen Lippman, and Leo's niece Janet Lerman-Graff. My own colleagues and friends also helped continually in this effort. I went for expertise and advice repeatedly to Gini Alhadeff, Christopher Baswell, Charles Rowan Beye, Micah Bucey, Cynthia Cathcart, David Cronin, Joan

Feeney, Christopher Gates, Lucinda Karter, Lisa Moore, Deirdre McCabe Nolan, Jane Sarnoff, and Tommy Tenhet.

For Knopf's expert handling of this very complicated book, I am particularly indebted to its editor, Robert Gottlieb; his assistant, Alena Graedon; designer Iris Weinstein; production manager Tracy Cabanis; and my production editor, Kathleen Fridella.

This endeavor lasted more than a decade. Some of the most helpful people have not, alas, lived to read it. Heartfelt thanks must go posthumously to Richard Hunter, for many hours of delightful reminiscence, and to Elian Pascal, for years of encouragement and deep insight.

Thanks, of course, but also truly deep gratitude go to Gray Foy. He remembered everything and withheld nothing. In preparation of this book, Gray was ever helpful, thoughtful, and frank—as he was for so many years with Leo. Without him, much less would have been accomplished, then or now.

# INTRODUCTION

When Leo Lerman appears in other people's memoirs, it is often as the host of some all-star gathering in postwar Manhattan. His parties began in the early forties, with dinners for a few smart friends whom he had met working as a Broadway stage manager or through reviewing books for the *New York Herald Tribune*. By the autumn of 1947, these gatherings had grown into a Sunday-night open house in his book-strewn apartment on East Eighty-eighth Street. Then a writer for *Vogue, Harper's Bazaar,* and *Glamour* magazines, he was earning only enough to buy jug wine and rat cheese, but Truman Capote and Anaïs Nin were not walking up five flights for the canapés. They came, as did scores of what today we call boldface names, for the conviviality, for Leo's ribald and mischievous fun, and to meet people they wouldn't meet anywhere else.

All his life, Leo minted new friendships at a brisk pace. Stage-managing in the Catskills and on Broadway he had met Imogene Coca, John Houseman, and lyricist John Latouche; a German refugee, Eleonora von Mendelssohn, introduced him to a stellar circle that included Marlene Dietrich, Noël Coward, and Luise Rainer; through writing a *Vogue* feature called "Before Bandwagons," he befriended avant-garde architect Frederick Kiesler and literary critics Lionel and Diana Trilling; a summer of late-night games (and very little writing) in 1946 at the Yaddo artists' colony brought friendships with Truman Capote, Carson McCullers, and Katherine Anne Porter. But Leo also knew how to work a room, and friends beget friends. On any given Sunday evening at Leo's, Jane Bowles, Gore Vidal, Gypsy Rose Lee, Dawn Powell, or Carl Van Vechten might appear. . . . Suddenly, that little one-bedroom apartment—and the stairway climbing to it—became a weekly attraction.

What made Leo's parties extraordinary was not only the caliber of the guests, but also the mix of them. He brought together different sets of people on a spectrum that included art, music, theater, literature, film, society, and demisociety, as well as the shopkeeper down the street. Parties were the laboratory in which he encouraged people to take an interest in one another's work. What friends often remember most fondly about Leo is how he changed their lives by a casual introduction or an offhand suggestion.

Among New York's movers and makers of art, Leo Lerman grew legendary as a man who knew everyone and had seen everything. For fifty years, it seemed he attended every debut, opening, and vernissage in the city and had the crowd at his place to celebrate afterward. He peddled his knowledge of the late great and the up-and-coming to a dozen publications. Through decades of reporting on art and entertainment and, perhaps more important, years of counseling, introducing, and prodding talent, Leo Lerman helped steer American culture. His lasting significance, however, may lie in his role as an observer of the lives and art swirling around him.

Shortly after high school (the end of his classroom education), Leo started reading the works of Virginia Woolf and Marcel Proust. Their novels forever altered his outlook and delivered him to a life of literary ambition and frustration. As many writers have done, Leo dreamed of becoming his generation's Proust, a seismograph of the social upheavals in his lifetime. Some of his earliest journals outline his imagined novel's content and plot, and a prime motive for his keeping a notebook for decades remained documentation, as he dashed down observations and quotations to use in an eventual tribute to his time and his friends.

But by temperament Leo was more a collector than an artist. His fragmentary attempts at fiction he himself dismissed as contrived and overwritten. He felt that the work he had published, if occasionally inspired, was largely second-rate, and the unlikelihood that a fashion magazine editor could equal Proust was not lost on one who spent so much of his life enjoying such ironies. He constantly wrote to space and against a deadline, and although he worked on his journals with alacrity and insight, he never summoned the perseverance and confidence to realize the modern historical tale he envisioned.

Yet Leo seems always to have viewed life in retrospect. To him, time was a thief, not a benefactor. A central theme of his notes is recollection, or, as he calls it at one point, "allusiveness"—creating continuity by finding the connections between events. He could see an entire personality in a single encounter, with all its ganglia of private and historical connections. He loved literature, especially the long novels of nineteenth-century England and Russia (and of course Proust's *Remembrance of Things Past*), but it is anecdote, more than narrative, that caught his interest. The manners, gestures, styles, and affectations of people fascinated Leo. Ironically, it was his propensity—and gift—for summing others up in a few strokes that probably made him ill suited to be a novelist. The journal—impulsive, frank, unrevised—was an ideal medium for him.

A sensualist and an extrovert, Leo left a uniquely sharp record of his time. He shows the cultural machine of New York as it actually worked, fueled by scores of talented and clever editors, agents, and producers. As someone immersed in this history, who learned most of it anecdotally, I know that many of those connections between the bright dots of celebrity are fading from the record. They were the real fiber of New York's golden age, and Leo was one of them.

By the time I arrived, Leo was nearing the crest of his lengthy career in magazines. In June 1981, Condé Nast Publications hired me to be his assistant at

*Vogue*, where he had been the features editor since 1972. Within that magazine's glossy confines, he maintained a fiefdom where serious books and painting could be discussed alongside snappy reports of the latest television shows or new restaurants. He ran the office as a sort of salon—or perhaps as one of his open houses. During my interview with him, editors wandered in with questions, article ideas, and gossip, while he took telephone calls from agents and writers, occasionally rolling his eyes and making droll asides in my direction. The interview scarcely touched on the present. Instead, we discussed what he called "Mr. Hitler's War" and the émigrés it had brought to New York, especially his adored friend Eleonora von Mendelssohn—heiress, actress, addict, lover of Rathenau, Reinhardt, and Toscanini. She had been dead thirty years, yet he was still talking about his "Ela" as though she had just left the room. I had never heard of her before, but had spent my college junior year in Germany and did know something about the powerful men she had loved. So I sat there at *Vogue*, amid all the laughter and interruptions, talking about Berlin in the twenties, unwittingly becoming one of Leo's tenuous links to his past. Suddenly he bellowed, summoning the magazine's personnel manager, Sarah Slavin. Leo extended his arm regally and, pointing at me, said, "Give notice where you are." Then, pointing at Sarah: "Work out the details." We were dismissed.

Leo often disconcerted people at first meeting. He was at once a fashion magazine editor obviously itching to spot the next trend, a wit—sometimes saucy and often very funny—and a collector, who would wax nostalgic over societies and cities he could never have known. His imitation regality was enhanced by a genuine elderly manner. From his start (out of the Feagin School of Dramatic Art in 1933) to his finish (in 1994 as editorial adviser to all the Condé Nast magazines), everyone thought of him as a generation older than he was. During that first meeting with me, Leo said of his going to work at *Vogue* and *Harper's Bazaar* in the forties: "I was their darling. They thought that I was this sweet old thing. Little did they know how long you can stay old!"

When he had entered the field, American magazines for women were changing rapidly. More young women were attending college, looking for jobs, and working after marriage. To many of them the life and fashion displayed in the pages of *Bazaar* and *Vogue* appeared chic, modern—and unattainable. As a no-nonsense alternative, a struggling serial-novel publisher called Street & Smith founded *Mademoiselle* magazine in 1934. From its launch, it set a new trend for frank writing about career, money, education, and health. From the start, *Mademoiselle*'s editor in chief, Betsy Blackwell, with an attitude that clothes were not enough, made arts coverage part of her formula. In 1941, she hired George Davis as features editor. This onetime novelist had recently made *Bazaar* into a venue for innovative fiction, and his daring soon gave *Mademoiselle* real muscle in the artistic arena. *Mademoiselle* was, for example, the first to publish Saul Steinberg's cartoons (in 1941) and a story by Truman Capote (in 1945). Then, late in 1948, the free-spirited and tempestuous Davis suddenly quit. On the way out, he telephoned Leo Lerman, suggesting that he apply for the job. Leo rang Betsy Blackwell and casually invited her to a party, then called in the troops. She was dazzled and signed him on as a contributing editor, starting on January 1, 1949. Within months, he was effectively editor of all *Mademoiselle's* arts coverage.

Leo created a monthly section in *Mademoiselle* called "Something to Talk About," a venue for him to announce discoveries to the magazine's audience of collegiate and young working women. Writing with delight and a dash of humor but without condescension, Leo sought to make these young ladies feel like guests at one of his soirées. In those pages, he would be the first to tell them about Margot Fonteyn, Edward Albee, Leontyne Price, Harold Prince, Jim Dine, John Updike, Liza Minnelli, Betty Friedan, and on and on. He worked very hard, scribbling endless pages of research for each piece, believing that he wrote well only when immersed. Fortunately, once under way he wrote quickly, producing a surprising number of articles and often meeting several deadlines in rapid succession. In the forties he also reviewed for *The Atlantic Monthly, Tomorrow,* and *The Saturday Review of Literature;* in the fifties he was regularly contributing to *Playbill, Dance Magazine,* and the *New York Times.*

Leo could have bylines in so many publications because he remained freelance throughout his career. His *Mademoiselle* contract only guaranteed him a small expense account and a monthly check ($500 in 1949, when his rent was $125. In comparison, the *New York Times* and *The Saturday Review* were then paying $25 per review). In return, Leo would produce several columns for each issue of the magazine. Later, his arrangement with *Vogue* was virtually the same. Although he worked until after his eightieth birthday, Leo never took employee benefits. Remarkably, he always regarded journalism as interim work, a way to keep afloat until he could dedicate himself to the books he longed to write.

He had been born in May 1914 into the thick stew of Eastern-European Jewish immigrants in New York City, with both sides of his family lower-middle-class but on their way up. The Goldwassers, his mother's relatives, had already (in thirty-odd years) gained a foothold in real estate and owned the house where he was born, on 107th Street (in what today is Spanish Harlem). The Lermans operated a house-painting business out of a small paint shop under the elevated railroad on Second Avenue. Leo's two grandfathers probably first met there over paint chips. By his parents' generation, the grandparents' Orthodoxy, tempered by America into holiday observances and kosher kitchens, no longer ruled the family. Moving even further from that background, Leo rarely set foot in a synagogue after his bar mitzvah and saw himself as "more Yiddish than Jewish." He was a secular Jew who vividly recalled family circles and household rituals and who felt richly imbued with the tumultuous, pleasurable life of his early youth among aunts and uncles crowded into apartments in New York's East Harlem.

For someone of this background, coming to maturity in the early thirties, Leo handled his homosexuality with remarkable ease. He writes frankly in his journal of being a highly sexual man and shows no shame or regret over preferring the same sex. Such gay self-acceptance, decades ahead of its general circulation, was surely rooted in his family, which was extraordinarily tolerant of an idiosyncratic son. Leo believed that his mother recognized his sexual preference early and possibly foresaw an advantage for her in his never marrying. "So he's a mother's boy," she once said. "I'm his mother."

In the mid-thirties, Leo's parents, uncles, and aunts welcomed his first long-term lover, the painter Richard Hunter, into their family. In the late forties, they accepted his new lover, artist Gray Foy, just as cordially. That each of these men was not only homosexual but also gentile seems to have caused no friction in his home. Leo's family, Richard told me, were pleased that Richard and Gray looked after him. In contrast, neither Gray's nor Richard's parents ever fully warmed to Leo. Although dissimilar in many respects, their mothers found his urbanity intimidating, his Jewishness foreign (Mrs. Hunter, a Methodist minister's wife, referred to Leo as Richard's "Hebrew friend"), and his evidently intimate relationship with their sons illicit. In forty years, Gray's mother, Maebelle Hughes, never openly acknowledged that he and Leo were a couple, although she grew to accept the arrangement.

In fairness, one should say that our society's notion of how to acknowledge gay couples has changed utterly in recent years. For most of Leo's life, people proved their tolerance by behaving as if they saw nothing. In the artistic circles of New York, homosexuals were hardly a rarity, of course, but it was well into the seventies before most associates and friends (even some gay ones) would treat Gray as Leo's spouse. Notably, hosts often invited Leo assuming he would come alone, and he did not press the issue. On the other hand, at the offices of *Mademoiselle* magazine, Gray and Leo's relationship was treated, Gray recalls, "as ordinary, with absolutely no impression or smirk—ever." Betsy Blackwell, whom Leo described as "the complete Republican lady," evidently set that tone from the start, having met Gray at the party Leo threw to impress her in November 1948. Although Gray had begun sharing Leo's apartment only a couple of months before then, to Blackwell they already appeared to be domestic partners.

Leo always required a great deal of assistance in the form of emotional support and household management, and he relied first on Richard and then on Gray to provide it. Richard did all the cooking and cleanup for Leo's first parties (and it was Richard's small private income that kept the pair financially afloat). Gray cooked, cleaned, and organized. He also sold drawings at a fine-art gallery and took on illustration assignments, but his works—hyper-detailed pencil drawings of intense, hallucinatory scenes—could never fetch enough for his hours of labor. Then Leo's journalism paid the grocer. Although in the beginning it was all very exciting and seductive to Gray, the unceasing social round that Leo followed was dizzying, and holding it all together could be exhausting. Leo once proposed to *The New Yorker* that he become its columnist on parties, and he could cheerfully have attended or thrown one every night. Gray fought, sometimes sharply, to keep Leo in the comforting home he had created and to stem the cascade of visitors. Leo's journal records his pondering whether he and Gray were temperamentally suited and of what their love and years together might have cost each of them. He sometimes felt that Gray was both his lover and his child. Yet it was Gray who shouldered all the real maintenance at home, thereby allowing Leo, in some ways, to remain the child. We have him to thank for fencing in Leo's driving extroversion enough so that he had quiet hours to write in his notebook. With all that they shared— sharp senses of humor, delight in eccentricity, romance with the innocence of childhood—Leo and Gray often lived on what one friend, the actor Simon Callow, has described as "the knife-edge of passionate incompatibility." Leo's last working title for his memoir was *Call It Friendship, Call It Love.* Call it what you will, these men had a marriage.

In a world that denied their relationship's legitimacy, Leo did see the irony of its conventionality. He enjoyed such career and social success that one can forget how many places and sets must have been closed to him, a Jew and an openly gay man. Surely he suffered bigotry or exclusion, even in the cosmopolitan circles in which he ran. In the summer of 1946 at Yaddo, for example, he learned that its director, Elizabeth Ames, had been gossiping about his homosexuality. Affronted and bewildered, he wrote to Richard Hunter that "being Jewish (and so exotic, flamboyant), being quite uneducated both socially and formally in any sense, it requires so little to shake the facade I've built up." The nonchalance with which he lived was shored up by a belief that others would respect his private life, and that *he* could determine where the boundary lay. Leo never disguised the fact that he was a house painter's son, but from an early age he practiced dressing for other parts. Leo picked up, chameleon-like, the manners, accents, and tastes of cultures (past and present) to which he aspired, ignoring the fact that the prejudices or restrictions of those cultures might have excluded him. With the upheaval of World War II and the arrival in New York of its refugee artists and aristocrats, the world seemed as open as Leo had once fantasized.

Leo's world became more and more "Europeanized." His view of Europe, which had been formed first by books and theater, became increasingly shaped by his contact with refugees. As Leo later recalls, those friends were so relieved to have found safety in America, that their outlooks were more positive than we might assume today. Still, it seems odd that Leo's surviving journals, which begin in 1941, scarcely refer to the war (although Leo's brother fought in the Italian campaign) and do not mention Nazi Germany's racial policies or concentration camps until long afterward. Perhaps, as with his later health problems, Leo simply denied something so fundamentally catastrophic as long as he could.

Young and optimistic in those war years, Leo also did not then fully appreciate how much of the artistic scene mesmerizing him in Manhattan was fueled by artists in exile. The émigré society in New York vanished with the end of the war. He mourned it, but—then barely thirty-one years old—he also took up the reins and made his own life and career as closely in its image as he could. In his last years, once again Leo saw the society and culture he loved disappear, overrun by vulgarity, discarded as obsolete, or simply reaching the end of its run. His notes are filled with tales of people, real players and creators of their day, who have vanished from stage, print, and even popular memory. So it goes. One person's legend is another's footnote, a fact that Leo understood quite well: At one point he considered titling his memoir *A View from the Footnotes*.

Random House had, in fact, signed Leo to write an autobiography in 1982. After nine years, when he had not written past the first page, Leo devised a plan: He would dictate reminiscences onto tape, without using notes or outlines (his time, he said, had grown too short for research). Having then worked a decade for him, I would serve as audience and tape-machine operator. On quieter afternoons at the office, with the door closed and his phone unplugged surreptitiously by me, Leo told his tales slowly and deliberately, obviously having incubated each passage mentally over the intervening days. For revisions, his failing eyes required that the manuscript be printed in a huge font on 11 × 14 sheets of paper. In his last nine months, with his legs too weak for the arduous trip to the office, I carried the pages to his bedside and read aloud for his corrections. Leo's health had always been fragile. Through a succession of ailments (plus a lifelong dislike of exercise and delight in being helped by others) he had often worked in bed. But at this point his body really had begun to give out. Gradually our work on the book came to a halt. He left it unfinished.

As he felt the end of his life approaching, Leo extracted a promise from Gray that after death his body would be kept at home for two days. He wanted one last party, a laying-out at which friends could bid him adieu. We were scarcely surprised—it was just another of Leo's ways of clutching every extra moment of pleasure and inviting us to share in the game. On August 23, 1994, word went out by telephone, Teletype, and a memorandum to the Madison Avenue offices of Condé Nast Publications that Leo Lerman had succumbed at last, aged eighty. He would be at home, however, for those who wished to pay their respects.

Home, since 1967, had been the Osborne Apartments on Manhattan's West Fifty-seventh Street, a ponderous nineteenth-century pile of brownstone entered through a lobby garnished by Hollywood-Byzantine mosaics. A towering pair of mahogany doors opened into the apartment's grand foyer, its mauve walls hung chockablock with gouaches of erupting Vesuvius. Out of habit, I took the role of leading mourners (and a few gawkers) down two corridors and a half-flight of stairs to Leo's room. There stood Gray, as he often had, a reassuringly still focus point. He embraced each visitor and then made the moment unexpectedly easier by turning to tell Leo who had just joined him. Leo, embalmed, seemed to sleep as he had in life, propped up in a mahogany sleigh bed, wearing a Turkish needlepoint cap, guarded by a pack of dog portraits on the wall above. His fingers were laced across his chest under deep purple sheets. His beard, snow white and patriarchal, brushed his nightshirt. For many of us it was an indelible, atavistic, oddly comforting moment, and one that interwove major themes in Leo's life—*le style ancien*, theater, family, royalist fantasies, hospitality, and, of course, a cavalcade of celebrated figures.

A few weeks after Leo's remarkable farewell performance, Gray mentioned to me that, while searching for Leo's tallis, he had discovered dozens of notebooks filled with "jottings." More surprises lay in store. Notebooks squirreled away by Leo over the years kept appearing—in the downtown warehouse where he stockpiled books he could not bear to sell, in an ancient wicker trunk under the piano that he had converted to a desk, in the attic over their pantry, at the back of his study's file drawers. He had filled literally hundreds of notebooks of all sorts, finishing in the late eighties with reams of canary foolscap covered in his signature purple ink.

Although it was a year before we realized it, the notebooks proved to be a remarkably continuous account of Leo's life, stretching from the months before his first *Vogue* assignment (in 1941) to a year before his death. What the diverse books had in common was illegibility. Leo's handwriting was always difficult to read; he may deliberately have made it worse in the journals to discourage prying. The difficulty was compounded by personal abbreviations, shorthand, haste, his failing eyesight, and an occasional jouncing railroad bed. Faced with this mountain of scribbling, Gray and I decided to tackle the books together, at first simply looking for enough material to complete the memoir.

Years of having to take action at the office based on Leo's scrawled notes had prepared me, yet on every page certain words might as well have been inkblots. That we came upon these journals out of chronological sequence was in a sense a blessing, because we began with the eighties, when I had known many of the players and events that Leo was describing. Still, one small notebook could take a week to untangle. For me to get through it at all—never mind understand what Leo was talking about—would have been unimaginable without Gray at my side to decipher names, arcane terms, and, most important, to provide context. Still grieving when we began, Gray naturally found reading chronicles of times they spent together, written in his lover's hand, both comforting and upsetting. He broke down over the job more than once but always came back for another try. As we continued to collate and decipher, our purpose changed. The writing in the journals was so immediate and sharp that we set aside the manuscript that Leo had dictated to me and began envisioning a more comprehensive book.

Gradually we worked our way back to the years before Leo had met Gray. Fortunately, Richard Hunter was often in New York while we were working and had superb recall. He and I spoke often and I taped hours of our conversations about his life with Leo. Patient with my queries, revealing, and kind, Richard became my good friend, and I was deeply saddened when he suddenly died in January 2001, at the age of eighty-eight. The following April, I received a cardboard box in the mail from one of Richard's nephews, Forest Hunter. Inside, I found 458 letters written over fifty years from Leo to Richard (the original frequent flyer) in cities all over the globe. They had been uncovered in various corners of Richard's house near Augusta, Maine. A cursory turn through this box showed Leo's tone in the letters to be unguarded, affectionate, playful, and remarkably close to his private writing. They also told some marvelous stories missing from the notebooks.

Richard was an artist and would-be actor two years Leo's senior when they met as fellow students at the Feagin School of Dramatic Art in Manhattan. Their friendship, initially a shared interest in theater, galvanized into love in the spring of 1936. After nearly a dozen years together (with occasional separations), Richard left Leo for another man, Howard Rothschild. Deeply pained by their breakup, Leo vowed to stay single and to direct his energy into writing. Then Gray Foy came along. On April 30, 1948, he attended a gala party that Leo was giving for the Parisian couturier Pierre Balmain. By summer's end, Gray was living with Leo.

Gray became the love of Leo's life. Yet Leo's letters to Richard seldom drop the flirtatious, bullying, longing tone of a separated lover. Peripatetic Richard is always being urged by Leo to return, reminded that he has a place to stay with him and Gray. Richard's frequent voyaging lent a very peculiar rhythm to their friendship. He might be out of touch for months, letters to him returned as undeliverable, and then abruptly appear on their stoop to occupy one of Leo and Gray's bedrooms for weeks. If he was in New York when Gray was traveling, Richard sometimes came to stay and cook for Leo. Did they sleep together? Leo never mentions that they had, and Richard never gave me the slightest hint of it. His letters to Leo, despite often saying that he loves both Leo and Howard and signing off with their habitual baby talk, always remain at a rather courteous distance—fond, somewhat paternal, and fatalistic about their separation. It was Richard who had left, after all. Leo never really ended it, never stopped missing the old Richard—his playmate. Perhaps if Leo had real-ized his literary ambitions, conceived in those years with Richard, he might have relinquished some of this nostalgia for their earlier life together.

Now that Leo's letters had become part of the project, I asked Gray whether he had kept his as well. He promptly handed me 166 of them, written in the first twenty years of their relationship. Many of these were romantic—raptur-ous, teasing, and beseeching Gray to come home from his travels—in a sweeter and less petulant tone than Leo took with Richard.

For his other friends, Leo was an erratic correspondent—in fact, many of the letters he received either complain of his never writing or exult in finally get-ting a few lines. Nevertheless, I searched. Leo did not keep carbons of personal correspondence. Business letters written from *Mademoiselle* or *Vogue*, when copies survive, are succinct. Fortunately, there were two major finds: his letters to the writer Ruth Landshoff-Yorck (most of them still owned by her friend, the poet Kenward Elmslie) and those to Marlene Dietrich (today in the Marlene Dietrich Collection in Berlin). Dozens of letters are now interwoven in this book, often filling in where the journal had skipped.

The earliest letter from Leo to Richard that survives, the first in this collec-tion, is dated April 14–15, 1939. Leo is twenty-four and living with his parents in the Jackson Heights neighborhood of New York. He and Richard have been lovers for almost three years, both of them pursuing theatrical work. Richard has tried acting, Leo stage-managing, and together they have been designing costumes for small productions. Leo is also critiquing manuscripts for agents, reviewing books, and writing *Leonardo: Artist and Scientist*, a biography for young readers that will appear the following year. In the autumn of 1939, he will launch into an affair with the costume designer Ladislas "Laci" Czettel. Leo's journals at the time speak of this romance's pitfalls, but do not really tell how it came about. For that story, we have only what Leo wrote about it some forty years later.

Inserted into the chronological flow of journal and letter are vignettes Leo wrote long after the events. These passages appear in italics, to alert the reader that here Leo is writing with hindsight. Many come from his unfinished mem-oir; a few he published as tributes or delivered as eulogies, and others he wrote later in the journal. They are placed where it seems readers will want to know more, particularly at the beginning, as the principal players arrive.

In the progression of excerpts, I have provided dates whenever possible. The location where Leo is writing his journal, however, is noted only if it has changed since the preceding entry. While writing, Leo—his thoughts quite freely associating—often interrupted himself by inserting a reminder, jotting down an overheard line, or recalling a similar event. As I am not a paleogra-pher, and Leo's papers are not the Dead Sea Scrolls, I see no point in torturing the reader by being overscrupulous. If moving a clause or a parenthesis could make a line more sensible, I intervened. When deletions would clarify or expedite without altering Leo's meaning or tone, I cut. These minor omissions are not indicated in the text. Small errors and inconsistencies (of date, for example) have been corrected without remark. More controversially, perhaps, I have occasionally woven pieces together when Leo split a story within an entry or between two dates, although I have made such shifts only when the parts fell close together in the journal. If the related passages were more seriously separated, I might put one, usually the later, in a footnote.

Leo's spelling, very creative and leaning toward Briticism, has been corrected and standardized to American usage. With punctuation, I have taken a rather free hand. Leo had little use for the full stop, preferring the dash in his journals and the ellipsis in his letters. In the original, pages can pass without a single period; semicolons are rare; colons are often misused. But frequently these ubiquitous dashes and dots are simply indications of Leo pausing for thought. When his thoughts are hurried, anxious, or random, I felt the dashes fit and left them. Elsewhere I have substituted more standard punctuation.

Annotation of Leo's busy life has proved a challenge. Wherever facts and grammar permit, brief information is supplied in brackets. When more is necessary to identify a person or understand a circumstance, details appear in a footnote. Leo's close friends also receive lengthier descriptions there, and occasionally a note sets the record straight or offers commentary by Richard Hunter or Gray Foy. Because Leo followed virtually every line of culture in New York and often pulled them together in his features, his parties, and now in this book, the notes are written for a general reader, not for the aficionado of any particular art. The editor apologizes to anyone whose substantial achievements have shrunken here to a meager word or two.

As one who came along long after the heyday of Leo's party-throwing, I had shrugged off most accounts of them as exaggerations. Then, while sorting out Leo's ramshackle files, I uncovered scores of yellowing guest lists, stretching from the late thirties into the nineties. Six of these remarkable documents of their time (and of Leo's web of acquaintance) are reproduced here. The invitees are not annotated, although many of them have notes elsewhere, and they remain in the order that Leo wrote them.

Each element—journal, letter, and memoir—contributes to this tale, but Leo's journal really drives the story and provides many of its most arresting moments. Therefore, it seemed fitting to let "The Journals of Leo Lerman" stand as the subtitle for the whole. The excerpts that comprise this book are only a fraction, perhaps 10 percent, of the original. Needless to say, any number of books could have been cut from this material. Other editors would have found different stories and characters more worthy of inclusion, as would I, no doubt, if I were to begin again. In making these selections, I have been fortunate in receiving frequent guidance from my editor at Knopf, Robert Gottlieb. He knew most of the people Leo mentions, by reputation if not personally—an inestimable benefit in editing such a crowded work—and offered abundant suggestions after reading each revision of the manuscript. Finally, it was he who persuaded me that I ought to publish before we all perish.

A lifetime of Leo's scrawling in notebooks and hunt-and-pecked letters to chums—can it come to more than all of his hard work for magazines? Yes. The trouble was that Leo idealized writing, but did not trust his own, although he saw its potential. He repeatedly compares himself to a lepidopterist, a butterfly collector, capturing and mounting rare specimens for display. A journal entry during the fifties recalls the boy Leo chancing upon a glorious butterfly—the Camberwell Beauty. He was transfixed by desire. The moment was transformative. That singular creature became Leo's version of Proust's madeleine. He continued to pursue powerful beauty, performance, and character through a long life, yet with a premonition from the outset that such things could finally be kept and re-created only through memory and fantasy. As a boy, Leo had paged through *Vanity Fair* magazine and scrutinized rotogravure supplements in the Sunday papers, aching to somehow slip into the recherché world shown there. He succeeded, transforming himself in their image, and he did so without disavowing his family, his ethnicity, or his sexuality. To many eyes, Leo Lerman achieved the glittering life that little Leo had dreamed of. But did his vehicle—the glamorous, ephemeral business of fashion and publicity—actually take him to a different place? Did so many years of trumpeting the latest starlet and hot spot trivialize his quest? Had he succeeded in transmuting himself into the golden image he had seen in childhood, only to find that world vanished, along with the rotogravure? Had his nerve failed? At the end, Leo wondered. The same appraising instinct, the collector's eye, that he had used on others Leo could turn on himself. But did he do so too late? These ambiguities are some of the beauties to be found in these pages. In his journal, Leo is at once the child bedazzled and the aging lepidopterist ready with his pin.

*—Stephen Pascal*
*January 1, 2007*

# THE GRAND SURPRISE

MAY 28, 1956 Some weeks ago, looking at [the BBC's weekly] *The Listener* in the early morning, I suddenly, upon turning a page, saw a photograph of a butterfly—a Camberwell Beauty. Instantly, I was about ten years old, on a hot, delicious day in early summer in Jackson Heights. We had recently migrated to Jackson Heights from Grandpa's in New York. Never before had I been anywhere in a world which was not Yiddish and not entirely composed of my relatives. I had been sent to a public school, where my odd accent and my individuality had incited a teacher to rouse up the boys against me, and one recess they had kicked me into insensibility, after which Momma had removed me for a time from that school. But now summer vacation had come. I madly collected insects and butterflies (desiring them for their beauty, the glamour of them) and also living secretly as Laurie (*Little Women*) or in the French Revolution as gleaned from the movies. Most of all, I desired to enter one of the great Victorian houses, which still ranged along Broadway, a cobbled and trolley-tracked thoroughfare between immense ancient trees, the houses set back, topping lawns where iron deer stood transfixed by the jets of water which sprung from their nostrils and gaping mouths. The closest I came was Dr. Combe's office. He lived in an 1820ish house in a park. I knew the office part of this house and that portion of the park, which stretched on the other side of the drive, a green and copper world of immense trees, a world of sudden sightings and creakings and splintered sunlight. Anything could happen there—and one day did.

I heard Momma and Poppa talking about how Dr. Combes had sold his enchanted park and his house. (I did not realize that this was the first crack in what was until then a perfect Victorian world, at least in appearance.) He had operated on me for a blood-poisoned toe, performing the operation on our dining room table, while Momma fainted in her bedroom closet, pulling her dresses down upon her, sinking into the painting of a male nude (back to the beholder, but still considered too indecent to display with our treasured lithograph of Wagner, tam-o-shantered at the keyboard, while his "characters" floated in a soupy green all about him). Now Dr. Combes, I heard, was to move into one of the huge Victorian houses, and Poppa was to housepaint it. Instantly I concentrated on how to go with him on this job.

We were the first Jews in that neighborhood. I never spoke to the children and they never spoke to me. We were poor, although I lived high and rich interiorly. But still I wanted to see, to be part of, the great elegant, laughing, safe world these houses represented. I could hear the children of these houses laughing or screaming in their gardens behind their hedges of althea and hydrangea, and sometimes I could see dresses pale as luna moths fluttering in the dusk, beneath the trees on the great old lawn. Never did any of these magical creatures seem to notice me, as I walked toward the local library, which sat snug and enticingly at the far end of the avenue (now Momma and Poppa live behind it). So, when Poppa said that he was going to paint Dr. Combes's new house, I had only one desire: to go with him on the very first day of the job. And magically, on the Monday morning when Poppa was to begin, he got into the truck and suddenly called out: "Leo, wanna come along?" Leo hopped right in.

It was an immense house, completely empty save for sunlight—so thick and moted that I tried to touch it. Poppa said for me to get out of his way, but not to open any windows, and so I wandered through the house, living my Laurie life, until I came to a little golden room, high up in a turret. And there I suddenly felt a presence. On a wall, near a diamond-paned, dusty window, a squint-eyed window, was a butterfly—wings flattened against the peeling, creamy, watery paper. It was a Camberwell Beauty—the butterfly I most coveted and had never before seen, save in butterfly books in the library. It rested, all spread out—plum-brown and buttery-golden bordered, its wings cut as if by pinking shears, its head furry like some fantastic beast. So still it was. And as I came closer I saw that its wings were not plum-brown, but the purple of marvelous ancient Chinese silk (later I knew that).

I wanted that butterfly. It was the most beautiful, and a book had told me that it was extremely rare. This butterfly, the life in the great Victorian house— I stretched out my hands, stealthily, to take the prize, and suddenly I knew that I could not take it. It was too beautiful. It made me feel the way I felt sometimes in synagogue, or at tender moments with cousins and Momma, or the way I felt one milky winter day as I crossed the railroad bridge from Aunt Rose Klein's house to our house, and suddenly I was rent and bereft by the trees, stark against high, thin, pale sky. (I had seen these trees many times before, but now they were something else. They made me yearn and ache and be confused and sad and lifted, and later when I fell in love, that feeling was identical with the one I had experienced on the railroad bridge.) So now I felt this about the Camberwell Beauty and, feeling so, desired instantly to set it free. Poppa had told me not to open a window, but Poppa, childlike and kind as children are, would not want me to leave this butterfly to perish. So I tugged open the window, and the room was inundated with the peppery fragrance of climbing roses. They were great yellow blossoms, buzzing with huge black-and-gold bees. Then I tried to shoo the Camberwell Beauty to the window, but it remained obdurate, clinging tenaciously, somnolently to its wall. Suddenly, as I stood, hands outstretched, supplicating, it raised its wings languorously (as later I was to see Margot Fonteyn raise her arms numerous times), fluttered onto my right hand. I can feel the kiss, the almost imperceptible kiss of its feet, and the sweet tingle of the little stirrings it made as it raised and lowered its mysterious purple-brown wings several times. Then I flung it from the window, worrying whether it would be hurt, alarmed because my hand was all dusty, purple-brown, the powder from the Camberwell Beauty's wings.

So sitting there, thirty-five or so years later, I read about this butterfly and discovered that it has another name. Sometimes it is called the Grand Surprise.

# CALL IT FRIENDSHIP, CALL IT LOVE

**RICHARD HUNTER** *The first time I saw Richard was in October 1933 at the Feagin School of Dramatic Art, in New York, where my in-theater life had started. Miss Lucy Feagin began our day, at 8:30 in the morning, with readings from the Bible. Miss Feagin, for all her activity on the gaudy fringes of one of the world's most ancient professions, was a god-fearing Southern lady. One day while we were all gathered in the greenroom, I saw a pair of brown-suede shoes and a young man whom I had not before noticed. There was something different about him: He did not look actorish. He looked removed, apart—there was no tempest in him. We became friends.*

*He wanted to be an actor; I did not. He was interested in designing for the theater, so was I. So he became part of a little group that sat up all night talking about the plays they wanted to do, or the plays they loved, and the actors they loved. We reveled in every aspect of being from, and almost of, The Theater. We fenced, we tap-danced, we painted our faces, we put on beards, we disguised ourselves according to play. We led strenuous theatrical lives. And, of course, I achieved one of the main goals of my becoming a scholarship boy at the Feagin School of Dramatic Art: I spent many, many nights in Manhattan and yet remained for a long time the respected, seemingly respectable son of an intensely organized Orthodox Jewish household.*

*Since the Feagin School, Richard and I have been devoted friends: First, my friend to whom I told all my love woes. Then, with a kiss (and a robin's song) in Central Park on Shakespeare's birthday, April 23, 1936, he became my permanent love woe. That lasted until 1948, with 1939 to 1941 the time of Laci. (1993)*

APRIL 14–15, 1939 • JACKSON HEIGHTS, NEW YORK
**TO RICHARD HUNTER**

I was listening to the Delius *In a Summer Garden* for the first time, which seemed lovely . . . a bit Debussy. I say "seemed" 'cause my bitchy relatives decided they couldn't shout at one another against so exquisite a background. They loudly said for quite some time, "I don't see what you hear in this noise! What do you get out of it! My Eddie listens to the [radio show] *Make-Believe*

*Ballroom* and does he shake! What do you hear in it?"[1] Since I didn't take the hints, they acted on their own behalf and done it in. I sat on the front steps and grouched a time.

It is now past midnight, and I am extremely sleepy, but they show no signs of departure. In fact, Momma is about to serve a midnight meal, after which they will go back to the carouseling [*sic*], and she will wistfully murmur, "I wish somebody"—with a bleeding look in my direction—"would do these dishes! I'm so sick . . . My head . . ." Howsoever, I will seal this missive, drop it into the mailbox, take me my pillow, and plant me on Jerry's bed. Fortunately, that monster is out dancing.[2] Good night. I'm starting a new set of verses—about being afraid of the dark. . . .

**LACI CZETTEL** *In the late autumn of 1939, while I was hanging a costume-design exhibit in the basement of the New School for Social Research, I saw a short, stocky, elegant—almost too elegantly dressed—man come swiftly into the room, moving with the pert steps of a boulevardier in a French play. Coming to me, he handed me a portfolio of sketches. His large, brown, amused eyes—slightly the eyes of a dog wanting to be loved—peered at me as through a veil, seeking some sort of information, flashing signals. Suddenly, he clutched me, drew my head down, kissed me deeply. Then, drawing away, "Come to dinner. . . ." I was already in love with the dress he had designed for Wendy Hiller in [the movie]* Pygmalion *(the white dress she wore to the ball). I was now enthralled. Some days later, as Laci looked down at me, he murmured, "How will this end?" his words coming, I realized years afterward, out of an immense sadness. I did not care. I no longer was able to care about anything except being with the strange, plump, exigent, manipulative, sex-ridden little man, being with him in the world he already represented and in which he was more and more involving me. So began my re-Europeanization (and that world's Americanization?) and my finding a new family.* (1993)[3]

JOURNAL • MAY 28, 1941 One should never pick himself up and go away in the night, after he has lain beside his beloved, his body all arranged until morning. It leaves an empty space. It is impossible to fill this space. It is how I so clearly see my life, and how it will always be, basically: no ability to pick myself up and

---

1. Eddie Goldwasser was one of Leo's scores of cousins. Samuel Lerman (1886?–1958), Leo's father, was one of eight siblings to survive childhood; his mother, Ida Goldwasser Lerman (1898–1980), had five brothers.
2. Jerome Bernard Lerman (1921–2002), Leo's brother, was seven years younger and his only sibling. After returning from army service in World War II, he would become a plastics entrepreneur who often worked with toy manufacturers.
3. Hungarian-born costume designer Ladislas "Laci" Czettel (1894?–1949) worked in Europe until 1938, then in New York at the Metropolitan Opera and on Broadway (in *Rosalinda*). In the mid-forties, Leo helped him begin designing women's clothes for New York department stores.

go away in the middle of the night. Laci is a magnificent example of how one can be a child, an infant, all one's life, and make a talent of it and survive.

I wish I could be a mother with these two men [Richard and Laci] for sons. I could then love them and they could always come and I would never have to choose. Laci is sick. One does not hate one's child for cancer. How can I cease loving him because of his sickness?

JUNE 12, 1941 • NEW YORK CITY
**TO RICHARD HUNTER** • MIDDLETOWN, NEW YORK

Ilse [Bois] and Eleonora [von Mendelssohn]'s performance [in *La Voix Humaine*] turned out the most conspicuously and brilliantly distinguished audience in the year, with Countess Yorck drooping about in her fur-lined bedroom slippers, and everyone unmentionable standing in [coves].⁴ The best were Hélène Fischer (an Amazon like unto the Empire State Building sans its erection) embracing Spivy [LeVoe, nightclub singer] and both shouting "Daaaaarling" and Noël [Coward]'s momma, Violet, looking like an old English duchess and scratching her rear, and Princess Paley in a hat that hid, completely, the front of her face but left her back hair naked, and [milliner "Mr. John" of] John-Frederics surrounded by gilded youths in golden chairs and really everyone who ever was, or tried, and a few will-be anyones. [John] Latouche reminding me that he met me six years ago, when I was about to be the white-haired boy of Broadway, but then I didn't have any hair at all.⁵ On the stage, Miss Scarlet Mendelssohn—unusual, frequently superb, and absolutely magnificent in the last two minutes—very uneven—no direction. Ilse bad in her act, but marvelously heartbreaking in the badly written scene which surrounded it. The audience yelled and screamed and it was a *succès fou*, a *succès d'estime*, and a *succès* good-evening-friends.⁶

**ELEONORA VON MENDELSSOHN**   La Voix Humaine . . . *I seem to have had endless years with remarkable women who waited for men by whom they were ensorcelled to call. There was Marlene Dietrich who waited for Jean Gabin to call. There was Penelope Dudley Ward who waited for Carol Reed to call. There was Maria Callas who waited for Aristotle Onassis to call. There was*

4. Ilse Bois (d. 1961) had been a comic actress in German silent films. Ruth Landshoff-Yorck (1904–66) was a novelist and playwright, a quintessential Berliner of the Weimar Republic. A 1930 marriage to Count David Yorck von Wartenburg (1905–85) had afforded her, a Jew, some protection from the Nazis, but eventually she immigrated to Paris, and then in March 1937 to New York. Leo and she disliked each other at first meeting, but they grew very close, and she became Leo's most trusted critic.
5. John Latouche (1914–56) was a lyricist (*Cabin in the Sky*), librettist, and poet (*Ballad for Americans*).
6. In *La Voix Humaine*, a one-act play by Cocteau, actress Eleonora "Ela" von Mendelssohn (1900–1951) played a woman pleading on the telephone with her disenchanted lover. "She played *La Voix Humaine* in her own bed linens, on furniture with which she had grown up. The telephone was an erotic instrument for Ela." *Journal, February 2, 1971.*

Alice Astor who waited, at the end of a tumultuous life, for John Latouche to call. Before all of these, there was Eleonora von Mendelssohn who waited and waited and waited for Arturo Toscanini to call.

Eleonora . . . Almost half a century I have been haunted by Eleonora. Death does not still, nor does it diminish, love. I exist every day of my life in her climate. Her life (which she gave bountifully, without seeking payment at any point for it—except love) was spent like the waters of a great river. In my life, she was such a river, and I have yet to see the end of what came to me on its floods.

Eleonora had flung open the door—apparitional, all glittering brown and gold, twined and twisted taffeta, lace low around her white, white shoulders, her hair tossed about any old way, tendrils floating freely and charmingly, her sea-green, shortsighted eyes tight with withheld tears. The door was in a room where Laci and I were sitting, in his apartment in an East Sixty-seventh Street mansion. "Liebling!" She advanced with a sort of duck-footed gliding step (she seemed to swim as she moved, more a water creature than a landlocked being) directly to Laci, peering at him closely, "Liebling!" Her voice had a sound of deep bells in it and, at this moment, they were speaking full peal.

"Liebling! What should I do? He's gone! He disappeared! Even his trunks are gone! They were in storage. . . . The storage is empty!" "You think," asked Laci, "that he went back?" "That is what is frightening me. If he goes back, what will they do to him?" "Nothing. They want him. He is one of the most famous of German stars. They need him. He will probably live in his little house outside of Salzburg, and they wouldn't dare to touch him. He will probably play in Vienna and in Berlin and he will make movies. . . ." "But they know that he escaped with me. They tried to get me. They wanted to kill me!" "But I am sure that they do not want to kill him. They want him to make movies for them."

She, who had heard of me but never seen me, suddenly in one swift swooping motion bent over and kissed me on each cheek. I was lost forever. "Do you want me to look for him somewhere?" I asked her. "Oh . . ." (This "oh" was more moan than expletive.) "Oh . . . I want you to very much. . . . He lived in Yorkville in an old, awful house. I have the address here. . . ." She opened a little bag made out of some intricate Fortuny fabric. "But, liebling, you do not even know what we are talking about. . . ." "Yes," I said, "I know a little bit. . . . You are talking about Rudolf Forster, your husband. I have seen him in the movie of the Threepenny Opera. I saw him when Max Reinhardt brought him here with the company. He is a great actor. . . ." I was not talking in the overemphatic, extra-loud voice one uses when talking to the hard-of-hearing or foreigners: I was talking in the comforting, reliable voice one uses to soothe, to assure a frightened old friend.[7]

7. The events Leo recalls probably occurred early in 1940, when Rudolf Forster (1884–1968) returned to make films in the Third Reich. Max Reinhardt (1873–1943) was the preeminent German theater director and producer between the wars, with whom many of Mendelssohn's friends had worked, including two of her husbands, Forster and the German-born actor Martin Kosleck (1907–94).

"But," murmured Laci, "such a child and so Austrian. He could not exist anywhere else but in Austria."

So, I—in many ways a craven beast—found myself in a very dark house in the upper East Eighties in New York's Nazi Yorkville. I stood in the shadowy, cabbage-smelling lower hallway, and on the landings above me so many frowzy-haired, scarf-headed, smoke-mired women leaned over banisters, all shouting in German, "Go away! We know nothing! We don't know what you're talking about! No Mr. Forster was ever here! Go away." Was this The Blue Angel or M? There is something exhilarating in being frightened. I went down the brownstone steps, and ran back to the house on East Sixty-seventh Street and told them that Rudolf Forster, I thought, had been in that house and was no longer there. Late the following morning I heard, "Forster got on a boat and he is on his way to Austria now." I did not know, then, that I was to have at least twelve sometimes terrifying, sometimes exhilarating years entwined with Eleonora von Mendelssohn's life.

I am jolting north, in the early-wartime forties, in a ramshackle cab driven by a Mr. Miller, whose head under a floppy black cap (I never saw him without that cap) was mostly two enormous jutting ears, his laggard speech a rich seedcake full of jokes and malapropisms. He waited day and night to serve Eleonora, no matter how penniless she was. He waited, he served. She was also his excitement. We were, stealthily, at one or two or three or four in the morning, on our way to sit under a tree in Maestro [Toscanini]'s garden in Riverdale.

Eleonora existed in a grand tradition of women madly in love. Such women breathe folly. They are protected. How else to explain Eleonora, who, having somehow secured a latchkey to Toscanini's house, would leave me sitting under a tree in his garden while she crept soundlessly into the dormant house, crept to his bedroom door, there to crouch listening to his coughing in the night, his breathing, his very being. Having accomplished this madness, she would return to me, under my tree, fall down beside me in what I could only call an orgasmic state, crying, "Liebling! Liebling! You should hear him! He is like a great storm! He is an element! You should hear him!" And, truth to tell, I did hear him, even there, out in the garden. I could hear him coughing, sometimes calling out, sometimes even moving about, sometimes—oh, ecstasy for Eleonora—coming to a window and peering out.

How to explain this woman? How to explain any legend, for she was essentially legend. Born into the fabled Mendelssohn family, descended from musicians, bankers, scholars, hostesses, madmen, collectors of prodigious works of art and of exquisite furniture. Generations mingled their blood with Italians, Basques, Russians, and fellow Jews (some of them converted) of many classes. Eleonora somehow became for us (and this "us" included some of the most distinguished minds and creators of this century's first six or seven decades) a symbol of European culture and civilization then fast being trampled. She assumed heroic stature, for we knew she could, in her frail, star-driven person, endanger herself out of loyalty, she having ventured, with her name high on

Nazi lists of those wanted, in and out of Germany, helping friends and ex-lovers in peril.

Duke or dustman's daughters, none of that much mattered to Eleonora. What mattered to her was genius. She was a pushover for genius and, of course, for charm. She was Duse's goddaughter.[8] She married four times, not even once for love. She married Edwin Fischer because he was such a glorious pianist; she married [cavalry officer] Emmerich von Jeszenszky because he bullied her into it; she married Rudolf Forster because he was such a great actor and charmer; she married her last husband, actor Martin Kosleck, because there was no one else around to sit up all night talking to her. She was a night person. She slept in dribs and drabs. Ela had a way of laughing uncontrollably, peal on peal welled up from somewhere deep inside. She screamed with laughter, until she cried hilariously. And sometimes, like Niobe, she was all tears. Her life was crescendos: The diminuendos—sometimes they were not pretty.

After she had been forced to flee Europe, Ela lived in one small rented room in a house where the back of the Whitney Museum now stands. The "great" crowded into this small room—mostly bed, photographs of Maestro, and cooking on a couple of gas rings. I remember a night after some event when there were Toscaninis in her little room, Barrymores sitting on the floor in the hallway, Morgans sitting on the stair, Astors at the front door, dancers of all kinds out in the street waiting to get in. They came like bees to suck up the sweetness of this frail flower of the finest European culture, clinging so optimistically, so irrefutably to the remains of her shattered world.

Later she lived in a larger room over a woodworking shop on East Seventy-third Street. This time she was somewhat affluent, for she had sold a Van Gogh and some other paintings that she managed to get out of Germany (by wrapping them around a broom handle and claiming them to be her own works). This time, she had a drawing room with piano, a bedroom, and even a rooftop with a screened-in dining room on it. In the house next to Eleonora's, to the east, in the basement, lived her brother Francesco—addicted to "drink," addicted to his Stradivarius cello, addicted to the glories of the theater—his basement rooms a welter of fine books in tatters, stage designs by Eugene Berman, letters from [music hall singer] Yvette Guilbert, a Picasso "Blue Boy" . . . much of this scattered about the floors.[9]

When the opportunity came her way, Ela was a hardworking actress. She was not a very good actress, but she acted. I think her best acting was always offstage. Onstage, on-screen she had extraordinary atmosphere, especially when she was

8. The Italian tragedienne Eleonora Duse (1858–1924) had been a lover of the banker Robert von Mendelssohn. He and his wife, the pianist Giulietta Gordigiani, named their daughter for the actress.

9. Eleonora's younger brother Francesco "Cesco" von Mendelssohn (1901–72), a cellist, actor, and theater director, suffered mental illness and according to Leo was eventually lobotomized.

*playing some poor victim, for in her life, although she never knew it, she was sometimes a victim. She acted because she hoped that would enhance her in the eyes of the men she loved. When, for some fifteen or so years, she was in love with Max Reinhardt, she acted for him. In all the years she was in love with Toscanini, she always hoped to show him that she was Duse's true godchild. The Maestro came to see her perform* La Voix Humaine *(in a translation by our friend John Latouche). I wonder whether he recognized that the heartrending words Cocteau gave to this poor character were in no wise different from words sometimes murmured by our Eleonora into the telephone from her own bed when talking to him, in the long, dark nights when she was alone—or almost alone.*[10] (1993)

**LACI'S OTHER MAN** *Resting my left leg on the right knee, removing my sock . . . and a sudden, stomach-wrenching sure knowledge that there was someone else. A bit of broken tie chain, which Laci's porter had thought mine and so given me, belonged to this unknown. I felt that my life was ebbing away, that I was bleeding inside. I could not sit. I could not stand. I went out into the street, a deluge of tears dammed behind my eyes, and I went to Elsa Snapper's rooms to seek some solace, some comfort—only to find that she already knew the supplanter, had even had him, Laci, and the supplanter's friends in these rooms that now sheltered me.*[11] *Suddenly, I was insane—that is, I knew the deepest meaning of that hackneyed "insane with grief." I saw in our past a whole series of betrayals—not only his of me, but, curiously, mine of him. That I had "betrayed" him did not now compensate. He needed me—but only for business, for his comfort. He needed the other person for all of the reasons—the sensual reasons—he had once needed me. Laci threatened me: "If I drop you, everyone will drop you. Eleonora will drop you. Lili [Darvas] will drop you."*[12] *But they didn't. They saw him as a "little" man, and by that time I was their American friend, never ceasing to amaze them with how I was "just like a European boy." I had charm for them. They found me useful, and they were ready, these women, to help me restore myself after this accident of love.* (1981)

NOTE: Leo had continued to live with his parents throughout drama school and several homosexual affairs. Richard had moved through a succession of rooming houses, leaving town whenever he felt too guilty about his relationship with Leo, his first male lover. During one of those voyages, when Richard went to Miami, Leo had fallen for Laci Czettel. When that affair ended, eighteen months later, Richard was living, lonely, in Greenwich Village. Their friend Elsa Snapper convinced Leo that he'd be

10. Toscanini had met Eleonora von Mendelssohn in 1935. In letters at the time, he complained about her persistence, portraying her as a constant, uninvited houseguest, but by the forties her devotion had prevailed in making him a lover.
11. The Dutch Jewish émigrée Elsa Snapper Czebotar was a painter and close friend to Leo in the forties.
12. Hungarian-born actress Lili Darvas (1902–74) was a star of Reinhardt's theater and was married to Ferenc Molnár, who wrote several plays for her.

happier going back to Richard, and he did, but it was some months before they lived together.

Leo had been reading manuscripts for the literary agent Elizabeth Otis and reviewing books for the *New York Herald Tribune*. In 1940, Bobbs-Merrill published his *Leonardo: Artist and Scientist*, a biography for young readers. Thanks to that income, Leo could afford by the summer of 1941 to move into the rooming house where Snapper lived on Manhattan's East Seventy-first Street. At the age of twenty-seven he finally left home.

JOURNAL · JUNE 14, 1941  One day returning from the doctor, Laci told me that he had said that any excitement in the next week would be fatal. He then forced me to do this thing, knowing that I could not resist when he said he could go elsewhere. This made me a murderer, which is what he wanted and needed. He constantly induced me to give him overdoses of sleeping medicine. He seemed to live in a constant state of terror, but only at night after his medication did he talk. He was frightened of death, for he expected to meet his mother. He loved and hated her. She had been married to a Spaniard. He had died on the honeymoon. The first year she had only their son, Laci. In the next two, she was in with Mr. Czettel. Thereafter she married him, and took Laci from all those things he loved—the pictures of his father, the medallions, his grandfather, everything—thereby murdering him. Sometimes at night, she took this three-year-old child through the house, sword stick in hand, and made him defend her by plunging the sword into the draperies and dark places. He became her councilor, but saw her rarely. He, however, listened when she was in bed. He knows he must kill himself with a razor or knife. He has once tried to kill someone, but never himself. He waits at night for his mother and death to come through the door.[13]

JUNE 16, 1941  When one is waiting, all sound is an enemy. The creaking of a door, a fancied step upon the lower stair, the delicate shuddering of the window glass, the moaning of the buses upon the avenue beneath the windows— everything is portentous. All the senses sit bound and tense, waiting. Yesterday I woke in the early morning and thought, even before my eyes were opened, when I was conscious of light and waking: This evening Richard will come. My heart and my stomach twisted within me, and I clutched the pillows to my breast, hung my face among them, burying myself in the very thought of Richard—the way his jacket smoothes upon his shoulders, and his trousers, through which I can always, thousands of miles away, feel his skin, but more than these—the smell of him. All day I ran toward evening, performing the mechanics of laughing and thinking and philosophizing and admiring, but all day I ran toward evening, and in the evening he did not come.

13. "I discover, this evening, that Laci was a morphinist. I never knew. Was that then the link with Ela? Were they all dope pals?" *Journal, January 6, 1969.*

JUNE 28, 1941 Toscanini saying: "If I weren't what I am I'd be a lust-killer."

AUGUST 10, 1941 • NEW YORK CITY
**TO RICHARD HUNTER** • PORT SEVERN, CANADA

You had better sit down now, because you will doubtless be upset. I am sitting with Elsa, who is growling over a bowl of cornflakes. I worked very hard all day. Somewhere about 7:30, I heard a noise and I turned. There was John, the man who runs the house—dead drunk. I asked him what he wanted, and he muttered about disliking my face and how he was going to choke me. I got up—I thought it would be more pleasant to be choked standing. Then, for two hours, he sort of menaced, and once we tussled, and he broke the lock on my door and tore my Chinese thing. I couldn't get out from the corner. It was an ordeal. He said he had a knife and he would throw me through the window. And so it went. Finally, about ten o'clock, when I thought I would faint, I heard Arnold [Hoskwith, theatrical agent] whistling. I managed to throw him the key to the front door, and he got me out of the house to his place. A fine policeman came and took me home to get my manuscript and some things.

I will want to move because I wouldn't sleep there again. Now, I wonder: Do you think we can manage Jo Washburn's place? Jo said she would give us some furniture including beds—but I could live and work there this month.[14] Please don't be too distressed and don't be pressed into this thing because of me. I feel like someone who's forcing a boy to marry because she's going to have a baby. If you feel all this impractical, you must say. Leave us not railroad ourselves into something we will regret.

NOTE: The troublemaker was sent away, and Leo returned to his room on Seventy-first Street.

The manuscript he mentions was his second biography for young adults, *Michelangelo: A Renaissance Profile*, which Knopf would publish in 1942. Leo earned $300 for writing it, and Richard did the illustrations for nothing.

AUGUST 12, 1941 • NEW YORK CITY
**TO RICHARD HUNTER** • PORT SEVERN, CANADA

I had to go to the army [draft-board physical]. I went. It seems there is nothing wrong with me according to the sloppy doctors, who looked up my rear and couldn't even find those pesky piles that gave me so much pain! Unfortunately my own doctor was one of them. I will go on Monday to ask for a deferment— so to try to put them off until next May. I had to stand, along with some fifty others—stark naked—from eight o'clock through 11:30, in the rear part of a store, which had not been cleansed in days. The Wassermann [test for syphilis] was painless. I got so interested in watching the others getting theirs—some

14. Josepha Washburn, a friend from Leo's stage-managing days, had married and was living in Connecticut.

boys passed out!!! They did not test my reflexes. I had a horrid doctor who said I looked pregnant while he gleefully patted my belly. I was not bashful about being naked—most of the boys seemed to have as small or smaller!!! If they send me away in some months (they said surely not before a month), I will be over thirty when I return, and all this striving will have been in vain—but leave us be happy now and not consider it. Oh—if I could tell you what trembles in my heart and flies to my lips so deftly—but these things are for you to hear—and letters are so goodly, but unsafe things.[15]

JOURNAL • AUGUST 20, 1941 It is by some casual and exuberant confession: "I have three rings. I put them all on in the morning and lie in bed and smoke cigarettes." Or by a gesture—slight—almost imperceptible. Or by the break and pitch of a voice. By such trivial tokens do revelations come. Many times it is merely sensed—the easy meandering along the avenue; a sudden, veiled inquiry from someone walking in the opposite direction; the somewhat veiled looks cast backward over shoulders while the attitude is one of disinterest but the body is too elaborately casual; the frequent pausing to look into shop windows, wherein repose objects utterly unrelated and unseen; the gradual reversal; one proceeds to retrace his steps while the other appears nonchalant, waiting or strolling leisurely onward—thus at times losing the reward of all his careful actions—but more frequently the words "Have you a match?" or "Do you have the time?" as though this had been the sole motive for a delicate chase of some ten or twelve streets.

Recently I have had no money at all, barely managing to scrape together the few pennies needed to go home to dinner. Only because of blithe faith I found an anonymous nickel in an old suit yesterday. My library books are now overdue—and no way to return them, for I cannot pay the fines. Hunger does not seem to bother me—only toward evening when I know that soon I will have oh so much to eat [at Momma's] I frequently feel that my stomach has been shrunk so much it will hold nothing. Soon after, when running eagerly down Madison Avenue or on the subway, my head aches—but oh the bliss of many rolls with butter. This seems to be my hunger—rolls with extremities of butter. A dinner composed of vegetables and meat and soup is nothing without rolls and butter—bread, not potatoes—but bread to stuff into one—and butter, fresh and salt, to savor. I love to eat. I love to read about food. I love to look into shop windows at food. If I were hungry this moment I could not write about hunger so energetically, but today I shall not be hungry—and tomorrow holds an excitement all its own, and this is why I will never commit suicide, for I am constantly curious about what is around the corner.

---

15. Eventually, Leo told the inspectors that he was homosexual. "I was turned down on Governors Island by the army ('Not pathological, but psychological')." *Journal, February 18, 1986.* Richard Hunter's asthma had disqualified him from service.

NOTE: On November 1, 1941, Leo and Richard moved into a one-bedroom, third-floor walk-up apartment at 64 East End Avenue (near Manhattan's Eighty-second Street). "Forty-five dollars a month, bedbugs and all," as Richard recalled.

**LUCIEN AND *VOGUE*** *Lucien Vogel was in love with Ruth Yorck, and she was in love with him. Lucien was the creator of the Parisian magazines* Vu *and* L'Illustration des Modes, *and he was the brother-in-law of Michel de Brunhoff, who was the editor of French* Vogue. *Lucien's wife, Cosette (called "The Duchess"), was formidable as both a woman and a cook. I preferred her as the latter.[16] My friend Ruth was strictly Berlin—the latter part of the Weimar Republic—intellectual, a woman of many arts, and avant-garde all the way. In the autumn of 1941, Lucien led me to Condé Nast. "You know," he said, "so much about women, Italian women in the Renaissance. Why not write about these women for* Vogue? *I will take you to [its editor] Mrs. Chase. She will be interested."*

*I went with Lucien because I wanted to see what Elsie Mendl had done with the Condé Nast Publications reception room, which I had heard she had decorated. Stepping out of the elevator, I was enchanted immediately with the inlay of gold (brass, actually) stars that paved the floor. When Lucien planted me in the empty reception room, I saw that, in true Elsie Mendl style, it was all "Fine French Furniture" or reasonable facsimiles thereof. I also saw that it looked out onto an ample terrace, fantastically verdant for New York on a mean November day.*

*As I sat there, I heard from stage right—for this was all theater to me—a woman's voice, high, carefully modulated, uttering one word, "Divine . . ." It trailed off. Then she came into view. She was tall, Chaneled, hatted, white-gloved, and she moved with a curious kind of hippy glide. Then I heard another female voice—postmenopausal, attractively sexy, sandpaper had worked it to a permanently growling invitation. This voice said, "Debauchery!" I instantly knew that a life of "divine debauchery" should be mine.*

*Lucien returned. I murmured, "Divine debauchery . . ." He looked faintly alarmed-amused. Then I found myself in a good-sized room unlike any office I had ever seen. At a table sat a sweet-faced woman, somewhat designed by Beatrix Potter. Her glove-encased hands were folded neatly before her on the table, and, from beneath a toquelike hat, large, kind eyes peered—demurely?—at me. There was an unoccupied chair in the room, to which I was motioned, and then I realized that all about the room there was a Winterhalter frieze of women—very fashionable women in hats, in gloves, in furs. Real ladies. All of them, including Edna Chase, were looking at my ankles. I looked at my ankles and saw that, as was my habit, one ankle was in a red sock and one ankle was in a green sock. I looked at*

16. Lucien Vogel (1886–1954) and Cosette de Brunhoff (d. 1964) had managed the French publications of Condé Nast, including *Vogue*, through the twenties and thirties. She was also sister to Jean de Brunhoff, creator of Babar.

Mrs. Chase, and Mrs. Chase looked at me. Mrs. Chase made a small, dry chuck-ling sound and said, "Stop . . . Go . . ." I said, "Right you are, Mrs. Chase." The ladies all laughed politely and faded away. I was alone with Mrs. Chase.

Mrs. Chase then said something into a telephone and soon in came an exotic-looking man and an even more exotic-looking woman. These were the art direc-tor, Dr. [Mehemed Fehmy] Agha, and his assistant, Cipe Pineles. She was the kind who smoked reflectively through a very long cigarette holder. She was tur-baned and done up in an excess of fine woolen fabric. (Many years later, she was the kind who dressed in artful hand-painted peasant clothes and was an Earth Mother.)[17] They looked me over, and Dr. Agha said something complimentary about my book reviews he had read in the New York Times and the Herald Tri-bune. Cipe said nothing, and they went away. Then Mrs. Chase sent for a small, rather plump, round-eyed, smiling woman who was ungloved and unhatted—very bouncy, very perky. Mrs. Chase said, "Allene, this is Leo Lerman. Lucien brought him in. He's yours." Mrs. Chase looked at me and I knew that she meant for me to get up. Allene said, "Come with me." So, fortified by Mrs. Chase's smiles, I went with Allene.

Allene Talmey's office was small and dark, tucked away. It consisted of a large desk, a heavy typewriter, a sturdy visitor's chair, her swivel chair, and books. She was the Features Department of Vogue. She seemed to me, at that time, a much older woman—meaning much older than I was: She wasn't much older, just some. She said, "What do you know?"

For the next forty years, I spoke to her almost every day and saw her sometimes almost every day and loved her all of the time to the day she died. I learned from Allene Talmey, and later from Carmel Snow, editor of Harper's Bazaar, more about magazine craft than from anybody else in the world. From [Vogue's edito-rial director] Alexander Liberman, later, I learned to take risks, to go all the way out on a limb until it almost broke under the weight of my certainty, and I learned to outwit.

I had arrived, I soon discovered, in a world of surface glamour supported by hard, almost unceasing, endeavor. I heard that [its publisher] Mr. Condé Nast had said that he believed in a Vogue that housed some—let us say arbitrarily—fourteen intensely singular people, each of whom held the key to something very special, and these fourteen would bring to Vogue the very being of that very spe-cial something, bring it all to perhaps seven intensely industrious, brilliant people who sat at their typewriters and pounded out the sometimes recherché fantasies and the increasing realities that Vogue sold. So many of these "fantasies" sump-tuously cloaked the hard facts of life—and merchandising. I found that I had been led by Lucien into a royalist world of practical make-believe. (1993)

17. In 1943 Cipe Pineles Burtin (1908–91) became one of the first women art directors when she took the job at *Glamour*, and in 1958 and 1959 she was art director when Leo was at *Mademoiselle*.

JOURNAL · DECEMBER 8, 1941 The president asked Congress to declare war on Japan some minutes ago. The national anthem was played. The wrinkle-faced woman continued to pin her crumpled and dripping clothes onto the line. I could hear the pulleys screeching, and the flimsy gray-topped, black-skirted dress flapping. The sun has come out in a blinding white-light glare, but the sky is gray with snow held back. Yesterday morning, a destroyer—battle-mented, turreted, and bristling (this word has become a convention) with guns went up the river. People looked at it with curiosity and delicious tremors of safety and vicarious danger—and some pride—not realizing it was the last truly free morning we shall know for a long time. Doris [Uhlman-Mayer, choreographer] said, later in the afternoon [yesterday], when we knew of this thing, that it could be no shock to refugees because they have been through this so many times. I rang Eleonora, and she had heard but was busy dressing to go to Toscanini's. And the world was the same.

When I was born, the first war was some days old. When I was to go to college, the Depression was here. Now that I am about to get on my feet—at last—having so carefully planned and striven, here is this war. But I knew it, and there is no shock or depression, for the accomplished fact is a point of departure, never a resting place.

NOTE: Virtually no journals exist for the following six months.

JOURNAL · JUNE 27, 1942 I want to write about a few days at Montauk [Long Island]. How we went there—the three of us—each with his sickness. The train ride out—Elsa was sick on it. We were excited at the green of the countryside, at the chocolate-splotched creamy white cows standing knee-deep in daisy-starred grasses, at the infrequent glimpses of the cobalt-blue sea, and once—ecstasy—a windmill, incredibly ancient in the rain-washed fields and gray-silver-green with haggard mosses. Drawing on the way out. The walk to the lodgings. Gray, gray-blue, cobalt, worn green—no bright colors save an orange scarf, a yellow-red scarf, the brown-red dotted cap. The sea and cliffs and white mist and Elsa's urge to go into the sea. The strange black heads and portents of magic. The dancing at night. The walk back. The broken English house. The walk alone. The Tyrian purple beach—not worn with age as in Wales—there had been no Romans here. The shells—naked. The *raffiniert* man on the way home. Going to the city, quite healed, carrying all the stones.

JUNE 28, 1942 I do not know what keeps me from writing this so important article.[18] I need the money. I need the prestige. Perhaps I have not tried hard enough. I make so many bad excuses about it to myself. Everything I have done seems to have been less difficult than this, and I do not think I am tired.

18. Leo was probably writing his article "Reading for Democracy," about books on that subject for young people. *The Saturday Review of Literature* would run it on July 18, 1942.

My drive seems also to be on a holiday. Now I will telephone, and then I will read in Ouspensky, just a little, and then I will write this piece—or bust.

AUGUST 2, 1942 The most important thing, perhaps, is how transitory all things are. Now Richard has been in a room where I have never been and lain in arms that I have never known, but he has given to me the major part, and I am troubled hardly at all, but his other's face intrudes when his lips press mine, and I hear him say, "His lips are soft and sweet to kiss, but I love yours," and I believe him.

**THE ACCIDENT** *I wrote my first "Before Bandwagons" column for* Vogue *and delivered it on July 1, 1943;*[19] *then went down to New York University to give my weekly lecture on children's books; then walked across Washington Square, where on what was once a parlor floor lived Bravig and Valeska Imbs. They were, that evening, giving one of their many, many parties.*[20]

*From the great tangle of white curtains drifting into the parlor, a tall, slender, youngish man I had never seen before advanced toward me. ("I found him sitting under a tree in a park in Los Angeles," Anaïs later explained. "He worked in a beauty parlor!") He stopped close to me and said, "You're going to have a very serious accident." I said to him, "I know. I've been hearing a crash for one week now. When will the accident be?" The man said, "I don't know that—maybe tonight . . . maybe sometime this week. . . ."*[21] *Someone strummed a guitar . . . someone Spanish and accomplished. Slowly Anaïs raised her bare arms, her emerald-green taffeta dress falling in ample folds about her, and she began to quiver, to swirl, her skirt making wide arcs. . . . So the night went on typically.*

*Eloise Hazard said, "It's after midnight, and I have to be at* The Saturday Review *at 8:30 this morning, and I have to go home." I said, "I'll get a cab and drop you." Everybody kissed everybody, and Eloise and I went down and out into the Square and into a taxicab. The taxi made off into browned-out (for that is what it was during these early war days—dimmed low down) New York, and I*

19. "Before Bandwagons" was intended as a regular column on artists in the vanguard. In the end Leo published only one further, unsigned, in the *Vogue* of February 1, 1947.
20. Leo was teaching a summer course at NYU called "Juvenile Writing." The American writer Bravig Imbs (1904–46) and his wife Valeska (1905?–49) had been part of the Stein-Toklas circle in Paris before the war. In mid-1943 Bravig Imbs joined the Office of War Information and began radio broadcasts of jazz to the French. He was killed in a jeep accident in France in 1946. Valeska then became a translator and, briefly, a restaurateur.
21. This professed clairvoyant, Pierce Harwell, also said Leo looked as though he "were soon to go into exile." Harwell (1916–85) was introduced to this crowd by the writer and diarist Anaïs Nin (1903–77). In her published diary for September 1941, Nin wrote: "I met Leo Lerman, who talks like Oscar Wilde, but has a warmth in his glittering dark eyes. Behind his constant game of wanting to amuse, I sense a sorrowful human being. But the door is closed to this aspect of himself. He parries with quick repartee, he is the man of the world who practices a magician's tour de force in conversation, a skillful social performance, a weather vane, a mask, a pirouette, and all you remember is the fantasy, the tale, the laughter."

*dropped Eloise. She said, "Don't drop the pot of basil that Valeska gave you, and, for heaven's sake, don't lose Wilson's Shock of Recognition! You're going to have to write about it soon." She got out. I stayed in.*

*We sped up Park Avenue. There was nobody anywhere in view. I said to the cabby, "Please stop, I want to get out." He did not stop. An enormous crash. I heard myself say, "Well, there's the crash." I know so little about mechanical things that my next thought, after the first oblivion, was: I must get out of this. Dimly, dimly I sensed disaster. I felt blood before I saw it. I clutched what was in my left arm—The Shock of Recognition. I hefted myself, out of what I did not know, into what I did not know, feeling that whatever it was would explode if I did not get clear of it.*

*Then, on this very hot July morning, I was very cold—freezing, and I had a secret. My secret was that my top teeth were in the top of my head and I must not tell anyone because to get at them they would cut my head open. I heard me murmuring, "Someone please hold my hand, or I will die." I heard a woman say, "We're not allowed to touch you. That is law." Somewhere in me was the thought that all about me surely there were friends, people who loved me, who would be delighted to touch me. . . . Then I felt a strong hand holding mine and a man said, "It's all right now." And I laughed, because I realized I was being covered over, and I realized that, unbelievably, I was almost naked, flat-out on Park Avenue. Then I went somewhere else. Then I came back. Then I went somewhere else again. This to-and-fro-ing and laughter went on and on for what seemed to me a very long time, until I saw flaring gaslight, which I believed improbable, but which later I was told lighted the way into the subterranean depths of Bellevue [Hospital] (Or did I make this up?). Then I went out—very far out. These little deaths, along the way, are most restorative. (1993)*

NOTE: This crash permanently scarred Leo's face, hence the beards that he wore for the next fifty years. How much else of him was smashed up is not clear today. Leo later often needed a cane to assist with what he called his "gimpy legs," and he blamed the 1943 accident. Richard, who went to the hospital that night, laid more of Leo's future difficulties on circulatory problems and his aversion to exercise. In any case, Leo had a lifetime of troubled walking after the accident.

On October 1, 1943, Leo and Richard moved to a somewhat larger walk-up apartment at 20 East Eighty-eighth Street (between Fifth and Madison Avenues), where they would live until the spring of 1948. Here, first by continuing the dinners that Richard had been cooking for six or eight on East End Avenue and then with open houses on Sunday evenings and increasing crowds, Leo began giving the parties that became legendary. Richard later speculated that Leo's Sunday at-homes might have been a replacement for his family's weekly gatherings in Jackson Heights. Richard, however, soon felt unappreciated by the many guests and tired of the routine.

JOURNAL · AUGUST 17, 1944 Today I lunched with Touche [John Latouche], whom I love very much for his gentle little-boy qualities, and we talked of our hauntings and of panic, each of us having such enormous panic.

The heat was intense, and in the late afternoon such a storm beat on my head. What other storms? In Interstate Park [near Jackson Heights], when a great oak flattened [cousins] Rosalie and Nonny's shoes and we all ran screaming through the torrents to hide in insubstantial privies. It was soon after Grandma had died[22]—all the women in black, with it dying their skins. And the storm when the children had got me to eat horse manure on Aunt Annie's farm.[23] That night I was anguished with pain, a doctor an impossibility, and everyone terrified in a house all lit by oil lamps and flickering, a great storm raging at the little-paned windows (but it helped my stomach). And the storm in Grandma's house—sitting on the kitchen table—oh, it is all so lost in gaslight and the feel of a scratchy wooden table, and the black shirtwaists and skirts she always wore. But she was so beautifully safe-feeling, and there's an elusive fragrance to her which I shall come upon one day. She was spare, with silver hair piled and twisted high upon her head; she had lovely blue, kind, bemused eyes and her skin was exquisitely wrinkled; she spoke no English; her fingers were delicate and long, remarkable for a woman who came from Jewish peasant stock (of her family I know little); she was fond of the diamonds Grandpa hung upon her, but she gave them away to women, daughters-in-law, of whom she thought more. We all loved her exceedingly, and, when we were terrified, she always knew what to do. In that storm, she tucked me away from the lightning flashes in a room that had no window.

AUGUST 29, 1944  As a small child, I was so hungry for flowers that I would beg them from people who had been fortunate enough to carry them into our stony, dirty street. There was an Italian family who brought masses of field flowers from some suburb. They kept them—daisies, black-eyed Susans, dandelions—on their parlor windowsills, and we would plead for them. They would fling them to us and that was heavenly. Even the most hard-boiled of us loved them. Once we stole carnations from wreaths being carried out to a hearse!

I laughed aloud in my sleep last night, or rather early this morning, and Richard said it was much better than the screaming I usually do. Richard is exquisitely pale and thin. Touche says he's so beautifully complete, and that is so, but intact is more accurate.

AN APPARITION  *One summer day, I went to see Eleonora. On entering her bedroom (above the cacophonous carpenter's shop), I found, stretched in*

22. When Leo refers to Grandma and Grandpa, they are his maternal grandparents. The names on their gravestones are Joseph (1852?–1930) and Edith Sugarman Goldwasser (1859?–1919), but the family called them Jacob and Yetta.
23. "I had believed (poor city child that I was) my cousins when they told me it was chocolate." *Journal, March 2, 1981.* Rosalie, Martin, and Norma "Nonny" Goldwasser were the children of Leo's uncle Harry and aunt Ida. Leo's father's older sister Anna Lerman Germain had a farm in Colchester, Connecticut.

*blazing sunlight upon a pale lemon-yellow bed, an apparition I had only seen until that moment upon the screen. The apparition was done up in tan army fatigues, rumpled pants, a rumpled shirt open at the neck, marvelous blond hair spread in disorder on a corn-yellow pillow, matter-of-fact blue eyes staring straight at me. The bone structure of the face, seemingly clean of makeup, was fantastic. And out of the pale crimson lips came a husky voice. "Sit down," she said. "Where?" said I. She said, "The bed, of course." So I sat down. And then it was hours later. Because the apparition was Marlene Dietrich. And she had for some time bewitched me on-screen, enchanted me, made me laugh with and at her. Later, I realized that she knew when people laughed at her and she knew when people laughed with her, and that she exercised, at all times, total control.* (VOGUE, JULY 1992)

NOTE: Leo swiftly wrote a piece describing Dietrich's work on a USO tour, which *Vogue* published on August 15, 1944, titled "Welcome, Marlene!" Their interviews began a friendship that grew closest in the fifties, when she was often in New York.

JOURNAL • NOVEMBER 26, 1944 Last evening we set out for a theater and found ourselves at Columbus Circle and the Ballet International, which, save for *Sebastian*, was outrageously bad and almost entirely peopled in the house proper with a particularly repulsive species of [homosexual] bitch—the over-plump, over-forty, baby-talking (they really talk so mincingly to be refined), gray-faced kind, who need not open their mouths to give themselves away, for their posteriors do it, but I don't want to tell about them, nor the unhealthy pallor which hung palpably on their faces and in the theater, that old-smoke pallor so omnipresent at theatrical and human disasters, nor the cankered yellow of the [company director] Marquis de Cuevas's face mounted over his extra-large dark bow tie. It was all too nauseating.

NOVEMBER 27, 1944 Maya Deren's film [*At Land*],[24] with Richard showing up in it: He is beautifully what he is—almost out of a [James Branch] Cabell *Sorisande* novel, and I with age, but not discretion, and the gestures of a rabbi exhorting or a ham actor of the old school, and Deren crawling her way through it all—but what sense to it? Lovely photography: A shot of great crystal chandeliers memorable, and the ocean surging on the shore, and footprints in the sand, their edges crumbling—these things are always effective—but what and why?

It is 1:15 a.m. Richard makes go-to-bed sounds in the bathroom, and I am tired, but so filled with things I want to set down, things I want to empty out of me: I am so wound up! I hear the bathroom light click off and a slipper scuffle

---

24. Avant-garde filmmaker Maya Deren (1917–61) cast both Leo and Richard in her works, including the fifteen-minute silent *At Land* (1944).

against the hall floorboard. I must get into bed. Sometimes a distant automobile on a rainy night makes an almost imperceptible fluttering. I ache to hear the summer wind in summer trees. "Nib-tip," says Richard, "aren't you goin' to bed?"[25]

MARCH 30, 1945 Richard is somewhat in love with V. He said that going to lunch with V made him feel as he did when he looked for a job in the theater and he was to come back the next day and that he would probably get the part. That is why this has to be: He almost never got those parts, but this part he must know that he can get if he wants it. Perhaps he will then be as secure as he can really be. Having no ability to feel jealousy about this makes me have the same amputated kind of feeling as when I knew that I had no feeling for any religion taught me. I just couldn't make bargains with God anymore, and I couldn't run to him. There was no refuge—none—jealousy is refuge, religion is a refuge. I have neither to sustain me here. I have only my profound curiosity in what happens and in recording it.

It will be late morning, in the fragrant spring rain, when he returns, climbing the stairs wearily, looking naughty—but he has to do this, I know it, and he must know it, too. It is only this way that we can have some measure of mutual respect, and so some little joy.[26]

APRIL 20, 1945 When I practiced the piano at home, the doors leading from the parlor (we called it that then; now Momma calls it a living room) were many-paned. (French doors they were called, and everybody had them put in.) When I banged on the piano, all the glass thrummed. Sometimes I thought there was a great gleaming horsefly in the room, but it was glass, always glass, and this enchanted me, and was one of the reasons why I banged away at made-up pianistics. The exercises never made as much glass shivering as what I made up. A curious thing about what I made up was that it was, and still is, very Yiddish-Russian, minor in mode and Slavic-Yiddish in rhythm and feeling even when in three-quarter time—atavistically. I can improvise nothing in any other style, and I love playing this. It is fun and relief and a kind of well-being-in-where-I-belong.[27]

---

25. Leo and Richard shared a love of nonsense language. Many of Leo's letters to Richard are sprinkled with such words: *snunc, ugh-wumph, topmiff, nib-tip*, etc. Most of his letters also close with "ity-ity-ity," probably an allusion to a robin's song heard when they first kissed.
26. "V" was Fulco Santostefano della Cerda (1898–1978), Duke of Verdura, an Italian jewelry designer. *Richard Hunter:* "Fulco was very amusing, very intelligent. It went on for a couple of months. Then he met Leo at a party, and asked Leo if he was in love with me. Leo said, 'Yes.' Then I never saw Fulco again."
27. Leo's familial heritage on both sides was mostly Polish and Russian Jewish. Leo said that the Goldwassers had originally been called Schneidover and the Lermans named Simon-Berghaus. Originally, "Lerman" (acquired at some point) had been spelled "Lehrmann," but "Grandpa could not write an 'h' and the extra 'n' was lost." *Journal, December 1970.*

NOTE: Leo reviewed *Wars I Have Seen*, Gertrude Stein's memoir about the Occupation of France, for the magazine *Tomorrow*.

**WARS I HAVE SEEN** ... *I was quite puzzled as to how I would really tell about this rich, good, homely, insistent, courageous, wise, ungrammatical, amusing, very personal book. And I thought of my mother's family meetings.*

*Some years ago, my mother formed her kinsmen into a family club. Three weeks ago, for the first time in two years, I attended one of their monthly meetings. My mother's family is enormous and noisy. They all have the faculty of listening to and carrying on several conversations simultaneously. This is extremely irritating to outsiders, but to those in the know, it is the essence of their special gregariousness.*

*Listening to the family in full flight, I heard long stretches of conversation which fascinated me because I knew the people, the anecdotes were personal and amusing, and I understood the family lexicon—that lexicon which each family evolves as its own shortcut to communication. Then there were conversational stretches which made no sense to me; they were so intimate in structure and thought, so derived from a wealth of experience in which I had not participated, that I found no basis of communication. These were stretches in which the participants seemed to enter into a conspiracy of willful obscurity. They began right where they had stopped a day or even a month previously, taking up right in the middle of a thought or a sentence, interlarding each phrase with allusions obscure to me but filled with apparently world-shaking significance to all the others. And, of course, there was a constant repetition—repetition for emphasis, repetition for insistence. And a lot of it was just talk for the love of talking, talk as a form of harmless exhibitionism.*

*Most of this talk was of war—this war, past wars, wars of which they heard or read, family wars, national wars, world wars. They talked of war in headline terms; they talked of war in terms of food rationing, bond buying, plasma giving, girdles, the draft, heat, and prosperity. They told one another the latest about young Cousin Eddie in the Air Force who has piloted a bomber for months and has only just learned to drive an automobile; about Cousin Larry who parachuted with broken legs into a German prison camp and who continues there to draw his designs for stage sets.[28] And they talked and talked and talked. It was all interesting, and in retrospect it all made sense. It was exhilarating, real, alive, courageous, very personal, sometimes very dull, and always as peculiarly balanced as life. It was direct, funny, malicious, uninhibited, and replete with matter-of-fact kitchen wisdom.*

*Gertrude Stein talks of all the previous parts of her life connected with wars, and of big and little happenings during four years of life in Nazi-dominated*

---

28. "Cousin Eddie" here is probably Martin Goldwasser (d. 1985), a cousin who became an Air Force colonel. Leo probably invented "Cousin Larry," the stage-designing paratrooper.

*France, and all of it—articulated in Gertrude Stein's lexicon—is personal and intimate, and some of it is obscure to the outsider but of world-shattering significance to Miss Stein. Both Gertrude Stein and my family talk of themselves in terms of the world and of wars, and of the world and wars in terms of themselves, and it is the same thing down to the trivial obscurity, the most boring repetition. Sometimes Gertrude Stein is more literate and more comprehensible, and sometimes my family are.* (TOMORROW, MAY 1945)

JOURNAL • JULY 16, 1945 Ruth [Yorck] met an old psychiatrist who attended Nietzsche during the last days of his madness. When she finally pinned him down, he said that Nietzsche had said only one thing, and this repeatedly during those days: "Where is reason?"

NOTE: Leo and Richard went to Siasconset, Nantucket. Hellmut Roder and Fritz Mosell, a couple introduced to them by Eleonora von Mendelssohn, had lent them a small rented house there for the month of August. Mosell wrote from it in July warning Leo that he might not enjoy it, as "there is no nightlife, only peace and quiet, and you will be the onliest [*sic*] person one will hear laugh miles around." Leo found it heavenly.

AUGUST 18, 1945 • SIASCONSET, MASSACHUSETTS
TO ELEONORA VON MENDELSSOHN • NEW YORK CITY

Last night Richard and I—and a man who seemed to know me but whose name I cannot remember nor probably ever knew—were crouched near a roaring fire, because of the winter in the evening, when suddenly there was a shout in our back lane. The door to the little drawing room flew open—and thirty-five people crowded in, headed by dear little Luise [Rainer] and her Bobby [Knittel] (she calls him Butch).[29] So then we were giving a party—but it's the only party we ever gave without anything to drink or eat. Three people—the Dreyfuses and an Egyptian princess with a very unreal name [Jacqueline Shohet?]—had appeared at luncheon and ate everything save us.[30] Why are people like locusts when they, the people, are on a holiday? But we all had fun.

We want you desperately because you would love it here, and it would be so healthy for you: no fishers—no conductors of any description—not even a trolley car—and some possibility of practicing witchcraft. To wit, yesterday I was sitting, minding my own and everybody's business, and suddenly one of those awful American women who have given the world such a picture of the American beauty came riding down a little hill, on a bicycle. Looking at her, I wished: "May something frightful happen to you. . . ." Just then a station

29. The Vienna-born actress Luise Rainer (b. 1910) had married the publisher Robert Knittel just a month before. Although she is the only actress to have won back-to-back Oscars, her Hollywood film career was over by 1943.
30. Richard Dreyfus (1913–2004) was a banker and art collector; his wife Denyse Mosseri (later Harari, 1918–91) had degrees in philosophy and mathematics. Each was descended from an important Jewish family: His were bankers in Germany and Switzerland, hers prominent and wealthy Egyptians.

wagon rushed across her path. She smacked into it. Loads of people flew out of alleys and houses, and she was carried off howling. Richard materialized behind me and said, "You did it!" All the people looked at me quite reproachfully. I smiled smugly. The people went away muttering. Richard and I sat looking at a gray dilapidated automobile. Suddenly, with an awful roar, it burst into flame. I immediately got up and hid behind a hedge. When the fire had been extinguished, I emerged rather triumphantly. Richard glowered at me and said, "What the hell do you think you're doing?" I smirked and we returned to our little nest.

There's one ancient female who lives out on a point of land who walks around every tree she meets three times, because she thinks it will bring her luck. For forty years she has been waiting for her lover. Darling—this is what it would be like if you or I went away to some other part of the world. It's awful without you—or even the daily possibility of hearing your old cracked voice croaking something appallingly sweet over the telephone. Don't write, just descend on us—that would be dreamy—and on the way you might look for our trunk, which has been missing for a week.

JOURNAL · AUGUST 23, 1945 One comes to the place where talking ends. It is like reaching the end of a street . . . the rest is a dirt track ultimately trailing off into meadows or the town dump. When talking ends there is only the first person very singular, a species of chaos, a progression rabbit-run in structure and shape. For the first time in some years, I find myself confined—that means no telephone and little or almost no possibility of escaping into bevies of people. I have consequently become curiously sex-ridden, or perhaps overconscious of sex, although I have enough, shall I call it, indulgence. . . . But I now know that it is not so much the sexual act, no matter what its form, but the sexual excitement which surrounds this act. . . . I must sublimate much of this quiet desperation in entertaining, in that sort of mass flirtation that I so enjoy. Giving parties, rushing about for people (really for myself), the endless telephone conversations, all must absorb so much of this lusting. This is the closest to those adolescent years when it was my habit to wander endlessly both in Jackson Heights and Lakewood [New Jersey] in the nights hoping to find somebody— just somebody—who would blot out everything, for this is the basic and very real potency of the sexual act. I know that I remained here, refusing to go with Richard and Franny [Wormser][31] to the film, because deep down I hoped that someone would suddenly materialize out of the night . . . perhaps a lot of someones . . . and then I could be very gay and make them laugh and I would feel "myself" again. But in this state, I work so hard at it. I am so very conscious of the bourgeois normalcy so deep all about me.

---

31. Frances Dewey Wormser (b. 1902) was a former musical comedy actress, a friend whom Leo had met through Imogene Coca.

# A "1926" Party

JANUARY 26, 1946  •  20 EAST EIGHTY-EIGHTH STREET

Max Ernst
Dorothea Tanning
Rufino Tamayo
Olga Tamayo
Lionel Trilling
Diana Trilling
Dorothy Wheelock
Rue Wheelock
Saul Steinberg
Hedda Sterne
Grace Zaring Stone
Ellis Stone
Hansi Janis
Sidney Janis
Rudi Blesch
Helen Hoke
Anaïs Nin
Ian Hugo
Harold Halma
Emily Hahn
Eric Ladd
Evelyn Gendel
Milton Gendel
Dawn Powell
Rev. Otley
Mrs. Otley
George Sakier
Kay Silver Sakier

Ruth Ford
Yvonne McHarg
Luise Rainer
Robert Knittel
Charles Rolo
Eva Gauthier
Julian Levy
Muriel [Draper]
Xenia Cage
Briggs Buchanan
Mrs. [Florence] Buchanan
Marion Greenwood
Elsa Neuberger
James Neuberger
Frances Dewey
Eloise Hazard
Imogene Coca
Bob Burton
Hazel Slaughter
Charmion von Wiegand
Peggy Guggenheim
Yul Brynner
Claude Alphand
Jon Stroup
Joan McCracken
Sono Osato
Kitty [Messner]

OCTOBER 19, 1945 · NEW YORK CITY  This is really Saturday morning—about 3:06 a.m. I am starting this in an effort to return into myself. It is as though a glass bell has dropped between me and myself. Extrinsically, it looks the same as it has before—the picture seems unchanged—but this is untrue. I am in danger of becoming one of the amputated ones—with all my days and nights given up to the pursuit of wages—not creation. I mean no writing that illuminates—and no true writing at all—not even book reviews. Into those I can work something seedlike. For *Bazaar*, I can give, thus far, only sterility. The surface coruscates, but it is sterile. How to live? I am so luxury-loving. Anaïs said today that she could only write a little book behind the door: She gave later; I give here and now. But this is no consolation. She said that she couldn't see how I would have anything left for a book because I was so flamboyant and prodigal. I said that is what's wrong.

FEBRUARY 11, 1946  I am impatient of any human relationship that falls short of intimacy. All others do seem to me a waste of time—save when they are business. If someone interests me, I want to know him thoroughly. When a person or thing becomes quite completely known, when there seems to be no mystery left, no intangibles, our pleasure is at an end, and disintegration, which subtly began quite unknown at the beginning of the enchantment, has inevitably come.

I always pay more for charm. If a waiter has charm or is good-looking, the tip is larger than usual, and if a waitress has charm or is lovely in some way, her tip is larger than usual. Charm and beauty should be acknowledged by some gesture of pleasure. We should pay for what we get, even if it's free. And we do pay—wittingly or unwittingly.

NOTE: Leo was admitted to Yaddo, a writers' colony near Saratoga Springs, New York, for May and June 1946. He would work there on a dual biography of the Renaissance leaders, patrons, and beauties Isabella and Beatrice d'Este. Leo pursued this project for years, never completing a manuscript.

Truman Capote was also to be at Yaddo that summer and they journeyed up to Saratoga together. The two had met earlier, probably in the autumn of 1945.

**LITTLE T**  *I went to visit with a dear friend, Mary Louise Aswell [fiction editor of* Harper's Bazaar], *and there, in a shadowy room, I found a strange, smallish creature—a sort of changeling, I thought, like the one Titania and Oberon fought over—fragile, but tough. He regaled us with gossip, jokes, little dances. Later when I went away, down a dim stair, someone suddenly landed on my back and with a high treble cry demanded: "Give me a piggyback ride!" I did. And that is when Little T and I became friends. He saw me as I saw myself, and I saw him as he saw himself. We each saw each other's invention and through the invention into our true, ever-loving hearts.* (1984)

MAY 1, 1946 • SARATOGA SPRINGS
**TO RICHARD HUNTER** • NEW YORK CITY

Soon I will go up to my room in the "mansion" and make myself presentable for my first dinner. I have a corner bedroom on the second floor wherein I nestle my downy ears on a little white iron bedstead, excessively virginal. Carson [McCullers[32]] greeted us at the door, and it was then Truman discovered that his manuscript plus his typewriter were lost. He flew back to the station. Later I heard him tell that he'd found them.

The house is something from the turn of the century, the inmates something from *The Turn of the Screw* . . . but it does seem lovely here. There are many trees and great gusts of sweet-smelling spring air. There are butterflies and birds twittering and palatial houses for them to inhabit. A little walk from the house I have a house all for myself called Hillside, and it's where I work. It is as large as your mother's living room and there are numerous tables, a chaise longue (!!!) and sixteen large windows. It's so light. I have drawn up a desk and thereon repose the first pages from which I hope to wrest a little masterpiece—also a moneymaker. Across the road and through a little glade Truman has his studio. Mrs. A [director Elizabeth Ames] is a tallish woman, a little plump but extraordinarily pale.

MAY 3, 1946 • SARATOGA SPRINGS
**TO RICHARD HUNTER** • NEW YORK CITY

Yesterday Marguerite Young arrived.[33] She is a heavy-faced female. Her book is fantastic. The chief character could be Eleonora. She told me that about a year ago she saw me in the lobby of the Royalton [Hotel] and followed me about there trying to hear what I was saying. She said my face fascinated her. She has a way of looking intently at one when she doesn't think you are noticing.

MAY 4

Late last night, Truman, Marguerite Young, and an old resident, [biographer] Howard Doughty, went into the main part of the mansion—peering at it by lighted matches. It was vast and very frightening and we didn't stay long. We all talk about murders and what a setting for a mystery—and Marguerite Young is somewhat monstrous. Carson coughs so. Today, walking to our studios, she had a dreadful seizure—and threw up.

32. The novelist (*The Member of the Wedding*) and short-story writer Carson McCullers (1917–67) was frequently at Yaddo during the war. Leo had met her previously through the writer Edita Morris.
33. The novelist Marguerite Young (1908–95) took some of Leo's features and experiences for the character of Mr. Spitzer in her magnum opus, *Miss MacIntosh, My Darling* (1965).

**TO RICHARD HUNTER • NEW YORK CITY**

Today I have done little work, perhaps because the first little spate of plunging into it is over. Also, I have been disturbed by Curtice [Hitchcock]'s death.[34] Any threat to income always sends me to the margin of despair, because I would hate being very poor again. Through my front windows the spring trees and the blue-white patched sky is absolutely a copy of that little Bellini [*Madonna and Child*] in the Bache pictures—the one with the tree of hope and the tree of despair.

I think that here I should tell you how much I love you—but again, as in May eleven years ago, I find no words to tell you. There is only one advantage this May: now you surely know; then you couldn't have known. Without you— or without the knowledge that there is you—I am so derelict—so lost. I suppose telling you this—which you know—is not good, for it places responsibility upon you who do not wish it.

MAY 5

I spent yesterday evening with Carson, who plays the piano very well. She was trained to be a pianist and she earned her living, while she went to Columbia, by playing in settlement houses. She told me much about her life—especially with Annemarie [Clarac-Schwarzenbach][35]—and she said that she disliked me violently that first time at Edita [Morris]'s[36] because she thought I had been a friend of Annemarie's. Now she seems to dote on me—but I think she must be quite ill—she coughs so much.

**TO RICHARD HUNTER • NEW YORK CITY**

Yesterday, after I ate my lunch with Truman and Howard Doughty—who is a very nice man (Harvard 1926)—I saw that the gardener had arrived with wood for my stove. So I ran across to my house, which is about a hundred feet from Truman's, and aided and abetted the gardener. . . . Quite suddenly I heard Truman shouting, "Leo! Leo!" So I went to my door, and I saw Howard walking across Truman's front yard and Truman standing in his doorway yelling.

34. In December 1944, Curtice Hitchcock (1892–1946), director of the publisher Reynal & Hitchcock, had signed Leo to edit a series of books on American highways and their regional histories. The project was never realized. For the publisher Julian Messner, however, Leo did begin editing a Cities of America series. Volumes on Chicago, Louisville, and Indianapolis were published.
35. A brief affair with the beautiful Swiss novelist and journalist Annemarie Clarac-Schwarzenbach (1908–42) had left McCullers obsessed and later devastated by Schwarzen-bach's death following a bicycle accident in Switzerland.
36. Leo had met the married writers Edita and Ira Morris on Nantucket in 1945, but dropped them a few years later, when Leo read her lips saying dreadful things about him at one of his parties. Leo's deaf cousins had taught him this skill as a boy.

Then I saw that Howard was holding something, which sort of writhed, and I saw that it was a snake . . . very gray and long . . . and I thought it's dead . . . it's dead . . . and I shouted, "You're mean and wicked. . . ." and ran back into my house and said to the gardener, "They're teasing me. . . . Please take it away. . . . Take it away. . . ." and bolted my door and drew all the blinds and lay down under my desk. I think I did that because it seemed so safe . . . and then I didn't know what to do. I knew that they hadn't done it intentionally because they are not bad, either of them, and they like me. They did it because they didn't believe that I was so upset by snakes . . . and because boys will be boys even if they're girls (a cheap remark). So then all afternoon I didn't know what to do, and I could hardly move, and everything was black, and I knew that if I lay on the floor, which was hard and reassuring and cool, everything would be all right in the end . . . but I thought I could never get out of it. I cannot tell you how lost and tired and distraught I was . . . but there was really nothing I could do about it . . . nothing. It was one of those times that in retrospect seem to have existed only in the most frightful of nightmares. The spirit, being so affirmative, rejects such times as improbable. There are parts of that afternoon that I cannot remember, for they were so lost, so black. Now there is a brown bird with bright red wings swaying on a bough and only the taste and the color of the afternoon remain and the memory of anguish and disaster and how tired my arms were when I tried to work and couldn't. I suppose I must be very sick where serpents are concerned, and I don't know why. At about five o'clock (after some four hours of misery), I suddenly knew that I was better. I drew some of the curtains and saw the sky and the trees and the rain and then I was quite better and I sat down and made myself work but I could only make notes and not write at all. Then it was time to go to dinner, and I went out and along the road. When I came to the barn where a green snake lives, I walked—I didn't run as I usually do—past it, but I didn't look. Then I went up to my room and sat on the edge of the bed and wondered why all of it had happened. Howard, who has the next room, came into my room and gave me a letter. It was from Mrs. Ames to him saying that she knew that Mr. Lerman was being "insistently persecuted by snakes," and that if he or Mr. Capote knew anything about it they must stop, because she knew that such persecution could be very dangerous. Howard was very upset, and when Truman heard he was very upset, not because of the letter but because they hadn't realized that I was so affected by all of it . . . and I never before had realized that either. Now Carson has made them promise that they will convoy me to and from my studio and carefully defend me from all disaster.

The day before yesterday there was a blue note pinned up where we get our mail and it said, "Katherine Anne Porter will be with us for dinner tonight." So then that evening we all spruced up, while Truman heckled us, and then when he came down to dinner he was more spruced than any of us . . . and there was Katherine Anne, who reminds me of Carmel Snow, and she laughs all the time. She is a small woman with the beautiful ankles, feet, and smooth legs of that generation. She has marvelous white hair, and she was a great beauty. She has the airs and graces of a former silent-film actress—and I discovered later that she was one—but most of all she is a Southern belle, with all that implies, and she is most like Bette Davis playing Fanny Skeffington. She's overvivacious. She talks well. She sat next to me at dinner, and she talked all the time very quickly, laughing nervously. She wears pastel colors, and she had on an emerald ring which she'd borrowed from Mrs. Ames (whom I like). She said she'd borrowed it for luck, because it was her birthstone. After dinner, someone put a samba or rhumba on the gramophone, and suddenly she jumped up and did what looked like the shimmy and made me feel as though I suddenly saw one of my parents quite naked and carousing. So, soon Truman danced with her, and she doesn't dance well, but she does give an impression of Lillian Gish making whoopee . . . and he wore her out. He dances very well. Then there was a lot of dancing, and she practically fell on her face—but it was all very *gemütlich*—after which she sat down to Chinese checkers. Truman and Howard and I went off to visit Carson, who was in bed.

MAY 15, 1946 • SARATOGA SPRINGS
**TO RICHARD HUNTER** • NEW YORK CITY

Last night, when I saw that there was a moon, I said to Truman, "Let's go for a walk." So I led him down through the meadow toward the great fountain, where the statue is covered by that tall wooden house, and looking back we saw a light, very dim and secret, in the attic of the mansion where nobody is supposed to be. This was mildly terrifying to Truman, but I was not afraid at all in the meadow, although the mansion standing in the cold moonlight and the wall of moonlit trees—motionless, dense . . . the mist rising at the foot of the meadow . . . the big blobs of radiance and mist, which seemed to be trying to form into some palpable shape . . . all these were the stuff of horrible nightmares. I led Truman into the rose garden, which spread out vast and inhabited by terrible shapeless horrors, all the parterres and white marble people in the moonlight. As I went through the marble gate, I suddenly ran up the path into the horror, dragging Truman with me. I knew that he was terrified but I ran because of delight. I wanted to run up all the paths because it was so incredibly beautiful. Then I walked very measuredly everywhere in the garden and Truman with me, and sometimes I stopped and stroked the white statues because they were so contented and so utterly secretly sly and smiling and alone. It became more monstrously dreamlike all the time . . . walking under the long, long pergola . . . standing with the white goddesses . . . becoming one with the trees. For the first time, last night I was too frightened to go to bed without my light, and Truman was terrified. He said that I had looked and walked so fantastically in the rose garden in the moonlight. He said that when I ran into the garden dragging him with me he knew that something awful could happen, and he was almost sure that it would. . . . He said that people turn into monsters—and they do[37]

No one said anything about my not being here [for a day] but Carson and Truman and Marguerite all said that breakfast had been a blight. No one had been happy or civil, and although no one said a word about my absence everyone was thinking about it—not angrily, but because there was no gaiety. It seems that when they are all alone without me they are unable to make one another gay. They were all at breakfast when suddenly the dining room door opened and everyone looked up at Esther [Rolick, a sculptor], who is so gay and Greenwich Villagey. Esther stood there with her face black—horribly awful and corrupt with darkness. She looked at them and ran out of the house. It then came out that she suffers occasionally from fits of manic depressiveness! She was suffering. When I heard this, I was so sad for her, and then looking out of my bedroom window I saw her coming up the path to the house. She looked like Elektra must have looked after all the horror and before she murdered. Her face was utterly, frightfully transformed. You could see misery eating at her. Carson said that sometimes, when Esther lived over there, she would hear a horrible weeping and sobbing in the night, but when she went to see what was wrong she found Esther's door locked and there would be no answer. At dinner I looked at her, and I saw that she wanted to be gay, so I set out to make everyone laugh, and soon we were all howling at Momma and stories about her. Then I saw that there was something strange about Marguerite.

Mrs. Ames isn't here, and she asked Marguerite to sit in her place and hostess. We were all pleased, because we all know that she needs wanting and tenderness. So, there she was at the head of the table, and it wasn't anything she did or said at first but the utterly slumped, abandoned, loose way she sat. Then she suddenly looked at Truman (he sits next to her), and she said, "Do you love me, Truman? Do you love me?" He said, "Yes . . ." just taking it for good fellowship, and she leaned over from her place to his and pulled him to her and kissed him right on the mouth. . . . Then she went back to eating as though nothing had happened. Everyone saw this, but everyone went right on. When we were serving ourselves from the sideboard, she went up and down the line asking everyone, "Do you love me? Do you love me? Will you miss me? Will you miss me?" Everyone murmured to her, and we all pretended that nothing unusual was happening . . . but we all knew that she was dreadfully drunk. Carson had given her some whiskey in the afternoon, and this was the result. After dinner she became completely abandoned and flung herself into Howard [Doughty]'s lap. He stroked her hair, and his face was the face of a criminal fas-

37. "Elizabeth [Ames, 1885–1977] said: 'I remember the thirties, when the leftists were here. . . . You couldn't get them to go into the garden.' I answered her clear, deaf-woman tones: 'And now, when the queens are here, you can't get them out.' Little T squeaked with joy." *Journal, February 1, 1986.*

cinated. It shifted, as he stroked her hair, from a horrible tenderness to a tender malignance. It was dreadful and eerie. Finally he escaped, but not until he had kissed her—or rather she had pulled his head down and forced her mouth and tongue, I presume, into his. She seemed to have no realization of what she was doing, and she spoke all the time about love and saints and murder and monstrosities, while Truman and Esther danced to the gramophone like two little children who play among the insane, brightly laughing and fluttering about, not quite understanding where they are or why they should be there.

Howard's life is more complicated than I thought. Every person here has something to hide—insanities fancied or remembered, aberrations assorted and portioned out variously, or just terror. All intensely creative minds have a core of sickness. I don't think that they should be permitted to live together. The sickness tends to grow, like exotic plants forced swiftly to blossom and corruption in a glass house.

MAY 17, 1946 • SARATOGA SPRINGS
**TO RUTH YORCK** • NEW YORK CITY

The maids and the cooks came to ask one of the people whether I am a rabbi. They said I was because 1) I wear black; 2) I have a beard; 3) I have the Bible by my bed. What do you think?

I have written and finished four little sections of B and Bella [Beatrice and Isabella]. It turns out to be B's book thus far and maybe it will never quite be Bella's—but do we care? It's gay and highly informative and really quite a drag. Anyone reading it will know immediately that only a sensualist could have written it.

CA. MAY 20, 1946 • SARATOGA SPRINGS
**TO MARY LOUISE ASWELL** • NEW YORK CITY[38]

Mostly we wonder whether we haven't been gently hoodwinked into a sanitarium. There are so many evidences, but my book goes apace and Truman probably will get into his soon. Carson lives in a house with Marguerite Young. Carson sits all day—a cup of tea in one hand and a cup of sherry in the other. Occasionally she puts one or the other down to write a few words of verse. Marguerite slumps all day over a large worktable absolutely snowed under sheets and sheets of discarded manuscript.

The house is vast and of its kind perfection—American William Morris or Seventy-ninth Street Gothic crossed with Indianapolis Renaissance. Two nights ago, we played Murder all through one wing of the house. I was murderer and I picked Carson as my victim, stalking her everywhere she went in the frightful dark. The lights were all turned off through the house. She moaned and moaned and, by and by, when she felt that the unseen was with her everywhere, she called a little bit upon God. Then she stopped, and I put my foot

---

38. Mary Louise Aswell (1902–84), fiction editor of *Harper's Bazaar* from 1945 to 1949, had opened that magazine to Leo by introducing him to Carmel Snow.

out on hers, and then she began to plead, and slowly I raised my arms and choked her. . . . This is what you do in that little grisly game . . . and these, my dear, are Yaddo's childish pleasures.[39]

Truman just rushed in to tell me that *Life* has commissioned Russell Maloney to do a profile of Carson, to defend her from her detractors. That's wonderful. I do think that the *Bazaar* should have an occasional piece about a writer or a painter or a musician, a kind of fantastic discovery sort of person. *Vogue* is running a whole piece on Marianne Moore. Marguerite wrote it for them. I find the book she's working on curiously intriguing. She's a strange, lovable girl with a great need for assurance. (I've been reading [psychoanalyst] Karen Horney.)

JUNE 1946 • SARATOGA SPRINGS
TO LIONEL AND DIANA TRILLING • NEW YORK CITY

You, Diana, were right.[40] This Yaddo is where any tact creates a situation, and two and two total perverse numerals. I wanted very much to talk with you when I came into town last week because of Bravig Imbs's death. Probably Elsa [Snapper] has told you that I've been among the living . . . but I adjured her to tell you nothing of this intellectual terror, this sort of psychopathic disaster that our Mrs. Ames manages to create. . . . Nothing you told me ever prepared me for her passion for the oblique, the indirect. Everything becomes so sinister once she has started her silly suspicions and accusations. She never accuses anybody directly, but does it through other "guests." The least thing she does, or anyone does, becomes distorted to monstrous proportions. Surely this is not a healthy climate for people who want to work creatively. While the upset lasted, it made me furious enough to start packing all of my trunks. It made one of the other "guests" take to his bed for a whole day. It helped Carson decide to depart, and it kept almost everybody from doing any work whatsoever for almost a whole week. And all because God's Angry Man decided that any hilarity, especially at breakfast, was a sign of abnormalcy![41] Unfortunately, among the newer

---

39. The players in the game Murder drew cards: The ace of spades designated one the murderer; the jack of hearts made another the detective. One night, Leo was the murderer and stalked Capote: "I lured Truman into my closet. I strangled him. He screamed, 'Oh, you, I'll get you for this! I'll never trust you again!' It was absolutely thrilling; his scream went up several octaves above and several octaves below: It was the full range of Truman. It was the manly Truman, the female Truman, it was the *works.* I think the scream haunts Yaddo still." (As quoted in *Truman Capote* by George Plimpton [Nan A. Talese/Doubleday, 1997].)

40. Diana Trilling (1905–96), essayist on literature and social issues, had been at Yaddo in the summer of 1931; Leo met the Trillings in the fall of 1943 by writing for *Vogue* about Lionel, who would become one of the country's leading critics.

41. Leonard Ehrlich (1905–84) had published a novel, *God's Angry Man* (1932), about the violent abolitionist John Brown. Leo's and Ehrlich's mutual dislike was instantaneous. On May 6, Leo had written to Richard that Ehrlich was "like all the Jewish boys who belonged to clubs in the local synagogue—serious and sallow visaged," and then on May 30: "I really find it difficult to believe that he has any Jewish blood in him whatsoever. He's so boche."

arrivals is [writer] Richard Plant, the one who caused me to depart from my column in *Tomorrow*, and just as unfortunately no one likes him, for he is belligerently German and horribly misinformed on everything. So, God's Angry Man decided that some of us had formed a clique against this precious literary talent, and that combined with the hilarity (for all of us enjoy one another very much) made a pretty mess when Ehrlich told Mrs. Ames that he would have to move from the mansion because his nerves were exacerbated by us. He paid me a grave compliment by calling me, according to report, "the life of the party." So it raged. I think it a great pity that this place, which could be absolute heaven if Mrs. Ames had never read a psychology book, should be, mentally, so mismanaged.

NOTE: Elizabeth Ames's habit of making indirect queries and admonishing residents with succinct notes ("Memo to Mr. Lerman: Rumor has it that . . .") certainly grated on Leo. What he apparently did not know was that Leonard Ehrlich was Ames's clandestine lover. Ehrlich's objections to Leo's joviality—and perhaps to his homosexuality, to judge from what followed—evidently had a special hearing.

JUNE 8, 1946 • SARATOGA SPRINGS
**TO RICHARD HUNTER** • NEW YORK CITY

I think that I have perhaps hit upon what is lacking in Truman's work. It's not his writing but his curiously sheltered life that makes for the lack. Although even at twenty-one he has had extraordinary experiences, he still has been kept from the sort of suffering that he looks upon as bourgeois. The other night when I was talking about homosexuality, I said—why I do not now know—how it was a sickness; how anything which deviates from the norm or the average must be or make for sickness, for the norm and the average do not condone deviations and put all who deviate outside. This outsideness—for all one's arrogance—does provide some little distortion or some anguish or some pain. This pain, this incompatibility, is part of sickness. As when one has even a slight fever there is some distortion. Not that it is bad . . . but I think that there must be some sickness, some melancholy, some suffering for any creation. There are almost no happy artists. When I said this, he was furious. He said that I had a distorted view of life, that everyone condoned homosexuality, that everyone knew about it and didn't even think about it. So I saw that this creature had a very immature and idealistic approach to life (at twenty-one one does. I did, and you did, too). I tried to explain, but he didn't at all understand. I wonder whether he doesn't need at least the terror of living in so dreadful a world as the army for at least a little time. I think he needs some experience in a wider life than any he seems to have known. His people know all about him, and his friends and publishers, and they all adore him and never seemed to have suggested to him that the rest of the world won't. To make him the great writer he should be he must not go on this way, or he will remain minor. Perhaps that's all he ever will be or should be. . . . But if Virginia Woolf didn't suffer or Dostoyevsky or even Hart Crane (he's not a good example) . . . When I tried to tell him that if he got into a sex scandal no one save avant-garde publications would publish him, he said that I really had the most morbid approach to life, that he couldn't believe that the *Bazaar* would not publish him. Do you think that this is how the younger people really all think? And is it quite healthy, or does it mark an acceptance, which is a sign of our increasing degeneration?

When I think of the suffering and of how hard I have tried and of the schooling that has gone to make the curious edifice—the facade that is me, I can only look upon this effort (even if I never do the enormous book I want so much to do) as well worth the struggle. It hurt horribly at times, and it will again, but this makes one feel alive. It enmeshes one in the deeps of living—the emotional deeps, not the abstract psychiatric deeps. I get so furious with these silly children playing with this wonderful abstract weapon, this panacea for all ills—even lumbago or rheumatic fever—psychiatry. Why do they never find their own adjustments? This place is the perfect example of how psychiatry can wreck lives, when it is so basically misunderstood and so promiscuously applied.

We must never forget that we are each of us chained eternally and relentlessly to our individual stakes . . . like beasts in the fields. Each of us has these chains. Perhaps we forge the links and so their length is dependent upon us, but we are chained to this stake, which is oneself, and all our living time we stumble or fall or move serenely about our stake. Never are we completely unfettered—never—but when we love or when we read sometimes or listen to music or do any creation or view any beauty.

JUNE 12, 1946 • SARATOGA SPRINGS
**TO RICHARD HUNTER** • NEW YORK CITY

Little Truman has had some hours of anguish, because Howard has sort of been preparing himself for Newton Arvin, who comes today.[42] He doesn't understand that two decades of experience or inexperience separate Howard from him. Also, Howard is educated and has been a teacher and Truman lacks almost all education. He is remarkably astute in contemporary letters—mostly fiction—but of the past he knows almost nothing, and when Howard says something to him using mythological creatures, Truman doesn't even know what Howard is talking about. He's very Southern belle that Truman at times. Howard gave Truman the synopsis for his Parkman, and Truman just didn't understand it at all, although he bluffed quite well. What Truman didn't

42. Although married, Howard Doughty (1904–70), biographer of historian Francis Parkman, had been the sometime lover of Newton Arvin (1900–1963), who was a literary critic and professor of American literature at Smith College. In the two weeks before Arvin's arrival in 1946, Doughty had begun having sex with Capote. When Doughty departed, Capote and Arvin started a romance that continued erratically until the summer of 1948. Arvin is also remembered for his 1960 arrest for possession of homosexual pornography. To escape a prison sentence, he named other collectors including two young Smith College colleagues, later convicted.

understand about that bluffing is that it would have been better to admit that he didn't understand it. . . . So it is all very sad. It would make a good short story, because it's really all about how almost impossible it is for two people of extremely disparate ages to love one another for a long time.

It is now 5:15 p.m. Howard came in and said he was bursting with news because he had been with Mrs. Ames to fetch Newton Arvin from the station. Howard said Mrs. A had asked him whether the homosexuals bothered him. So he said to her that he wasn't so heterosexual himself, but she didn't listen at this point. She said that Truman was such a nice boy, that he was so talented, that he would have such a hard life, and then she said how I was so amusing but she implied that she didn't think I was really very serious. Why should she make judgments about intelligence and one's private life, and why should she discuss any of us in this provincial fashion? Oh, I am so upset I want to go right downstairs [to telephone] and ask you to take me home. But if I went and did that, and you did, I would probably indulge myself in a nervous breakdown . . . because I have tried all these years since knowing you to be careful . . . that is, as careful as possible within the confines of our world . . . and nobody ever discusses this with me who hasn't the privilege . . . and if they do think or talk about it they do it when I'm not there . . . and nobody makes an issue of it . . . and this blundering stupid pig of a small-town bitch . . . It makes me feel so unsure. It makes me feel as if that's all anybody thinks of when I come into a room. This is how Negroes must feel—and outcasts. GOD HOW I HATE THAT WOMAN! I know that this is hysterical, but I had better be hysterical with you than in public. Howard said that he wanted to bash her head in, she makes him feel such a hypocrite. I think I'll lie down and read the Bible, or I'll sit and look at the hills. I have been so careful—more than usual here, because I know how things get distorted. I haven't been unduly attentive to anyone. Am I crazy or is she? Am I so obvious, so transparent after all these years? Has my life been just as insular and sheltered as Truman's? Has all the effort come to nothing? This would be such a failure.

My head aches so, and dinner is almost here, and I can't think how to manage to be gay and amusing. . . . I suppose if one makes a reputation for being amusing and gay no one ever thinks there's anything else. . . . This is no place for me or for any people who have managed to adjust themselves precariously. Being so,[43] being Jewish (and so exotic, flamboyant), being quite uneducated both socially and formally in any sense, it requires so little to shake the facade I've built up, the security I have been amassing. Even Christians in a Christian world are insecure, so how much more must I be. The worlds of anguish I have put behind me, the torments for having been me . . . and now suddenly all that is with me again and it consumes me with sickness. If I did not believe in life, if I did not believe in the you of my living, there would be nothing. But now I

43. "Being so" was then gay slang for being homosexual.

must take up the little rituals of living here. I will wash my face and my hands and my ears (for these are sacred);[44] I will put on a tie and a jacket; I will go downstairs . . . and since I am such a good drawing room actor this evening will pass.

NOTE: Leo left Yaddo in the last week of June. He stopped keeping his journal for six months.

It was probably during the time Leo had been in Saratoga Springs that scenic designer Ben Edwards, once their classmate at the Feagin School, introduced Richard to Howard Rothschild. Recently out of the army, Rothschild was four years older than Richard and, although not one of the famous banking family, wealthy; a dilettante artist who lived on Park Avenue with his mother. What began as a sexual dalliance grew in a few months' time to be passionate and drama-filled. Leo was fully informed and chose to wait it out. For eight months the men were an uneasy trio.

During the winter of 1947, Richard, Leo, and Howard spent about six weeks in Richard's mother's house in Middletown, New York, while the Hunter family wintered in Florida.

JOURNAL • JANUARY 19, 1947 • NEW YORK CITY Howard [Rothschild] is so Jewish, so hypochondriacal, and a good lover. It's the only time he can relax. He's spoiled, frightened of his servants, always worrying, always insisting his life and others' conform to little plans and routines. He's dated by his language and his sentiments, Aryan looking save for his nose, a poor little rich boy. He thinks, or is ready to believe, that nobody really likes him, that everyone is out for what they can get from him. He is the conventional neurotic Jew carried to the extreme perfection and as such becomes fascinating (see De Quincey on perfection). He came and kissed my hands and said we must both help one another, because troublesome times were coming—and how apt.

JANUARY 25, 1947 Laci told me about how upset he was, and how this seemed to him to sum up the changed world in his lifetime, when, last summer, on the train to Canada, going through to the diner car, he suddenly saw a gaunt, pale woman sitting in a day coach (he was in a Pullman). She was dressed in an ancient black woolen gown, very long, and very high under her chin. It was loose in the fashion of 1915 (or 1920?) and belted. She leaned her head on a little black pillow, and she looked very nervous, very hungry. When she saw that he recognized her, she shut her eyes. It was the ex-Empress Zita.[45] He had seen her coronation in Budapest. Hundreds of women had labored a year to embroider her robes in real gold and pearls and diamonds. As he sat eating, she came in very awkwardly, nearsightedly, and sat down trying to hide her nerves and shyness. She sat at a table for four. The steward came up and told

44. Richard had an erotic fascination with men's ears.
45. Zita (1892–1989), last empress of Austria-Hungary, had married Archduke Karl in 1911. They were crowned in 1916 and dethroned in 1918.

her brusquely that she would have to move to a table for two. She obeyed, quite frightened, as though she thought she might even be deposed from this chair. She ordered only a roll and a cup of coffee. It cost 75 cents. She left 75. She did not come in for dinner, but he saw her standing in the heat, in the steaming dirt by the train's side in a station, swiftly eating a thick sandwich from wax paper. She had bought it from the porter. Laci's doctor was her doctor and [her son] Otto's. Fritsch told him that they were absolutely impoverished, that Otto had had ulcers for a year because he ate so frugally and badly from tins, that the two grand duchesses [*sic*, archduchesses] worked incognito as typists in New York offices. In Montreal, Zita got off and was met by a dowdy elderly woman, ravaged. It was her mother, the duchess of [Bourbon-]Parma, who lived in the country in a small poorhouse, not far from Montreal. The little money she has comes from the church.

Today there was a sudden announcement that Grace Moore had been [killed] in a flying accident in Denmark, along with "a prince of the royal Swedish house."[46] Now what is the lesson to be learned from this death? Is it that, again, no person escapes without paying for every single thing, and the price is in careful proportion? A good moment is paid by a bad. A life of fun, pleasure, happiness is paid for by premature death, by the incipient agony that one must suffer when one realizes that one is about to die suddenly in an accident. There is always a moment that becomes all time—a brief and horrible eternity. When [I nearly] drowned[47] and when I had the cab accident, it was this way. This is the astonished heart: How can this happen to me!!! No, No, No! The blackness and then possibly gray blackness—and then possibly the hilarity of living again, of reprieve.

Grace Moore's death (which means little to me, for she was not an artist, just a good-time girl of the arts, meaning music) takes a little from each person's security because she seemed so secure, so chosen. Since she could meet so abrupt and disastrous an end, every person knowing her golden life feels the void closer. It was announced between advertisements, ones for a new bread and a new wine. A few years ago, the announcer said, only the titled and the wealthy could afford good wines. Only a few years ago Grace Moore could not have died in the company of a prince, unless she was unofficially connected or strictly backstairs.

The irritating qualities of the living become marks of individuality, and sometimes ciphers of genius, when those who have inflicted them upon us are dead. That [Alexander] Pope falsified letters is an endearing characteristic, for it shows him to have had vanity, shows him to have been weak beneath the

46. Grace Moore (1898–1947), a soprano who sang at the Metropolitan Opera, also appeared in Broadway revues and in popular films (*One Night of Love*).

47. Leo could not swim. On a visit to Miami early in their relationship, Richard coaxed him into the ocean, inadvertently leading him beyond his depth. Richard had to pull Leo, who fought him all the way, back to shore. Leo believed that Richard had saved his life.

sharp-edged armor of his scorn and invective. That [Samuel] Johnson was filthy in his person is another mark of character. We then prefer our giants to show us marks of weakness and sins of human failings—but in retrospect.

JANUARY 27, 1947 Looking at Léon [Kochnitzky],[48] you would never suspect that Nijinsky had loved him, stroking and kissing his shoulders, saying they were the most beautiful in the world. Or that as a child he had been photographed and his person displayed on chocolate boxes all over Europe. Or that Diaghilev had been jealous of him (Diaghilev with his dictatorships and his tyrannies and his enormous jealousies, tastes, and talents). As [composer] Reynaldo Hahn made love to him one day, Proust had been kept waiting a full fifteen minutes, and finally had gone away, slamming the door angrily. Marguerite Clark, the silent-film star, had loved him. His long love with a Belgian prince was internationally famous.[49] He had been stabbed by a ruffian he'd picked up in Vienna, and Ruth [Yorck] had first met him as he convalesced in a hospital there. Later, she had gone to the opera with him in Paris and had startled everyone by displaying a huge diamond on her left big toe. He had been a cabinet minister under D'Annunzio in Fiume.[50] He had several doctorates—one from Bologna. He had gone through three fortunes of his own and at least a dozen others. He was ingratiating, charming, malicious and, now fifty-four, utterly believes all the lies he heard, especially his own. He has a marvelous way of putting things together, securing conclusions, all erroneous, and disseminating them as the truth. He owed everyone, and people continued to "lend" him money. He was an anti-Semitic Jew, but boasted of his descent from [Rabbi Eliyahu] the Gaon of Vilna. His father had been a converted Catholic. He looked as though he could be a cardinal one day.

In certain circles, a man is déclassé who sleeps with women, but homosexuals are always interested in men who sleep with women, especially if the man is suspected of being himself homosexual. It has come to such a pass that certain men say they sleep with boys just to be socially acceptable, while all the time they are having affairs with women!

How you can know so much about people you do not even know. Howard told Richard about how [scenic designer] Stewart Chaney was in bed. He'd say, "Don't you want it! You know you want it. You know you want this fucking cock shoved up your ass!" Now to know that a man is excited—seeks his

48. The Russian-born Belgian poet, art critic, and journalist Léon Kochnitzky (1892?–1965) introduced Leo to many refugees (including Bravig and Valeska Imbs) and art world figures (such as gallery owner Kirk Askew). To escape the Nazis, Kochnitzky had reportedly disguised himself as a nun.
49. According to Richard Hunter, the affair was with Prince Charles (1903–83), the king's brother.
50. In 1919 the Italian writer Gabriele D'Annunzio declared a revolutionary government in the Adriatic port of Fiume. Kochnitzky served as its foreign minister until December 1920, when the Italian government ousted the rebels.

oblivion—this way is to know him more intimately than most of his best friends. Yet I know him only most casually. When we meet, we do not even greet one another.

"I wonder if it's true that the Jewish race has a greater capacity to love," said Richard. But this capacity is in proportion to the basic insecurity. "This is the only glorious moment of my life for me," said Howard [to Richard]. "There has been nothing before. I can see nothing after. Only this single moment of loving you."

JANUARY 28, 1947  Ela resorts to drugs at the least suspicion that any crisis will be approaching, and since her crises never remain long absent, her drug taking is almost continual. It must be cured, for her to go on at all, at intervals of about three years. These cures are dreadful, but after them she immediately begins to grow fat and full of life, prodigally. Just before, she has become dreadful, her eyes hooded and glittering, her hands like talons. She looks utterly predatory, malignant, evil. She is emaciated, shifting from one dream to another with little rifts between when she perceives what has transpired. Cloud image—and light rays between tall buildings—"Those moments of madness which had the grandeur and vastness of years" (Edith Sitwell on Pope).

Looking at Howard, who says, "I no longer have a home. My only home is where Richard is," it is impossible to try to keep Richard—but when he is drunk he is so pathetic that my heart breaks and I do not think that Howard can cope with him. I do not know where there is room for me when they are together. I feel and become so effaced. No matter how long one has been alone with someone he loves, the absences (no matter how brief) are longer. I must be content with writing. It must be my beloved and my lover. It must be the center of my life. Nothing else is dependable—not lovers, nor friends, nor anything. When I lie here scrawling, I am safer than in the arms of any lover, but when I stop to think, I am more alone than when I turn my face to the wall to sleep. This aloneness pays, perhaps, for being able to write anything, but oh, how quietly desperate the heart becomes, rebelling. The heart is an anarchist. It can always overthrow the intellect. The heart knows what it wants, which is to feel against it the heart of its beloved beating the world away, vanquishing its own aloneness.

FEBRUARY 1, 1947 · MIDDLETOWN, NEW YORK  Cesco [von Mendelssohn] throwing himself on the floor to blackmail Ela, saying can't they say their mother is mentally infirm to get her money, telling people Ela was incestuous with her father. He now blames her for all of his unhappiness, and Ela says he must be committed for half a year at least, not because he needs to be, but because she's frightened of what he might say that will reach the Maestro.

The steady clicking, probably a leaking drain, all through the night sounded like someone in high heels walking up and down the walk. The going-to-the-bathroom woke me up and made me count the number of times "they" probably bedded. The first time I had thought of Howard and Richard as "they."

Howard: "Isn't it curious. I could never love two people at once like Richard does. I could desire two people. I think Richard will always love you." Richard and his running away. He does not realize his obligations. He must hate being home. Howard says the great lack in his life is love. He offers no responsibilities, save the responsibility of loving him.

FEBRUARY 5, 1947 Noël [Coward] on Mary Martin: "The only two grown-up things about her are her ego and her son."

FEBRUARY 7, 1947 Howard always talks about his diseases because he has nothing else to talk about. These and the trivial afflictions (from waiters, other servants, clerks) make up the highlights, along with his paid-for pleasures— concerts, theaters—and of course his amatory desires. This makes him so important to himself, this talk of sickness—imaginary mostly—and so boring to others. "I had an old German maid for years, who taught me how to pack with tissue paper—stuff the sleeves of jackets, between trouser creases." He did it all through the war—even on battlefields.

FEBRUARY 9, 1947 When I first saw Richard, I wasn't impressed. I even thought him ludicrous. I remember how he wanted to be seduced, and wore those sexy nylon pajamas, but I didn't realize it. Finally he kissed me in the park, and I fell deeply. This is all so female—how I tried to get him interested in Billy, or someone, and how he fell for Winnie.[51] Richard was in love with her, and how he used to cry, and how I tried to help him. Ten years later she came back twice to marry him, but she was dull.

Richard says: "I need people to love me so. . . ." Howard: "I have such a sense of being lost—without love it doesn't mean anything." How conversation shifts from these deeps to the trivial. Richard: "Did you put your toast down?"

FEBRUARY 11, 1947 Atavism in people: How Jewish Howard and I become. Yet he never was Orthodox and I do not practice Judaism. Proust compares Jews' essential loneliness and separations to that of the inverts—because both are never sure when they will become the mob's victims. Must study the bravado this engenders. I do not agree with Proust that one loves only an illusory idea. I love Richard, but I know what he is. You must know the bad or weak parts. Then you must love despite these things. Being faithful—what difference does it make? There comes a time when one loves with eyes wide open, and this is the best kind of love—but I do not think I love normally.

51. Billy Price and Winifred Ingalsbee were both female classmates of theirs at the Feagin School.

Howard is more normal in his love. He wants to possess—oblivion in his lover's arms always.

Most people seem to need continual anxiety to nourish their love (which they confuse with sex). But there comes a time when even love suffers a mutation, and this has happened to me with Richard. I no longer am consumed with love for him—although I have no ability to live smoothly the inner life when he is absent—as I am living it now here in this attic room, which I love, for it is so temporarily safe. I know suddenly that probably I am happier over Howard, because this love between them protects me. I do not need to give myself always and so utterly. I can give myself when I am wanted—and more intensely (I do not mean only sex)—and so have these emotionally quiet times in which to lead my own inner life, while they lead their love together, grateful to me. And I am grateful to them.

Richard: "It's amazing the things people that love you say. I was thinking about Howard lying in bed. He said that he wished I could come all day—all over him—because it was like a fountain of me, and that he wished he were a vine to twine all over me." I said that I would rather be roots. Richard: "They're underground." Me: "I like the idea of underground." R: "That's the trouble of being like us. You can't touch the person you love in public." Me: "But that's a good thing." R: "But sometimes, like in the movie last night, I have to." Me: "And you did . . . but touching out of love in public is like talking too much. You dissipate yourself."

FEBRUARY 14, 1947 Richard goes back to reading Proust, Howard to lying on his bosom sleeping. R: God, Leo there's a lot of stuff in here that should have been cut out. (Richard's in the last book, the annoying dull part, which Proust never cut. Occasionally Richard kisses Howard's forehead and murmurs something inaudible.) Richard: What time is it? Oh, just nine. Howard: I want you to scratch the top of my head. No, further over. Yes, thank you. How much longer are you going to read? R: This is such a bore. H: I thought you loved it so. R: I do, but, as Leo said, it hasn't been cut. Your head is too low. H: Yes, open the top of your trousers. R: No, I won't. Someone might come in the door. L: Who's going to come in the door? R: What did Proust die of? TB? L: No—everything. H: I thought asthma. (R strokes H's chest. H lies in his lap.) R: I think [the character] Elstir is a combination of Renoir and Monet. He speaks of Monet here as a separate artist—and Renoir—and he speaks of big nudes, and that's certainly Renoir. L: It's getting warmer and warmer. H: The winter's fairly over. R: Are you sad? My God—this one's got a semierection again. H: (laughing) I'm never without it. (The radio advertises Eichler's Beer. Yes, "Everybody has a good word for Eichler's Beer.") R takes H's thing out: Look at that! H: Go away. L: It's a pretty thing. H: Thank you. Don't they ever play anything else? (Tchaikovsky introduces the John Wanamaker Music Hall.) R: Did you ever hear Rachmaninoff play? H: It was like iron. R: He was so temperamental too. H: No, he wasn't. He just came out and played and got it over with. (Long pause.) H: I like it between my cock and my legs. (Stroking.) R: Why are you covering it all up? (Opens H's fly more.) R: Howard's perspiring around his testicles. I can see these five pages are going to take me a long time to read. Is your brother as nice as you to stroke? H: I never stroked him. R: Is Harold hairy all over? H: Who was it said, "Where he wasn't hairy he was pimply"? Too bad he's not attractive. R: Oh some people think he's attractive. H: I mean I wouldn't want to go to bed with such a hairy person. I'm too hairy for myself. R: I used to hate hair. Now I like it. Howard says he's sure his brother is good in bed, because he loves sex so much. H: Most people love sex, unless they're just pigs about it. R: Howard Rothschild is a sensual pig. I like circumcised cocks. H: You're supposed to have more fun fucking women if you're not circumcised. Before the war I would have come ten minutes ago. I don't want to get back to that. R to H: You look about fifteen now. I think you're going to have tufted eyebrows. (Stroking them.) Your eyes look strained. Are your glasses all right? H: I think Rimsky-Korsakov's very nice, very gaudy, but nice. R: The first music I ever loved . . . I went to my first concert when I was eighteen or nineteen years old. H: The first concerts I went to were [conductor] Walter Damrosch's. I must have been about eight or nine years old. L: I loved them. H: I didn't enjoy them. They were too long and heavy for a child. H: I love to tickle Richard under the armpits. But Richard doesn't like it. R: Yes, I do, but sometimes it tickles too much. H: He really looks like one of the medieval saints on the cathedral of Chartres. It really has a mystical quality. R: How do I look with my eyes closed? H: Wonderful. R: Some people look awful—like corpses.

FEBRUARY 17, 1947  Howard [to Leo]: "Your whole role is wrong. You should always be more dignified and grand—Zeusian—much more august. You've got the inner dignity to do it, and not be the Jewish Restoration comedy figure you try to make yourself out. You shouldn't camp and make rude remarks to be amusing. You don't know when to stop."

For over a week, the three of us have seen no one save one another and the few people who serve us. It is still a little curious to see Howard doing so many things I used to do, behaving so like me. I have lain in Richard's arms so frequently. Perhaps, tonight, I am not so valiant. "What are you writing, Tibis?" asks Richard.[52] "Some notes."

Howard kisses him—triplets of sweet, little, loving kisses, making wet clicking sounds, like snow against windowpanes. Richard looks tenderly upon Howard, holding his face in his hands, while Howard peers at the *Tribune* and

---

52. "Tib" or "Tibis" was an affectionate name between Leo and Richard. Usually it referred to Leo, whom Richard's letters greeted as "Tibi" or "Tibface" or "Tiblabel." For Richard, Leo often used "Reezl," a nickname from childhood begun when a brother dubbed the asthmatic Richard "Wheezer."

Léon's piece, which I wanted to save, but Howard wants it for his Diaghilev collection.

I feel so sick suddenly, as though I can't get out of this room. That's because I never let anyone see me depressed—never—it would be like telling a secret name. You should never show despair, not even to those who love you, perhaps especially not to those who love you. So I have been deceitful for many years now, but why share despair? Nobody can help too much with this. It is the manure which makes the soil rich and the tree to grow more lavishly. (They are both behaving so giddily right now. Howard says: "God, what a bunch of camps we're turning into." Howard always is impersonating someone—maids, foreign characters, types from plays, friends—needing to project himself somehow.) The root of my despair was surely that Richard and Howard seemed so attached in love. I probably felt outside, but now Howard, before going upstairs, has kissed me very sweetly and said some sweet words, so I feel gayer.

FEBRUARY 18, 1947 Howard says I accept this situation because I must have a masochistic pleasure in it. Now everything has this "taint" to it. But how much in me is this?

FEBRUARY 25, 1947 Madame [Henriette] Pascar, says Richard, is very like an old Odette.[53] Her husband, Mr. [Simon] Liberman, was a sweet little man who had been intimate with Lenin and was minister of forests or some such thing. He wrote a good book about it, which had some success (published by the University of Chicago) before he died. His son, Alex, is art director of *Vogue*. He is married to Tatiana du Plessix, hat designer of Saks—rude, big, handsome, blond. She was a comtesse or something.[54]

MARCH 4, 1947 Last night when I went upstairs I found Howard in hysterics and tears with bag packed. He said he couldn't bear it, that he loved Richard so much, that it seemed wrong because of me, that I was so good, so understanding. I felt awful because of my really wicked private thoughts and tried to make him feel better and laugh. It was quite dreadful, but I did. I told him that only profit accrues from his love of Richard and explained this and the personal

53. In Marcel Proust's *Remembrance of Things Past*, Odette is a beautiful courtesan who eventually marries Swann and bears him a daughter. Henriette Pascar (1886–1974) was an occasional chanteuse and actress who had frequent affairs during her marriage to Simon Liberman. She was devoted, however, to their artistic son, Alexander.
54. Tatiana Iacovleva du Plessix (1906–91) was the Russian émigrée widow of Count Bertrand du Plessix (a French aviator killed early in World War II) when she married Alexander Liberman in 1942. Lucien Vogel, one of Liberman's mother's past lovers, had persuaded Condé Nast to hire him as an assistant art director at *Vogue* in 1941. Alex Liberman (1912–99) became art director at the magazine in March 1943, a post he held until becoming editorial director of all Condé Nast publications in 1962.

motives, and he said he loved me and it was easier when he had hated me. And he put [Richard's sister] Nancy's pistachio satin and salmon-pink-lined comforter over him because by this time he was cold, and he looked very sweet and like a decadent prelate. I made jokes about it. It looked like a [cleric's] cope.

9:50 a.m. Just now, Howard came in and said, "Well, did you have a good time last night?" I was embarrassed. "I slept well—" "You know what I mean." "Yes, but you can have a good time going to the theater or eating chocolate or eating anything you shouldn't." "You can have a bad time or a good time making love." "But loving somebody can't be a good time—the language is wrong." The car came, and he went away. I felt as though I had been too harsh. I really didn't wish to debase the great escape—release—I had been swept into. Having a good time made it sound so cheap.

MARCH 7, 1947 Lost my temper. The result of Richard's telling me that Howard had said the evening hadn't been a success. This brought back all those years when Richard always told me when I hadn't been a success, and this hurt when I had tried so hard to please, brought back some of that anguish and insecurity. I still cannot seem to be entirely emotionally reconciled to this arrangement—no matter how I know intellectually I must be for our welfare. I continue to feel upset at times and left out.

We were all in moods tonight. Howard said he would sleep alone and that Richard should sleep with me, but Richard didn't want to, and I felt that this kind of arrangement had nothing to do with love. Now I feel better, because I inadvertently scared Howard by hissing down the stairs when I wanted to drop a surprise love note to Richard. It's full moon—perhaps that's the explanation.

MARCH 1947 · MIDDLETOWN, NEW YORK
TO RUTH YORCK · PARIS?

Ballet Society is the only new thing of any consequence.[55] I went to one evening and it was delightful only because they seem to have a passion to do something. What they did was pleasant but not new. This could be good, although the people who head it make it almost impossible. *Les Enfants du Paradis* [*Children of Paradise*] I saw twice before it was played for the public, so I saw it uncut, and it is probably my favorite movie. Also saw *Le Retour*, which Cartier-Bresson made, and it is magnificent, but it was only shown twice in one evening so most of the people who should have seen it didn't. He photographed me. It is the best I have ever had. Cartier is such a curious creature. . . . Know anything?[56]

If you see a *Vogue* with a picture of little Truman in it, I wrote the article,

55. Ballet Society was founded by George Balanchine and Lincoln Kirstein in July 1946 to perform new works. Two years later it became the New York City Ballet.
56. The French photographer Henri Cartier-Bresson (1908–2004) took several impromptu portraits of Leo during the late forties and early fifties.

but I would not sign my name because *Vogue* bitched up what I wrote.[57] A new book *Under the Volcano* [by Malcolm Lowry] is not uninteresting and, of course, *Tower of Babel* by Elias Canetti, called in England *Auto-da-Fé* and published in Vienna pre-Hitler, is magnificent, but the reviewers don't get it. The great triumph of the season is John Gielgud and Oscar Wilde.[58] Penelope [Dudley Ward] still reigns as the town beauty and when I go to town we go to town, and everyone is envious. People say, "That's Penelope Ward, but who can that be with her?" and they all look quite alarmed. You see, I have temporarily a full beard—very black and big and some white hairs in it. Richard has a reddish beard and looks more goatish.

NOTE: Leo probably met the actress Penelope Dudley Ward (1914–82) in the autumn of 1937, when she performed in the Broadway production of *French Without Tears*, as he was assistant stage manager. They became friends, however, after they were reintroduced at a party in the fall of 1946, during the run of Cecil Beaton's production of *Lady Windermere's Fan*, in which she played Lady Windermere. Offstage, she was pursuing the British film director Carol Reed (best known for *The Third Man*). Ward had asked Beaton to make her the most beautiful woman in New York, because she wanted Reed to hear she was the toast of the town. He would soon divorce the actress Diana Wynyard to marry Penelope. Through that winter and spring, Leo and she spent many evenings in the Plaza Hotel's Oak Room, planning and commiserating. Possessing great looks and gentle manners, Penelope Dudley Ward also had a family history irresistible to Leo: Her mother, Freda Dudley Ward, had been the lover whom the future Edward VIII jilted for Wallis Warfield Simpson. According to Richard, Penelope was second only to Eleonora among Leo's favorite women, but his "Pempie" soon returned to England and ceased acting. Only one letter from Leo to her survives (written April 6, 1968), but the first call and last good-bye on any trip he made to London was always to her.

JOURNAL · MARCH 11, 1947 · NEW YORK CITY Yesterday morning, Truman told me so many dreadful things about everybody. It's wonderful how Truman acquires bits of information and then passes them off as his own.

Ela told me that she'd had a to-do with Noël during the Maestro's concert two weeks ago. She says she's always had a hankering for this, for years. She did it gaily, making him think he'd done it. She thinks it's the first time with a woman for him. Interesting how he's always been drifting to this quasi-*Vortex* relationship (she being both mother and his theme).[59] How she drifts to "the boat" [homosexual men]. How could she get anyone from the boat? She wants to know. [Photographer] Horst proposed to her.[60]

---

57. Leo is referring to the February 1947 "Before Bandwagons" column, which ran unsigned. Others mentioned in the piece were Robert Davison, Paul Bowles, Valerie Bettis, and Riche Pereira.
58. Gielgud was starring in *The Importance of Being Earnest*, which played concurrently in New York with Cecil Beaton's production of *Lady Windermere's Fan*.
59. *The Vortex*, a play written by Coward in 1923, portrays a son attracted to his mother. His jealousy of her affairs leads him to drug use.
60. According to Richard, Leo also once proposed to Eleonora, but she took it as a joke.

MARCH 21, 1947 · MIDDLETOWN   Saw Ela this morning, looking voluptuously beautiful, but her eyes made her grotesquely ridiculous at times. Laci was there. She is going off with Kosleck. This is the fitting evolution, to mother, especially someone [Kosleck] as mad as Cesco and as queer. She owes everyone, but has bought a car. She looks like vampires are supposed to look after feasting on rich red blood the night through. There is something wicked in her voluptuousness, but she is beautiful and stately. Perhaps some new drug, definitely some evolution in her madness. She's almost never still, rushing about to and fro. I am here in Middletown [at the Hunters'] again. It is heaven, but only for three or four days.

MARCH 22, 1947   Ela's life is motivated, according to her, by Maestro's making fun of her bed habits in front of people in his house. He is eighty this month.[61] She has resorted to queer boys—"the boat"—but not because of this reason. She goes on much about being out of "prison," about how her friends don't want her to be so happy because they love her to be sad, tortured like themselves. She seems to misunderstand many things, leaping to conclusions like the old and deaf do.

MARCH 23, 1947   What does it do to hear another's orgasm? Today, for a moment, it quite undid me. I lay here gasping, almost in tears, but only for a moment. I wonder if Richard realizes that he's been living with Howard, and not really with me. This inability to go away must really be linked with the Jew's inability to leave unless forced to. We are so afraid, we Jews, having been terrified for thousands of years, first by our God and then by his people.

APRIL 2, 1947   It has been so long now that anyone has made love to me. Yesterday Richard said he didn't know whether if I shaved off my beard and became thinner it would help, but I will diet, and at the beginning of summer shave off my beard.[62] If Touche and Peter [Lindamood, antique dealer] hadn't called and made the time pass, I would have been in a more wretched state. It is raining and the light is all skimmed milk, white-blue like milk on farina.

So the pendulum. I feel pleasant. I am drinking tea. Richard came this afternoon and lay beside me, and loved me, and fell asleep on my shoulder. Even the painfulness attendant upon a portion of the body having fallen asleep was joy—unadulterated—with no bitterness. Joy like lovely dreams—and even better—but Howard is gray with depression and sits playing the piano—quite well.

61. "A friend, subletting Ela's flat over the carpenter shop, demurred at the two flights of stairs. The owner of the building said, 'What's wrong with you? Toscanini climbs 'em twice a week.' " *Journal, February 22, 1971.*
62. Leo had become heavy and didn't appeal physically to Richard. When he shaved that summer, everyone agreed that Leo looked much more benevolent with the beard. He wore it the rest of his life.

Then by seven Howard had packed his things (after escarole-chopping lessons), had said he couldn't stand it. Richard was bored with this new outburst. Howard said he was insanely jealous. I sat drinking my tea and said nothing. And in half an hour it was over. We had our dinner. I made jokes. Howard and I played Pounce. Now I am in bed with the beginnings of a cold. Howard said it was a judgment.

APRIL 6, 1947 · NEW YORK CITY · 6:30 A.M.   In bed at last. I stayed the whole night at Peter Lindamood's party. It was pleasant this staying awake the whole night and talking. It had been a large party, and Iris Barry got very drunk, talking avidly about her time with Yeats, and how Ezra Pound had made [bedded] her (1919–23), and how they would have nothing to do with her when she had a baby. They didn't approve.[63] The colored lamp globes at Peter's in the dawn, so lucidly beautiful, holding all the gay night—green, red, pink.

When [costume designer] Connie De Pinna had been asked by a census taker on a London street what had she done the first two years of the war, she had answered: "Stitching paillettes on my silk stockings." This sums up a world that should now be dead.[64]

**PETER LINDAMOOD**   *Peter and his parties on East Tenth Street: Klaus Mann, Moravia, Italian Surrealists, Grace Stone, Stravinsky, Edith Piaf . . . and his great friend, Oliver Smith . . . and the Bowles[es]. "Let's get 'them' or 'her' or 'him,' " Peter would say, and the parties went on all night long, among the Victorian fripperies, with Touche singing fake lieder. We would eat fried chicken and stumble out into freezing dawns. The sexual underskein of his parties—all the worlds were entertained at Peter's. By the time I was in 1453 [Lexington, in 1948], Peter had come up into East Fifty-eighth Street and his party world was finished. He held a special quality and was so much a center. Little, infinitely curious, wonderfully observant, hilarious, and needle-sharp in his accurate assessments, Peter was a fantastic, and he had the great gift of making life fantastic for others. Peter is the postwar world.* (1984)

JOURNAL · APRIL 19, 1947   Richard is very contrite, but there is almost nothing he can do. He is sexually so attracted to Howard that he has become 99 percent impotent in all other circumstances. But when he was very drunk and spoke with that profound lucidity which drink seems to bring to otherwise incoherent creatures, he said he loved me beyond anything in the world. I believe him, and this knowledge helps, but only if we lived so as I wouldn't

63. The father of Iris Barry's child was the painter Wyndham Lewis. Barry (1895–1969) was the first chief of the Department of Film at the Museum of Modern Art.
64. "First glimpsed Connie as a little girl, when I sat on the polished wooden countertop in her father's store, where my uncle Irving was a 'coming' young clerk. Then as John Huston's mistress." *Journal, July 21, 1972.*

have to lurk in the street until Howard goes home. Howard was so angry with me that he asked me if I didn't have any pride—but this was tactless. And so it has been—save for the three days when Howard was in the hospital, and those were very pleasant.

APRIL 21, 1947   Richard says that he will go away quite alone, and that will solve everything, but what he doesn't realize is that it will solve nothing for me, and for a long time it will be a punishment—while he escapes—although he will also be miserable. Howard, having plenty of money, will probably follow him. Richard tells me that Howard is even now making plans to go to the West Indies next autumn, because Richard said he wanted to go there.

Ela went to the Maestro on Thursday and cried the whole night after it. He gave her back the Millet [painting]. She has given him $70,000 worth of paintings up to last spring. Now she's gone to tour with Lizl [Elisabeth Bergner].[65] Koz [Kosleck] is living in her apartment.

MAY 12, 1947   Sunday was warm spring and that commercial invention of the flower merchants—Mother's Day. Momma said wasn't I coming out, even if I didn't bring her something. And I went, taking her the little box of two gold shells, a pillbox, which Fritz [Mosell] and Hellmut [Roder] gave me. It was somewhat gaudy, but I liked it very much. I wrote on a bit of paper, "love— Label xxx" and put it in.[66] And when I gave it to her, she didn't look at it. She was sitting in the yard with relatives, but later in the kitchen, she did. And she said: "What's this? What do you do with it?" very nastily and seemed very unhappy to have it and was lousy about it and hid it away and never even said thank you and the bit of paper fell on the floor and that was that. She is truly a stupid, selfish, nasty woman, and sometimes I dislike her utterly. She also told me that I had better make sure I make some money to pay for her operation.

NOTE:   Richard, Howard, and Leo rented a house on Nantucket Island for the summer, this time in the village of Quidnet. Leo and Howard usually rotated their visits; Richard more often stayed with Howard.

JUNE 11, 1947 • NEW YORK CITY
**TO RICHARD HUNTER** • QUIDNET, MASSACHUSETTS

I miss you very much, but I do not miss the difficulties of these past months. I am very lonely, and it is like being cut off from breathing fully to be without you—like seeing only out of one eye—but I would be even more adrift if these

---

65. Elisabeth Bergner (1900–1986), great star of theater and film in Germany and Austria, was a friend of Eleonora von Mendelssohn. Her 1935 stage and film performance in *Escape Me Never* launched her American career in the thirties and forties.
66. "Label" was Leo's familial nickname. He preferred it to "Leo," which he thought sounded like a cat's cry.

last months had been happy ones—or if I knew that I should never see you again—this is not a complaint, just fact—I love you very much—but I am not essentially sick, so I don't wish to go through life like the last months. Also, I don't intend to live a life without you if I can manage it. Howard has moments, sometimes days of sweetness, but for me these never make up for his selfish-nesses. I can get along with him—and I will—but somehow the last weeks when he was here were too much, and I do not intend to repeat them. Do not be alarmed by this. He will never realize how I feel, and anyway I won't have time or energy for much emotion this summer. The kind of emotion he seems to need isn't my kind. I think you, too, must feel somewhat relieved to have only one of us about—the strain on all of us is considerably less. I intend no strain (if possible) this summer, so don't worry your hatless head about it.

JULY 14, 1947 • QUIDNET, MASSACHUSETTS
**TO RICHARD HUNTER** • PORT SEVERN, CANADA

All the boys came and they take very good care of this house and of me and it is very cheerful here and I do my work and the house is filled with enormous bunches of wonderful red roses. Newton [Arvin] and Truman came over and stayed an hour. [Christopher] Isherwood arrived yesterday and Newton is in a state. These boys are tarragons [*sic*] about work. They all spurn me if I dally, and they all lecture me about eating too much, so I am thinning. I wrote my *Vogue* (staying up a whole day and a whole night) and it is very long but I think not bad. Today I am finishing my thing for Ruth Stephan. It's called "Notes for an Historical Novel." I do hope she likes it. It's $250, and that would be lovely to have.[67]

**JOURNAL** • JULY 24, 1947 • QUIDNET, MASSACHUSETTS • 6:00 A.M. I am sitting out on the porch overlooking the sea and the sunrise, which is splendid, with great brushes of cloud overhead directly, then thick darker clottish streaks and the sun, well above the middle horizon, diffused and shy. Blackface gulls everywhere, and our single post on the edge of our cliff, lonely with the loneli-ness of single objects in a vista. Rays of light as in religious or "spiritual" paint-ings and movies, radiating through the clouds on the water. Where it meets the sun's rays, an island, all rosy and quite palpable. The sun is gradually drawn upward, behind the cloud streaks. Now its path on the water is dull beaten pewter, and the whole vista has become watery like those in Turner watercol-ors. Two black crows very silent. Swiftly, leisurely, suddenly two of our house swallows, like acrobats opening a vaudeville. There is no wind this morning, just the faintest stirring in the grasses. The Queen Anne's lace nodding gently like very aged ladies in heavy Nottingham lace caps. I love sitting here this way,

---

67. Poet and art patron Ruth Stephan (1910–74) published a quarterly of art and literature called *The Tiger's Eye* from 1947 to 1949. Leo's work never appeared in it, although pieces by many writers he sent to her did.

quite alone, and this would content me, this life, if I had some servant within to care for things, and some money, so as not to worry.

JULY 29, 1947 I just woke up, but not unpleasantly. Many insects are butting and fluttering and sizzing against the window screens. Yesterday, R came in while I was trying to dress, and suddenly I had some kind of crumbling and went into the closet and clung to the clothes and wept a good deal. I hated that, and tried not to weep, but it did me great good. Also, R seemed to see, for the first time—for a time—how it was. But I thought I was going out of my head yesterday, and sometimes I was. Lying here now I feel better again, as after a long illness. If only this feeling will last. When I was a small boy I hid in closets and cried—so reassuring, so wombish—but I won't anymore. I must not add anything more to R's burdens. He is beginning to work, and he must go on.

AUGUST 1, 1947 • QUIDNET, MASSACHUSETTS
**TO RUTH YORCK • PARIS**

All the boys came to stay with me for two weeks, while Honey and his Rothschild went away.[68] It was heaven and gay here. I forgot to be sad, and I had fun, and they took care of me, and we laughed twenty-four hours and more a day. We mourned for you and said constantly how you would love it here, with the sea with this house's own private beach and great moors and winds and sea-island skies.

But now Honey and Mr. Rothschild are here again, and he is bored with Mr. Rothschild's scenes and complaints. Mr. R has lots of money and is a drip, is loathed by everyone (even unsolicited by me), and is generally bad news. He is always telling about how this year his income is better than last year, but how things (to eat, etc., etc.) are not as good anymore. Mr. Honey poses for him and cooks for him. So he has gained little in this venture, save it has made him grow up a little bit. There's much more about Mr. R, but all of it the same boring ilk. He was a mistake on Mr. Honey's part, but it is disagreeable to have people ask me how I feel about it, and others acting as though a royal marriage that was a love-match had had a bad finale.

Lionel Trilling's first novel, *The Middle of the Journey*, is coming out. It is superb, really, a novel of the American intellectual during the thirties, beautifully and simply written, but which opens the skull and shows what ticks so punctiliously and with such sure, smooth craft. Truman's book, *Other Voices, Other Rooms*, is coming in January. This one reads as though the child of Carson [McCullers] and Katherine Anne Porter and Eudora Welty and a few drops of Faulkner's sperm (I am in *Moby-Dick* land, so I think of sperm) had precociously done it. And in a sense he has—horror, horror, horror artfully pruned. The prose is what we used to say about Gypsy Rose Lee: She keeps her

68. Ruth Yorck called Richard "Mister Honey."

garden prettily weeded. That's how Truman and all those girls keep their prose. He has a house about five miles away from here—with Newton Arvin first, and now with Mary Lou Aswell. He is writing the last words of the novel there.

My deaf cousin [Lew Goldwasser] suddenly appeared—in black-satin drawers and a cerise-and-emerald-green shirt. He is a raving queen, and with him came a little boy also of the same persuasion. Because they cannot hear, they never realized that some people could understand what they were saying. So all Nantucket trailed them up and down Main Street and was horrified and delighted to hear them shrieking at men that they would want to go home with them.

This is a Nantucket mosaic—make of it what you will. . . . Christopher Isherwood came for a week, part here and part with Truman. I found him quite delightful, with strange eyes and a delight in malice and in hurting himself.

I have written a wonderful article. I know it's wonderful because no one will publish it. Title: "A Marriage Has Been Arranged."

JOURNAL · AUGUST 18, 1947   Howard is packing furiously this afternoon to leave—his toilet paper and all—already having called up his mother. This morning he spent with a boy he picked up the other day. Howard hissed at me: "You've won, just as I told you!" And he said to Richard, "So the beautiful dream has ended."

NOTE: Within a few days, all three men were in New York City. Richard and Leo then went back to Quidnet. After Leo departed Nantucket, Howard returned to spend the last part of that season with Richard.

JOURNAL · AUGUST 29, 1947 · 6:50 A.M.   Richard says, "It will be a good day. Well, I'm gonna try to sleep some more," wraps himself in his sheets and sinks, save for an ear tip and a tuft of hair, from sight. Now his breath is the regular, emphatic breath of sleep—and far-off crows, shrill and distant, sound like asthmatic breathing. The sun is valiant in repeated efforts to find a crevice in the clouds. Last night he was drunk and rambling on about sex, said he was calmer these days, because it had been a week since he had had any, and it was better for his work, and that he had done no work when he was here with Howard, because for those three weeks they had been in bed two and three times a day—almost constantly, he said. I was enraged. But in the dark, pride (which can be a blessing) balmed the rage. This then was another manifestation of R's candor, which is somewhat insensitive. But I would rather know all the truth and be strengthened by it. It has also made me realize that I must no longer look for this from R. With me he is as psychologically impotent as Edwin Denby is with all men save toughs in dark places.[69] I must live on the remem-

---

69. Edwin Denby (1903–83) was a poet and influential dance critic.

brance of it now as a diabetic lives on memories of past feasts. Yesterday I thought it is better, perhaps, to have dreams than ever the realization of them—to dream but not to dream true.

SEPTEMBER 21, 1947 If only I could meet my *House & Garden* deadline here I would stay.[70] Staying is really cowardice. I am so unwilling to go where I shall inevitably be disheveled by New York, by the competition there. Here, with not much money, I could go along—reading, writing, conjecturing. There is no repose in cities. To make repose requires all our energies and then what remains in us for joy in the repose? Blossoms flowering in hothouses are frequently even more fantastically beautiful than those that grow gradually and naturally. But hothouse beauty is artificial and, while I am interested in it and it brings me pleasure, I have never had lasting sustenance from it.

OCTOBER 1, 1947 · NEW YORK CITY I get hungry just to talk to Richard. Nobody has his place. But I will not call [Nantucket], because that would only upset us all, and there is nothing in that. I will sit talking to myself—and soon, soon, I will be writing that piece and that will occupy me quite fully. But how cruel and how thoughtless for Richard to say that I have done nothing to hold him. It is, however, apparent to me that some of the actions I thought of as helpful were merely selfish. I must not interfere. It is when he is faced with both of us that he really suffers, and I must not complicate his life anymore. Whenever he is with me, I must be gay and bright and careful—and perhaps one day he will be either here or there. I know that I must remain here in this city, because if I left I would be fearfully insecure, and here people love me— lots of people.

OCTOBER 17, 1947 The heart could not restrain itself. It spilled over. I make scenes—little niggardly stupid scenes. I do not seem to be able to avoid making them. I know that I must not do this. I do it. All the time I am doing it, I try to undo it, but I continue in my perversity—inevitably saying things I have never intended to say. I know that it would be better if I lived alone or left this city. Then both of us would be helped. This situation is intolerable. I must alleviate it somehow. This morning I will ring up Norman Cousins [editor of *The Saturday Review of Literature*]. Perhaps he will want me to represent them in London. The danger there is of my writing badly because I am such a chameleon.

OCTOBER 20, 1947 Idea: The difference between the world presented by *Bazaar*, *Vogue*, etc., in its pages (and in the outer persons of its editors and personnel) and that which really goes on in it—the sordid, competitive, cutthroat

---

70. Leo was writing "Fresh Paint," a feature article about recent paintings by a dozen contemporary artists. It would run in the magazine's December 1947 issue.

world—the breaking of hearts and spirit—the really Fascist setup. A microcosm of the great U.S.A. world?

OCTOBER 29, 1947 "I have a sweetheart, but I don't have any beaux." Little T.

**LITTLE T AND THE PROF** *We are sitting in the all-night cafeteria on the west side of Madison Avenue, between Eighty-fifth and Eighty-sixth Streets. The time? That sere autumn of 1947, those cliff-hanger months before* Other Voices, Other Rooms *was published, our long autumn of cafeteria nights. A life I had had for some years was breaking up, and Little T, who listened patiently to my plaints, was, he said, in love with the Prof up in Northampton. So we sat in the vacant, skim-milk, nullificator light, facing one another over a gouged, splotched tabletop, and I got through quite a few soggy grapefruits, and T sipped tepid coffee from chipped cups, and we talked the nights away.*

*I think that Truman was less physically enamored of Newton than he was over-whelmed by his prodigious intellectuality, his sensitivity to all things aesthetic, and his position in academe. "What do you do up there all of that time?" I asked one very early morning when Truman had been back on campus for a couple of weeks. He hunched back in this chair, gave me his tortoise grin, crunched himself into his corncob-pipe-smoking little-old-man self: "Weeelllll . . . I sit in this little rocking chair, which I love, and I drink hot chocolate, and he reads to me—every day,* The Odyssey *or* The Iliad *in Greek, the original Greek. And I don't under-stand a word, but I love it. . . . I love the sound of it. Then he plays records for me . . . beautiful. Do you know the more recent quartets of Beethoven?" "More recent than what?" "Oh you!" he yelped. "I'll never tell you anything again!"* (*VOGUE,* SEPTEMBER 1987)

JOURNAL · NOVEMBER 4, 1947 Richard is going through the books and removing those that are his. These, he tells me, are to be put away into a trunk. Most of them, or many of them, are books that I gave to him. But it is the con-crete action—the first visible, on-the-surface action of parting, of separating. He needs to take his books away, to hide them, to separate them from mine. This is another step to his independence. "Isn't this one mine?" "Which?" "*The Arab Island* by Freya Stark?" "Yes, I gave it to you." The book slams to the floor. [Richard:] "You have [collected] many stones." "Yes, I have to throw some out." "You're silly. You shouldn't try to change your life. You like to live this way. If I liked to live this way, I would. . . . Isn't this mine? . . . Now one of these *Caesar and Christs* is yours. . . ." And the books that are his are flung down—flat, slam on the floor. "There are none in here," opening the glassed-in bookcase, sniffling because the dust gets into his nose. . . . "I should think you'd keep some of your better books in here. . . ." I don't think. I find it diffi-cult now to distinguish between tactlessness and subconscious vengeance. The dust blowing away continues—off the Phaidon *Botticelli* and three volumes of the Fogg [Art Museum] drawings. These I love very much. I gave them to Richard because I wanted them so much myself. And the Hogarth I bought in London. "You haven't written that in a long time. . . ." "What?" "This book is Richard Ford Hunter's to be his very own." This is upsetting. I wish he had done it while I wasn't here—but perhaps it strengthens me.

NOVEMBER 11, 1947  "Such a pity. I have so many sailors, but only one Tchaikovsky." Czar Alexander III, when he heard about the composer's death, which, according to Léon [Kochnitzky], Pavlik [Tchelitchew][71] was told by Diaghilev. The police told the czar. It seems that Tchaikovsky was so large, he tore a sailor, who had to be treated and died. Tchaikovsky, out of conscience, committed suicide. This was at the height of the cholera, so it was arranged to seem as a death from that plague, not the other.

I sit at my desk writing, because this is the only solitude left to me. I am like Nicole in *Tender Is the Night*. This notebook is in my bathroom, but even it has been invaded, and that is hard to forget. Nobody should be on exhibition all the time. No, I cannot even communicate here. I must go inside and try to plunge into darkness. If I lie down, he [Richard] will come in. I don't want it. I do want it. Soon I must go out.

NOVEMBER 23, 1947  "I prefer the baths," said Edgar Kaufmann [MoMA design curator]. "Nobody there knows I have any money."

NOVEMBER 25, 1947  Richard went last night. Today I am ill with a trying-to-be cold, but resting here in bed is pleasant, and I have my melted-sherbet-pink bathrobe to comfort me.

"I saw the most beautiful dancing," I told him. "Alicia Alonso [with Ballet Theatre] . . . footwork as precisely beautiful as hieroglyphs upon ancient tombs," I told him—making him a gift of all the loveliness I had that week seen, all the beauty I had known these past few days of separation. "Yes," he said, not looking at me, not by any little gesture of hand or face assuring me that he had received my offering. "Yes . . . but . . ."

NOVEMBER 30, 1947  Pearl [Kazin] is so bright and feminist and desperate to remove the yoke of Alfred, she occupies herself with queer boys, where she can feel dominant. This is a typical American female character.[72]

The D.C. Club: An army major came on Thanksgiving and said he wanted

71. Pavel "Pavlik" Tchelitchew (1898–1957), a Russian-born set designer, painter, and draftsman, was the lover of editor Charles Henri Ford (1908–2002). Tchelitchew's 1940–42 painting *Cache-cache (Hide-and-Seek)* had enormous influence on Gray Foy's work.
72. Editor and book reviewer Pearl Kazin (b. 1922) and Leo were friends in the forties, when she worked at *Harper's Bazaar*. He called her "Cultured Pearl." Her brother Alfred Kazin (1915–98) was a literary critic and memoirist.

to be beaten, so the head of the D.C. got two sadists, and after Thanksgiving dinner all three beat him with whips. He loved it, and yesterday the major called the D.C. head and said it was so wonderful that he now couldn't even walk.

DECEMBER 1, 1947 When I hear a piano playing old, gay, sad tunes, then my stomach turns over and I ache. These fourteen years [of knowing Richard] made me rich, but I have paid for them. When Hedda [Sterne] asked me what I was thinking when I looked at my portrait [painted by her], I could not tell her, because I was thinking: "Richard gave me my ears. He made me beautiful."

DECEMBER 9, 1947 The Tamayo party[73]—the kind all out-of-town readers of fashion slicks think New Yorkers give and go to all day and all night: a duplex with a huge triplex window—a few pieces of almost peasanty furniture—modern, of course, the painted primitive innocence of the Mexican bibelots—the cows, the bulls, the artwork, the one or two Tamayos, the huge pewter-silver lamp rearing two stories on a standard as thick as an exotic stalk, (it is a symbol of terror—it swayed), the tortillas and the very elegant cocktail food (cress—memories of England). Some eating because they would have nothing else to eat. Olga [Tamayo] with her ex-sanitarium face. Rufino with his Mexican peasant elegance and his libidinous charm. The eager women. [Silents star] Dagmar Godowsky, with her self-satisfied self-love but how-delightfully-repulsive-I-am wit.

NOTE: Hoping to sort out his feelings, Richard went away to paint—first to his family's house in Miami, then to Cuba and Haiti. After a few months, Howard joined him. Richard and Howard then remained a couple (frequently apart for months at a stretch) until Howard's death in 1989.

Richard's family owned property in Buffalo, New York, which provided him with a small income (about $110 per month during his years with Leo). That check, plus a few investments, allowed him to be a dilatory painter and a continual traveler.

Through the years, Richard and Leo remained close—although Richard never set anchor in New York for long. Howard and Leo's relations, however, were always strained and sometimes icy. Howard often had a querulous and disapproving air that rankled Leo. He may have envied Leo's easy social manner and the life and friends it brought. According to Richard, the difficulty was Howard's great insecurity: "He was easily hurt and just so afraid that he'd be left alone."

DECEMBER 22, 1947 • NEW YORK CITY

**TO RICHARD HUNTER** • MIAMI

Change is good—having people on Sunday nights shows me that. So many new and interesting people—and many people we've known for a long time—

73. The Mexican painter and sculptor Rufino Tamayo (1899–1991) and his wife Olga, a pianist, lived in New York from 1936 to 1950.

and the new and the old quite happy with one another—and all offering and reaching out to one another. The New York growing up now has a chance again—a real chance. All the young people who come, especially the girls, make me feel very optimistic again for the future—and having them here permits us to have a hand in the changing world—and that's very good. We must not live too much with death and dying. Nobody, not even the very strong, can resist the gravity that death and dying exert. They pull from below and wear us down and it is like an undertow. We are gone before we even realized that we were. I do not think New York City has changed for the worse. I think it is changing to something quite wonderful—and I want to be in it—where I can really help.

**PARTIES** *In the forties, fifties, way into the sixties, so many of us saw one another weekly in one another's houses. We did not have, in the sense of an earlier time, "days," but we did have definite places where we knew we would meet: Along Fifty-seventh Street, from Park to Fifth, on Tuesdays late in the afternoon, for vernissage day; at the Askews on Sunday afternoons; at Dorothy Norman's where under the guise of parties she held "meetings" (political thinkers, Nehru, the Pandits, [watercolorist] John Marin); at Grace Zaring Stone's (that was at lunch in the corner of the Plaza Hotel's Oak Room on Sundays); at the Van Vechtens', where under the silver-papered ceiling of their drawing room there was a constant to-and-froing of great theater, ballet, literary, and motion picture stars (everyone from Nance O'Neill to the Lunts and Lenore Ulric, from Harlem to Truman and Gore); at the Sonnenbergs, in their ever-expanding treasure-crammed house on Gramercy Park, where the illumination from the silver and brass and the mix of personalities was at its most intense; at the John Gunthers, where John inevitably introduced you as somebody even more important than you were (here was always a chance of Garbo); and at our house—open on Sunday evenings and for random huge parties for all sorts of special reasons.*[74] (1993)

DECEMBER 29, 1947 • NEW YORK CITY
**TO RICHARD HUNTER • MIAMI**

Monday morning four a.m. and after setting some of the house to rights, here I am quite solitary—in your bed—thinking, as usual, of you. People stayed a lit-

---

74. R. Kirk Askew, Jr. (1903–74), owner of Durlacher Brothers, who showed neo-Romantic and Surrealist artists (selling Old Master drawings to pay the bills), and his wife Constance (1895–1984) were known for their afternoon cocktail parties. They gathered many literary and musical leaders in the thirties and forties, plus a few of Askew's painters. The socialite Grace Zaring Stone (1891–1991) also wrote novels under the pseudonym Ethel Vance. Benjamin Sonnenberg (1901–78) was a prominent publicist and philanthropist. John Gunther (1901–70), the author of best-selling sociopolitical studies (*Inside U.S.A.*), married Jane Perry Vandercook (b. 1916). Leo describes the Askews, Normans, and Van Vechtens in the journals that follow.

tle later tonight because it is a holiday. Droves came, and it was the most successful yet. You would have enjoyed it very much. And now here I am quite
here I am, as Gertrude Stein probably once said. I wore my beautiful new
jacket, which Edita and Ira [Morris] gave me. It's deep maroon-wine-
burgundy—velvet with black satin lapels. Everybody is so delighted with your
postcards. I am stealing as many as I can, because I want them. Do not worry
about me. If anything happened you would know, and nothing will. I will be
here in this place when you come up these stairs—or I'll know the reason why!

DECEMBER 30[75]

Eleonora has arrived! She says she will stay in New York if somebody gives her
a job—any kind of job—but she looks awful, and she really hates Hollywood.
She loves Kosleck, but really not enough or in any ways to comfort her. She is
the same—in spirit. She came back because the Maestro asked her. She says
she has no money, but there is still a million owed her by Holland, and she can
get it if she can prove that her mother wasn't a Fascist. I hope she does.[76] She
says she has [not] taken anything (you know) at any time in Hollywood. I suspect she has—but it is heavenly to have her in the same city.

JANUARY 2, 1948 • NEW YORK CITY

**TO RICHARD HUNTER • HAVANA**

When I receive a letter as happy as the one that has just arrived from Cuba, I
am so very pleased. I must say, I am very curious about your brothel activities
and I think, which is even more curious, that any activities therein are probably good for you—but remember that syphilis is intensely rampant in the
Indies.

JANUARY 5, 1948 • NEW YORK CITY

**TO RICHARD HUNTER • HAVANA**

It is about 3:30 a.m., for I have been carrying glasses in and here we are again,
you and I, but I decided to sit at my desk to talk with you. This *soir* was even
huger and successfuller, it seems, than any heretofore. Someone said 150 people came, but it seemed like more. Everyone you know—and loads of their
friends. I never give them more than four gallons (about $9) and the cheese
costs about $1 or $2. So this is inexpensive—and fun to them—all sorts of gay
and attractive people.[77]

---

75. A peculiarity of Leo's letters to Richard is their frequent continuation over days, even
weeks, while Leo awaited a mailing address for his wandering friend.
76. Leo doesn't elaborate. There may have been Mendelssohn money in Holland, but
Eleonora's mother, Giulietta Gordigionia, had reportedly been an early supporter of
Mussolini.
77. By "gay people" Leo meant carefree and lively ones. He later disliked the use of the word
"gay" to mean homosexual.

**TO RICHARD HUNTER** • HAVANA

I went to Dorothea [Tanning]'s opening. Her painting is better, but what she paints seems so mannered, so trivial, and somewhat dated. I liked two of them, one of which I would like to own, it being two mermaids (you can tell by their tails) all dressed in crimson 1880ish little girl coats, bonnets, muffs, and faces—sort of going calling in a snowy winter landscape—quite delightful.

I went to visit Peter [Lindamood], because I didn't feel like coming home. There were several marchese and marquises there, and the painter Mangini. I fell fast asleep for about ten minutes. Now I feel wide awake. I guess not eating, not having any sex, not looking at one's beloved—and only being half here—makes me fall asleep in company and be wide awake this moment talking to you.

I always sound so busy; you must wonder when I have time to be lonely. I am always lonely—when I wake, when I sleep—but this is only a temporary thing, for one day the door will open and there will be a Tibis. I sort of feel like those old-fashioned heroines who lived all their lives in one place, never changing a thing, because they eternally awaited their heroes who had gone off, and of course never returned. Please do not permit me to join their ranks. I would like to live some other place one day.

**JOURNAL** • JANUARY 9, 1948  Truman went to address the [publisher's] salesmen. They squabbled over what he should wear. They treat Truman like a thing rather than a person: The exterior looks like an act and the interior isn't.

**TO RICHARD HUNTER** • HAVANA

I must go out now, and just as well—it's cold here, and I have to find some money. I've asked Ruth Stephan for the few dollars she still owes me. I need some desperately. Oh me—it's my own fault. If I hadn't been such a pig all those years, I would never have become so huge, and I would never have needed to diet, and I would never have impaired my enormous vitality, and I never would have not had enough strength to will myself to work. Money never seems to materialize as I see it. But it was fun to spend it as I did—and it will be fun again.

**JOURNAL** • JANUARY 12, 1948  Aunt Pauline in her great grief—when I was holding her—realizing that her hat was disarranged, even while she wept, "Do you know what happened to my Charlie?"[78] arranged her hat very precisely, almost coquettishly. This was not a cynical gesture, only a reflex one. When people—no matter how old—are being comforted, they instantly assume the pliability and trustingness of children. Their bodies become childlike.

78. Her husband, Leo's uncle Charles Goldwasser, had died suddenly the previous day.

JANUARY 12, 1948 • NEW YORK CITY
TO RICHARD HUNTER • PORT-AU-PRINCE, HAITI

Lots of people had been reading Truman's little piece about me in *Vogue* and saying how lovely but wasn't the last paragraph horrifying, and even if it were true why did he have to print it. It's the one where he says that I can be easily destroyed if one day somebody shows me that all the people who seem to love me really don't—and that I'm like a child playing in a playground and believing that the audiences love me but there is really no audience at all. I guess that's upsetting. And I guess I really became quite fed up with his little-girl act during his predeparture days—especially with his complete inability to take any criticism.[79]

I went to a party with Phoebe [Pierce of *Bazaar*] for a girl going to England (her name is Joan au Cour—it really is), and there were all the Bizarres. Pearl [Kazin] spoke only Yiddish—so I saw she was drunk. Then she played "Für Elise" and she fell on her stomach—so everybody saw she was drunk. I discovered that everyone had been upset by T's little-girl act this last week and that, although we all love him, we are all pleased for him and us that he has gone. He behaves somewhat stupidly, but he always will. Andrew [Lyndon] is going home, and perhaps that is over—I wonder.[80] My, how people's lives evolve and evolve and no one knows on which corner he will next find himself—and with whom. I'll tell you what really upset me—for him. Truman told Robert [Davison][81] that he thought I was wonderful but that he would outgrow me. Now, that is really outrageous. He will never, never be capable of feeling what I feel, which ultimately is the thing that will debase anything he does. I guess it upset me because I hope that he will not be limited, but it seems that he may be. If he really thinks this way, I am sure that he will be. You are not to discuss this with him, because he is utterly incapable of understanding any of it. I feel better for having told you. Phoebe says he's blatantly cast her aside many times, but he always comes back for more. He's really a selfish little beast—but who isn't? I am, too.

79. Capote had recently departed for Haiti on assignment for *Harper's Bazaar*. His collection of vignettes titled "Call It New York" appeared in the February 1, 1948, *Vogue*. In it, the section "Tea with Hilary" depicts a character clearly Leo: "Playing host is his cure-all. [ . . . ] Hilary, with his large, spectacular appearance and roaring, giggling monologues, gives even the dreariest occasions a bubbling glamour. Hilary so wants everyone to be glamorous, to be a storybook creature; somehow he persuades himself that the greyest folk are coated with legend-making glitter."

80. In the summer of 1948, Capote's confidant and fellow Southerner Andrew Lyndon (1918–89), an unsuccessful writer, would have an affair with Newton Arvin. It brought an end to Capote's relationship with Arvin, but not his friendship with Lyndon.

81. For "Before Bandwagons" in the February 1947 *Vogue*, Leo had interviewed and swiftly befriended scenic designer Robert Davison (b. 1922). Then living on West Fifty-sixth Street, Davison soon moved into two floors of an Upper East Side brownstone at 1453 Lexington Avenue. By the spring of 1948 he would be sharing them with Leo. The two men enjoyed each other, but their attraction was never physical.

JANUARY 14, 1948 • NEW YORK CITY
**TO RICHARD HUNTER • PORT-AU-PRINCE**

My first book came to review from the *Times*—Marya Mannes's [novel] *Message from a Stranger,* which I like. But if you were here it would be easier to review, for I trust your sense about what I write much more than mine. I think that I get $25 for this. I'm not sure. I'm reading a novel, *The Left Hand Is the Dreamer* [by Nancy Wilson Ross], which is pleasant while placing no strain on either my mind or my heart—such a relief. I completely upset *The Saturday Review* by a big intrigue against their stupid, malignant review of Little T's book [*Other Voices, Other Rooms*]. It worked so well that they have withdrawn the review! And they did that after the lousy magazine was in print! But it wasn't out yet. It was really a most irresponsible review, and I felt that it and the people who write things like it are a menace to all of us. So I waged an afternoon's war and thus far it's a victory.

Oh yes—I have a new beau. You'll never guess who—[novelist] Glenway Wescott! Little T, who says he and I are really Myrt and Marge, says that I have more beaux than anyone else he knows.[82] It's pleasant having Mr. Wescott come to fetch me for dinner. I hope you get this—and that you are keeping your nubbin clean in them islands.

JANUARY 21, 1948 • NEW YORK CITY
**TO RICHARD HUNTER • PORT-AU-PRINCE**

Glenway Wescott came to make friends with me last night. He is an extremely lonely creature who exists in the most complicated surroundings. I like him, and so he seems to have become one of my children. He guessed my age right off, so I didn't say no I wasn't thirty-three. My, he's a troubled man. I think you will like him, too—not wholly—nor do I like him wholly.[83]

JANUARY 22

Now I am riding in a cab—the first I've taken in weeks—to meet Allene, and I am of course late, but I warned her. I continue to be gay. The *Times* apparently liked the [Mannes] review, because this morning they asked whether I would review the new John Moore [novel, *Brensham Village*]. I am so pleased. I reviewed his last, *The Fair Field* for SRL [*The Saturday Review of*

---

82. *Myrt & Marge* was a radio serial (1931–46) about a chorus girl (Myrt) and her chorus girl daughter (Marge), who competed for men and roles. Leo and Capote often addressed each other as "Myrt" (Leo) and "Marge" (Truman).
83. The novelist and critic Glenway Wescott (1901–87) and his lifelong companion, Monroe Wheeler, had very open arrangements (including a ménage from 1927 to 1943 with the photographer George Platt Lynes). Although Leo never knew why Wescott pursued and then promptly dropped him, a letter dated January 21, 1948, from Wescott to the artist Bernard Perlin explains: "I have committed an act of darkness, at last—with one most undesirable [Leo] whose desire for me I chanced to observe; [done] in my way of cool decision, not good though well meant. . . . With also the characteristic problem of disentangling myself from further engagement without wounding the self-esteem of my poor friend."

*Literature*]. Maybe they will pay me $25! If only this could be a long-lasting literary relationship.

I am very tired of having to live up to my apparent age—anywhere from forty to fifty. I want to be thirty-three—and no more for a time. It would be such a relief. This does not mean that I am frightened of growing old, but that I am tired of being old.

JANUARY 24

I am here—writing and reading and leading my indulgent wealthy man's life. It's fun turning into a new shape and a thin man. I love it. I am having this quite enormous vogue right now, wherein everyone wants me to come to parties or to come here—literally everyone. This is fun—and exhausting enough to make me sleep—and food for my future work—and I go out extravagantly.

JANUARY 25

I went to a little gathering at Libby Holman's[84]—and that is one ugly mess I can do without. I became depressed the moment I entered her apartment. I think because she is so vulgarly, sordidly ugly—but it was all so awful feeling. Well, it was good to see. I hope she doesn't come here. Now I must sleep, for I must work in the morning and go to Momma's and then Eugenia [Halbmeier]'s[85] and then broadcast and then my *soir*. [Elisabeth] Bergner and Luise [Rainer] and Stella Adler and Wendy Hiller and Eleonora are all coming.

I've finished Gore [Vidal]'s book. I loathe it, for it makes all things dirty. The meretricious—soap operas, slick fiction—always blacken whole areas—like locusts—and this is because in these works there are always some echoes of truth. If they were totally false, they would have no effect on anyone, but their partial truths make them so monstrous, so insidious.[86]

JANUARY 30

A missive just came from you in Haiti. But please tell me more details—all about the interiors of the brothels and what you did and saw there, about the routine of the Haitian day—what they eat and all that. Oh, I am so pleased that you are there. I am not really so pleased that Little T is there, because he will,

84. Libby Holman (1906–71) had been a celebrated torch singer on Broadway in the twenties and early thirties, until her trial (and acquittal) for the fatal shooting of her tobacco-heir husband. Jane Bowles, then a lover of Holman's, may have taken Leo to meet her.
85. Leo had met lifelong friend Eugenia Halbmeier (b. 1916) during a showing of the film *Dracula* in 1931, when he and his brother terrified her by leaping into her row over the seat backs.
86. The novelist, playwright, and essayist Gore Vidal (b. 1925) met Leo through Anaïs Nin around 1946. The Vidal novel that rankled Leo is probably his homosexual-themed *The City and the Pillar* (1948). His unhappiness with Vidal's novel did not long dampen Leo's gregariousness (or perhaps it inspired mischief). According to Robert Davison, "In 1948, Leo took a table at a Halloween drag in Harlem given by Phil Black, expressly inviting both Gore and Truman Capote." The famous jealous feud between the two writers had probably begun earlier that year.

without even wanting to, try to usurp your day. You mustn't let him—and remember he loves to stay up all night.

JOURNAL • JANUARY 23, 1948 The writers who give us only chaos can lead only to vaster chaos—unless they, like Faulkner or Dostoyevsky, make a moral comment—elevate us. To present horror is insufficient—but to present an organized vision of evil, which is also a comment, is probably the most important work an artist can do. The little boys in Dickens all had sordid childhoods but evolved into splendid men—they had a moral structure—a social structure to palliate, to use as a yardstick, but the little children in today's novels will remain forever misfits and figures in a pathologist's report.

Last night, after the *Far Harbour* opening, Lincoln Kirstein was at the Everard baths, a place where he could lose himself in sex and in no one knowing him—anonymity after a $25,000 disaster—and he, married and situated at the center of a species of Ring One.[87]

Most of our friends fuck Negroes and say it's social consciousness.

"That's no little boy—or if he is a little boy, he's dangerous!" A woman looking at a picture of Little T in Doubleday.

FEBRUARY 2, 1948 Truman cannot help betrayal. It is in him and something he cannot control. I guess I'm hurt at what he told Robert [Davison] (that I was wonderful but that he would outgrow me). I doubt that he will—but he will think that he has. T is the most totally selfish one—but I know this, therefore it cannot scar me.

FEBRUARY 4, 1948 • NEW YORK CITY
**TO RICHARD HUNTER** • PORT-AU-PRINCE

Robert [Davison]'s landlord asked him did he want to buy the house (a good brownstone) for $4,000. The two top floors are rented to [fashion model] Dorian Leigh (with whom I went to [high] school). It is situated on Lexington Avenue, between Ninety-fourth and Ninety-fifth; its back windows look out onto a series of terraced gardens, which are enchanting. It is really on the summit of Goat's Hill and will be valuable. It has oil heat and has recently been fixed up. I wish that I could have it.

FEBRUARY 5

It does sound lovely in Haiti—save for the mosquitoes and the squalor. Haven't you been to the other side of the island—and the Toussaint-Louverture part—

---

87. *Far Harbour*, an opera with music by Baldwin Bergerson and book by William Archibald, was a failure that had only two performances at Hunter College in New York. It had been produced by Lincoln Kirstein (1907–96), the influential dance patron, historian, and critic. Kirstein had brought George Balanchine to New York in 1933 and with him cofounded the New York City Ballet.

and the Christophe Citadel? I wish you would go and tell me all about it. What do you do about sex—or don't you want to talk about that? I am so wicked with myself—and so very-very rarely with anyone else—only three times since you went away, and what transpired was not exactly my idea of release at all. I guess I really don't need as much sex when I am really dieting—ho-ho. Your room sounds horrible—but that doesn't matter really, as long as you paint and are as contented as possible. Even drinking doesn't matter as long as you don't make a fool of yourself. This is a time for you to get a perspective. At least we know that the only happiness is acceptance.

FEBRUARY 5, 1948 • NEW YORK CITY

TO RICHARD HUNTER • PORT-AU-PRINCE

Yesterday a girl came from [the newspaper] *PM* to interview Mary Lou [Aswell] and Pearl [Kazin] on Truman. She is profiling him, and she said what a wonderful journal T kept. So Mary Lou and Pearl couldn't believe their ears and kept straight faces, because we must all protect one another—that's class solidarity. The girl (one Selma Robinson) asked had Mary Lou read any of it, and ML said no she hadn't. Selma said T had shown her, and she had copied out of it such a brilliant analysis of Sartre and Gide and wasn't T a brilliant intellectual. Pearl left the room, ML looked stunned, and Selma went away. Of course we wonder from whom T cribbed it, and is he really silly enough to think that ultimately he can be less than a laughingstock if he continues. When she comes here, I will tell her about his love for quartets and how he's a dreamy cook—and that should delight him, because he knows just as little about music and cooking. I hate this part of T because it reminds me of Touche. It's so unnecessary—he has so much without it. He has a success—a big one— commercially. That and the knowledge that he has written what he wanted to write should be enough. Ah, well, he's excessively immature and selfish and very like the U.S.A. in his adolescence. He needs to be hit on the head, and I guess this time none of us will prevent this being hit on the head because if we do it will mean that we value ourselves more than we value him.

Little T has written me a beautiful letter about how wonderful you look and are, and I am so pleased.[88] The little displeasure with T is subsiding—leaving a deep scar in most of his friends—because they love without looking. You must always know the most awful part of anyone you love. Then if you go on loving that person you can possibly help yourself and help him. T's friends, some of them, will not go on and so they, perhaps, were only more intensely interested in themselves than in T. This is in a degree a definition of friendship.

88. Capote's letter described Richard as obsessed by his entanglement with Howard and Leo: "Indeed we discussed practically nothing else. He talked of you with a heartbreaking tenderness . . . meanwhile H. remains something of a sexual idée-fixe. . . . But [Richard's] ego, still a feeble thing, draws from it some poisonous nourishment." Howard would arrive there in two weeks.

JOURNAL • FEBRUARY 14, 1948 What is there in leaving Richard completely (this relationship) and going to live with Robert [Davison]? There are many good things: Among them would be his decided loyalty. Most of all, I love him—quite uncomplicatedly by sex or anything impetuous—maturely, with a great element of paternity. I could go on with my life, having assumed a new suit, realizing that all suits are basically identical. One must not be whimsical in purchasing a suit, unless one can afford to have many. I can afford to have only one. I wish to return to a life uncomplicated by any sundering love, in which love is an integral part and not a galloping consumption. I want a strict monogamy—in work, in living, in loving. I feel that [in] reassuming my life with Richard, I would be assuming an old suit—somewhat refurbished albeit, but an old suit, and since it has been mended, it must wear out sooner and must be split again. I feel that Richard would be tired. Also, I feel that it would be better for him if I went. He could then truly be on his own.

CA. FEBRUARY 21, 1948 • NEW YORK CITY
TO ROBERT DAVISON • SARASOTA, FLORIDA

The town is somewhat amazed and scandalized by Noël's curtain speech after his [*Tonight at 8:30*] opening last night. He preached to the most hard-boiled and ambivalent audience anywhere that his new love (also the lead [Graham Payn]) was and is the world's best actor. Since he is merely a somewhat charming boy, the audience was rather bewildered. How could a man of Noël's experience be so silly? It's such a pseudo-Wilde gesture. And since he really loves this boy, why didn't he consider how awful it would be for him if he did this?

JOURNAL • FEBRUARY 28, 1948 I became instantly depressed when Eleonora said didn't I think she should go immediately to Vienna, before the Russians got there. It seems to start all over again—the dangerous journeys, the midnight talks and terrors, the world closing into a small pregnable space—and this time all is dilemma—everything.

MARCH 2, 1948 Ruth [Yorck], when she was seventeen (in 1921), made a film with Murnau.[89] She was walking home from school with her governess. A man stopped her and talked to her governess, and the governess didn't tell him to go away. That night, he rang up Ruth's mother and said he was Murnau, and so Ruth became a film actress in this version of *Dracula*—in her mother's best Irish lace nightgown! Yesterday, after all these years, she saw it in its entirety for the first time. (She was not old enough to go to the premiere; you had to be eighteen to go at night.) It had meanwhile been a success with the Surrealists in Paris. This she never knew. How much has happened to her—from that

89. The film was *Nosferatu, eine Symphonie des Grauens*, the first of several landmark silent films that F. W. Murnau (1888–1931) directed.

moment of walking home on her jazz-baby legs with her governess to this moment in her thrift-shop coat in the Museum of Modern Art.

"The faggots' *Huckleberry Finn*." George Davis on Truman's book.[90]

CA. MARCH 10, 1948　All my time is consumed with trying to arrange this house [with Robert]. The leasing of it. I want it very much.

MARCH 17, 1948　This morning I have been very much upset by a letter from Richard. In it he says that he is coming home, giving specified hours, and that he has missed me very much, especially when he saw things that I would have loved. This is cruel because it is tactless. Tactlessness is always cruel. I could have seen them. I could have loved them. But he did not want me. Writing dramatizes despite even the most sincere attempts to suppress all emotion. Nothing is factual, not even numbers. Rage is instantly born when illusion is threatened. Richard has threatened my illusion and destroyed some part of it.

90. George Davis (1906–57) was a novelist, fiction editor at *Harper's Bazaar* (1935–41), then at *Mademoiselle* (1941–48), and features editor at *Flair* (1950–51). He was the act that Leo would follow at *Mademoiselle*.

# I KNEW I HAD COME HOME

**1453 LEXINGTON**  *I came to 1453 when my friend Robert Davison found an apartment in this tall, gaunt, pigeon-desecrated, 1870ish brownstone "town house." In 1948 the family brownstones of my childhood were coveted town houses. It stood on the east side of the avenue, third [south] from the Ninety-fourth Street corner. It was, as it had then been, one of a row of typical brownstones, but now they looked leftover, left behind, some almost abandoned to roomers, impecunious lost descendants, young dwellers on their way to more presentable elsewheres.*

*From the moment I climbed 1453's crumbling steps, pushed open its heavy wooden door (more a memory of black-green than a color), and smelled its close, thick, overripe atmosphere I knew that I had come home. I had been born in just such a house, a typical Manhattan brownstone side-street house, thirteen blocks north. 1453 was an avenue house and wider than Momma's father's place. But the floor plans were identical citywide.*

*Robert and I raised two or three thousand dollars one morning. I found in my mailbox an envelope containing a note: "Darling Leo. Please accept this [$1,000] check with my love. Pay it back when you can or don't or give me essays for The Tiger's Eye. You must have your house." Ruth [Stephan], born Walgreen, was our fairy godmother. She looked the part: a spare blond beauty, she brought radiance into our lives. She lived for literature (especially poetry), art, the sharing of her wealth. She "helped" where she could. She had an enormous joy in life and letters, and I became a part of that life and joy.*

*We bought the lease from the dubious little man who had owned it, and for $125 a month and a signed promise to keep this house in good repair and pay our utilities monthly, there we were—beholden to the family who really owned "our" house, Czechoslovakians rumored to have been in the fur business. To our house, on April 1, I brought from the fifth-floor walk-up where I lived some oddments of furniture, a battered family-office desk, a chaotic mess of files, a typewriter, a heterogeneous mass of objets trouvés, boxes of photographs (loves and hates—I had papered two of my bedroom walls and the ceiling with these), the enormous research for a book about the d'Este sisters (which I would never write, but of which I would reap and even play forever), and I brought books, books, books. We did not have much to sit on until, two weeks after I moved in, Carmel Snow gave* *me a wall-long, screaming-red-lipstick satin sofa from, she said, "a brothel in Paris!" But what we brought most of was spirit, a sense of the ridiculous, fantasy, curiosity, and delight. We both loved to work hard, and we each had lives fat with work we loved.* (1993)

JOURNAL · APRIL 20, 1948 Now begins my new regime in this house. It is deeply pleasant here. Early in the morning, even in the current unfinished, dishabille state, with echoes of cook and maids in caps and uniforms—I love it. Now it is warm and private. I must make it rich in work and love and goodness.

NOTE: During the forties and fifties, Leo tried several times to write a novel with a central character based upon Eleonora von Mendelssohn. Passages for it are scattered in his journals, and the following is one of them. The "she" in it would be Leo, "E" is Eleonora, "E.B." probably Elisabeth Bergner, and "S" possibly the risqué nightclub singer Spivy LeVoe.

JOURNAL · MAY 1, 1948 So she perceived that once having discovered someone took dope or was homosexual or had been institutionalized, she soon met or found someone linked in the same aberration. This was the ancients' birds-of-a-feather, but these feathers were from darkling birds, and almost always unsuspected—until some initial evidence briefed her for the clues, which were everywhere to be found. When she knew that E doped, she discovered the reason for E's passionate devotion to S (who was ugly, vulgar, rude) and her three-decade devotion for E.B., the actress. A great network, as secret as veins—and as busy—was exposed to her awakened perceptions. She could follow their tortuous meanderings as easily as cartographers read maps that were quite obscure to uninformed eyes.

NOTE: Gray Foy had been an eighteen-year-old studying art at Los Angeles City College when he and fellow student Robert Davison fell for each other in 1940. It was Gray's first romantic affair. "I learned," he has said, "more from him than almost anybody—the neo-Romantic painters, García Lorca, Gertrude Stein, ancient music—Robert was encyclopedic." That relationship ended with Robert's army induction and the outrage of Gray's mother, who intercepted some of his letters to Gray.

By April 1948, both men were living in New York, but they hadn't seen each other in some five years. Robert was designing scenery for the theater, including *Galileo* for Orson Welles and *O Mistress Mine* for the Lunts. Gray was taking art instruction at Columbia University, living on $75 a month, and showing his visionary, minutely detailed drawings at Kirk Askew's gallery, Durlacher Brothers.

When Gray and Robert met again, Robert sought a rekindling, but Gray didn't pursue it, feeling disenchanted by Robert's then life, which he recalls was "very untrammeled, to say the least." Gray was growing lonely in New York, however, and resolved that his life had to change. At about this time, Askew introduced him to the modernist architect Philip Johnson (1906–2004), then better known as the founder of the architecture department at the Museum of Modern Art. Johnson began pursuing Gray avidly, if discreetly. Then Robert invited Gray to a party that he and his new housemate were giving.

**GRAY FOY**  *On April 30, 1948, Robert and I had a party at 1453. As the years went on the pattern became a familiar one—inexpensive flowers to fill the rooms, multitudinous candles to make a glorious glowing, and not, at least until much later, notable refreshments. No one came for the drink or the baked meats. For a very long time all that was served—and that is a euphemism—was a huge block of cheddar-cheese-in-port and gallons of jug red wine. People came because they wanted to be with us and with one another. That first party was to honor Pierre Balmain, the Parisian dress designer, canonized by Gertrude Stein and passed on by her to [music critic and novelist] Carl Van Vechten.*

*I can smell the cheese, lilacs, candle wax, and perfumes. There is a certain moment in party-giving when the host knows that this will be a momentous, memorable, talked-about occasion. This moment happened to me when I came upstairs to the landing on the first floor and saw in the front parlor a young man standing shyly. He stood there—looking. I said to him, "I know who you are." Then I said, "That's a very good blue blazer, but I don't think you should have those silver buttons." Since I am writing some forty-five years later, I must tell you that I have those silver buttons in a box in my bureau's top drawer. I have cherished them for those forty-five years.* (1993)

**JOURNAL · MAY 8, 1948**  Now there are footsteps above me, and it is Robert on naked feet, and I know that, after seven years, he has been lying beside the only one he has ever loved, and this is as it should be. Now there are voices—and laughter—and I wish him the serenity he deserves—but I cannot dissever that long winter of sitting in the attic room [in Middletown] and hearing love at its tide in the room beneath me—but what complaint have I save that induced by self-pity? I have a home and its security. I have the possibility of work. Richard loves me and of this love I have all that is possible. He cannot give me more. Why do I then begrudge the little payment that his love for Howard demands from me? It is because I do not work enough, because tonight Robert and Gray lie above me and, without even knowing it decisively, are entering again a common future. For me there is no common future—not really with anyone—and I must accustom myself to this. For a month now this house has helped me. Now it must take its proper place in proportion, and my writing must again usurp any other thing. This is my only salvation. I love Richard: He is part of the blood which flows in my veins, part of the veins themselves. But I am not utterly good—useful—to him unless I work.

The little creakings a bed makes when it is occupied by lovers . . . How to become accustomed to the central solitude? How to be alone in aloneness without being lonely?

NOTE: Robert Davison has said that it was apparent from the first moments of their meeting that Leo intended to woo Gray. Leo worked at it throughout May 1948, and by the end of the month a romance began. In the meanwhile, Gray's involvement with Philip Johnson continued.

## To Honor Pierre Balmain

APRIL 30, 1948 • 1453 LEXINGTON AVENUE

| | |
|---|---|
| Pierre Balmain | Dora Vertès |
| Hermione Gingold | Marcel Vertès |
| Mary Boland | Gypsy Rose Lee |
| Truman Capote | Julio [De] Diego |
| [Alexandra] Choura Danilova | Dorothy Norman |
| Alvin Colt | George Davis |
| Isa Jennings | Diana Trilling |
| Jennie Tourel | Lionel Trilling |
| Ruth Yorck | Allene Talmey |
| Friede Rothe | Dick Plaut |
| Antonina Valentine | Frances McFadden |
| Dorian Leigh | Stark Young |
| Virgil Thomson | Kay [Silver] Sakier |
| Marlene Dietrich | George Sakier |
| Oliver Smith | Jan Struther |
| John Garfield | Mr. Plectheck |
| Robbie Garfield | Anita Loos |
| Carmel Snow | Albert Kornfeld |
| Nicki de Gunzburg | Tonio Selwart |
| Marquise de Casa Maury | Edith Lutyens |
| Iva Patcévitch | Barbette |
| Fania Marinoff | Hazard Short |
| Carl Van Vechten | Muriel Draper |
| Saul Mauriber | Dolly Haas |
| Diana Vreeland | Dorothy Wheelock |
| Eleanor Perényi | Lincoln Kirstein |
| Louise Dahl-Wolfe | Glenway Wescott |
| Irving Penn | Martha Raye |
| John Latouche | Peter Lindamood |

| | |
|---|---|
| Margaret Anglin | Cornelia Otis Skinner |
| Ellen Goreson | Phoebe Pierce |
| Luise Rainer | Marya Mannes |
| Rita Romilly | Betty Penrose |
| George Freedley | Buffie Johnson |
| Miles White | Ruth Ford |
| John Gielgud | Aaron Copland |
| Mary Lou Aswell | Beatrice Kaye |
| Pearl Kazin | Harvey Breit |
| Esther Pallas | Nancy Reid |
| Elisabeth Bergner | Pavlik Tchelitchew |
| Charles James | [Eugene] Berman |
| Olla Kent | Donald Saddler |

JOURNAL · MAY 25, 1948  Gray would lie down beside anyone who offered him affection—because affection is his deepest need.

MAY 29, 1948  Philip Johnson, a very evil man, has come to the end or a termination in his relationship with [*House & Garden* copy editor] Jon Stroup (who was a "good" boy when he took up with Philip). Philip is now seeing Gray. He needs his freshness, his energy, his goodness, his unspoiled youth, his creative talent, his very soul (the old Mephistopheles-Faust-vampire ratio). Gray, like Jon, has strong scrupulous reactions, but he is attracted. Philip commissions a portrait, also one of Theodate [Philip's sister]. He tells Lincoln [Kirstein] that he is in love with Gray. Lincoln commissions a painting. So the net is drawn over the "unspoiled." Philip and Lincoln represent the museum world, the world of "names" who will be Gray's patrons. Kirk [Askew] dislikes this, but he is powerless. Gray is almost in great danger.

Glenway had an affair with Bernard [Perlin, silverpoint artist], but Bernard could not continue. Now he [Glenway] has the atmosphere of a retired stallion. [The painters] Jared French, Paul Cadmus, George Tooker, and Mrs. French [Margaret Hoening] all live together. French paints such obscene pictures so exquisitely that he cannot even show them. Lincoln Kirstein is married to Paul Cadmus's sister, Fidelma, but he loves boys.[1]

Lincoln Kirstein and Philip Johnson seem to be great friends.

1. Fidelma "Fido" Cadmus (1906–91) was also a painter. Lincoln Kirstein was homosexual and subject to bouts of depression and violence, and she was recessive and troubled, but they remained married for fifty years.

MAY 31, 1948 Howard Rothschild attempted a relationship with Ward, the [Rothschilds'] new gardener, who had been a lineman and has a wife and two children. Howard does not love Richard, but wants him so as to satisfy his ego by discarding him, and he behaves exactly as Swann with Albertine[2]—goes to queer bars to tell Richard, so Richard will be jealous, and all Richard is concerned about is venereal disease and blackmail, while Howard wants him to be bug-eyed with passionate jealously. Howard inflicts constant hurt on himself in an effort to hurt Richard.

JUNE 9, 1948 Mondrians are unbearably lonely, because they depersonalize. It is the depersonalization I hate, and this is why I am against so much of "modern" art and psychoanalysis.

JUNE 14, 1948 I shan't be able to sleep—even though I am tired—and I wonder whether I shall be able to sleep alone in this house again. At about fifteen to eleven, someone broke the window to the right of my bed. It apparently was done with a stick or bludgeon of some sort. It has frightened me. I can't believe this was done to me—for who would do it?—but the idea that there is some unknown malevolent person (or persons) who would do this—seems to make sleep impossible. I reported to the police. Two came. They asked did anyone dislike me in the neighborhood. I thought instantly of the three boys in the upholstery [shop], but said nothing. I have nothing really to say about them. They jeer—but since I have done nothing wittingly to offend them why would they do this? Perhaps it was a drunk or some malicious boys—or someone who hates [the previous tenant] Drawant and thinks that he still lives here. I was hurt that Gray wouldn't come over and stay, but now I am pleased, for this is something I must do my myself—as I have tried to vanquish darkness—but tonight I shall leave one light burning.[3]

JUNE 15, 1948 Laci is ending as a *Steckenkünstler* [costume tailor], as he started—traveling over the country, playing fifth-rate theaters with his girls, sticking pins into them because he hates them. Laci is rouged, sleeked up, still has some of his "good things."

JULY 1, 1948 1:15 A.M. This has been a wretched three hours again: Gray hasn't come home; Richard is with Howard. I think that something has happened to Gray—but perhaps he is staying with Philip. How can I continue this life of crumbs? I have been in pain as hurting as last week's toothache. Empirin [painkiller] relieved that, but what will relieve this? Resolution? How can I do this to myself? I am sick—but . . . There is more to living than this.

2. He is probably thinking not of Swann's relationship with Albertine in Proust's novel, but of the narrator's, which is filled with insecurity and jealousy.
3. Leo was afraid to sleep alone in the dark for most of his life.

Now he's here and life begins again. I must protect myself against myself—I must do this—I must not burden others—I have no right.[4]

JULY 4, 1948  I came to Momma and Poppa's last night and stayed here. Surprisingly it is quite pleasant. The room is brilliantly light, wonderfully airy, and it smells with all the summer smells I had lost these years. I am stuffed with my favorite dishes, surfeited with Momma and Poppa singing and quarreling, and I read Ouida incessantly ([the novel] *Moths*, which I adore). There are beautiful leaf shadows. If this house had just a little more privacy in it, I would stay a bit. It is lovely to be waited on, fed, and to make believe there are no worries— for at least this day. The radio blares old operetta tunes. There is a fricassee cooking. I am quite pleased. There is a wire screen on the windows. This makes all the outside look as though Seurat had painted it. Now the sunlight diminishes. The air has the tint of a new copper kettle. In this room, I have fainted; I have first been in love; I have almost died; I have planned dream houses and dreamed dreams that have now been realized. I first came into it when I was about nine and a half or ten. That was twenty-four years ago. Again, it is we who pass, but not ever time—and soon, in two or three months, this will all be gone—ah well.[5]

The flowering hedges remind me of all sorts of young agonies and loves and hungers. Now I begin to worry about Robert's return, and how can I give up my life with Gray—such as it is. I begin also to want for myself a strict morality. Perhaps being in love makes me feel this. I have never, in many years, been promiscuous, really, but now I should prefer a single faithfulness to Gray, but this is premature, and I must not plan it now. I risk nothing, for what have I to risk? I wish that I could go away to write—and Gray with me. I know that we could be contented. It is only natural to want this now, but still I love Richard. He must know this, but I cannot go on with the wretched part-life we have, where everything is measured and tainted by Howard.

4. *Gray Foy:* "I met Philip Johnson at a party at Mina Kirstein Curtiss's apartment, to which Kirk Askew had taken me. Philip was the first affair in which I felt equally attracted. Very sexual. He wanted to keep me, but as a kind of secret, because he was determined that people not think him homosexual. We went on for that summer, while he began clearing the land for his famous glass house in New Canaan, [Connecticut,] until I learned from Kirk that Philip had been involved before the war with the Silver Shirts, the Union Party, American Fascists. That ended it. And Leo offered me a home."
5. Leo had been born at 71 East 107th Street (between Madison and Park Avenues) in a house that his grandfather Jacob Goldwasser owned and where his parents were living. When he was a toddler, the Lermans moved to an apartment in the Bronx on the Boston Post Road at 165th Street. They returned to Manhattan, when Leo was about five, to live with his mother's father in a tenement building that he had recently purchased at 66 East 106th Street (again between Madison and Park). In 1923 they moved to a small house in the New York neighborhood of Jackson Heights, Queens (37–31 Seventy-fourth Street). In the summer of 1948, his parents were selling that house to move to the adjoining neighborhood of Elmhurst, where they would then share a duplex with Leo's brother Jerry, his wife, and, soon, Leo's two nieces.

I love knowing that Momma and Poppa may buy that place back of the library. I love it there, and I have a feeling that it may provide a little something for my old age and Jerry's. That would be heaven to know. Now I shall read some more of *Babbitt*.

JULY 20, 1948   I will stop a bit from writing *Bazaar* captions and rest in this notebook. I would like to rest my back by lying down, but I can't because deep inside I am frightened. I don't quite know of what. It's since Robert's insane tantrum on Friday morning, and it is because I see that he is not quite balanced. He is in Detroit, but I am frightened of falling asleep—with the same awful terror I had when I was younger. Twice today, someone has rung up on the phone and not said a thing when I answered. If only someone were here, I could sleep. But could I sleep, if I were alone with Robert in this house? As I feel now, I could not. Now it is four a.m. I must finish this work. Somewhere the house creaks, settles; a fly zooms through the rooms; in the garden a branch taps; a cat screeches—I shake with terror. I am horrified. It is a steaming, torrid night. I am wet with icy sweat—these are the saltwatery beads of terror. Juliet glittered with them when she remembered Tybalt. How can I continue to live here? At least there was nothing incomprehensibly terrifying at Eighty-eighth Street [with Richard]. I will stretch out the writing of these two captions until the sun has risen. The reflection of my hand in the window glass—seen out of the corner of my right eye—startled me—my heart jumped. I must control this. I must somehow rest my back. It is all pain. I wanted this house because it was the surest out—the swiftest—because I was greedy for a house—because I could no longer remain at Eighty-eighth Street. This house is a bad bargain. I must turn it into a good bargain, must manage to master it rather than permit it to master me.

NOTE: Gray had continued to share an apartment on First Avenue and Forty-seventh Street, but spent much of his time with Leo or (until the beginning of August) Philip Johnson. Relations with Robert Davison predictably chilled. One July morning at breakfast, when Leo or Gray hinted that they preferred not to look after Robert's cat, he erupted and yanked away the tablecloth, shattering much of Leo's prized Chelsea porcelain. After that they avoided Robert. He moved away in November.
    Robert intended never to speak with either man again, but his resentment soon faded. In May 1950, he went to live and paint with the American painter Charles Blum in San Miguel de Allende, Mexico. Occasionally returning to New York to paint backdrops for shop windows, he sometimes saw Leo, and by the time Robert left Blum and moved to Paris in 1956, he, Leo, and Gray had become long-distance friends.

AUGUST 7, 1948 • NEW YORK CITY
**TO RICHARD HUNTER** • OCRACOKE, NORTH CAROLINA

Your apartment is such a haven.[6] I stay there at night, and it makes my cellar days here [at 1453] pleasant. Robert has never yet realized that I do not sleep

6. For about a year Richard kept the apartment that they had shared.

here usually, he is now making snuffling and washing noises in the bathroom. He wants to know why I am so quiet these days, but I pretended I did not hear him. I am trying to make him see—without telling him—that I want to work, alone in my workroom in the morning. I no longer eat any breakfast, for I have to be here to answer the phone by nine. He trails down at 10:30—and tries to converse—but I just ain't agoin' to. Gray is painting in your house. Robert has just departed above, I think coffeepot in hand—so perhaps it has sunk in.[7]

SEPTEMBER 18, 1948 • NEW YORK CITY

TO ELEONORA VON MENDELSSOHN

Every day, these last weeks, I woke thinking that I would hear from you: This morning it came true. You know, my dear, I lust for you—actually lust. Isn't that odd? This has been an awful summer—with illness and money worries and house worries and love worries (but I don't have these anymore, having reached a situation somewhat like yours—or is it a position?). I have been wretchedly ill and had one little operation and will probably have three or four more, when I find money with which to pay for them. That accident [in a taxi in 1943] that gave me my beard also cracked my right cheekbone, and this is now infecting my face, the remaining teeth, other bones. . . . Oh darling, I am a mess. I've lost eighty pounds, and you had better come home before I dwindle away. It's really not that bad, but it has been hell. I grow cysts, the pain is agonizing, and I am such a coward. I took fifty-three Empirins in three days. All the doctors said that I was a miracle, and that I should be dead from it, but I thought of you and smiled, because they did not know the wonderful example of strength I have had for such a long time. I am so awfully homesick for your not unattractive face and for your dainty, not unfeminine ways. Oh darling, as unhappy as we were, I do miss those secret trips north, and the time I took you to hear the sap running in the trees of Central Park and [the driver] Miller was so shocked, and all the big and little secret pleasures and pacts we had, and you always thought that I would tell, but I never did.

I have a new friend. He is really one of the greatest draftsmen I have ever seen and wonderfully beautiful. You will adore him—everyone does. It's pleasant to love without too much agony, but one misses it at times, like when a sore tooth has been pulled. One frequently misses the pain. Or is it that the pain has been so shocking that we wait for the shock?

SEPTEMBER 25

I've been to some parties (all dull) and, best of all, I lured *Glamour* into paying for me to go to all the theaters and music in town for the next month. So, I feel gay and put black ink on the rather large spots in my black suit which quite a

---

7. GF: "When I arrived, we lived downstairs, with Leo's bed in the front room of two and a makeshift kitchen without a sink (dishes we washed in the bath, shared with Robert). I first slept in the back room on a chaise longue. When I met Leo, he said, 'I can't love you because I'm in love with somebody else.' "

few enterprising moths industriously managed to convert into moth luncheons and dinners. With the black ink covering where the lighter lining shows through it almost looks piggishly new—at least I hope nobody can see that the suit is really curiously chewed into intricate and unlovely designs.

Marlene asked me whether I would ghost her memoirs, but I thought it over and decided that she would never really tell what the public wants to know. So, I intimated, couldn't we just be friends.

**MADEMOISELLE**   *George Davis on the telephone—his sleepy lethal voice. His is the deep, quiet voice of frozen rage. "I am giving up my job at Made-moiselle and I want you to have it." "Why?" "Don't ask questions! Just tell Betsy Blackwell that you have heard that I have given up my job and that you would be interested in having it."*

*I called Kay Silver, fashion editor for Mademoiselle, and said, "Kay, why has George left Mademoiselle? He has the best job in New York: He's made the feature department into a glory. Why has he left it?" "I can't go into that now, but if you want the job I'll tell you what to do. . . ."*

*So, late one autumn day, I sat on a window ledge polishing up the front windows at 1453 and jumped back into the front parlor when down the street I saw the first guest advancing—that was Kay. The bell rang and my new life began.*

*The back parlor was candlelit, but the candles, although densely placed, did not illuminate the faces of the closely packed crowd. Upon the flaming-red sofa sat a small, plump, much-hatted, mottled-faced, bird-eyed woman whose feet overflowed her tight shoes. These feet did not quite touch the floor. There was something appealing about her, for a very young girl peeped out of this plainly middle-aged, imbibing woman. The small woman, peering through the gloaming, asked, "And who are you?" "Marlene Dietrich." There was no air around these two words. Then Marlene jumped up and insinuated herself about, emptying ashtrays, while Truman and Tennessee beamed. The Trillings, the Van Vechtens, Dorothy Norman, John Latouche aided and abetted. And the chums all piled in, making much of Betsy Talbot Blackwell, the editor in chief of Mademoiselle, the small, plump woman who sat on the sofa.* (1993)

NOTE: Blackwell was impressed by Leo's connections and forecasting talent. By the end of December, after having him followed by a private detective, she offered him the position of contributing editor. Leo consulted Talmey at *Vogue* and Snow at *Bazaar*. Both advised him to sign, but to remain a free agent, an arrangement he would keep with *Mademoiselle* throughout his work there.

CA. NOVEMBER 20, 1948 • NEW YORK CITY
**TO RICHARD HUNTER** • NEW ORLEANS

*Mademoiselle* sent me $400, so I can pay off some of my debts and pay you $90 and next week when the Philharmonic $100 comes you can have that,[8] and so

8. Leo wrote program notes for the Saturday children's concerts of the New York Philharmonic.

I will owe you only quite a small fortune besides . . . but if all goes well and more comes from *Mademoiselle* next month and from the Philharmonic, you can be paid all the extra monies I borrowed!

CA. DECEMBER 4

Todd Bolender and Jack Dunphy (who wrote a good novel and was once married to [dancer] Joan McCracken but isn't—and now is a friend of Todd's) came, and Little T arrived and was quite pathetic and lonely and spoiled-acting. We all went to inspect his premises. Mr. Jack D said wasn't it all full of echoes of a powder room, and that's a good description.

NOTE: Within days, Jack Dunphy and Capote had been to bed. Bolender, a New York City Ballet dancer who had been Dunphy's lover, soon called Leo to say that he had been abandoned for Capote.

DECEMBER 22, 1948 • NEW YORK CITY
**TO GRAY FOY** • GLENVIEW, ILLINOIS[9]

The shortest day of the year has been and gone, and in its celebration the furnace has decided to rest itself a while—right in the middle of my shower. The water suddenly was fluid ice. I instantly knew this to be a judgment, but I am unreconciled to it. Now the house is nasty with cold, and I am pleased that you are not here—you would hate it. The snow was beautiful—especially in all the gardens where it almost obliterated the fences. Upon the trees, it invented incredible fantasies, and all this backyard world was wreathed in white. You would have loved it, and I was sad because I wanted you to see it. It is deeply quiet here—and lonely—very lonely—especially in the mornings. Good night. (I love watered silk but not in great quantities.)

DECEMBER 23

I am done up in gloves and shawls and blankets. The house is ice. You would be miserable here, but not as miserable as I am alone in this winter. The oil-man has been and said that it is a matter of oil—but the oil remains an abstraction. Meanwhile I have a sore throat from the intense cold; my nose is a beetroot; my hands are numb. Writing to you warms them, but I am in such a temper that it is difficult to write. I wish that you were here. I am so frozen. Light is thick and golden on the houses all down the hill. There is something so Italianate about those houses and the sky.

MAY 6, 1949 • NEW YORK CITY
**TO RICHARD HUNTER** • MADRID

Suddenly I understood some mornings ago, what [the clairvoyant] Pierce Harwell meant when he told me that I was going into exile someday, for a very long

9. Gray's aunt Alice McKay lived in Glenview, near Chicago. Gray would meet his mother there for holidays.

time, and now I understand about exile meaning one day one returns. That makes me optimistic. I understand all about these Elbas of the heart, which I have been resting on.

I saw Eleonora (who has been having a cure again) and there she was, rallied, and—when I did not peer too closely—amazing to look at.

MAY 10, 1949

I had an enlightening but grim (that should be vice versa) experience yesterday. Allene loved my book piece. Then she said that she wanted to talk to me about my writing—the actual technical aspects of it. She gave me an hour's lesson in elementary composition. It was wonderful. It also made me feel that I really do not know how to write the English language. Now I am starting all over again, trying to write simply and substantially. Gosh . . . She really knows, although she explained that all she was telling me was what she had been taught in freshman composition at Wellesley. I wish that I were a Wellesley girl! The gist of her message signified to me that I am extremely sloppy. I always manage to get away with hasty jobs. That is why I write badly. She merely said technical things: too many imperative sentences, too many sentences constructed identically, too many inactive verbs, too many crowded sentences, good critical phrases or telling characterizing words buried in all sorts of verbal rubbish. . . . She's right, of course. She said that I say such wonderful things about books and people, and that when I come to write it's all gone . . . and she's right there. Thinking over what she said, I realize even more intensely that if I am ever to write anything worthwhile I shall have to sit and write it. I shall have to stop making believe and making attempts—just write it and then rewrite it until it's good. What a difficult life that is. But since I want to write . . . and I do it shabbily now . . . I must set myself to it all over again.

MAY 23, 1949 • NEW YORK CITY

**TO RICHARD HUNTER • MADRID**

This is a day of sudden bursts of brilliant sunshine, then lowering clouds—and that is how I feel. It's quite unlike any birthday I've had these last fifteen years. But why be sad? I have three pretty presents: a small bird with a red breast (made in Sweden), a large white cup and saucer (very pretty, white Limoges), and a big pleated lantern from Denmark—Gray gave me these. The Trillings gave me a copy of Lionel's [first book] *Matthew Arnold*—and Mary Lou and Pearl are taking me to lunch at the St. Regis—and Dorothy Norman is having the mayor [William O'Dwyer] to dinner with me—and Jacqueline [Errera] and Rut [Ruth Yorck][10] and in all about nine people are coming here at eleven —and [high school English teacher] Maggie Henning and Momma are com-

10. Leo said his friend Ruth's name in the German way—"root"—and usually spelled it "Rut." Jaqueline Errera was a wealthy Belgian Jew in New York in the forties.

ing at 4:30—but none of this seems to mean very much, which is wrong but that's how it is—oh, well. Now I must get dressed. It all reminds me of that song about "Greta Garbo's had me to tea. . . ." I guess—superficially—my life has turned out the way I dreamed of it when I was young, but essentially it hasn't. I shall have to accustom myself to what it is and build on it. Now I must stop. They [at *Mademoiselle*] renewed my contract for the rest of the year!!! Isn't that fine?

JUNE 11, 1949 • NEW YORK CITY

**TO RICHARD HUNTER • PARIS**

It was a pleasant Saturday morning until about thirty minutes ago when my "roommate" [Gray] threw his erstwhile familiar tantrum. Since he hasn't tantrumed for quite some time, this was unexpected. It's because last Saturday afternoon Pearl [Kazin] came over at five—and [literary agent] John Schaffner and Sylvia Wright [a magazine editor]—and it was so very pleasant sitting up here that I said why didn't they come today. I still have white wine left from my birthday [May 23], and all I do is put it in the icebox and then they sip it, so it hasn't cost anything or made any dirt. So I said for them to come—and also Mr. and Mrs. Fritz Peters, which newlyweds I haven't seen since they became just that[11] . . . and [editor] John Lehmann called up and Diana and Lionel [Trilling] . . . and also Jeremiah [Russell] . . . that makes exactly nine people. He scowled when I said about Jeremiah, and he threw the fit when I said about John Lehmann. And now he's locked himself in the bathroom and says he's going out because he doesn't want to be in that little group or even on the fringes of it.

It's lovely sitting up here over the garden in these two big vacant rooms, the sunlight buttering the leaves and flagstones and gilding the wisteria vines. There are no flowers in the garden, but it is beautifully green, and Gray keeps it so pretty-looking. . . .

Sometimes I think that Gray's living here is not too good—especially right now. He has just departed, indicating that I am a monster of selfishness and without even saying good-bye. It was pleasant mostly these last weeks. Perhaps it is selfish to ask anyone to come here on Saturday because, perhaps, the outside world should be kept out . . . but I do spend all the time away from business with him, and it's good for me to see Diana and Lionel and Mary Lou and Pearl and . . . Oh, well . . . It occurs to me the chief selfishness in life is perhaps the focusing of attention on one person, because it is surely the attention that one gives a looking glass. You wish to see the image you create returned to you.

11. Mary Louise Aswell had married the novelist Fritz Peters (1913–79). The marriage did not last long. GF: "About 1950, Mary Lou came and rang our bell, said he was trying to kill her, and hid in our house for about ten days. Ken Tynan once said that Mary Lou was always 'marvelously aghast.' Anyhow, she often looked terrified." In 1956 a divorced Aswell left for Santa Fe, where she lived with the tapestry artist Agnes Sims until her death in 1984.

E. M. Forster has been here [in New York], and he had dinner at Lionel and Diana's and he loved the baby and held him, and then he autographed a book for the baby and signed, "With love," and said, "I guess he won't resent that until he's fifteen or sixteen." Diana says that he's a good sad man. When he inadvertently dropped a bit of food on his lapel, he said, "I guess I'm becoming one of those old men who drop food on themselves." He seems to be very sad at growing old and also very bitter at losing the house, four years ago, in which his family had lived for over a hundred years. The family who own it decided that they had to have it for some connection, and they threw him out. Cambridge took him in, but this has almost been a mortal blow. He wrote a book about it and says that he will never publish it. He's a very private man.

JOURNAL · JUNE 18, 1949  Robert Lowell said to [poet] Allen Tate and the police before he was taken away, "I know I am God and they cannot cut my balls off."

NOTE: Gray went to visit relatives in Chicago and Los Angeles for six weeks.

JULY 3, 1949 · NEW YORK CITY
**TO RICHARD HUNTER · PARIS**

It is so intensely hot that the garden is all seared; the earth actually hot and scorched, for this is the fifth or sixth week of the big drought. Now I am quite alone here. Everyone I really love dearly is gone: you, Gray (he went last Friday), Eleonora, Rut. . . . It doesn't quite seem being alive without you here. Sometimes I think I shall sell all the books and depart . . . but only for a moment. Every day I am lonely for you—isn't that absurd? Now, to be truthful, it is somewhat of a relief to have Gray away. There is no strain, and what heaven that is. Gray is a very good boy, and I am devoted to him. He can be extremely sweet, and he has tried very, very hard . . . but he forgets or can't control his surly disposition and his wicked temper, and life can be hell.

This is a lovely free time and, since it is a holiday, I am in bed (11:20!), and yesterday was a real lazy cat-stretching of a day . . . lovely. With Gray here I can't stay in bed because he thinks I am sick or something—anyway I can't. I have been working very hard—so hard that last Sunday I sort of passed out. I am all better now, but recently I haven't been well. I guess I was scared, because I bled for about eight days from my inside, but it stopped . . . and then Gray wasn't being very pleasant all during that time. The difficulty of not having money, feeling that he is being sort of kept, and the strain of going home to his family—all combined to make him bad-tempered. Then he is so impractical about business and does not realize that to keep a job you have to work very hard, especially with business so bad. Ah well . . .

I don't think that it would be fun with all those old dreary faces in Paris. I am not surprised about Truman. Didn't he say anything unpleasant about me? He's a little monster like Pope, but I am fond of him, and until he does something horrible about me I guess I shall continue. I began to write in my notebook yesterday. I can't do that while Gray is here ever since I realized he read my notebook, and I am not secretive and can't write in it and hide it. It stops me.

I guess I might as well tell you . . . Gray didn't have any money, so I bought a drawing from him the day he left. It's that good one with all the naked bodies, very beautiful, and I paid him $100. I wanted it, and he wanted to give it to me, but I wouldn't accept it that way. So, I'll have to make some extra money and not take taxis and all that for about four weeks.

The telephone has not even squeaked all this day and the garden flecked by brown leaves looks as if it were under glass. The heat is so intense that it seems to cover everything with a thin glass surface. Here I have been all this long day, lolling in this now quite wet bed, and now I am beginning to feel that the world is dead. I am lonely for you . . . and why shouldn't I be? . . . There is no rancor in this . . . just a little sadness that I have to be and will probably always have to be . . . just a little, for I know that you will always be errant . . . and I am not.

And, as always, midnight is here, and so am I—bleary-eyed, for I have read over 250 pages of [Virginia Woolf's] *The Years*. This time I find it even more beautiful than before. It is so exact and so sad, because it is all about time. These last days have been an oasis really, despite aloneness, because they are like weeks I breathed away before January last, when I went to work. Reading, writing a little, brooding, eating little nothings, listening to the radio, little plans and projects forming like clouds then melting and merging or just drifting away, lying abed the whole day through, telephoning just anybody at all . . . such a lovely, lazy, rich man's life. It's so pleasant to live it for a day or two again and make believe that tomorrow night, the holiday ending, you will be returning from Middletown . . . and I shall be sitting waiting for you and almost dying of excitement and breathlessness, just to hear you come up the street a little after midnight—or earlier. How rich I am and happy in memories, and these do not sadden me or depress me. I am sort of drowsy with heat and reading and remembering.

You are asleep at five in the morning, which is what it must be where you are, with your foolish mouth wide open and a thumb in it and an ear clutched? My lovely ears . . . nobody ever pays them any mind . . . but I do. Good night. Be a good child and come back safely—yowyow . . . snufit . . . twhow . . . yimp.

JULY 6, 1949 • 5 P.M. • NEW YORK CITY

**TO RICHARD HUNTER** • PARIS

Such a curious thing has happened: Mrs. [Grace] Vanderbilt has asked me to tea! I couldn't be more astonished. First, she asked me to dinner tomorrow night, and I said I was engaged. Then she asked me to lunch, and I said I was engaged. So then she said, "Well, you must be an exceedingly busy man. . . .

Can you come to tea this afternoon?" and I said yes. So, in ten minutes I am going. I kind of have stage fright because, after all, I've been curious about her and her house ever since I've been a small child.[12]

9 P.M.

So I went to tea with Mrs. Vanderbilt, and I had a good time, and now we are buddies. How we used to conjure over her torn curtains and her headbands. She's really so very amusing and sweet and kind—like anybody's great-grandmother!

Now it seems that I'm actually supposed to go to stay with the Astors at Rhinebeck next month. I was very kind to a gawky young man who was brought to my *Mademoiselle* party [on June 20], and he turned out to be Ivan Obolensky, son of Prince Obolensky and Alice Astor.[13] So now his mother and his grandmother have asked me to come and stay with them, and it's very funny to me. My being very kind consisted of introducing him to a flock of girls, and he told his family, and they were so pleased. All the time I was sitting at Mrs. Vanderbilt's, and she was holding my hand, I thought of Momma and Aunt Silly [Celia Goldwasser] . . . and I couldn't explain, if anyone had asked me, why I was so amused, but you would have understood. This is really the first time I've felt gay in years. . . . I guess I needed a little glimpse of a world completely unlike my world to set me up.

JULY 18, 1949 • NEW YORK CITY
**TO RICHARD HUNTER • PARIS**

It doesn't matter much to me what people think about us, because I know the truth, and this truth is mine utterly and it is good. . . . When I die—now don't be angry at this, because you are the only person whom I can tell these silly things to (and anyway it won't be for years)—please see that I am buried in that yellow bathrobe, the one with the slit and the moth holes, which you gave me. I love it dearly and I have been very happy in it, and it feels like you to snuggle me for all eternity—not that I feel quite comforted about eternity—and won't it look gay on Judgment Day? How lucky I am to have one real deep love and to have it complete now within me, not to want anything from it save that you should be contented. How many people ever have that? I shouldn't have involved Gray, but I was weak, and I think that I do him more good than harm. When he returns, I know that I will make him grow more independent, because I am strong enough for several people. I guess I really feel that he's my

12. Grace Graham Wilson Vanderbilt (1870–1953), the widow of Cornelius Vanderbilt III, was in her later years arbiter of the New York social scene.
13. Alice Astor (1902–56) was the heiress daughter of John Jacob Astor IV. She had four husbands (with whom she had a total of four children): Prince Serge Obolensky, Raimund von Hofmannsthal, Philip Harding, and finally David Pleydell-Bouverie. Two other passions in her life were choreographer Frederick Ashton and lyricist John Latouche.

child. I get rebellious about that sometimes, but I have a feeling that he's going to turn out. I don't really resent Howard anymore, and I have, at last, become sorry for him . . . because now I know, in some little measure, what contentment can be. I have it, and he doesn't, really, because he is the way he is, and that makes me sorry for him. Do you know that now, at last, I really love you, without jealousy or anything acquisitive to impair or mar this love? And for the first time I do feel free in it, and right now I am deeply happy? You know, I don't mind living alone [these weeks]. . . . I wouldn't mind at all if there was someone to feed me and care for the house and the knowledge that one day you would appear.

JULY 29, 1949 • WOODS HOLE, MASSACHUSETTS
**TO TRUMAN CAPOTE** • TANGIERS, MOROCCO

You have probably never received those delicious epistles which I never wrote—let alone sent. But there you are selling grain in the marketplace with little Jane [Bowles]—and now both of you adored by Berbers and strange wide-eyed men such as have never adored me.[14] When are you coming home to your sweet old bald-head mom? When I pause to think, I realize that the me has gone out of my life, and then I realize that you've been gone ever so long, but, of course, each to his own hell and far be it from me to covet another's hot coals. I read a little story by Paul Bowles in George Mayberry's new anthology [*A Little Treasury of American Prose*], and it is about where you are. For heaven's sake and mine, too, please keep away from camel bladders.[15] It's an awful, malignant story. Are you writing precious little words—each worth a small fortune—very small currently what with taxes. I've been here at the Normans these last ten days at Woods Hole, and it's heaven—loads of servants—and several yachts—and such magnificent food and witty conversation (this last is my contribution), and it's even more heavenly because *Mademoiselle* pays me while I loll and sparkle and display all my lovely finery, which I borrowed from some friendly sewer rats. Oh my dear—N.Y. has no *ton* (a French word meaning class) *sans* (a French word meaning without) *toi*—(a French word meaning you, but very familiar!). Now I must go in to breakfast. Gray is in California—so while the mice are away the cat is *all* play!—love, Myrt—meaning love *me*. Write!!! I collect stamps.

JULY 29, 1949 • WOODS HOLE, MASSACHUSETTS
**TO RICHARD HUNTER** • VENICE

Do you remember that point of land which you see on the right as you leave Woods Hole on the Nantucket boat—that long point on which there are some

14. The married writers Paul and Jane Bowles began living in Tangiers in 1948.
15. In Paul Bowles's story "A Distant Episode," a traveler in North Africa asks where he might buy boxes made of camel udders. He is led away, captured, and driven mad by brutality.

huge houses? Well, I am sitting in a big bed, looking out over the water, the Nantucket boat has just wailed, and I am here for ten days in one of those houses. The house I am in is owned by Dorothy and Kiddo [her husband, Edward Norman]. Allene and Dick [Plaut, her husband] are here, and it is really heaven, because it is not modern, but beautiful, full of flowers and lovely old furniture and pictures and maids, who turn your bed down, and a superb cook, and a gardener, who wheels your lunch down to the beach. I am luxuriating in this lovely rich life—with nothing to do except eat and be waited on and giggle. You would love it here—if you liked Dorothy. I have a wonderful brown-tan face, and my forearms are a little sunburned, but I feel absolutely well for the first time in years. Oh, what bliss: Through all the windows you see water—like my room at Nantucket. This is a kind of storybook house.

JULY 31

The ten-minute bell has just been clanged by Sarah (an old, dyed-black-haired Irishwoman with very dark red, high cheeks), and Dorothy, sitting in a light blue bathing dress in the lower garden, dictating to her secretary (also in bathing dress, white) both on a long bench beside the big lily pool, has not moved. Edward, across the harbor has possibly heard the bell, but only as a ghost bell. The great bees bumble among the spotted Turkish lilies—and the sprinklers whoosh—and all the world is rainbows—and glittering drops—a little wooded island in the foreground fixes it—makes it by its isolation, by its permanence, forever. I have put a peaked blue cap on my head, and now here comes Edward, rowing swiftly, for he has heard the bell or he is hungry, and now Dorothy rises and pats her shoulders, and Simone gathers their papers. It is lunchtime. Sarah clangs her bell again, again, again.

JULY 31, 1949 • NEW YORK CITY
**TO RICHARD HUNTER** • VENICE

Now it is night rushing beside this train with everyone riding doubly in the night—inside the lighted train and outside in the dark. I had forgotten how one is always attended by an almost perfect reflection of oneself in the window during night rides. Over Providence the sky was filled with magnificently terrible (meaning awesome) colors—blood in all shades—from fresh red to black clotted. There's autumn in the sunset sky these days. I am always amazed at looking up and finding a bearded, spectacled, interesting-looking middle-aged man in the dark window beside me. And it's me—there—and I feel as though I had dressed up to be that person—because inside it's yesterday in Central Park on a spring evening with a robin singing[16]—and all sorts of other days and nights when I wasn't middle-aged and bearded—but it's fun, too.

16. A reference to Leo and Richard's first kiss.

**TO RICHARD HUNTER • VENICE**

There is never a moment when I am not you and you not me. It is as though we existed not at all beside one another, but in one another. That is why when we are apart each is a little less vivid—each of us is diminished, vague in certain areas, for each of us is there and still not there but with the other. It sounds complicated, but it isn't. The only pity of it is that we have involved other people—and we must not hurt anyone—there is too much hurt, please don't let's add to it. Anyway, who can plan his future save in dreams, and how many dream true in the way they expect?[17]

**TO RICHARD HUNTER • FLORENCE**

Here I am in my untidy bed, where I have been since 10:30 p.m., exhausted from a day at the Lerman Picnic Grove—familiarly yclept [called] Lerman's Folly. Poppa has been insisting that he was going to move the house himself—with Jerry—and since this would probably cripple them both—and since he is obstinate—the only way I could get him to promise not to do it was by telling him that I would give him the $200 needed to have it moved. So, now I'll have to think of some way to make this up. I guess the powers that watch over me will help. But I had to do this, to save Jerry, really. I'll give them my *Vogue* money, which I had planned to use for other necessities. Momma revealed that they have spent the $40,000 even before they got it, having borrowed on it. Then Momma said that she hoped I would finish a book soon because they really needed quite a lot of money. I instantly decided never to write another if that was to be the consequence. I guess I am in quite a temper. Then she announced that she was going to have her hair cut and to get a permanent and that I was going to pay for it. I told her that as far as I knew I wasn't. Oh, well—this is the same story. If I had lots of money and had paid my debts, I wouldn't mind—but if my job ends in January, will Momma give me anything? That's a useless question.

**TO RICHARD HUNTER • FLORENCE**

Eleonora is back! She made *The Knife* with Gene Kelly. She played a mad Italian woman.[18] In six weeks she returns to make another. I always said that she'd become the grand old lady of American movies. Most of all, she returning means soon you will be here. It's more than half over. Isn't that mean of me to be so selfish? But what a desert (the kind with sand) this has been. In about two hours G. Foy will be here. I have stage fright. Gosh—how I used to sit and wait

---

17. *GF:* "In my early days with Leo, when we went to visit Richard in Middletown, I slept in a guest room while he and Richard slept together. Leo really loved him; I didn't want to make him do without."
18. The MGM film, directed by Richard Thorpe, was released as *Black Hand* (1950).

for you—all over this city—breathlessly—until I thought that I would perish of suffocation—and my heart pounding and way up in my throat a huge lump. And that time at Yaddo when you came through the doorway, and I got up and moved out from the table as though a string pulled me straight to you—and that, strangely enough, was a turn in the screw which finally made us what we are today. But what a heavenly life, so full of happiness and agonies. I wouldn't have changed any of it—save to have had a larger or two apartments on the same floor—and a maid.

AUGUST 28, 1949 • NEW YORK CITY

**TO RICHARD HUNTER** • FLORENCE

Gray has returned determined to be happy and good and he is really trying very hard. So far it's very pleasant having him here—so happy and sweet—and I do hope that he can continue this way. It's heaven. He did three and one half drawings, while he was away, and part of a small painting—very pretty—like an explosion of thought in a bee's brain—all golden-silvery-brown. I hope though he gets some money from that monster Kirk [Askew].[19]

OCTOBER 10, 1949 • NEW YORK CITY

**TO RICHARD HUNTER** • PARIS

This is a sad letter so read it slowly, Tibby dear. I am sad about [the sale of the Hunter house in] Middletown, and if I knew where to call you I would. Well, we all do get forced to grow up, and now this house will have to be our home for a time.

I guess I had best tell you now, so it won't be too much of a shock later: I have had to sell all my books. And it broke my heart a little bit, but you would have been proud of me, because I didn't show it. I did it to get Jerry money he had to have because Momma and Poppa mismanaged. It was selling a little bit of my future and a great part—really almost all—of my visible past. I got $2,000 and gave it to Jerry. This was most painful. I lost fifteen pounds—which is good. It's too complicated to tell all. Gray was wonderful, but I wanted you like a small child wants somebody he knows is good from the past. Darling Tib— now we are quite grown up. I stole some of the books while they were being packed. Gray and Eugenia [Halbmeier] helped. It was like Southerners hiding their treasures because the Yanks were coming. I saved the Stanislavsky you gave me (Gray hid it) and the Virginia Woolf and the Proust. When they really took the books away, I only cried when I remembered all the times and places we bought the books—but that's growing up, and I am sure I'll have others— and it will be fun again.[20]

19. Leo thought Askew sold Gray's drawings too cheaply and withheld advances and payments.
20. Later, Leo was enraged to discover that his parents had not truly needed the money raised by the sale of his library. Ida Lerman was notorious in the family for using many ruses to get cash.

**SADLER'S WELLS AND MARGOT FONTEYN** *The most beautiful party I have seen in Manhattan? The American debut, opening night, of Sadler's Wells Ballet. Stars, corps, supers, conductor, and the guiding dragon leapt from our city's old yellow school buses, the Ballet transported from their fairyland on the stage of the old Metropolitan Opera House to a Manhattan— just for this one fragile night—on the lawn of the mayor's mansion. Dozens of tables on the green lawns sweeping toward the moon-glinting river, crimson-seated golden party chairs ringing the pink, flower-decked tables, red-coated waiters, a cross-hatching of held-high silver trays, shrubberies twined with fairy lights, eddies of men in white-tie, black-tie, women in whatever newly revived Paris had sold them. The lights blazed again, at least in Manhattan, jewels all out of heirloom vaults, effulgence, sparkle, and the band played on and on. This is all about hope and rebirth, a possible glorious future: If England, so devastated, could produce this gorgeous magic, this life-assuring triumph, then all was right with "our" world, at least for this radiant moment.*

*For months I had been hearing about the splendors of this* Sleeping Beauty. *"Wait until you see what Freddie [Ashton] has done with the Apotheosis. Wait!" Alice [Astor] told me over and over. I had heralded this "dream" in* Mademoiselle, *talked endlessly about it with Allene at* Vogue, *plotted with Carmel about it at* Harper's Bazaar, *for I was the only one who had a persuasive tongue and a hardworking hand simultaneously at all three, and now I knew that the embodiment of that "dream" was Margot Fonteyn. From the moment we perceived this pink flower-petal child rushing, remote beyond Oliver Messel's high-flung baroque arches, balustrades, rushing to a Grand Surprise, to Love, to Life, this small, piquant-faced, wide-eyed, dark-haired girl in her pink tutu was immediate assurance. The world was good, at last again, the world was good. Goodness emanated from Margot Fonteyn like a perfume. There was always this about the Margot I came to know—no matter what mean streets she walked.*[21] *(1993)*

**JOURNAL · JANUARY 2, 1950** Why are [soprano] Jennie Tourel and [harpsichordist] Wanda Landowska interested and delighted by scatological humor? It leaves me absolutely untouched—isolated. Why does it do this to me? I almost never see any humor in copulation or procreation, for it is so sublime— the emotion and sensation which arises from the act of love—why debase it? The robust Italian treatment—that is something else, for there is nothing snide or behind-the-barn about it. It is all natural as the act itself. And so with

---

21. The full-length *Sleeping Beauty* of Sadler's Wells was a triumphal beginning for Margot Fonteyn (1919–91), remembered by many today for her hugely successful partnership with Rudolf Nureyev from 1961 to 1976. Leo met her through Alice Astor after the ballet's New York debut. His remark about "whatever mean streets she walked" refers to the Panamanian politics of Fonteyn's husband, Roberto "Tito" Arias. In 1955 Fonteyn would be briefly arrested in Panama during a botched revolution organized by Arias, who was later paralyzed in an assassination attempt.

## Welcome, Sadler's Wells Ballet

Margot Fonteyn

Mr. [Roberto] Arias

David Webster

Alice [Astor Pleydell-]Bouverie

Freddie Ashton

Ruth Yorck

Bobby Irving

Anya Linden

Sol [Emma] Hurok

Mrs. Sol Hurok

P. W. Manchester

Anatole Chujoy

Lee Anderson

Cathleen Nesbitt

Oliver Smith

Viveca Lindfors

George Tabori

Julie Harris

Manning Gurian

Carol Channing

Ax Carson

[Alexandra] Choura Danilova

David Hersey

Brigitta Lieberson

Goddard Lieberson

Saul Steinberg

Hedda Sterne

Ruth Ford

Zachary Scott

Philip Bloom

David Shearer

Cornelia Otis Skinner

Geraldine Page

[Alexander] Sascha Schneider

Arthur Penn

Sono Osato

Victor Elmaleh

Siobhan McKenna

Bill Inge

Nancy Ryan

Wystan Auden

Chester Kallman

Constance [Hope] Berliner

Theo Berliner

Muriel Francis

Harold Clurman

Stella Adler

Truman Capote

Jack Dunphy

Mary Lou Aswell

Imogene Coca

Carl Van Vechten

Carson McCullers

[Arnold] Saint-Subber

Maria Tallchief

Paul Magriel

Buford Chisholm

Allene Talmey

Eugenia Halbmeier

Pat Neway

| | |
|---|---|
| Rouben Ter-Arutunian | Irving Penn |
| Mark Shaw | Lisa Fonsaggrives |
| Geri Trotta | Jeanette MacDonald |
| Norman Cousins | Walker Evans |
| Betsy Blackwell | Maggie Carson |
| Tobé Coburn | Tanaquil LeClercq |
| Robert Whitehead | George Balanchine |
| Virginia Whitehead | Diana Adams |
| Roger Stevens | Aileen Pringle |
| The Apfels [Iris and Carl] | Harry Abrams |
| Cecil Beaton | Mrs. Harry Abrams |

Elizabethan and Restoration comedy, or the French formal farces and come-dies, or the limericks of Norman Douglas. But dirty jokes are not amusing to me, and I do not think that this indicates thin blood.

APRIL 29, 1950  In bed again, because of being tired—and probably because I have a couple of deadlines. I am so resistant to writing that if this goes on I should find another way to exist. The idea of meeting a deadline becomes increasingly horrible. I am almost too weary to hold this notebook and pencil—but this must be mental, because of not wanting to write the review and the piece. I'll rest a bit and then try to work. . . . Such laxity—no one who wrote anything put off this way. The moment I have a deadline I do nothing save end-less research, but the writing—oh, no—even little memos or notes or paying bills, anything which means shouldering a burden, giving up just existing, just riding on the tide from moment to moment . . . I'll try now to drift into work-ing—gradually—pampering—ugh.

So this whole day, during which I have been so intensely depleted, has been an intermeshing of time past and time present: a band suddenly quivering the window glass as they thumped this morning, calling up those bands thirty years ago bringing heroes home from Armentières and the Marne and what was left of the Argonne. But the past is multiplied by the present and surrounds it like that quivery haze of heat that shimmers everywhere—on pavements, walls, flowers—and is a thin, tenuous pulsing veil between window frame and win-dow ledge on a hot summer day.

When I was a small boy I slept and dreamed and was frequently ill in a brass crib. One side could be lowered or raised by my elders—all bars intricately knobbed and golden. I knew these bars to be fairy wands, so it was my desire to work one loose—then I could transform, make magic. One morning I man-aged this—only to have it snatched by one of the elders and to receive a stinging slap, but it pained only the skin upon which it fell—the spirit, still inviolate, continued to believe in the knobbed wand and the magic. Sometimes I saw the loveliest beings—people aureate and elms gorgeously distorted—in the plump, glittering knobs. When I drowsed, I slipped away into the brass-bars-and-knobs land—becoming something as elusive as the burnished light, being that light. No one ever knew. It was a simple escape, especially if I licked the brass—but this somehow seemed to give away my secret, with disastrous consequences to my corporeal. Thus I learned soon that any escape to fairyland must be a secret one. And it was.

NOTE: Leo again shifts into a narrative past tense in desribing Eleonora von Mendelssohn.

JOURNAL · APRIL 30, 1950 Ela—From two sources she nourished herself—narcotics and love. For weeks she lay twisting in the arms of a lover not there—for a night he was. But where did the poppy dreams begin? The lover vanishing leaves the dream never ending? The needle—its thrust of release—and the lover—identical. The wonderful Italian lace bedcover with ducal arms upon pale green silk (the green of pressed spring leaves or faded, young green straw), the fabulous Mendelssohn jewels in cold-cream jars, the hats and veils, the furs, the ostrich coat . . .

MAY 2, 1950 What are the roots of these people—behind Grandpa, what fairy tale figure or legendary character? Behind Aunt Minnie, what lady in romance?[22] My reading was *Pioneers and Patriots of America*, fairy tales, and nursery rhymes—but the people in my life (save for certain Prince Charmings, like "Uncle" Herman [Wald]) had little connection with what I had read.[23] Did I then have deep atavistic Yiddish archetypes backing these people? Also, I was taken to the movies. "Cousin" Selma [Rosen], who did the shimmy in the kitchen the day Grandma was buried [in 1919], surely she represented some early jazz-baby movies siren—so the world of this sort of American child evolves—not from [medieval legend] Geneviève de Brabant, but from Douglas Fairbanks and ogre Germans and Jew haters and the boys playing epic figures in a pageant at school and the movie of Lincoln's assassination and death.

The situation of the world in 1914: the crossroad of displacement. A child born, as I was, in May 1914, got in right at the beginning of this displacement,

---

22. Minnie Poliner (1894?–1960) married Jacob Goldwasser's son Isidore (known as Irving, d. 1983), who prospered as the merchandising manager for men's clothing at Saks Fifth Avenue. Aunt Minnie was not always kind to young Leo, but she and Irving were the messengers who carried much Jazz Age culture into the Goldwassers' Orthodox home.

23. "Tall, dark-suited, plump, smiling, beautiful blond (then silver) wavy hair, round-faced, marvelous blue eyes. We were all in love with him. I can hear Uncle Herman's voice this moment—deep, Yiddish-inflected beneath a New York overlay, but charming. His face was litmus paper for our love, because he adored us, had been Momma's beau, and was Poppa's best friend." *Journal*, February 1, 1971.

but since the predisplacement world did not entirely vanish immediately, as Atlantis is said to have vanished, my world had islands, promontories, sometimes almost continents of pre-1914 world imbedded in it, as whole scraps of previous ages are to be found by archaeologists and students of history and decoration everywhere today. So, in the aging face of an old friend—when a birthmark or a scratch or a blond hair is suddenly encountered—it is possible to relive a moment long past. A single drop of the liquid of the past instantly drops into the liquid of this moment's impression, so muddling it that we do not for a time know is it now or yesterday, until the face before us reassembles as it is believed to be now, and we realize that memory, the repository of all, has beckoned us and we have followed.

MAY 12, 1950  Momma, about a plane shot down over the Baltic: "They were carrying that new thing they invented—personnel."

NOTE: In May 1950, Leo stopped working for *Vogue* and *Bazaar* to concentrate on *Mademoiselle*. Editor in Chief Betsy Blackwell provided secretarial help and expected him at *Mademoiselle* editorial meetings, but usually Leo worked at home. When he could find assignments with magazines that did not directly compete with *Mademoiselle*, he often accepted them. For six months in 1951, Leo was supervising editor of a short-lived New York monthly called *Park East*; in the late fifties, he wrote a regular column for *Playbill* magazine; and the *New York Times Book Review* occasionally commissioned a piece. One of the latter was a review of a biography of the nineteenth-century novelist Ouida.

JOURNAL · JUNE 25, 1950  Hearts—that was Ouida's business. She was monstrously ugly, this small swart female, and desperately in love—with that desperation that only the hideous must sustain—relentlessly. Her heart broke and tears fell upon the endless pages, watering them so well that fortunes grew and blossomed magnificently. She made it—spent it. Who knew more about broken hearts in this period of perpetual semicolons? George Eliot with her illicit Mr. Lewes? Miss Barrett with her runaway Mr. Browning? Lord Tennyson with his amiable home life and the grief of *In Memoriam*—long passed?[24] Compare Henry James's picture of society with Ouida's. Do they not overlap, especially in such books as *Portrait of a Lady* and *Moths*? The locales inevitably do, for fashion frequented the prescribed resorts. James's Madame Merle [in *Portrait of a Lady*] and Ouida's *ultra-dames* surely brushed gowns—perhaps even were intimates.

JULY 4, 1950  As I sit here writing, it is not known whether we shall be dead now, unexpectedly-expectedly. The headlines about [outbreak of war in]

24. The writer George Henry Lewes was the married lover of George Eliot. The dedicatee of Alfred, Lord Tennyson's *In Memoriam* was Arthur Henry Hallam, the poet's Cambridge friend, travel companion, and perhaps lover.

Korea make it so immediate. But if the Russians suddenly decided to do it with one bomb this would be Hiroshima—not knowing annihilation at all, just experiencing it. Gray will not even talk about it. I, the fatalist-optimist, have it here residing in me, and I abide with it—what else is there to do? It is waking high up in a house and hearing far below the persistent gnawing of a mouse.

NOTE: Gray went to Glenview, Illinois, to stay for several weeks with his aunt Alice to help her prepare for the wedding of her daughter, Barbara Cockrell.

AUGUST 17, 1950 • NEW YORK CITY

TO GRAY FOY • GLENVIEW, ILLINOIS

Goddard [Lieberson] took us to Sardi's tonight,[25] and I saw a memorial table full—Margaret Truman,[26] Jeanette MacDonald, and Jennie Grossinger!!! Three genuine pig-pusses. Margaret T is real common—or maybe it is just local. As for Jeanette MacD—you can't believe it. I wondered where Marion Davies is. I flirted with Jennie Grossinger and she looked angry-pleased. Finally, I told her who I was, and she said to the Mesdames Truman and Mac-Donald, "Isn't he a naughty child!" They looked real hard—in every sense of the word—and smirked. She got up and kissed me, and said again, "Oh—you naughty child!" Everyone in Sardi's stopped, and I felt like I should yell: "It's just my ma!" But I didn't. It was awful—and funny. Good night. I turn all the lights off. If anybody comments on letter frequency, this one came so soon because of sending you your mail.

**THE GROSSINGER**  *I can see myself sitting in what we called, when it was new, Radio City. I am sitting in an office, in a pool of warm electric light, waiting. I am waiting for a job. I am some two or three weeks out of acting school and I have heard that there could be jobs for a willing boy in a hotel called the Grossinger, way up in the Catskills, the star hotel on the Borscht Circuit.[27] I wait patiently and, by and by, a door opens, and a thin, grayish man comes out, peers at me with tired, knowing eyes. He is followed by a woman whose composure seems slightly ruffled, but whose attire is immaculately correct—a very pretty, beautifully cut, delicately patterned-in-flowers silk daytime dress; a little, brimmed, dark straw hat perched firmly on her tight profusion of blond hair; a plump face, generously lipped. When her blue eyes look in my direction, they smile at me. The woman says, with a familiar Yiddish inflection to her soft, care-*

25. Goddard Lieberson (1911–77), president of Columbia Records, commissioned Gray Foy to design record jackets and Leo to write liner notes for classical music albums. In 1946 Lieberson had married the ballerina Vera Zorina (Eva Brigitta Hartwig).

26. Margaret Truman (b. 1924), daughter of the president, became a best-selling mystery writer.

27. It is likely that Leo had heard of this Catskills theater from his cousin Frieda "Flo" Gold-wasser, who had married Jennie Grossinger's brother Harry in 1927. The couple operated an antique shop at the resort for many years.

fully modulated voice, "Are you waiting for me?" "Yes—I think I am." The man says, "Jennie, do you know this boy? He probably wants a job. . . ."

"What sort of job do you want?" asks Jennie. "I want to work in your theater. I hear it's a wonderful, growing theater. I want to work there." She laughs; her eyes crinkle. "Oh, you already heard about our theater. . . . What can you do?" "I can sweep the stage floor. I can design scenery and paint it. I can design costumes and paint them. I can act if I have to. I can do anything in the theater." She laughs. The man says, "What kind of experience do you have?" "I'm just out of acting school." And the woman says, "Which one?" "The Feagin School of Dramatic Art . . . I had a scholarship there for one year. . . ." They both laugh. They laugh quite a lot. The woman says to the man, "He's very funny—isn't he?" "It's going to cost you something, Jennie. . . ." Then he smiles wryly, and she says, "You could come to work for me, if you want—room and board, good kosher food—probably just like your mother's—two dollars a week . . . and everything you can possibly do around the theater you have to do." I ask nervously, "Who pays for the bus trip up?" They both laugh again, a lot. He says, "You better watch out for this one."

So I went to work for Jennie Grossinger. Those months that I stage-managed the Grossinger Playhouse could be subtitled "The Pleasures of Adversity." I was envied by everybody else, all my classmates and all of their friends, because they were all hunting for jobs. For three seasons—1934, 1935, 1936—from before Memorial Day to after Labor Day, I lived, literally breathed the world of the Grossinger Hotel. Grossinger's was, when I first became a summer inhabitant of this cyclonic world, on the verge of becoming the greatest, indeed the grandest hotel in the Catskill Mountains. And in fact, in my first summer, the Grossinger enjoyed what was known as its first "1,000-guest" weekend. It is difficult today to think what an enormous, flourishing, intensely Yiddish enterprise, what a Jewish triumph the Grossinger was.

The core of the Grossinger was its main building, containing its check-in desk, executive offices, some of its most desirable apartments, a jumble of rooms in which to relax (lounges with English sporting prints on the walls, country furniture), a dining room with an enormous breakfast menu, which I really believe began "Good Morning, Pickled Herring," and in which madam musicians sat playing during every lunch and dinner—potted-palm music, the kind that came from Vienna and Budapest and Old Broadway. The main building looked out over a big grassy place centered with English medallions of flowering plants, each looking like an aging opera singer. Then there were the buildings which seemed to grow each season and which contained an ever-increasing number of guests. As sunset approached on Friday nights, Jennie and her mother always stood on the landing above the front steps of the main house, looked heavenward, and moved their lips in prayer. I believe that part of this prayer was for the greater success of the Grossinger.

None of the health-giving amenities the Grossinger provided—the golf course, the tennis courts, the ploys of all sorts—really were for me. My life centered in the playhouse, where all summer long we did weekly concerts, revues, a big Saturday-night musical, and "dramatic plays," these last by a resident company which came up seasonally for that purpose. The entire aggregation of "entertainers" sometimes numbered some 125 people. They included stage crew, scenery painters, costume ladies, and assorted agreeable or malevolent personalities, who had "things to do" with the proceedings.

The playhouse was run by a small, cartoon-faced gnome of infuriating energy: he "wrote" the shows. Much of the material was based on burlesque sketches, popular Broadway shows, madcap impressions of current events—basic revue material. The Catskills had, indeed, never seen such shows. A typical Saturday-night revue included a whooping overture, half a dozen comedy sketches played by Hank Henry (the top banana already famous on the burlesque circuit and later a big star in Las Vegas) and his diminutive partner Al Parker (he frequently worked in drag and was sometimes given to dancing on tables or even on drums in dark blue light). The show also included Sylvia Sims, not the one who became famous for her jazz later but a monologuist who did "dramatic" scenes and recited Dorothy Parker to the utter joy of the audience.

Then there was the opera wing. It consisted of three people. I think they were called Lazarin the Basso, Mario the Tenor, and Brema the Soprano. They did trios from Don Giovanni. Sometimes the trios had not started out as trios, but they ended up as trios at the Grossinger. They did an abbreviated version of Faust one season. This was done with slides. The basso was hidden below stage. Being somewhat unsure of when, as Mephistopheles, he should materialize, he would frequently raise the trapdoor, peer out into the audience—they seeing only the whites of his eyes—and mutter in his Russian-Yiddish voice, "Now?" Marguerite ascended to heaven backed by angels who were headed to hell, since I had put the slide in upside down. The 1,000-member audience screamed and shouted and wanted an encore. They loved Grand Opera.

The Grossinger audience got Cockney songs, a tryout by Danny Kaye, Yiddish theater with Jennie Moscowitz (a great Jewish tragedienne-comedienne, who had started her career when she ran away to join Sarah Bernhardt's troupe), even bits of Greek drama, sex talks, and six chorus girls done up in lavish beads and hand-painted grosgrains (we bought these at the Ziegfeld auction) swaying and stroking themselves to the sound of "Temptation," or swirling girlishly to "Alice Blue Gown."

Jennie Grossinger was fond of me, and sometimes in the late afternoon we would walk together down a path toward the playhouse, which sat there on the brow of a hill like some great ark. On a hill opposite the Grossinger eminence, in the late-afternoon light we could see an orchard of flowering apple trees. Under each tree was its prone shadow. One afternoon, I said to Jennie, "They look like ballerinas upside down. . . ." Jennie turned her blue eyes at me and said, "I love *dancers. . . . I never had time. . . ." Then she looked around, and she smiled and she looked at me: "But look at all of this."* (1993)

**JOURNAL • AUGUST 20, 1950** I am in bed—perhaps for two or three days— even a week—before the slight excuse of this cold evaporates and the magazine realizes that I have not appeared for some days and inquires whether I do not wish to work there anymore. A slight cold, when accompanied by a little fever, makes a legitimate oasis in the tumult of living from day to day. These few days in bed bring an illusion of forever, as when I was a little boy—ill for a year at a time—in the great brass bed set upon a platform so that Momma could see Fifth Avenue and the park beyond when she was ill, which was almost always.

**NOTE:** In January 1951, *Mademoiselle* sent Leo to London to research a feature on the British Broadcasting Corporation (BBC).

His only previous trip to Europe had been with Richard to England, Wales, and Ireland in the summer of 1937, for which Leo had taken a monthlong break from stage-managing a Broadway production called *Behind Red Lights*.

JANUARY 11, 1951 • LONDON

**TO RICHARD HUNTER • NEW YORK CITY**

I have just been out walking on Piccadilly and over all those streets which we knew so very well fourteen years ago. So many whores still, and Berkeley Square almost utterly modern apartment houses—but here I am in London, and I do truly love it more than New York. It again is coming home. I feel absolutely alive and marvelous here. Why is that? Oh, how I do love luxury! And no offices to go to. And how I do love flying. I am a bit tipsy, for I have had an excellent dinner at the current rage—Les Jardins des Gourmets. David [Webster, head of Covent Garden] and his friend Jimmy [Bell] took me—and then to something called the Buckingham Club (full of willowy English teeps), and, before all that, Peter [Wilson] came and fetched me to his huge eighteenth-century amazing house where he lives with a friend, Harry [Wright] (a charming boy).[28] His little son Philip was there, because it is still holidays here, a sweet, beautifully mannered boy as only English children can be—very pretty, long-lashed blue eyes, blond, sort of Gray-like. We went to a wonderful circus, one-ring—and that is how it should be, not too complicated and huge. The Henry Greens are giving a party for me Saturday night.[29] I feel

28. Leo and Richard had met the British cataloger and auctioneer Peter C. Wilson (1913–84) through Denyse and Richard Dreyfus in the early forties, just as Wilson's career took flight. As chairman of Sotheby's from 1958 to 1980, Wilson would lead the auction house's global expansion, and it was he who, in the mid-sixties, would arrange for Leo to write a history of the firm. Harry Wright had been a servant in one of the lofty country houses when he and Wilson met. By the mid-fifties, he had become host in Wilson's house in Kent.
29. Henry Green was the nom de plume of British novelist Henry Yorke (1905–73). His wife, Adelaide Biddulph, was called "Dig."

like a regular little picture star. Peter sends his love to you. They are divorc-
ing—and his house is large enough for all of us. He is giving a party for me on
the twenty-third and David is taking me to the country all Sunday (and I think
Brighton) and my head is in a gay whirl. This is exactly what I needed. Tomorrow I [interview with the] BBC. What a strange, wonderful-lucky man I am.

This is just a good night note to tell you that I could not come home without going to Clarges Street. Everywhere I find us—and somehow it is long ago
and now all at the same moment. Only Virginia Woolf knew exactly this.[30]

JANUARY 12, 1951 • LONDON
**TO GRAY FOY** • NEW YORK CITY

Baby dear—It is very early in the morning, almost three, and after coming into
this pretty room, with its enormous bathroom (such a luxury), from a party at
Peter Wilson's, I sat reading the newspapers to bridge the interval wherein being
alone makes me absolutely sick with longing for you. This is the awful time, the
lonely time—but all the day long as I go about this really extraordinary city,
which I do love so very much, you are with me, and I talk to you constantly—
comparing and pointing out. So many things here you would love, but it is chilly
almost all the time, because they have so little coal, and the [rationed] food is
brave, and the women in the streets do look shabby, and places like broken teeth
show where bombs fell—but so much has been all built up again. I went to the
opera tonight—*Pique Dame*. It was so very good, so integrated. Why can't the
Met do this? It is so shameful what we have. The English was all understandable, none of it embarrassing, and the Messel decor excellent, so accurate—
1792ish, a period almost never seen on the stage. This opera house is something
out of Pollock's [toy theaters]—smaller than the Met, all pinkish, white, and
gold, and everywhere the feeling of royalty, such a feeling of elegance with
many people "dressed" and dukes and their ladies. Next to me—unexpectedly—
Freddie Ashton, and not far off [theatrical designer] James Bailey.

I was occupied almost all day with BBC people. They are spread in some
forty buildings throughout London. I visited some in what was formerly the
very fashionable Hotel Langham, where Ouida lived when she was in London.
I was terribly pleased to see it—even as it is now—all offices, but each office has
a fireplace. People here unconnected with BBC—the public—seem so apa-
thetic to radio, and some of them feel that it is too controlled. One never hears
a radio here, as in New York, although over eight million have them. How still
it is. My pen stopped scratching and the silence was appalling. Oh darling, I

---

30. Richard and he had stayed in a cheap rooming house on Clarges Street in 1937. "That
freezing winter of 1951 I was living at the Ritz. I had not even dared to enter it in 1937, a war
and fourteen years away, but stood looking longingly. When my sack split and fat green-
gages, bought from a barrow back of the Queen's and Globe [theaters] on a hot July afternoon, rolled into Piccadilly, I lost my dinner. I was very poor in 1937, but happy beyond
sanity." *Journal, December 27, 1970.*

wish that you were here and could see London, because if you also loved it I would try very hard to make it possible for us to live here. I can't understand why it seems like coming home. It has big disadvantages, but so very many compensations. The eye always finds something to enchant it, and the city is filled with so many people out of books and with those who wrote them. It is so much all the past 250 years, with evidences of them everywhere, and the people are so very courteous. When I came into the lobby this morning, the lights were all dim and the porter asleep in his chair, and someone with violets had just passed along the passage, for perfume was heavy on the air. My key is huge and silver, the elevator is all gilt-and-looking-glass cage, the stairways circle huge wells, and the carpets are flowery red. You see, my love, why I am so enamored. I am still living like a very rich man—and it is fun, but how much more it would be if you were here, because I can just see your dear beautiful eyes—enormous with delight.

JANUARY 17, 1951 • LONDON

**TO GRAY FOY** • NEW YORK CITY

I have had a beautiful evening with Elizabeth Bowen in her genuinely lovely house.[31] It is the corner house on Clarence Terrace, which is a great terrace and crescent of early Regency houses actually erected in Regent's Park. So it stands heartbreakingly Palladian and utterly detached from this world, like architecture in an old colored engraving—mysterious, remote, frozen in its own time. She and her husband [Alan Cameron] (who is usually too ill to see people) live there and—because of conditions now—Philip Harding has their top floor, but this is a very large house, and he is wonderfully charming (the only one of Alice [Astor]'s husbands for whom I can see any reason whatsoever, and I suspect that he still loves her. I must say that watching him I did begin to think that she is a pretty shabby woman).[32] Elizabeth has a wonderful cook, a deaf Frenchman, her only servant. The house is spotless. All of the plaster, which she says was original and exquisite, was shattered by bombing. But the great windows from floor to ceiling with vistas of porticos and lake and piedmonts (all classical, like in illustrations for early nineteenth-century Russian tales)—most of them are intact. And she has the most beautiful china and glass I have yet seen. She genuinely lives with grace—even her broken chairs are

---

31. Leo had been sent to Elizabeth Bowen (1899–1973), author of novels (*Death of the Heart*) and short stories, by the Askews and Grace Zaring Stone.
32. Alice Astor had been married from 1938 to 1943 to the British soldier and journalist Philip Harding (1906–74?). They had one child, Alice's fourth, Emily Harding. She had taken five-year-old Emily to America in 1946, and Harding did not see his daughter again until after her mother died in 1956. GF: "Alice had such varied tastes—Hofmannsthal to Obolensky to Harding. She was very asexual looking—elegant, brittle, very beautiful, almost like a Chinese painting. She had very black hair usually slicked back. I never heard her raise her voice, not even in laughter—very controlled, muted, but her passion was not and was misplaced."

lovely. We talked and talked—about Virginia Woolf and novels and her work and one another. I do love her dearly. All the time, the shadows of branches and lamplight from outside (when she drew the heavy, mossy green curtains aside to show me the park stretching away).

Before this the Greens gave a lovely festivity. I met [novelist] William Sansom who is very neat and well-tailored and soft, but precisely spoken—and it was fun. Penelope [Reed] is flying back to see me before I go—so that is a joy—and Dame Edith [Evans] called to say she was giving a small dinner for me, Alec Guinness, and his wife [Merula Salaman], etc., on Thursday. She lives in Albany, a place I have always wanted to see.[33] So I have two old, old wishes come true—to go into a house in Clarence Terrace and to see inside Albany. All those dreams when I read novels long ago and wondered. If only you were here to share it.

JANUARY 17, 1951 • LONDON

**TO RICHARD HUNTER** • NEW YORK CITY

Just a quick good night scrawl to say that this is the loveliest experience. London is cold (always), rainy, monotonous, and sparse in food, dirty . . . everything you hear, but it is lovely. I adore it.

I just wanted to tell you this—and to say that I try very hard here not to be unhappy. We should be fulfilling these dreams of our youth together. You see, my dear, I do love you very much, and I will always. I am desperately sorry for what life has done to us—but at the core of all my joy here is our joint young ghosts—and sometimes it is too much. I can never even have the somewhat dubious solace of saying, "Why did this happen to us?" for I know. Well, now I feel better—but it was too awful for a moment jumping out of a taxi in Clarence Terrace right into a July fourteen years ago. I can even remember what you wore. Good night, my darling, sweet, pig-headed boy. Maybe in our next lives we will be wiser.

**AN END** *When I was flying home from London that January it took almost three days for some reason, and I, who can so frequently know when "something" will happen, did not even feel a hint. But when Richard and Gray looked at me, as I came toward them in the airport, I knew—but to whom and what? They did not tell me until we were going into my downstairs, through the gate. "It's in the papers." Gray's voice was hidden. Then I knew: "Eleonora . . ."* (1993)

**JOURNAL** • JANUARY 30, 1951 • NEW YORK CITY Constantly I question how can she be dead? And I do not believe it—not at all. In the vestibule of the

33. Formerly a house of Lord Melbourne, in 1802 Albany was divided into bachelor's apartments. It has housed a distinguished succession of politicians and artists, including Edith Evans (1888–1976), a great British stage actress known primarily for her comic character roles (including Lady Bracknell).

church, her friends clutched one another, pressed cheeks to one another's. Laci's coffin had been small, green, dark, and compact. It rode on a wagon.[34] Ela's was large, lighter green, womanly—it rode on the shoulders of eight men. When the coffin came up the aisle, I thought that the organ had burst into the Mendelssohn "Wedding March." I heard it distinctly. In the gutter, two bright scarlet roses twined together with wire, some of their petals scattered.

The bad people got her in the end. (Laci got himself—his past, his sickness got him.) How can it be that I can't ring her up—her clutter still there in her room?

FEBRUARY 1, 1951 • NEW YORK CITY

**TO RUTH YORCK** • MUNICH

I am still in bed with the flu aftermath and the bottom falling out of our world. As you now know, darling, I do love you very much. You are in my blood. You know, of course, that Ela did not kill herself. At first, at two in the morning, when I finally got into this house and was exhausted from coming home by way of Iceland and Gander [Newfoundland] and they told me, I believed that she had killed herself, but then I was too incredulous to think of anything save believing. The next morning (and I still wait for her to call up), I knew as I looked at a photograph of her, which I saw accidentally, next to my bed where I have always had it, that she did not kill herself, and that either this was an accident or she was murdered. For a long time I thought: What is the lesson to learn from this? Then, last night, I realized how the pure and the good will always be done in by the bad and the weak and the corrupt, if they (the pure) do not take care always. . . .

This is worse for Hellmut [Roder], in many ways, and for others than for us. We have lives so totally ours and such capacity for living, and they do not have our resources—although sometimes we do not want our strength and would wish to be weak with the weak, and to lean upon and not be the ones to support.

One never, never believes in death, but that is strange because it is so definite. Did she not die as she had lived? Turbulently. Mysteriously. Did she kill herself? Did she die by an accident of a pillow falling as she drowsed into love? Did that horrible man [Kosleck] murder her? Without you it is almost impossible to separate anything. . . .[35]

34. Leo's lover of a decade earlier, Ladislas "Laci" Czettel, had been found a suicide on March 5, 1949.
35. The police made an investigation of Eleonora von Mendelssohn's death, but never brought charges. Leo recollected later that both her husband and his younger male lover were there when Mendelssohn died. A pillow was found over her face, and a bath mat in the apartment had been soaked with ether.

When Cesco came to the coffin, he saw the Maestro medal on her and he took it, but then he was made to give it back. How like in life this was—taking from her everything . . . and of course she also took—always. Now the wrangles with Twardowski persuading Kosleck to hire a lawyer on his own to get money from the estate, saying that if Koz needs three nurses a day, not to hire them, because he will take care of Koz, if they give him the money. This is so murky.[36] When she lived, her life was surrounded with dirty, shabby, shoddy people, and because she was pure—above this muck—it inevitably came out good. Written in a newspaper, her life would not read with the beauty we know it to have had, with the sporadic generosity and the vast energy of love. It would be ugly, with the bare so-called details of her everyday living set down by a reporter. But she rose above this, making it a richness and a vitality and a dazzling thing—invigorating all who genuinely loved her. If only we had a recording of the little sounds in that room that morning, we should then know what happened. All summer, neighbors heard them fighting. Frequently, she would scream that he would kill her. The most incredible part is that we did not expect her to die before we did.

I asked Touche to read the first Rilke elegy, and some Beethoven and Bach were well sung . . . but only the greatest music and the most magnificent production could have touched its central figure. The world having fallen on poor days, we did not have this, and without you to feed such tributes they do not happen.

Darling . . . do you know whether Ela and [Rudolf] Forster were ever actually divorced? This could now be important. I have their marriage license here among some of her papers that she sent to me to keep some months ago. . . .

JOURNAL · FEBRUARY 11, 1951  Ela seems to be fading. I look at her only with delight, a sweet delight, and see her always in one of those wispy sheer nightgowns, her hair flying and that smile, that one-third shy, one-third imp, one-third womanly-wisdom smile.

FEBRUARY 16, 1951  Faulkner didn't want to go to Sweden to accept the Nobel Prize. The State Department called him and said because of the delicate international situation wouldn't he go. He said no. His daughter (in the local high school) said she would want to go. He said yes. Called Random House, his wife did, and said Bill was ill in bed with a cold, would Random get him a cutaway and trousers? What size, they asked. She didn't know. She asked Bill. He didn't know. Random then had to know. She said couldn't they take a chance. No. She said Bill said to go to a place named Brooks. So finally they

36. Shortly before Mendelssohn's death, Kosleck had injured himself by jumping out the window of their apartment above the carpenter's shop. Hans Heinrich von Twardowski (1898–1958), also a German-born actor, was a friend of Kosleck. They often played Nazis in Hollywood movies, which intensified Leo's aversion to them.

said they'd chance it, decided why be extravagant, and hired it for him. He went off to Sweden with it. Came back, said they'd let him down in only one way. The king of Sweden's trousers had two stripes, Bill's only one. He wanted to keep the suit, he liked it so much. But would they please have another stripe added? They have. They think he wants it to save to be buried in. Recently they sent him $10,000 for a tractor. He gets any money he wants.

Yesterday [publicist] Leonard Myers told me that the day Maestro heard about Ela he wouldn't let anyone near him. He was in a rage. Now he plays his farewell concert abruptly—tomorrow.

FEBRUARY 18, 1951 It came to me at Maestro's farewell that Ela was everywhere in the hall, because her existence was now entirely in the hearts and minds of those who knew her. Maestro is at last an old, old man, grasping with his left hand a rail (set around the podium for this purpose) to support him. He is erect and rigid with age, conducting with his baton hand (right), until he cannot control himself and breaks out with his left hand. The audience, very small and nondescript, wept. No applause at any time. He stepped off the podium and stood a moment as though to make up his mind, as though to resume some other more prosaic self. Unsettled. Then he walked away among the musicians, slowly, a lonely, sick, dying old man. The silence roared. Ela would have been heartbroken. He will probably conduct no more. But she sat there shaking her head incredulously, soaring with the tumult, deflated, less than vapor when he finished.

FEBRUARY 26, 1951 A strange illness seems to have purged me of a wave of eating. For me eating is so much what drinking is to others. I become an eato-maniac, as Peter [Lindamood] becomes a dipsomaniac. Only a shock makes me pause. All cravings which are satisfied to excess are maniac and must be treated by the same general curative: Shock alleviates it for a time.

MARCH 13, 1951 Last night at the Olivia de Havilland *Romeo & Juliet*, I realized that the Nurse was a wicked, genuinely immoral, lazy woman, and that she is, actually, the Mrs. Danvers who permits Juliet to undo herself, and even abets her, in what the Nurse must know is a fatal act. This Nurse lives in the moment, is spoiled, lewd. In the park, even today, nurses and chauffeurs of this astonishing irresponsibility are to be found. Edith Evans came close to playing her, but I have never seen a production which has been staged to present her this way. Perhaps it would be anticapitalist.

MAY 3, 1951 · NEW YORK CITY

**TO RICHARD HUNTER** · ATHENS

Remember about the hideous poison pen letters *Park East* [magazine] has been getting from some maniac? We turned them over to the postal authorities, and they haven't been able to do anything about them yet. Today, one of them, on an open penny postcard, came addressed to me. It is a most unpleasant one—making references to sex, etc. Of course, I am very upset. It is quite frightening to feel—and know—that some crazy or malevolent person is interested in one. Also, what if they or she or he sends these things to *Mademoiselle* or the *Times*?

MAY 15, 1951 · NEW YORK CITY

**TO RICHARD HUNTER · ATHENS**

We went to a screening at the Modern Art—an awful movie, but we came early, and pretty soon a big dark-haired woman came in and spoke to me and it was Nita Naldi. Then a blonde, very pretty, came in and bounced up, and it was Gilda Gray. Almost at once Carmel Myers, Patsy Ruth Miller, Lila Lee, and Leatrice Joy joined our circle . . . and it was like old-home week and all the girls back for class reunion. Gray and I loved it, because they all fell on one another with refined shrieks of enchantment and gave us glamorous looks and were so genuinely glamorous and good-looking and more fun than these twerps today. They all said wasn't it wonderful about Gloria [Swanson]? And had anyone heard from Aileen Pringle? Nita Naldi said she'd had a letter from Betty Compson and Aileen was just grand.[37] Then she turned to Gilda, pointed at Gray, and said she didn't know this child's name . . . and Gray sat there round-eyed and blushing. Then Luise [Rainer] and Josephine Hull [of the movie *Harvey*] came in and none of these ladies paid them any mind at all.

MAY 31

Miss [Elizabeth] Bowen came to dinner on Monday and Allene and Mary Lou and Maggie Cousins (the *Good Housekeeping* [managing editor] woman) and later Louis and Emmy Lou [Kronenberger][38] and Alice and Touche, and it was loads of fun. Miss Bowen told somebody that this is her favorite house in New York, and she loves best to come here. I was pleased because something like this is still unreal to me and it's a long way from Momma's.

So I had a tea on my birthday [May 23]. It was a nice tea, which Gray and Eugenia [Halbmeier] provided. I contributed the cake, one of those big strawberry ones from Long's, and twenty-five people, including us, came and I

---

37. These women were all stars of silent films: Nita Naldi appeared frequently as a temptress, famously opposite Valentino in *Blood and Sand*; Gilda Gray is said to have introduced the shimmy; Carmel Myers often played vamps; Patsy Ruth Miller had many leading roles, notably with Lon Chaney in *The Hunchback of Notre Dame*; Lila Lee was a demure actress whose career lasted into the talkies; Leatrice Joy was a favorite player of Cecil B. DeMille; Gloria Swanson had resurrected her career by starring in Billy Wilder's *Sunset Boulevard* in 1950; Aileen Pringle made more than sixty films, retiring in 1939; Betty Compson was a top star, memorable in *The Big City* and *The Docks of New York*.
38. Louis Kronenberger (1904–80), a drama critic, novelist, and translator, was married to Emmy Lou Plaut.

didn't get many presents because I didn't tell anyone it was my birthday, but I didn't mind, mostly I minded that you and Eleonora weren't here. Those horrors had her secretly cremated. She was terrified of that, and they knew it. I wonder whether they wanted to destroy some sort of evidence. But what's the good of worrying now. It can't bring her back.

JUNE 11, 1951 • NEW YORK CITY

**TO RICHARD HUNTER** • ATHENS

So now I've seen all the remaining great country houses in [New York's] Dutchess and Columbia counties, and I've had the perfect weekend at Alice's. It's like the dream prewar English country houses—endless nannies, dogs, friendly servants, flowers everywhere, wonderful food "created" by a great chef, such privacy, space, and fun—and so many books and beautiful things and your shoes and clothes all cleaned and pressed every day and breakfast in bed or on the terrace, which looks out over the Hudson—and scones for tea and elevenses (but nobody is down that early save I). Did you know that Mr. Astor wrote bad Jules Verne stories for a hobby?

My deep anguish over Eleonora has been transmuted to an acceptance now. Marlene did this by telling me that had she lived it would have been dreadful for her. The narcotic squad was about to put her away. It's a bizarre story—and such a Lily Bart end.[39]

**JOURNAL** • JUNE 13, 1951 Yesterday I was fired from *Park East*. "You set the magazine up and did very well for us. Now we feel we can go on without you." I gave a party and everyone had a lovely time, even the day was beautiful.

JUNE 17, 1951 Early this morning, at about 1:45, I went to lock the iron garden door, as we always do before taking to our bed. I looked out into our garden. To the right—halfway or so out, I know the exact spot—a man stood. He was in a pale-colored (perhaps white) summer suit. I saw distinctly (all in a moment) how it was cut—with the jacket corners rounded instead of square. His hands and arms were hanging down straight at his sides. He wore black shoes. He stood dreadfully still. I looked straight at him—but suddenly screamed—such an almost strangled sound: "Gray! Gray!" As he came running from the closet and latched the door, I ran through the bedroom to the refrigerator, here I hid my face and wept and shivered. All the time, I repeated, "A man in the garden—standing in pale summer clothes—" I did run before I saw this man's face. I was terrified. I sat on the bed and wept. I had a feeling

---

39. In Edith Wharton's novel *The House of Mirth* (1905), Lily Bart commits suicide after a succession of misalliances and scandals end her chance for success in fashionable society. "Ela's dear absurdity—toward the end this grew wearisome, for the world had changed. We were no longer behind walls, and we had to earn our livings." *Journal, December 14, 1970.*

that this had something to do with Richard. I did not tell Gray, but I have had little flashes of uneasiness about Richard these last two or three days. This was a small, neat, slender man standing silently, diagonally in the garden. When we looked later—as I knew—he was gone. It gave some sort of solid comfort to stand on the same stone where he had stood. Gray and I were both shattered by this experience. I told him I would tell him next week with whom the man was connected. I will not say now because saying frequently makes a suspicion—all too true.

JUNE 18, 1951 Today, almost all day—or rather yesterday now—I was so close to tears. I suppose that this is what is known as "a highly unsettled state." Now this morning, after Gray lowered the bedroom blind, I was forced to raise it, so the poor ghost—whoever he is—and oh please, please that he isn't who—but I wanted him to know that he is welcome here, and that I love him, and that yesterday morning I ran away because it was so unexpected and sudden. Not even in a private notebook can I write what is deep within me. When Gray asked what would make me certain of what I don't know completely, "Time," I said, "time."

11:50 P.M. The weight seems to have lifted a bit, almost as though Richard were now coming out of danger—or free of it.

NOTE: For *Mademoiselle*, Leo wrote an article about the "lady editors" who had created or were running the leading women's magazines of the day. Betsy Blackwell, Edna Chase, and Carmel Snow were included. The following are his notes from an interview with Diana Vreeland, then fashion editor of *Bazaar*.

JOURNAL • JUNE 20, 1951 Diana Vreeland on Carmel Snow:[40]

The best glands in the world.
Terrific early-morning clarity.
She's not like a person who lives in actuality.
A contemplative, mystical woman.
The thing that makes her tick is her mystical Catholic quality.
Her mystical essence is the beginning and end of Carmel Snow.
Whatever the Catholic Church gives in its complete essence.
Those miniature bones, which attain elegance.
The most divine knees.
There's very little elegance in the world, and you can't acquire it.
She doesn't have great elegance of mind.

40. A legendary flamboyant personality of the fashion business, Diana Vreeland (1906–89) was fashion editor at *Harper's Bazaar* (1937–61), editor in chief at *Vogue* (1961–71), and ultimately became a special consultant to the Metropolitan Museum's Costume Institute (1973–85).

She's still a child.
Her Irish characteristics.
The Blarney Stone's her desk, her bed, her everything.
The best sense of humor.
Her wonderful sense of gossip.
She's educating herself all the time.
Her cleanliness, her sweetness, her naïveté.
When you lose your naïveté, God has left you.
Carmel is the most divine woman.
It isn't respect, it's kind of like spoiling somebody—or thing—to upset her.
People keep her so carefully.
She does needlepoint, reads everything, is voraciously interested in all.
She's always in the midst of a great flirtation.

JUNE 28, 1951 • NEW YORK CITY

**TO RICHARD HUNTER • PARIS**

Tibby, we had a bad happening. Gray received a special-delivery late last night from his aunt Alice. She told him that his stepfather has been trying to divorce his mother for some seven months now, and he seems to have lost his mind or something, and Maebelle has lived away from her house for a month, and now Earle [Hughes] (Gray's stepfather) has disappeared, and it is such a mess.[41] So Gray must go to California next week, and he doesn't know how long he will be gone. Ah me. It's most upsetting, and I am exhausted from working so hard. So, it is a consolation to think of you having a beautiful time. This broken-down house has been offered to me for $20,000, but I can't think of that now. What a year. I'm worried about Gray going out there. What if Earle is jealous of him, as I know he is, and tries to do something to him?

**JOURNAL • JULY 1, 1951** This evening, Gray said that I was such an impractical dreamer, always saying I would get $10,000 for an article or some such thing and never doing anything about it, and I'd better stop. I was so depressed at dinner that I could not eat for a time. It was as though he had wiped away all my substance for a moment, for I know how much I am of dreams made. My whole fabric is of dreams. But he meant it well, and it is because he feels that I do too much work. I've tried to explain that this is how I must do, but he doesn't understand this. I am utterly selfish, for all I do is to assure my own comfort, my own ego. Is there such a thing as a selfless action? I doubt it. The

41. Maebelle Durfy Hughes (1898–1991) was Gray's mother. Raised in Dallas, at seventeen she married Frederick Gray Foy, Sr., an alcoholic, whom she divorced in 1926, when their only child was four. Within a year, Maebelle and her younger sister Alice Woodyard (later McKay, at the time also recently divorced) moved to Los Angeles. There, Maebelle married Francis "Earle" Hughes around 1933. Maebelle worked for many years as a salesclerk at Magnin's, a fashionable department store, and lived in Burbank.

good is when the action accrues to another's constructive benefit. We're all of us cannibals. But nobody has the right to destroy another's dreams, unless the dreamer and his dreams are destructive to others and even to himself.

JULY 1, 1951 • NEW YORK CITY

TO RICHARD HUNTER • PARIS

I wish I could recapture the wonderful safe feeling I used to have years ago when I knew where you were resting your head and where Eleonora was resting hers and Rut [Yorck] hers and Sylvia [Hunter] hers.[42] In so short a time all dispersed, all gone . . . but if I go on this way it becomes bathos and self-pity . . . and that's silly and life is less difficult for me than for many others so I should be trusting and believe that always sooner or later happiness descends. The most depressing and most uplifting thing one learns as one grows older is that time really moves more rapidly than light. Lo—you are here; lo—you are not. The longest moment is nothing, absolutely nothing, and the briefest hour is forever. This may be corny but it is true and reassuring and, as I say, depressing.

I wonder if I have anything cheerful to report. . . . I shall get some money from the *Times*, inasmuch as they asked me to write 1,200 words on the new Cecil Beaton book [*Photobiography*]. And they said that I was the person who did the best social history pieces they had. So that's indeed a gay thing to report.

JULY 14, 1951 • 6 A.M. • WESTHAMPTON, NEW YORK

TO RICHARD HUNTER • PARIS

I am sitting here at a little writing desk, before a little window that is so very similar to Quidnet, because from it on one side is a vista of tumbling ocean, and on the other is a bay, beach grass, sweet little birds, and dawn. I am in Alice's house in Westhampton, and it is so relaxing. I couldn't bear to sleep tonight because of being right beside the ocean—for this is a long, old, big, rambling house right in the dunes. The fragrance of salt and wild roses and sea grasses all commingled is so wonderful. This is a genuine Mary Roberts Rinehart house.

11 A.M.

Now I am awake again in a light by-the-sea morning. Waking, the sound was autos rushing and whooshing along a highway—far away—coming closer—close—right here—and fading. Then I realized these motors were all waves rolling in and breaking on the shore. Then I heard long, high-up voices calling only as voices sound at the shore, and, my eyes still shut, I thought: Soon I will open my eyes, and Richard will be here in the bed next to me—all scrunched up, maybe holding one of his ears. Then, for this was suddenly unbearable, I

---

42. Richard's sister-in-law Sylvia Hunter had been a close friend in the thirties, when they were all pursuing theater work. She moved to California in 1949.

opened my eyes—and, of course, you weren't, and the seashore voices went right on calling. And I thought: How can anyone live too long, for life is intolerable, and even the medicine that one knows he must take is, still, medicine. I must tell you, and it is best to tell you when you are far away, so as you will not forget this when you are here, that I love you as I never could love anyone else. Gray is a child to be protected and loved in another and—God forgive me— unlike way, but you are my true love—and now, like a man who has once lived in a paradise (or so it seemed to him, though he saw the poisonous plants and vipers in it) and has been forced by life itself to leave it, I am always walking there—all the time—while apparently I am here, or in my office, or lying in bed at home beside Gray, whom I do love—but not in overwhelming, annihilating passion. I am telling you this because you already know it—and probably even surmise how many times I sit miserably in a room or a train or at a meeting—because I find life so relentless and hope so in danger—know that I carry it within me like some precious globed fruit—treasuring it, eating of it sparingly but incessantly.

But now china clatters, ice tinkles in glasses downstairs, and I know that I must put on a shirt and trousers and socks and shoes and be sure to take my wallet—and hide this letter away—and go downstairs where other people, who have probably been miserable in their rooms, will also sit waiting and being every day beside the sea, now meekly creeping up the shore and just as silkily, suavely creeping away. I must tell you briefly and without being a would-be writer while doing it, that I love you as deeply and madly and painfully as the first time you kissed me in Central Park—while that bloody beautiful robin tootled. And I am so very pleased about it, because each life must have a continuity and this isn't a bad one—is it?

JULY 19, 1951 · NEW YORK CITY

**TO GRAY FOY** · BURBANK, CALIFORNIA

Did I write to you about Brigitta and Goddard [Lieberson] and the magnificently situated house in which they summer rent-free with butlers and maids and a vista like a Patinir [Dutch landscape]?[43]

Brigitta looks tan and lovely and the little boys are wonderful. I ate a sparse dinner and came home and ate a little more. It was a pleasant, unfraught evening during which I discovered Brigitta and her mother had once been befriended by Rut, who had them living in her [rented] palace in Venice, where they were broke. Brigitta seems to like Rut very much and didn't know that she was [nowadays] always broke. Isn't that odd? Just now Marlene calls. I

---

43. As Vera Zorina, Brigitta Hartwig Lieberson (1917–2003) danced with Les Ballets Russes de Monte Carlo (1934–36). Her appearance in the 1937 London production of *On Your Toes* led to a contract with MGM and roles on Broadway. Zorina's choreography was usually by George Balanchine, to whom she was married (1938–46). Soon after their divorce, she married the record producer Goddard Lieberson.

mean I am typing with one hand and listening to her with the other. She's in a state of being over that Siamese [Yul Brynner], and she's upset, and she talks about you a great deal. She wanted to know whether you would spend any time with her if she comes to California.

**YUL BRYNNER** *Marlene asked: "Who is this Yul Brynner?" "Oh, he is very big at Columbia television, and he is going to be the lead in the new Rodgers & Hammerstein show, the one with Gertie Lawrence, and I've known him a long time, and you know very well who he is because Claude Alphand was his mistress. . . ." "Oh . . . Claude . . . all of those white curtains . . . She really needed all of those white curtains.*[44] *. . ." The next day Marlene called, "Noël knows your Yul Brynner, and he feels I must know him, so he has arranged it. . . ."*

*So then she got to know Yul Brynner. She was lost in a deep, lady-waiting-at-the-telephone, all-pervasive passion. This amused me very much, for the Yul Brynner I knew had been so like the silky boy, Chéri, whom Colette's aging courtesan Lea had adored, and who had not only given himself to her, but had even more enjoyed wallowing in her pearls. This began my life as an emissary between her and Yul, whom I had known ever since he had come to America with the Chekhov Theater Studio.*

*The boys and girls of the Chekhov Theatre had burst upon me one late afternoon when sitting in Eleonora's room, her single crowded cell on East Seventy-fifth Street in a converted town house. I heard a hullabaloo across the landing. There in two large rooms lived Ilse Bois, once the reigning star of Berlin vaudeville houses. Ilse was a small, faded fiery redhead, compact, tightly muscled, and as Berlin as her neighbor Lotte Lenya. Lotte kept the tiniest room, a pied-à-terre where she led a life she thought private, between Ilse's spacious quarters and Eleonora's meager housing. There were no tempestuous sounds from Lotte's lair. Eleonora was securely in her bed, attached to her telephone, plotting ways and means to share in Toscanini's whereabouts—the closer, the better. But Ilse's rooms seethed with wild, enthusiastic greetings.*

*I crossed the landing into the tumult and found a tall, loquacious, keen-faced, bright-eyed boy, who said his name was Hurd Hatfield.*[45] *I also saw a catlike young man, sinewy—was he Oriental? Part Oriental? Kurdish?—something so exotic I could not say quite what he was, but what he definitely was, and knew it fully, was a charmer. He had dark, flirty eyes and an attractive, sullen, come-hither-if-you-dare manner. His friends whirled about, but he sat cross-legged on the floor. Ilse had known them all in England.*

44. Claude Alphand was a beautiful patrician Frenchwoman who had a brief career in the forties singing Parisian ballads to her own guitar accompaniment. She was married to a French diplomat.
45. Leo learned later that Hurd Hatfield (1918–98), best known for playing the title role in the film *The Picture of Dorian Gray*, had had an affair with Yul Brynner when both were starting out at the Chekhov Theatre Studio.

Soon after meeting Yul at Ilse's, I went, one evening, to visit two young women who lived in what I fondly believed was the last house in Manhattan lit by gaslight. Jonatha and Paquita lived on the parlor floor of an old brownstone just off Fifth Avenue, west on Forty-sixth Street. A strange, mythical beast, very large, carved in stone, guarded the steps of this erstwhile mansion.

Paquita played the piano—a very concert-jazzy piano—under a gaslit chandelier. Jonatha looked as if she knew all the weird spells of the world.[46] The atmosphere in that very large parlor (furnished, I think, only with the grand piano, since we all sat on the highly polished floor) was equivocal. It was in that gaslit room, a great fire leaping in the fireplace, with shadows so dark and so deep, that I found Yul again, sitting on the floor plucking at a strange stringed instrument and singing a slow Slavic song. Years later, when the legend of Yul had convinced vast numbers of paying customers that he was some exotic from a far-off place, I understood it. Yul was always more legend than self.

Marlene could not get enough of him. She could not give him enough. She gave herself, of course. She plied him with shirts made specially to his measure. She bought him expensive trinkets. She baked him wonderful German doughnuts full of apricot jam, and these I carried to the stage door of the St. James Theatre and these he ate voraciously. There was an awful time when his wife, [the actress] Virginia Gilmore, rang me up and laid me out for being a go-between. But I was Marlene's friend. I was her Rosenkavalier. I was amused by Yul, and I was even more amused by Marlene's entanglement.

To the best of my knowledge, this passion of Marlene's for Yul had little of the intensity of her love for Jean Gabin. It was her love for Gabin that transformed her into a true slave who sat in bistros of his choosing, who took any crumbs he would fling her, who felt that she had no life other than one with him. I knew that Yul never wanted to marry Marlene. I knew that it would have an end. It did. I never knew when her obsession ended. I do not think that Yul was ever obsessed—with her. (1993)

NOTE: In early July 1951, Gray went to California and Texas for five weeks of visits with relatives.

JULY 26, 1951 • NEW YORK CITY
**TO GRAY FOY** • BURBANK

Now, for a world-shaking bit of news: Our little Pearl [Kazin] will leave us come late August. I hope you are sitting, or even reclining. . . . Pearl is getting married to Victor Kraft in Brazil in late August! She is flying there to do this and living there forevermore! He photographs for a Brazilian magazine called *Vision*! Pearlie is now to be our aunt from Brazil, where the nuts come from. So, that's

---

46. Paquita Anderson (1911–84) was a pianist, composer, and actress. Jonatha may have been her sister or her lover; Leo didn't say and Richard could not recall.

quite a bit of news. I bet she's doing this, at least partly, as a reaction—on the rebound sort of—from being disappointed in love with *Harper's Bazaar.*[47]

JULY 31, 1951 • PHILADELPHIA

**TO GRAY FOY • BURBANK**

Some nasty mosquito bit me and it itches so that I woke, and now I can't sleep—what with that, the heat, being alone, being still so stimulated by Nancy Mitford's [novel] *Love in a Cold Climate* and also baffled by parts of the Faulkner [play *Requiem for a Nun*]—I think that it's real dopey. A child seems to have been murdered by a dope-fiend, drunkard Negro governess. It's set today and Ruth [Ford will play] the mother of the child, the only other female being the governess. It's all so fraught and written in some sort of pretense at verse. It seems arty and foggy and the parts between the three acts of the play frequently make little or no sense. Sometimes the writing seems to have a hot beauty . . . but it don't communicate to me. Then again, I am so illiterate. Maybe it will be a big success.[48]

**JOURNAL • AUGUST 6, 1951 • NEW YORK CITY** Suddenly desolation, like the irrevocable clang of a tower bell. Heed this hour—one. Loneliness is this hour. The sound is definitive. It confines. The radio sings: "I love you so much; it's a wonder you can't feel it." But I have had many solitary nights. And I should be accustomed to them. No, all the rich nights of being loved and sharing sleep do not prepare for these vast solitary nights. I must read, or try to sleep, or keep on writing, writing. Six more days [until Richard arrives] and at least the solitude will be ended—for a time. But I want Gray here beside me. This is selfish, but that is what I want.

AUGUST 9, 1951 • NEW YORK CITY

**TO GRAY FOY • BURBANK**

Truman came home today [from Italy], and I saw him. He looks fine and sends his love and he brought us a lovely present—a *putti* head, replete with wings, from a church in Sicily—sort of iridescent metal. You will love it. He is much better than he used to be.

---

47. Part of his astonishment was owing to the photographer Victor Kraft (1915–76) having previously been the lover of composer Aaron Copland.

Leo's friendship with Kazin ended abruptly in 1952, after publication by the literary magazine *Botteghe Oscure* of her short story "The Jester." It ruthlessly depicts a sharp-tongued, corpulent adviser to magazine editors, with a "spongey availability to shifts of taste and favor"—unmistakably Leo—and his lonely demise. Capote wrote before its publication asking Leo to go easy on Kazin, assuring him (January 1951) that he was "only the springboard for the main character," and afterward (July 1952) saying it was "a disservice—but mainly an artistic one." As Capote had recently republished in *Local Color* his own unflattering depiction of Leo (as Hilary), he might have been excusing himself as well. Certainly, for other friends Capote's defense was premonitory.

48. A success in London, the production failed in New York.

Then Truman called to say that I should go to California. He would get me the money—a sweet idea. It's pleasant to think about. Truman is so improved and I think that we will like Jack [Dunphy]. You would have been most amused to see Truman unpacking his toys and running over to the bookshelves—peering—saying, "Where's the American edition of my book?" He's getting deaf.

AUGUST 22, 1951 • NEW YORK CITY

**TO GRAY FOY • BURBANK**

When I came home today, I found Howard [Rothschild] here. This evening Richard announced that he probably would never see Howard again. Ten minutes ago, he dashed down here, having fully dressed, and said he hoped that I didn't think ill of him, but he was going over to Howard's and would be here before his model gets here at nine. Oh—little Gray—couldn't this house be restored again to its proper inmates?

**JOURNAL • AUGUST 25, 1951** Marlene: "My life would have been so easy if I had really been sexy."

**SEPTEMBER 3, 1951** Marlene says Garbo has only two suits of underwear. They are made of men's shirting. She wears one for three days, then washes it, does not iron it. Then she wears the other. Marlene says she doesn't mind the not ironing, but three days! Garbo uses only paper towels in her bathroom, has two pairs of men's trousers, two shirts, and little else in her wardrobe. She is very stingy. Marlene says John Gilbert hated Garbo.[49]

**SEPTEMBER 23, 1951** Gray comes, at last, and suddenly spring is in the air, all fragrant and new green. The house is spruced up. Marlene says, "If I were going to sleep with someone, it wouldn't be between five and seven (*cinq à sept*). I would be in love, and I would stay the night. I am too vain for five and seven—all the curl gone." Gabin was said to be so suspicious, to tear the clothes from her and try to choke her, and his gold (like all the French) buried in the South of France. Then six days after he met this model brought to a party by a garage mechanic friend, he married her, got her with child (his?). She looks superficially like Marlene, and she turned out to be a violent collaborationist—the final irony.

On a Sunday morning, rain, fresh and early, and going to meet one's love. Train time an hour away, so leisurely savoring every rich moment. What were these past fourteen weeks? Nothing. Everything—but now passed.

---

49. A leading man of silent films (*The Big Parade*), John Gilbert (1895–1936) made four films with Garbo and almost married her in 1927.

Abruptly, I see a hero-sized but sodden figure, flung down before the change booth—one hand clutching an oozing something—sprawled—inert. Is he breathing? Doubt—then confirmation. A small boy stealthily moves from behind a pillar. He is in his go-to-Sunday-School clothes, and in his hand is a toy revolver. He grins, looks about for adult approbation, points his revolver at the fallen man: "Bang-bang, bang-bang. He's dead."

Waiting in the station. The anonymity is satisfying. Meeting Little T adds to it. In ten minutes, my summer life of sleepless nights and terrors is ended.

SEPTEMBER 26, 1951  Two different ways of life—or motivations. Richard says how can anybody make plans; I say I can't live unless it's forever. So it is a final irony: that which I thought to find in Richard—permanence, a sense of forever in residence now and always, living in each moment as forever—that I have more than he. And he is rootless, a wanderer, impermanent. To know this after eighteen years, having known it somehow always.

OCTOBER 5, 1951  When Alice saw Eugénie [widow of Napoléon III] in Spain, the year before Eugénie died, Eugénie was a little, spry, blue-eyed (but cataracted) woman who had a man and a maid, Carlotta, with her. At a great state dinner when she wished her orange peeled, she threw it the length of the table to Carlotta.

OCTOBER 5, 1951 • NEW YORK CITY
**TO RUTH YORCK** • FRANKFURT AM MAIN

My darling—guess what—I have a check for you—$150!!! I scrounged it out of *Park East*. They fired me months ago, but at last I have this money for you. What to do with it? Please let me know at once. These last months I have been poorer than in a very long time, but we cling to this house and one another. So, I am a rich man hungry for you and Ela—with the possibility of you—which is reassuring. *Please do not die.*

Here, in town, the season slowly begins—a fat bird, somewhat growing extinct—a dodo?—an auk?—preening itself, gently ruffling what looks to be glittering costume-jewelry plumage.

Darling, I haven't written anything save to earn a living, captions and all that, in over eight weeks. It is lovely to write, but having a job is mostly a pain in the bottom and almost nonpleasurable because of how appalling people frequently are. Also, money is practically out of the pocket before it is in the hand. But this house is extremely pleasant. You will love it in its more recent evolutions.

Gray was gone all summer, and so were the tenants, and Richard was in Istanbul and Greece and France and the Netherlands and Italy, and here I was alone in this big house with the rats and Marlene. The last was a great help—and very pretty. She cooked and tried to be Ela—so the summer passed, and I did not quite.

JOURNAL · NOVEMBER 6, 1951  Ours was a house in which extremes were all. Grandpa [Goldwasser], in the left bay window in the front room, sat the day through—and most of the night—frequently swigging long gulps of whiskey. This bay was his lookout, his point of advantage. From it, he noted the comings and goings of his enormous family. With a sudden, startling rap upon the pane he could alter or foil any plan, no matter how ardently desired, how long pre-arranged. It was the canniest, luckiest son, daughter, or in-law who could slip past his sharp bleary-blue eyes, and into this house after midnight (his imposed curfew for inhabitants of all ages). Many times, Momma and Poppa burst into our bedroom, tumbled into bed, tugging their feather bed up over their heads and breathing with exaggerated rhythm, the way people do who are trying to convince that they are and have been asleep for a long time. Then Grandpa opened our door (the gaslight on the landing outside flickering, distorting his huge shape). He stood listening. Sometimes he even came into the room, car-rying his glass of tea (or was it whiskey?) with him, and stood over their bed as they lay there feigning sleep. Finally, when he went away, they lay beneath the feather bed giggling and chuckling and kissing. They loved one another very much, and like all the family, they demonstrated this best by kissing, hugging, and bitterly quarreling.

NOVEMBER 8, 1951  Alice said that last year her mother [Lady Ava Ribbles-dale], having bad circulation, had to lie in a bed that was gently kept in con-stant side-to-side motion by a little motor. Somehow the gadget went berserk and gave off a noxious gas of the kind used to gas cities—deathly. Lady Ribbles-dale woke, struggled out of bed, opened a window, and went into her sitting room, where she sat reading the night through—until her servants, wakened by the smell, rushed into her room. . . . Her bed vacant, the window open: They thought that she had jumped. But, of course, she had not. No matter how many strokes, she totters to teas and society lectures, and rages against fate, which has brought her to this pass—beauty gone, friends and contemporaries all dead. She reads everything, tyrannizes over her family, sometimes suddenly calls into being a ladies' tea. She judges all things as to whether they will be fun for her guests.

NOVEMBER 11, 1951  Our family quarrels—they were nothing, everything. They happened abruptly, crashing into whatever other humor or mood pre-vailed. They were only a suggestion one day, a sort of heaviness in the air. A week later they exploded, involving everyone. Sometimes only carried on fiercely in whispers between two members. Frequently Grandpa instigated them, enjoying the whole course—from distant cloud in the sky to the torrents of tears that finally flooded, quarreling from floor to floor, doors banging, the screams and rages out of the house and into neighborhood houses. The neigh-bors, in the big quarrels, always participated.

DECEMBER 2, 1951   The usual crazy thing happened yesterday. Speed [Lamkin] called. Then Mr. Huntington Hartford. He wants me to run his New York modeling agency and such.[50] He will pay all my expenses to Hollywood and back, so I can talk to him there. I am much tempted to go, for I have long wished to see California, and I love traveling. But I do not think running a model agency is for me. Maybe this is the rescue I know must happen, but not the exact shape of the rescue. I will listen and then try to make him open an office for the Huntington Hartford Foundation in New York. If he were to do this and make me eastern director, and pay me ten or twelve thousand plus expenses, that would be fine. Perhaps he could pay the rent for the house as part of the expenses. This office could supervise the model agency and serve as an eastern focus. Eventually we could get out a magazine.

DECEMBER 7, 1951   On train now pulling out for Hollywood and Mr. Huntington Hartford. This is even more of an adventure than flying to London, for this is more improbable. Out into the night and smoothly fleeing over the Jersey marshes. What luxurious privacy this room, to be my home for the weekend.

DECEMBER 7, 1951 • EN ROUTE TO CHICAGO
**TO GRAY FOY** • NEW YORK CITY

I have just come from my little turkey dinner, served in the dining car some three blocks behind. The car was (and is) full of menfolk. That is the only descriptive word for them. All of them wear these wildly patterned and colored ties which my uncle purveys at Saks. Now we know who wears them. Also, they speak to one another about "trips down to . . ." and muchly about "the boys" and "They entertained us. I mean—they entertained us at their home." This seems very important. Sometimes they grasp one another's large and paradoxically well-tended paws in tight, man-to-man friendship. This is, of course, a side of America which I almost never see, so I am fascinated—a naturalist naturalizing. These men have all either been to conventions or are going to conventions—have just got it in the bag, are just on the verge of pulling it off, are having lucky breaks handed out mostly by these "boys" down and/or up there (who are these deities?). Sinclair Lewis, in his best work, knew it all. It is raining sparsely as we leave Harrisburg and "Austins—The Gilded Leaf" in raw green and phosphate orange makes a bleary smudge. . . . Now it is night again—black pinned together higgledy-piggledy by electronic lights. We ride smoothly, soporifically—and, oh, the lovely, solitary privacy of this room with not a telephone nor a doorbell nor even a radio to disturb—the pulsing monotone rail-wheel sound.

50. A philanthropist heir to the A&P supermarket fortune, Huntington Hartford (b. 1911) was a friend of the novelist and playwright Speed Lamkin (b. 1927). In addition to making Leo a job offer, Hartford wanted his counsel on other matters, including opening an artists' retreat near the Southern California coast.

The train is grunting in Altoona [Pennsylvania]—real pig grunts—and I am sitting in my bed with the blind up and porters giving shocked looks as they pass. But I don't want to miss anything—even "Blatchford's Park Lane Furniture for Better Living" directly opposite, all in white letters on a scarlet ground. So many houses are lighted, over doors and on porches, with curious virulent yellow bulbs. These must be to fend off summer insect hordes. It's lovely to crouch here in this little bed and hear a big hog grunting beneath this train. Being in this room is like being in a secret box—so soothing—and soon the mind perfects a Braille, reading the variations in sound. Now we are leaving Altoona—now crossing a trestle—now rushing through wide open countryside—now approaching a town—rain slaps the windows—while all the houses, patched in window lights, seem something in a Russian novel—but towns burst like rotted fruit—with neon colors—rain makes it all even more lurid—for color runs everywhere through the deserted streets—and taillights fleeing down anonymous highways seem portentous. I will stop now while the whistle signals ("Coming—coming—"). How lovely to be part of the whistle—of the dream. Good night—my love—I found your letter—and of course I cried.

DECEMBER 8 • 7 A.M.

For the past half hour I've been peering at Indiana in the pale pink dawn. Quite flat it is, with little towns of widely spaced, dirty-white houses. The street-lamps (they are globes—replicas of the full moon or sun—very beneficent looking) are still aglow. Just beyond a town named Plymouth, in a stubbly field, live many black-and-brown-spotted pigs!!! They were having a fine time and sent love. Here is a delegation of white geese. They are too intent on committee meetings to do anything save give level, sharp looks. Now I must dress.

I've been breakfasting through the Chicago environs. Isn't it dreadful, how ugly most American cities and towns are from a train window? This—and ever since Gary [Indiana]—is just like Long Island on the way to Momma's, perhaps even uglier. Only industrial architecture has some distinction—and even beauty. This is a smeary sort of morning—Love to little Richard—"Chicago! Chicago!" I have my Bette Davis [*Beyond the Forest*] wig on.

DECEMBER 9, 1951 • BETWEEN CHICAGO
AND GREEN RIVER, WYOMING
TO GRAY FOY • NEW YORK CITY

Terrific snow! Forests deep in it, cows all huddled together in it, and all the meadow grasses flowered white with it. Suddenly it is winter—like in [Willa Cather's] *My Ántonia*.

Later: I guess I have just seen the Mississippi—very brown, prolific, and islands riding it like many-masted ships. I am in my bed, peering out at the deep snow. And now this train wails ever westward. I guess the train wails so much because of the snowstorm, and it must be very cold, for the train men, when we pause, have little breath balloons attached to their mouths. We travel through Nebraska all this night. I read Leverson.[51]

8 A.M.

Now, here in Wyoming, all rivers and ponds are solidly frozen, and the plains and mountains winter-locked in frost and snow. A solitary watertower is a single lambent icicle, a frozen flame, for the sun has undone its icy heat and transformed it so. Now the sky is every shade of blue—from forget-me-not to the deepest delphinium. In this world only flower colors describe. Here horses and cattle stand in the snow—and now automobiles begin to appear more frequently on the single highway, which parallels our route. All houses (not many to be seen) are as dripping with icicles as a [Radio City] Music Hall production of *The Night Before Christmas.* We are passing through a vast plain—with the sort of mountains I have heretofore seen only in glorious Technicolor Westerns.

It is the Wyoming landscape that I think most boring—only an occasional distant mountain range relieves it, or a cluster of ochre-yellow painted shacks and houses—so desolate—and sometimes brown-red cliffs whose crests have been expertly turned out by a French frilling or ruffling iron. Now we are passing through a vast gray-silver-white waste—perhaps in summer it is more beautiful. Everywhere the minute tracks of beasts crisscrossing.

DECEMBER 9, 1951 • BETWEEN GREEN RIVER,
WYOMING, AND SALT LAKE CITY
TO GRAY FOY • NEW YORK CITY

I think we are entering Utah, for we are veering southwest and we are in mountainous country, apparently high up and following the crest, with even higher ones in the distance. Wyoming grew endless—great, unrelieved fields of snow coruscating—and only one flock of gray sheep tended by a little covered wagon like in a children's storybook. Then, just before Evanston [Wyoming], a lovely valley with many trees (poplar, like home, I think) and some children sleighing and two dogs. What relief to the eye's tedium.

The trees and grasses are all encased in ice. The snow is all shadowed blue. It is twenty-nine minutes past five, according to Mason the porter. We are crossing a great flat place—but how different from Wyoming and Iowa. This is so "friends." Even in this winter twilight, far-off lights, way away over the blue snow, those winking red kind that palpitate in the dusk, signaling radio stations, airports, civilization. The trees now have a heartbreaking loneliness—each twig defined in the dusk, just before night consumes tree and twig and world. On the left, even higher mountains—just discernible and lunar in this evening light.

51. Ada Leverson (1862–1933), a novelist who wrote comedies of manners in London society, sheltered her friend Oscar Wilde during his trials.

Out in desertlike country. The sun is just risen, and here the colors are all washed reds and earth colors—like the first sculptured hills I ever saw. The vegetation is different—strange sorts of pine and sagebrush. Everywhere in the distances stand worn-out hills. The architecture is similar to the twenties in Jackson Heights and other New York suburban areas, because it is Californian—which is where I now am! In the distance, wonderful snow-topped mountains. Everything is brown—all the shades of brown.

I have seen my first really growing cactus, and we are coming down into the San Bernardino Valley. The mountains are beautiful, but I would not want to live in this part of California (around Victorville), through which we have just been riding. It's so mangy and so impoverished looking. Also, there must be so many serpents. Strange black foothills all creased and folded like heavy carpet flung down and not set in place. Above the black hills, the snow-topped mountains. A flock of startling-white birds (perhaps pigeons).

At Cajon, just passed, many Indians, mostly looking like my cousin Sadie and Marguerite Young—and smelling probably the same. As we descend farther and farther into the valley, trees are all green (or touched with autumn) species of willows, but straight like poplars, flashes like silver-backed green ribbands in the wind. I have run the whole cycle of seasons in these brief days. Now we seem to be running into a terrific dust storm, through which the distant mountains are just washed-in—their tops visible—as fine lines are in Oriental watercolors. This is the land of the jerry-built, the trailer come to ultimate rest and rounded by two barrels—one for water, one for fuel. I would not want to live here either. It's hideously ugly and ramshackle. And here are many palms! No camels. Much foliage of Robert Hichens's novels![52] "Parks Dressed Poultry—Dressed While You Wait." Ugh. Loads of Indians. And the station—four squat Islamic (really Shriner) towers holding down an oblong gray building. I don't really believe that I am here. "Crane Pacific—the Preferred Plumbing." I wonder if Mrs. Crane puts little instructive messages on the back of each seat?[53]

**TO GRAY FOY** • NEW YORK CITY

So I went to Paramount and lunched with Jane Wyman and Bing Crosby and [choreographers] Donald [Saddler] and [Helen] Tamiris and others. At the next table was Cecil DeMille and his entourage, and it was all just like in *Sun-*

52. Robert Smythe Hichens (1864–1950) was the British author of *Bella Donna*, *The Garden of Allah*, and other popular novels of the early twentieth century.
53. "Mrs. Murray Crane writes (or her secretary does) little directions to her luncheon or dinner guests. These appear on the backs of their place cards. On Thanksgiving Mary Colum's said, 'Talk about Colette,' and Truman's asked, 'What is your favorite play?' " *Journal, December 1, 1951.* Her family's money came from the Crane printing and stationery firm.

*set Boulevard*, and the place full of all sorts of men and women in elaborate formal dress. Actually it looked like some strange, surreal ball for charity. Jane Wyman is sort of giggly and razzmatazz. Bing Crosby talks a lot, very seriously, and almost always in a sort of *Variety* argot.

The extravagance of making movies—those sets of rooms in the home of a successful composer! Not even Mrs. Vanderbilt's Breakers was ever that ostentatious (later I saw a "real" house which was). I saw everything at Paramount—a whole building full of period paneling and fireplaces, a whole shed full of lamps (some very beautiful). And all the time it was hot, blazing summer.

About Jane Wyman again: She seems fundamentally a most unhappy girl, so full of a kind of gayest-girl-in-the-senior-class vigor and is sure to say: "It used to be better when I was a whore in Peoria." Or "hot as you can scald a cat." She has a twelve-year-old daughter whom she adores. She took this child and some of her little friends to a sneak preview of *Blue Veil*. The little girls sat there sniffing and saying how sad. Later, at home, Jane Wyman picked up a telephone and heard her child say, "Well, you know, Momma doesn't really understand much about drama." Bing Crosby's sad because of his wife [singer Dixie Lee], who took to drink when he was away entertaining the troops. She had previously helped him cure himself. A friend of their young and poorish days came to live opposite, and when Crosby was away Mrs. Crosby took to visiting her and taking a little drinkie. So, she became a dipso, and one day she kicked one of her little boys in the stomach so hard that he had to have an operation. I tell you all these gruesome things because I am always interested in the disparity between the surface and what goes on underneath. Crosby likes to sneak off and drink beer in bars while watching television.

Cecil B. DeMille and his entourage were obviously the royal family—the emperor or president of some Latin American country (not too big) with his cabinet and henchmen surrounding him at luncheon, with equerries and messengers coming and going all the time. He sits not at the head of the table, but, in true old-fashioned regal style, center. It all has a semimilitary atmosphere, his world. He seems to have long silences while his followers sit looking at him lethargically, and then the great man says something and everything's all carefully weighed, judicious animation about that unfestive board.

At one table sat most of Paramount's "Golden Circle"—starlets both concave and convex.[54] Those starlets—oh, so typical American boy and girl—plus. The whole commissary was actually more like a lunchroom at a big, good college. You could even pick out the school stars and the dullest boy in the school and the female cheerleaders and the popular professor and the coach and his

54. In the forties, Paramount began promoting a group of rising young stars as "The Golden Circle."

team. Then those hundreds, all in elaborate dress and makeup, just standing or sitting and waiting on those supermagnificent sets.

JOURNAL · DECEMBER 14, 1951 · BEVERLY HILLS Those tag ends of time— the oddments of minutes between leaving a hotel room and the moment when one should be on the way to the car that carries one to the train or plane. At such times—the open seams, the unmortised joints—depression seeps in— anarchy—for the continuity is broken. This is a little limbo: a bird making its morning toilette in the gutter of this hotel, the sounds of breakfast carts wheeling-jinkling, crockery clattering over the garden paths—but death creeps in the betweens. The light in the palms is so Winslow Homer. All those months when Ela was here—miserably—and how wonderful if she had been here now.

DECEMBER 15, 1951 · EN ROUTE FROM LOS ANGELES Diner—The head- waiter is a foreign gentleman with the rimless, round-spectacled look of being engaged in some concentrated, studious enterprise. His accent is German. He could be in cahoots with the tall, thickening-in-the-midriff, gray-suited, nonobjective-patterned tie. They give me another abrupt reading-between-the- lines (or is it sheets?) looks. The tall one is the dark-skinned, curly iron-gray-hair sexy type so popular since Pinza [in *South Pacific*]. Something slightly vulgar about him—perhaps his ruby ring—and the show-off way he holds his cigarette.

A funeral in a desert pueblo—the burnished winter sun on all the brown adobe; the little houses attended by corn shucks baled on high ricks; the brown church and the thick skein of people, in dark clothes, moving into the church, while the black hearse waited. This, seen wholly for a moment, framed in the dining-car window, which reflected luxury tangible in linen, silver, and rich breakfast food was not sad. It was tragic.

Pueblos do not seem mean and poverty-stricken, the way all those little hor- rors do in the San Bernardino Valley (trailers, shacks, etc.). Pueblos are indige- nous and exactly right. I love their compactness—everything belonging to each house right there—but I would rather not live in a pueblo.

DECEMBER 16, 1951 · EN ROUTE FROM CHICAGO "North Philadelphia!" John the porter cries, which returns me, having been thousands of miles. . . . What comes first to mind: the hours at Marion Davies's [in Beverly Hills], for this was the seamy side of a certain kind of high life—the inside story.[55] She looked like an advertisement for the Carlin Comfort Shop [at Saks], for she was all in tufted and quilted blue, velvet crepe de chine, and her blond (surely fixed) hair every which way. Her mouth and chin Carol Chan-

55. Once a Ziegfeld star, Marion Davies (1897–1961) is remembered as the Hollywood actress whose pictures were usually bankrolled by newspaper magnate William Randolph Hearst, her lover of thirty years. Shortly after Hearst's death in 1951, she married Horace G. Brown, a former studio bit-part player.

ning's. Her complexion good. Her eyes sharp and secretly gay. She had been drunk for years and had Marie Dressler's gestures, but she knew what was going on. Nothing escaped her. Drink had addled her gestures, but sharpened her wits, there in that little leftover room, in that huge leftover house—empty glasses and overflowing ashtrays on the huge "Renaissance" table before her, its wood scarred and stained by drink and cigarette. In the chairs about her: thugs, millionaires, a novelist, a society reporter, her new husband Mr. Brown, in brown clothes, wordless, glowering. And always traffic through the room, "characters," and the telephone clangoring in the kitchen beside it. A nurse instantly helped her out of her chair and bore her into the kitchen. "Yes, Hedda—yes." "No, Louella—no." The house felt as though many parties of a low character were going on in many other unseen rooms.

In a huge, long hall, decorated by double-life-sized portraits of Marion Davies in her best-known screen roles (for fun and diversion she nightly showed these movies), all sorts of hangers-on and visitors walked about or talked in groups. (Old carpets, massive furniture still about, the gold dinner service said to be in the cellar, and millions of dollars of diamonds in vaults in the Bank of America at the foot of the hill.) Off the huge hall, little rooms, dressing rooms. In one, a brazen blonde (peroxide) in Prussian-blue satin pajamas, shrilling at a trim but drunken woman in tight black skirt and white silk shirt. Perhaps this woman was Marion's mother.

A man who had constantly ambled through the rooms saying, "Has anyone seen my basket?" appeared. "I found my basket!" he exclaimed. His wife, a well-known radio entertainer, grabbed it—a white covered basket, decorated with canceled American postage stamps on its handle and pansies (in full color) on its white sides.

Then Marion talking endlessly at the table, and finally her husband saying something sullen. She replied snappily, gave a look of disdain. He rose, went away. The phone rang. Marion's secretary whispered to her. The nurse and the secretary guided her into the kitchen. The secretary returned and asked Hunt [Hartford] to come in. In five minutes he returned. "She wanted me to listen in. Her husband's laying her out." Then the phone clattered. Marion returned. In a few minutes so did Mr. Brown. He sat opposite her, glowering. Then he went into the kitchen. He called: "I want to speak to you!" She pretended not to hear. He called again. She continued her pretense. He grabbed her arm. She shooed him off. With the majesty common only to drunks and playacting children and Negroes, she went into the kitchen. In a moment, a sound like a slap. Then she hoarsely chanted: "How dare you! How dare you!" Silence. The secretary said she'd had to retire. Would we forgive her? Would we care to wait and see [her 1933 film] *Going Hollywood*? A hooligan said, "Come on back, folks, wanna see you. . . . A party's going on. . . ."

We went back through the servants' rooms into a small room filled with the kind of people you see when Hollywood does Raymond Chandler (all L.A. and

Hollywood seems written by Chandler). On the bed, another big dyed blonde with skirts above her navel, and a tall dress-extra kind of run-down sexy man (later he would be a bum; now he was a drifter) stroking her between her thighs. She singing: "Nothing wrong. We're married. He's my husband. He's good. That's why I married him." And thick smoke and nasty laughing and smell of rye and vomit. It was evident that a fight was in the making—and all sorts of nastiness. We went—under protest. In her garden, rose trees—pink and yellow and crimson—bloomed eerily beneath synthetic electric-light moons.

In the car, Speed [Lamkin] said: "They found a scorpion in Marion's bed last week. Luckily she decided not to sleep in her own bed that night. Something she'd never decided before."

NOTE: Upon his return, Leo wrote to Huntington Hartford saying that he was ill-suited to run a modeling agency. He suggested that he represent Hartford in other business, but nothing resulted.

JOURNAL · JANUARY 19, 1952 · NEW YORK CITY  How [society columnist] Elsa Maxwell looked at Truman's reading of *The Grass Harp*: a Kewpie-doll face left out in the rain and snow these last fifty years and now lost in a vast flabby face. Her velvet blouse top was embroidered with sequined and diamantéd butterflies. She is an old woman, almost at the age when male and female appearance blur together. She has the appearance and atmosphere of a well-to-do abbot, just right for Robin Hood plundering. She said: "This is the last refuge, dear Mrs. Crane, the last refuge. You have the only saloon [*sic*] left in New York."[56]

Carlo [Van Vechten]'s tale about Isadora [Duncan] at the Plaza: She had danced at Carnegie Hall, and then she gave a dinner at the Plaza in her suite. The round table was so vast that it almost filled the room. She said she would dance naked on the table. Mrs. Walter Damrosch instantly told Mr. Walter that it was time to go home. Isadora later danced, naked in her bedroom, a hymn to the sun as it rose over Central Park. Then everyone crowded into a cab, Isadora in her nightdress and a fur coat (chinchilla?) and off to the sailing, with everyone clinging to the cab, atop and astride it—shrieking and singing.

JANUARY 20, 1952  Ela killed herself a year ago. Some evenings ago, at midnight, Alice came here and she told me how Ela had come to lunch to meet Dr. Rinkle a year ago. She had been in a dreadful state, and while the other guests had talked amongst themselves, Eleonora had poured out in German to Dr. Rinkle, a stranger, her agony: She didn't sleep. She had taken dope—many years—now she couldn't sleep. She seemed to be asking him to help her. He

---

56. A reading of the stage adaptation of Capote's second novel was given by Mrs. W. Murray Crane to attract backers. Leo bet its producer, Arnold Saint-Subber, that the show would close within a month, thereby winning four antique chairs from its extravagant set.

said he would see her when next he came from Boston. He returned in a week, to find that she had killed herself. I did not, a year ago, believe that she had killed herself, but I do now.

JANUARY 23, 1952  Plaza Dining Room 1:15 p.m. Having come full cycle, I find myself quite by accident (or are there accidents?) at this corner table in the big dining room where precisely a year ago we came—Gray, Richard, Eugenia, and I—to lunch, in memoriam after Ela's funeral. The trampled crimson roses in the cruddy gutter . . . petals shocking the eye to attention . . . Now I do not talk to Eugenia; Richard has, at last, been unfaithful to Howard; I love Gray every day more, and he is working hard.

MARCH 3, 1952  I have wasted my life. A sloppy, sloppy life—mostly notions and remarks and little achievement. My reason for being seemed, until about three years ago, to make other people feel wanted, gay, confident—to make them laugh and feel able to go on. These last three years, I have permitted my personal gloom and tension to show, and more and more I have become self-ish—so selfish that the "I" has swamped all else. Of course, in those years of being private while helping (or whatever it was), I was repaid magnificently, for my ego was nourished, and I battened upon the reciprocity of it all. It has been a long sickness, which I have not realized, and somehow this morning it begins to lift. Or is this the little calm before greater rigors? One fact: I must not sit in gloom and give myself away. This is spoiled and childish and so horribly unattractive. Even jotting this way is more negative than positive. I murmur the surface.

MARCH 10, 1952  In the night, at four, screams and then terror mounting the stair, horror in the hall—but little Gray, all tousled and rosy, rushed to my rescue. I read Proust until six and so to sleep again—slipping the Méséglise Way, among pink hawthorns and lilacs.[57] The body remembers pain that the mind, asleep—anesthetized—did not let one "feel." I mean, when I woke screaming, I felt, in all those places from which teeth (etc.) had been removed, the dimmest, most vestigial ache—an ache I remembered from those times when teeth had been pulled without anesthetic.

APRIL 29, 1952  I called Peter [Lindamood]. He was drunk—lucidly, vociferously drunk. "Do you remember when you first found me?" he asked. "On Julian [Levy's] sofa? In the back room? That was the beginning." He is brokenhearted over a man. Peter as a character is a real study in degenerating.[58]

57. In Proust's *Remembrance*, childhood strolls on the Méséglise Way come to symbolize innocence, natural beauty, and maternal affection.
58. Julian Levy (1906?–81) was the first dealer to show many of the Surrealists in America. As a soldier, Lindamood had befriended many Surrealist painters in Italy.

**TO RICHARD HUNTER** • HAMBURG, NEW YORK

T. S. Eliot is an odd-looking giant. He made those little semidry jokes (like a second-best, watered-down-for-the-children pale sherry) and the audience played right along—rapturously. He said things like he could give them a soprano cough and a bass cough and that his poem "The Hippopotamus" was hated by Edmund Gosse, who thought Eliot's talent declined then and there, but that Arnold Bennett loved it, and this provoked titters.[59] It was all so sycophantic, like kids in school buttering up the teacher. Then he read some poems—"Prufrock." Some fifteen months ago, when he was asked to read this, he said he thought it too immature . . . but now he read it, saying that he thought that he was now ready for it. The hall was packed. He said that his two best poems were "Dry Salvages" and "Little Gidding." That sounded like a parody. He reads in a light, faintly self-ironic voice, and he drinks lots of glasses of water (rendered golden by the stage lights and so seeming some precious light golden wine) . . . and he stoops and wears heavy black shoes. Right in the middle of his reading, I thought how indecent this all was—this reading of passionate poetry by its author. Marianne Moore, googly-eyed like the crusty (but popular) professor of a girls' college (one of the big ones), flanked by Monroe Wheeler (that little simian).[60] So that was T. S. Eliot in the Theresa Kaufman Auditorium [at the YMHA].

**TO RUTH YORCK** • WEST BERLIN

I will hastily write this little note to you before I go off to my operation. I can't remember whether I told you that my face (bones and teeth) is infected from that old cab accident, and this year has been hell. I had one big operation about two months ago and now, today, I am to have a bigger one. They will take out bits of bone, all remaining uppers and roots, and some in the bottom and bone. Of course, I am scared. Constant pain and intimations of pain make one more frightened as it goes on. I now dread anesthesia, needles, and dope more than I did six months ago. This is odd, for I now know that after the initial pain (the needle prick, the eternal but miraculously swift suffocation—with that feeling of having solved all the riddles of the universe) after this pain—painlessness and return, recall. But I miss you: You would (said he selfishly) mainstay us.

**TO RUTH YORCK** • PARIS

This is the first typewriting I have done in over two weeks, the last being to you just before I had my last operation. This was hell. But what hell. I woke up

---

59. Critic Edmund Gosse (1849–1928) introduced many foreign writers (Ibsen, Gide) to English readers. Arnold Bennett (1867–1931) was a novelist (*The Old Wives' Tale*), playwright, and diarist.

60. Monroe Wheeler (1899–1988), was MoMA's director of exhibitions and publications (ca. 1938–67).

right in the middle and could not let them know, and they went right on cutting. Finally, I fluttered my eyelids very fast, like a jazz-baby Clara Bow. They all stopped and said, "He's awake!" and quick they needled me . . . but it was awful. Then I was out, but, oh, the agony and shock when I came to in Gray's arms. So, he had the problem of coping . . . and he did. I was taken home, and for three days and three nights I was delirious from drugs not mixing right. One of these drugs contained something which is used in the truth serum, and so there was truth here all those days and nights. I flung myself about, and made like I was riding a bicycle, and was a windmill, and I looked at Ela's photo and said, "Such a pity . . . You were such a silly girl" and other such truthlike sentiments. Darling, you would have been impressed with my four-letter vocabulary, or so Gray says. I really went to town. And all the time, all those nights and days, it seemed a bright blue, white, and lilac enamel day. Now I have not an intact bone in my face, not one upper tooth, and many lowers departed, and I look pretty much the same. The details (save the teeth) are more emphatic.

JUNE 10, 1952 • NEW YORK CITY
**TO RICHARD HUNTER** • SIASCONSET, MASSACHUSETTS

Gray got two covers to do, from Columbia Records. So, he and Pavlik [Tchelitchew], [Eugene] Berman, and Stuart Davis are the chosen ones. Gray gets $500 for the two. The contract is now signed. Hosanna! We saw Choura [Danilova], and she looks wonderful and is so gay and asked us to come to visit her in New Jersey, so we probably will. Gray has always adored Choura, and she and he will now have Dallas in common. She said, "But Dallis is de cruss-ruds uf de woild."[61]

**JOURNAL** • JUNE 12, 1952 Yesterday, in the evening, to the Van Vechtens for dinner, and after this excellent repast, in came Frieda Lawrence (now married to an Italian).[62] She is en route to England to see the children she abandoned when she ran off with [D. H.] Lawrence. She will also see her grandchildren. In all these years, she has not seen any of them. "Should I take with a ham to hot them up?" she anxiously asked. She is the most German of women. Not since [contralto Ernestine] Schumann-Heink have I seen a woman so *Frau*-ish. At any shopping moment she can be found in quantity, string bag in hand, in Yorkville, or wherever Germans exist. She is frumpy with age, but her ankles are slim. Her longish, narrow feet were in black wedgies, single strap (Gertrude Stein always wore Mary Janes). She wore a gray cloth suit, white-polka-dotted

61. Alexandra "Choura" Danilova (1903–97), ballerina and teacher, had left Russia with Balanchine in 1924 and performed with Diaghilev and then, from 1938, with Ballet Russe de Monte Carlo. After retiring in 1952, she taught for four years in Dallas, where Gray had been born and his father still lived.
62. Frieda von Richthofen (1879–1956) left her husband and three children for D. H. Lawrence, marrying him in 1914. After Lawrence's death in 1930, she married Angelo Ravagli.

long skirt, a heavy-cream satin (much folded and detailed around the collar) blouse, and great quantities of turquoise and silver Indian (New Mexican) jewelry. Some of the stones were beautiful, but all of the jewelry was touristy. Her blond-gray hair—in a longish bob—looked as though, when she rose in the morning, she inevitably exclaimed: "What should I—*ach*—do with it!" She uses *ach* as punctuation, as temporizing, as padding. She has a country-clear complexion, a nervous *Hausfrau*-hostess laugh (a sort of chuckle, out of wanting to appear convivial), a matriarchal air of complicity (to be found in all Earth Mothers), and nowhere the dynamic beauty that inflamed and inspired Lawrence. "All the time—*ach*—Lawrence grows. I who after all knew him—everything—how he sat at table—everything—am finding constantly new things in Lawrence. I hate the Viking *Portable* [*D. H. Lawrence*]. It is awful. This woman doesn't know anything about Lawrence. How should she? She knows only what she hears. Lawrence is too big for these little books—but she has a talented son. He is a good writer. She is not altogether bad—but she doesn't know." Frieda Lawrence met Diana [Trilling, the *Portable*'s editor], and thought Lionel was her son. She was interested in everything, especially the beautiful lamplit vista of the park. She said Lawrence would have been so pleased about the enormous Penguin sales. He always wanted the man in the street to read him.

JUNE 22, 1952  On Friday evening, the college editors being here and a party being given for them, it was necessary to go to MacDougal Street [in Greenwich Village].[63] It has been over three years since I crossed Washington Square and walked along MacDougal Street, and in that time all the houses, in which Valeska and Bravig Imbs and their world lived, have vanished, leaving emptiness. The Imbses are dead, and all those who lived in these houses are dead, divorced, or gone from this city. I thought: Not even the solid fact of a dilapidated house to which to cling—were any of them to return—not only at the vacant, debris-cluttered lot upon which once their house and dreams stood, but all about the square whole blocks have been torn down to make way for a pseudocolonial law-school building, an aerial apartment house. In the square itself, the human flotsam and jetsam still drifts and clots, but always I see Valeska limping across the square, her arms loaded down with books. Valeska in a suit—five or ten years old (blue, it seems) and still good. And the Imbses, long, pale room, with night seeping in on summer-breezy white curtains, moth-pale and fluttering, and outside the summer evening gaiety of the square.

NOTE: In September 1952, Gray and Richard sailed to Europe. The two would be together for several months before Leo joined them in December (coming to Italy from Copenhagen). They began with a stay in Paris, toured the Loire Valley, and then

---

63. For decades, *Mademoiselle* bestowed paid summer internships upon some twenty college students, who then worked on the magazine's August collegiate issue. *Mademoiselle* (and sometimes Leo) would host a party to introduce these guest editors to New York.

went on to Venice and Rome. Gray and Richard's nearly two months in Rome fell during a time when Truman Capote, Marguerite Young, Ruth Stephan, Carson McCullers, Frederic Prokosch, Stark Young, Charles Henri Ford, and Pavel Tchelitchew were all nearby.

SEPTEMBER 17, 1952 • NEW YORK CITY

**TO GRAY FOY** • PARIS

I went to the Balinese [musicians and dancers] and it was ravishing—the most beautiful and gay theater since the very first time I saw [sitarist Ravi] Shankar on a rain-blotted Sunday afternoon many, many years ago. This was such rapture—almost mesmeristic—obliterating theater and audience. Oh, the beauty and the humor of it—and the love without any debasement. Now, as though to complete it all, someone (perhaps on a record) is tootling a pipe down at the far end of the gardens. I sit here quite naked (a mountain—or a series of rolling hills at least—of flesh). Only the thin, serene, restful tootling— and the hurtling cars on the avenue—and the almost imperceptible breeze intimating autumn among the ailanthus leaves. It is sometimes solemnly beautiful here, and the house seems disposed to friendliness. I hope it means to be.

SEPTEMBER 27, 1952 • NEW YORK CITY

**TO GRAY FOY** • PARIS

The ballet has been so dreary save for Markova,[64] and she does not have her former brilliance, but she does have something to take its place. She somehow manages to create the most marvelous period atmosphere, so that when she dances *Giselle*, you feel immediately that this is how Taglioni did it. She projects an almost lithographic representation of this. What a clumsy way to say it. . . . And then, of course, she dances with the greatest delicacy—almost tact. And her feet are more akin to swans' feet, trailing through reedy waters, than any other dancer's.

Oh, dear, darling, well-meaning little Foy Boy, why ever did you tell Eugenia [Halbmeier] that she was to watch after me? Don't say anything to her, for she also means well, but she now insists that I give her a key so she can come in whenever she has time to tidy. She says that she has to have one so she won't have to make arrangements with me, and also then she can come in and stay over. Ugh. It's no fun to be alone, but being alone is much pleasanter than having to cope with this new, emancipated career girl. It is nice of her to want to tidy, but when I come home exhausted I don't want to have to talk to her or anyone except you, and this I do by letter. I can't bear thinking about invasions of privacy. I like trudging about our happy home without clothes and so forth. Well, I will have to think up ruses.

---

64. Alicia Markova (née Alice Marks, 1910–2004), the first British prima ballerina, founded the English National Ballet. Her last season dancing was 1952. Ballerina Calotta Grisi, not Taglioni, created *Giselle* in 1841.

**TO GRAY FOY • ROME**

You would love it here right now, for this is your favorite weather—snappy, crystalline—all blue and gold and autumn hazy with flottilas of leaves moving through the air—leaf smoke . . . Oh my baby . . . Well, I guess seeing the treasures of the ages is important, too.

Yesterday I dined with the Liebersons and then I took Brigitta [Lieberson] to Bea Lillie. She, Bobby Clark, and Charlie Chaplin are the three greatest funny people I have ever seen. She is marvelous. Something (life, I suppose) has happened to her. Now she is sweet, touching, and so miraculously, effortlessly funny.

Marlene moved into another apartment while waiting for still another—all at 410 Park. Her nemesis [Yul Brynner] is off to Hollywood for a week—with wife. She even bought him luggage to go—what a sucker.

The other night we had a citywide "real" practice air raid. All up Forty-second Street to the Hudson, fire trucks stood steely-crimson, spraying huge jets of blue-sequin water high into the air, the whole floodlit by the sort of light one sees when good moonlight is used on a stage—endless flourishing fountains, stories high, pluming Forty-second—fantastically beautiful. [Theatrical director] Mary Hunter and I were late for the ballet—it was so beautiful.

**TO GRAY FOY • ROME**

This has been a most upsetting day. . . . But first I must tell you some wonderful news, and you must think how Richard should know about it without his being upset. You are in the Met [museum's] show! They will be hanging your drawing in December![65] But Richard's wasn't accepted, and that makes it awful for him. He wrote me such a sad letter. I am so delighted about you.

About today—I went to a lunch for the Italians (who are here having their film festival), and I sat down with Dorothy Wheelock [*Bazaar*'s theater editor], who said I had to meet the woman who owns the Obelisco [modern art gallery] in Rome. Dorothy looked up, said, "There she is," and I practically fainted dead away. My heart actually stopped for a moment . . . and then I realized that Dorothy was looking at me with alarm. You know, my love, it was Eleonora! Madame Brin, in some moments, looks exactly—but exactly—like Eleonora, and since I never quite believe that she is dead, it was easy for me to believe that it had all been a dreadful fantasy . . . but then I studied her closely and I saw that she wasn't Eleonora, only very like at times (her very trick of

---

65. The show was "American Water Colors, Drawings, and Prints." GF: "My drawing *Summary* won a $500 prize, which paid for our return passage on the SS *Liberté*, second class." In 2005 this drawing (retitled *Dimensions*) was purchased from Gray by Steve Martin and given to New York's Museum of Modern Art.

peering at writing closely, for she is just as nearsighted). This was all a great shock.[66]

Then I went to see [De Sica's film] *Umberto D*, and I haven't wept so much in years. Even now, typing here in this office, I am beginning to tear. It's a very simple movie about what happens to old men with little or no money, whose friends have all died. I was on my way to a party (for it is evening now), and I walked toward it, two streets, and then I came right back here because I had to talk to you. I guess when we have finished this junket, we will begin to save for our old age. I couldn't bear it if you ever, ever had to want. Do you know what you mean to me? Do you know how grateful I am that you came to me at a time when you were most needed? Do you know how very much I love you and kiss your little shirt, which hangs, smelling of you, in your cupboard? Oh, my darling, usage has hackneyed words—and even gestures—but the heart's tongue is never time-worn. I will send this to you now, there among fountains and monuments and antiquity. . . . Please take care. . . . I love you.

OCTOBER 10, 1952 • NEW YORK CITY
**TO RICHARD HUNTER • ROME**

Sweet rabbit: Please, please do something to guard against being a lonely, penniless old man. When I think of you alone and lonely . . . ah, me. You should make up with Howard, no matter how depressing he is, because at least he fills your days. And you must sit and work. I guess you should come home sooner because here are people who love you. Today I see that life is a bitter, bitter thing, and the sorry days are longer than the happy ones, as death is inevitably longer than any living. Oh, Richard, please don't go on being such an obstinate fool. You have so much to give. I have tried not to talk about Eleonora, but I guess you knew what a blow her death was. But do you realize how much more devastating would be anything happening to you? You have been so reckless with those who have loved you. Please don't be anymore. It gets later and later. Today I am genuinely frightened about life, and this is so strange for me. I am quite naked—terrified—seeing everyone grow older, friends dying, becoming time-worn, oppressed by life and fear. . . . I think you must come home to those who love you and not go solitarily and obstinately by yourself. Life is a lonely business anyway, so please be with those who love you while it is still possible. You know, that day when you came from Buffalo and I was delirious, you hurt me more than in all the years I've known you. I had been waiting for you all that day, even in my delirium, then you went away—but this doesn't matter because think how long we have been growing up together.[67]

66. "Marcello Guidi [an Italian diplomat] said casually, in talking about Irene Brin, 'Oh, she doped even when it wasn't fashionable.' So even that was parallel to Ela." *Journal*, October 15, 1972.
67. GF: "Richard appeared after Leo's dental surgery, when we had to cope with his hallucinations. Richard said, 'I just cannot deal with sickness,' and sped off."

Truman and Jack have an apartment in Rome where you are, and Carson is there, writing a movie [*Stazione Termini*] for De Sica. Doesn't all this thrill you? Thank you endlessly for caring for Gray. See, you are good, not wicked like you always try to make out—a genuine rabbit, not a fox. Do you need money or anything?

OCTOBER 10, 1952 • NEW YORK CITY

**TO GRAY FOY • ROME**

I took Hurd [Hatfield] to Goosey's party for his sister Mina (the Proust female), and she told me many interesting tales of Proust and Montesquiou.[68] Especially I liked one about the Whistler portrait in the Frick. Remember that Montesquiou is carrying a cloak in that? Well, this cloak is one he borrowed from the Comtesse de Greffulhe (just died), because [Whistler] felt that he needed something "light" there. She loved her cloak, but she doted on him, so she loaned it to him. After a year, she thought that it would be nice to have it again, so she asked him for it. He was amazed, and said he had had his friend (Yturri—the original of the boy [in Proust] who had all the men turn up at his funeral) return it, but of course that one never had, for he was a crook of sorts. Whenever he and Montesquiou went to visit friends and Montesquiou admired some bibelot, he was sure to get it in a day or so, with the boy saying that that friend, learning that Montesquiou loved it, wanted him to have it. Of course, the boy had just taken it, but M never discovered this—until the cloak. M is buried next to the boy. The comtesse said to Mina C: "Isn't it awful that Robert is buried next to that crook!" That's how Mina C heard this saga.[69]

OCTOBER 29, 1952 • NEW YORK CITY

**TO GRAY FOY • ROME**

This morning, in the Fifty-ninth Street station, I came up and ran right into Brigitta. I think that this neighborhood is her wyck. She was dressed in a little blue Valentina suit (very nice), Ferragamo shoes (beautiful and simple), a sweet sweater from Lanvin, a little hat from Mr. John, gloves from Basle, and carrying a package wrapped in Mark Cross. These contained binoculars as a going-away present for the Gunthers (off tomorrow to darkest Africa—with accoutrements by Valentina).

OCTOBER 30

I am off to see Marlene's new apartment, and then to *Dial M for Murder* (Maurice Evans), and am Brigitta-ing, and then we go to supper with Gielgud. Oh,

68. "Goosey" was a familial nickname of Lincoln Kirstein. His sister Mina Kirstein Curtiss (1896–1985), biographer and teacher, shared with Leo a passion for nineteenth-century literature and art (particularly Marcel Proust and his circle), which became the basis of a close friendship.
69. Gabriel Yturri (1868–1905) was Count Robert de Montesquiou's secretary and companion from 1885. Montesquiou (1855–1921) was brilliant, handsome, and insolent—an outstanding figure of Belle Époque Paris and Proust's model for his Baron de Charlus.

I am tired . . . but everyone says how wonderful I look. Today I flew off to lunch at Kay [Silver]'s with the Tamayos. Such simple delicious food and interesting talk about Mexico. I love Olga Tamayo. She is fascinating-looking in that Spanish way—tight-wound, knotted black hair (the Cézanne woman has it this way), beautiful matte white skin, a red fruit of a ripe mouth, and such restrained, clear, chic color in her dress. . . . Also she has the charm of the genuinely mad.

Yesterday, at Alice [Astor]'s mysterious large festivity in the library of the St. Regis, that [lawyer Lillian] Rock at least talked to me, and she announced that Kosleck has stated that among Eleonora's papers sent to me were valuable Beethoven manuscripts. I laughed merrily and said that there weren't. She said that he and the estate would sue me to get them. I said that they could, and that furthermore they would have to sue the N.Y. Public Library to which I was giving them.[70] . . . Also that these things were mine because I possessed them, they were given me. I was in a pet. I have rarely been as autocratic (a Howard word) and I think she was amazed to find me so angry, because she tried to smooth everything over and blame Jakob Goldschmidt [Eleonora's financial agent]. I said if he were interested he could discuss it with me, but that this junk was mine to do with as I pleased. They are dreadful people, and she is even worse than we thought. Marlene says that I should have said I had burned everything . . . but I think I was right.

OCTOBER 31, 1952 • NEW YORK CITY

**TO GRAY FOY** • ROME

Marlene's apartment is indeed all blond and the bedroom (the only complete room, naturally) is extremely handsome—save one *cocotte* kitsch touch: When all the lights are doused, light filters into the room from under the enormous bed, outlining it. I queried, "When you put the nickel in, does it play 'Too Old to Cut the Mustard?'[71] She beat on me and threw me down on her beautiful blond carpet and we just lay there laughing. . . . Then she turned on her side toward me and said, "Gray will like this room?" I said yes you would, because I could only think how very beautiful you would make it by being in it.

**MARLENE**  *There was always a high time with Marlene, whether times were good or bad. . . . I discovered that to love Marlene meant that you sort of gave up part of your life. You could not open your mouth and say, "I really don't feel quite well," because she became an instant infirmary. She practically killed you with affection. She anticipated your every want. She pampered you with too much*

---

70. Leo soon donated the papers of Eleonora von Mendelssohn in his possession to the New York Public Library and Brandeis University. Neither donation included Beethoven manuscripts. He will recall in May 1984, however, having once given Callas a copy of Donizetti's *Lucrezia Borgia* "left to me by Eleonora."

71. A Marlene Dietrich–Rosemary Clooney recording of this song had been one of the hits of 1952.

*food, which, of course, she cooked herself. But best of all she made you laugh always when you needed to laugh. She always had humor—gallows humor, outright street humor, late late night humor. She could laugh at herself and tell you about how she had been a plump girl, and part of her mystique came from being hidden behind furniture, so moviegoers couldn't see how plump she was. And she was wonderful at takeoffs of other actors and actresses. But I think she was best at takeoffs of herself: Marlene the insolent, the impossible, the spoiled greatest beauty in the world. Marlene the supplicant. Marlene the loving heart. To hear her murmur "mon amour" on the phone to some anonymity (male? female? octogenarian? child?) was to believe you were hearing Marlene in love—love all abiding, forever, igniting, pealing. Adoration nourished her the way health food sustains others. Marlene so needing money—not able to stop lavishing . . . family, lovers, friends, self. So to Marlene the giver . . . Marlene the sexual symbol.*

*I think of a midnight discourse during which she matter-of-factly observed, "Men want it. I'm not interested in it, but if men want it, why should I refuse?" Marlene, overcome by admiration, devastated by charm, undone by enthusiasm, felt she had only one tribute to offer: the remarkable gift of her beauty. She gave it unstintingly. The "great" were her "peer group." What did her conquests mean to her? She thought that she was giving. She was taking care of all of them.* (*VOGUE*, JULY 1992)

**TO GRAY FOY • ROME**

Baby dear, sweet darling, I do love you so much. So, Marlene just called. She is very happy (fool's-paradise kind) these days because Mr. Y. B. seems to be deeply in love with her (she says), and his wife's new analyst has told him that he must leave his wife soon. I wonder whether Marlene would actually marry him. If only she would get a movie to do, one which would take her far away, she would be saved from all this.

I am sitting here in my writing chair, drinking coffee (made by me on the pilot light)[72] and eating shortbread, still some of that old tinned kind, very good, and reading the Sunday papers before I set to work writing a piece. It is curiously pleasant in this house. It sits here surrounding me with you. This is where I first saw you, and this is where I picked you up from that chaise and carried you into my bed, and this is where I grew to love you so very much that now I cannot conceive of a life that does not center about you, loving you, you loving me. Oh my love, I sit here, shivering with love for you, shivering on the hottest day in November. How very close deep life is to popular songs. Manhattan is fallen beneath a still sea of fog. Remotely voices blear in the fog. This is a soundless city in a soundless time.

In the autumn, all the world reveals its heartbreak side . . . shape of fallen curling and clutching leaf—shape of hands remembered—hands flung up and

---

72. Leo was frightened of striking matches and would not light a stove.

away and curling at the fingers to grasp—what? Dreams . . . love standing beside the love-rumpled sheets . . . and the wisteria vine, having persevered throughout spring, summer, foams acidly green, against the windowpane . . . trembling, stirring faintly. So I saw you one early morning when I stood by our bed and wondered for a moment did you still breathe. . . . How the heart stops, the stomach turns painfully even at remembering—but you trembled slightly and, turning from left to right, raised the lovely curtain of your exquisitely veined eyelids (What master craftsmen fashioned these. You know, my love, I sometimes play a game of wondering whether artists when they die are then employed to create in people, in nature what they did most perfectly in life. So, perhaps your eyelids were fashioned by Leonardo, for only in his boys have I ever seen eyelids so beautiful.) . . . first the fringe, those improbable lashes which lie in the hollow above your winged bones . . . and then the lids . . . and you looked at me and smiled. When you smile I have blinding sunlight in my heart. I can feel it tangibly, this sunlight, I can taste it and even hold it in my hand. Then I kissed you, creasing your lips with mine, inhaling you, breathing you with every pore. Sometimes you are fragrant like a sun-baked wall or biscuits freshly baked or a garden of hot summer flowers buzzing with fat black-and-gold bees. I have read that extreme cold, such as it is to be experienced only in the highest altitudes, burns like fire. When I am in your arms and you look down upon me, I am in those high places . . . the sweet, sure dizzying gradual obliteration of self . . . oneness . . . then the hand touching, finding of one another. . . . Oh my love, it is always morning in my heart because of you . . . and somewhere within me a beautiful consistent sun is always rising, moving in rainbow slippers across the white walls and ceiling of our room. . . . Oh my love, oh my love, oh my love . . . in each lovemaking the entire cycle of life repeats, the cycle of the seasons, the hours of the entire day . . . a sun rises, a sun sets, and the moon attended by its stars and planets is here, is elsewhere . . . the tides of the seas return, recede . . . first the womb, then the death . . . time diminishes, time enlarges. . . . I sit here typewriting to you . . . and I am as full of secret places as a nougat—those honey-colored nougats . . . and in all those secret places what makes richness? You, your loving me, my loving you. I wrote two days ago, in a caption, that the Golden Gate Bridge is the longest in the world. . . . This is untrue. . . . We are. It is also, I discovered, painted red because of visibility during fogs. I know this to be true, for I also am red, crimson, burning like a beacon with love of you. . . . I suspect that if you are looking toward upper Lexington Avenue, you must be seeing me loving you.

NOVEMBER 3, 1952 · NEW YORK CITY

**TO GRAY FOY** · ROME

About Touche's Halloween film showing: He asked, and Maya [Deren] asked, and somehow I got to go to see her film there. Within was a dispirited group of

ABOVE LEFT: With Poppa, 1914
ABOVE RIGHT: Brothers Jerry and Leo with a family friend
BELOW: *Front seat*, Sam and Ida Lerman; *back, right to left*, Leo's grandmother
Yetta Goldwasser with his uncle Irving and aunt Minnie Goldwasser

ABOVE LEFT: Momma and "Label" on Fifth Avenue
ABOVE RIGHT: Friend-for-hire, probably on 106th Street
BELOW LEFT: Leo playing, *center*, perhaps with Poppa and Jerry
BELOW RIGHT: Middle school graduation, 1928

ABOVE LEFT: Stage manager of the Grossinger Playhouse with chorus girls, ca. 1935
ABOVE RIGHT: Leo's uncle Irving, buyer for Saks, kept him well dressed.
BELOW: Elsa Snapper, John Latouche, and Leo
on her Greenwich Village rooftop, ca. 1939

RICHARD HUNTER    ABOVE LEFT: Beachcombing on Nantucket, 1947
ABOVE RIGHT: In Middletown, New York, ca. 1940
BELOW LEFT: In Quidnet, Nantucket, with Leo, 1947
BELOW RIGHT: On the Nile, with Howard Rothschild, 1960

ABOVE: Robert Davison in Sneden Landing, New York, 1948
BELOW: "Laci" Czettel with a costume from the *Ballo en maschera* he designed for the Metropolitan Opera, 1940

**ELEONORA VON
MENDELSSOHN**
ABOVE LEFT: This
photograph's inscription
to the Yorcks translates:
"For Rut and Soni,
Christmas, 1932."
ABOVE RIGHT: Eleonora
the actress
LEFT: "Ela" and Moko,
1942

**RUTH YORCK**

ABOVE: In France at Lucien
Vogel's country house, ca. 1952
LEFT: At work in Greenwich
Village, with Oskar
Kokoschka's portrait of Ruth
above, early sixties
BELOW: Ruth, *right*, with
Arturo Toscanini and Eleonora
on the Kammersee in Austria,
ca. 1936

GRAY FOY
LEFT: On a friend's rooftop,
ca. 1950.
BELOW: The twenty-five-year-old
Gray who met Leo in 1948

ABOVE: Long Island shore, mid-fifties
RIGHT: Marching to protest nuclear arms, 1984
BELOW: Visiting the Cloisters in Manhattan, 1969

ABOVE: As the Dirty Old Man, restrained by Tom Aldredge,
ninety stories up in Ted Flicker's film *The Troublemaker*, 1963
BELOW: Competing against artist Larry Rivers on
*The $64,000 Question*, 1958

ABOVE: Directing a photo shoot of the New York City Ballet
for *Park East* magazine, 1951
BELOW: Previewing a show in rehearsal, late sixties

While researching the history of Sotheby's, Leo, *far right*, observes an
auction—"Magnificent Jewels"—in London, 1964.

ABOVE: The freelancer at work—in the Eighty-eighth Street
apartment he shared with Richard Hunter, ca. 1947
BELOW: In his basement workroom at 1453 Lexington Avenue, ca. 1966

In the upstairs library of the Lexington Avenue house, 1966

*Leo Lerman, New York, 1977*
Leo described Irving Penn's making of this portrait as "a two-man meditation."

dancerines [sic], but no one of any sex had ever laid even a frigid hand on any one of them. Mostly their eyes were kohl-rimmed—at least that is how it seemed. So when I saw one creature of indeterminate gender covered with milk containers (they were hooked together by string), and he said (in a squeak and cracked trill of a voice) that he was the Milky Way, I realized that maybe it was a costume showing of Maya's opus. So it transpired it was to have been, for soon Mr. Latouche arrived, streaked with what I took to be his breakfast and in a sort of space suit. He was livid because I also was not similarly arrayed. Then I waited until 3:30 a.m. to view the cause of all this horror, and when it was finally unreeled I fell fast asleep.[73] Waking, I crept away before anyone could discover. It was awful. That girl [painter] the avant-garde is trying to zoom sat Groke-like,[74] swathed in blue tulle and tarnished tinsel, looking as though she had swallowed Peggy Guggenheim whole and was now unable to digest her. Her name is Jane Freilicher.

NOTE: Leo sailed to Copenhagen on November 18 to research a piece on the Royal Danish Ballet. Instead he ultimately wrote a two-installment article on Denmark itself for *Mademoiselle*.

During the trip he met Baroness Karen Blixen-Finecke, the writer better known as Isak Dinesen. As he would write in January 1971: "I met Blixen through [the actress] Ruth Elizabeth Ford. [Her brother] Charles Henri Ford had written to Karen when he was still a boy in Columbus, Mississippi, when his momma was the hostess in the local hotel coffee shop and Ruth Elizabeth was the campus queen, singing with the bands."

NOVEMBER 30, 1952 • COPENHAGEN

**TO GRAY FOY • ROME**

It is four o'clock, and the chimes and bells all over Copenhagen are sounding and re-sounding—the one from the great church (a baroque marvel which once seen spins in the head for hours) and the one from the Russian church (with three golden-green onion towers and glittering ropes draping its curious crosses) and the clocks in the Amalienborg—a great octagonal square. The palace surrounds its cobbled vastness on all sides—every inch of it completing the inch preceding, the one succeeding, and all garlanded and scrolled—with maids in white nurse-cap-like hats peering from between snowy curtains, and men in uniforms only worn elsewhere in operettas about *Alt Wien* also peering out, but on the floor above. A maid setting the table, dimly seen to be lit by pink-shaded candles. Many doors have china plaques on which an owl sits on two keys crossed—he and the keys are blue, the plaques white.

Here the queen goes shopping like anyone else, and the king loves to conduct the symphony orchestra. The Danes all stop whatever they are doing

73. John Latouche was probably screening Deren's *Ensemble for Somnambulists* (1951).
74. The Groke, a character in the Moomintroll children's books of Tove Jansson, leaves a damp, dark spot wherever it passes.

when the quite modest royal car passes, uncover their heads and smile sweetly and fondly at it—like people who have some oldish friend whom they love—a sort of half-smiling-at-a-child protective smile.

Today I have been walking from 10:30 until a few minutes ago—oh, the beautiful, unexpected, remote-in-time sights I have seen! Here the sets for the royal theater—the big one where ballet, opera, plays are performed—are dragged in by two beautiful ancient horses—from the shipyard where they are kept. Also, it being Sunday, almost no one is on a bicycle or in an auto—but on foot—and more friendly dogs (of all kinds) are about—also sweet-faced blond children, some in white goatskin coats like little girls used to wear at the turn of the century. They look like old-fashioned white poodle fur, and with Kewpie-doll hats of the same fur. But most in blue—all of the blues in the world—embroidered in scarlet—and now and then a scarlet one worked in blue.

It is on Sunday that every child (it seems) in Copenhagen and many dogs and quantities of adults flock to the Amalienborg Square. There an elaborate changing of the royal guard happens. The guard about to work lurks in the entry of its guardhouse (like a chorus in an operetta in the wings) now in long black coats and white-and-silver trim; sky blue trousers peep from beneath, on their heads even larger busbies than the guards at Buckingham. All the while, through the great gate more and more children arrive—all sizes, girls and boys both, dogs and gulls and large black birds—but not performing bears. (They have one in *Petrouchka* which was wonderful last night—with the [Diaghilev Ballets Russes'] original Benois decor.) Everyone is in great good humor and no one shoves and the police make jokes and pick up the littlest children and give them friendly kisses—it is *lovely*. Now everyone has made an irregular circle from the Frederick Quintus statue in the center of the square (a huge flourish of an equestrian statue—high baroque—it echoes and echoes as you look at it), so they all are in fanned line with one opening at the gate and the other near a door to the palace. It is an octagon, broken in four places by passageways, but giving an illusion of continuity—save where the harbor is to be seen through one passage—and the great cathedral surmounted by its shattering star of a spire (oh, how beautiful, topping the green dome) and garlands. Faint music—and a tremendous influx of people (like in any opera when the crowd comes on), and this means the people who've been marching with the guard through the city are arriving. Then in come the guard—to very gay and silly toy-soldier music (very Von Suppé), and they march and do formations. The music is so spirited, the children all so serious, and the dogs stand or some sit smiling and wagging (what well-behaved beasts)—I thought of you even more, and suddenly I began to cry, so then I made believe I had something in my eye, in case anybody was looking, but nobody was. Then the doors of the palace opened, and a majordomo in scarlet and gold (early eighteenth-century costume and cockade, with a great gleaming staff of office) held doors open, and out came the king in the palace windows (deep-silled—all windows here are, and all have great quantities of plants on them) and the Danish royal flag. Loads of presenting arms, and a dignitary, with a huge, felt-looking, sky-blue sash across his shoulder, took the Danish royal flag. (The steps of this man and his companion were the same as we have seen in movies showing royal personages following royal coffins.) And so more marching, and the king retired, and then still more marching—always to ever-changing gay music. Then within all the guards all the people stood in a hollow square, within this a double set of musicians and—do you know what?—for one half hour they gave a program of music which surely Von Suppé, the Strauss boys, and Offenbach had collaborated on. It was ravishing—and all the children and dogs and the policemen and the guardsmen just stood there visibly loving it!!! Then the whole previous ceremony was repeated at each of the guard booths, those narrow kind, four pairs, Danish red with white royal initials. After this, off they marched with everyone following them through the rest of Copenhagen.

**ISAK DINESEN** *A large, square, highly polished room, and there she sat, incredibly elegant, behind her lace-draped tea table. She had never before seen me: I had never seen her. Almost two hours later, I realized that we had not stopped talking from the moment she said, "Sit down here, Mister Lerman," beckoning me to a huge chair beside the table. What did we talk about? Friends. Those she did not know, she knew about. She was a mesmerizing listener. It was impossible not to tell her the sort of detail you note in a very private diary or do not dare to set down at all. Her immediate and singular magic transformed you into a teller of the tales she wanted to hear. There she sat, swathed in pale woolen stuffs, minutely perfect, erect like czarinas and empresses in nineteenth-century picture books, her enchantress eyes so alive that it was impossible to imagine them still even in sleep. Within their luminous depths, an ironic humor glittered. Her wizard hands poured out tea, dispensed buttery little cakes filled with preserves. "These cakes, what are they called?" "Jew cakes . . ." She had the voice of a great diseuse. You could hear Paris of* La Belle Epoque *in it. Yvette Guilbert sounded this way when she sang, Colette when she talked. "Jew cakes," she said again, suddenly looking not at me but into me. "Oh," I said, "my mother makes them. I have known them always. Her mother made them." "Yes," she said, "I know because your mother and her mother must have come from Russia. Russian Jews make them. I had the recipe many years ago from one of them." (She had the power of evoking a long-lost moment in time, a host of people, not only by what she said but by what she did not say.)*

*From the gray wall opposite, a small, storybook-dressed boy of amazing presence came. He was, obviously, not a real little boy, but a child out of a Gothic or a Winter's Tale. He wore the garments of some long-ago day: Children in* The Nutcracker *are dressed this way. Put him in a Kate Greenaway [children's] book and you could not find him. He bowed to the baroness. She said something in Danish, giving him a smiling look, which overflowed into love and pride—as though she had achieved him and was deeply pleased. The baroness beckoned the little boy to the cakes. He took one, retreated, said something in Danish, looked at me merrily. "He says you look like the men in the paintings." Her walls were covered by enormous nineteenth-century canvases of military formations and battles, interspersed with small paintings of flowers. "He admires your beard," the baroness continued. The little boy backed away to the hidden door, made his little antique bow, and vanished. She gave me a mischievous look. "You are mystified, are you not." This was not a question but an expression of pleasure. "And you are a curious man . . . so curious. Well, this little fellow is not an apparition. He is not an automaton. He is the son of my cook. Some years ago, soon after she first came to me, I was at my dinner. I felt someone was in the room. He was. Lurking in a dark corner—watching. So I told his mother that he and I would dine together every Thursday evening. We would have an evening suit made for him and have champagne and make the social graces. And we do, every Thursday evening at eight o'clock."*

*Much later, I went away out into the November night, out into the falling snow, which cascades from the skies in Denmark as it did when I was a child in New York . . . or even now when* Petrouchka *is danced upon the stage of the Royal Theatre in Copenhagen. There was not a light to be seen in Tania's house, not a sound came from it save the high, thin tinkle of a bell—a silvery tintinnabulation. Then nothing. Did she write her tales first or live them?* (FROM ISAK DINESEN: A MEMORIAL, 1965)

NOTE: On December 6, Leo left Copenhagen by train for Florence, where Gray met him. After a few days, they went to Rome, where Leo did interviews and research about the Italian film-studio complex Cinecittà.

DECEMBER 25, 1952 • ROME
**TO BETSY BLACKWELL** • NEW YORK CITY

Rome is resplendently beautiful today, with more theater and opera transpiring in the churches than on any stage, ever. I have been laboring over our features here strenuously, so this has been my first sightseeing day. I have filled some fourteen notebooks with material for use in the three features and later "notions." This *albergo* is freezing cold and I am writing to you clothed in four sweaters, a flannel pajama top, my hands in knitted gloves, two pairs of socks on the usual appendages (obviously all four of them).

**BETSY BLACKWELL** *Mrs. Blackwell was that old-time American lady, a thoroughly modern woman, superbly hatted and impeccably gloved. She believed that her readers should be informed, delighted, surprised, cultivated— admonished when necessary—literally from foot to head, inside and out. The complete Republican lady, she was one of the most curious women I've ever known, and she loved to be first. That made life as one of her editors a frequent* *paradise. She had that superb editorial sixth sense that told her when an editor's most freakish notion would work to the advantage of her magazine. Her door was always open, and I would rush into her office. "Mrs. B," I would shout, "Copenhagen is going to be the place next year." She would look at me quietly and say, "Does that mean a trip?" "Sure," I'd answer, and she would say, "If you can keep the expenses down you can go." That trip was typical of all our decades together, because it eventually evolved into traipsing from Copenhagen to Rome (to write about the then-flourishing Italian cinema), to Venice (I wired:* MRS B CANT COME HOME WHEN PROMISED MUST GO TO VENICE TO HEAR WONDERFUL NEW SOPRANO MARIA MENEGHINI CALLAS WE WILL BE FIRST*). The years went by and we were first, to her utter delight, with Margot Fonteyn, Sadler's Wells, Dylan Thomas's* Under Milk Wood *(published entire), the Beatles.*[75] *The excitements piled up. Mrs. B loved gossip and a joke. I remember coming back from a fashion sitting in which we used Manhattan's most famous nude model, and Mrs. B said, "How did it go?" and I replied, "Well, it went very well, but the naked lady seemed so prim. When she saw us slapping paint on the girls, she firmly said, 'You can look, but you can't touch.'" Mrs. B laughed so hard that she fell into a paroxysm of coughing. The coughing always terrified us, but Mrs. B's laughter was pure, unadulterated, forever-young joy. (1985)*

JOURNAL · DECEMBER 30, 1952  Tuesday. Having been ill since Sunday evening, I now feel well enough to go out, and sun makes it more desirable. Gray has also been ill with the current Roman cold epidemic. I read *Out of Africa* and fell deeply, painfully in love with it. I know of no other book like it.

Here in Rome, I am constantly beset by an at-sea feeling. The baroque churches, with their facades in sea-wave curves, seem indeed sea waves at the very moment of their breaking, tumbling, topping the churches of Rome. And the many bells are, especially at night when I lie awake, forlorn bells of the sea, and everywhere, even on a windless day, great sea winds fill the billowing, swaying draperies of the statues, while cupids (*putti*) clutch them, hoping to restrain them from being blown by these winds from nowhere, save the hearts of those who shaped them invisibly. And here, in this city, Triton reigns, not the eagle or the wolf, but Neptune and his Tritons, his Nereids and seahorses and the very fish of the deep sea—all limey and salt-sparkling and seaweed green in the fountains. Nowhere are there so many jets of water iridescencing [*sic*] a city.

In the [Protestant] graveyard, the small cats that guide one stand discreetly among themselves while you stand weeping, in the rain beneath black umbrellas, reappearing when the moment of departure comes.

75. Some news magazines beat *Mademoiselle*'s January 1964 Beatles story by a few months.

On the marble-topped bureau in this room:
a feather-framed photograph by Sheila [Ward] of Gray and me in their pool
    in New Hope (and Peter [Lindamood] sitting beside it); it is also holding a
    postcard view of Sleeping Beauty's château (Blois)
a little insect playing a cello, mounted atop a flower (its base a calendar)
a double leather frame containing Ela and Maestro, Cecil Beaton's snap of
    Ela at Kammerschloss, and Louise Dahl-Wolfe's photo of Penelope [Reed]
a little rabbit peering at the Sheila photo
a *befana*[76]
six vegetable dolls
the little bear from New York
a flashlight
two kaleidoscopes
two bottles of snuff
a large plastic bottle of bay rum
a jar of fixing cream [mustache wax] from the Ritz in London
a peasant riding a white cow
the hair and eagle top from [a marionette] Tancred's helmet
a bobbing, long-necked, blue-hair-bowed bird
seven painted-tin flower trees (three sizes) in gold pots
a little colored holy card from the Bernini church on Christmas Eve
an 1840ish bisque figure from the junk shop on Via del Babuino
a lovely green-flowered carton of chocolates from Perugia
a hairbrush, black-tail comb, beard brush, two beard shears, and nail scissors
Dorn's capsules for colds
a baby-faced sphinx from the Piazza Borghese junk market, with a bit of
    mistletoe offering from the Piazza di Spagna
a two-faced hand looking glass found in Ela's boxes
a ball-shaped and an egg-shaped wooden sock darner—very beautiful
seven tangerines—orange with gold lights and interior skins like honey and
    ivory-colored nougat, some with green leaves at their hearts
a folder from the American Express about Hotel Amstel in Amsterdam
two linen handkerchiefs marked R
a first-aid kit and a thermometer
a chocolate pear and a chocolate lime, each wrapped in tinfoil and leaves
my engagement book
my little account book
four bone-colored rods
a white-spotted, large blue bandana, folded
a balancing Pinocchio

---

76. A *befana* is an ugly old woman expected by Italian children to come down chimneys
with presents on Epiphany.

a large wooden Pinocchio
a gay Buon Natale card
a pack of *doppie Tedeschi carte* [playing cards]
a pile of notes, reminders, and Perugina candy bands
a glass jar in the form of a grape cluster
a basket of yellow beans
a little pig, a little cat, the Negro Magi, and a cupid from the Piazza
  Navona—all of these say "Buon Natale"

And one Ray Co. #2 pencil—in yellow painted wood—that I took and am
  using—and will now replace because we are going out to lunch![77]

NOTE: According to Leo, the first report of a new singer named Maria Callas came to
him in 1947 or 1948. More rumors followed, and in him a "hunger set in, like Marcel's
for Berma" (*Journal, July 18, 1981*). While in Rome, they spotted a placard announcing
a gala *La Traviata* in Venice with Callas on January 8, 1953. After Twelfth Night, always
their favorite holiday in the Christmas season, Leo and Gray took the train to Venice.
Gray recalls that they made their way to the Hotel Bauer-Grunwald in a gondola, with
excesses of luggage, and Leo in a homburg hat and shearling-collared coat, holding a
walking stick. They swiftly pulled themselves together and went to the performance
that evening at La Fenice.

**CALLAS**  *Upon a stage thronged the surging crowd of laughing, chattering,
wildly gesticulating ball-goers—women's wide skirts making a sound like leaves
on a windswept day, their steps as they twirl and twirl heard above the mounting
waltz-beat lilt in the orchestra. Upon the stage, downstage left, quite apart, in
solitude to be found in dreams, sits a monumental, Titian-haired, marmoreal figure, encased in her flounced but simple white gown, as she sits there casually,
almost indolently, tossing white camellias toward the dancing guests. Am I imag-
ining her? From her . . . the most haunting voice I have ever heard. It is filled
with lost joys, permeated with present despairs. Here is desperate frivolity, and
here is unavoidable tragedy.*

*I do not think, on this night of that early January day in 1953, the 100th
anniversary of* La Traviata *being celebrated in the theater where it encountered
disaster (for it did, at its premiere in Venice), I do not think I saw anything or
anybody save Maria Meneghini Callas.[78] Only when the lights came up, Act I
ending, after I had lived with Violetta through her tumultuous falling in love,
only then—it was a matter of some minutes and considerable nudging from
Gray—I came back to see all about me the glory of* La Fenice. *Here was an opera
house obviously scooped out by mysterious seaborne architects . . . all green and
pale gold, brimming with aqueous light—a sea-washed grotto, a secret place in a
coral reef (for this gala occasion festooned top to bottom with blush-pink and
blood-red carnations).*

77. GF: "We traveled with everything except a parrot."
78. The theatrical billing she preferred.

*Then, Act II, and we were in some country French place and the enormous woman was the essence of a young girl transported by her love for this so obviously charming, but not quite steadfast, young man. The opera—one I knew intimately—unfolded and I clung to it as if I never before had heard it. In Act III, this Violetta's great size completely vanished and even the voice was already in the other world and all dreamt. The destruction of this monumental woman by her monumental passion for a weak, conventional man: How much more devastatingly huge Callas made her destruction than did any more fragile Violetta. We went away, exhausted, into the dark Venetian winter night, a night full of retreating footsteps. We could not talk, for each of us knew that we had seen the greatest operatic performance in years, for me years which had included Flagstad's Isolde, Lehmann's Marschallin, Welitsch's Salome. I had seen Bori, Sayão, Albanese . . . but indisputably Callas's Violetta was—greatest is inadequate.* (1993)

NOTE: After Venice, Leo and Gray visited Paris, then sailed for New York.

JOURNAL • JANUARY 27, 1953 • SS *LIBERTÉ* EN ROUTE TO NEW YORK
Lucien [Vogel] and Cosette [de Brunhoff] took us to lunch in a small marvelous restaurant in Les Halles. Here the proprietor, a brisk, pigeon-breasted man, looks fifty, but is seventy-one, and the food and drink are magnificent. When I asked Lucien and Cosette why they did not come to America, Gray and I fell into one of the terminal tragedies of our time: He cannot get his visa because our State Department thinks him undesirable, thinks him a Communist. He went to Russia in the thirties and did an issue of *Lu* or *Vu* about Russia.[79] He and Cosette are both violently anti-Communist. He has a daughter who was in the Underground and at Auschwitz (she is crippled) and is violently pro-Communist. She does not live with her parents because of their political differences. Her younger sister is violently pro-Communist, and doesn't live with her parents. Their brother, in the movies, and befriended during the Occupation by his older sister while his father and mother had to flee to America, is torn by devotion to her, devotion to his parents, and noninterest in politics. So this family is sundered and Lucien is kept out of America because they think him Communist. The mother is a heartbroken woman. All this played against a Faubourg Saint-Germain, *Vogue-Jardin des Modes*, high Paris life background, Lucien looking, as always, a French Pickwick, Cosette a *grande dame*. It needs Racine to write it.

79. Launched by Vogel in 1931, *Lu* was a weekly roundup of press articles from around the world with many points of view on subjects such as armament. In September 1936, Vogel's photo magazine *Vu* had published a map of Germany's concentration camps, including Dachau. For obvious reasons, the Vogels had to leave France when Hitler invaded.

Oh how beautiful Paris is. Rome has big moments—hours—of beauty, but Paris *is* beauty. Venice exists in the mind, a transfixed moment, the only city to retain the freshness of a dream, to hold the nostalgia for the unexperienced even after it has been experienced, for Venice is improbable. It cannot be, yet it is. Venice, even when one is in it, is improbable. Paris is forever probable—an *actual* beauty.

# EVERYONE'S GIVING PARTIES

JOURNAL · FEBRUARY 8, 1953 · NEW YORK CITY Mina Curtiss translates Proust's letters and now goes about among the very people of the *Remembrance*. For she is writing Bizet's life, and with the money left her by her parents (they having made it with Filene's department store, the basement of which store is famous for its bargains) she lives in Paris. "You can always reach me through the Ritz," she says, and goes to visit Strauses and Mante-Prousts and Gramonts and Montesquious and all those others who are to be found along the Guermantes Way,[1] becoming herself, this Mina, a figure in that world which perhaps some *enfant* Proust even now admires from afar, tracking after her along the rue d'Anjou, along the St. Honoré. Will Mina also say, "Fitzjames is waiting?"[2]

Last night, watching Brigitta in her house, at her table, listening to her, I thought about how the glittering world de-tinselizes when one is within it. Brigitta, a Norwegian-German girl, telling of the hardships of her early life. Listening to Brigitta tell about her impoverished childhood, her terror in a Norwegian boardinghouse in Paris, her hunger, how the two lovebirds she and her mother bought out of their little savings had to be given away, because in a French newspaper they read that parrots spread a malign disease, and these little beloved birds were their only companions.

How delighted she is when she tells about the only good time she and her mother had in Paris. This was when her mother fell sick with some horrible ear infection and a doctor, after a week of misery, ordered her to the hospital. Brigitta must also go, for she also was suddenly suffering from earache. After her mother had had an operation lasting four hours, Brigitta had her eardrum pierced, and they then had spent long days convalescing in the clean, good hospital, and they had been fed.

1. The Guermantes Way, an occasional boyhood walk in *Remembrance*, winds by grand houses and symbolizes social progress. In Proust, the Méséglise Way represents the innate, familial self, the Guermantes Way the acquired self.
2. In *Remembrance of Things Past*, the Duchesse de Guermantes answers "like a parrot, with 'Fitzjames is waiting for me' " to the narrator when he tries to engage her on the Avenue Gabriel.

Then, when she was sixteen, Peter Vollmoeller took her to Venice. She barricaded her door every night. There she met Rut and Sohni—all penniless, but living in the Vendramin.[3] Swimming to a raft off the Lido, Brigitta tore her leg so that it was all covered with blood. Flopping onto the raft, she was greeted by a male voice: What was wrong? he wanted to know. In this way, she met [Serge] Lifar and danced [the divertissements] with him at a great ball in Venice and became famous, dancing in a negligee and a cutoff ball gown of [Russian princess] Natalie Paley's (now Mrs. Jack Wilson and so beautiful then, but now a painting by Albright, because of dope).[4]

In between, Brigitta and her mother had gone to London, and after an audition in [Anton] Dolin's studio, a large bright room in Chelsea, Brigitta studied with him. She was thirteen. Three months later [in 1931], she became his dancing partner, much to the disquiet of [British ballerinas] Markova and Wendy Toye.[5]

Now she is married to Goddard (a Jewish boy from Seattle who has climbed) and they have two children and the only bathroom with a bidet and a *Spy* cartoon, numbered 69, and a soundless Frigidaire in their bedroom. She has had a glittering career, and is now having a more esoteric one [as an orchestral narrator]. She still yearns to dance Nora [Kaye]'s ballets,[6] and in their house is not one evidence of good (what a snobbish remark) taste.

All this, as she told about her past, made me wonder how much of it had been improvised when she was very young, and now was true in that she had believed it for so many years. During the war, social barriers dissolved, and it is easier for unknowns to climb or even step into so-called high places. I am reminded that for a long time, in my childhood, in my adolescence, I made up histories about myself, my family, my "friends." I still believe some of these stories and even find myself telling them, and those who hear them also believe them, for the fantastic world of the "smart" magazines and social columns of

3. Karl "Peter" Vollmoeller (1878–1948), a German screenwriter and playwright (*The Miracle*), was a lover of Ruth Yorck's in the thirties. In 1933 he rented two floors in Venice's Renaissance palace Ca' Vendramin Calergi for six months. Ruth and her husband, Count David "Sohni" Yorck von Wartenburg, came to live there with Vollmoeller. (The Yorcks divorced amicably in 1937.)
4. Serge Lifar (1905–86), formerly of the Ballets Russes, was then leading the ballet of Paris Opéra. Princess Natalie Pavlovna Paley (1905–81), granddaughter of Czar Alexander II, married fashion designer Lucien Lelong, then producer John C. Wilson. Ivan Le Lorraine Albright (1897–1983) painted the transformed portrait of Dorian Gray for the 1943 movie.
5. The British dancer and choreographer Anton Dolin (1904–85), formerly with Diaghilev's Ballets Russes, was then principal guest artist with the Vic-Wells Ballet. He and Brigitta Hartwig danced together in a West End play called *Ballerina* in 1934, after which she joined Les Ballets Russes de Monte Carlo as Vera Zorina.
6. The ballerina Nora Kaye (1920–87) danced many roles of dramatic intensity created by Antony Tudor.

the rotogravures of my childhood—what is left of them—are now as open to me as those ruins that one finds everywhere in Rome. Like those ruins, some of it has disappeared—forever; some of it has been used to erect other structures or for ornament; some of it is lived in.

FEBRUARY 12, 1953  Great flashes of searing white light to the east at about two a.m. woke me. They continued with ever-increasing brightness, a white glare like that which was formerly made by the powder that photographers ignited. These, too, terrified me and always at weddings, which I loved and feared, even as I now fear entering even the most familiar group of friends at a party. Poppa and I went to those big family weddings almost always without Momma, for she was ill, or perhaps she did not wish to go. (This is difficult to believe, loving parties as she does.) Always, if she were not in a hospital, she would be in her bed waiting to hear all about the festivity. She had that special delicious Momma fragrance—a white-flower, flour-white fragrance—coming partly from the linens of her bed, a great brass confection in which I was permitted to snuggle early in the morning or when I had night terrors, running across the frigid, uncarpeted, splintery wooden floor, and, oh, the warmth and security, the pleasure of that bed. Mine, a brass cage, was almost always wet and icy. I did not know how to control my bladder, and this brought continual anguish— beatings, starvations, confinements in black closets, rubbings—violently—of my face in the wetness. I did not mind this last, rather liking it—sexually I suppose—but I protested, for the intention of debasing me was so apparent, and anything obviously a punishment demanded a set-piece reaction: howls, wails, screamings, kickings, a convulsion, which led to demonstrations of affection. But always I knew this was tinged by frustration in my parents, a feeling that they did not know quite how to cope with this awful, ugly, perhaps stupid (retarded would be the word today; then no one was retarded, for we did not know the word) child.

FEBRUARY 14, 1953  Valentine's Day—Heaped the breakfast table with old Valentine cards and little presents, some given before, and laughed very much.
About Frankie Merlo: One Saturday afternoon (perhaps four or five years ago?) when Peter [Lindamood] and Touche had been drunk for several days, they went to Everard's [baths]. There, after much sport, Peter told Touche that he had seen an attractive young Italian. So Touche went up to the room in which this boy was (with others)—and for about a year Touche and the boy were intimate (Blanchard [Kennedy, housemate of Lindamood] said: "There they were, riding tandem as hard as they could."), until Touche took Frankie to visit [painter] Buffie Johnson in Provincetown. Here he met Tennessee and now there they are. Frankie, who had been a bricklayer, wondering who to have arrange his taxes, really telling Tennessee what to do, and having definite

opinions on everything. Also, he's rather fat now, but likable in the way a mobster can be. He gives the impression of running the numbers racket.[7]

A fragile young man rose at Elizabeth Bowen's lecture and asked: "Miss Bowen, What do you do when you find your style hardening?" She suggested that the work be put aside and the writer read someone diametrically opposed.

FEBRUARY 18, 1953 Yesterday Elizabeth Bowen came to lunch—thinner, more haggard, with a cold-in-the-nose look about her and her good black clothes unsoignéed by train travel and time. She was dressed too thinly for a cold February day. But nothing dims the fine, intelligent, kind, mildly inquiring look of her eyes. Always I see her in medieval garments, a lady in a fortress-castle. She said how very lonely she is at Bowen's Court [in Ireland], talking swiftly and almost without stammer about Alan [Cameron, her husband] and how deeply she felt his death.[8] For, as she explained, she had always been free to go and come and he was always there—for twenty-nine years. So now she did not feel, as so many women do after the initial grief has worn away (what clichés I write), that she was free. The most boring years of her life, she said, were those between thirteen and twenty-three, the year her mother died and the year she married Alan. But she intends to continue at Bowen's Court. It is to her what Africa was to Isak Dinesen.

11:10 A.M. At Strang, in men's locker room, waiting.[9] A genuine locker-room atmosphere, with stories of a mildly "naughty" ilk being swapped by a knot of men, in gowns, sagging, open at the back, loads of warm convivial laughter, with some of them laughing long after the joke is ended, and strung in thought to it—as stations mark the progress of a journey, so their laughter marks the joke's route within each of them.

FEBRUARY 21, 1953 The doctor appeared in red-rimmed, heavy goggles, and as he massaged my stomach (very pleasant on a workday to lie in the dark with a man massaging my stomach) and inserted the tube up my bottom, he said, "You know, we've met before. About a year ago, at the Ballet Ball. I was at Nancy Norman's table. You were at Mrs. Bouverie's." He went on in this high-fashion, social tone all the time he gave me the enema.

NOTE: In late April 1953, Eleonora von Mendelssohn's personal effects were sold by the auctioneer Tobias Fischer.

---

7. Frank Merlo (1922–63), a Navy veteran, was the lover (1949–63) of Tennessee Williams.
8. GF: "Elizabeth had a dreadful stammer, utterly stopped by words until she could substitute others."
9. The Kate Depew Strang Clinic specialized in cancer prevention and treatment. Leo had several cancer scares.

JOURNAL · MAY 6, 1953 Her purse, the two black coats she'd "lied" about, the black ostrich-feather bedcoat hanging still with her perfume—at Tobias Fischer's—always the furs on that final rack and the sable gone for $160.

NOTE: Gray went to California to be with his mother, whose upset over her divorce the previous year had led her to a breakdown. Gray stayed for a couple of months to help her recovery.

JULY 27, 1953 · NEW YORK CITY
**TO GRAY FOY · BURBANK**

I waited almost an hour for the bus, and then it cost only ten cents so it was worth it, I guess. I've been with Marlene, and she fed me a bountiful, excellent dinner of rich, savory lentil soup complete with frankfurter slices, and cut-up steak, peas and little potatoes, and cheese and fruit and wine . . . all lovely. Then we went window shopping in all directions and to Howard Johnson, where she was pursued by ravenous autograph hounds. She is writing a lovely piece. When we returned, she read Goethe (proverbs and poems) to me for about an hour. . . . I didn't realize that Goethe was so humorous and human.

JULY 30, 1953 · 5 A.M. · NEW YORK CITY
**TO GRAY FOY · BURBANK**

Oh why am I such a craven! A sundering, tearing, stabbing storm (I am writing just to try). It's a regular Puss-in-the-Corner tempest, right overhead. All I can do is sit and quiver and say "Oh dear." I suppose I could pray—a mean stab— Oh, Possums!—The worst storm of the year. I don't dare go up and close the windows. It has sickening moments, when it gathers itself together, and then it leaps. . . . I am trying to be brave—not successfully. What torrents. What battles aerial and shattering violet light. It's funny—even I can see that. Every time I try to creep up the stair to shut the windows, the flash-and-crash comes, and I run back into this room and crouch, a fat creature in that exquisite, sleeveless creation I favor when the heat's on, which it indeed is. I try to think of happy lovely things—like the beaded-flower store in Paris opposite Marie Antoinette and Louis's graveyard or Sainte-Chapelle. . . . Ah me . . . I'll think VENICE.

If I were a genuine writer, I would utilize this time for minutely describing the storm, rather than crouching here with a terrified heart and an aching stomach . . . but this is a baroque storm. If one has the serenity to listen, the sound is all flourishes and curves, arabesques of sound, then great whorls of sound. Blessed deaf Beethoven—but he heard even more terrifying sounds. . . . An interlude, while others are permitted to cower. I wonder if I dare crawl up. I trust that you are not being terrified by anything or anyone. I feel like a small beast, who wonders whether the great hunter and his wrathful hounds have passed. You can't reason with them, best to hide and be discreet.

**TO GRAY FOY • BURBANK**

Marlene called. She seems to have had another of those dreadful attacks like she had three years ago. She promised that she would go to the doctor. Her mind blanks out and she can't even remember to whom she's talking. This happened while she was talking to me. It is terrifying. I wonder whether she shouldn't be X-rayed. This could be a brain thing. It would be awful if it happened while she was on the stage. Tomorrow I will hound her into going to the doctor. I told her that you might come home a few days later than we had first planned, and she had a genuine fit, saying hard, true, but unrealistic things about parents in general.

Of course it's helpful for you to be there, but also parents, like children, have to cope with their own problems. Maebelle's are not going to grow easier and she will doubtless make an adjustment to them. All this is painful and will continue to be painful. It's been that way with my family always. Although the pain and problems are not similar to yours. All I know is that no one prepares children for the fallibility of parents.

**JOURNAL** • AUGUST 15, 1953  For almost a month I have been unable to write in this notebook. The center of my life having gone away, I lacked a center from which to write. Now, suddenly, perhaps because it is less rather than longer until the return of my center, I can write again. George Sand, or rather André Maurois in *Lélia* [*The Life of George Sand*], writes: "No woman in love regrets that she cannot offer lost virginity, an untouched body, and an innocent heart to the man of her choice. . . ." This may be true for women, but it is almost utterly untrue for men. I regretted deeply not having a whole heart to give,* but did not realize until recently (a little over five years) that my heart would again become whole through giving it once again. As one can tell the age of a tree by the lines in its trunk, so surely one can tell the heart's age by some similar line.

*(not even thinking until this moment of the body—the virginity)

**TO GRAY FOY • BURBANK**

I think I must write to you about something which only in these last two or three years I have come to realize. When you first saw me my heart was mortally hurt—crumbled or whatever it is when one's heart (one's inner being) has been blasted. I thought that I had nothing much to give anyone—affection, yes, and some knowledge—but nothing of the deep within. Now, my heart (I use this only as a shorthand, a sort of representation) is whole again—richer, fuller. It has been made whole for me, because I have been and I am loved—and I love—totally, without reservation. Oh the duality of all living: the healer is healed—the healed is the healer—in each of us it's the universe, complete, minutely—mountain ranges, sea deeps—precisely as these are in the great world. Each thought we have—the shape of that thought is identical with some shape in nature. So it must be true that when I see stars and moonlight and sun shimmering in leaves I do truly see my love—the shape of my love—my love—my love—my love—I cannot help but think that no matter what enormities a man commits, if he has love truly, even for a moment, he has been God.

For a long time I stopped praying because, although I believed in godliness, I knew that prayers were inevitably requests. One always asked for something, like "Bless Momma and Poppa" or "Make Inky well." Now I pray again, because I realize that one only asks from the great force of loving (of giving) in the world to give, and that one gets nothing but that giving is miraculous. So I ask that although my heart is whole again—and loving—that the bestower and creator of this be as safe there as here in my heart—the heart which has been made whole by the one who lives within that heart.

AUGUST 29, 1953 • NEW YORK CITY

**TO GRAY FOY • BURBANK**

Today I called up Bill Inge to break a date with him and was astonished to hear him say, against a background of jazz (it was like opening a little secret window on a fever-bright concentrated vista): "I'm drunk, Leo—I've been drunk for three days—I'm gonna clear out now—I'll call you next week—So long, pal—" I worried a bit, but decided that I had troubles of my own. So he should cope with his. I guess he's put himself away. I hope so.[10]

NOTE: In October 1953, Leo made the first of three autumn visits to Chicago. The first was a trip promoting *Mademoiselle* in various department stores. Then, in 1954, he would attend Maria Callas's American debut at the Lyric Theatre of Chicago. He returned again for her performances there in 1955.

OCTOBER 8, 1953 • CHICAGO

**TO RICHARD HUNTER • PARIS**

Here I am in Chicago where I have been for four days. I have a huge room looking over that barbaric lake. What a curious city—the last genuine frontier town. So much wealth and very like Buffalo in a way. I've been seeing it on all levels—and oh, the rich are rich. Everybody gets into expensive cars at evening and runs home to the North Shore. In all the expensive restaurants are many Mary Bolands[11] drinking champagne cocktails and acting like they had gold nuggets for teeth. Art galleries here are incredibly awful—junk jewelry, ceramics, and "abstract" paintings (almost all bad). I have been to all the "best" houses (called homes, as in New York)—the McCormacks, Piries, Bordens,

10. Earlier in the year, playwright William Inge (1913–73) had won the Pulitzer Prize for *Picnic*.
11. The actress Mary Boland (1880–1965) is perhaps best remembered today as Countess de Lave in Cukor's film *The Women*.

Scotts, Carsons, and Epsteins have fêted me. The food is marvelous, and this week I have not dieted. On Saturday, I go home via the *Commodore Vanderbilt* [train] and that is even a better thing.

Oh, how I lust to be in Paris: It is incredibly beautiful—a poem. Venice is a dream; Rome a succession of sonnets; Florence a bouquet of pale flowers— spring flowers; Copenhagen a box of wooden toys, a jar of hard candies; London the books one has read—where will this end?—But Paris—those full moons, one after the other, in the arches of the rue de Rivoli, in the dusk . . . I'll just be sick and have a fit if I think about it more.

NOVEMBER 3, 1953 • NEW YORK CITY

**TO RICHARD HUNTER • PARIS**

We had a little Halloween do on Saturday night last, and Martha Spider [*sic*, Speiser] arrived looking like an elderly Carmen, complete with a huge, light green, heavily embroidered in colored wools Venetian shawl—also with a young nephew from Philadelphia. He interested various creatures, but she intrigued even more.[12] We also had a regular rash of blondes (as someone said: "Blondes from the Cradle to the Grave"). These included Angela Lansbury (so English cockney and nice) and her aged mother [Moyna MacGill] (she was the very funny drunken woman in [Minnelli's film] *The Clock*), Stella [Adler], Carol Channing, Brigitta, Marlene, and a girl yclept Missy Watson (brought by [lyricist] Adolph Green—he was not blond). We had cakes from Café Geiger and coffee and red wine and grapes. The house looked fine, with pumpkin faces carved by Mr. Foy everywhere, and autumn leaves decorating the fireplaces.

NOTE: In late November 1953, a very rare form of conjunctivitis blinded Leo for weeks. The schedule of drops and compresses that ensued marked the beginning of many eye troubles. During his temporary blindness, Leo dictated some personal correspondence. The following is one of only two letters to Capote from Leo that this editor found.

DECEMBER 7, 1953 • NEW YORK CITY

**TO TRUMAN CAPOTE • PARIS**

I cannot write this with the usual flummery. I am having eye trouble and currently cannot see, so I am lying fatly in the hospital and dictating. Gray says it has been like being on a two-week party here. Everyone descends on me and it is exhaustingly fun. Mostly you would think that I operate a goodies ring. I think I am holding a perpetual cake sale. Do not worry about me because I am getting better. I have a room in this hospital, which I am told has a fireplace and a real fake fire in it. This room feels like London. Also there seem to be

---

12. Martha Glazer Speiser (1880–1968) and her husband (who had been Leo's lawyer) Maurice Speiser (d. 1948) were leading Philadelphia politicians, modern-art patrons, and hosts.

quantities of attractive nurses. They smell nice anyway. As you can tell I am inhabiting and enjoying a new world. I think the ancient creature in the next room is not enjoying my world as much as I do. Among the events: a complete Chinese banquet brought in by [artist and historian] Mai-mai Sze; an elaborate multilingual get-well song recital by Jennie Tourel; Hurd Hatfield reading me three acts of a play about a decrepit toreador; Julie Harris and Edna Best calling up and *Colombing* at me[13] . . . In my old age I am turning out to be a regular Ned Sheldon. I always suspected that he got up in the middle of the night and jumped about his room and saw everything. What a wicked wise heart I had.[14]

DECEMBER 20, 1953 • NEW YORK CITY
**TO RICHARD HUNTER** • MÁLAGA, SPAIN

Poor Gray has an infected wisdom tooth and it will have to come out. He is in pain. That is why, what with having to give me five treatments a day—and all— and cooking and Christmas, for which we have little relish or money this year, Gray has not been able to write. He has headaches.

I write so very big! That's because I can see this size—sort of. Oh, Reezl, I can't get your Christmas present, the check, into the bank until later in January, and Gray planned to give you a check, but I've used all the money up, and I am so sorry. If you were here or I was sure where you are, I would send you products or some things from stores where I have credit. This is the first time in almost twenty years I haven't given you anything, and I can't even cry about it because it hurts—the salt, I guess. Anyway, in two weeks, I should be able to do things, and I have much to do, unfortunately, with lots of research. Oh—it's lovely to write words. These are the first I have written. It was good and awful to hear from you [by telephone]—and so clear. I loved it and it made me weep. I was lying there utterly in the dark and there you were in Spain!

**JOURNAL** • DECEMBER 20, 1953   Peter [Lindamood] came and read about Mrs. Lydig out of Cecil [Beaton]'s ill-written "new" book [*The Glass of Fashion*]. It is always intensified, reading or being read to, out of a book about people one knows. Now Gray asks, flinging open the bathroom door, "Is he writing? He's a busy one! I caught him writing!" So, I must stop and have drops and salve. But—oh—I can read better with my sick eyes today!

This morning the *Times* published my Misia Sert review, and some ghostly hand had deftly added two paragraphs![15] I resent a takeoff in the use of

---

13. Julie Harris (b. 1925) and Edna Best (1900–1974) would open in January 1954 in Anouilh's play *Mademoiselle Colombe*. Leo had gone out of his way to meet Harris earlier in the year after seeing her as Frankie in *Member of the Wedding*.

14. Playwright Edward "Ned" Sheldon (1886–1946), stricken early in his career by arthritic paralysis, continued to collaborate on theatrical productions and entertain from his bed.

15. In his review of the memoir by this beauty and hostess of pre–World War I Paris, Leo wrote: "To know her would, I am sure, have been to loathe her."

"quaintly" in the second of these paragraphs, and I loathe having my name on work which is not even in one word or punctuation point mine, but where else to review? I enjoy writing about books. I must make so much money, to pay all the debts I have incurred, because of sickness and extravagance and the passionate desire to live pretty. I just told Gray I was putting on my house socks. "You must be a centipede," he says.

DECEMBER 21, 1953 Monday—But just then I had to stop, because of drop time and eye cleaning and ice cottons, all of which Gray does angelically and with painstaking delicacy. These are such darning-needle notes. I mean like those gleaming, darting, summer-winged creatures, precisely the sweep and the in-this-moment time of them as they shot brilliantly through sunlight, a green sunlight, skimming the dark pool, beneath the little waterfall, long ago at Grandpa's in Englishtown [New Jersey], at the end of the white-dust road.

Yesterday Marlene called from Las Vegas. She said that making $90,000 was a lonely business, and she was amazed that her dress was considered immodest.

DECEMBER 22, 1953 Lincoln called, rattling along in his voice with its perpetual echo of amazement and delight, a sort of perpetual resonance of naughty wonder. He wanted to bring Christopher Isherwood here. Christopher has with him the youngest boy ever. "Twelve!" says Lincoln with that wonder and delight at the naughtiness of the world.

DECEMBER 24, 1953 Last night to dine at the Berliners[16] and Alicia Markova to take in, with Jeanette MacDonald to sit in my lap later (her chair having broken). She's Penelope-like, and, of course, to a small boy (now bearded and aging) blissful dreams come true. How she amused us all those years. I had a proposal of marriage from [press representative] Helen Deutsch! All she wants is a man to talk to, someone who sees that she eats and who will take her to the movies twice a week. I told her the story of Carmel Snow and the sailor whose cab she tried to hijack. "But lady," he said, "I have a girl."

DECEMBER 27, 1953 Christmas elaborately for days.[17] Eight to lunch yesterday and visitations from the Jerry Lermans. Gray exhausted and rampageous. The tree wondrous—and such splendid presents—but, oh, the agony involved. Tomorrow I will go ask Fuller may I borrow another thousand [from the bank].

16. Leo's ophthalmologist Milton "Theo" Berliner (1893–1981) and his wife, Constance Hope (1908–77), an agent for musical performers, frequently hosted large parties filled with opera and concert personalities.
17. Both Leo and his brother had always celebrated Christmas. He told a story of one childhood Christmas Eve when he and Jerry put out stockings for Santa to fill, only to find in the morning that their mother had washed and hung them to dry in the bathroom.

This would see me through. I could then return the borrowed money to Gray and pay some bills. Oh the happiness of being able to do that. It's too much to consider. Everyone loved the Christmas here, saying we had the most Christmassy—and it was beautiful, with a delicious luncheon. The cost is too much. I hate scenes, and it is not worth having any visitors if scenes must precede them. Better peace than parties. If I had not borrowed the money for Momma [to have a thyroidectomy], I could more easily get some to help now. I am exhausted in every bone, but not in any corner of my spirit. If only I could work again. This morning I tried to read, but my eyes pained too much. I must be patient.

I had to stop abruptly. My nose bled—two huge handkerchiefs-full. I hid this from Gray. He is sufficiently upset—all these weeks of actual hardship, then Christmas, and tomorrow his tooth to be pulled. This nosebleed could have been the straw. In trying to fix the electric light on the landing, he received a bad shock. Now I must stop again, dress, go to Billy Inge's and then to the ballet.

DECEMBER 30, 1953  Tonight is the music. Now to get the stollen. The little darkness is trying to get in, but I know that it will not—the moment people begin to arrive, I shall be safe again.

NOTE: Conductor Noah Greenberg, in gratitude for a piece Leo did in *Mademoiselle* and to cheer him after the preceding difficult weeks, brought his Pro Musica Antiqua ensemble to a party at 1453. Later, Leo recalled that people crowded in so thickly that no one could get upstairs or down. Suddenly, during the recital, he found the repetitive medieval music on period instruments ridiculous. He pressed out to the front stoop, where he howled into his handkerchief, unable to stop his laughter. It had been a tense time.

JOURNAL · JANUARY 1, 1954  The blackness, or actually the gray, gray melancholy left, vanished. Glorious, glorious bright day when even clouded skies seem brilliant. Not for one moment did the horror return. So, one day passed without sorrow, and this was the first day of the year, an omen, I pray.

JANUARY 11, 1954  The house is filled, like a water glass, with the flat white light reflected from snow, for all of the pavements and the ugly wintered earth in the garden are obliterated by snow, metamorphosed. It streams—a glittering winter hair—snow, the beautifier, with a harsh kindness, and the world is still beneath the snow, even street sounds, the voices of children, the chunk-chink of shovels are stilled, fined-down to a muffled purity. Gray cleared the pavements and came in overcome by asthma.

After a little scene on Saturday evening, just before Stark [Young] and Wales [Bowman] came, something happened to me, almost a rigidity or hardness, as if a leather skin formed. As I knew, it was a mistake to have Stark, Wales, Mai-

mai [Sze], and Irene [Sharaff] to dinner.[18] Having them caused endless drudg-
ery for Gray, and this was wrong, but we owed them dinner. Now, if we accept
dinner invitations, I must somehow repay by lunches in restaurants. This will,
of necessity, limit our accepting invitations, for I cannot afford much repay-
ment (not any right now). Saturday's dinner here cost about $15 (with wines,
etc.). At the Plaza, this identical do surely would have cost about $70 or $80.
But it is very wrong to expect Gray to cook and all that. I will try, really try, not
to ask anyone to come here. Scenes, which I loathe, inevitably ensue, and
those I cannot cope with at all. Gray does not even know what he says.

I am difficult for someone of Gray's temperament. It is a situation that, in a
normal marriage, would probably end in divorce. Since I am too settled for
divorce—and too fond of Gray—that is not involved. Also, we are not married.
And what would become of him? Now I will try to avoid causing scenes. I will
also go to my office at least three days a week. When I am here all day, Gray
cooks and fritters away the day. I must try to remove any excuses for his not
working. Also, I must watch when in company, and see that I do not rattle on.
Gray is absolutely right when he points out that I am always rattling on, not
even waiting until the person speaking finishes, but jumping in with some trivial anecdote about me. Again, I write here, only as though I peer into my looking glass, and the glass is filled with me, but life goes on outside my glass. I am
such a taker—such a greedy, avid taker.

What we need is to live remote, in the country—on Nantucket—with the
seasons eating into our bones—even to have the attic room in Middletown
again—not any of the misery, but the room, with its eternal snowy vistas—and
the two red lights in the gelid evening sky, and the intricacies of tree
boughs—and the scrunch scrunch of tires on Highland Avenue—and the
endless days for writing and reading—but then, when I had that, I wrote nothing and read *War and Peace* over and over and "suffered." I would not want
any of that ever again—only the room and the warmth and the *time*—the infinite precious moments in which to do something—nothing—to read *War and
Peace* or Proust or V. Woolf or Dostoyevsky over and over again and to write
and write.

JANUARY 19, 1954 • NEW YORK CITY
**TO RICHARD HUNTER • PARIS**

Today, New York has sunk beneath a sooty, milky sea and even people in the
streets are subaqueous. Paris is beautiful in such a winter fog; New York is
hideous, for all the vertical splendor—the soaring of the city—is vanished. I

---

18. These were two same-sex couples: the theater critic and novelist Stark Young (1881–1963)
with the traditionalist architect William "Wales" Bowman (1895–1966), and Irene Sharaff
(1910–93), costume designer for some sixty plays and forty movies (*An American in Paris, The
King & I*), with the art historian and artist Mai-mai Sze (1910?–92).

guess I must stop now because my eyes ache. I know that the world will seem more cheerful when my eyes are healed. You know, I seem to have lost or mislaid that happy feeling I had years ago—about waking up and finding unexpected good news (or a check or something) in the morning mail. Oh, how I used to run down those stairs to find the check or the letter asking me to write something or go to a party or . . . I get loads of invitations, but I know that each and every one means criticism or a wry face or a scene—and slowly a certain joy has been leaving me.

The doctor says my eyes are acting up, and I must have treatments every day the next three days, on the hour—at least ten times a day. It may take eight months. Ah, well . . . Don't be alarmed. He says all will be well.

JOURNAL · JANUARY 21, 1954  Truman's reaction to [his mother] Nina's suicide. "Life is *so* bitter, my darling," he repeated and reiterated. A new view apparently for him. And after all the worldly, or actually "sophisticated," depraved legend he had built.

JANUARY 24, 1954  I want to write a novella, set in a party, carrying the action from person to person as one sees a party, the mass impression, then the breaking up and the horrid isolations—all of it—the ebb and flow.

As we sat lunching, idly listening to the 2:05 news—Hemingway's death by plane-crashing into the remote Ugandan jungle, not far from Kilimanjaro. So I went instantly to Marlene. She had just been told by Tatiana [Liberman], but did not yet believe it. She drank big gulps of neat whiskey, paced, and searched for his last letter. It had come about two weeks ago, while she was in Las Vegas. It told how he had loved her more than anyone save his "Pocket Venus" by his side (Mary Hemingway). The life he has been living, he wrote, was one of casualties. This was a bitter, sad, he-man-tender, loving letter, and now the radio supposed him dead in the jungle, while off shooting beasts. But tonight the radio gives some hope, the plane having settled in the treetops. But the place is dreadfully dangerous, beasts and all that—inaccessibility.

JANUARY 25, 1954  Marlene calling happily in her little, tired-but-happy girl voice—now that Hemingway is saved, and she, of course, has the letter. What a splendid finish! An exhausting day. Hemingway wrote in the letter that he hoped Marlene would consider marrying him (if his Pocket Venus died) even though he was "a fucking bore or a boring fuck." Also he passionately desired the days again when they had lain close together during the last war. But they had never had an affair—the comradeship of those days.

JANUARY 27, 1954  How much simpler living would be if I could ask some people in. Mary Garden is here. I have always wanted to watch her close up, to talk to her.[19] [Writer] V. S. Pritchett, also. I would want Speed to bring [salonière and beauty] Mrs. Rhinelander Stewart. [Political humorist] Art Buchwald's another. So many interesting people right now, but I cannot do a thing about this save continue to lunch or tea some. I know that when the bill comes from the Plaza, I shall be wretched at not knowing how to pay it. Surely, I am sufficiently bright and inventive enough to solve this. I cannot ask anyone to lend me a place. And now the problem of Richard returning. I must ask him to stay here, until he finds a place. He hasn't any money. He has always helped me (with money), no matter how he has behaved in other situations. I know that this will make Gray wretched, but Richard is my only friend. Perhaps for this there is no solution. What with piling up debts, Richard's return, not being well, and being so far behind in work, I wonder about the easiest way out of it all. I speculate whether the little tough wall within me will not suddenly crumble like some sea wall, staunch until the unexpected moment of its destruction, crumbles abruptly. So I try to make writing, even out of this—pretty shabby writing it is, too. What to do? This morning I even wondered whether I could disappear—go away, cut off my whiskers, get a menial job, live in a room, and write. But this is adolescent and self-pity.

While I think death and disappearance, I think of columns and stories to write, plan next week's luncheon with [*The Saturday Review*'s] Norman Cousins (how adroitly I must try to lure him into promising me a page every two weeks titled "The Midnight Reader"—people, books, trivia; how I must get $200 for it—or even $150), and he will doubtlessly cancel luncheon. So I must get out of bed, go to the bathroom, brush my teeth, dress, think how my shoes are shabby, how fat I've again grown, how my hair grows grayer, how it is not easy to admit to forty (I always thought this would be heaven) and all my books unwritten, my essays, my stories—none of them written, for writing has not been the center of my life—loving someone has. But the bliss of scribbling like this—quite like being a secret drinker. Isn't every writer a secret drinker?

I put a foot tentatively out into the cold morning air. I see that dappled, minnowed stream, crystalline, icy, far away above Kingston [New York], all those long, brief years ago, with Grandpa cooking messes in his bedroom beyond the wood, and an old man from Union City synagogue singing heartbreaking Yiddish songs. We wept, [Cousin] Rosalie and I, not quite understanding (we were only ten years old) but tearful and heartbroken at the pathos in his ancient crooning voice. He sat at the end of a nasty oilcloth-covered table and sang from his heart. We wept, and Momma and the other women looked at us proudly and lovingly through their tears. We were all mothers and children and grown-ups together.

---

19. Leo had written about Scottish-American soprano Mary Garden (1874–1967) for both *Bazaar* and the *New York Times Book Review* in the previous six years.

FEBRUARY 15, 1954 Ruth Draper [the monologuist] is the most fascinating phenomenon in the theater this season. I can find no explanation for her prodigious impact. She is a lady, essentially a lady of old New York family (the Danas on one side) and so Jewish[-seeming] (the Drapers on the other—were they Jewish?). She has a rigid middle, as such gently-reared ladies always had. She is almost nondescript in coloring, pale, aristocratic, would be unnoticed in a crowd, and yet she peoples her stage with myriads. She is by turns, almost in the same moment, a girl of sixteen, an old woman of ninety, and no makeup, no excessive costuming, the basic straight up and down long brown dress, shawls, a jacket, some period hats, accessories, a twentyish evening coat, and her indefinable genius. It is impossible to pin down the genius of her magic. Only the greatest have this: Toscanini, Raquel Meller, Argentina,[20] Margot Fonteyn, Yvette Guilbert—but not an actor in my experience—yes, Duse. These transcend the art in which they are supreme, transporting all beholders beyond this art and its mechanics, transporting them out of themselves. Stark and Wales say that Miss Draper does not read, wears good quiet clothes, lives quite elegantly. But when she went on a journey to Istanbul (I think they said Istanbul), a friend reported that always Miss Draper seemed to be the well-known Miss Draper's maid. She met Lauro de Bosis and fell instantly in love with him. He seems to have been typical *jeunesse dorée*. Later, he flew his plane out over the ocean and fell to his death, having opposed Mussolini. Miss D was inconsolable.[21] Meeting Stark, she reproached him with not having written her a condolence. But all of her friends believe her to be a virgin. And they said of her long ago: Ruth is a genius, but watch her love scenes. She doesn't know a thing about love. She's never had any. She had wired from Paris to a friend that at last, with Lauro de Bosis, she had love. No one believed this.

The sound heard as one climbs to the party[22]; the lesbians in hordes; Carol Channing in the briefest of white, diamantéd dresses, murmuring, "I feel so overdressed." Carlo [Van Vechten] bellowing and squeaking, rushing through the densely packed rooms, tossing aside little faggots. The lesbians in white cable-stitch sweaters, even on their heads! Ruth Elizabeth [Ford]'s shrieking about how utterly loathsome [T. S. Eliot's play] *The Confidential Clerk* was and turning to a quiet, big man lurking near her. "Don't you agree?" she demanded. "Well," said he apologetically, "I produced it." Farley Granger, minty [effeminate]. The female bartenders from the Flanders looked like girls

20. The singer Raquel Meller (1888–1962) was a top-billed act in the twenties with a repertoire of Spanish songs. The Spanish dancer Antonia Mercé (1890–1936) had been known as "La Argentina."

21. Seventeen years Draper's junior, Italian poet Lauro de Bosis (1901–31) disappeared after dropping anti-Fascist leaflets over Rome when his airplane ran out of gas over the Mediterranean.

22. In the following, Leo is describing Oliver Smith's closing-night party for *The Summerhouse*, by Jane Bowles, which set designer Smith (1918–94) had designed and produced.

at a Yiddish wedding. Judith Anderson playing Herodias[23] and Jane [Bowles] yearning at her. Nora [Kaye] to Oliver [Smith], as she swept out: "I thought at your parties, Oliver, I would always be safe." Janet Flanner saying that it all reminded her of Paris in the twenties.[24] Oliver furious, because he had planned this as a small party. "Just thirty of my best friends to meet the cast." (!) Touche mystical. Jerry Robbins like the older boy who had worked hard on the prom committee. And the noise! And the breaking glasses. And the little queens screeching: "That's [actress] Ona Munson. She's married to Eugene Berman who makes the gorgeous designs." [Jeweler] Maria Volk, suddenly tragic, murmuring "Angelica . . ." Jack Dunphy quiet. Mary Lou [Aswell] quiet. They were the only ones quiet.

FEBRUARY 17, 1954    Harold Arlen and the two who wrote *Finian's Rainbow* went with Marlene to see *The Blue Angel* and made funny jokes, such as, "I've got an angle on the *Angel.*" German pronunciation (*Engel*) making it funnier. This infuriated her, for they were not taking it all seriously. They went to look at it because she hopes a musical can be made from it. *Tovarich* would be better for her—but I should hate to be the producer. Arlen does sit and think only of himself, knowing almost nothing about anything, save the writing of popular music. That he does brilliantly.[25]

Brigitta's filing system at the Ritz. Under W she had all the letters from Orson [Welles]—also many other men.[26] Brigitta always made Nora [Kaye] sleep in her room (twin beds) when Nora went to stay out on Long Island. She would say: "I don't want that man [Balanchine] in here with me." When [director Otto] Preminger asked Brigitta, at the ballet or theater, did she want to meet [Elisabeth] Bergner, Brigitta turned to Nora and said, "You take George to Sardi's." Balanchine said, "But I would like to meet Bergner also. . . ." Brigitta: "Go to Sardi's with Nora." He did.

Now Nora is at the apogee of her power. A great artist in what she can do. The portrayal in dance of drama-haunted women. This tremendously disciplined artist has no place actually where she can show her art. Nothing much with the City Ballet. She can return to Ballet Theatre, but "facing Lucia [Chase, its director], every day" would be hateful (there is a character that must be written). Where can she go? If I were producing, I should arrange "Nora

23. The actress Judith Anderson (1898–1992) excelled in tragic roles, notably as Lady Macbeth and Medea.
24. Janet Flanner (pseudonym Genêt, 1892–1978) was Paris correspondent for *The New Yorker* from 1925 to 1975.
25. Harold Arlen (1905–86), the popular song composer (*The Wizard of Oz*), saw a great deal of Dietrich in the mid-fifties, while his wife was institutionalized. When Arlen himself was hospitalized at one point, Dietrich was discovered in bed with him.
26. Zorina and Welles had an affair (platonic, says her autobiography) in 1938, while Balanchine was repeatedly asking her to marry him, which Zorina did later that year.

Kaye and Her Company in an Evening of Dramatic Ballets." This would make money. Not a big company, but a beautiful one, with beautiful decor, and a small orchestra. Even this could be prohibitive.[27]

Marlene talked on this telephone from midnight until two, consuming my reading and writing time. She went on and on about Harold Arlen's egomania, but never once did she realize that she is just as great an egomaniac in talking about him in relation to her for two hours. She does concern herself with the exterior world. Harold, of course, is sunk in himself, is a deep neurotic, and apparently quite uninterested in reading—in anything which has not to do with himself.

FEBRUARY 21, 1954  Truman said, "You're the kindest unkind person I know."

FEBRUARY 24, 1954  I lunched with Lincoln, who was vituperative and "honest fellers" about almost everyone. Mina, his sister, came up with a fistful of Offenbach memorabilia. "Nora's finished," he said. "Diana [Adams] is the comer. Balanchine adores her. Her arms get better, says Balanchine. It takes a long time to get over [Antony] Tudor arms.[28] Jerry [Robbins] is a shit—a meanspirited, opportunist little bastard. Gore [Vidal]'s horrible. . . ." So he went on, gaily demolishing.

Marlene rang up, crying how depressed she is because of reading Virginia Woolf's diary, and how she longs for the cut-out parts. Still I am amazed at Marlene and her reading. She heartily agreed with Virginia Woolf on Katherine Mansfield.[29] I feel that [Woolf's novel] *Between the Acts* must be a good book, but resent the pageant rushing off with it. I want more of the people. Always, in Mrs. Woolf's novels, ambivalents creep in. She is most sympathetic to them. Why, I wonder? "I hope that you are not going to make me look ugly in those notes," says Gray, settling back with *Peepshow into Paradise.*

Truman called. He is alone at 1060 [Park, his late mother's apartment], and ill (flu), and says Bunker [Blue, his bulldog] grows rigid, glaring into the dark of the adjoining room where Truman can hear someone moving about, but he knows that no one could be there, for he is utterly alone in this apartment. I wonder whether Nina haunts it. Quite possibly. T also wonders. Jack is off dining with Todd [Bolender]. "They are very old friends," explains T, trying to make us forget that he met Todd right here in this house on Carmel's red satin sofa.

27. Nora Kaye was a founding member of Ballet Theatre in 1939. During a three-year interlude (1951–54) with Balanchine's New York City Ballet, she had recently premiered Jerome Robbins's dramatic ballet *The Cage* and Antony Tudor's *La Gloire* (1952).
28. Ballerina Diana Adams (1926–93) created many roles, first for Antony Tudor at Ballet Theatre (1945–50) and then for Balanchine at New York City Ballet (1950–63).
29. Woolf found Mansfield's experimental short stories "hard" and "shallow."

Truman said that he wished Marlene would go away. She interferes in his *House of Flowers*, through Arlen, of course, who is a *shmegegge*, a dope, a man of limited inference.[30] But why expect a man, because he writes beautiful tunes, to be a great literate? Why expect any refinement? This is a common mistake, to expect persons of background to be literate, to expect masters in one form to be cognizant or informed in others.

I read Mrs. Woolf's *On Being Ill*. In this she deplores the curious lack of illness as a main literary theme. I feel more than competent to utilize illness as a major theme—as a *sole* theme—but this is because my back actually aches with the day's labors.

FEBRUARY 25, 1954 Reading Colette, *My Mother's House*. Feel as though I've walked in a summer garden rich with roses and strawberries (Royal Sovereigns and Early Scarlets), and then rolled in the herb garden. Oh, most savory, most country-sweet of writers. She is France's greatest living writer, and of women who write, the truest woman. More robust than Mrs. Woolf; more intelligently female than George Eliot; Elizabeth Bowen is a writer for big women's slicks, when one considers her against Colette; Isak Dinesen, in herself, has it, and in *Out of Africa* she reveals it, but not as richly, as savorily as Colette does. What other woman has the deep humanity, the very stuff of women's existence? Hers is the richness of life itself—and nowhere desiccation.

FEBRUARY 28, 1954 I continue to buy things—the disease of acquisition, with its attendant pleasures and despairs. I never have regrets, only pleasure and worry. This does make me somewhat inhuman, I feel.

MARCH 3, 1954 I finished off my Tynan-Beaton review for the *Times*, saying sometimes what I really meant.[31] Oh, the difficulty of actually writing what is in the mind—and the easy way of writing just for ornament. I found a word today—"brankie." Scottish—gaudy, spruce. I used it to describe Tynan prose. But never once did I say that he was a smart aleck, and that is what he tends increasingly to be. And I did not say that he cribs continually and ever increasingly from himself. But he does say some sparkling things. Anyway, it's done. I trust that I have earned $50 or even $65, which we need desperately.

I rang up Madame Lynn [dressmaker at Hattie Carnegie] and Ken Elmslie,[32] asking them to give Rut some money. This was difficult for me to do, but

---

30. The musical *House of Flowers* (book and lyrics by Capote, music by Arlen) opened December 30, 1954, after months of backstage fighting.
31. Leo was reviewing *Persona Grata*, with biographical essays by Kenneth Tynan and illustrations by Cecil Beaton. Through the fifties and sixties, Kenneth Tynan (1927–80) was arguably Britain's most influential theater critic and writer.
32. Kenward Elmslie (b. 1929), poet and lyricist, was the lover of John Latouche, then of the artist Joe Brainard, and a close friend of Ruth Yorck.

I did it and, actually, asking Dorothy Norman yesterday was more difficult. I wonder whether I could ask for money for me? Ironic that I need money so desperately right now. But at least I have an earning capacity.

MARCH 6, 1954 Reading Christopher [Isherwood]'s new novel *The World in the Evening* (a lovely title), I wonder: Do loyal people necessarily have to have a big dollop of masochism? To take (using this verb colloquially) what one's beloveds give—or how they give—does necessitate being hurt in myriad intangible ways (the big hurts have drama, so they are easier to endure). Here, Chris has a man very like Laci. I think love must be strong in masochism, but loving one person over the years is loneliness so much of the time—the need to be needed even stronger than the need to need. Chris is right: In the deeps, love is total, whole, only the surface ruffles, muddles, ambiguates. Chris has written quite a good novel, actually much better than most, and the homosexuality he handled very well indeed—candidly, as a part of life, not as something special—but the book lacks in the central character. The focal, first-person-singular character is a hollow man. He's spoiled, self-indulgent, always running off to please his own little egocentric self—reminding me somewhat of Richard—and Chris makes no definite comment on him, actually never takes a stand. So, the book remains good, but not more than that.

MARCH 16, 1954 In the evening, a Maxfield Parrish sky—cerulean dusted, glittering stars, and a plump moon. We went to the Kochs'.[33] At the lift gate, Gray suddenly made a scene saying he was not going out anymore; why did I want a house if I was never in it? I felt almost as "gone" as I did Christmas Day, resolving then never again to ask anyone to visit us, which resolution I have kept. There I stood at the lift gate, wildly wondering how I could go up and be gay and fool the Kochs. Now I know that I shall never again accept an invitation for Gray, nor shall I ask him to go. This could make a serious difference in our lives, but I cannot cope with scenes of this intensity, and while I do this work, on which we live, I must continue to see people. It is a serious handicap, not being able to entertain. I cannot go on about it. He must surely realize how stupid he is being. He does not have to go out every night, nor should I have to go out every night, but he must, living in this world, know that he cannot be a hermit. He will not answer the telephone; he does not want people to come in; now he will not go out—that is his life.

MARCH 17, 1954 Because of having lunched with [Count Lanfranco] Rasponi some weeks ago a "new" world opens. With no effort at all I could

33. An adept painter of realistic New York City interiors, John Koch (1909–78) painted Leo several times, including a solo portrait in 1953. He married Dora Zaslavsky (1905–87), a highly regarded piano teacher.

enter it. Two days ago, at Mrs. [Nathan] Milstein's party, the countesses, etc., were delighted with me. I knew that I looked shabby, so I enjoyed myself to make up for this, and oozed charm. It was heavenly, being admired and being made much of. Now an invitation comes from Rasponi to meet Prince Henry of Hesse. This interests me—but I cannot begin to enter this world, for I would have even less peace here. I try to learn to look before I leap—at least to look and leap anyway. The upsets in my life have all come from impetuosity. I have been the most self-indulgent of creatures. Now I must pay. It is not important for me to enter that world—but the richness of my book would be benefited by this last, ten-years-later look.[34]

MARCH 21, 1954  Fania [Marinoff]'s birthday party was fun and did lift me out of myself, doing for me what dope or drink does for others.[35] The Lin Yutangs [of UNESCO] and other U.N. types sat together. Ruth [Ford] had on a costume more suited to the Mardi Gras, but her face is pretty. Zachary [Scott] is so *bien élevé* and made it his business to talk to the U.N.[36] Irene [Sharaff] had a beautiful Basque coat which [costume designer] Karinska had given her. Nora Kaye continues undecided and wants to go to a fortune-teller (I am tempted, but I should so implicitly believe every word). Alvin [Colt, costume designer] is somehow sexier in this early middle-aged look. Donald [Saddler] has been made even more of a person by his [choreographic] rigors on *By the Beautiful Sea*. Judith Anderson was paunchy-faced, serpent-eyed, musty-dusty on an epic scale. Lillian Gish in a big pale woolly coat, very Eleonora in some mysterious way—her mouth? Very aqueous. Dorothy [Gish] very medieval in a flat, crownish, black hat held on by a black scarf tied under the chin, and with her Rover, most pouting and dearest of Pekes. "He's so dirty," she cried, as they, these orphans of many storms, went away.[37] Dear Fania in a great, heavy gold skirt and some sort of sweatery greenish top, a sumptuous Yiddish lady in a big house, her face Ariel-young. She is such a love. Carlo much benefited by the awful spectacle of Stark prone and peeing at Ruth and Zack's, now seems to

---

34. Count Lanfranco Rasponi (1914?–83), a prominent social figure, was a writer and public relations agent. As Enrico d'Assia, Prince Henry of Hesse (1927–99) worked as an artist and stage designer. Leo went to the party after all: "The Rasponi party: How that old 'glamour' world, the remnants of Café Society, looked—some of the women still making token curtsies, a little collapse to royalty." *Journal, March 27, 1954.*
35. Fania Marinoff (1890–1971), married to Carl Van Vechten, was an actress whose last Broadway role had been in 1937, an attendant on Tallulah Bankhead's Cleopatra. *GF*: "Fania was a Russian Jewish woman—small, perspicacious, flamboyant, given to brocades— who came poor and sold newspapers, then became an actress. She had a fiery disposition, but was full of great kindness. Carlo and she happily disagreed about almost everything."
36. Zachary Scott (1914–65), an actor (*The Southerner, Mildred Pierce*), was married to the stage actress Ruth Ford (b. 1915).
37. *Orphans of the Storm* (1921), directed by D. W. Griffith, had starred the sisters Dorothy and Lillian Gish.

have blossomed unalcoholically, and speaks of it always. Aileen [Pringle] thin-nish, thoughtful, slangy, withal a lady. I had fun and was admired and petted (which was needed) and flirted and laughed and felt better for all of it, taking it for what it was worth.

MARCH 22, 1954   In the evening to Prince and Princess Gourielli's to hear Aaron Copland's opera *The Tender Land*, as dated as selling apples in 1930 and WPA projects. Aaron talked and talked and said much nonsense, such as: No contemporary work has a real love scene. He asked Gian Carlo [Menotti, com-poser], he told us, whether in any of his works a real love scene occurred, and Gian Carlo thought this over and said no. What rubbish. The princess [Helena Rubinstein], a squat, bejeweled Jewess (she fits this designation more than any-one I have ever seen) is dark, smooth, pummeled, shrewd-faced. She has seen everything, knows everyone is rotten, wants to be amused, but does not think that she can be—withal is nice! And so professional. Her much-praised apart-ments are full of miscellaneous beauty and banality mixed. "I'll take a hundred of those," she surely has said, whether it be French Impressionists, Mexican or African Primitives, blue Bristol glass. She looks as though she said: "Prinsk, com inta da kitzen, and I'll cook us up a tup uh borscht." When I asked did she have any hamantaschen, she acted out that she didn't know what I meant, but always affable with power. The Prinsk [Artchil Gourielli-Tchkonia] is a sexy, compact, younger-than-the-Prinskess man. She could be hawking fish in Orchard Street and relishing their heads like Momma and Poppa do.

Patrick O'Higgins, the Prinskess's factotum, showed us the apartments, deploring her bad taste and frugality in enhancing the beautiful things she had. Examples: magnificent silver Venetian "shell" furniture and in the same room a "fixture" like an office; on a French (I think) Empire table a huge bowl of glass grapes, such as my aunt Minnie had years ago on her dining room table. Minnie's were lit from beneath by electric bulbs and when we went to visit her in her Bronx, Jerome Avenue, apartment ("Just off the Concourse, so convenient," she always pointed out), we thought that dish of electric-lit grapes the last word in beauty and chic. They were *Die Elegante Welt*.

The singers, who were impersonating farm types, sang "Give me your ha-and," always giving us that phoney "A" singers dote on. Aaron has the voice of a seventeen-year-old, and at this time in his long and heartily overpraised career has written an adolescent's talented opera. From the first note we are back getting the apples out, the Depression is here, and so is that tenth-rate tal-ent Agnes de Mille (who did write a delightful book). Touche sat thinking up puns. Ken [Elmslie], a Pulitzer Prize given only to Touche, looked askance.[38] Harold Arlen went into the WC and remained there one half hour, piling up a

38. A joke: Elmslie's grandfather was Joseph Pulitzer, endower of the Pulitzer Prizes.

line of resentful females, who wanted only to comb their hair, they said. Finally he emerged, folding some paper. "I always get ideas in the bathroom," he told us.

So we went off to the [New York City] Ballet's closing-night party on the fifth floor of the City Center, and was that a surprise. A real orphanage, settlement-house blowout. Very funny. Lines of rigidly smiling ballet mothers, rats dancing together,[39] a band from the local boys' high school (surely), balloons and crêpe-paper festoons, and disheveled trestles of salami and corned beef and kegs of beer and a general atmosphere of mustard by the ton. And wild noise and disorder. Women saying: "I must shake your hand, Mr. Balanchine, and tell you how much I admire . . ." while other women stood gimlet-eyed and jealous-headed. "My Susie should be the next," you could see them insisting. We went to the Andros [coffee shop] where Peter [Lindamood] fell asleep and I ate Westerns. So that was Sunday night. I told Gray about it, rocking with laughter, and fell into bed at two, read Su Hua Ling Chen [*Ancient Melodies*], and was asleep soon.

I must remember Lennie Bernstein's brown-velvet little suit with the Edwardian cuffs; [soprano] Pat Neway's frontier gauntness; Jessie Daves's gentile-woman-who-lives-next-door-and-is-so-nice-but-so-shy—and so distrustful and dowdy—shockingly.[40] When Peter told the Prinskess that he had beautiful things for sale, she immediately asked: "You got many things? How much?" And, oh, the depraved, corrupt faces mounting that stair. Peter said that the women all looked as though they had to have rich viands all day. One of them sat making chewing faces constantly. I said she was receiving messages from pheasants and grouse who had passed on. You knew that the roar of stomachs would drown out the opera. Tommy Schippers played the piano brilliantly, and everyone sat on hired gold folding chairs in a pleated (ceiling and walls) picture gallery hung with genuine horrors—or really immaterials.

MARCH 28, 1954 Yesterday Osbert [Sitwell] came to lunch, shaking more than ever, but, somehow, looking healthier.[41] He has been in Hawaii, but I did not gather that he adored it. He becomes so difficult to understand. And when going through the streets, he runs. He has to run. Poor, poor man—and so lovable. We went to Knoedler [art dealer] where Lelia [Wittler] showed us a Poussin, *Creation of Adam*—very softly blue and green and liverish in color, beautiful and fantastic; a great Rubens of Christ and the thieves on the cross, so unlike the fleshpot Rubens; a Fra Angelico prelate as carnation-colored as the day it was born. Gray wanted the Angelico for the beautifully painted lower

---

39. In France, child ballerinas were called *les petits rats*.
40. Jessica Daves (1898–1974) was editor in chief of *Vogue* from 1952 to 1962, between Edna Woolman Chase and Diana Vreeland.
41. Edith and Sacheverell Sitwell's brother Osbert (1892–1969), the poet, novelist, and autobiographer, suffered with Parkinson's disease in his last years.

skirt and the color; I wanted the Poussin for its fantasy and Leonardesque color; Osbert wanted it also—$8,500. She also showed us a friar—very Zurbarán—but it was not—and a dear, little, whiskered, blue-green backgrounded Corneille de Lyon. None of these are wanted by museums, yet each is a great treasure.

MARCH 30, 1954  This morning Marlene called, in her voice of sorrow at passion gone: Yul had been with her and was now gone with no plans for the future, and she was lonely and footloose. I read *La Princesse de Clèves* all day.[42] How immediate, vital, and alive it is. "So many lovely women and handsome men have never been gathered together at one court; it seemed as if nature herself had taken a particular delight in bestowing her most coveted prizes upon the most exalted personages." Fireworks, understated and utterly alive. She had a story to tell. She told it.

I want to write "Emily and Lizzie" (Dickinson and Borden), a study of their two childhoods, because they represent "good" and "evil," how a person can take one path or the other despite similar backgrounds. I always think of them as identical, actually as one woman. They represent to me the two schools, as do Duse and Bernhardt, of the same art.

Last night [press agent] Phil Bloom picked me up and, all black-tie and pleated shirts, we went off to the Players Club "Pipe Night" [tribute] for Mary Garden. She is astonishing. What a marvelous time she has—black sequins, black-net adjustable voluminous sleeves, a little black hat with a rolled-up brim (sort of thirties), great quantities of diamonds on wrists and flat at the base of her still beautiful columnar throat and on her fingers (so clever to wear all these magnificent diamonds; [jeweler] Harry Winston lends them to her, I hear). For they distract from her (still beautiful) face. And what magnificent eyes! Honest, straight-to-the-heart eyes. With this fabulous getup, a leather strapped, ordinary, man's wristwatch! But she is fabulously fascinating. Great blue-violet eyes, hooded and wise, a fresh complexion. Peerless, constant gestures. A voice which hypnotizes, and a body the instrument of her thoughts. A small, vibrant woman who speaks her mind, having always spoken her mind. She began a star; she continues a star. Her hands are cool and smooth, and she clings to one a long time. Her interest is constant. Her vitality astonishing. She demolished Sarah Bernhardt and Mrs. Pat Campbell. Debussy and Mary (as the old and venerable gentleman called her) went to London to view *Pelléas and Mélisande*.[43] "It was awful," Mary says. Mrs. Pat throwing masses of dirty black hair down over Sarah Bernhardt. "Those two old women wouldn't know

---

42. Novel by Marie-Madeleine Pioche de La Verge, Comtesse de Lafayette (1634–93).
43. The preeminent stage actress Mrs. Patricia Campbell (née Beatrice Stella Tanner, 1865–1940) was famous for sharp comments, eccentricity, and bewitching G. B. Shaw, for whom she created Eliza Doolittle in 1914, when she was fifty. Bernhardt and Campbell were playing the 1892 tragedy by Maeterlinck. In 1902 Mary Garden sang Debussy's operatic adaptation in Paris, and she premiered it in New York in 1908.

what they are talking about," said Debussy. "Is there a train back to Paris?" Mary Garden speaks with wonderment and passion and amusement. She seems a Druid witch, and in her gestures one can see whole generations of movie vamps and wicked women.

**MARY GARDEN** *I was the most fortunate young person in that I got to hear opera early on. In Uncle Maxl [Goldwasser]'s house at High Bridge,*[44] *there was a wireless set of the kind that had earphones to clamp over my ears, and which poured into those ears opera from Chicago. That is how I heard Mary Garden. I did not realize then how this would set me apart many years later when almost nobody was left who had heard her. Mary Garden was, of course, Debussy's great Mélisande and Charpentier's first Louise. Mary Garden was also one of the scandals of the early part of this century. She attracted scandal the way fragrant flowers attract bees, and, as bees carry pollen, her scandals were carried, long before the days of quick transmission, from opera capital to opera capital of the world. When, in the mid-forties, I contrived a series at* Harper's Bazaar *titled "Living Legends," Mary Garden was among the first living legends I had photographed. She was then living modestly in Aberdeen, Scotland, and she still was the mysterious, deep-throated, woodsy-voiced heroine, a Morgan le Fay who turned you into a part of her legend.* (1993)

JOURNAL • APRIL 12, 1954 Marlene read me a letter from Hemingway. In this one he was his usual he-man, cussing self, telling of his sickness (sphincter muscle), and how even when both he and she were broke, she helped him, and now she receives $90,000 for three nightclub weeks, and he's got the Nobel Prize. Hemingway seems to adore her. But why must he always be such a "he-man"—the foul language and cock strutting?

APRIL 20, 1954 Marlene called to tell me what a marvelous, unexpected day she had had with Yul. Then she fell to discussing Mrs. Woolf, insisting, as Gray does, that Mrs. W wrote this journal seriously, but to be published, and that because we have only these portions, Mr. Woolf seems a Narcissus, and it all becomes too one-sided.

APRIL 22, 1954 Lunch with [editor] Bob Linscott, where—surprise—was Faulkner—minute, silent, grinning shyly and secretly at odd times, wracked by back pains. He said that he did not like to put things down, but that he went to his typewriter when a job had to be done and did it. He had just been working three months in Europe with [director] Howard Hawks on a film [*Land of the Pharaohs*] about the building of the pyramids. "The same story he always does," Faulkner explained. But he never goes to the movies. He did not know

44. High Bridge is a Manhattan neighborhood near 173rd Street.

who Marilyn Monroe was, but he remembered Garbo as beautiful. Faulkner is one of the most withdrawn of men, coming into our world only when I talked about dogs. He has some twenty. His eyes seem hazel. He ate scrambled eggs, coffee, one martini, and sat silent for endless minutes—this silence making our talk seem utterly superfluous. He doesn't seem to read. He exists—drinks—writes. I could not say that he was happy to see me. Later Bob called and said: "Bill was very pleased to see you again."

MAY 10, 1954 Today Rut rang up and said that Lucien [Vogel] had died—a stroke. So all of her people are gone and only Cesco [von Mendelssohn] remains, in his sanatorium. I went to her, her face mottled and in tears. I had no consolation to offer, for she is beyond consolation. Now she has no future. She gave him her whole heart. . . . But we ate. Lali Horstmann came in, and Max and Nina Jacobson, and Gray brought food.[45] I felt that this must be done, and I left ten dollars by the telephone, but what consolation could this be? Poor, poor Rut. She is all alone and no one can comfort her. Lucien made my fashion magazine career. He took me by my hand to *Vogue*. I remember as though it happened today. I think of Ela welcoming him—in heaven, of course. So they have gone, Rut's protectors—the Comtesse de Noailles, Peter Vollmoeller, Ela, Luli [Kollsman], Louise Salm, now Lucien.[46] She has nothing, nothing left. I must somehow help her.

Carson's monstrous exhibition at the Y last night with Tennessee. Carson said: "Poetry must make sense; prose must make poetry." Ugh. This was all so humiliating and the packed house loved it. A dreadful exhibition on both sides of the footlights. Carson witchlike with a silver-headed stick—disjointed, her depravity open, again proving that the best crooks show their hand all the time and charm their victims into applause.

MAY 13, 1954 My afternoon with Cary Grant: the gentleness of him, the deep charm and flirtatiousness. His admiration for Noël Coward. He has eight Boudins [French seascapes] in a ramshackle whitewashed house. And he seems to have a definite philosophy of being contented.

45. Lali Horstmann (d. 1954) was a Jewish Berliner married to a wealthy German diplomat, with whom she had lived in the German capital through World War II. Dr. Max Jacobson became notorious in the early seventies as "Dr. Feelgood" when it was revealed that he had injected drugs, often amphetamines, into many celebrities. Leo later blamed him in part for the deaths of Ruth Yorck, John Latouche, and the photographer Mark Shaw. "Jacobson made Ruth feel good and bad for years; even Marlene went to him for a time, and Touche did for years. Perhaps this is a medical science for the new frenetic world. But I doubt that." *Journal, March 25, 1971.*
46. The first of these is probably Countess Anna de Noailles (1876–1933), a poet; Austrian Luli von Hohenberg (1901–51) briefly became the Hollywood actress Luli Deste before marrying Kollsman, a wealthy aviation-industry inventor; Louise Salm (d. 1951?) was a translator, an aristocratic German with whom Ruth Yorck had been enamored in the late forties.

MAY 26, 1954  Poppa had two strokes yesterday. This, selfishly, panics me, but I must hold on optimistically and know that if I need money, somehow money will come.

MAY 28, 1954  A sullen day and the leaves suddenly enormous, midsummer size. Poppa's speech seemed, last night, a bit thick, but his appearance was rosy, rested, and childishly belligerent.

Richard came to gather the things which he wished to store. He seems very hurt at putting these things away, but all I wanted him to do is store the huge packing case, which was blocking up the entrance on the basement floor. He was so hurt that he wanted to buy back the *Tempest* painting [by him]. Also he intends to take away the portrait of me with all the books. I am very fond of this.[47] He will lodge it in his mother's attic. But this was all in vengeance. I think that, without even knowing it, he is hurt by the apparent harmony here. Richard's behavior is the most predictable in the world. He is a genuinely depressed person—basically—and then he has a certain childlike joy and delight, but inevitably he is depressed.

JUNE 2, 1954  I spent the evening with Marlene and Maria [Riva].[48] I became so upset over viewing the McCarthy [anti-Communist] proceedings that I drank a glass of brandy. I felt claustrophobic, like being in a jammed lift.

JUNE 11, 1954  This evening was the first I have actually been at home with Gray and Maebelle [Hughes, his mother]. Gray never keeps his hands off her. This is touching and upsetting. That she permits it is astonishing. I almost rang up Eugenia to ask was this procedure normal among young men, but I do not think that it is. *Fin de race* [last of a line]: Gray has this. But their life together was surely a horror and a delight. I wonder whether her husband was as much to blame as I was told. If Gray's behavior distresses me, surely Mr. Hughes was in a state all the time. But perhaps Gray didn't behave this way at that time and now does it only because he is sad for her and wishes to comfort her? I do not know any answers to this. I am not sufficiently wise.

JUNE 15, 1954  I am alone for a brief moment and sit here pleasantly, in the basement, on the old sofa. A sullen green fragment of the yard is visible

---

47. Leo's favorite portrait of himself by Richard depicts him reading in an easy chair, surrounded by towering mesas of books.

Until Howard inherited his mother's apartment in 1974, Richard and he seldom kept a residence of their own in New York. Richard would stay with Leo and Gray, sometimes for months, using two rooms on their third floor, where he also painted.

48. The only child of Marlene Dietrich and Rudolf Sieber, Maria (b. 1924) became an actress, married the scenic designer William Riva, with whom she had two sons, and published a biography of her mother in 1992.

through the glass of the door. Rain falls—a secret, afterthought rain. As I scribble, the gay, lid-off me comes out to jounce about again.

Lunching with Glenway [Wescott], he described how he spent his father's last six days in the hospital, beside him, holding him in his arms as he died, and how a flame seemed to burn in his father's body, and the wound made by the operation upon him was all healed—beautifully, neatly—while the black blood oozed from his mouth. How angry Glenway became when I said that Louis [Kronenberger] and Lionel [Trilling] referred to the [American] Academy as the Sewing Circle.

Glenway told me how Katherine Anne [Porter], [novelist James] Farrell, [Allen] Tate, and he all stood waiting for Faulkner to talk to them, in Paris where they all represented America at an international arts conference, and he never even looked at them, but stood accepting the applause of the adoring French. Then he went away. Monroe is apparently intensely jealous of Glenway's escapades, although they haven't slept together since 1929. He is so very unfriendly, Monroe, Glenway says.

I feel alive and slightly ashamed for being so happy.

JUNE 25, 1954  Monday night last [June 21], I was in agony—howling, groaning agony such as I have not experienced since I woke during that operation. Gray fetched a "new" doctor, who jabbed needles and diagnosed a kidney stone. So, I have been here [at home] all this torrid week, and still the stone remains mine. Today I had pain, but I will not drug myself against it. Ela started that way. I read Proust and more clearly realized that what the Guermantes and the Faubourg Saint-Germain were to Proust, Europe was to generations of Americans.

JUNE 29, 1954  Danilova in her just-off-the-ground walk, sharp daintiness, and long arms recalled Karsavina and 1911 and the whole impact of Diaghilev, as she ate in the Russian Tea Room. Her gay gloves, this time red and white, her caressing accent, and general "sweetness."

CA. JULY 8, 1954 • NEW YORK CITY

TO MARLENE DIETRICH • LONDON

Glittering glacier dear—or even Serpent of Hollywood—or by this time Dame Marlene . . . Your hysterical notices arrived at last. Why, dear, doesn't the government wake up and let international relations alone, and by so doing permit you to take over? Also, what incentive could you have to make you want to come home? In America that sort of reception could never happen—even if you did show as much as American papers said that you did last year. Or can it be that the English have shrewder eyes? I suspect that is it.

I passed my stones! Isn't that wonderful? I did want to add them to your rock collection (mounted appropriately by some small-but-sure jeweler like Verdura, since these were stones not jewels), but, alas, they were taken from me because the doctors seemed to need them—maybe to add to the piles upon the graves of victims. What a painful sickness this was, and how wonderfully slender I have become. Now I am on a strict and limiting diet. This is to go on one year, and then we shall see. It seems that stones can return. So now I no longer eat the delicious unnecessaries but the delicious necessaries (ugh). . . . Here all is desolation and not even actually real summer, because I no longer believe summer to be real unless the doorbell rings and there are you in an old cotton dress and little summer shoes, somehow looking cool and hot simultaneously.

Not one word in any paper I have seen about the King [Yul Brynner] nor any King followers. The town is having a little flurry over the somewhat unexpected marriage of [fashion designer] Charles James. She [Nancy Lee Gregory] is a twenty-seven-year-old, very rich, Kansas City girl. He is, of course, a slightly-late-fortyish Chicago girl. She has money, and he some talent, I believe. (Boys can't ever help being bitchy about other boys—can they?)[49]

My father is recovered. My mother says that on good days she feels worse than on bad days . . . always a new approach. Why doesn't she go into television and support us?

JOURNAL • JULY 11, 1954  The childhood vision of glamour presented by the young people upon a pile of lumber in the street at Rockaway that long-ago summer when we went to stay in a rented room at Aunt Ida [Lerman]'s, in the early years of her widowhood.[50] These young people in contrived fancy dress marched glamorously, self-consciously toward the beach, one of them a king in bathing dress, a great portiere—purple or deep scarlet, I think—billowing from his shoulders, this borne by his faithful. He crowned by a large straw hat and the others turbaned in towels. All this was most glamorous, a sudden vision of what I wished my life to be—carefree, regal, a composite of gaiety and regality, affability and richness.

Summer memories: Aunt Annie's farm near Colchester, Connecticut, and various gardens in New Jersey; the empty lots upon the little cliff behind our apartment on the Boston Post Road;[51] the Palisades and picnics; Aunt Ida and Uncle Joe [Lerman]'s hotel near Monticello [New York]; boat rides to Rye and Coney Island; days on the beaches of Coney Island (being lost; terrified of water) and in the water at Starlight Park; walks in Central Park and in the zoo;

49. *GF*: "We went to the wedding at the Sherry-Netherland. All of his ex-boyfriends were there and astonished." *LL*: "Charles James: His features—part gothic, part prune. His figure—a brief elongated oval, spare, on pipe-stem legs. His manner—*vieux élégant*. His dark eyes, always mischievous, veiling a deep melancholy. His purpose—single. His wit—all-pervasive. His dressmaking—genius." *Journal, January 6, 1990.*
50. Leo's aunt Ida had been married to Joseph Lerman (d. 1920), the oldest sibling of Leo's father.
51. In the Bronx, where the Lermans lived for some three years in his early childhood.

playing on the street and seeing scenes in the heat lightning; sudden rain and then a cart of bananas; going to a Coney Island job with Poppa in a horse-drawn wagon; trolley rides; an early auto on a ferry coming into a dock; running away at a very early age and hiding in an alley while the family looked for me . . . All this was before we moved out of Manhattan. After we moved summer memories were of the green world in which we lived.

AUGUST 1, 1954  During this week now passed I went to lunch with Carson in Tennessee's apartment, a disheveled, unloved, transitory place over Nicholson's [café] on East Fifty-eighth Street, where the autos on the Queensborough Bridge–approach shriek inconsolably, insensibly, incessantly. Carson, paralyzed (or is she?) in hand and apparently on one side of her somewhat malign face, sits and makes even greater disorder. She said to Rita [Smith], a loving patient sister, who seems to be supporting her, "My neurosis is as important as yours."[52] The moment she hears of something someone else has—a dress, a book, a room, a pleasure—Carson wants it. Her annoyances and jealousies are perpetual, even though they disappear, as does the sun on a day of cloudiness. "Sister needs love," Rita explained. "She can't live without love."

AUGUST 6, 1954  Two mornings ago Gray told me that Colette had died, and I had to work at keeping the tears back. How curious that both Gray and I were reading Colette at this time. The world now seems a poorer place. Although I did not know her to talk to, I feel her death a private loss. But, of course, having read only *Sido* and *La Maison de Claudine* one knew her intimately. This is the mainspring of her great genius, this intimacy that she sets up instantly and with such dignity. This dignity elevates above pornography such works as *The Gentle Libertine* [*L'Ingénue libertine*]. So the triangular cat face with its mop of music-hall hair is gone, but do not think that one smitch of the spirit of that loving heart is lost. I felt this way when V. Woolf died, but furious, for that was a self-destruction in wartime. This saddens me: Colette's death is like the dousing of a little dependable potbellied stove that miraculously heated you all your life.

AUGUST 9, 1954  In bed, making notes on Colette, and a spittling rain making this room, beneath these lamps, an island in the vast summery, autumn-touched night. Gray works at his table, painting snowflakes on a Christmassy red ground. In between the notes I think of Judy Garland, and all the things Irene Sharaff told us, especially Judy G crying: "Am I such a monster?" as the zippers on her dress burst because drink fattened her, thickened and coarsened her overnight, sometimes as much as two to five inches. And how she delayed

---

52. Margarita "Rita" Gachet Smith (1922–2005), Carson McCullers's sister, was fiction editor at *Mademoiselle* (1944–60).

and delayed the last moments of her movie [*A Star Is Born*] because of her terror while she was making a movie that she would never make another. She would only work at night, keeping hundreds of people waiting an hour and a half. She and her husband, [Sid] Luft, have no money at all, having to borrow all the furnishing from the Malibu scene when they had people in. She had nothing to wear when they went to the party the Jack Warners gave for Franco's daughter, so Judy G tried to borrow one of the dresses Irene had designed for the movie. At that party Judy G fell flat on her face.

Seven carloads of people would go to her house to fit her. When she came to fittings she always had one of her children with her, and sometimes several people who would reassure her, make her feel the star. But then suddenly, drunk, fat, worn, she became the great obliterating star—a twelve-year-old girl, a marvelous raw current, an elemental force—making all those who had suffered from her caprices, her insanities, her drinking adore her, acclaim her, weep over her—her vile language forgotten, her tantrums, her wastefulness all forgiven. They loved her and the force she became. Her mother fed her Benzedrine when she was twelve. She was drunk in her teens. She hated her mother, who died doubled over in a Hollywood parking lot. I think that Colette would have understood this utterly.

AUGUST 22, 1954 • NEW YORK CITY
TO RICHARD HUNTER • HAMBURG, NEW YORK

Well! That Bible! That Jacob! He married Leah and Rebecca, and they, filthy girls, gave him their handmaidens, and he just begat with all of them. How can Christians be against bigamy or whatever it is, when a man has many women for wives and concubines and children from all? I asked Gray about all this, but he says that he just accepts the Bible and doesn't try to explain it. I do not understand how any person of intelligence can believe in a man-made God.

JOURNAL • SEPTEMBER 26, 1954  The Duchess of Kent [Princess Marina], dowdy but literally ablaze with jewels, in a white-chrysanthemumed box at the Met . . . Alice [Astor] gave a posh luncheon for the duchess—only nobilities—such as Nin Ryan (!), the duchess's local hostess.[53] (I wonder if Nin was given Wit's End [Alexander Woollcott's apartment], where once Saint-Subber kept Robbie [Campbell, his lover] and later Johnny Ryan kept Eartha Kitt?) Alice brought her butler and chef down—and what splendor. All the royalties assembled, and this time Alice was even [there] beforehand. After everyone had gathered, a message came that the duchess was unable to attend. She was at the dentist!

---

53. Margaret "Nin" Kahn Ryan (1901–95), the socialite daughter of financier Otto Kahn, was the mother of John Barry Ryan III.

SEPTEMBER 29, 1954  Sometimes I suspect that I have ruined my life, in the way a life or two lives can be ruined by a bad marriage, bad signifying the attempt of two more or less incompatible persons to unify themselves. I wonder if most marriages are not between incompatibles? Most marriages, I am sure, are premature. A bad marriage is hell on earth, for it deteriorates the persons involved, embittering them, diminishing them, exaggerating their sensibilities, making them ugly.

OCTOBER 19, 1954 • NEW YORK CITY
**TO RICHARD HUNTER** • HAMBURG, NEW YORK

Yesterday, early in the morning we trundled off to the Paramount Theater to preview (I had already seen it) *A Star Is Born*. Mobs poured in. This time we were the guests of Irene Sharaff and Mai-mai. I found the movie even more fascinating the second time. I think it a most important document, a sort of elaborate, perhaps unintentional look into what the American mind (especially the Hollywood mind) thinks America lives like. The mise-en-scène held me as much as did Judy Garland's and James Mason's performances. They are wonderful, but the surroundings really are a triumph of contemporary mediocrity. Millions of people dream of living that way—and Judy G is so much the product of today in America.

Then I went to my office for a bit and then flew home in time to dress up in my old dress-up suit, which is now much too large (!), and off we went to dinner at the Sharaff-Sze ménage and so on to the gala opening of *On Your Toes*. I had Diana [Forbes-Robertson] for my partner and Gray had Mai-mai.[54] Irene, who designed the costumes, flitted about. So very gala it was—because *A Star Is Born* was opening simultaneously at two theaters and the biggest fashion event of the year was being held at the Waldorf, so all through midtown life seemed like the twenties—enormous limousines jammed with expensive furs and tulle and glittering with sequined and diamonded ladies and even white ties.

*On Your Toes*, you will remember, was years ago a great favorite of mine, and I used to delight you with my interpretation of it. All those years ago, I saw the show from a hard-earned seat high up in the balcony. I scrimped and saved while working at the Grossinger, came to town, bought an inexpensive ticket, and saw it. Now here I was in an orchestra seat for which I did not pay, all dressed up, and surrounded by people I know and "friends" with most of the people in the show, and I thought all about this and did not feel gay, because life does not turn out quite the way one expects and hopes, and who is there to say whether this is good or bad.

The show is not terribly well done, but Brigitta is much better than I

54. Journalist Diana Forbes-Robertson Sheean (1915–87) was a friend with many theatrical associations for Leo, including being the niece and biographer of the great stage actress Maxine Elliot.

thought she would be . . . actually dancing better and acting well. Some of Irene's costumes are good but all of them look awful because of Oliver Smith's dreadful sets and horrid lighting by untalented Peggy Clark. Balanchine didn't do so well, either.[55] The songs are heavenly, as they always were. So, backstage and into Brigitta's room in time to see a nondescript, housewifish woman dash up to Miss Zorina (who disports herself more licentiously in the "Slaughter on Tenth Avenue" number than any burlesque harridan ever did), and this housewife was clutching Brigitta and saying, "I never would have dreamed anything like this in the playground in East Sixty-seventh Street. . . ." That was where Brigitta took her little children. Goddard looked an easy sixty. I do not think that he is happy with all these developments.

Then we had a lovely surprise—Judy Garland had asked Irene to bring her friends to a party she was giving in her suite at the Waldorf after midnight. So, the people who own some enormous whiskey enterprise took us all to the Plaza, and then we all went to Judy G's party. She is very small and immediately reaches out to you and makes you feel that you are the most important person in the room and that she is deeply delighted to see you. She has wonderful manners and puts herself out to be a marvelous hostess. All the while, as the night grows on, she becomes more and more frantic, and when everyone decides to go she seems wildly desperate, implores you never to go, setting up new attractions. She cannot remain alone—even with her husband. Also, she seems to be drinking. . . . But none of this impairs the original impression she makes: a warm, loving girl with devastating charm. She sang a lot, and Lena Horne, whom I like, sang, and little Truman and Harold Arlen whimpered numbers from *The House of Flowers*. So far I don't much like the songs I've heard. There were lovely viands, and [British actress] Leonora Corbett, who has become a horrifying frump, and a few dozen Wampas Baby Stars[56] and [prizefighter] Sugar Ray Robinson and Mrs. Sugar Ray Robinson—a chocolate baby-doll type. I had a very good time . . . and Judy G seemed to take to me and gave me kisses, and Lena Horne gave me cuddles and kisses, and Moss Hart shook my hand dankly and repeatedly, and Kitty Carlisle looked like a wound in a rumpled bed,[57] and it was that world—always reminding me of Eleonora but not really her world . . . and always reminding me of how I used to conjure over it and wonder at what seemed to be their marvelous and glittering lives. . . . So now I know that world and how very seamy and fragile it is . . . and how desperate. Maria Riva was there, enormous in one of Marlene's

55. The 1937 London production of *On Your Toes* had been Brigitta Lieberson (Vera Zorina)'s big break. The choreography in both productions was Balanchine's.

56. From 1922 to 1934, "Wampas Baby Stars" were those deemed most likely to succeed by the Western Association of Motion Picture Advertisers (WAMPAS).

57. Moss Hart (1904–61), playwright (*You Can't Take It with You*) and director, married the singer and actress Kitty Carlisle (b. 1910), who after his death would become chairman (1976–96) of the New York State Council on the Arts.

white-beaded dresses, and when Maria telephoned Mummy in Las Vegas, where she opens tonight (Judy G said, "My, think of calling her Mummy . . ."), Mummy was in a state—bored, with a cold, lonely, firmly convinced that she, Mummy, was doomed to a disaster this time. . . . Everyone talked to her and it was more like one of those embarrassing broadcasts late at night when someone requests a record to be played for someone and all the names are mentioned. These people stay up all night. When we left, at about four, Adolph Green and Betty Comden were just getting down to performing burlesque opera. At one point I said to Irene that next on the program was square dancing. . . . Everyone had taken to clapping in rhythm to Judy G's singing (she has marvelous sure pitch, innate rhythm, and such a sense of dramatizing a song) and snapping their fingers—real homefolks-having-a-party-in-the-kitchen sort of antics. Part of the atmosphere at that party came from a curious fact: Almost nobody there was born into a world rich enough to make them think that they could ever afford the sumptuousities of dress which they all now wear with such aplomb.

NOTE: *Mademoiselle* presented Maria Callas with a merit award in the autumn of 1953, probably at Leo's suggestion. Dorle Soria of Angel Records wrote to Callas explaining the honor.

**CALLAS'S AMERICAN DEBUT** *Dorle Soria, sometime early in 1954, rang. I was in my office at* Mademoiselle. *She was in her office, probably at the New York Philharmonic Orchestra. Dorle said, "I'm not calling to ask where your program notes are. You're always late, but somehow you always manage. I'm calling to tell you that Maria Callas asked me about you this morning, and I told her that you thought she was the greatest person on the opera stage. She said that she had heard, and she would like it if you called her one day. Here is her telephone number in Milan." Dorle's husband was the head of Angel Records: Angel recorded Maria. By and by, I got my courage up and I called her in Milan. The voice was rich in varied associations: Manhattan street twang, Italian musicality, girlishness, a touch of diva resonance, a kind of Greek harshness. She told me that she would be coming to make her United States debut with the Lyric Theater of Chicago. I told her I knew that. "How do you know that?" The voice was surprised, delighted, instantly intimate—she knew that she had hooked her fish. "Larry Kelly told me." "Oh, Larry. You know Larry." Then she laughed. "Only for Larry would I come. . . ."[58] There was a pause. "You will come to Chicago, no?" "That's a silly question, isn't it?" "I am sometimes silly. . . ." This was flirting. I enjoyed this game very much. I had played it many times before. So had she.*

58. Giving Callas her American debut was a coup for Lawrence Kelly (1928?–74), manager for the Lyric Theatre opera (called the Lyric Opera after 1956) of Chicago. In 1957 he would found the Dallas Civic Opera, also bringing Callas there for some of its first productions.

*Scene: Autumn in Chicago. Larry Kelly called: "She's already here! She came, as usual, with a retinue and enough food to feed an army. You cannot believe it! She wants to see you." I went to the opera house, into a dressing room, and I did not see the woman I had seen in Venice. She stood up, twirled about in imitation of a model, or what she fondly believed was an imitation of a model. Then, impulsively, she hugged me. She said, "Surprise!" I was not surprised: I was shocked. Here was a suave, utterly feminine, in a sense freshly seductive figure (of course, she had played those parts so very well, even as a very big woman).*[59] *So, then I did several radio broadcasts in Chicago, all about the greatness of Maria Meneghini Callas.* (1993)

NOTE: In November 1954, Callas sang *Norma*, *La Traviata*, and *Lucia di Lammermoor* at Chicago's Civic Opera house. The response was rapturous, launching what would soon become the Lyric Opera of Chicago into international visibility.

JOURNAL • NOVEMBER 2, 1954 • CHICAGO  The opening of the Lyric Theatre of Chicago, Maria Callas, the Angel Ball and all my broadcasts:[60] Callas sang, especially in all the embroidery and in the genuine coloratura passages, exquisitely. The upper, upper tones wavered a bit, but the voice has great heart, brilliance, ease. It is produced with such ease that at times it seemed to float in the air, an entity in itself, quite independent of any human agency. She has become extremely slender, a twenty-two-inch waist, and she is very girlish— not repulsively—with enormous, darkly outlined eyes, an archaic Greek profile, dressed at the ball tastefully in a pale blue slightly bouffant gown, and magnificently diamonded. These diamonds are given her by her sweet-faced (but a touch of Scarpia) elderly, non-English-speaking Italian husband, [Battista] Meneghini.[61] The Callas diamonds are named after each of her triumphs, for she receives them for them: The "Puritani" is a huge stone. ("Dirty," she said, "I must clean it.") She also had on "La Scala," a great brooch, and others. She has the same warm, affectionate hand, strong but womanly, that Judy Garland has. The contrast of her peering through ornate, gold-rimmed, and jeweled harlequin glasses at the ice show, which formed the entertainment at the ball—this gaudy, noisy, fleeting-for-over-an-hour "show" so antithetical to the glorious *Norma*, which was its excuse. Callas is very reminiscent of artistic girls I have always known. There is a suggestion of Audrey Hepburn about her, and you know that she can be a beast when she wishes, but oh those prima donna smiles, wiles, and graces.

59. Callas had lost some sixty pounds since Leo had first seen her in January 1953.
60. Six radio shows had interviewed Leo, representing *Mademoiselle*, regarding Callas.
61. During his marriage to Callas from 1949 to 1959, Giovanni Battista Meneghini (1895–1981) was also her manager. In Puccini's opera *Tosca*, Baron Scarpia is the treacherous chief of police.

**A REFUGE FOR MARIA**    *How to tell about the twenty-three years of our loving, to-and-fro friendship? There is no point to recounting the pyrotechnic public life. That can be found, in various stages of truth, in dozens of publications—in newspaper headlines the world over, in books. . . .*

*Here is Maria, sitting in the back parlor of 1453, on her first, very private visit, when she found it a refuge from reporters and all of the clamor that her Metropolitan debut was causing. She is meticulously correct in a black tailleur, closely hatted, sleekly shod, discreetly jeweled, furs flung back—but she is raging: "Why would they not let me alone? Why, oh why, all this with my mother? What did she ever do for me? Why can they not be content with what I have to give them?"[62] She is all fury. Then the darkness is gone. "What are these?" She reaches for a very large piece of cake, takes up the plate on which it reposes, peers at it nearsightedly with her gleaming eyes—pokes about the rich cake with a fork, smiles roguishly, and says, "You eat it: I'll taste it." I eat or really manage to eat a very small bite, and suddenly the rest is gone: She has eaten it all. In years to come, I would discover that when she asks me to order, in a Dallas restaurant, fifteen different varieties of ice cream, she will taste each and every one and I will scarcely get a chance to eat any of them. Maria was a prodigious eater who thought she never really ate anything. Finishing the cake, she was relaxed and all eagerness for news, any news, of rival divas, although she never admitted that she had any rivals at all. She was merely interested in what the other girls were up to.* (1993)

DECEMBER 5, 1954 • NEW YORK CITY
**TO RICHARD HUNTER** • MIAMI

Everyone is giving parties—and I find that I am having a small birthday party for Osbert Sitwell, who practically asked for it. He's dying, poor man, and I like him very much—but his sister! Edith [Sitwell] says there are noises in the walls of her room at the St. Regis, and she cannot sleep. So she went down and told the people behind the desk that she was sure that a nun was immured in the walls of her room: They now think her crazy—what a monster.[63]

**JOURNAL** • DECEMBER 7, 1954    Dame Edith fell on Marlene saying, "You are the great revelation of my life." And went away in a green brocade tunic— clamped to her bosom by an enormous, gold-mounted, oblong jade brooch, topping a black satin skirt—murmuring, "About 'woman,' Marlene Dietrich . . . I will send you my *Collected Poems* on Saturday. You have a wonderful thing for me." Marlene ecstasized: "A great woman, that one." Wystan

---

62. In October 1956, two days before Callas was to make her debut at the Metropolitan, *Time* magazine ran a cover story about her, which quoted a blunt letter from Callas to her mother; telling her to make her own money or "jump out of the window."
63. "She descended to the desk, at four a.m., in full Edith Sitwell regalia—black-and-silver dogeressa robes, five-story turban, a loot of barbaric jewels." *Journal,* July 20, 1978.

[W. H. Auden] buttled. He was dressed in real work clothes, browns, torn, unpatched. Osbert was teary when the cake came down and Wystan led the singing.[64]

DECEMBER 11, 1954 • NEW YORK CITY

**TO RICHARD HUNTER • MIAMI**

I have gout—that means I have uric acid in my blood which helps make kidney stones and affects the liver. The idea now is to diminish the uric acid, so as to prevent kidney and gallstones and liver sicknesses. That means I am on an even more rigorous diet, being permitted to eat only 1,000 calories a day. Also, I have various medicines. I find it consoling to know that I, myself, have earned all this—gorging my way into it—and I am not sorry, because I think back on all the good things you ever cooked and I am rapturous. The evening after hearing this report, I had a real old blowout—an enormous dinner at the Canton Village (which, alas, will see me no more for a long time) and a sundae at Schrafft's (my first since mid-June). Now I've settled down to getting well.

JOURNAL • DECEMBER 12, 1954  A gentle morning with the mellow gleam of a bird's wing, some blue-green bird, and the river in the distance an icy light blue, the palest blue in all those blues flaring in a lighted gas jet. I lay in my lavender-fragrant bath reading *Memoirs of Hadrian* [by Marguerite Yourcenar] and sometimes the writing slipped quite away, such marble, slippery writing, but sometimes a great chunk of marble, an idea, a concept, a characteristic— and, ah, a toehold, something on which to pull oneself up.

Yesterday, after a morning of looking in the shops (oh, the hard, set, rapacious faces of women shopping), found an oasis in Bergdorf's antique rooms. No one there save some Staffordshire and a porcupine—not too expensive. We rushed home.

Then Bill Inge and a nice boy to drive came—and Lesley [Blanch], very pretty[65]—and off we went through the early green twilight, the tremulous apple-green moment that almost annihilates with memory and nostalgia. Along we went, high above the marvelous Hudson (always imposing Indians and Henry Hudson upon any talk or other inner vision). Lesley suddenly realized that Bill was the author of *Come Back, Little Sheba* and *Picnic* and she was in rapture. All the while, the lighted towns on the New York side were so many glittering promises. I think we live too close here, in this house, in this little world of friends and acquaintances and business—and one another. I think we need the air of long rides into the country and walks not on pavements, but most of all a long, deep breathing out of city fumes. Mrs. Nature

64. Osbert Sitwell lived until 1969.
65. Earlier in the year, their friend Lesley Blanch (b. 1904), a British biographer and historian, had published what would be her greatest success: *The Wilder Shores of Love*, about adventurous women finding their fortune in the East.

whooshing down the mountainsides, not the Lexington Avenue bus moaning down the avenue.

Nyack was in the deep, intensely glass-green twilight, with the churches outlined in colored Christmas lights. Lesley thought that Carson [McCullers] lived in one of those churches, but Carson, when seen, was crouched in a corner of a dowdy sofa. She glowered evilly at us, and did not seem at all pleased to see anyone. She clearly intended for us all to disappear promptly at six, and we wanted to. This was the most un-party party I have been at. A television showed football all the while in an upper room.

FEBRUARY 26, 1955 This is a first-person-singular book. Yet I have always distrusted "I" as a beginning, preferring this "I" to be tucked away, to be slipped in unobtrusively. Feeling about it much the way I do about exposing the title side of any book I carry. To do that seems to me to be advertising oneself, to be showing off, to be revealing one's secret name, and with those "savages" about whom I read long ago, those South American savages who don't tell their true names, I feel superstitiously . . . And here I stopped, marveling at the clumsiness of what I had written, questioning how, after so many years of writing, can I write so badly? Then the music seeps in—the sounds of birds, the chiming of Marcus, the little glass-walled eccentric clock. Light bruises [the night sky], and I am suddenly sleepy. So I make excuses to stop this scribbling, to leave once again a little pile of words, of promises, stillborn. "The house," Gray said, "is filled with abortions. How he can stand it, I don't know. Little heaps of promises." I burrow down beneath the blankets and scrunch the sheets, exulting: "I am thin—at least I am thin." I feel this without thinking it, so much of what we say we "think" is not thought at all, but felt.

NOTE: Gray went to spend a few weeks with his mother at her sister Alice McKay's home near Chicago.

MARCH 26, 1955 • NEW YORK CITY

**TO GRAY FOY** • GLENVIEW, ILLINOIS

This chilly room heaves with Auber [French opera music]—so faded and tinkly and nursery-tunish. We are deep in sleet, and all the world is frost-crusted (sounds like amateur advertisement-writing for a sugar-coated loaf). The light is that employed by seventeenth-century artists of the north countries, who seem to have lived perpetually in a sleety world—winter the year round.

*Cat on a Hot Tin Roof* is remarkable for never, not even for one moment, touching any sensitive speck in one—save that area wherein revulsion lurks. The play never emerges from the privacy of the bedroom. We sat there feeling that we were peeping into their bedroom, and with no reason whatsoever save voyeurism. Everyone knows that everyone has scenes in the bedroom, but why should anyone be interested in these scenes unless they are raised to general applicability and so reveal us to ourselves and elevate us in so doing? This is a private, dirty-bedroom play which pretends to poetry and heart and universality and never, never gets beyond the dirty-sheets mind of Tennessee. According to him, life's still a mess on the old plantation and Big Mama always knows best. Bill's play [*Bus Stop*] is a work of delicacy and sympathy, the outpouring of a loving heart compared to this murk. *Cat* has been endowed with a smooth, orchestrated, shadowy production. It is acted magnificently—with Mildred Dunnock [as Big Mama][66] the image of Muriel Francis and utilizing a voice of such stridency that she seems to have swallowed Ethel Merman and is regurgitating her Southern-style. Barbara Bel Geddes is very good (but how extraordinary Miriam Hopkins would have been), although she seems always too rectitudinous and Aryan to be mixed up in sexual exhibitions—and this play really never omits anything pertaining to the closet, including moths as large as condors. The huge audience adored it. Lesley [Blanch] and the Valentines[67] and I seemed the only ones to hate it. I resent Tennessee's evil, sure masturbating of audiences. He literally milks them dry—ugh. So on to other voices in more pleasant rooms.

NOTE: In May, Gray and Leo departed New York for several months in Europe. Leo would write three long articles for *Mademoiselle* based upon this trip: about Holland, Belgium, and Salzburg, Austria.

JOURNAL · MAY 4, 1955 · LONDON  Sotheby's was just locked up by a dapper, gray-suited man in a black bowler as we came to it, so off I went to Claridge's, where I surprised Aunt Minnie and she laughed and cried and looked lovable and told me in a confidence burst that she had arranged to take care of the girls because she was so worried about them.[68] This made me too late for Noël Coward's party, so I flew home and into my bib and tucker and off to the opera, just in time. The great arrangements of lilies and peonies on the stair—the men more "dressed" than the women—the friendliness of everyone—also the extreme air of privacy. We talked with John Gielgud—somehow his face looked more disenchanted but quite beautiful. He introduced us to [singer and actress] Gwen Ffrangcon-Davies, who was smaller than I had imagined and in a gown of Mediterranean-blue silk with a lilac satin scarf. The women were not dowdy, but also not intensely elegant. No one was chic, in the French or American sense. They were, most of them, suitably well dressed.

Then David Webster came and introduced us to Sir Hugh Casson, who had

---

66. An agent for musicians, Muriel Bultman Francis (1908–86) was from a New Orleans family made wealthy by an undertaking business.
67. Helen Valentine (1893–1986), founding editor of *Seventeen* in 1944, had recently revamped *Charm*, Street & Smith's rival to Condé Nast's *Glamour*.
68. "The girls" were Minnie's nieces Rosalie (1913–2000) and Norma Goldwasser (b. 1918), unmarried daughters of Leo's uncle Harry. Leo thus learned that his well-off uncle Irving and aunt Minnie would leave him no money.

carefully designed the *Troilus & Cressida* (in "Trojan Modern," as Gray said). The colors were lovely (Cressida wore a pale lilac Alix [Grès] robe)—all purples and earth reds and shades of lavender and pale yellows—with the camp scene against a great, pale, burnt-out sky. Magda László [the soprano] a beauty, a lovely figure, and almost always a ripe voice. She should sing operettas because she is just too good for them—that is the sort of voice operettas need. I saw [William] Walton looking like a Sitwell family member.[69] His opera is very good—the music not thick enough always, but beautifully written and proportioned, especially a storm-and-passion orchestral interlude while Troilus makes love to Cressida behind a drawn curtain, a quartet of maidens robing Cressida. This is a first-rate work—really all Walton, no discernible influences like one finds in Menotti—an intricate, tidy, intensely disciplined work.

Now I must to bed—and work in the morning—but these notes do not give the color, only some of the meager facts. The carpeting everywhere is worn and shabby—but every window is curtained.

MAY 5, 1955  At the opera, I wondered whether the Frenchwomen were so elegant, even many of the poorest, because the French were essentially a cynical nation—bone cynical—and whether great elegance in dress, or even elegance without "great" was an outward sign of cynicism. Does one then have to be cynical to be elegant? I think that this is probably true. Englishmen are, many of them, elegantly dressed, and Englishwoman are almost all dowds—albeit their suits are beautifully cut. They are sensibly dressed. Englishmen (I am not talking of the lower classes) are basically cynical—perhaps even amoral—certainly, sexy men are given to their pleasures. This is so vigorously a man's town and such a city of business. Not brash business, as New York, which seems effete when viewed from these male-teeming streets.

MAY 6, 1955  About Margot in *Firebird*: This is a performance in the great Diaghilev tradition and, since [Ballets Russes dancer] Karsavina coached her, some of the miming is dated—but the bird is magnificent. Her fingers seemed taloned—yet she wore nothing on them—and her face was both evil and caressing. The great strength of her back and arms has never been so beautifully apparent and so exquisitely employed. This is a long work compared to the Balanchine version. Maria [Tallchief] is dazzlingly brilliant and sharp; Margot is a multifaceted creation.[70] The Goncharova *Firebird* sets [here] seem so dull after the Chagall [for New York City Ballet], and the orchestra sounded

69. British composer William Walton (1902–83) had been a protégé and dependent of the Sitwells in the twenties and thirties, living in Osbert Sitwell's house for more than a decade.
70. *Firebird* was a 1910 creation of the Ballets Russes and was Stravinsky's first commissioned ballet score. Leo is comparing Fonteyn's dancing in Serge Grigoriev's 1955 revival (with the original Fokine choreography) to Tallchief's performance in Balanchine's 1949 production, which had been a sensation in New York.

unbrilliant. We are accustomed to a more impetuous, coruscating, briefer *Fire-bird*, but this is the original and as documentation was fascinating. Here we saw the beginnings of much decoration—i.e., grill and trellis decoration as on tin chocolate boxes (inevitably gold on dull blue). Some of the choreography so very kitsch today—and the peasant women in what looked like nightgowns and moccasins. . . . Could they have led to Chanel? And the groups like *Les Noces* (they seemed to dote on thick groups).[71] But the Balanchine monsters are more monstrous. This must be seen, as the Copenhagen *Petrouchka* should be seen, for its historic value.

MAY 8, 1955 The Tynans live at the top (reached by a small, self-run lift) of a converted early nineteenth-century house in Hyde Park Gardens. The general impression is that it's all been hastily brushed up, things thrust under furniture. You feel that their wardrobe is all out on pegs—such a dressing-room feeling everywhere in their flat—a bath (here they fix drinks: it is closer to the "living" room than the kitchen); a nursery chockablock with stuffed beasts and toys and baby books; a small room crammed with books and papers—one end, his writing place, backed by a montage he has improvised of bullfight memorabilia, a chair heaped with review copies, and the floor piled with things and books (like home); a bedroom with the clothes even deeper on pegs, a wall shelf in which are some of [his wife, novelist] Elaine [Dundy]'s favorites—Benchley, at least five or six volumes, Jane Bowles's play [*The Summerhouse*] (Elaine loves this play), some photographs—one of Ken and Elaine leaning enthusiastically out of a box or bleacher at a bullfight and another of Ken with some heavy, swarthy men at a terrace table, some café, and on the table a large wine bottle (all very Hemingway, but in the French translation). A beautiful pink toreador cloak stands in one corner of the living room and books are on Italian sort of "modern" shelves, which stand out into the room—the whole impression is of rooms in the Village at home.

MAY 10, 1955 • LONDON

TO RICHARD HUNTER • NEW YORK CITY

We've been to the first night of the *Firebird*—re-created by Grigoriev and Karsavina for Margot Fonteyn. She is superb in it, but it is not a great part for a great ballerina. David Webster sat us right behind the queen, the Duke [of Edinburgh], and Princess Margaret—so close that unavoidably my foot sometimes poked the duke's bottom. The queen is remarkably like (in face) Queen Victoria at times—sort of that same lowering, reproachful, bad-little-girl look. This is in repose, but when she is animated she becomes quite pretty. She actu-

---

71. *Les Noces* (1923), premiered by the Ballets Russes, is a ballet with music by Stravinsky that depicts a Russian wedding. Scenes in Bronislava Nijinska's original were laden with revolution-of-the-proletariat implications.

ally looks like many English girls. The princess is pretty and a pet and everyone seems to dote on her. When the apotheosis happened at the end of "Homage to the Queen," the duke leaned over and gave the queen a little kiss. They are very pleasant together. Some parts of *Firebird* amused him into comments, across the queen, to the man with Princess M. The queen did some wifely shushing.[72] She applauded everything diligently. The people love her. We became local celebrities because we were seen sitting, it seemed, with the royal party.

JOURNAL · MAY 10, 1955 Osbert [Sitwell]'s house is smaller than ours in depth—actually the right size for two people. It is crammed with all sorts of fascinating *objets*—drawings, paintings, and some delightful furniture. It is a bright house complete with a happy cat named Ally (after Alice, probably Bouverie), tiger in kind and great-lady in temperament. Miss Noble [the housekeeper] had the *Cornhill* [magazine] on her kitchen table and Edith's *Gardeners & Astronomers* at the telephone. "Can read a verse or two while waiting," she explained. She has beautiful, honest, blue eyes and came to Osbert some twenty-five years ago. "Mr. Walton was here then." She loves dusting the house, taking one hour for the drawing room (all full of blue and pink Bristol glass, Pavliks [works by Tchelitchew], shell fantasias, glass sailing ships), because she always finds new things in what she's known. She says the house has become better and better as Osbert has "gotten on." Osbert's bedroom—the floor one below the top—has paintings by a Chinese, done after Osbert had been to China, and these are unique because they included fruits and untypical Chinese subjects—also a wardrobe painted to represent clothes, etc. "I thought that a pity," said Miss Noble. "It was such a good piece of walnut." In the morning room where Osbert does his personal mail—a Magnasco [painting]. David Horner's room seemed secret. It was the only room in which I felt that I was invading privacy. It had crucifixes and rosaries.[73]

This stood all through the Blitz and only the glass clapper of one Bristol-glass bell was flung out among the glass. Not one object was harmed, although Miss Noble herself picked up incendiaries in the little back court between the house and the dining room, a room quite apart from the house proper. She has to come up from her basement kitchen and out into the open when she serves. The dining room is like a deep sea grotto—Venetian shell furniture, shell

72. "The prince got the giggles at the girls throwing golden globes—oranges?—at one another. The queen gave him A Look and A Mutter, her diamond earrings trembling in her ears." *Journal, February 23, 1985.*
73. David Horner (d. 1983) and Osbert Sitwell were lovers for more than thirty-five years. "Edith Sitwell's lunar face as she cried, in the dining room of the St. Regis, over her luncheon, moonstone tears over David Horner's treatment of Osbert and how Osbert had taken him back. She was feminine in an epicene way, the way some high churchmen are." *Journal, July 8, 1981.*

things everywhere—all dark and mysterious, this dining room made from a shed.

MAY 11, 1955  We went to Peter Wilson's to dine. Peter talked about Miss Margaret Jourdain and how Ivy Compton-Burnett had all the money, and how mean I C-B was to MJ.[74] One day at tea, with a lavish table, I C-B demanded to know where the quince jam was. MJ said that what with several varieties already set out, she didn't think the quince was needed. After about ten minutes, MJ asked for tea, but I C-B said where was the quince? And not until MJ brought it did she get her tea. MJ was bitter because [her sister] Miss Jourdain left a sizable fortune to [medieval-art historian] Joan Evans, who already has much money, whilst Margaret Jourdain was very poor. Margaret said of her sister, the *An Adventure* one, "She was not a good witness." Of I C-B's writing she said—"Oh, she just scribbles away. . . ."

MAY 12, 1955  The "guests" of Fleming's [Hotel] are strung about this dining room's outer edges, like *objets untrouvés,* and the bandstand, at the far end, backed by its wall of looking glass, is, as usual, full of clamorous morning emptiness. How very audible are vacant places dedicated to noise. This is the special charm of amusement parks and summer pleasure grounds in winter, their animated ghostliness. And how footsteps sound on London streets: They do sound here like footsteps. In New York I am never aware of footsteps in the street. So, again I perceive that I hear and see and even feel through a literary scrim.

This morning, we have several waitresses I have heretofore not seen. One pale, red-lipped, and quite unsure but willing. "Will you please bring the toast and tea now?" I ask. Flustered, she darts a look, gathering herself. "Actually, the other girl"—the oldest and most wild-haired and the smellingest of them all—"is bringing the order up." "The other girl" does, giving tumultuous Irish glances. I believe that Fleming's must be a station on the Underground Railroad to Schrafft's in America.

The American middle-aged couple has stopped to talk to the shyish, throaty-voiced, unhappy-at-going-home-looking girl in gray suit and tousled hair, neat small-collared blouse and little string of pearls. They tell one another where they're from and how long they'll be: "But we're going on to Paris," says the man, while his carefully coifed and waved wife (in woolly cardigan, skirt—gray and neat, white blouse piped in blue), her maquillage slightly twenties, dimples and smiles, thereby suddenly almost vanishing into a perspective of

---

74. Margaret Jourdain (1876–1951), a prominent authority on British furniture and decoration, had lived for three decades with the novelist Ivy Compton-Burnett (1884–1969). Her sister Eleanor Jourdain (1864–1924) coauthored *An Adventure,* an Edwardian tale of two English ladies seeing ghosts at Versailles, a story Leo wanted very much to believe.

tango teas, racy talk, and smoking in public. "That's nice," says the girl, adding that she's been working in Germany. We have with us, this morning, some of *Separate Tables*'s own[75]—including a pocket edition, quite abridged, of the woman in furs. This version is very small-town American, eats mincingly, looks lost in the eyes, is without doubt a widow, was once told by her father that she was pretty and now can't believe that she will never be told again, wears a dark plaid suit, a small black-green tight-to-head peaked cap, an orange pullover, (only a small v shows) and a string of pearls, also rimless spectacles to shield the shyness and disappointment and even, perhaps, through which to see the world more clearly. Which, unfortunately, those ladies sometimes do.

Gray came down and I told him about the greetings and getting-to-know one another of the Americans abroad, but midway he said that he didn't like verbatim reports and what was the point? I was sharply hurt and said there wasn't any point. Living so closely must produce these little aggravations. But it occurred to me that a basic difference in temperaments must be my seeing everything as a story, as interesting about people and life, and his not viewing the world this way. I am still upset, but I try to think as much as I can how the other person feels, that perhaps he didn't feel well. Also I know that in conversation one of my great faults is going on, in too great detail, about anything. This makes me, frequently, a dull talker. I have tried, for years, to learn how to hold my tongue in check. Sometimes I talk so much, with such surge and senselessness, that even my nose goes dry and my right ear fills up— providentially, in a way, for I at least cannot hear the sillinesses I trumpet forth.

MAY 13, 1955 Margot was superb in one of the most beautiful ballets in the world—[Frederick Ashton's] *Symphonic Variations*. At moments she rose straight off the floor, as though plucked up by some powerful force. A cool, calm, soothing, frigid work to sentimental watery music, a combination as satisfying as sweet-and-sour. In the interval, Margot sat in her dressing room, in a deep red, minutely paisleyed wrapper, her jet black hair tumbled down, undoing her ballet slippers and surrounded by admirers. The telephone rang. Margot said how she'd been to banquets and both menus were identical. "Like being a lecturer, dearie," I said. Why, she demanded, had *Symphonic Variations* been such a flop on the first American tour? "Why? . . . It laid an egg, a great big egg, an ostrich egg," she went on. But I had to go back to my seat. John Gielgud and two young fellows (very sissy) sat next to us and we talked and he sent love to Karen Blixen. "I'm just in the throes of *Lear*," he said to me, ". . . in the throes." Later he strode away, incredibly slender in a dark straight coat and black homburg, a flower in the coat and a handkerchief jutting from

75. *Separate Tables* (1954), by Terence Rattigan, consisted of two one-acts about characters staying at a rather tired English seaside hotel.

its pocket, a general air of being Graham Robertson.[76] The two sissies ran along, one in front and one behind. It was like a Beardsley as they vanished down a little Covent Garden street.

MAY 15, 1955  In the morning yesterday we were off to Charing Cross and into the train for Ashford, down through Kentish valleys. Kent is the beauty of countryside in storybooks, written with great love by delicate minds for children of any age whatsoever. Here Beatrix Potter and Kenneth Grahame live, and all the hedgerows, as one nears the sea, ripple with news of noble refugees from the Tribunal—Calais-to-Folkestone. You can see the Scarlet Pimpernel without even lowering your eyelids, and poor Beau [Brummell] on this last journey to exile and poverty and disorder in Boulogne just across the Channel, but forever away from the world he made.

In the station at Ashford, a tall, sort of diffidently gangling, white-haired but balding, most distinguished man came up to us. He wore a battered, tan raincoat, but with great style, more like a sumptuous but negligible (because he had so many) rich coat, a yellow-and-brown-and-red scarf loosely knotted at his throat. He had a long mouth, rather loose, but fully lipped and quite ready to tremble or turn down or lend introspection to his angular, quite thin, high-cheeked, enormous-eyed (blue they are and sad, but brightening suddenly to amusement) face. He was browned in the open a lot. His hands were long and capable. He waved them and fluttered them, more in the manner of an epoch than in femininity. He was purposefully languid. Immediately one felt that this was the tail end of Regency bucks, Edwardian beaux, bright young people. "I'm Bobby Howard," he said, "and you must be Peter Wilson's friends." His voice was quiet, and he enunciated his syllables, caressing some and eliding others, making a pattern so akin to the prose of Wilde in his plays, making contractions here and carelessly-carefully putting in all verb parts there. This speech pattern is so individual that it is surely the last gasp of Edwardianism, of twenties very-high society. At this moment Martin Wilson came up, in gray flannels and what we call a windbreaker, looking very young.[77]

MAY 17, 1955  In a moment, summer vanished; autumn chilled the air and leaves almost unborn go sailing in argosies, armadas to gain the world for winter.

This is an unsettled time—with peace in Austria and terror in cinemas everywhere. The hydrogen bomb had been exploded in an American desert—

76. The British illustrator, costume designer, and dandy W. Graham Robertson (1866–1948) had been portrayed full-length, wearing a slender black coat, by John Singer Sargent.
77. Martin Wilson (1910–92), an antique collector and dealer, was Peter Wilson's (of Sotheby's) older brother. Bobby Howard was his good friend. GF: "Martin Wilson should have been carried around in a sedan chair. The most ineffable eighteenth-century fop I have ever met, with the most glorious silver and a man to take care of it."

trial houses peopled by waxen facsimiles of people (children, dogs, cats, all cupboards meticulously stocked with tinned foods), a "test" village, exploded off the earth. I saw the dreadful ghastly sweep of the air and sucking up of the air with it everything torn up, more dreadful than cyclone or tornado, more dreadful than any natural force, and then the broken waxen people, some quite vanished, others deadness among shattered possessions—all too monstrous. This we saw, unexpectedly, at the tail end of a newsreel, just before Carol [Reed]'s not-too-good movie, A Kid for Two Farthings.[78] Oh—the dreadful rush of the air as it swept up the houses and burst them open, tore them to splinters in less than a moment, tossing their contents into nothingness or into bits, which in their familiarity made it all the more horrible. Seeing this, why can't people everywhere put a stop to the avalanche, the now almost inevitable nothingness of tomorrow? This is comprehensible, not a dramatic statement: "1,000,000 killed." No one comprehends one million. Everyone instantly understands an accidental or even an intentional pinprick. What we saw was personal. Still a quarter hour later, watching Carol's little boy and a goat in situations made unreal because they were too movie-made (as opposed to Marty's just-as-it-really-happens atmosphere), the hydrogen bomb and its utter devastation became only the shadow of a cloud. There are thunder and torrents and lightning in that cloud. We know that, but who is to fear a cloud? There it is behind us. . . . Here it is right overhead. . . . Oh, dear Lord, please send a wind to drive away that awful cloud. Who wants a cloud, even a little cloud, on a holiday? There it goes, the shadow, to spill and bluster and roar and shatter elsewhere. Thank you, Lord. This, then, is how we do not want to believe in clouds and hydrogen bombs, in life ending. It is far easier to fear pain than it is to fear death, especially death from the skies, death by man. I think of Fania [Marinoff], so terrified of dying that she sleeps in a blue-walled room, her blue-and-white glass Venetian chandeliers brilliantly lighted, light blazing from floor lamps, light pouring upon her bed, making it into a stage, upon which she tosses restlessly, fearing death, sometimes leaping from her bed to rummage among the brilliant scraps, which make it almost impossible to shut her drawers and cupboards, there are so many remnants of Poirets and bargains and embroideries and beaded bits and feathers and flowers plucked from barrows in the flea markets of the world.

MAY 18, 1955   Martin Wilson talks "sister-in-law" talk about Harry Wright [Peter Wilson's companion], gently doing in the rise of Harry, and with such diffidence, such style. Then Martin ran off "to dash more powder all over himself," said Peter, before going out into the pelting cold rain to meet someone on

78. Leo had probably seen an excerpt from Damage and Destruction, a film made by the U.S. military documenting the effect of nuclear-bomb explosions on soldiers and test models of civilian life.

Duke of York Street. Bobby Howard's house is in precise and exquisite Regency and eighteenth-century style—lovely *Vieille Russie* objects and satin bedcovers. "They do make such good dog benches," Bobby said, pointing to a low fuchsia-satin-covered Regency bed, upon which Puffy (a large Alsatian, like a dog on a Berlin wool carpet) had rested.

Then luncheon in a large, light dining room with birds in cages—a cardinal-red bird, parakeets, and a trilling canary who flew about and was excessively vocal. Lunch bountiful, beautifully served, during a great thunder and rainstorm, with the magnificent dramatics of the skies so enthralling that I forgot to be afraid, and the silver so curious and beautiful—probably early eighteenth, late seventeenth—and china of great delicacy and beauty. When I asked what Bobby did with himself all day (he is fifty-six) I was told: "Oh, he finds occupations—the birds, the flowers, his hair, walking."

We went off in Bobby's Rolls to Sissinghurst, where there were many trippers and the gardens were not at their peak, but were nevertheless quite beautiful and one could see how marvelous they would be. The great hedges were wonderfully kept, and two urns pouring purple clematis were as lovely as ornaments in eighteenth-century books. Vita Sackville-West stood talking with some visitors. She was in a battered, tannish, weathered, country-felt sort of *pot-cloche*-with-brim, a baggy skirt and warm sweater and coat, gardening gloves, leaning on a garden broom. She is very tall, still retains some of the beauty that won Virginia Woolf. She vanished before I could talk to her. The dog, Rollo, bounded out, friendly and gay. We went off to tea in a shop in a nearby village—awful tea, but fascinating to see the trippers (the men not removing their hats, guzzling it down with relish) and great shelves of candies with names I had never even imagined.

MAY 19, 1955   Last night we went off to dine with Dig and Henry (Yorke-Green) in their minute Trevor Place house. Henry seems older, gradually becoming stooped. His eyes enormous and velvet, but more and more fixed in their unclouded whites. His color is compounded of rich browns and deep reds and pallor. And he drinks quietly, unobtrusively, incessantly, wine mostly, never quite betraying his state, but quite plastered all evening long. This does not impair his conversation, which is good, but causes him to reiterate moments of it, sort of making a Greek chorus of himself to himself. Dig has the atmosphere of a woman who has given up struggling against this inevitability. She has humor and curiosity and a sort of properly-brought-up girlish vivacity. She was once lovely, probably in the season she came out she was thought beautiful, and that was more the vitality of the moment and good bone structure than actual physical beauty. Dig is good, the way Penelope is good, and Henry is a good man, but alas he is an alcoholic. He says that he now finds taking up a pen even to write a letter impossible. He has started several books, and written one page. Then they stop.

He spoke of David Cecil[79] going to stay at San Simeon and being flabbergasted by having the plane in which he traveled pass over a blue desert, and after having been met by a fleet of Rollses, Bentleys, and other mythological motors and swept off to [William Randolph] Hearst's fairyland, being told that he would have to carry his own bags up. Cecil, accustomed to hordes of servants and the *politesse* of Hatfield, could not believe this rudeness and was utterly put out by it. Only to be overwhelmed again, when he had carried his bags up, by luxury such as he had never imagined any contemporary could summon. In a great garden, furnished with a battalion of Greek temples (actual ones, brought block by numbered block from Greece and erected in this California fantasy), he discovered that each altar, within its temple, was, when a concealed button was pressed, a fully stocked bar.

Henry's conversation flickered over Cecil, over L. P. Hartley ("He is now considered by many our greatest living novelist. I can't abide children in books, but I did think [Hartley's] *The Go-Between* good."), over Ivy Compton-Burnett. ("Cannot abide her. Can't read her books. She was awarded a little honor, the OBE, but she said 'too late,' for her companion had died."[80]) I told him how mean she had been to Miss Jourdain, and he said he was sure that she, Ivy C-B, was a monster. Then he talked of Evelyn [Waugh] and how he had heard a rumor of Evelyn now becoming sporadically unbalanced, how Evelyn had got on a boat to go to Africa or the Mideast and had demanded his letters after the boat had been at sea a long time and became absolutely black-faced with rage when the captain told him he could not possibly have letters at sea. Ultimately, his rage having subsided, he asked the captain whether he, Evelyn, was having hallucinations, and when the captain told him that he thought he was, Evelyn retired quietly to his cabin. His wife came out and took him home. Henry also told of spending a weekend with the Waughs, during which Evelyn flew into a black-faced rage at the table when, having given Henry permission to smoke between the courses, Henry did. Evelyn became so furious that he went off with two bottles of champagne and locked himself into his library. Henry says Mrs. Waugh enjoys all this. My experiences with Evelyn and Mrs. Evelyn [Laura Herbert] do confirm all this. Evelyn brought Mrs. to lunch at the Chateaubriand, which he had chosen, ordered only the most expensive foods, said to the waiters that the food was "filthy, positively filthy," and threw the basket of biscuits off the table.[81]

79. Lord David Cecil (1902–86), scholar and noted eccentric, was one of a distinguished English family that includes the earls of Exeter and Salisbury.
80. "Herman Schrijver [British decorator, 1904–72] said that Ivy Compton-Burnett came storming up his stair shouting, 'My man is dead! My man is dead!' on the day of Miss Jourdain's funeral, saying that she could not bear to go to it and would he have her to lunch." *Journal, August 2, 1971.*
81. "He iterated to his pale, pretty, cold wife (only pearl gray and washed-out blue), 'Don't stint yourself, darling,' as he sent expensive dish after expensive dish back. He was a beast— more sarcastic than witty." *Journal, March 2, 1969.*

Henry went on about wanting to come to America. He could pay his way, but would have to be kept there, perhaps by lecturing. "But no one night stands. They do me in. I require one half bottle of gin a day—that is all."

MAY 20, 1955   Lesley told about traipsing all the way out to Flushing [in Queens, New York,] to see a cousin of Lady Burton's—a huge, well-poitrined, educated seventy-five-year-old woman married to a night clerk. There she sits surrounded by mementos of Lady Burton.[82] She says Lady B was beautifully dressed, gay, not a prude, and that there is a little grave beside the big one, because Lady B insisted on having a tumorous growth which had been cut out buried there in anticipation of her remaining remains. Lady B said that it had been with her very long and suffered and grown within her. It was now a part of herself and must be buried.

MAY 25, 1955 • COPENHAGEN   I finished my Carlo—almost two days of industry and the bliss of sitting and writing and choosing and shaping and patting into place and finding some of it almost what I wanted to say.

NOTE: Leo's seventy-fifth-birthday tribute to Van Vechten was not published. The following is an excerpt.

*As a nation, we were musically benighted at the turn of the century, but Carlo [Van Vechten], along with his vanguard-minded precursor, [critic] James Gibbon Huneker, did not intend that we should remain a country of mandolin strummers and piano-piece players. So Carlo did his best to make honest women of American jazz, blues, and Negro music; the iconoclastics of Stravinsky; the unorthodoxies of Satie; the tunes of Gershwin; the folk music of Iowa (he was born in Cedar Rapids). He passionately interpreted the new interpreters—singing-actors such as Mary Garden, Olive Fremstad, Geraldine Farrar, and Chaliapin. He prophesied that movie music would be written by leading—even great—modern composers, not jingle-jangled out of stock "mood-music" collections by marathon piano players. Then in 1920, when he was forty, Carlo said that the time had come for him to give up music criticism and explained why: "Because after that age prejudices are formed which preclude the possibility of welcoming novelties."*

*At least one generation has matured without wittingly realizing that his extraordinary erudition, his enthusiasms, his great gifts as an agent évocateur and agent catalyst, his disdain for the trite and the conventional, his dedication to the exquisite in the most exact sense of that designation, his lavishly documented frivolity, his carefully calculated insolent willfulness, his delight in incongruities and in the unexpected, his seventy-six-year-long, shameless, public*

---

82. Isabel, Lady Burton (1831–96), wrote a biography of her husband Richard Francis Burton, the renowned explorer and translator of erotic texts.

*love affair with glamour have made today's living in America gayer, richer, and altogether more worldly—if you want it that way and have the capacity to take it.*
(1955)

JOURNAL · MAY 26, 1955  The terrace of the Stephanie et Porte, across Kongens Nytorv [the opera house's square] now blossoming with lilac trees and blooms, huge, pale lavender and white, and looking as all flowers do in the north, more delicate, more fragile. Here crowds sit all the long afternoon and into the evening, despite the disadvantageous weather. They hide their tea and coffee beneath cozies, and they wear bits of fur and mittens and, women, antiquated hats. Especially one antique female in a flat-brimmed, brown-velvet, high-crowned hat (like Momma wears in the snapshots, taken of us in about 1918 or 1919. Here many women look like Grandma and my Goldwasser aunts). So they sit on the terrace of the Stephanie et Porte, like so many egg-cozies and tea-cozies, and the bicyclists flash and flit by and the trolley cars lumber along—and horses. Too lovely, this makes me feel inside: All the pleasures of childhood and almost none of the fears.

MAY 27, 1955  Yesterday felt the first day of spring, when the sun actually warmed this world diligently and all day long. Morning flowed through the twisting, narrow streets and the helter-skelter squares of Copenhagen on the gentle, creaking croonings of pigeons—a coolish, amaranthine morning, which the ping-ping of trolley cars burst open like a great golden orange into torrents of sunlight.

I went off to tour the ballet school and the Royal Theater with journalists. We trooped through the classes: a men's class in the beautiful haunted rehearsal room, with the blue-and-tan walls and the portraits and the windows (curtained, fan-shaped at the top, and sunlight meshed in the white curtains), and the boys in great form at their barre work and the piano tinkling operetta tunes. I dote on practice pianists, for they are vast repositories of old operetta and show tunes and ballet music no one has heard in years—or ever. All of the boys have the long, straight, precise line which Roland Petit uses so marvelously, and all of the boys, in practice, seemed better than a similar group in New York, London, or Paris. So to Vera [Volkova]'s girls' class, and here the high caliber of form was not so apparent. But Vera is today the greatest teacher we have, and it is delightful to watch her—compact in a dark skirt and little shirt, her hair piled on top of her head and held in place by a little black ribbon—gently straightening a foot into the proper degree of turnout in relation to the leg, here talking in a quiet low voice to a dancer who, having done the same exercise since she was a small girl, is not now doing it.[83] The lightly lilting operetta

83. Vera Volkova (1904–75), the foremost teacher in the West of the Russian Vaganova method of ballet, was a Russian-born dancer and artistic adviser to the Royal Danish Ballet.

tunes tinkled on and we went to the paint shop and the little theater and through the school where the little children are taught other things than ballet—very cheerful and sunny and high-up, a whole separate suite arranged as a day school for towheaded little boys and girls. All of whom seemed very gay and amused at us, coated and foreign and wintry and gape-eyed. Overlooking the two rooftops upon which these children relax (one for girls, one for boys) is a great ledge, each corner held down by enormous seated-on-their-haunches sphinxes, 1870ish, a decoration of masks, comedy and tragedy, and everywhere against the sky the green-corroded fantastic towers of this city. If you know the principal towers of Copenhagen, you need never be lost.

MAY 29, 1955   What a lovely Sunday at the sea with Margrethe Schanne and Kjeld [Noack].[84] They fetched us at eleven (in a convertible) and we drove north along the coast [by Kattegat], past Queen Alexandra [of England]'s house (white, with caryatids upholding the roof of the second story) and past Isak Dinesen's (still looking unoccupied, so she must be in Rome). We left Kjeld at the Marienlyst [hotel], where he is staging a revue, and then Margrethe drove us out to Holbæk, where we lunched in an inn with the sea light brilliant. We talked and talked and compared and compared. Margrethe explained Bournonville.[85] I see that this style is direct, uncomplicated, simple, and full of strength. The Russian style is essentially theatrical (the difference between Bach and Tchaikovsky). Margrethe has enormous eyes, a Luise Rainer voice, an utterly mobile face, and hands which only a ballerina could have. She weighs about eighty pounds! (She has had the lung sickness, water in the lungs, I believe.) She sometimes has money sent by the Tuborg brewery. When in London she lives at Margot [Fonteyn]'s. Margrethe is unhappy and fatalistic, having too little to dance, but still is the Danes' greatest Bournonville dancer. She says there is no one to teach Bournonville anymore and the tradition is dying out. This must be true, for the company is definitely not as good as it was three years ago. It lacks discipline. How sad that they no longer love what they do best, but wish to do "modern" works for which they have no talent whatsoever.

We went to Tivoli, arriving just in time to see and hear the boys guard marching, and the music was so gay, the little boys so serious in their red, white, and black replicas of the King's Guard, and a lovely young white horse in the center of the procession. I saw a little blond boy in a coat the color of the summer morning sky, this child held aloft in his father's arms with fingers jammed into its ears and an expression of interest and rapture and trouble on

84. A couple, Schanne (b. 1921) and Noack (b. 1924) both danced with the Royal Danish Ballet.
85. In the mid-nineteenth century, the choreographer and teacher August Bournonville (1805–79) had made the Royal Danish Ballet into a top company. Margrethe Schanne was a major exponent of the Bournonville repertoire.

its face. I felt that way at the approach of drums: I still do. I had to gulp to keep from crying, I was so stirred. We walked about among the orderly Danish people and finally chose La Belle Terrasse, which has a dining room where time stood still circa 1910, the atmosphere of boat dining rooms with trellised walls. Shanghai Chow-Chow on the menu, and its little dishes filled with raisins, grated coconut, pickle, chutneys, pickled beets, bananas, chopped hard-boiled egg (yolks and whites separate). Also a good papadum and rice and fried chicken and curried beef, and onion and curry powder to add. The best Indian curry I have had in years.

MAY 31, 1955  Last night, the king and queen of Denmark attended the ballet, for it was Bournonville's 150th anniversary. (His great-great-granddaughter was present, but no one could point her out to me.) The queen [Ingrid] sat as today's queens sit, with great dignity, a rather pretty woman because of her blondness and clean looks, in a royal-red satin stole and a flowered formal summer gown, almost no jewels, not even earrings. The king [Frederick IX] was of the boyish variety. He sat quite bent forward, eagerly looking at [Bournonville's ballet] *Napoli* and apparently enjoying it very much. They quickly vanished in the intervals. No ceremony attended their comings and goings, unlike that attending Elizabeth's when she went to the ballet at Covent Garden— unannounced. There the audience stood at attention whenever she rose and went out or she came in. The queen of Denmark applauded wanly—token applause; the queen of England had applauded with dutiful determination. The prince consort had applauded boyishly; the king of Denmark applauded with evident pleasure. The only moment of Royal Family, old-style feeling here was when the king and queen left the Royal Box. Then a uniformed (but not splendidly uniformed) man, in blues and silver, medaled, swiftly opened the door, inclining his head. This seemed a moment of glory, but more in recollection than in the present, more reminiscent than contemporary. These are the heads of a middle-class state and they are also middle-class. Denmark is a family state, a place where middle-aged and older people should be very happy, and children joyful. I saw black velvets with added homemade lace collars, a little sailor-suited boy nestling his head in his granny's blue-brocade bosom— that kind of atmosphere of our world of thirty or forty years ago up in Harlem.

NOTE: In Copenhagen, Gray developed a fever and then a persistent streptococcal throat infection that kept him in bed for much of the next weeks. Dietrich's doctor in Paris ultimately delivered antibiotics of sufficient strength to finish it.

Meanwhile, the pair went from Denmark to Austria. Leo had arranged their tour to coincide with performing-arts festivals in Vienna and, later, The Hague. In the Austrian capital, Russian, English, and American forces still occupied sectors.

JOURNAL · JUNE 4, 1955 · VIENNA  The types here in Vienna: twee, sad, ancient persons with packs on their backs; the well-dressed, smooth-mannered people; the Viennese high-style ladies; the big city hairdos . . . Sometimes, the Vienna one expected, the magical, haunted Vienna, suddenly reveals itself— in the way a fountain falls; in the fragrance of lilacs in a carriage racing along the Graben; in Haydn played under a full moon *in der Burg* [the imperial palace]; in the lighting up of the Rathaus [city hall]—window after window, spire after spire, while a big orchestra lilts *The Blue Danube* and dancers whirl through it, and the Viennese, by the thousand, applaud; in the way the enormous crowd all went to walk along the Ringstrasse and through the courtyards of the Hofburg and peered at floodlit monuments; in figures silhouetted in windows, high up in the Burg; in the manners of the patricians behind the desk; always in the decor of the Sacher [café], always in the decor and confections at Demel, always in the baroque ecstasy of the churches, always in the endless functionaries through which one's life oozes away before one gets to do what he has come to do (the procrastination here is worse than in Italy. Viennese officialdom are old, old hands); in the moldering palaces and in the glimpses of crystal chandeliers (cascades of congealed petals and frost and raindrops and stalactites); in the waltzes discreetly tinkling at the Ambassador [hotel]; in the very delicious food; in the little winding streets and in the decorations on windows and cornices and over doorways; in the street café life; in the gardens with lilacs and peonies and chairs (white and carnival-decorated with dagging, quite different from Paris or London); in the enormous *Burg* seeming to spread over a great city; in the groups of singers, talking and emoting on the sidewalk at the Sacher or the Café Mozart; in the tinkling of a piano heard late at night; in the booming of an organ heard from the far end of a square while light faded from the sky behind the turbaned steeple; in how the clock chimed ten while the orchestra worked away at Haydn, the clock shredding it, diminishing it, for a moment. (Glamour here is still opera stars, more than stage or screen.) How quietly the enormous crowd went away, and how unlike the Vienna of Laci's dreams this city almost always has been.

JUNE 7, 1955  As I sit at breakfast, the sound of the wind—as if huge wet sheets are flapping. That's what I like about being up in our bedroom at home when there's a great wind: I feel closer to God then. When the world is still, the world is a bit frightening.

JUNE 8, 1955  The Russian soldiers walk like bruisers, after years of plodding. They look sidewise at one and seem so cut off. When I inadvertently went toward the soldiers stationed at one wing of the new Hofburg, they laughed and looked up and so did I, there seeing the Soviet sign with Lenin and Stalin shoulder to shoulder. I realized from their gesticulating and laughter that they were reminded of Lenin when they looked at me. Going away, I asked a pretty blonde in German (she was boxily, heavily dressed, but in a nice light-colored woolen tweedy suit) where to go. She laughed a lot and tossed her head and answered in Russian. Then she went to the soldiers, and they all laughed and looked at Lenin and at me. She vanished into the Soviet part of the Hof.

JUNE 12, 1955  Last night's *Intermezzo* was superb. [Soprano] Hilde Zadek gave the sort of performance Lotte Lehmann gave in *Rosenkavalier*. I have now heard eight [Richard] Strauss operas. He is the greatest and most delicate of our contemporary opera composers. I love Puccini, but Strauss seems to have written more that plays today; Puccini's repertoire is less than Strauss's. This opera is such a construction, such a delicate structure for robust and ravishing sounds. He is the composer who best knows regret. Sometimes I was reminded of [Charpentier's] *Louise*, but I like this better. Strauss knows middle age. Arabella, Christine (in *Capriccio*), the Marschallin [in *Rosenkavalier*] all are ladies who look at themselves. How imperative to sing Strauss in German, for the music absolutely follows the line of the speech, the rise and fall of the inflection. Christine sung and spoken is so similar to the inflections of those Viennese women who sit in the Sacher or at Demel chatting lightly with one another and occasionally bursting into robust words or tinkling laughter. This is charm made palpable. In *Intermezzo*, the people sometimes talk, sometimes sing, sometimes do both almost in the same word. This is so beautiful and so "real" in giving the dimension, which is always in life, between the lines. Also the episodic design, upon which it is all strung, is a fascinating one.

JUNE 21, 1955 · SALZBURG  Turning the radio on and hearing an old Ray Noble recording, I sit here with the world caved in—longing for the telephone to ring and Ela to whisper swiftly "Darling." But this can never be. And now the song ending, a female German announcer makes the world brighter. We arrived in a great storm. Salzburg is always dripping—wet and gray and dripping—but I love it here, for it is like a toy (the old town) and so comprehensible after Vienna. Although, peering into streets in the early morning and watching the Salzburgers stepping along swiftly with their baskets and briefcases—aproned and lederhosened—they seem secret—like people in stories about villages where something goes on beneath the "holiday resort" surface—something almost *Golden Bough*, ancient rites and beliefs and ceremonies. These are a reserved, carved-dark-wood sort of people.

The Mozart industry is rushing into high finance here—windows full of *Mozartkugeln* [candies], boxes and bags with Mozart in peruke on them, a Mozart *Kino* [movie theater], a Mozart Café, of course. We came upon Mozartplatz near the Residence—vast-seeming in the watery evening light. (The rain pelted all evening as we trudged. How very Italian this town is at times—the outskirts with tan and buff and cream-colored villas set as they are in Italian towns of similar size, and then the narrow streets and vast-seeming squares.) A large Mozart dominates the Mozartplatz. He is in robes and glorified to a sort of elder statesmanship, looking more judicial than musical. There is a Café Figaro—mostly U.S. servicemen—and a Mozart Bridge and a Così Fan Tutte *Konditerei* [café] run by one of the men who makes *Mozartkugeln.* There is Mozart on gingerbread and Mozart candy boxes and Mozart on braces (I saw that today) and Mozart at six shillings per in his Geburtshaus and the Mozarteum—and probably children named after him and horses and dogs after him and his works. In Salzburg, of the Mozart industry there is no end.

JUNE 24, 1955 · PARIS  In no state to make notes, but notemaking will soothe me. Gray being ill again, and the expense of all this, disheveled me. Our hotel is made for lovers who want to be clandestine and have the curtains down, the bed, and the bidet. It is a very inexpensive, very young-people's hotel; for the middle-aged or old it means disaster. Only the very young or incontestably transient could be happy there. It has the atmosphere of being the last jump, or being a hideout (despite a great profusion of flowers in the entry and the pregnant, sweet-faced, forever sleeping, fat gray-and-white cat named "Sit On"). I loathe its part of the Left Bank, as I loathe Greenwich Village and all that it signifies. That life is for the young, and I am no longer that young.

JUNE 26, 1955  I think that Clouzot [director of *Diabolique*] thought this "hotel" up. It is designed for the discomfort of its "guests." . . . But the Quarter's life is fat around us: A soprano, quite good, with a dark, rich voice, practices over and over some French art-song phrases; some little boys toot on high piercing whistles, like French trains (when I didn't know that they were made by little boys, they seemed the music of strange birds); then there are the clatterings of pot lids upon pots; the shuttings, groanings, and creakings of doors; the constant sounds and tumults of water and water closets; the tinkling of metal on glass; the wild, disheveled clatter and clanging and tumult of too many church bells all clamoring simultaneously and producing one of the most horrible discordances I have ever heard; the rattling of keys; the rutchug-putt-putt of motorcycles; and, late last night, shouting and fighting and screeching of "American go home!"

Édouard [Roditi] lives in the heart of a little market.[86] Here one sees Paris of the lower classes mixed with Bohemia, squalor, and dirty-faced children. There a supper table set out neatly with a checkered green-and-white cloth, and napkins folded primly on green-and-white plates and even a little bunch of flowers, all very precise and almost like an advertisement for country table settings. Leaning out of a garret window, naked as far as one could see, the handsome, utterly masculine torso of a man, dark and rosy and vigorous. When a young girl came to lean beside him, she in a slip, you knew that they had been in bed together, for she leaned against him with the catlike satisfied languor that means only one thing. He placed his big arm around her, drawing her

---

86. Édouard Roditi (1910–81) was a critic, translator, and Surrealist poet.

against him tightly and passively. In the trembling blue twilight, they leaned upon the casement ledge, looked down from their mansard into the narrow rue St. Gregoire, saying not a word to one another. Occasionally he brushed her hair or ear with his full, red, passionate mouth, and we did hear her sigh with pleasure and see the tremors which agitated her sleazy slip. His hand pushed down under the stuff of her slip. We could see his knuckles outlined as he pressed her breasts. They vanished into the oblong of pale yellow light. Much later he returned and again leaned, naked as far as the eye could see, against the casement ledge. Sometimes he smiled . . . and sometimes he murmured a little song, for now there was music in the rue St. Gregoire, a violin and an accordion, bal musette music, and children jumping up and down to it, and fat, worn, coarse women sitting in the doorways, enjoying the hot night air and the stenches and the music, and the young man up in his mansard close to the wavy night light and the pallid stars.

Édouard lives in his usual sloppy way. His Arab, whom he loved for seven years, was killed in a bar brawl while Édouard was abroad interpreting. When Édouard returned and discovered that the Arab had been murdered, he had a nervous breakdown, but now, after "help," he seems better than he has been in years. He writes diligently—now about Maurice Saxe, or was Herman Melville homosexual (no, says Édouard), such exotic subjects. He has a general air of doing jobs for anyone who will pay and for some who won't or can't. I thought of how he had written forty pages on how he had not met Proust.

JUNE 27, 1955   Ran off through Sunday streets yesterday to lunch with Édouard, a comte who has written a novel and edits the *mondanités* [society-news] page of a magazine, and a rather nice pickup of Édouard's. The pickup is a manservant. He said he had been *"mal baisé"* [badly laid] by Édouard, who said, "That is how it is the first time with me, always."

I bought some cherries from a cart for Gray and some for Édouard. The cart man spoke English and gave me some extra cherries for myself, because he seemed to like me. I was pleased because I needed someone to like me just then. I also bought, from a cart man, a bunch of poppies—many-colored: papery white, pink, orange (like lanterns for twenties pajama parties), red, mauve . . . all for a few cents. The market in which Édouard lives was just closing—butchers in bloody aprons pushing stands in, women with [fish-] scaly hands, the sun whipping them into jeweled hands (you could see full fathom five), and carts blazing with cherries and autumnal with apricots, like the banks of the Hudson in a good October, and everywhere families decked out in Sunday clothes and carrying packages and bags, which could only mean visiting relatives in the country, and the sun like fresh country butter.

The pickup wore a blue-purple speckled silk dressing gown and smelled of a peculiar powder or toilet water, the kind one imagines is used by certain whores in French movies and novels, like melted candied violets mixed with a more belligerent purple smell. This was so unpleasant as to be exciting, but not enticing. Certain foul smells have a potency that excites. The comte had turned-down eyebrows, liquid, brown, almond-shaped French eyes—like those to be seen in Boldini's portraits of French "society" women—also like Anaïs Nin's, but kinder. He had manners verging on tango-tea daintiness. He was slight and gay and wanted to come to America because "American boys are so wonderful," enunciated like a slow masturbation. He can come to teach a summer session at Harvard and probably will—French conversation. "In New York, there are many sailors?" he wanted to know. The pickup's name was Lucien— a very polite, fine-featured, virile type, but with a delicacy, almost female, which one finds in very virile men. He had a snub nose and smiled very prettily. He will probably marry, but this is more convenient for him now, and probably he picks up easy comforts this way. So they all spent part of the time trying to get into conversation with the naked torso of the night before. He is Spanish and wasn't interested in talking with them. The pickup was tender with the Siamese, and one could see that he and the cats were kindred.

NOTE: Marlene Dietrich saw Leo in Paris and asked for his editorial help with something she had written. He returned it with the following cover letter.

JUNE 28, 1955 • PARIS
TO MARLENE DIETRICH • PARIS

I have read the piece, as you will see, many times. I have made many minor "fixings" and some suggestions. What you have to say is pretty much there, in your rough piece. But what is not there, is your own special rhythm—the flow of imagery and the rhythm of your other writing. Take this piece, sit down at your typewriter, and let what you have written sieve through—always *hearing* it, for the sound of the phrases. Elaborate—or make it flower, as you do so beautifully. Make images—not too many, but just enough to give the prose your own color.

This piece, yours, as it now stands, is too impersonal, too "set." The reason no one else can write it for you is that, as you know, no one else is you. No one could possibly capture your inflection. The facts are all here: Sieve them through your fantasy. You can run this through your machine in one *good* day or two, at the most. Then please send me the carbon. Please try this piece, letting yourself go. Let the images go. Look in the looking glass—you will find the most nourishing image in the world there. *Merde.* ["Break a leg."]

JOURNAL • JUNE 29, 1955 Paris is one of the most uncomfortable cities in the world, unless you have lots of money. You walk blocks in search of a mailbox or chemist's shop. Comfort consists of endless cafés, but you must have money to sit in one. The city is enormous—a teeming, feverish, shrieking metropolis like New York. Yesterday, in the morning, we went out and along the rue Bonaparte and to the Seine. The people in the streets of St. Germain des Prés were like dogs in a dog show. The people took on unexpected shapes, guises, haircuts, malformations, and arrays. They became freaks. The atmosphere here in this quarter is more intensely freakish than that of Greenwich Village.

We went to ask for letters and to breakfast at the [Hotel] Quai Voltaire, sitting out in the hot sun while we ate our bread, croissants, *fraises* jam, and good butter, and sipped our not bad tea. Gray lamented the obliteration of the old parlor, now replaced by a "cocktail lounge" and a *"salon de thé."* But I do not think that this recent arrangement can dispel the charm of the little hotel, not even the constant influx of tourists mars the atmosphere there. I know that if we had been able to stop in the Quai Voltaire rather than in the flophouse, we would have been much happier with Paris.

Nevertheless, Paris seemed more beautiful in winter—the color of the city mellowed to mauves and grayness, its buildings mere lines softly looming in the fog or suddenly overwhelming and rigid on a black freezing day—a day which rings in the ears like cast iron flung down on cobblestones. That is the Paris I love, the Paris of gray and lilac washes—winter Paris, the Paris of twilights, and the Paris of late, late night and early morning—the great *places*, the Vendôme, the des Vosges, the Concorde as still as when all the world is finished, put away, and the gods have gone on to other business and other planets. No other city has this teeming vacancy, late, late at night—not London, not New York, not Vienna—this thick velvet beauty. But yesterday, even in tourist-thronged summer, Paris was frequently beautiful—a robust, thriving, blowzy beauty—a rampaging beauty—but beauty undeniably.

JUNE 30, 1955 · THE HAGUE  The sun shines hotly through the big windows of our room [at the Hotel Des Indes] above the tree-topped square. Swift impressions: utter cleanliness, dignity, the quiet beauty of the old houses (many now embassies) which surround this large green, for it is more a town green than a square. The houses seem early Georgian, and some are in fact earlier (and one has a step-front roof, which should make the heart of any New Yorker beat with joy, for at one time Nieuw Amsterdam was composed of houses precisely like this one). The houses are of brick—different tones of red—flowering into beauty at their fanlights (never have I seen such a variety, never such beautiful ones) and at their white shutters. Sometimes they are washed with buff or yellow as in Austria. They are always spotless, formal, homey, and look comfortable.

JULY 3, 1955  Claudio [Arrau, pianist] stepped out of the lift last night as I was about to go in. He had been to Paris for the day and looked at the Picasso show. He thought it wonderful; great crowds as usual, he said. Just then John Gielgud came up. He has a kind of dazzle about him—like silver ribbons, he gives a light—bright and tinselly. He is neat, slender, tall—a charmer with a heart-breaking, feather-in-the-wind smile. An air of knowing something wickedly gay and entrancing—a good-humored, high-comedy devil. How I doted on his *Hamlet* photos in *Theatre Arts* years ago, up in Richard's furnished room on West Eighty-eighth. I thought, knowing neither, that in the rain he looked like Marlene. John said they'd not had good notices in Vienna (he made comparisons with the German way of acting Shakespeare), but were an enormous success, with huge mobs at the stage door, shouting in that way peculiar to Vienna. Not many actors or theater people had come, and anything to do with officialdom had been woeful. He thinks this is so because of the different parts—for U.S., English, and Russian—among the Austrians. This makes for three complete sets of officials, each watching the other and undoing the other's work. He said that he could slap Ruth Gordon, because she was so good [in *The Matchmaker*], but always the same and such a vaudeville. He would like to see Ruth play Beatrice [in *Much Ado About Nothing*]. He envied Claudio playing the Fenice, because he has always hoped to play there. He said he could never go abroad on holiday because of finances; he had spent two months in Jamaica and that had broke him. He'd heard of a Hofmannsthal play in which he was told that he would be very good—high Edwardian life. Neither Claudio nor I had heard of this one. Claudio is marvelously read. He seemed to grow tired and pale. He wilted so. I wonder if he's well. We talked of plays and theaters. John talks in sentences—complete and punctuated.

I do love what I have experienced of Holland. The sky is magnificent, with volleys of clouds and the special gray-silver light one sees in Dutch paintings. Oh, the pleasure of seeing paintings in life as one rides to the museums and then seeing the same life in paintings. So Holland is double-imaged (like Venice), to be seen reflected in the green waters of its canals and rivers and lakes, to be seen again (as in looking glasses placed opposite one another) into perpetuity in its paintings. Between Haarlem and Amsterdam, Holland is very flat and very green and very beautiful, with trees blown all in one direction— away from the sea—and the beasts of Holland fat and placed in their green paradises. A gray-haired man sharpened his scythe at the margin of a field. He had a finely, vertically blue-striped shirt, black pants—very flared out, caught tight just below the knee, really like certain tulips, black long stockings, and bright yellow wooden shoes. The shipping cranes of Amsterdam, like raised dinosaur heads on long, long necks, over the meadows and haystacks—also factory chimneys, but none of this industrialization "hurts" the timelessness of the vistas. To keep the birds away from the fat, small, good, rich little kitchen gardens in which vegetables, fruits, shrubs, and flowers commingle, they put out tiny windmills, like those we used to have on houses in country places years ago, all busily revolving, better than rag strips or strips of newspaper or tin foil to blow in the wind.

JULY 5, 1955 John Gielgud says that Ustinov, Welles, and Laughton are all very good but not what Mrs. Patrick Campbell and that generation were. They don't fill the stage, although large. This *Much Ado About Nothing* is one of the most lucid performances I have ever heard or seen. John has directed marvelously. Of Peggy Ashcroft [touring with him], John said, when we went back: "She is not really a comedian, but she gives it such dash." Brilliant in a sort of dart-and-tickle-me manner—delightful. The audience loved it, the Dutch obviously seeing more than something in it. John, with his nut-brown makeup half off and his wig off, looked an American Indian. Many good dresses in the house—Dior, Balenciaga—good Paris haute couture. The audience stood up to cheer. John said plaintively, "I wish I could take this to America." But I suppose he won't be permitted in. He was in frisky humor after the premiere. He spoke of knowing that there are some clubs here, but he said he thought he'd better not.[87]

JULY 7, 1955 John says Edith Evans thought that she had cancer, but that wasn't so. Then she decided to do this play—awful *Nina* [by André Roussin]. She couldn't remember her lines. She became very ill and left for two weeks. She hated the other actors. Then she returned from the nursing home and got into the play's dresses, went up onstage. She just couldn't do it. Went offstage, put on her own clothes. Went onstage, stood silently there for two minutes, and left the theater. Later she said that was saying farewell to the theater. This was a magnificent exit, but she wasn't leaving. She's genuinely ill, sits in bed crying that she's lost her religion (Christian Science). If she feels that she has, she's indeed lost, for she had nothing else—no real friends save the daughter of the rich woman who sent John [Gielgud] and Edith, mysteriously, twenty-five pounds [sterling] every so often, because they had given her such pleasure. The daughter (the woman is now dead) has taken Edith off somewhere to try to help her. Edith has had only two good friends (one is Betsy [Thurman]).[88] John says she's so larky and gauche and unhappy. She even took dancing lessons because she wanted to be popular. This is all very sad, when you realize that she is the greatest living actress on the English-American stage. She has been unhappy in her work for years and loathes the idea of getting old, character parts.

John's trying to behave. This is just as sad as Edith. He says that if he hadn't gone on the stage to perform two years ago—that night—he could never have acted again.

JULY 8, 1955 Diana [Adams] came after dancing [Balanchine's excerpts from] *Swan Lake*. She says the stage is so impossibly narrow that she can almost not do an extension on it. She looked younger and happier and alto-

---

87. In England in 1953, Gielgud had been arrested and convicted of soliciting sex in a public restroom. It made a major scandal.
88. Betsy Thurman (d. 1974), the actress Elizabeth Farrar, was also a good friend of Leo and Gray (and the grandmother of Uma).

gether like one of those pink-yellow sort of tea roses just opened a little bit—and after what she's been through. She loathed the Left Bank but Hugh [Laing] made her live there when they were married.[89] At dinner we went to the Bali Scheveningen, and there the *rijsttafel* was elaborate, including baked bananas, fried peanuts, and all sorts of dark meats in darker sauces and something which was surely broiled Brillo, but delicious, and we made jokes about Fania being in the kitchen, for this is the sort of food the Van Vechtens tend to—and how delicious it is. During this she asked sort of tentatively and a little tremulously about whether Hugh had a success and about Nora [Kaye], and she said how happy she was about it all when we told her that they had. Diana has a good heart, and although they all gave her a rough time, she finds it impossible to be mean about them, and really does wish them well. She says that Maria [Tallchief] arrived twenty pounds heavier and seems to be suffering some sort of private grief and has become strident and loud—very vulgar and also very discontented—what with all she has, technique and success—again like Edith Evans.[90]

JULY 10, 1955  John's *Lear* too hysterical in the way a young man is hysterical—too fretful and pettish. Lear needs to be heavier, to fill out the vast tides, not to be a cockleshell upon them. Lear is overwhelmed by the tides; he is also their instrument. Through him they speak. Also this Noguchi[-designed] production is too desiccated, too Japanese. There is no reason to play Lear in an abstract Japanese decor and in a lion's wig and beard, both of which got into John's way continuously. There is nothing epic about this portrayal. You never once feel sorry for Lear.

JULY 14, 1955 • EN ROUTE TO BRUSSELS  Isn't it horrifying, to discover at forty-one that if I had my life to live over again I would not have lived these last seven years as I have lived them? I have had much to be joyful with and about, but this evening, because joy has collapsed, I see again even more relentlessly that the cost has been prodigious. I must be tired, for I have been able to take outbursts over nothing for what they were—nothing. But this evening's outburst seems to have struck me dumb and sent me into some awful deep place. No blood, no pain, no visible scars, only inability to make conversation and isolation, in which I feel secure, but uneasy. It is not in my nature to be still like this—silent—and it is not in my nature to talk when I have been deeply wrenched. In these last seven years I have been given much pleasure, but the cost has been too great. I have indulged myself in a luxury, and now there is no

89. Diana Adams had been married (1947–53) to the dancer Hugh Laing (1911–88), a principal at Ballet Theatre in the forties, who created many dramatic roles in ballets by Antony Tudor, his lover for some fifty years.
90. Maria Tallchief (b. 1925) danced with New York City Ballet (1947–65) and was married to George Balanchine from 1946 to 1952.

way out. I should never have remained, for in essence that is what I have done. This was unfair to the other person from the very beginning, and I have only myself to blame for permitting my masochism to be so bountifully nourished.

NOTE: After a day's wandering in Bruges, Leo and Gray learned they had missed the last train back to Brussels and were stranded. Finding no hotel room, they finally stopped a policeman to request help and were offered beds in the city's jail. In a nearby cell, a drunken older man, arrested by the police, died during the night.

JOURNAL • JULY 17, 1955 • BRUSSELS Each of our journeys has its mysterious heart-cracking and probing experience: in Italy, at Caserta, a little lost dog; in Belgium, at Bruges jailhouse, a drunken man suddenly dead. I said my prayers and asked God to help his soul. I returned to saying my prayers after the little dog in Caserta. That dog made me miserable for days.[91] This man seems to have some significance yet unrevealed to us. I am sad for him, and in this sadness is anguish for myself, for all of us, but I am not undone as I was by the helplessness of the dog, and our helplessness to do anything save run away on the bus and be miserable at the unjustness and cruelty of the world and at the trust of the little beast.

The man was conclusively dead. We saw him drunken and—not knowing this—dying. He probably did not even know that he was dying—or that he died. . . . The abruptness of this death and the pathos of an old man, dying drunk—with roars and vast sighs and writhings and tumult—on a miserable cot in a room behind a door (half glass and half wood, like one leading to the yard at home) . . . the pathos of this, the immediacy . . . this must surely have a deep, still, somewhat submerged effect on us.

All of my dealings with people in the streets have been good here. Only trying to get off a train, coming into Brussels, I had to push men out of the way. They insisted on getting on. I lost my temper and, for the first time in my life, shoved a man in the chest and made a mob stand back. I do not think that travel improves manners or graciousness or any of the amenities. It broadens one's comparisons and enriches one's experience and appreciation, but it is hell for the temper and the everyday morale.

NOTE: Marlene Dietrich met Leo in Belgium and then flew Leo and Gray to London round-trip to see her perform at the Café de Paris.

JOURNAL • JULY 22, 1955 • LONDON The words which I thought as I watched Marlene's performance were: insolence, efficiency, token. Also she seemed

---

91. GF: "Walking to Caserta, we met this small tan dog, lots of terrier in him. He danced on his hind legs at meeting us and then accompanied us for hours. No one knew to whom he belonged. At the end of the afternoon, we had to board a bus, keeping him off, and he stood watching, apparently brokenhearted, as the bus pulled off."

during the earlier part to be rushing. And she was, for she had to go on to a big ball at which the queen was to be present and where she, Marlene, was to sing. Before the show, she looked scraped, tired, emaciated. Then on she came, looking incredibly youthful and beautiful—especially during the latter half and dressed in tails. The audience's enthusiasm gave her youth and beauty, nourished it until she blossomed visibly before our eyes. Her range of gestures is a limited one. Her voice, save when she sings in German, is even more of a freak than ever before. But she makes you feel that she is the woman of the world's lewd dreams, the unobtainable always beckoning and promising, but insolently. Her accent is more marked during this performance than it is in her everyday life. She removes the glitter drapery for one set of encores, has the wind machines turned on, and seems even younger when less clothed. Everything she does she does camp, save the real heartfelt—by her heart— bits. She says to the audience: See how good I am? She kids the audience and her songs, but not ever underlining that she is better than her material—like Pearl Bailey and Paula Laurence do.[92] When Marlene sits or rather strides a chair and growls "One for the Road" she is very beautiful in two sexes simultaneously. This is a performance, in this number, on a par with Judy Garland's at the Palace. Sometimes she's fun. Always she's beautiful. Too much she makes token gestures and expressions. And always she is fascinating to watch and so very professional. I have never seen a performer take bows in such an efficient way.

JULY 23, 1955  A bright Saturday morning. We came up Piccadilly in a pale gray mist—like fine French suede. Looking up from our deep and scattered chortling—sometimes howling—could it be called talk?—we saw dawn standing like still, pallid pewter, waiting for life and color from a somewhat vagrant sun. We left Marlene at six in the morning, left her pointing to the vastness of the egg-yolk-colored bed Oliver had designed so optimistically for her, and crying hoarsely, "I lay here, in this small, little, tiny corner."[93] She ran down the long passage of the penthouse to help us out. Her white-trimmed cloak, which created the sensation at Las Vegas and Blackpool and the Café de Paris, lay under a dustsheet, on the bed we should have occupied, and the "naked" dress was folded like Medea's fatal veil on a large case top. So we came away in the dawn light and were asleep by seven, and I was awake, feeling fine, at eight.

92. During the previous theatrical season, the singer and comedian Pearl Bailey (1918–90) had starred in Capote and Arlen's failed musical *House of Flowers*. Paula Laurence (1913–2005), the actress and singer married to producer Charles Bowden, was a friend whom Leo first met in 1936, backstage during her performances in the Mercury Theatre production of *Horse Eats Hat* .
93. Stage designer Oliver Messel (1904–78) had decorated a suite for Dietrich in London's Dorchester Hotel.

**PAL JOEY AND MARLENE**    *Marlene knew who she was, who the public thought she was, who she could have been, and sometimes succeeded in making [herself] believe all about herself: "Cohn, at Columbia, was casting* Pal Joey, *and he asked me would I come and see him, because he had a wonderful part in* Pal Joey *for me. And at that time nobody was offering me any wonderful parts, so I went to see him. So he said to me, 'Marlene, you play this part, you will be a bigger star than ever.' So you know what he wanted me to play . . . ? He wanted me to play that woman who was always chasing after that awful boy called Pal Joey. I said to him, 'Harry, who would believe that me, Marlene Dietrich, would chase after any man?' And I went away and that was that." Actually, who would believe that Marlene would chase after any man, or that Marlene would be a woman attached to a telephone. . . . Who would have believed the Marlene on the screen would be a real woman? Of course, she was a real women, any number of real women. (*1993)

# THEY HAVE ALL HURRIED AWAY

NOTE: Leo and Gray went to the opening of the Lyric Theatre of Chicago's 1955 season, where Callas would sing *I Puritani* and *Il Trovatore* and Renata Tebaldi performed *Aïda* and *La Bohème*. Afterward, Leo returned to New York, while Gray stayed through Thanksgiving with his aunt and grandmother in Glenview, Illinois.

NOVEMBER 5, 1955 • CHICAGO

**TO RICHARD HUNTER • PARIS**

You would have been muchly amused. I did two television shows and four radio shows, and headwaiters in the Pump Room asked for my autograph, and elevator boys asked wasn't I a moving-picture actor or one of those opera stars—and, of course, I've been lapping it all up, ham that I am. It has been bliss being in a "foreign" city, in a hotel room alone and being able to leave all the lights on and taking cabs everywhere—because *Mademoiselle* was paying—and Brigitta is here (because she is doing a Monteverdi at the opera) and Alicia Markova and Callas, of course, whom I adore with a real star-smashed, little-boy passion. Even when she sings making ugly sounds, she is fabulous to watch. What a marvelous stage personality she is. She knows exactly how to handle the audience, whether it is 4,000 (in the huge *Welt* of an opera house here) or, one, me in a little room. I do hope that you can meet her one day, because I think she will give you that Gone-Garbo feeling we once had. Did I write and say that that one [Garbo] had pounced on me a week ago, at the Gunthers, and wrung my hand? I couldn't say a thing because she had aged so, and I resented having now to see this line-meshed and leathery face along with the beauty of Camille.

**JOURNAL • NOVEMBER 6, 1955 • CHICAGO** The revelation of Maria Callas's art—her acting—or stage-presence artistry: No stage personality can be truly great unless, in the beholding of that personality on the stage, one receives not only the impact of the present but also the past is revealed concurrently. Maria is a great example, for in viewing her Leonora [in *Il Trovatore*] last night, I felt (and so did Brigitta) that here was the [French tragedienne] Rachel we had glimpsed in spotted representations, in written descriptions. Here was the classic tradition in stage art, at its present greatest. I told Maria this, this morning, and she laughed and said she didn't know what she did onstage. But this is perhaps what she believes and does have happen to her. There can be no art as powerful as hers without the art of knowing what one is doing and then transcending that knowledge and that technique.

NOVEMBER 7, 1955   I have been joying in and noting in *Jean Santeuil* since 4:15 a.m., grudging every word because I shall never again have this first delight.[1] It is seeing the chrysalis grow more fragile as one reads—sometimes so transparent, so filled with the beat and stir of the life within it, that the reader is able to discern the minute flutterings and stirrings, to catch the vibrations, dim but suddenly flashing, of color. Is this to be a great luna moth or a peacock butterfly or a curious amalgam of both, not a hybrid but a new breed? We know the answer, for in this marvelous, rare instance, we have had the full, vast spread of the creature, seen in all of its unique colors, known it to be part luna, part peacock. In *Jean Santeuil*, Proust works with a whitewash brush, in frequently crude strokes and slashes. In *Remembrance*, the brushes used are the finest sable, the most expensive in the world, so sensitive that the fiercest storms are minutely impaled. Here we move gradually through milky Whistlers of damp fog and starry lights, glowing sharply in the blue-white, skim milk light. This is Proust's sketchbook and should be exhibited with Degas's and Manet's and Saint-Aubin's (the one in Chicago).

Gray said, "No one sits in circles anymore." The horror when I see that guests have formed a circle in the back parlor. This usually means constraint and formality. Spontaneity falls panting for breath, and the air of free exchange, on the flowered carpet. The flowers instantly become garlands sent to a funeral.

NOVEMBER 19, 1955   Maria is the most gimpy-legged Butterfly, but indisputably the greatest singing actress in the world. Then her Medea, the greatest performance, but quite unseen by an audience, save that few lurking backstage, when the process servers (eight) and the U.S. Marshal advanced on her. Claudia [Cassidy, Chicago critic] with her atmosphere of a silent-film star (this is her relationship to Katherine Anne [Porter]) said, "For three and one half hours I sat through her Butterfly, and then to hold Medea in your arms for half an hour!" Maria is so similar to Marlene in ego, in detail, but Marlene sells beauty and style; Maria sells style and the greatest artistry.[2]

---

1. Marcel Proust had written the novel *Jean Santeuil* before *Remembrance of Things Past*, but it was published posthumously in 1952.
2. After singing *Madama Butterfly* on November 17, 1955, Callas was presented with a summons. A former manager, Eddie Bagarozy, had sued her. Callas excoriated the process servers in operatic style.

**TO RICHARD HUNTER** • NAPLES

I went down to pick up the newspaper at about seven a.m., two mornings ago, and then I got some gramophone records to take up. I was walking slowly up the stair from the parlor floor to the next, when suddenly, I guess, my slipper caught, and down I fell, hard, and hit my head on the edge of a step, cutting my face from the corner of my left eye, about an inch diagonally away from it. The amount of blood was terrifying, but after the shock, thinking that I had to do something about it, because no one else was going to since I was all alone, I gathered my records and slowly mounted higher. On the stair to the bedrooms, I realized that I was going to faint, so I dragged me up to the bathroom to get smelling salts—all the while bleeding like a stuck pig. I reached the smelling salts and then everything happened at once. I tried to get to the telephone, thinking: Even if anyone comes, he can't get in right away, because the chain is on the door. The oddest thing was that I wanted to get to the telephone to call you, even though I knew that you were far away, but I was going to call you—probably at [our old apartment on] Eighty-eighth Street (do not mention this). I heard quite a big crash, and I thought: I never got rid of all those letters. Also: I never remade my will. Also: Isn't this a funny thing. At this moment, I felt that it was touch-and-go as to whether I was fainting or maybe dying. Also: Suddenly I have to go to the bathroom. The next moment everything seemed marvelously clear and peaceful. Then I came to and found myself in the most awful mess of blood and filth. (I didn't know that the bowels became uncontrollable sometimes when one faints, did you?) The bedside table had turned over, and the books fell everywhere, but miraculously nothing was broken. So, after reviving, I crept into the bathroom and cleaned everything up. I guess I dragged myself while trying to reach the telephone. I didn't quite know what to do about stopping the bleeding. So I trusted my instinct and made a mixture of cool water and iodine and used it, and it hurt fearful, but I told myself that I was a grown forty-one-year-old man, who had to accustom himself to taking care of himself. Anyway, I climbed into bed at last, and the bleeding went on until about three o'clock, when Poppa, Jerry, and Janet [Lerman] arrived.[3]

When Momma heard about this, she announced: "It is a well-known fact that no one passes from consciousness when they are alone." I inquired where she had learned this "well-known fact," but got no information. She got angry when I reminded her that she frequently called frantically saying that she had just fainted and that no one was in the house. So now I have an interesting wound, which I don't think will leave a scar—if it does it will only be like a little wrinkle. But it was all quite a shock. Why do most of my accidents involve

---

3. Leo's brother Jerry had two children, Janet (b. 1952) and Nancy (b. 1954).

my head? It is very frightening to know that you are becoming unconscious and that you are all alone—a little glimpse of death, which at the last moment, before I went under, showed me a lovely, calm, nonpainful state. Could that be death—with no waking up in a welter of blood and excrement? Maybe. I wonder whether you had a flash that something was happening?

JANUARY 9, 1956 • NEW YORK CITY

**TO RICHARD HUNTER • CAIRO**

Don't tell a soul but I'm about to try to adapt *Jane Eyre* for [the Irish actress] Siobhan McKenna. I'm doing it with Stanley Young (remember when we designed Regency dresses for a Byron play he wrote—a bad play?) because if I do it with someone I'll do it. Maybe it could open in London. Please pray that this really comes off and brings some funds, because then I can get out of the fashion-magazine world. I think I would go to The Hague for eight months and live in the Hotel Des Indes (this is a blissful dream) and write my book, now titled "Lament for a Potted Palm."[4]

A doctor says that I must cut all my activities in half because I have a common complaint—a spastic colon—and this means that I am too tense and too rushed and do too much (all of which we all have known ever since . . .). So he says I will be a very sick old man if I do not take precautions now. My grandpa Goldwasser died from this complaint (or complications caused by it), but he died when he was about eighty-two. I am not worried, and I am trying to slow down (hoho).

Are you on a barge with peacock-feather fans fanning you? Keep away from strange asps.

A Christmas card arrived from Leningrad, from little old Truman. Such a curious postcard with a girl, very blond and in matching accessories—red-and-white banded knitted scarf, hat (pointy), and mittens. She's blue-eyed and carries boxes of what could be candy—a round fruitcake tin and a sort of bunched-up package—maybe a babka—or an H-bomb . . . who knows. He wrote that we would "love this city" and the snow and black palaces and that he was freezing. His rich friends now call him Bunny. Gray said, "I guess Bunny's freezing his little ole cottontail off."

**JOURNAL • JANUARY 26, 1956 • NEW YORK CITY** What's bad about me? I am dilatory. I have a Jewish conscience—an equivocal goading thing at best. I am overgregarious; this could be looked upon as vanity—and the overweening necessity of nourishing this vanity. I have an unkind tongue, which means an envious heart. I have understanding but am too sloppy in applying it. I cannot say no purely. I seek the easy way and am spendthrift in almost all things. I

---

4. Playwright Stanley Preston Young (1906–75) and Leo did complete a *Jane Eyre* script, but it appears never to have been staged.

make enemies or inimical situations for silly reasons. I am thoughtless—and very selfish—although I do not seem this to many energy-blinded people. I rankle and do not speak out. When I do, everything is disproportionate.

FEBRUARY 15, 1956 • NEW YORK CITY
**TO RICHARD HUNTER • ATHENS**

Gray is currently jealous of Mina Curtiss, and that's funny because he should be pleased that I see her maybe once every ten days or so and not others. She's so harmless and fills a certain need, but not the one Eleonora filled. I like being with Mina because she amuses me and feeds me and talks and I can think about all sorts of other things and she makes no demands and is wonderfully well read.[5]

Gray's poppa is better, but mine isn't and I worry about that, and what will happen if anything happens. I know what will happen . . . unless his insurance is not borrowed on heavily. I am sure that it is. He had an attack last Saturday night, because he behaved like a hog.

FEBRUARY 29, 1956 • DANBURY, CONNECTICUT
**TO RICHARD HUNTER • ATHENS**

The ballet (New York) opened, not too auspiciously, this evening. The pleasantest thing was Mrs. [Eleanor] Roosevelt (not dancing) who held out her hand to me, saying, "Good evening, Mr. Lerman . . ." etc., and I met her over nine years ago, briefly. What an extraordinary memory. Her hair is still fair and she looks Dutch-Scottish, holding herself erectly. She has a very warm, friendly, understanding hand, and a smile that comes from way inside—a golden smile—quite obliterating her homeliness.

MARCH 11, 1956 • NEW YORK CITY
**TO RICHARD HUNTER • ATHENS**

I am peeping at *Richard III*, the movie having its television world-premiere or, rather, American debut. This is the Gielgud scene—and he is marvelous and curiously beautiful and so like pictures of [the great British actress] Ellen Terry. I wanted to compare. With this sort of movie, if it is made with the crystal screen in mind, there will be no reason to leave one's house. For it is so wonderful to have this in this house, to hear the lines and be able to think about them.

The Whitney sought Gray out last week and bought a drawing [*A Saprophytic Landscape*] for the big spring show. They even had a special meeting so that they could buy it for a high price ($125). He is the luckiest boy. Things come to him.

---

5. Gray found her overbearing. What Mina Curtiss thought of him is not recorded, but she never invited Gray to her home.

APRIL 23, 1956 • NEW HAVEN, CONNECTICUT
**TO RICHARD HUNTER • ATHENS**

I am on the train to New Haven, rushing through a bright, sunny day. I just wanted to say happy day, now that we are in the twentieth year. The only thing I mind about age is sickness. I loathe that and going to doctors and taking medicines every day and always being apprehensive of pain—and being frightened when pains come. All that I hate, but age itself I like.

People have been dying—not close to us people, but the kind I saw at theater and in restaurants, knew professionally, and liked. It's so odd to see one's world—the clutter of it and the endless smiles and greetings, and those to whom you do not have to explain about who you are—dropping away. But spring is trying to burst through, although winter lingers.

MAY 22, 1956 • PHILADELPHIA
**TO RICHARD HUNTER • ROME**

Here I sit in the Bellevue-Stratford in Philadelphia, where I have blissfully been for two days and now two nights while [Gray's mother] Maebelle arrived. I haven't had one unhappy moment and not one sour face nor one complaint nor had to live by anybody's notions save my own—and what peace—it's wonderful. How do men manage to stay married to the same woman for all the years without busting out? Tomorrow Maebelle and Gray come here, so she can see Philadelphia, and then we return to New York. I take them to a preview of *High Society* (Crosby, Grace Kelly—the musical made from *Philadelphia Story*) and to supper at Michael's Pub. Then on Wednesday, for my birthday, I take them to lunch at the Ambassador, to the new revue at the Phoenix, and to supper at Luchow's. On Thursday, I take them to dinner at the Canton Village or the Three Crowns and to *The Matchmaker* and probably to supper at the Plaza. Then I think, if I can find the money, I'll depart again—maybe back here (I write so easily here, and it's so quiet) to wait out Maebelle's departure. It's heaven not answering the telephone. Ah me—I never was meant to be a parent and probably not even a loving mate in any square sense of that designation.

I bought loads of 10-cent books—a real binge, like years ago. I'll get hell when they begin to arrive, but I thought: If I spend so much on Maebelle, I should have something tangible.

NOTE: Instead of returning to Philadelphia, Leo went to stay with Mina Curtiss.

JOURNAL • MAY 27, 1956 • WILLIAMSBURG, MASSACHUSETTS  Mina has the life—the time part of it and the money to keep the time. The bliss of not being interrupted for five hours at a time! I do almost nothing save revel in it— bathing in it, hoping that this immersion, despite its brevity, will wash me clean for a long time. Oh, the bliss of being here, in bed, in the early morning and knowing that any problems are not mine. As much as I love sharing a bed,

I do, honestly, wish that I could have the early mornings alone in it. This is my best work time. And Gray doesn't wake early—nor graciously—and why should he?

MAY 29, 1956 • NEW YORK CITY
**TO RICHARD HUNTER** • LAUSANNE, SWITZERLAND

I am now on a little old-fashioned-feeling train chugging southward—homeward—from four heavenly days with Mina. She lives about twenty miles from Northampton—such pretty, unspoiled country and not frightening or spooky. That is the house you would love to have—mostly very old, very American—very beautiful, clean, and fragrant—with six old-fashioned country servants, a fine stream with beavers busily building dams, bees, such quantities of books, heavenly furniture, eighteenth- and (early) nineteenth-century American and English paintings, and dozens of unpublished Proust letters and photographs. Sometimes the feeling was very like 150 Highland [in Middletown], when I first went there with you. I worked marvelously, because I woke at 5:30 a.m. every morning. Mina never appears until 11 or 11:30, so I sat in my four-poster and breakfasted on strawberry jam. Everything is homegrown and homemade. I scribbled and read and never worried about one thing all the four days. She never intruded or tried to make me do anything—and she did me great good and gave me a birthday present of the Gavarni illustrated (very rare) *Camille*, the earliest edition, and some Proust photos (and you know how very much that pleased me) and an eighteenth-century cookery book (the best I have seen) and a Victorian cookery and household book. She's half-finished with her huge life of Bizet. I read it, making notes for my own fell purposes, and it's very good—you know how related this all is to Proust. But best of all, she said so much, so wisely about my would-be books, and that was the greatest help. She was, I am sure, the good teacher former Smith [College] students always say she was. I know that she seems overbearing, but she's so very good for me. Since Eleonora died, I haven't had any female who talked to me this way—and since you have become a traveler I haven't had anyone, actually, to give my life the continuity it seems to need. I love Gray—but, as you know, this is more the conventional, hysterical, husband-wife business than I ever realized could happen between a couple of boys. I missed you these days because so many things to see and eat and feel were related to our common past, a past I shall never have with Gray because he is younger and temperamentally unsuited to much of it. We were also unsuited to one another in many ways—but we were growing up together. Gray adores me—although this would be hard to believe sometimes from his behavior, and he will always be in my life because I guess he is my child—and I do love him.

**JOURNAL** • MAY 31, 1956 • PHILADELPHIA Thinking about Maebelle and Gray, how very similar he is to her, in so many views—minor but making for misery in his relationships with people. She is more outgoing—seemingly. He must have the misanthropic streak from his father and that side. But the vanity and prestige needs, the scorn must come from Maebelle. The disdain of others' frailty and of the need of people to make believe they are what they are not, that need he so seems to despise, comes from his father, I suspect. I should see his father, but I dread that. The temper (Maebelle has pique, not temper) [comes] from his father. The genius part of Gray—that is unaccountable. I do know that I am deeply grateful for those thousands of miles between Maebelle and us.

AUGUST 6, 1956 • NEW YORK CITY

**TO RICHARD HUNTER • LONDON**

I am writing a letter to you, which you will read looking out, perhaps, over Cadogan Square, where Wilde was taken, and where I walked in a January long ago and so caught my death—but as I remember, I did not die.[6] Everyone, almost everyone else seems to have picked up and gone away. Alice now [dead on July 19], and that undid me, but not like Eleonora or Valeska [Imbs]. Now they seem to be more on that side than on this. So I sit here scribbling away to you, where my heart is—in a green, dusty, and stripped square—more imagined than actual. I see you in rooms—all gray in the rainy London light—wavery and subaqueous. Here my room is also beneath a tumultuous wave. The tide is running high in all the treetops from here to Sankaty Light, and great moon-eyed fish nuzzle the windowpanes. Little Gray wrenched his back, suddenly, as we hoisted a heavy filing cabinet. He is flat upon a pad of heat—a lily blossom awaiting confirmation of its ethereality from some sparkling-eyed frog with the airs and fretful graces of a prince—my, how literary the light is in this room. With the windows open, I feel the sea buffeting this crumble-house, but with them closed and clamped, nightmares prowl, perceiving in the clasps intimations of victory. In each of us terror and triumph await animation. I cannot bear for friends to go away. I cannot even bear walk-ons to walk on and on and on and so over the edge of the world. Have we ever known one single lovely person to become more lovely or even lovable because of having put on infinity? No. Time does not fonder anything—especially absence. What slothful fibs proverbs and old saws are.

AUGUST 7, 1956 • NEW YORK CITY

**TO RICHARD HUNTER • LONDON**

Gondor is besieged and Pippin is listening intently, standing behind the throne of Denethor, for Faramir has at last returned. Gandalf rescued him

6. Leo's January 1951 stay in London had ended with him in bed for several days with a "Norwegian Rat Flu."

from orcs, I think. The Great War is on and the tides of Darkness everywhere. Aragorn & Co. have come up through the Paths of the Dead. So you see what I am about, in this flickery morning. Oh–that amazing Mr. Tolkien. I have a copy of volume three for you waiting here. Maybe this will lure you faster. I do not doubt that Mr. Tolkien has immense fountains of lovely hair gushing from his mothy ears. That is only logical, for surely he could not be the chronicler of *The Lord of the Rings* without hairy, lovely moth ears.

AUGUST 8, 1956 • NEW YORK CITY

**TO RICHARD HUNTER • LONDON**

I must tell you something that will possibly upset you a bit. Touche is dead. Teddy [Griffis], Alice, Touche—and before that Valeska and Bravig [Imbs] and Marian and Harry Dunham.[7] So almost all of that world gone and nothing to explain it—nothing. This happened in Vermont at four a.m. yesterday morning, without any warning—save what seemed an indigestion attack—and then he was dead. His heart stopped. Harry [Martin] had been with Touche in Vermont.[8] But it is Ken [Elmslie] who will suffer the most, for he has nothing save his future and this little high-time past. I have always had the rich possibility of you not gone out of this world, but poor Ken—his one golden egg he furnished to this basket—and lo—not even the fabric of the basket will remain. I think only the energy remains at large—certainly not the intelligence. Sometimes so intense is the energy that, granted certain conditions, this energy can even assume shape, become visible, but not palpable—and of course, the energy can be wicked or good and used by angels or devils.

How they have all hurried away—one chasing after the other—that world of little friends. How eagerly they ran to catch up. Now I must stop—what with Gray's illness and this, which has picked me up and set me to flapping like Monday washday sheets to beat the world and fly the wind to scorn. This is also bad for Rut. No matter how they fought, he inevitably helped her. So Touche is dead—passionately dead, I am sure—and rebelliously—and as ever unable to resist an invitation—and mostly not too sure of keeping it on that date and at that moment.

7. Theodora "Teddy" Griffis (1916?–56), of a prominent investment-banking family, a lesbian, had married and divorced John Latouche. Latouche's friend the photographer and film editor Harry Dunham (1910?–43) was killed in World War II. Dunham's wife Marian (1889?–1951) then died from polio on a transatlantic crossing.
8. "Touche took handfuls of quieting pills and goblets of brandy—Did Harry kill him?" *Journal, February 22, 1971.* Leo speculated that something untoward was involved in this death, particularly because Harry Martin (a painter who was one of Latouche's lovers) admitted burning a bloody mattress. An exhumation and autopsy, demanded by Latouche's relatives, confirmed a coronary thrombosis.

**TO RICHARD HUNTER** • LONDON

It is so fantastically hot that even the blank-faced full moon is vaporous, trailing heat clouds all about like fading beauties do veils, and probably for much the same reason. What happens to the moon as one grows older? (How exact that phrase—grows older is precisely what happens.) It becomes and is all things— fear—science—beauty—but not the symbol of passion so frequently confused with love when one is very young.

I went out into the garden. Looking up at the skies decorated with still, leafy branches, pricked and primped with stars, the moon—her highness—so collected—so superior—so round—I could not resist admiring her assurance. Then I saw that Mrs. Blum's bedroom was lighted. Off they went last Thursday, and those lights had been running since then—for four days and four nights! I could cheerfully strangle them. So much for the moon.[9]

**MARLENE AND MARIA**   *Marlene was curious about Maria, and Maria was curious about Marlene. So one Sunday afternoon, some days before Maria's first* Norma *in her first season at the Metropolitan Opera house, two ladies came to meet each other in our parlor.*[10] *Maria arrived first, attended by her husband and her father. Maria was perfectly dressed, as usual, this time in a very plain, beautifully cut black afternoon frock made by expert Italian hands. It was ornamented, in exactly the right spot, high on her left side, with an intricate diamond brooch. Maria had no ancestral jewels, but her genius acquired them. She was hatted neatly. As she sat down she drew immaculate white kid gloves from her hands. On her fingers were at least two severely cut diamond rings— nothing ostentatious, but they spoke for themselves. She folded her hands neatly in her lap and looked like a very sweet young girl. I thought: This is a dangerous situation.*

*Doorbell rang, and Marlene came in. Marlene had chosen to be sportive. She was all done up in tweeds. She was very jaunty. She was very hail-Maria-well-met. She relaxed into a corner on the same sofa on which Maria sat and extended endless legs. Maria, obliquely, looked at the legs and smiled. Marlene laughed. Both girls seemed to be getting on very well. There was a finishing-school atmosphere about that sofa. They fell to chatting.*

*Marlene was curious about Maria's career. Marlene, I could see, was eager to give advice. Mother Marlene could never resist taking over. Soon I heard, while the teacups tinkled politely, Marlene say, "But, liebling, you should*

9. Leo and Gray had rented out the top two floors of 1453 to a psychologist and her female lover. Later in 1956, they took the entire house for themselves.
10. This tea occurred on October 21, 1956, eight days before Callas opened the Metropolitan Opera's season in Donizetti's *Norma*.

*really not have such hair. . . ." My heart sank. I heard Marlene say, "But,*
*liebling, I know exactly the right hair for you. . . ." Maria just sat stirring her*
*tea. Nothing was coming from Maria, except a look in my direction. Marlene*
*noted no signals whatsoever. "And, liebling, I will make for you the most won-*
*derful thing. It will preserve your voice. I will make for you beef tea. . . ." I knew*
*Marlene's beef tea. I could have thrown up on the spot. I could see in Maria's*
*eyes a gleam of amusement. Marlene could see nothing except Marlene-being-*
*mother. She inched slowly toward Maria, put her hand around Maria's shoul-*
*der, and said, "I will help you. Leave it to me. I will fix your hair. I will see that*
*your voice is all right. I will bring you beef tea." Marlene moved back into her*
*corner. Maria sat in her corner. Both ladies sipped their tea. Marlene was radi-*
*ant. Maria was amused. Maria by and by said, "I think I must go now because*
*I must preserve everything for Norma." Mr. Meneghini rose. Her father rose.*
*They had said nothing throughout this scene. Maria got up. The gentlemen*
*helped her into her furs. Maria bent toward Marlene. Marlene got up and*
*kissed her on both cheeks, and Maria went away with her father and her hus-*
*band. Marlene sat down and said, "She doesn't have much conversation, does*
*she? . . ."*

*And then by and by I had a call from Maria. "Your friend Miss Dietrich was*
*here. She brought me this awful stuff. What should I do with it?" I said, "Throw*
*it out and say you liked it very much." "Then she will bring me more," she said.*
*"No," I said, "she won't."*

*A little over a month later, the night of Maria's first* Lucia di Lammermoor,
*at the Met, I stood in the wings just before the mad scene. There was no one on*
*the stage at all. In a faded, dusty, shimmering, paraselene light, Maria stood at*
*the top of a long flight of steps, miserably moving to and fro, her right hand mov-*
*ing nervously up and down her left arm. She moved incessantly, a kind of caged*
*movement, then the flute struck its note, and Maria, who really could not see*
*where she was going, the voice pouring out into the vast darkness of the audito-*
*rium, carefully flowed down all those steps, not at all a human but an apparition*
*with a disembodied voice making humanity of abstract sound, making form out*
*of madness, clarifying beastliness.*[11]

*Later in her dressing room she sat exhausted but smiling, and when she saw*
*me she lifted up from a low stool by her side a hank of hair. "Your friend Miss*
*Dietrich brought me this. She thought I should wear it in the mad scene. What*
*do I do with it?" I looked at it and I said, "You keep it. You keep it forever. You*
*cherish it. . . ."*

*Marlene and Maria never became friends; they existed in a state of mutual*
*respect.* (1993)

---

11. "The audience so devastated, that I could hear their horror, although not a sound came
from them—the soundless shriek of frozen terror." *Journal, May 20, 1984.*

## Chinese Supper for Maria Callas

NOVEMBER 18, 1956 • 1453 LEXINGTON AVENUE

Maria Callas (plus 7)
Dorle Soria
Dario Soria
Soria's sister [Faie Joyce]
Soria's brother-in-law [William Joyce]
John Hershberger
Carmel Snow
John Woolford
Ania Dorfmann
Francis Robinson
Ruth Yorck
Reginald Allen
Helen Howe
Felicia Bernstein
Leonard Bernstein
Thomas Schippers
Tilly Losch
Samuel Barber
Lillian Gish
Viveca Lindfors
George Tabori
Jennie Tourel
H. Gross
Gian Carlo Menotti
Celeste Holm
Goddard Lieberson
Lili Darvas
Stark Young
Nancy Wilson Ross Young
Philippe Jullian

Contessa Castelbarco [Wally Toscanini]
Roger Stevens
Mrs. Roger Stevens
Arthur Laurents
Tom Hatcher
George Weidenfeld
Lincoln Kirstein
Jean Stein
William Faulkner
George London
Mrs. George [Nora] London
Cathleen Nesbitt
Janet Rhinelander Stewart
Rouben Ter-Arutunian
Leontyne Price
Gid Waldrup
Leueen McGrath
George Kaufman
Simon Burgim
Julie Andrews
Tony Walton
Maggie Smith
Muriel Francis
Colonel Bugner
Friede Rothe
Federico Pallavicini
Mrs. Sulzberger
Feliks Topolski
Dave MacElroy
Larry Kelly

| Siobhan McKenna | [Baron] Henry[-Louis] de la Grange |
| Gjon Mili | Michael Redgrave |
| Tom Clancy | Eugenia Halbmeier |
| Mrs. Tom Clancy | Tyler Redd |
| David Hersey | Bill Riva |
| The [Alexander] MacKendricks | |

NOVEMBER 25, 1956 • NEW YORK CITY
TO RICHARD HUNTER • HAMBURG, NEW YORK?

Last Sunday I had my Callas supper—Chinese food, eighty-five-plus came, the oddest food-line ever. They all had to line up to be served—and they loved it. The line stretched from the living room down and around through the parlors—Maria and entourage, Carmel Snow, William Faulkner,[12] [baritone] George London, [producer] Roger Stevens, Lillian Gish, Mrs. William Rhinelander Stewart, Celeste Holm, the Toscanini "girls,"[13] Jennie Tourel, Lennie Bernstein, Gian Carlo Menotti, Sono [Osato], Siobhan McKenna, [actress] Leueen McGrath Kaufmann (unspoused), Stanley Young and wife [Nancy Wilson Ross, a novelist], and so very many others—but I missed those elsewhere or gone forever. Ania Dorfmann played the piano. The party cost under $125 and several days and bad tempers all around domestically, but I guess it was worth it. If only people did not bring people—if only.

JOURNAL • JANUARY 17, 1957 On January 16, I heard that Maestro was dead, ninety years old. Gray and Richard kept this from me. Gray and Howard [Rothschild] lurked around a man reading a newspaper with this news in it. But when I did glimpse the Maestro's name, the photographs showed him most active. I concluded that the paper was running a story on him.

So now he is dead, and in my weeping I thought, "At last Ela has him." But when Gray said this to comfort me, I said, "There are so many there ahead of her." I wonder whether Ela is hiding behind a cloud or has she brazenly and daringly rushed up to him and kissed his darling face at last? Whatever she's doing, she must be radiant with that special radiance which only she had. In all of my life, I loved her most. And when the Skater's Waltz came on the radio, just a little while ago, I found myself crying again, not for Maestro, who had a long and most glorious life, and who in these last months was, Rut told me,

12. Of Faulkner's visit to a previous party at 1453, Leo wrote: "Faulkner stood in the center of the back parlor, while the literary world grew more and more timid and only Henry (Green) Yorke braved him." Journal, March 16, 1982.
13. Because of his history with Eleonora von Mendelssohn and Toscanini, Leo never ceased thinking of the conductor's daughters, Wally and Wanda, as "the Toscanini girls."

quite gaga at times, not for him but for me. For now I realized that Ela would never return—never. So that forlorn hope is ended. I can see her smiling and giggling in that way she had, so sweetly demented. Now the night program is playing some of his Wagner. How vital. How full of life. No, not full of life, but life itself. So the glorious ones depart, and the world sinks into a long gray time. Not the dark ages, but the gray ages. To my aunt Minnie this is a marvelous time in which to live. "If only I was younger," she cried on Sunday last while watching her color television set. "If only I was younger! What a wonderful time we live in!" But she sees only the surface, the glittering, telescoped surface, when she joys in her color television, in all the miracle soporifics, the magical cozeners. . . . Oh, what a bloody synthetic time. What a swindle this time is. What a bitter joke—especially in this huge stony city, this airborne congeries, which has had to rear its head so very high. One story lower and it would have mud on its face—permanently.

I lost $200 a month today. My expense account was cut totally. So now I must think how to supplement my dwindled resources. Next, the whole job could vanish. I must somehow prepare against such an emergency. I have no savings save those in the tin boxes—pennies, loose change. I must fortify myself, and that means work for the outside. Also, I must keep my ears and eyes open for another job.[14]

The house is so empty feeling now that Richard's gone.

JANUARY 18, 1957  The struggle to write in this notebook—the unwillingness and then the pleasure of writing in it. But the time of procrastination, the resistance? Perhaps because the fear of failure goes so very deep in the bone. I must work to eliminate this fear, for it corrodes and ruins. Deep down I'm frightened that I'm about to lose my job or that I'll be asked to cut my salary still more. But most of all I'm frightened that I'll lose my job.

FEBRUARY 12, 1957 • NEW YORK CITY
TO RICHARD HUNTER • GRENADA, WEST INDIES

A week ago, on a Sunday evening, I was rushing into my clothes because I was late for the Toscanini memorial concert (very good—[Charles] Munch, [Bruno] Walter, [Pierre] Monteux each conducted) when the telephone rang and Gray answered it. Then he said, "It's Knox Laing, your schoolboy crush." I said, "Stop kidding! Who is it?" I thought wildly that maybe you were playing a joke—or Ben [Edwards] was. But no one was—it was Knox. I told Gray to get his number. The next morning I called. There he was, stopping in the Dakota,

14. In eight years, Leo's monthly salary had only gone from $600 to $700, but it had been supplemented by a $200 per month expense account (plus $50 to buy recordings). Street & Smith had been tightening its belt, however. Two years later, the struggling company would be sold to Samuel I. Newhouse.

with [British actor] Eric Portman, with whom he has lived for many years.[15] So I arranged to go there—to lunch I thought. I met this man of seventy in whom I could discern a boy we had once known! He is obviously an alcoholic. He lives in a "pretty" house—Portman's in Cornwall—sometimes, rarely, in Portman's London house. He does nothing save cope with three bull terriers—and he drinks! He burst into tears—and thereafter he had frequent torrents of weeping. He knows so very well what has happened to him—and oh how awful to see it. He said I looked wonderful and that I was the only good thing that had ever happened to him, and that he thought of me constantly, but knew there was no purpose in writing. If he hadn't gone with Portman (a strange, tense, nervous, somewhat forbidding man—like someone in Samuel Butler or Thomas Hardy) to a party on the eightieth floor (!) of the Empire State, a party given by Roger Stevens, he wouldn't have called. It was a dreadful afternoon—something out of an Elizabeth Bowen novel—sometimes comical, but not really. He seems to live much in the past and remembers incidents and people I've forgotten. Then he doesn't remember what he has just said. How dreadful to see someone who seemed to have so much and have it so easily become this. I couldn't ask him about his family or anything because I didn't feel that I should. So that's what became of Knox Laing. How fortunate we are—you, Ben, I.

NOTE: In May 1957, Gray went to California to visit his mother.

MAY 21, 1957 • NEW YORK CITY
**TO GRAY FOY** • BURBANK, CALIFORNIA

Richard housekeeps, so I don't worry about that, and he sits lilacking—[drawing them] diligently and doggedly. But, oh, how intensely cold these days and nights are. Below forty degrees. I am done up in my gray sweatshirt and Chinese hat and wool scarves and mittens, and my feet (in socks) are ice. . . .

I'll tell you about Nora [Kaye]: I thought she seemed worried, so finally I asked what the matter was, and she said she was frightened because as soon as arrangements could be made she would, sometime next week, go into [the] hospital and have an operation. Her doctor says it is some sort of growth—or woman's trouble—but, of course, she worries about cancer. You can imagine how upset I was, although I told her all the things I've ever heard anyone say—

---

15. Scenic designer Ben Edwards (1916–99) had been a classmate of Leo and Richard at the Feagin School of Dramatic Art. Although British, Knox Laing had studied in America and also enrolled at Feagin. It's unclear when his affair with Leo occurred, but when Laing returned to Britain in 1936, Leo was saddened and turned to Richard. RH: "Then we began to be interested in one another."

Leo had a penchant during his acting school days for older British men in the theatrical trade: Playwright Hubert Osborne, director Teddy Fitzgerald, and actor-playwright Emlyn Williams also had affairs of varying brevity with Leo in his twenties. He met all of them through the Feagin School. "I was irresistible because I gave myself so completely. All of me was hunger, desire," he later said.

but, of course, that didn't help much. She's still frightened. Also, she does love Kenneth [MacMillan] very much and he loves her. She says they are very much suited in all sorts of ways, but she is ten years older and an aging dancer who does not know how long she can continue to dance. If they married he would have to give up Sadler's Wells—so it's all a mess—and what with her illness and love and all she feels older than old. She was extremely sensible about it all.[16] How relentless life is—with its seesaw of delights and darknesses. I told Arthur [Laurents] this morning and we both cried a bit—suddenly—and I said if you were here you would be tuning up, too. So then we laughed.[17]

JUNE 10, 1957 • EN ROUTE FROM BOSTON TO NEW YORK
TO GRAY FOY • BURBANK

Dr. [William Carlos] Williams burst out passionately to Robert Lowell, about death: How he didn't mind dying, but he did mind not knowing so many things and having no time left in which to learn them—so many books he hadn't read. When he publicly thanked his wife for being so good a wife, she gave an angry look. When I came up to her, she said, "All those weeks and months when I didn't even know where he was . . ." And [novelist and critic] Elizabeth Hardwick Lowell said, "I deserve some praise, too. . . . Why doesn't Cal [Lowell] get up and sing a song about me!" Poets' wives . . . Seems I heard Mrs. Shelley and Lady Byron laughing grimly in the ether.

NOTE: Richard Hunter and Howard Rothschild had rented a house in Connecticut for the summer of 1957. Leo spent a few nights with Richard there on his return from a visit to Boston.

JUNE 15, 1957 • CORNWALL BRIDGE, CONNECTICUT
TO GRAY FOY • BURBANK

I must tell you about last night's dinner guests—Jane Grant, once Mrs. Harold Ross (together they founded *The New Yorker*), and her now husband [William Harris] and an elderly woman (very Boston and crusty, belongs more in a herbaceous border than a drawing room). Jane Grant is a Lucy Stoner.[18] She and her husband (he works for *Fortune*) live up here and have White Flower Farm nursery. Remember their wonderful catalogs? It is strange to see this woman, once the center of the Algonquin Round Table set (Woollcott lived in her house, so did Benchley and almost all of that world), here in remote Connecticut and wrinkled the way country women are wrinkled, as though each

16. Nora Kaye did not marry MacMillan (1929–92), a dancer who in 1953 had begun an important choreographic career with the Royal Ballet. Kaye would retire from the stage in 1961.
17. Playwright and novelist Arthur Laurents (b. 1918) had been Nora Kaye's lover intermittently in the forties and wrote his screenplay for *The Turning Point* (1977) based on her experiences.
18. In 1921 entrepreneur and feminist Jane Grant (1892–1972) had cofounded the Lucy Stone League, a women's rights organization.

line, each wrinkle held earth—the sort of skin you could grow something in—herbs rather than flowers. I like her and she is, of course, writing a book about her dead world.

JUNE 27, 1957 • NEW YORK CITY

**TO GRAY FOY • BURBANK**

Poppa is in the hospital. He had to be rushed there for a blood transfusion and oxygen. Oh, Pussum, he's so pitiful.[19] I've never seen him look so awful—all nose and huge scared eyes, sort of like a lumpy sack. When I was going away, he sat up and said, "I want to see how you look. Be a good boy and take care of yourself." I don't think that he wants to live . . . but he can linger on and on. I found out that each blood transfusion costs $80. I wonder where the money comes from, and I guess I had best start scrimping some together. Momma sits by his bedside from early morning until closing time. She behaves very well, and seems bright and even gay—such a show.

I talked to the doctor at eight a.m. He says that Poppa has unregenerative anemia. That means the marrow in his bones doesn't make red blood, and that means he can only be kept alive by receiving his red blood from outside sources. Poppa, to live, may need at least one [transfusion] a week. They don't know yet. Also, they don't know whether he can come out of the hospital. He has developed a congestion in the right lung. He's had three heart attacks, and his diabetes is dreadful. He's so frightened and looks like a child who has been through bombardment.[20]

JUNE 30, 1957 • NEW YORK CITY

**TO GRAY FOY • BURBANK**

I went out there [to the hospital], and Momma was on the telephone almost every moment (poetic justice) while Poppa was immersed in a baseball game (television)—emerging only to get hurt when in answer to his asking me wasn't I going to stay there over the weekend (where I wonder?), because he wants his sons around him, I said no, why should I be uncomfortable there when I had a big house with quite a few beds in it? He acted as though I had hit him while he was wearing at least six sets of eyeglasses and had diminished to baby-size. Oh! Anyway, I'll let this go on a wee bit longer and then I'll absent me a while. Give them a bit and they show themselves for the cannibals they essentially are.

Yesterday, Al Greenwald [secondhand-furniture dealer] (I was there) said he would drive me home. Coming up Lexington, when we stopped for someone to get out, we were fixed in our tracks, wordlessly, by seeing Mr. Millhauser emerge from his [mortuary] place of business—face front, hands attached to a

---

19. Leo's affectionate nickname for Gray was Pussum or, more frequently, Puss.
20. Sam Lerman was then about seventy-one years old. A lifelong exposure to lead-based paint may have led to his developing blood ailments.

stretcher. As he moved out onto the avenue (the little Chinese girl twirling up and down the curb, dogs with women attached passing along the street), quite apparent beneath a bright scarlet blanket was a human shape, a man it seemed. Attached to the other end of the stretcher was a male (elderly, countrified, in a straw hat and short shirtsleeves). They trundled across the pavement to an estate wagon, named "Sunset Lodge," and carefully thrust their burden in. Then Mr. Millhauser shook hands with the straw hat, and a lurking female in a countrylike blue-and-white print and a dark blue straw hat, shod in blue sneakers, came up and shook Mr. M's hand. All three were quite jolly, like acquaintances parting after a pleasant afternoon. There were suit jackets and shirts hanging in the wagon part, as in cars going on holidays along Route 17. I got out and went across to get some suits, thereby encountering Mr. M (as I knew I would). So, I said brightly, not intending levity, "Anybody we know?" and Mr. M thought that was about the funniest thing ever. He split his sides. "No," he said. "You know, those two came in a couple of hours ago with their father, and it's a hot day, so I went to work, and just about when I got going, they came back, and they said they hoped they weren't being a trouble, but they just didn't feel right about the East Side. No—they wanted him on the West Side. They just couldn't get used to the East Side. So, I said okay, and we went to work and got him out of here. You never know, do you?" That was my first glimpse in these almost ten years of Mr. M's business.

JULY 9, 1957 • NEW YORK CITY

**TO GRAY FOY • BURBANK**

I have just heard Momma say to Poppa, "Remember when you could fall asleep on a picket fence? You could fall asleep on anything. You even fell asleep when making love." I was startled to hear this. Said Poppa, "You even remember that. It was fifty-two years ago, on the sofa at Auntie's on Ogden Avenue. . . ." So then they gave one another loving looks and continued to hold hands, which they have been doing for some three hours. Poppa seems somewhat better in this enormous hospital. He is in a room with two other men. Perhaps this cheers him, since he has no resources. Constantly I find myself in a state of amusement at being the child of these parents. There is almost no relationship mentally. Emotionally, yes. Hysterically, yes. But mentally . . . Well—we've known this for years.

NOTE: Virtually no letters or journals survive from August 1957 through March 1958.

**MAKING AN ENTRANCE** *Marlene sat in a gray Rolls-Royce, leaning back against the gray velvet upholstery, while I sat beside her in a black coat and a dark homburg. She gnawed on an enormous liverwurst, and I laughed a lot and said, "Your public should see you now." And she said, "They would like it,* wouldn't they?" This was no question, it was a statement. We were on our way to Philadelphia, where she would receive an award for being the most glamorous woman in the world, and I would give it to her at the top of the grand staircase at the Philadelphia Museum of Art.

As we came to the Hotel Warwick, we heard a murmuration. Marlene pulled a blind down over the window on her side. The car stopped. The chauffeur opened the door. On the pavement was a pulsing mob of women and some young men, each one holding a rose. They all fell silent. Marlene extended one trademark leg. The crowd sighed. Marlene extended another world-famous branch. The crowd moaned. Marlene, the liverwurst, and a garment bag all went out together. She sashayed across the pavement and the women all screamed. I got out in my black coat, my black homburg—a sober, bearded, portly, older man lumbering after a flashing, laughing, fleeting young thing. There was instant silence. One woman blurted, "Is that her rabbi?"[21] (1993)

**GYPSY AND GERI**  *Bonnie Cashin lives in a two-layer penthouse in the West Fifties, intensely New York, with the new pie-tin crusted Fifth Avenue skyscraper dominating the flowering cherry trees on her south terrace and a vista of rivers and shipping, east and west, from the windows of her top layer. . . . When I first saw Bonnie Cashin she was deep in Rockettes, for she was designing costumes.[22] That was many years ago. When I last saw Bonnie she was deep in chums, canapés, and convivialities. That was yesterday, on her terrace. The occasion: a cocktail party for friends from India. I loathe cocktail parties, those SRO corridors between exhaustions, but this was unusual. It had an excellent story line, was brilliantly cast, and the decor was masterly. Also, everybody sat on something. I sat on Gypsy Rose Lee. Miss Lee, with massive straw and wheat sheaves on her head and a casing of ombré stuff up and down her frame, talked a good streak. She usually does, mostly in Baroque, a tongue peculiar to her. "Oha," she says, "aha . . ." She adds an "uh" here and an "uh" there. The result is irresistible and sexy, even when she was so relentlessly buttoned up as on Bonnie's terrace, with Bonnie peering up into her nostrils, her Brownie (so help me!) ready to fire when she sighted the whites of Gypsy's eyes. "Gypsy," we inquired, "Gypsy, what about that barn tour?" "Barn tour! I'm goinga to London. . . ." "Whatever for?" "To helpa," said Gypsy, "with the translation of my book into British." So then we got off Gypsy and went to another party.*

*In his hotel room at the Lombardy, visitor-to-Manhattan Ken Tynan, mental ecdysiast, the neon-eyed youth who writes drama criticism rather than reviews for London's weekly* The Observer, *was talking* Hamlet *with Geraldine Page and*

---

21. The Philadelphia Fashion Group honored Dietrich for "continuing impact on the world of fashion" on October 26, 1957.
22. Costume and sportswear designer Bonnie Cashin (1908–2000) had designed for the Grossinger Playhouse when Leo stage-managed there in 1936.

*Eli Wallach. "How," asked Ken, clipping it out and stammering just enough to make it all suspenseful, "how how would you plllllay the Quee quee—queen, Geri?" "Wellllll," drawled Miss Page, whose syllables were suddenly and unexpectedly airborne, as though on an especially sunshiny day children are seesawing in her larynx. "Welllllllll, I would be (here the seesaw jumped breathlessly six stories up) FAAAAAT. (The seesaw instantly descended.) I would be very, very FAAAAAAAT. I would EAAAAAAAAT SWEEEEEEEET things (the seesaw soared gradually and sneakily up) all the time, all the timmmmmme. I would be a PREEEEETYYYY FAAAAAT WOOOMANNN (seesaw down again) very (seesaw way down) sex—y." "Like Maxine Elliot latterly?" I asked. "Never knew her," from Geri. So I recollected [Edwardian beauty and comic actress] Maxine Elliot grown enormous, sitting fabulously on the edge of her Riviera swimming pool, consuming huge chocolate cakes, surrounded by admirers of all ages—including Sir Winston Churchill. Her beauty, as it became immersed in fat, grew more concentrated, her exquisite face diminished to coin size and set in a vast flabby medallion. "Yeeeees," Geri said. "Yeees . . ." And as she drawled she became a pretty, fat woman, a queen right there in Ken Tynan's hotel room in midtown Manhattan.* (PLAYBILL, SEPTEMBER 1957)

**IN THE NEIGHBORHOOD** *The undertaker who lives and works opposite is, appropriately, the historian of this neighborhood. Having been in residence over half a century, he relates the local past . . . how carriages stood two deep along the avenue when No. 14 entertained at an evening party, and how the corner house was once the dining room of the Republican Club, and the brownstone just north of it housed the club's ballroom, where every Saturday night the band played on and on. The delicatessen proprietor, his wife, and their many sons, the woman who runs the little stationery and lending library, the corner druggist and wife, all have occupied their premises for several decades, but they almost never recollect the past, preferring current local events—what the Kronenbergers are having for dinner, and that Marlene has just gone by in her white nurse's uniform, pushing the new Riva baby [her grandson] in his beautiful car, and that Betty Field has just been in to buy a toothbrush or a nail file, and that Al and Dolly Haas Hirschfeld's Nina is growing into quite a young lady with hair the identical color of her mother's. When Viveca Lindfors, in her new plaything-sized foreign station wagon, came around the corner from Ninety-fifth Street where she also lives, there were fascinated eyes at every shop door. Even the drugstore cat, a diffident beast, was interested—for a moment. Sometimes there is talk of Alfred Drake's beard, June Havoc's new coat, the color that the Vincent Sardis are planning to paint their front door (red). When the [George] Axelrods moved in and painted their front door—but the Axelrods are moving out of their brownstone and away from East Ninety-fifth . . . Curious that in the midst of this world of very public persons there live two, three, possibly four people about whom almost nothing save suppositions is ever related. They live in a brownstone* *whose upper floors have, these last ten years, fallen into ruin, windows quite disintegrated, wisteria vines tangled with remnants of once white curtains. But the ivy in the basement windows is carefully tended, and when one or the other of the sisters emerges she is usually wearing fresh white gloves. The contrast between their time-wrecked house and their neat, little white gloves, their tidy Edwardian lady ankles . . . Some mornings ago I went out to pick up a package, when suddenly I saw coming up the street a most fashionable figure, hatted, gloved, carrying a bouquet—chrysanthemums. So singular was this cavalier, on this ordinary weekday morning, that I stood watching him. Jauntily he passed my house, then neighboring houses, and he stopped. For a moment he considered the flooded areaway of the brownstone before him. Then he leapt over the stagnant water and pushed a button. After a long time he vanished, bouquet and all. In a moment he emerged, regained the pavement, gave a puzzled rueful look at the house, and moved nattily up the street. He had left his chrysanthemums behind him. I looked to see whether any of the local chroniclers had observed this most unique current event. But there were no interested eyes at any of the shop windows. For some low reason this gave me pleasure until, later that morning, I went into one of the shops and its proprietor said, "Did you see the man who brought the flowers for the recluses?" And now that is news up here in our neighborhood on the border between Yorkville and Harlem.* (PLAYBILL, JANUARY 1958)

CA. MARCH 31, 1958 • NEW YORK CITY
**TO RUTH AND JOHN STEPHAN** • OLD GREENWICH, CONNECTICUT

Please forgive the long silence. Life has been complicated because Poppa died [February 26] after much hideous suffering—so you know how this has been these weeks. What to do with Momma's long empty days and nights, I wonder.

APRIL 29, 1958 • NEW YORK CITY
**TO RICHARD HUNTER** • HAMBURG, NEW YORK

Poor Gray did the best [Columbia Records] cover he had ever done, and they paid $350, and suddenly yesterday morning the salesmen said the cover had to have a female—an exciting female—on it or they could not sell the *Sacre du Printemps* to the hilt. When will America wake up? How adolescent we are made to be. So now Gray is trying to make a bosomy female.

Oh—please don't breathe a word to anyone—but [the family's Elmhurst] property may be sold for $75,000. Momma bought it for about $11,000. If this happens, she should have enough to live on for the rest of her life, in a small apartment. I go there and sit around looking businesslike and commercially wise, while real estate people and Jerry Lerman talk endlessly. It all seems clear to me, but they do ritual dances and courtships and such. I am not going to get any of it, so I had best not get to feeling aggrieved.

MAY 9

I'm in a fit of delight—A girl here told the [*Mademoiselle*] meeting that at "our" Hawaiian-theme boat ride the Guest Editors would stand at the top of the gangplank and lei the men guests. When I fell off my chair, all the ladies gave me dirty-boy looks. Also, a new editor asked me to bait the trap by getting, for the same boat ride, Pablo Casals and Christian Dior. I said that my planchette would work miracles. But I think that she thinks Planchette is a new French painter or diseuse.

JOURNAL • JUNE 14, 1958 Leaving the Russian Tea Room, suddenly there was Rut calling my name, and with her Cesco. Ela's features in Cesco's face, he now very large, fat, and quiet—amputated—removed. He smiled his and Ela's smile. I dropped him, neither of us ever talking about all of the overwhelming matters. How could we, without drowning? We talked of books— Colette. And did he look out at anything? "No, nothing." Nor did he want to look out. Later, Rut told me that he has a lovely Renoir still, the last of the Mendelssohn pictures from Grünewald, and he has the portrait of Moses Mendelssohn.[23] When I kissed him, his skin was salty, not at all like Ela's—not at all.

NOTE: In January 1958, Leo had appeared as a contestant on the television quiz show *The $64,000 Question*. He competed against the artist Larry Rivers, answering questions about the last hundred years in art. In the decisive round, their challenge was to identify all of the real-life models for the men in Renoir's *Luncheon of the Boating Party*. Leo correctly named all but the painter and collector Gustave Caillebotte. Rivers couldn't identify him either, so they split the $8,000 prize. All Leo's winnings went to pay his father's hospital and funeral bills.

In August 1958, a former contestant on the television quiz show *Twenty-One* revealed that the game had been fixed. Scandal and investigations followed. Although *The $64,000 Question* had also been rigged, no one had coached Leo.

OCTOBER 3, 1958 • NEW YORK CITY

**TO RICHARD HUNTER • VENICE**

I am writing to you from a most peculiar situation—The [State] Supreme Court, I believe—where I sit in a green-walled (dirty, drab green), maple "furnished" room along with a truculent, frightened, fear-eyed, big-lipped Negro girl (now she droops as though she needs immediate watering) and a thickset, angry, white-socked middle-aged man. He disciplines his anger by chewing measuredly.

Several days ago I innocently answered the house bell. A little apologetic

23. German Jewish philosopher Moses Mendelssohn (1729–86) was the grandfather of the composer Felix Mendelssohn and the great-great-great-grandfather of Eleonora and Francesco von Mendelssohn.

creature thrust a grimy envelope at me. "Please, please take it," he urged. So I did. It was a subpoena from the district attorney, telling me that I was to appear here as a witness in the action brought by the People of the State of New York (of which I thought I was one—and for forty-four years!) against John Doe. "Who," I inquired from the little man, "is John Doe?" "I'm not allowed to tell yer," he whispered. I gave him a hard but charming look, so he, with more apologies and beseeching me not to blame him and protestations that he knew I was OK, told me—quiz show. That is why I am here, feeling intensely miscreant, and gradually feeling sure that I'll not come out of here for forty years, and then everyone I love will be vanished, and I'll beg in the streets—or deliver subpoenas. A tall "lady" replete with tam, fake pearls around throat and in ears (threaded with glittery stones—the necklace is), a kind of macintosh, and general look of *bon voyage* despite a good week of rich *mal de mer*, has just queened in. She blows her nose a lot—a very red nose which her mummy assured her was truly aristocratic.

So you see, my Tib, fame and some fortune does not pay. We were even woken out of soundly restless sleeps at about 5:30 by *New York Post* reporters hot for the big story. Maybe I should have stuck to blowing (I think that is the correct word) sages. I am told that for each day of my visit here I am to receive 50 cents plus 8 cents for each mile over three that I must travel. My little brother tells me that I am, at this extremely high remunerative rate, to get $1.06. Would you lunch with me, dear Tib, and we'll blow the sum on a tip to the hatcheck girl—thereby winning at least one friend among the people?

Along with the lady who told me that she had studied with [Italian soprano] Marchesi "right after Melba," I was ushered into the assistant D.A.'s office—a young man obviously come up the hard way. He has now asked me quite a few "background" questions and is baffled that I am not specialized in any one art. Now I am sitting outside while he talks "personally" on the blower.[24] The light is awful—I feel more and more criminal. In an office nearby, a man drones, "She says she make representation. . . ." The guard downstairs told me that many "sick" and "crazy" people come here. The guard at the desk up here is reading *The Life of Warden Lewes*. I asked him was it a textbook. This made him angry.

OCTOBER 7

I've had time to cool off. I was "grilled" for over three hours. They knew nothing about me and never understood anything I told them. They never believed that I hadn't gone to college. They said, "Name five things in your past that will tell us what you do." Such things. It was hateful and funny and depressing and

---

24. Leo's frequent term for the telephone, "the blower," is British slang originating in the twenties.

wasteful. Mr. [Sol] Hurok called about Marlene and Maria Callas (who is here).[25] Ah, well—If my phone is being tapped that should make headlines. I've been in the tabloids almost every day for a week—sometimes on page two with the call girls. Such is fame—ugh. They didn't prove anything and finally they sent me home, telling me to stand by.

OCTOBER 23, 1958 • NEW YORK CITY
TO RICHARD HUNTER • PARIS

I am sitting and awaiting guests for a small party which I am giving for Mrs. Curtiss's *Bizet* [*and His World*]. I invited twenty-four, but I think ten are coming. She is not exactly a public favorite—but I like her. Little Gray is leaving the premises while this transpires—where to I do not know—but he does seem cheerful(?). He has been painting and "touching up" the house for several weeks. I asked him was the Whitney going to hang the front hall.

You will be amused to see your little fat friend (me) caricatured on the walls of a new restaurant, which hopes to take the custom away from Sardi's. Al Hirschfeld did the murals, and I look like a billiard-ball fiend with a dead cat around my throat (my fur tippet).[26]

JOURNAL • OCTOBER 24, 1958  Fourteen people came to my Mina party— including [writer] Anne Lindbergh and her sister Mrs. [Constance Morrow] Morgan—little wren women with sharp eyes for the most unobtrusive worm and a manner more Concord of Louisa Alcott's earlier days than of Manhattan now. Mrs. Morgan lives near Portland and Mrs. Lindbergh lives mostly in Darien [Connecticut]. I like them—and, of course, they loved my home. These small women are the strongest of the race.

NOTE: At the end of October, Leo went to the Dallas Civic Opera to hear Callas sing *La Traviata*, directed by Zeffirelli, and *Medea*, directed by Alexis Minotis of the Greek National Theater.

OCTOBER 29, 1958 • EN ROUTE FROM NEW YORK TO DALLAS
TO GRAY FOY • NEW YORK CITY

Here we sit in a vast plain, not having come to St. Louis but having passed through Terre Haute. The only memorable sight there being enormous clumps of chrysanthemums—parti-colored and deep purple in a garden. My, the Midwest is flat, and there is nothing to distinguish any one place in it from another. (We are racing again.) I read and read (*The Proud Possessors* [by Aline

25. Sol Hurok (1888–1974), the Russian American talent agent and impresario, produced tours for many performers and companies. He arranged all of Callas's domestic tours.
26. The mural, of New York's opening-night audience departing a theater, decorated the Manhattan Hotel's "Playbill Room."

Saarinen]) and when I have read seventy pages, look up and out at precisely what I have seen all day long. There is beauty in the farmlands and in the trees and streams, but nowhere is there any architectural beauty save in functional structures—barns, corncribs, silos, railroad buildings. As for fantasy, I find level vastness utterly unrewarding: It neither feeds the eye nor nourishes the soul. Oh, for a hill. I didn't know that so many people lived in trailers. Impermanence breeds irresponsibility. What monsters of men and women trailer children will be. Here there was surely, in prehistoric times, a great lake—and just as surely there will be one here again

Now the train is wailing and slowing down. You would think that the nation is being invaded and no hints are to be given the enemies as to where they are. Not a station sign ever visible—nothing, ever, to tell where one is. Even small Austrian stops loudly proclaimed who they were. Here we stop in a station— where ponytailed or babushka'd females await someone and clouds of *Anna Karenina* steam obliterate what must be scenes of joyful greeting. I can hear this through two thicknesses of window glass, so they must be joyful. Maybe we are in Arkansas—it all sounds so southern. We passed through [Little Rock], your momma's birthplace (and Lorelei Lee's) at about three a.m. States seem endless out here. Sleep well, my own beloved Possum-Pussum.

OCTOBER 31, 1958 • DALLAS, TEXAS

**TO GRAY FOY** • NEW YORK CITY

It's a very pretty day . . . kind of smeary blue and smokey and quite warm. But, oh, the desolation of America . . . the enormous uninspired miles of America . . . nothing, nothing to nourish one, nothing, not even picturesque debris . . . only dead-car grounds with parking lots crammed with future dead cars right close . . . and the same neon-lighted nights all through the land . . . and hovels . . . bleak, nasty hovels in which only the most puny lives could possibly be eked out. Could anything save rock 'n' roll worship come from this? Could anything save debasement of language and spirit come from this wanton vast waste? Oh me . . . "The Waste Land"—and could he have written it if he hadn't sprung from St. Louis?

I listened carefully to people in the dining room of this excessively quiet and proper hotel, and I am amazed and appalled at the ignorance. They don't even know what *Traviata* is, many of them. The women seem well dressed, conservative even, but the men go all out for design(!) and color and those hats—they really wear them. Still, Dallas seems so worn-out, even the newest buildings, not like Chicago, which, no matter whether one likes or dislikes it, is full of spirit and bluster and is, as I thought, still a real frontier town . . . with more a cattle feeling in it than here. . . . Ruth [Lindley] showed me all those enormous *House & Garden* houses, and she says they just don't have collections in them. . . . Maybe when Neiman Marcus puts in an art department Dallas will collect pictures.[27] I still can't stop feeling that this whole city isn't here. It's not quite the same feeling that I had in Hollywood: There I felt that I could see through everything; here I feel that it's all not here. There is not even a rim of low hills on any horizon. The world seems to obliterate itself here, just levels itself into nothingness. What a situation for agoraphobia.

A curious detail: While lunching at the S & S tearoom yesterday there was a continual dreadful bombing sound, distant but massive and terrifying—jets. How odd to see all those costly ladies eating things they shouldn't have been eating, while their annihilation boomed in the near future.

Your stepmother Faye [Lockett Foy] just was on the blower—Puss, how can you ever? Oh, me . . . She means so well. She talked and talked and we are luncheoning (despite her migraine!) tomorrow at the Zodiac Room. Sunday morning, she and your poor father will be showing me nearby Texas (I can just see your pretty face). I told her about how hard you worked, and she told me about how much she loved you, and how it worried her that you had no steady girl, and I told her about how very popular you were and loads of girls just swooned at the mere smutch of your look, and she told me how Ruth was the only girl for you and vice versa, and I opined that you had a deep feeling for Ruth and vice versa, and so then she told me that all over again, and she could easily, with her good intentions, drive anyone to dissipation, just as a reaction. She has the sentimental approach to everything. Faye is pathetic the way some of Bill Inge's people are—the pathos of being middle class and perceiving life more glittering in the very near but quite inaccessible distance, like seeing the most glamorous party going on in the next block and not even knowing how to get to it.

NOVEMBER 1

Your father made me deeply sad. I wanted to cuddle him. There you are . . . your beautiful hands quite aged and your cheekbones (which, I do believe, I have told you are as beautiful as the *Winged Victory* in the Louvre) and so many similarities, but all drawn differently. He is one of the most touching people I have ever seen. How, how did things go wrong, I wonder. He talked quite a lot. I was surprised. He says that he and all sorts of other men in your family and, I guess, you, all derive certain characteristics, such as the recluse strain, from your grandpa.

Now, about Faye: She is everything I knew that she would be but plumper and dowdier. She and her ambitions and her hen parties and her whole morality and all of her "values" contrasted to this extraordinary desert, this reekingly rich Dallas-Texas world, are the true American play. For I should think that this is a synthesis of all such American regions. I am sure that despite regional variations here is the American dream and tragedy inextricably entwined. I sit here in the dusk looking out over the vast plain with lights glittering and the

27. Ruth Lindley was a friend of Gray Foy's from his young years in Dallas.

superhighways not yet in full fluorescent blaze and the neon blossoming like plastic signal fires all over this vast desert . . . and nowhere do I perceive the future . . . only the present as though viewed from the future. They have invented a new tense in America—the present past. To be trapped here . . .

Last night, the ball . . . $1,500 of camellia-pink satin ribbon festooning the Adolphus [hotel] ballroom(!) . . . and the Paris dresses from Neiman's and Magnin's and Marshall Fields and New York stores and even from Paris . . . and the jewels which even made *La Superba*'s [Callas's] look kind of niggardly . . . and that fat slob Elsa Maxwell so subdued that one wouldn't have known she was there . . . and the kind of smug discontent in that room . . . and the ambiguity of some of the males—so male that one suspected them as one suspects Hemingway's prose . . . and the rapacity of the women— it's all quite true about [Tennessee Williams's] Big Mama and Big Daddy and their slobby children.

The performance [October 31] was the most extraordinary *Traviata* I have ever seen. It is the only genuinely created *Traviata*. [Director] Zeffirelli is amazing. He did it strictly 1852, having all of the costumes made in Rome, and he did it much the way it is in Dumas's novel. During the overture the curtain rises and there is Violetta dying as in the last act. Then, quite suddenly, when the music requires, up blaze the lights (all very gaslit somehow, quite a miracle of stagecraft). Violetta is in her own past, receiving her guests and quite pathet- ically pleased not to be on her deathbed. All through the act you are constantly reminded by many subtle touches in her characterization that this is gaiety rec- ollected. It is never tricky; the magic never betrays the magician. The illusion holds as it did in Venice [in 1953]. This is never for one instant out of period. The chorus walks correctly; the hair is accurate; the rooms are the right size. Not the *haute courtisane* world, but oh so Balzac. And the dresses are each indi- vidual and each superb—all those 1850ish colors—autumnal, just off—the kinds you read about in old books and wonder about. If only you could see it. The diva sang better than I have heard her sing in years, and she looked so right. I know of no other diva who would wear her hair (a wig) this not too attractive way.

**FRANCO ZEFFIRELLI**   *Between the Callas* Traviata *and her* Medea *some days later, I wandered onto the stage in the early evening. There was Franco industriously snipping, tearing what looked like an animal skin. He was care- fully pasting bits and pieces of it onto the walls of his scenery. "What," I inquired, "are you doing?" "Needs it," he said . . . "Texture," he grunted. "But what is it?" "Fur." "Where did you get it? Looks like mink . . ." "Found it . . . in the house . . ." gesturing out into the darkened theater. "Just what I needed." (1984)*

**MARIA AND MEDEA**   *In Dallas, on the day preceding the evening of the* Medea *dress rehearsal, when I came to Maria's dressing room I found her in a* *rage such as I never had seen. She was clutching a telegram from Bing.*[28] *Time came for the rehearsal to begin. We sat out in the house, a small group of disconsolate Maria addicts, as the orchestra began and the opera got under way. Medea enters late in the first act. The opera builds and builds and builds and then slowly, gradually, Medea enters. Medea-Maria materialized, a cloak held up to just below her eyes. As she advanced on a platform above some steps and faced the orchestra, the orchestra stopped playing. The eyes were so full of hatred that it became apparent immediately that, if Mr. Bing were anywhere about, they would strike him dead. Slowly, the cloak began to descend. The mouth opened and out poured a volume of sound, and this was a Medea that no one had ever dreamed could exist in life or onstage. This was Maria complete—the Maria who could become Medea and the Medea who could become Maria—the essence of theater.*

*At about four in the morning, we were going home, Maria, Meneghini, and I. I sat in the middle. And Maria had not a word to say. We were holding hands, and her hand was very quiet and very warm. By and by a small voice said, "Who is this Rachel of yours?" "She was one of the very greatest French tragediennes. She began by singing in the streets, a poor Jewish girl, and she became the greatest actress of her day, before Bernhardt." "Oh," she said, "before Bernhardt . . . hmmm."*
(1993)

**JOURNAL · NOVEMBER 8, 1958 · ST. LOUIS** I should write down everything I remember about these eight Dallas days: the enormous emptiness of Dallas— the flabbergasting richness. Mrs. Lambert's maid, calling out to the pre- *Medea* supper party guests (about sixty), "Come and git yeur plate of knickknacks!" (Gumbo was served.)[29] Mrs. Louise Roberts's maid, in head cloth, receiving the lost *Italian Girl* guests (about seventy) at the foot of the drive and then, with arm and hand upraised in a gesture reminiscent of the Beckoning Fair One, leading each party all the way up the drive and onto the terrace (the house is a replica of a plantation mansion) and into the party— she did this with each group of arriving guests.[30] Mr. Leo Corrigan [real estate executive] pointing out that at least four of his male guests are billionaires, and one has at least a million dollars a week; the parties, parties, parties—and how Mary Reed and David Stickelbar (from Kansas City) never want to go to

---

28. Rudolf Bing (1902–97) was general manager of the Metropolitan Opera (1950–72). A notorious autocrat, he sent a telegram on November 5 insisting that Callas commit by the next morning to his proposed schedule for her at the Met. Callas responded the following morning with a counterproposal, but that telegram crossed another from Bing that canceled her contract.

29. Leo would meet socialite Evelyn Lambert (1918–99) again in Venice in the late seventies, when she had become one of the Veneto's busiest hostesses and preservationists. She did everything on a generous scale.

30. Rossini's *L'Italiana in Algeri* ("The Italian Girl in Algiers") was also presented in Dallas that season; "The Beckoning Fair One" is a ghost story by Oliver Onions, in which a feminine spirit gradually leads the protagonist into madness.

sleep.[31] He said suddenly that he wanted time to stop and then threw out of the window of the speeding car his $600 wristwatch; the lunches, dinners-after-party parties at the Cipango, the Imperial Club, the City Club. The woman who said, "Ah have to have at least thirty ball gowns a season, Mr. Lerman," with the inflection upward on the Lerman. The hundreds of women shaking hands with us when we were guests of honor at the Dallas Woman's Club—Mrs. Roberts finally saying, "It's lucky that you weren't doing this last year, you would have been blinded. Jewelry's changed in a year." Mrs. Vera Hart Martin (very Big Mama), who entertained five hundred for the debbie niece of Temple Phinney, at an eleven a.m. coffee and then entertained another six hundred of us at a tea on the same day—"People are always saying, 'Vera, Why don't you git married again,' and I'm always saying to them, 'I was married, honey.'" She's been a widder twelve years. Mr. Graf in his showplace, the Stone House, as empty an extravagance as ever the world has known, pressing buttons that illuminate each tree—and how many there are—hundreds—and saying in his Berlin-accented, *mittel*-European-charm, soft voice, his worldly eyes amused, "*und* we have walls all around us—like a prison—but it is comfortable. . . ." Then he showed me his dressing room, where some one hundred suits hang splendidly—also a couple of early Mondrian flower watercolors—all other "art" strictly from the calendar (nowhere in Dallas did I see a single genuine painting, save in the museums). When Nancy Howell and I were leaving, and she asked for a red rose from one of the flower arrangements (all placed precisely where [the decorator] Robsjohn-Gibbings had placed them the day the house was finished) and Mr. Graf was about to give her one, the butler in tailcoat said, "Mr. Graf, Mrs. Graf needs them for tomorrow." Nancy did not get the rose, and Mr. Graf looked regretful but accustomed to it all. Mrs. G was [formerly] a waitress near or in Fort Worth—a blonde and dressed like a carhop. She'd been done up in purple, but five minutes before we came Mr. G had forbidden her to come down in it, for it was too décolleté—so now she was in red pants and jeweled pull-on.

Do not forget Maria's temper—how this is a nourishment to her—an outlet and absolutely important, for it is the result of her superb genius. She breathes through temper as the earth breathes through volcanoes.

People at *Medea* were listening with one ear to the opera and the other fixed to election returns coming over transistor radios.

NOTE: In the winter of 1958–59, Leo wrote the screenplay of George Balanchine's version of *The Nutcracker* for a *Playhouse 90* broadcast produced by John Houseman. However, Leo took another prolonged break from journal writing in this period, resuming in July 1959. Although the *Nutcracker* project passed without comment, following are two reminiscences by him about other experiences during these months.

31. Mary Reed Carter and David Stickelbar were heirs to family manufacturing firms. GF: "Mary Reed caught up with Maria everywhere. She was known as Maria Seconda."

**TANIA AND MARIA** *"Isak Dinesen is coming to New York," everyone told everyone else, "to tell her stories." So, the legend arrived, with retinue, of course—a cousin, a secretary-companion. Female royalty was always attended, in its palmy days, by at least two nobly in waiting. She was even more fragile than she had been years ago when I sat at tea with her in her gray and gold room. I would take her to hear Maria Callas sing* Il Pirata *at Carnegie Hall [on January 27, 1959]. Yes, she would like that. She had never heard or even seen Callas. She loved music, opera. . . . She looked at me speculatively, her I-know-exactly-what-you-are-thinking look.*

*We went to Carnegie Hall. The mobs on the pavement were the kind you see in movies about Hollywood stars attending their own world premieres. When our taxi finally drew up to the curb, the mobs were busy looking this way and that way and shouting. I helped Tania out of the taxi. She was so thin that the weight of her garments made it almost impossible for her to move. She stood a moment, resting against me.*[32] *She seemed a design by Beardsley: In her youth she had surely known the Marchesa Casati, for here were related twistings and windings of tulle and chiffon, lace and fur, black and deep brown mingling.*[33] *Beardsley, the Casati—she had assimilated them years ago. Now she was herself, unique, a personage of very great quality and astonishing individuality. Automatically the mob became silent. It made a lane along which I half-carried, half-led her and so up the steps and into the hall.*

*During the second act, she whispered, "Yes. She has something of Pellegrina Leoni . . . yes. . . ."*[34] *She continued to peer at Callas. When the aria ended, still staring straight at the stage, she murmured, "It is not always possible to see even the shadow of one's own invention and hers is someone so closely related to . . ." It was never necessary to explain to Tania.* (FROM *ISAK DINESEN: A MEMORIAL*, 1965)

**MARLENE AND GRETA** *Walking across town late one evening with Marlene, after we had hidden ourselves in the top balcony of the old Paramount movie palace on Times Square (where we had gone to see the remake of* The Blue Angel *starring May Britt, and had not sat through the whole thing because it was agony for Marlene, who could not believe what had happened to her* Blue Angel), *Marlene said, as she stepped into the gutter, "Dear, what would have become of me if I had not really been a cold woman?" I took her to Café Geiger, that very German bakeshop and restaurant on East Eighty-sixth Street, and fed her* Kaffee mit Schlag *and rich cakes. We laughed a lot, and the little string orchestra played Marlene's "Falling in Love Again" and "Johnny" and "Peter"*

32. In his own manuscript, Leo later inserted here: "Her facial appearance—skull, kohl-lined eyes, all white face."
33. Italian heiress Marchesa Luisa Casati (1881–1957) was renowned for her eccentric style. In her younger years, she was lavishly dressed by Fortuny and Poiret.
34. Pellegrina Leoni is an opera singer in Dinesen's short story "The Dreamers."

*and other Marlene songs and "gems" from* The Student Prince. *Marlene whispered: "I always wanted to play Kathy in that, but who would ever let me play an ingénue? Who would believe me as Gretchen in* Faust?" *And we both cried.*

*Then we went back to Gray and my house, and she, who really did not like to go to sleep ever, sat in the back parlor and laughed and talked and impersonated. She settled down at about five in the morning and said, "Did I ever tell you about the time I went to see Miss Greta Garbo?" She laughed, "Yes. You know that book by Isak Dinesen,* The Angelic Avengers, *you remember what it's about? You know, two sisters . . . two sisters who really love one another very much . . . about their life . . . and about a beautiful sister and the other one wasn't really so beautiful . . . two wonderful, wonderful sisters . . . I thought what a marvelous movie, if Greta would play it with me. So, I went to see her. I took the book. Do you remember the cover of the book? It had the two sisters on the cover? You knew right away what that book was. So I took the book and I went to see Greta. And Greta said, 'What do you want?' and I told her all about these two wonderful sisters, one so beautiful and the other not so beautiful. And Greta said, 'So which one should I be?' And I said, 'What do you mean, Greta, the one who's more interesting, the one who's not so beautiful. She's the most interesting person in this whole book. She's the real star.' And Greta said, 'I don't think I want to make this movie with you.' And she got up, took me to the door, and that's the last time I ever visited Greta Garbo."* (1993)

SEPTEMBER 15, 1959 • NEW YORK CITY

**TO RICHARD HUNTER • PARIS**

This is like the first night of winter—cold, rain—the leaves almost all gone. My, how I've selfishly wished that you were home these last weeks. They've been hell. Only seven of *Mademoiselle's* staff are left now: I am one of the seven! Cyrilly [Abels, managing editor], the art department, Kay [Silver], etc., etc., all fired . . . Today Mrs. B assured me that I would be with *Mlle* for a long time to come. But who can believe? Anyway I still had the job today—tomorrow?

This evening I've been to a large dinner at Helen Hoke's! And there was Kitty Messner . . . just like years ago.[35] When she arrived she looked untouched by time—even better than she used to look. Then as the evening went on, her face fell apart and that was awful. I could see age obliterating the younger woman I once knew . . . age and dissipation. She still drinks incredible amounts. She immediately asked after you . . . and when I said that you were abroad for a year again, she looked aghast and asked how was I eating? Very well, I told her, but she did not seem to believe me.

I'm doing a job for the State Department. They've asked me as the leading authority on the American musical to write them a piece, which they will have

---

35. Helen Hoke (1903–90), writer and publisher of children's books, was married to the publisher Franklin Watts. Kitty Messner was head of the publishing house Julian Messner, for which Leo had edited several books in the early forties.

translated into Iron Curtain languages, especially Russian, and then will distribute there in *America Illustrated*—not on the moon yet! So now I'm a leading authority! They pay $300. For $30 I'd be a leading authority on pigs' trotters!

SEPTEMBER 23

The office situation seems somewhat improved. . . . I have had two meetings with the baroness and those henchwomen.[36] They move as one, a sort of blunt, obstinate, and ignorant flying wedge. They refer to themselves as "The Team" and as "The Brain Trust"! Thus far I've been able to cope, but I never know from day to day what next. Mrs. B seems to cherish me. I have a feeling that she has to because she has just about eight or ten of us left. Isn't that appalling? Also I seem to have an extraordinary reputation in this little world.

NOTE: In 1959, Samuel I. Newhouse, founder and owner of Advance Publications, a media empire built on regional newspapers, bought first Condé Nast Publications, including *Vogue*, and then Street & Smith, including *Mademoiselle*. One motive of the latter purchase was capturing *Charm* magazine, Street & Smith's rival to Condé Nast's *Glamour*. On September 30, 1959, Leo wrote to Richard that Advance had shut down *Charm* and "almost its entire staff has usurped *Mlle*'s." The new ownership was improving *Mademoiselle*'s financial stabililty, however, and hence Leo's own security. He soon ceased worrying about being out of a job and began a thirty-five-year working relationship with the Newhouses.

JOURNAL • JANUARY 5, 1960 I was up and away to the Plaza to take tea with a Mr. [Herbert] Breslin. Mr. Breslin [a publicist] tried to "sell" me Joan Sutherland, but I told him he did not have to "sell" me her, for I had heard her—and she sings carefully with all the passion of an English miss who has suddenly been set free from her country school.

Then we had a Schwarzkopf harangue and I told him why I'd never heard her save on disks—and he did not like what I told him.[37]

AUGUST 27, 1960 Dipping into diaries—Louisa Alcott's kept in that sun-splattered red house at Fruitlands, with its poor little truckle-bed attic where she prayed and wept. I just want to sit and sit and sit, but time runs out of the glass now. This is almost—why almost?—the other side of the hill. Mrs. Woolf,

---

36. Eleanor Perényi (b. 1918) had recently replaced Cyrilly Abels as managing editor at *Mademoiselle*. She had married a Hungarian baron as a teenager.

37. Soprano Elisabeth Schwarzkopf (1915–2006) had been a Nazi party member during her wartime years at Berlin's Deutsche Oper. When Leo attended Callas's Chicago debut in 1954, Schwarzkopf was also in the audience. He wrote then: "I sat looking with hatred at Schwarzkopf. One of those cold, pale-moon beauties, whose voice is ravishing, especially in *Capriccio*, but how can she produce anything of beauty after that Nazi life? How can [record company executive] Walter Legge, a plump, benign English Jew, be married to her?" *Journal*, November 2, 1954.

Katherine Mansfield, Rev. Kilvert, even the Gloomy Dean—all [diarists] writing away, breathing through writing.[38] Almost all that I have earned is by nonwriting. That is why I am so ecstatic when I feel that I have written something. So these years of dissipation during which my "talent" has slowly drained away . . . that must be the reason for these empty, writingless days. Bill Inge said that "the pattern" of my life has changed radically. What then has this change done to my writing? If only the change could be complete—meaning money sufficient to sit home and write only what I want to write—but I do want to write about Rev. Kilvert: To be precise, I want to write about how he was so in love with living that he was able to surmount anonymity. He picked himself up out of the river and became an island and the beacon upon this island, illuminating the world about it. This is what I want to write—for if we do not affirm that we live, we are dead things. Strength comes from affirmation of continuity. Knowing that a thousand years ago some poor creature sat scratching upon his tablet—while his world smashed about him—makes going on possible.

AUGUST 31, 1960   How can one know the depth of a wound? The injury inflicted by a phrase? No marks, no blood—almost nothing visible. These are wretched days—interior all messed, stoppage, breakdown—nothing moves from heart and head to paper. And the busiest time of the year. "Are you a writer?" the Israeli novelist asked. I can never answer, because I know how inadequate any answer would be. "Not for some time," I heard Gray say, and I was an aching, amputated mass. I know the truth in this—but to hear it was to know that, despite a life shared, no living closely ever permits the other one to know most of what goes on within. My sleeplessness came in the early dawn. Even knowing the cure does not help, for I do nothing about it. Hedda [Sterne, a painter] answered the Israeli by saying I write reviews. This compounded the depression. If I had written what I should have written these years, even failing at it—but no one is to blame. I am the only one—having written and published millions of words for some twenty-three or so years and to no deep, abiding avail. This is no time to waste with self-humiliation, feelings—but what wrongs I have done to such talents as I have (had). What self-indulgence and waste. The only cure is writing. So simple to blame others—I must somehow climb out of this muck. I must become not myself again [sic]. I must stop fumbling for words here and get to work. I lack all discipline. This comes of wanting to be loved and admired and be made much of. If only I could go talk with other people who have these problems, these inabilities to work. But if you cannot

38. The diary of British clergyman Robert Francis Kilvert (1840–79) provides a detailed account of Victorian provincial life. Leo found the innocence and observation of it quite moving. "The Gloomy Dean" (of St. Paul's Cathedral) was William Ralph Inge (1860–1954), journalist and author, a pessimist about progress and democracy.

talk to the closest being to whom can you talk? Oneself—like this—not saying all, because who can say all without hurting?

NOVEMBER 15, 1960 • NEW YORK CITY

**TO RICHARD HUNTER • CAIRO**

That long review I wrote about the Rev. Kilvert's diaries was printed on the front page of the *Times* [*Book Review*]—and such a lovely hullabaloo—letters (even from Agnes de Mille, signed "Your Agnes"). It is a good piece—really a kind of cry from my little heart. So, I am pleased that some people heard. Martha G [Graham] says that she knows that something wonderful will happen because of this review—and, oh, how patiently I waited for the *Times* to publish it.

The Blond Divinity [Dietrich] suddenly rang up to be friends again.[39] She says she's $40,000 in debt to the bank, because she has to pay so much to unions. Now she's off in Las Vegas replacing Sammy Davis, Jr. Then she plays a huge Philadelphia club and opens at the Palace in January. That last is scary.

DECEMBER 8, 1960 • NEW YORK CITY

**TO RICHARD HUNTER • BOMBAY (FORWARDED TO MIAMI)**

I shall know on the twenty-first when the doctors take the cast off whether I must go into hospital to have an operation and be evermore gimpy-legged. You see, that taxi accident has caught up with me again. The cartilage in my right knee is gone—all broken—and water-on-the-knee has set in. So I have been encased in a huge cast from my ankle to my thigh all the way up. I sprawl here (in the basement—I can't move much) like a beached whale. The past ten days I was all alone, for Gray was in Dallas. His father is fading away—down to 107 pounds and coughing all the time.[40] And his uncles are ill. All this is too grim. I am cheerful, but furious about my leg, since I don't think that I have earned this curious disaster. It is excessively painful—a little less (I try to believe) each day. I always have awful sickness when you are away. Sometimes—especially when I was alone and couldn't move—it was awful. I wished and wished for you all to be home, selfishly.

NOTE: Mina Curtiss owned a house in the Georgetown district of Washington, D.C., at this time. During one of Leo's stays there, the director of the Harvard research center at Dumbarton Oaks invited them to a concert and dinner.

JOURNAL • APRIL 10, 1961 • WASHINGTON, D.C. Of Dumbarton Oaks: A high "queen" (but likable) demi-camp runs it, Jack Thacher. The audience was invited and almost all in black tie. The British ambassador—a neat,

---

39. Marlene Dietrich's friendship with Leo occasionally lapsed, usually when she had taken umbrage at something he had—or had not—written about her. Leo does not say what this recent rift had been.

40. Gray's father had emphysema. He did not die, however, until April 1969.

businessman's compact, bargain-shrewd, polished face—and his wife, an American, in nondescript black, the dress very plain, reminding me of Sophie Guggenheim (they have in common the female athlete's look). The [James] Biddles—he with a rat-that-ate-the-cat face, and she I do not remember. "The oldest people in the world come to Dumbarton on Sunday nights," said Catherine Shouse. She, née Filene, but having determined never to be a Jew has almost no Jewish characteristics, save the slight atmosphere of certain very elderly, rich, Jewish men, a sort of dry-sweetness. You can hear the paper money and coupons being totaled.[41]

Maureen Forrester sang Schumann (the "Lorelei") and Brahms especially well, everything else not well, and looked a frump. The music room is perfection in the manner of the twenties re-creation of the Renaissance.

In the station I said to Gray, as we listened to two grubby Russians, not understanding a word, of course: "What a funny character, who eavesdrops even when not understanding a word of what he hears, but just because he loves to eavesdrop."

The full realization of my grave misstep in writing even a word for fashion magazines, years ago, has come upon me recently. I accept this—no anguish— but I must do something about it. How weak that last is. Surely [the actress] Signe Hasso meant, when she read my writing, that my fashion magazine earning-a-living has been the long detour, that this would be over, and I would write my books? (Such a lovely bacon smell now, but not for me. I hope not . . . save the teensiest hope, because if [the maid] Mae brings it, I shall have to eat it. I am very like Kchessinska, who had to accept emeralds and villas, so as not to hurt the givers.)[42] Perhaps the Grand Surprise isn't finding oneself in the "great world" of society, fashion, arts, and entertainment, but discovering that one has made an almost comical mistake, which for years has deflected one from his true purpose. Am I frightened of failure? I wrote that bad little novel some years ago, but all the while knowing that I need never show it to anyone, and so being protected.[43] If Proust had never written, I should not be what I internally am, nor should I be inhibited. But why use Proust as an apology? I know that I could sit and write. This novel would happen—no? Reading one of my many beginnings last week, I was appalled at the fancy writing, the overwrought, feminine, sensitized writing and feeling. I do not want to write that way. I want to write solidly, beautifully. The transfixed moment, yes, but not an enormous book of them.

41. This cousin of Mina Curtiss, Catherine Filene Shouse (1896–1994), was a philanthropist and activist who would establish the Wolf Trap Foundation in 1968.

42. The *prima ballerina assoluta* of Russia's Maryinsky Theatre, Mathilda Kchessinska (1872–1971) had been the mistress of Nicholas II when he was tsarevitch and then of the Grand Duke Andrei, whom she married in 1921.

43. In the summer of 1953, Leo had written a novella around an Eleonora von Mendelssohn character. The manuscript does not survive.

APRIL 13, 1961 "He used to treat me like his mistress. Now he treats me like his mother." Mina about [her brother] Lincoln.

APRIL 20, 1961 · NEW YORK CITY Just to note an unexpected evening with Maria Callas yesterday. She came off the [Onassis] yacht, having telephoned Dario and Dorle [Soria]. This was very family. Maria is leading the sort of life any woman lives, her timetable being totally controlled by the whims of her man who is apparently more loved than loving. "I'm an Oriental," she said. But there is so much more of this: Her new smile—very young, sweet, hurt; her softness; her vulnerability. She would not remain on the yacht alone with [Winston] Churchill: "So boring." How defenseless and inappropriate she looked, like an apprehensive schoolgirl, as she went up the steps of El Morocco going to meet Onassis. This person is the center of her life, not music.

APRIL 29, 1961 I feel that the adventure, in living, is to follow the strings (the Minotaur's thread) with surprise and delight, even when the climate is that of despair. When I feel, then there is hope, but when I am very still inside, when everything is suspended, frozen, transfixed, soundless—then that is a dangerous time. I am very primitive in my reactions—like a beast—but what is the sense of all this? Nothing—save writing to keep courage. Some people whistle when in a fix. I write, that is, I scribble.

MAY 13, 1961 I become more and more pent up. My ability to speak out diminishes. I know that much of what I want to say can make no difference save a destructive one. "If only once we didn't have to have something set . . . You must spend hundreds of dollars for food—dinners and lunches at the Plaza. . . . Who paid last night? Schiaparelli didn't pay. . . . And she wasn't even for business or a friend." "She's interesting. I wanted to know her." But I think that he never realizes how easy it would be for me to have these people in—on Sunday afternoon, just for wine and biscuits—no fuss—nothing—simple. "If you had the kind of life with a staff . . ." But I had the kind of life sans anything—very little money—none sometimes—and still the world came and loved coming and was grateful. I am now timid about saying that anyone has invited me anywhere, reluctant to say that I have gone anywhere, really quite frightened of telling what happened when I do go, for there is such a scoffing, such a ruthless criticism. This cannot be healthy. . . . Now everything becomes tangled.

So much happened this week. Carmel [Snow] died.[44] Richard came,

---

44. GF: "Leo was in bed with a cast. Carmel had got herself together in a beautiful Balenciaga outfit, and she came and visited him for about an hour, never alluding to her illness. She was definitely in the last weeks of her life and really very gallant."

departed, came again, and departed again—but I do not feel like scribbling about any of it. I can live upon myself, alone—but not when the aloneness is cracked wide open. I don't even think that he realizes: If he did he would be a monster: "What's the matter—does something hurt?" he asks. . . . Hurt! I am twisting into a strange root of an old man—afraid to be myself.

Now I have scribbled from my side, but what of his needs? He obviously needs to be alone with the one person he loves, but he cannot stand anything repetitive (save sex and his drawing) for a long time. He seemingly dislikes most people and does not especially want to be with the ones he likes. What he should never have had is me. The "bad" accruing from me far outweighs the material and creature goods. If only I could come by money enough to take us away into a small world while we are still young enough to try such an experiment. Soon there will be no time—the effort of being becomes more and more tiring. I refuse to face my own weakness. I am so easily broken down—and right now I am on the edge again. Any show of violence would topple me over. He never knows when not to say something to me. . . . I had to stop scribbling and hide away this notebook. That is wrong. We each need a secret place, but that secret place should be inviolate even when others know about it.

MAY 15, 1961  Yesterday at Poppa's grave, when Uncle Sam [Goldwasser] offered me the prayer book, thinking that I would read the prayer (in English), I could not even take the proffered book let alone read the prayer. I was never able to talk to Poppa when he was alive.

AUGUST 12, 1961  Schrafft's at Eighty-eighth and Madison. All of the women have creaking voices like ancient rocking chairs, homely, of no singularity save that they have survived lovelier rocking chairs. Each of the creakers orders a Manhattan and the Diet Lunch. Crockity-crickity they go. One bravely summons the male manager and suggests that more fish be added to the menu. The headwaitresses are close kin to women who supervise "rest homes." "Not in the dining room," says the most rigidly haired one. The one with glittering spectacles in place of eyes and old 5-cent pieces in her throat. "We had that one out before, Mrs. Pomerantz." Mrs. Pomerantz is large and could blubber. Her three companions diminish in size, each a replica of Mrs. Pomerantz: whitened, carefully set hair, and pale, carefully set smiles; wide, wondering, have-lived-for-years eyes huge and aquatic behind glass; mouths satisfied by things, not love, by respect from servants, not admiration. The supervisors have utterly dissatisfied mouths. They hate the "ladies." "Do you have that lovely," one of the ladies' voices suddenly cascades, young and girlish, "black raspberry ice cream I had the other night?"

NOTE: Gray received a Guggenheim Foundation award in 1961. He went to his mother's in Burbank, where he remained from September through December, producing a large drawing in addition to some covers for Columbia Records and illustrations for *Mademoiselle*.

SEPTEMBER 4, 1961 • WILLIAMSBURG, MASSACHUSETTS
TO GRAY FOY • BURBANK

I finished reading (not having read it for years) [Michael Arlen's novel] *The Green Hat*. It is quite a document, and how apparent is its power and the reason for its great impact. Iris March is, indeed, a gallant lady—and what a rotter is Boy Fenwick. Do you know why Iris March led her "dissolute" life for twelve years and why, finally, she crashed her yellow Isotta with its silver stork cap against Harrods (the great ash on the Harpenden estate)? Because there will always be an England. You must read it. I think of that little man [Arlen]— suave, smooth, beaked, sallow-faced, with hooded, huge, worldly eyes— looking as if he had a head full of pearl-gray spats and was to the silver-headed walking stick born—an anachronism in the late forties and fifties—not given to saying much, but always watching—a sort of revenant—and never as much Michael Arlen as whatever his Middle East [Armenian] self had been before he became Michael Arlen. Then his mother-in-law—smaller than a Newhouse and always in princely Catholic black, but cut so beautifully—and such a ransom of pearls—and seemingly tipped in diamonds—and her old, old wise eyes amused but kind. Those eyes had not only seen Eugénie and Carlota and Victoria and Elizabeth of Austria but looked into their eyes. What that woman knew—the wit and sorrow she had heard, for she was fantastically old when I met her and was waiting to be amused for the brief remainder of her many days.

SEPTEMBER 24, 1961 • WILLIAMSBURG, MASSACHUSETTS
TO GRAY FOY • BURBANK

Last night, as we sat reading in the immense but sibilant rain (the waterfall beyond the wood, the tides in the trees—a great Robert Louis Stevenson nightrider wind was vociferously driving away), we became gradually aware of a dog baying in the near distance. Soon we went out into the night to peer through the watery moonlight (that one passed through the sky like Garbo all deeply veiled in *Susan Lenox: Her Fall and Rise*) at an array of bright flashlights seemingly moving in our direction. We could hear men's voices—rough voices. And many dogs—hounds—were in full cry. The Goddess [Mina Curtiss] immediately went quite frantic with terror and boomed into the night, "Who are you? Who are you?" Then she rushed into the house to call the gardeners. I stood in the night quite fascinated by all of this—calm with that sort of quiet which always seems to fill me when I am not frightening myself. (That's because I do not believe anything will happen or even can happen.)[45] So then she rushed out, bellowing and screeching, and I knew that I was about to get

45. GF: "Leo could be fascinated with his terror. He would dissociate himself and see it in a comical or satirical way, almost as a cartoon not actually happening to him."

the giggles, but just then there was hollering from the flashlights and gunshots (such a curious flat, final crack, a gunshot—like the slap of a body against water, but no alleviating splash follows) and all of the hounds bayed wildly— and someone shouted, "Huntin' raccoons . . ." and the gardeners appeared, in bathrobes and spectacles, carrying rifles—and an ax and a club. It was all so other century—so like paintings and engravings, there in the hurtling moon-light, beneath the furious trees—that I never giggled at all, just stood there con-founded and delighted. Later the Goddess said how brave I had been, so I did not tell her that it was not bravery but having a literary experience that kept me from lighting out for safety beneath my bed. All through the evening, I could hear the distant shouts of the men, the transports of the dogs, an occasional flat, sharp crack—but I do not think any coons were done in. It was a glimpse of an America I have never known—frightening only when I suddenly thought that men, too, are hunted this way.

OCTOBER 4, 1961 • NEW YORK CITY

TO GRAY FOY • DALLAS

The [Metropolitan Opera] opening was marvelous, with Leontyne [Price][46] singing gloriously, but not quite as gloriously as she did at dress rehearsal. *La Fanciulla* is such a strange opera musically, Puccini so deep in wondering whether Debussy and Fauré and Wagner and R. Strauss couldn't be right.

[Composer] Chuck Turner turned up backstage and asked wouldn't I like to drop in at his apartment. Lennie Bernstein's chauffeur (!!!) would drive me. He has a beautiful gray, upholstered in scarlet, huge foreign (I think) motor (could only be called that) and a liveried, huge chauffeur, and he [Lennie] dragged himself about conspicuously, of course, in a Dracula outfit. So off we went to this tenement very like the one you lived in years ago. As we were climbing the stairs to the top floor (naturally), Lennie, demonstrating how like Dukas some of *La Fanciulla* is, sang out—at which a door opened, and a wiz-ened, rightfully wrathful man shouted, "People are sleeping! We have to get up in the morning. You don't have to go to work!" By this time, no one in the entire house was sleeping, I am sure. Lennie said, "Who doesn't have to go to work?" as we vanished into Chuck's very neat railroad flat. Here was a cold "spread" and [art patron and collector] Henry McIlhenny in white tie and a very nice man (fortyish) with him. So we sat and chatted. Henry asked why did we (you and I) never call him in Philadelphia, and I said that we were shy, and he said not to be. Soon, in came [pianist] Earl Wild and a jazz piano player, Paul someone, apparently an important jazzman, who sat down and talked to me about his wife and little girls. Then Marc Blitzstein [composer and lyricist] appeared and four or five young "people" and [actor] Mindy [Wager]. So I saw

---

46. The soprano Leontyne Price (b. 1927) was a superb performer of Verdi roles, particularly Aïda. Her 1955 television performance in *Tosca* was an African American milestone.

what this was going to be and got my coat, just as a large bed, upon which were seated and sprawled those luminaries and some of the *jeunesse dorée*, crashed to the floor. They flopped behind it, legs waving in air like overturned insects. At this I fell into loud, manly blasts of glee, thus momentarily incurring wrathful faces, more red from blood rushing to their heads. So Earl Wild and the jazz pianist said, "We'll drive you home. . . ." As we left, Lennie was clutching his hammy head and mourning, "Why did I do this—why?"

OCTOBER 21, 1961 • NEW YORK CITY

TO GRAY FOY • BURBANK

I did bills and chores and picked up Rut and trundled off to Maya Deren's funeral service in a huge, enormously high, Corinthian-columned hall. A most peculiar but fitting service—voodoo rattles and a long eulogy about her and quoting from her writings on voodoo and moviemaking and a small but ample-haired versifier reading his "Ode" to M.D. and her request that Haydn's "Trumpet Rondo" be played carried out by a "live" trumpet—brazen and corrosive. Her husband thanked everyone for coming, and that was deeply touching. I sat looking at the profiles and backs of heads of Antony [Tudor[47]] and Hugh [Laing]. They looked like Edward Gorey people—that was awful. Then Marguerite [Young] materialized, looking like a bloated caricature of Herodias in the Wilde play, but done by a provincial Dutch company, and she told me that Ruth Stephan had divorced John, and that Ruth was in India. Then Carol Janeway came up and proffered her cheek—raddled and worn.[48] Others out of the long-ago appeared, and Rut and I flew out into [Washington] Square and went to Ken [Elmslie]'s house. I like it—old, buried away behind another house, once a brothel, now the mansion of that beautiful [whippet] Whippoorwill, who cuddled against me and made sleepy-dog noises. So to an Italian dinner in a little, ugly place—inexpensive but good and the people friendly and all remote from New York. A place with a table around which sat the habitués— all middle-aged and elderly Italian men—singing softly, talking, reading papers. I longed for us to be in Italy. It is the routine of these days—getting up, brushing my teeth, clump-clumping downstairs, dressing, no one calling, each day identical—that does me in—the barren, necessary, unadorned, solitary, aging routine.[49]

47. Antony Tudor (1909–87), the British dancer and choreographer, worked after 1939 primarily with American Ballet Theatre and is best known for ballets that explored psychological motives (*Lilac Garden, Dark Elegies*). He was the lover of dancer Hugh Laing.
48. Ceramist Carol Janeway (1913?–89) had been close to Leo and Richard during World War II, when she was the lover of the sculptor Ossip Zadkine. Leo had sent Maya Deren to photograph Zadkine for his 1943 "Before Bandwagons" feature.
49. In a letter dated September 7, 1956, Deren had written to Leo: "You should do a book on 'Our bunch'—this pressured bunch that is dying off so early because upon them lay the burden of bridging over from the exhilarations and spectacular rebelliousness of the 'Lost Generation'—to the ones who are coming after us now—the first Cosmopolitans in the best sense of the word. . . . We are the *atomized generation*."

Last night I rang [Tatiana] Mrs. Liberman (you don't like her and she is a horror) and found her weeping like a huge, badly made building falling apart. At about this time Alex is having his [stomach ulcer] operation; it takes a minimum of four hours.

The Goddess of Massachusetts [Mina Curtiss] writes (in strict confidence) that [Marcel Proust's niece] Suzy Mante-Proust has sold all of the Proust manuscripts to the University of Texas for $300,000. The French scholars who know about this are in a state. The only possibility they have of keeping them in the Bibliothèque Nationale is by raising the money to buy them for France. How strange—Proust in Texas, and how fascinated he would have been—horrified—I am not so sure—but absolutely fascinated, yes. I see how possible it is to live in a fantasy world and become stranger and stranger. See! I've lived that way all of my life.[50]

**JOURNAL · NOVEMBER 1, 1961** Leontyne sang gorgeously [in *La Fanciulla*], but all during Act I her voice had an underlying unwell sound, especially phlegmy in that sore spot in her lower register, although the performance was magnificent. A jammed house adored her. Then suddenly, toward the end of Act II—rasp-rasp and her singing voice was gone—only a sandpaper ghost talking the piece. Tremendous, successful dramatic intensity sustained her through the card scene and the end of the act. I have never felt such horror in a theater—the entire, huge, audience breathing with her, willing her to finish the act and find relief. Torrents of applause for her. She was absolutely gray—her face and arms literally gray. But the needless gallantry of finishing that act. Dorothy Kirsten was routed out of sleep and dashed down and into the house for Act III. Not bad, but certainly no atmosphere—more Doris Day than Minnie [the heroine].

Geraldine Page had missed Act I. I found her in her seat when I returned after the interval. Although she had not heard a single note, she was weeping. "I always weep at Puccini," she said.

NOVEMBER 4, 1961 · NEW YORK CITY
**TO RICHARD HUNTER · LONDON**

You must promise me that if I die first there is to be no me left exposed in a gruesome coffin, and I must not have a funeral in a small, sordid room with plain, impersonal prayers. I would like to be buried from home or Millhauser's [mortuary, across the street] if I live here. I want the "Ode to the West Wind" and "Oh World I Cannot Hold Thee Close Enough," and someone who really knew me—or lots of someones—to tell little happy things, the prelude to the last act of *Traviata*, the two arias from *Figaro* (on the gramophone), and cheer—not horror.

---

50. The Bibliothèque Nationale did gather enough money to acquire the Proust manuscripts.

[Dancer and actress] Joan [McCracken]'s funeral was dreadful—with this wax creature exposed in what seemed a party dress. You could not avoid it—the room so small, many could not get into the mediocre, awful place—the sick sweet stench of perishing flowers—an utterly ordinary-voiced, black-smocked preacher reading prayers and nothing about her—all lasting some fifteen minutes—oh, it was awful—all save the turnout: Richard Rodgers, Agnes de Mille, Jerry Robbins, [Theatre Guild producer] Lawrence Langner, dozens of dancers who had been in shows with her (so many older), [actress] Mabel Taliaferro, the [Robert] Lantzes (whose [production] *Kean* opened last night), so many, many aging actors, wardrobe mistresses, and men who looked like stage-hands—everyone weeping—but most pitiful was the boy who lived with her, all alone and comfortless, and her mother. In church you can, at least, remove yourself from the weeping and, perhaps, be comforted by the church itself—but not here. I stood in the street until her coffin was tucked into a poor hearse—but why go on about it all? I am still baffled—what are we to profit from all this? And did you know that Vertès died in Paris? I am sad, thinking of that long-ago Northport summer when we first knew him and [his wife] Dora and sat upon the beach and he reminded me of Pat Dolin as [Fokine's] "Bluebeard."[51] So many deaths this week and last. I dread to open the morning paper. Joan died in her sleep. Many seem to think this a good way, but how do we know the terror in the night?

Dear, please write me a long, gay, legible letter, full of cheerful tidings. Please comfort me with laughter the way we used to laugh years ago. I always think of the mornings when we polkaed. Oh, we were gay in our unhappinesses. I cannot believe that those who die go before us to prepare a lovely house, as I heard today—but now I am too disturbed to go on about it all. I signed your name in the book at the funeral, because of our youth together. I signed yours and Gray's and Truman's and Jack's, because I knew that was what Joan would have wanted, but I signed yours and Gray's with mine because I knew that we should all be together in that book.

NOVEMBER 10, 1961 • NEW YORK CITY
**TO GRAY FOY** • BURBANK

Today girls who never heard of Joan McCracken look the way they do because she looked the way she did—bangs; sometimes a ponytail; full, full skirts; flat, flat slippers. It was the ballet girl look Degas loved. Agnes de Mille launched it [with her in *Oklahoma!*]. Joan McCracken epitomized it, gave it a sort of sad-eyed, flapper appeal. Beneath her gaiety, her funniness onstage and off, there was always this sadness. You cannot be a clown without it.

You are so very patient with me when I ring you and chatter away, but this is

---

51. Marcel Vertès (1895–1961), a Hungarian illustrator, designer, and painter, frequently contributed to *Bazaar* in the late thirties.

my only lifeline to certainty—my mooring rope and anchor. I know that you cannot talk freely, and how difficult that must be, and how uncomfortable it must make you. But selfishly, I persist, so as to be able to breathe from day to day. I went to see Alex [Liberman] this morning, and he seems fragile, but almost recovered, and he asked me how I could bear it here without you. I was surprised at this question. So, I said that time was cement-footed indeed.

NOVEMBER 15

I am so happy to have talked to my own Puss. Please, please do not weep. Something lovely will happen. You went to Europe twice and got a Guggenheim and found me (or vice versa) so you should believe in lovely things happening. Do not work so hard. All that matters is for you to keep well—and for us to be together again! I think of you every moment of the time—and worry about you—and try to think of how we can help Maebelle. Maebelle has earned something lovely, and I know that it will happen, so do not despair.[52]

JOURNAL · DECEMBER 11, 1961 Lincoln came to lunch and we chatted along amiably. He telling me that everything I had prophesied about his Chinese venturings came true—an attempt at blackmail, all of it—but this had resulted in a happy ending. He'd met (through all of this) a boy who gave him "bliss," was a "god," was "not very bright," but has an amazing conception of life: thinking that since he was useless, he was the kind who should do the dangerous things, like sea demolition. He did it. Lincoln took him to Dumbarton Oaks, and there he is now a gardener. He had been in gardening for a year while in the service. We chatted along and got to talking about Wystan [Auden]—oh, yes, through Lincoln saying that Lennie had lost some of what made him; Aaron [Copland] hadn't; Virgil [Thomson] was utterly deteriorated. I said Chester Kallman had grown but Wystan had deteriorated.[53] Lincoln flew into a quiet passion, almost weeping, saying that I shouldn't talk about my betters, that I wasn't an intellectual (which I never thought I was), that I couldn't analyze anything, that I was a very stupid man, that the only reason he ever saw me was to gossip, and so on. Then he leapt up and said I should pay for his lunch (which I had intended) and flew out, still teary and enraged. I felt deeply quiet, and this means I was having a bad time. I wondered whether this precarious "friendship" is now ended. I doubt it. I also wonder why he flew into this passion about Wystan and whether that is what it was about.

NOTE: Leo joined Gray and Maebelle Hughes in Burbank for Christmas and headed north on his own to New Year's Eve in San Francisco. He went ultimately to Seattle, where for *Mademoiselle* he toured preparations for the 1962 World's Fair.

52. Gray's mother, after working many years as a saleslady, was approaching retirement age.
53. The poet, librettist, and translator Chester Kallman (1921–75) was for thirty-five years the companion of W. H. Auden.

DECEMBER 18, 1961 • EN ROUTE FROM CHICAGO TO LOS ANGELES
**TO RICHARD HUNTER** • LONDON

I lunched with the opera people and heard all about opera in Chicago. Then I trundled to the Blackstone, where I was drowned in cups of strong tea and plied with cookies made by Orson and Virginia Welles's now married child, Chrissie (she lives in Chicago) and regaled with news and gossip and screams by Paula [Laurence] and her Chucky [Bowden] about their vicissitudes with *The Night of the Iguana*,[54] having now, at last, discovered that Frank Corsaro (a Method director and Tennessee's choice) is no good (I could have told that to them months ago). Having rid themselves of him, they seem happier. Also Bette Davis has calmed down, and Margaret Leighton and Alan Webb behave very well, and only the Method actor who is their lead [Patrick O'Neal] behaves badly. So they are optimistic. Chucky has taken over the direction. Tenn and Frankie [Merlo] came in and visited, and the great American author and I disagreed about all sorts of things. Why are those creatures—T. Williams, Carson [McCullers], etc.—so contrary-minded, so really degenerate-minded?

DECEMBER 28, 1961 • SAN FRANCISCO
**TO RICHARD HUNTER** • LONDON

It was immediately and pathetically clear that Maebelle intended Gray to stay as long as possible. So to lessen the tension, we abandoned our carefully made plans, and here I am jaunting north quite alone and desolate. Gray has been under incredible strain these five months and is in a state for which he cannot be blamed. The result—one huge, incredibly beautiful scroll drawing such as he has never before accomplished, related in little ways—very little—to [Charles] Demuth and the Chinese, but totally and characteristically his own. It is a masterpiece, of that I have no doubt—all rocks—deriving from that Sands Point shore [on Long Island]—quite without life but suffused with it. He has developed a taste for strong drink, but this will depart, and I know of at least two in love with him. My curious reaction is that of a parent who wants the best for his child combined with the knowledge that none of it matters because I am the most important creature in his life—actually the tough thread which binds him to it.

Surprise—Anaïs Nin gave a party for me. She lives, as Mrs. Rupert Pole, in Los Angeles high over Silverlake, in a large Japanese–Frank Lloyd Wright house (bare and beautiful and comfortable) with a good-looking youngish husband, who adores this "new," blond, quite pretty Anaïs. Back in New York she is still Mrs. Hugo, spending time there and time here, and although everybody knows of this bigamy no one seems startled.[55] The view was a mountainside,

---

54. Charles Bowden (1913–96) began as an assistant to the Lunts and, after this Tony-winning production, worked closely with Tennessee Williams on much of his later writing.
55. In 1955 Anaïs Nin had married Rupert Pole (actor, forest ranger, science teacher) in California, while still married in New York to Hugh Guiler (banker, then, as Ian Hugo, an experimental filmmaker). She would have her marriage to Pole annulled in 1966.

like a Christmas tree superimposed on a thirteenth-century Chinese screen and seen double—in the lake and above it—the reversed constellations like seeing the heavens from above them—extraordinary. But the surprise of Mrs. Rupert Pole was not finished. All week long I had heard of Tracey Roberts—a young, beautiful, vigorous actress-director who conducts a thriving acting, directing, playwriting unit on the Desilu lot. So, then Tracey Roberts arrived at Anaïs's. I automatically said to Puss Foy, "That is a woman named Blanche Gladstone who was in *Behind Red Lights* twenty-five years ago. . . ." And Puss said, "You're wrong. She's too young. . . ." "That's her daughter, then," said I. So then the creature came up to me and it was Blanche Gladstone! Just the same but tougher and resolute. Now I do believe that everything—bric-a-brac, Marie Antoinette's writing table (a man said it was when I visited him in a paneled nest high somewhere), bodhisattvas—everything ends up here.

Oh—what I've seen!! A day at MGM: We saw the big party scene in *Two Weeks in Another Town* being shot. A fantastic re-creation of the Corso in Rome, with dozens of women in Italian, French, and American haute couture—and international, sullen, and insolent expressions, while Edward G. Robinson makes a speech to Claire Trevor (eighth anniversary) and Cyd Charisse (all *coq* feathers and sequins, a very Marlene getup by Balmain) smiles spiritlessly—also Kirk Douglas and an Italian "find" with a most beautiful back, looking more Boldini and Lina Cavalieri than the originals.[56] "Who's that man looking like Erich von Stroheim?" said Gray. "Erich von Stroheim, Jr.," said I. [Director Vincente] Minnelli, older but somehow nicer. [Costume designer] Walter Plunkett acting as though we had been boyhood chums on the same block. A copy of Harold Clurman's *The Fervent Years* on the cameraman's shelf. Joan Houseman playing class in black velvet.[57] All of this make-believe somehow more real than the city around it. So it went. . . . Suddenly finding Barbette coaching a troupe of girls and boys, marvelous balletic acrobats for *Jumbo*.[58] The tremendous *Bounty* awash in another studio. A menu featuring Louis B. Mayer Chicken Soup and Lana Turner Salade!!! And hidden in the hills Fritzi Massary, with Galli-Curci nearby.[59] Streets suddenly thronged with last-minute Christmas shoppers—but in summer sports clothes, over which sable or chinchilla clutches and shrugs were flung.

56. Leo is thinking of a dashing painting (ca. 1901) of the Italian soprano Lina Cavalieri by the society portraitist Giovanni Boldini.

57. Joan Courtney Houseman (1916–2001), Countess de Foucauld, was playing a small part in *Two Weeks in Another Town*, produced by her husband, John Houseman. He had invited Leo and Gray onto the set.

58. Barbette (né Vander Clyde, 1904–73) was a female impersonator and high-wire artist. Born in Texas, he had a great success in Paris before World War II.

59. These two sopranos were contemporaries: Fritzi Massary (1882–1969) was a great star of operetta in Berlin and Vienna before Hitler; Amelita Galli-Curci (1882–1963) was an Italian coloratura.

**JOURNAL · DECEMBER 29, 1961 · SAN FRANCISCO** The constant clang and tinkle and crash of trolley cars. This was a big part of the sound of Manhattan when I was young. . . . Cary Grant called. (Sounds like Mary Astor's "diary"!) What a flirt.[60]

JANUARY 1, 1962 · SAN FRANCISCO
**TO GRAY FOY · BURBANK**

I came in at 3:30 a.m. from a pleasant breakfast party given by two boys whose names I do not know, having gone there from that party from which I called you. I think I probably behaved badly over the telephone. I am deeply and truly sorry—but suddenly the world seemed to collapse when I heard your voice, and I wanted so tumultuously to be with you—holding you and being held—that I became utterly undone with selfishness and I guess jealousy. I was angry, thinking that if you were not spending the New Year with Maebelle what reason then not to be here with me? Ah, well—I am a fool. So please forgive me if I sounded awful and upset you. Now I am all right. Hearing your voice undid me and then did me all up again. These last weeks have truly revealed the depths and intensities of my feeling. I thought that I knew, but I didn't know as fully as I do now.

When I came in, the lobby looked like the beginning of the last act of any Viennese operetta: everywhere the floors deep under confetti and mashed-up party hats and favors; three passed-out belles of many balls, with shoes flung off, dresses torn, one sodden man trying to shepherd them; a table with a big apple pie and coffeepot on it for the many Oriental domestics cleaning. What an opening chorus they would make, commenting in supernal Oriental ways upon the mores and customs of Occidentals. From the wide-open elevators cascaded Viennese waltzes.

The foghorns give cries of pain and longing (really like a brace of kine in heat) in the bay. At eight every morning a sound like a demon lover wailing for his mate shatters the thick, impenetrable air—and again at noon. A curious, unlovable city.

**JOURNAL · FEBRUARY 5, 1962 · NEW YORK CITY** Arnold Weissberger had a birthday party at his mother's apartment for Stravinsky, celebrating (all year long) his eightieth. This "relationship"—Arnold and Stravinsky's—must be rooted in Arnold's legal representation of the "Master."[61] I want to remember

---

60. In 1936 the actress Mary Astor's diary detailing indiscretions in Hollywood and New York made a sensation when read in a divorce court.
61. Entertainment lawyer L. Arnold Weissberger (1907–81) and his lover, talent agent Milton Goldman (1915?–89), were known for hosting parties filled with famous faces. GF: "If you wanted to meet stars, that's where they were. Arnold was usually their lawyer, and Milton was the one who found jobs for them."

Alger Hiss,[62] Rita Hayworth, Ethel Merman, Noël Coward, [actress] Cathleen Nesbitt, [writer] Cleveland Amory, Paul Scofield, etc. All of them there. Arnold said: "Rita Hayworth, I want you to meet Alger Hiss." Mrs. Weissberger tried to get Virgil [Thomson] to play "Happy Birthday" on the piano while a moppet bore in a cake. This was all frustrated by Virgil. The cake was finally borne in after Stravinsky left. It was infinitesimal, surmounted by a huge blue plastic "80," and sat abandoned on a little wall table. Rita Hayworth and Alger Hiss and Ethel Merman never got to sing "Happy Birthday" to Stravinsky. This aged, very small gnome seems obsessed with himself and his importance, always having his eye on the main chance.

FEBRUARY 7, 1962 • NEW YORK CITY

**TO RICHARD HUNTER** • LONDON

The doctor says that Gray was born with some sort of bone missing from the bottom of his spine, and that now (because of growing older) this has a bad effect. Gray is in pain all of the time. The doctor does not recommend surgery, but also says that this could be necessary later. Now Gray will probably have to wear some contraption and do exercises. This has thrown Gray into an even more depressed state. He has been in a state ever since we came home [from the West Coast], and rightly so, because this house and this city are filthy. This house is too much with which to cope. The pain is mostly on Gray's left part. This makes it all worse: That is his drawing hand. Now for some good news: *Mlle* gave me an unasked-for raise—a basic $10,000 a year [salary]. So that is a help. I have enough money for us to come [to Spain in April].

**JOURNAL** • FEBRUARY 15, 1962   Franco Zeffirelli's *Romeo & Juliet* opened. Mercutio's death was one of the great staging masterpieces. Always in the text, but nobody has ever done it that way. Franco has little ear for English verse, but this does not matter, since his stage sense is genius. At the Strasbergs' party afterward for Franco, it was wonderful when Franco said to Marilyn Monroe as she teetered away: "And come see the show!" He never understood why this is so funny.[63] Marilyn Monroe: "I can't remember anything—even words." Once she's finished with lines or "words" she doesn't remember them ever again. She with her small, compact, very pink-tipped (surely rouged) bosoms plain to see through the black lace of the short, skimpy black dress. She is part child, empty-headed, narcissistic—always looking into a wide-awake looking glass deep inside—a sleepwalker, utterly defenseless and appealing. Gray and Wanda

---

62. The case of Alger Hiss (1904–96), a former State Department official convicted in 1950 of perjury for denying his involvement with Communists, had dramatically divided public opinion in the fifties.
63. In the fifties, Marilyn Monroe had attended the Actors Studio, where she was instructed personally by its director, Lee Strasberg, and his wife, Paula Miller Strasberg.

Toscanini twisted. "Do you do the Twist?" I asked Marilyn Monroe. "I do the Twister," she murmured, smiling and twitching at her inner image. "I put something else in it. Jack Cole did the dances." "For *No Business Like Show Business*," I said. "Oh, I don't remember." "That's when you picked the boy's chin up, as you were dancing, and said, 'What's your name, honey?'" "I did?" She was delighted. Then the Hollywood good-bad, all-little-girl-and-as-wise-as-Eve face clouded, like a summer's day suddenly gone sunless and dull: "I don't remember. . . . I don't remember anything—even words." Later, before leaving, "Marlon, Marlon . . . *Macbeth*." She was being told that she should play Lady Macbeth. The machinations of the Strasbergs, wanting to use Franco, and Franco wanting to use them. It's a classic farce played by the Yiddish "Art" Theatre and the Commedia dell'Arte.[64]

MARCH 17, 1962 • NEW YORK CITY

**TO RICHARD HUNTER** • MADRID

I lunched with Dame Rebecca [West] today. Alone, she seems to have a passion for me. It was like lunching with the most brilliant gossip column in the world—everything from hating George Bernard Shaw to the sex life of the Askews—staggering.[65]

We sail on the SS *Atlantic*, April 4. No cabin was available on anything—even tugs—because the whole world seems to be going to the Holy Land for Easter and Passover, etc. This American export ship is chartered by some Yiddish organization and our agent managed to get this first-class cabin ($350 each)—very posh. But Gray will apparently be the only non-Jew on board. We plan to ride up the gangplank on piggies. Of course, immediately after leaving Ambrose Light [New York Harbor's edge], the SS *Atlantic* will doubtless reveal that it is the SS *Exodus*. We are busy making our crepe-paper gypsy costumes and arranging to hire tambourines, so we can work our way through *Espagna*. Do we get to go to the fair in Seville? Do we learn the fandango? Shall I have time to have a dinner jacket made in Madrid? Are you a snunc [*sic*]?

**JOURNAL** • APRIL 6, 1962 • SS ATLANTIC EN ROUTE TO ALGECIRAS, SPAIN

On the fourth we sailed. Here I sit, having eaten my breakfast, feeling the ship, like a tamed beast heaving and breathing not too far below the floor. I have not been in so extensive and deep a Yiddish atmosphere for about thirty-five years. As I was in the bathroom, a burst of hymn-singing from some sort of public room adjoining our cabin, and there we were, caught between that and the Jews (they were at early morning services in wonderful silver-collared taleisim) across the gangway. I laughed a lot—such a religious voyage.

---

64. A year later, Zeffirelli would cast their daughter, Susan Strasberg (1938–99), as Marguerite Gauthier in *The Lady of the Camellias* on Broadway.
65. Leo had become friends with the novelist, historian, and critic Rebecca West (1892–1983) after an introduction by editor Pascal Covici during the fifties.

APRIL 8, 1962  Very windy, but balmy, making me think of flying fish. Two nights past—horror! We sailed into a gale such as no one of the crew had ever experienced in these lanes. Poor Puss was terrified. He cast himself on the floor, seeming to find some sparse comfort there. Sometimes he said: "Shouldn't we get dressed?" For he seemed to think that we should take to the lifeboats at once. I tried not to giggle. I feigned sickness to distract him, but although I did feel odd, I couldn't even by sticking my finger down my throat bring up any sign of seasickness. The next night was a nightmare. I hope never to spend another like it. By yesterday evening, comparatively calm. Puss continues in the berth, but does not seem to be sleeping too much.

A sea voyage is always filled with sound—not a moment of stillness, not a soundless second. I stood out in the damp balminess, savoring the sea, the chrysoprase-colored wake, the sea-horse manes racing, the sea-witch sprays riding, the gray, opaque skies, and everywhere tumult—the ship's power, the ship's little creakings and quakings—people talking and calling one to the other—the tidal winds—the sea itself, roaring and screeching and crashing. Now, sitting in the glass of the sunroom—a typewriter, footsteps, voices, a chair skittering on the floor—and always the sound of shuddering.

NOTE: Leo and Gray met Richard to celebrate his fiftieth birthday with a tour of Spain and Provence. Richard hired a car and drove. They were joined during the trip by Howard Rothschild and for some days by Peter Wilson with his friend Harry Wright.

JOURNAL · APRIL 24, 1962 · MÁLAGA, SPAIN  On Easter Sunday, in Seville, we went out to Italica—many wildflowers and a large amphitheater ruin, masses of fallen stones and trippers hallooing to one another midst them, while the daily life of the nearby olive orchards went on, with only moments of looking at the "foreigners." I sat on a "ruin" while Peter and Harry and Gray went to look at the mosaics and a room. Ruins (save beautiful ones, like Ostia) depress me; flowers and brilliant sunlight, naturally, do not. While sitting, feeling like Winckelmann in a line drawing or a Rex Whistler bookplate or tailpiece,[66] [actress] Mildred Natwick came up and we exchanged pleasantries. Then my chums appeared and off we went.

Peter, Howard, and I trudged off to the bullring in a late afternoon of sunlight so dazzling that there was a coruscating blackness in the air. The mobs quite orderly. The girls in creamy white mantillas, draped over high combs, which are rooted in red or pink carnations. The pageantry and color of the opening procession. None of it alleviates the brutishness of the event. I loathed it—not emotionally, but with a heavy, dead coldness. Little art (at least in this fight) and no sport whatsoever. What sport could there be when the beast is

66. The writings of archaeologist and art critic Johann Joachim Winckelmann (1717–68) were seminal for eighteenth-century Neoclassicism. Painter and illustrator Rex Whistler (1905–44) was a fanciful *pasticheur* of eighteenth-century style.

actually murdered? I sat with Howard, and he says in all the three or four times he has been it has always been this way.

MAY 11, 1962 • BARCELONA  St. Ponce's Day, with a great street fair, stretching the full length of the Calle del Hospital, eddying into all small squares and into the plaza fronting the church. Everything orderly. St. Ponce ladies (rock-crevassed faces and twinkly eyes) cheerfully selling all sorts of herbs, honey, and honeyed fruits, also containers in which to carry away the *frutas*. Some of the Ponce ladies had glitter and sequins on their aprons. The procession headed by *gigantes* [giant puppets] in periwigs and a snaggletoothed witch. Then dancers doing a wand-against-wand dance, their costumes out of antiquity. Roman? Carthaginian? Little red-and-white embroidered skirts over continuations. A boy's band—later these serenaded the dignitaries (including a woman in a straw high hat. She obviously always had her official face on and never had fun). The serenade was "Never on Sunday."

MAY 27, 1962 • SS *CRISTOFORO COLOMBO* EN ROUTE TO NAPLES  On boat, in a sumptuous cabin. I must scribble, or I shall be so melancholy that I shan't be able to hide it. I have been so close to tears (and have overflowed), but I try to think consoling thoughts, such as: We will all be together very soon; Richard will be all right; Naples tomorrow! But my heart (or whatever we have within which cannot be fooled into a lie) is flooded—brimming over—inconsolable. I see that white handkerchief waving until its factuality is obliterated by space, by time, by inevitability. And so this becomes memory—and aches worse than any physical pain ever does or can. Now the loudspeaker is blaring safety instructions, and so on we go. But this has been the most glorious voyage ever, and part of the joy has been being together—all three of us, so closely, all of the time. At lunch today we sat outside and ate, watching the "freaks" of fashion—both males and females. Now I will finish *Dead Souls*.

JUNE 1962 • NEW YORK CITY

**TO RICHARD HUNTER** • LONDON

Coming through customs, I was suddenly greeted by shouts and cheers from an official who said, "Leo, why didn't you tell me you were coming in, I would have arranged everything!" (or some such I-have-a-crush-on-you dialogue). I didn't know the creature, but made signs of pleasure and recognition, so he scribbled some strange symbols on our landing things and told us to give them to the head customs man and all would be well. We did this, and Gray's declaration was immediately signed, but since I had so many boxes, bundles, baskets, bales, etc., I had to open some. He put his nose into the carpet and sniffed and sniffed. "Why do you do that?" I wanted to know. "To smell the age," said he. "Can't it be faked?" asked I. "Sure," said he. "You spray it." Gray and I looked at one another with wild surmise. Then he signed it all, and I found a huge longshoreman who came to put it all on a [hand] truck. When he discovered that we were going to 94th Street, he said he was born on 108th. I said that I was born on 107th. He practically kissed me. We discovered that we had both seen movies at the Garlic Opera House when we were little boys.[67] He found us the biggest taxicab in New York. He and the driver put all of the things (sixteen!!) in the cab.

But before this, I was traipsing behind the longshoreman and the truck, Gray walking behind me—when suddenly I realized there was no Gray. Turning, I saw Pussum in the midst of a flying wedge of customs officials, being pushed and shoved toward a little shack. "Hey!" I screeched. "He belongs to me!" They vanished into the shack, behind a glass door. I could see moving shadows. In about fifteen minutes a wild-eyed Pussum emerged—furious. It seems that as he was about to pass through the gate, a Negro stationed there said, "What you got in your raincoat?" Gray said, "Kleenex, other such things . . ." The Negro said, "We'll see about that. Take everything out." The first thing Gray took out was one of those little cellophane bags of saffron we bought in Barcelona. "What's this?" shouted the Negro. "Saffron," said Puss, and instantly he realized that the Negro did not know what saffron was, thinking it "dope." "You come with us," said the Negro, and Puss was then hustled into the shack where the Negro proceeded to grab his coat, in which he also discovered one of those ampoules of ammonia, the one Puss carried all those weeks, in case I fainted. The Negro was triumphant. "Well—here's something!" he shouted. So, a lot of other men surrounded Puss, while the Negro felt in Puss's pockets—even his pants! "Why don't you break it open and smell," Puss demanded. But the Negro was keeping it for evidence, I guess. Just when things were getting to Puss having to strip to the buff, a writhing craven was thrust through the door. He had been found trying to smuggle a gun. So they dropped Puss, told him to get dressed and out, and he did, falling into my arms in a fury. Now he is known as the Saffron Smuggler. The taxi man was especially nice. He would not permit me to touch a thing. And finally after we were in the house, Puss revealed that the taxi man said "what a nice rabbi" I was.

JUNE 9, 1962 • NEW YORK CITY
**TO RICHARD HUNTER** • LONDON FORWARDED TO NICE

I have been reading the ex-Duchess of Westminster [Loelia Ponsonby Lindsay]'s memoirs and here are Alice and Salzburg and Dr. Kommer[68] and

---

67. "Garlic Opera House" was a common name when Leo was young for movie theaters in immigrant neighborhoods.
68. Rudolf Kommer (1885–1943) had begun as director Max Reinhardt's managing agent, parlaying very little real expertise into a web of influence. By the time of his death in wartime New York, Kommer was Alice Astor's business manager and rumored to be a Nazi spy.

Eleonora and all of that world into which I so innocently and avidly stumbled because of a white evening dress in a motion picture and an insane Hungarian kissing me after a union meeting, while the creature I truly loved was being fugitive far, far south. How clearly one sees in retrospect. At fifty, I will write all about my life—as much of the truth as possible.

Puss came in and exclaimed over the gala candle lights [in the next yard]. I said that we had had many such events. He said that he has always told me that he would "even" help me have a party if I cleaned up the basement. How very safe he is. He never seems to realize that to clean it all up would take longer than eight weeks—that is, if I were to do it the way I should. Cleaning up the basement means picking through forty-eight years. I do not know whether I could bear that—I love my loves so deeply—you, Eleonora. . . . Ah, well— I was one to want the impossible, and sometimes I have had it given to me. I began life that way: No one believed that I could be made to live and live I did.[69] (Although sometimes I do wonder whether we are the living or the "ghosts"? Don't you, at times, suddenly think that we may be ghosts and that those we feel are here, or think are ghosts, are the "real" ones, who must, then, think of us as ghosts?)

JULY 8, 1962 • NEW YORK CITY

TO RICHARD HUNTER • OSLO

Did I tell you that Marlene is moving all of the Rivas [her daughter's family] to Switzerland and Italy for four years? They have rented their house to some art dealer (male) for $10,000 a year on a four-year lease! His houseguest is to be Van Johnson, so we all know about that tenant. Oh, yes, my movie-idol admirer [Cary Grant] rang me up this week. He was passing through, and he said would I be here in two weeks because he would return. I laughed merrily, and said that life was simple when conducted over telephones and telegrams. So, he laughed even more merrily. He said that he wasn't planning to be Professor Higgins opposite Audrey Hepburn. He does have the charm he seems to have on the silver screen, and I do get amused with this strange little flirtation. I guess it's fun because it seems almost so safe—also it's fun because he does it so well.

AUGUST 5, 1962 • NEW YORK CITY

TO RICHARD HUNTER • COPENHAGEN

We are melancholy because of Marilyn Monroe's death. We doted on her— and it does seem that the Strasbergs are to blame in part, for it was apparent that this girl couldn't take all of that "intellectualizing." She should have been left alone. So what we always felt about her was, alas, true—so near the edge. This suicide seems to add *pathétique* stature to her. I see her, gay and sad and

69. Leo was reportedly stillborn and only brought to life by the delivering physician's strenuous efforts.

wide-eyed—like a sort of depraved child—looking at St. Peter and God, and those two finding her irresistible as we all did. What has happened to her has happened to the world. Everything has been overmechanized, over intellectualized, carried beyond its natural capacity.

AUGUST 13, 1962 • NEW YORK CITY

**TO RICHARD HUNTER • HELSINKI**

Yesterday, Momma was talking about cooking and she said suddenly, "I don't make it anymore, because I can't remember the recipe, and I never wrote it down." This seemed infinitely sad, but she didn't seem sad about this—to her it was an inevitable fact. I am constantly amazed at how valiant people are— those who do not go on out of habit. I had Eileen [Herlie] to lunch at the [Plaza's] Edwardian Room. She is sad. Her beloved brother died. Only forty-five and he died suddenly, leaving three children and a wife. Eileen seems so capable, and really she is so good.[70] I find, as I grow older, that the goodness in people matters to me more than almost any of their other virtues or even defects—real goodness—the kind that is outgoing and helpful to both others and oneself.

SEPTEMBER 3, 1962 • NEW YORK CITY

**TO RICHARD HUNTER • LONDON**

I have read and reread your sad letter—and that is how life sometimes becomes, especially when one is sick in body and soul, one sometimes nourishing the other into total misery. Also, the drugs today inflate sicknesses of the spirit as they, presumably, alleviate those of the body. My dear darling Reezl, there is only one way to go on, and that is to think of those who love you and depend on your being. I do, and although he does have peculiar ways of manifesting, so does Howard—selfish, spoiled—but still, there he is. I am sitting in the big red chair in the back parlor, having done all of the bills and written to the shipping people for you, and . . . What if there were no you to write to? All about me are the presences of so many who are not here anymore. There Eleonora sat, and over there Alice and even Helmutt [Roder], and my dear Poppa slept over there many times—but I could go on and on, for this has, indeed, become a house of memories. I cannot believe that all of the people who came here ever did—so many, many people and so many of them went away feeling better than when they had come. For some reason I see [film actress] Elsa Lanchester on the front steps in a long-ago dawn—and Dame Edith Evans gorging herself next to the fireplace downstairs—and Maria in a corner of the sofa up here with Carmel Snow and Lillian Gish—and Alma

70. Actress Eileen Herlie (b. 1919) and Leo met in London in 1951, when he was dazzled by her in *The Second Mrs. Tanqueray*. She is now best known for a three-decade run on the soap opera *All My Children*.

Clayburgh [soprano] and Muriel Draper[71] and [actress] Margaret Anglin and Carmel all in one long, curved seat (all dead now)—and Osbert celebrating his birthday with Auden pouring champagne as sister Edith and Marlene ogle one another—and Isak Dinesen eating pistachio ice cream while Carlo [Van Vechten] beaus her[72]—and the first time I found Eileen Herlie here, like the beautiful heroine in an Edwardian drama while Puss sat transfixed—and Melina Mercouri and Geraldine Page comparing how each played *Sweet Bird of Youth*—and Maurice Goudeket talking about Colette to Anita Loos[73] and Margot Fonteyn and Nora Kaye and Alicia Markova and [French dancer Jean] Babilée and Choura Danilova . . . But why go on?

Well, because I have been thinking of my life and realizing that ever since I wrote the Rev. Kilvert essay I have not written one word which I can say is writing as I honor it, not one word which I can say realizes my basic gifts. I have also failed because I have not even helped people as I used to do. So, I have been taking stock—and the shop is pretty empty.

71. Although she worked as an interior decorator in the twenties, Muriel Draper (1886–1952) was better known as a hostess and patron of artists and then, in the thirties and forties, as an advocate for causes of women and the left.
72. GF: "Carlo acted as though they were in love. Always flirting with her and nuzzling."
73. Author Maurice Goudeket (1889–1977), Colette's third and last husband, would have known Anita Loos as the adaptor of Colette's novels into two Broadway plays, *Gigi* (1951) and *Chéri* (1959).

# THE MIGRATION OF TREASURES

NOTE: In the autumn of 1962, change seemed in the offing for Leo, both at work and at home. On October 2, Condé Nast's president Iva Patcévitch promoted Alex Liberman to editorial director of all the company's magazines. Then, on November 29, Patcévitch announced that Diana Vreeland would become *Vogue*'s editor in chief the following January.

Meanwhile, the landlord at 1453 Lexington threatened not to renew the lease, then relented. Although Leo and Gray would continue living in the house until July 1967, Leo saw that the days of living there might be numbered and looked at alternatives. Richard Hunter, with a modest inheritance from his mother, began shopping for his own place. He soon bought a nineteenth-century Greek Revival house near Augusta, Maine.

OCTOBER 7, 1962 · NEW YORK CITY

**TO RICHARD HUNTER** · BERN

I was reclining depressedly—what with Gray ill so many weeks, ten now, and new managing-editor worries,[1] and the rent being raised and [the landlord] Dancik wanting some $500 extra in a lump sum, and worrying over Maebelle's retirement (a year off, but still a worry), and worrying over Puss not having any money (but as long as I can make it that isn't a real worry), and such taxes . . . I had to pay around $3,000. Luckily, I had saved for this, but my income has been considerably reduced—no Columbia Records money (that came to about $4,000 last year), no *Doctor's Wife* (that came to about $800),[2] and *Playbill* cut in half—Woe—Ah, well—I feel in good health. Also, I have two things to write for the *Times* and some LP notes (*The Nutcracker*) to write for Mercury Records, and something lovely will happen now that you've called.

This is Yom Kippur, so I don't go to *Mlle* tomorrow, but work at home. Soon I must arise and get ready to retrieve Momma from the synagogue. Last night I spoke to her, and she said I should call up Aunt Ida [Lerman] and tell her what time services are today. Since Aunt Ida lives only two streets from Momma, I

---

1. Leo had perennial difficulties with managing editors, whose task it was to force frugality and compel him to meet deadlines.
2. In 1960–61, Leo had written a column titled "Down the Avenue of Arts and Letters" reporting current happenings for that bimonthly magazine.

asked, "Why can't you?" She said, "I don't use the telephone on Yom Kippur. . . ." "But Momma," I wailed, "you are talking—" "*You're* using it," she said. What could one say to that logic? She seems well and announces that she has more than enough money for the rest of her life. Why, then, must she have any from me monthly? What are all of these mysteries?

DECEMBER 9, 1962 • NEW YORK CITY

**TO RICHARD HUNTER** • LONDON

Mina is about to put [her Massachusetts farm] Chapelbrook on the market. At least three houses, a wood, all sorts of lovelinesses, thirty miles north of Northampton [on Ashfield Lane]. I wish that you could see it. Maybe this is a solution for all of us. I don't want to make a move until you return, because we must all be near. Life is too short for separations. Now we must try to make a real base for ourselves—somewhere. I feel like the lost boys in *Peter Pan*. Who is our Wendy?

I am trying to think of cheerfulnesses to tell you—we went to a party Arnold Weissberger gave for Vivien Leigh. Oh—she is beautiful. She said to me, "You never say anything to me. . . . Everyone says how witty you are, but you never say anything to me." I said, "How can I, when all I can do is look at you . . . etc., etc." So she was pleased and I felt like an oaf. Dolores Del Rio [screen actress] looked beautiful and hothouse, but Vivien Leigh is a genuine little girl beauty—such eyes.

DECEMBER 10

Last week was one of the worst in my whole life. I guess I had some sort of mental upheaval. Finally, Friday morning, Gray took me to the doctor, and he talked to me a long time and gave me an injection (which still hurts) and pills. These do seem to calm me, for I feel removed and controlled. My sin is pride. I could talk to you face-to-face, but not write about any of it. The house [concerns], it seems, did help to do me in. I am going to try to hang on until spring. Then we can all decide about the future. I think that I must move out of this whole world—but, of course, I must think of how to make a living. It was so good of you to think of coming home, but that would not be good for you. Be true to your heart. I have been so long away from my true center. I should never have walked into this jungle. Now I must somehow find my way out. Do you really plan to live in America part of the time? When I know what you really plan, then I shall be helped to know in what way to go. Was life similar for our parents? Poor, poor Gray—such a burden—what with his own troubles and sorrows. He has not been given a job since we returned from Spain (don't mention this) but luckily I earn enough for us both. Also I seem to have become so stingy and miserly. I imagine us in Spain and France and that helps. But I think that the drugs help the most.

DECEMBER 12, 1962 • NEW YORK CITY
**TO MARLENE DIETRICH** • MONTREUX, SWITZERLAND

Never, never listen to anyone save your own instinct about your work. You are a natural writer. You cannot be told what or how to do. When you try to be someone else—try to lie—you cannot be anything save a disaster. You must not worry or be worried about what someone else could or would do. Emlyn [Williams]'s book is his—good or bad.[3] Colette's books are hers. You write you. If you cannot remember the war, then you must write about not remembering. That is your world, your climate, that is what makes your writing uniquely yours. Please, please do not let yourself be worried with externals. Write from within yourself. Do not distrust what you know.

**JOURNAL** • FEBRUARY 10, 1963  Gray made a triangular hat—very neat—out of a newspaper, and this was my madeleine for today. What an upheaval of memories. Poppa made them, and we made swords of box pieces—and, oh, the wars, duels, and carousing.

MARCH 4, 1963 • NEW YORK CITY
**TO RICHARD HUNTER** • LONDON

About a week ago Puss had a dreadful seizure, seemingly a heart attack, but thus far, the various tests show no condition. Then, during the week we were (on a very cold evening) walking down Broadway, to view *The Hollow Crown*, and he had an asthma attack such as I have never seen—not yours nor any. He literally almost smothered to death in the street. I was frantic and carried him (sort of) into the Henry Miller [theater]. Soon after, two fingers on his right hand seemed almost paralyzed. Then a night or so later he had another asthma attack. I cannot get him to return to the doctor, but somehow I will. He seems better, but I am in a state. Reezl, I am (deep inside) really very frightened about Puss. He seems to have lost almost all of his hope.

MARCH 6

I have been asked [by Holt, Rinehart and Winston] to write a book, and the advance offered is close to $12,000!!! It is a history of taste and collecting, centered on Sotheby's, and it would be wonderful to do—London four months next year and Vienna and Paris and then home. I would try to arrange a leave of absence from Condé Nast.

NOTE: In the spring of 1963, Leo underwent a complicated and painful procedure of stripping his varicose veins. It took months for him to walk—even as well as he had previously.

3. Emlyn Williams (1905–87), the Welsh actor and playwright (*The Corn Is Green*), had published an autobiography two years before.

I am propped up on a long chair on the pool's edge at the Newhouses'[4]—
lovely, annihilating sunshine, a bellyful of strawberries, and I am being cherished. It is good to be alive, especially since I was in the way of possibly being
dead. When they opened my leg, a blood clot was forming. So my instinct to
have the operation immediately was good. A complicated business, taking
from ten in the morning to three in the afternoon. Going under the anesthetic
I was heard to murmur, "What a sneak!" and coming out, I raised my right arm
and declared, "Did I do it like royalty?" Eight incisions and over a hundred
stitches—incredible pain at times ever since—forty-three pounds lighter.

Look what happens when you go away: Item—one drastic but triumphant
operation. Item—one poor Gray with a bad ulcer, and he suffers desperately.
Item—one Richard buying a large house you will adore—four miles from
Augusta, Maine, a Greek Revival house (five columns) on the Kennebec
River. We saw it twenty-five years ago, and now he is buying it. Built circa
1810–20, it is a marvelously preserved example of its genre—six bedrooms,
thirty-five acres, one apple orchard, a day's drive from New York, and very
beautiful. Item—Gray and Leo are coming to live in London, because Leo has
a book to write (excellent contract), which requires him to research in London, and the book must be finished by March 1, 1965. Please do not tell,
because only Alex [Liberman] knows at Condé Nast, and we are trying to make
a plan whereby I can do some work abroad, so as to get paid by Condé Nast
while away. I will need that money.

You know when I missed you intensely? On my birthday, which was in the
hospital. Sixty people came, three enormous birthday cakes, more flowers than
for the opening of a Hollywood shopping center, presents endlessly, a twenty-
four-hour celebration. Ruth Gordon recited, Jennie Tourel played the cas-
tanets, Martha Graham made a speech, Eileen Herlie sang, wires came from
Fonteyn, Markova, Danilova . . . all the actresses. Callas sent a pressing of a
new LP. But the ones I wanted most—you and Ela—ah, well.

JOURNAL • AUGUST 4, 1963 • SANDS POINT, NEW YORK At Sono [Osato] and
Victor [Elmaleh]'s,[5] two p.m., and the pewter light streaming from water and
sky suddenly livened into a blinding, flaming boldness by sun. The radio beats

---

4. Samuel I. Newhouse (1895–1979), owner of *Mademoiselle,* was married to Mitzi Epstein
Newhouse (1902–89), whom Leo had met separately by the early forties. Their sons are
Samuel I. ("Si"), Jr., and Donald (born in 1927 and 1930, respectively). Si Newhouse would
become chairman of Condé Nast Publications in 1975.
5. Sono Osato (b. 1919), a dancer with the Ballet Russe de Monte Carlo, then Ballet Theatre,
and a musical-comedy actress, had married the businessman and painter Victor Elmaleh
(b. 1919) in 1943. During the sixties, Leo and Gray often visited their house in Sands Point,
on Long Island, and were sometimes invited to stay there alone.

a constant popular, syrupy beat. In the kitchen, Sono and Puss sit at table, lingering over crumbs, and settling world, children. . . . Sono is wonderfully graphic when she talks. She's a natural talker, as Vivien Leigh is a natural screen actress and Marlene is a natural writer. (Do I know what I am "natural" at? I seem to me to be so made-up.)

Sono and Ballet Russe [Monte Carlo] danced in Berlin in 1937 and 1938. Goebbels came to the Scala [theater] where they danced. Sono: "He sat there in the Blackshirt uniform—all black with the terrible insignia. Every night those Mercedes would drive up. I lived in the pension next to the theater, and those Nazi bigwigs, they gorged themselves. Then every Sunday, we'd go to the White Russian place, the Troika, and in would come the Blackshirts, shaking their cans and standing there till you gave them money. Oh, it was weird. It was an ugly town then. There was no butter. We ate whale blubber. I bought a jacket made of wood. I thought it was fun. One day, I thought it would drop off. Then, we were driving down the Rhine. . . . I always had thought that it was beautiful. It wasn't cozy. It wasn't intimate—unlike the plain, where the sky opens up near Avignon—not even cozy like that great flat plain. It was ugly. No, it's not my country."

NOTE: Leo played his only film role in director Ted Flicker's *The Troublemaker*, which told the story of a naïve chicken farmer who moves to Greenwich Village to open a coffeehouse. Leo's scenes were filmed in one day on Long Island.

JOURNAL · AUGUST 11, 1963 · NEW YORK CITY   In our yard at home, I have been rereading *David Copperfield*: "When I saw him going downstairs early in the morning . . . it appeared to me as if the night was going away in his person." David, about Uriah Heep. This is so devastating an image, that all of Dickens's touches—his dark revelations—pale, and the reader suddenly sees—actually sees and feels—the concentrated awfulness of Uriah—the black horror of Uriah spreading more and more through the book. What depths Dickens reveals—sometimes in a descriptive word or phrase so brief that it almost is lost in the mass of detail, yet lights the scene like a great burst of flame.

Last night I met Gore [Vidal], younger looking and tan and thin. He's here en route from Rome to Hollywood, where his play (the political one, *The Best Man*) is being made. He said that he had finished his novel, *Julian*, and asked, "What about Troosey?" When I told him that he was trying to finish his book [*In Cold Blood*] in a house in one of the Hamptons and would have to go to the execution in Kansas, Gore said, "Little T, baby ghoul . . ." Gore says that Tennessee's Frankie [Merlo] is dying of cancer, but doesn't know that he is dying.

I talked to Truman this morning. No news save that there has been a stay of execution, and a new trial will be held. Truman will have to go to Kansas for that. Tennessee and Frankie go to Key West. Frankie told Paul Bigelow (a revenant, a spook who does not fade[6]) that he weighs only 108 pounds. I can't believe Frankie doesn't know. But did Poppa know? Yes. When he saw the robin hopping in the early autumn and he said, "Even the birdies will be here in the spring," he knew—but did he believe?

On Friday morning I became a movie actor, and by Saturday morning I was in the depths at it all—no dignity to it. It is an emptying and empty business, acting. I understand the exhibitionist motive, but still I don't understand why people persist in acting, and no one can tell me. I played three scenes, the first two well at the first try, but badly when having to repeat them. These were scenes on a ledge high above the city. The third scene I did wretchedly. This was shot after seven, and I had been at it since midmorning, having been trotting about since six a.m.

This work is not for me. I do want the money from it, and it is a change from writing *Mademoiselle* copy. Even in the midst of making this movie, Tom Aldredge (who plays the "hero" and is an excellent actor) and Joan Darling (a wonderful stage creature—alive, talented, versatile) worry about their next jobs, not having a notion of what they can or will be. There is a lack of strain in the studio, but that is unusual. There is a heavenly doggie (Waggles, Tom's dog), who is a lesson in patience, obedience, and devotion. The people are friendly, charming, intelligent. The expertise is staggering and all for this ephemera—nine minutes and some seconds were shot during the long day, and this was thought remarkable. When I think of how many words I force out on some days. It was intensely exhausting. I fell into bed at eleven. But the long waits between scenes were relaxing, specially those during which I sat alone, the make-believe world going on all around me. That was soothing. But I am not an actor and I shall never be one, no matter how many movies I make. The agony of trying to remember lines—that alone would keep me from being an actor.

**THE TROUBLEMAKER** *It was awful. Tom Aldredge just opened doors, slid through rooms, said his lines as if he were making them up. I didn't know how to open doors suddenly. I didn't know how to walk across rooms suddenly. I certainly could not remember any lines. But I did it somehow.*

*When I, sitting on the edge of Marlene's beige bed, told about how it was, she roared with laughter. Then she got out from under her covers and onto her knees and hugged me and said, "Darling, darling, there never was a Marlene Dietrich . . . or a Greta Garbo."*

*Then came the big preview in a big movie theater in Manhattan, and Gray and I went. There I was. And people roared with laughter at whatever I did: When I, the "Dirty Old Man," held out, from a dark alley, an ice cream to a lit-*

6. Paul Bigelow (1905?–88), a consultant associated with the Theatre Guild, edited several of Tennessee Williams's works.

*tle girl; when Tom chased me along a ledge—presumably ninety stories up, only two or three feet from the floor, I was terrified, but did I show it? No. I wanted to go home! I was quite fascinated with this large creature in that beautiful Max Beerbohm-ish gray suit and a beautiful white hat on the screen and felt utterly detached. And we got outside and people asked for my autograph and Gray said, "I think you were dubbed." And I almost hit him.* (1993)

NOTE: Leo went to London in the fall of 1963 to discuss with his friend Peter Wilson, Sotheby's chairman, writing a history of the firm. Leo also had an assignment from *Mademoiselle* to supervise photographs and do research for a feature on Britain's National Theatre, which opened its first season that October.

JOURNAL • OCTOBER 19, 1963 • LONDON London, despite changes, as wonderful as ever. I pelted off to Penelope [Reed] and stopped there until ten at night—lovely Penelope is very beautiful, and we talked of being fifty. I thought of the great shock of discovering that one continues to be vaguely virile. (The absolute self-possession of the pages here, through which peeps little-boy rogueries.)[7]

Gina Lollobrigida came in, wearing an "old" Chanel, her black hair in a short full bob, chains and jewelry à la Chanel, a pale-blue silk blouse (not for this Chanel, for another). She loves Chanel: "She was the only one." She is very beautiful, tired, and discontented with her movie career, wanting something else: "I would give half of my money for memory, to be able to read and remember, to remember names. . . ." She has *morbidezza* and dreadful depressions. She is radiant when she talks about "my son." Or the publishing house her husband has bought and the triumph of their Dalí-illustrated Dante. She says the Dante title as though she has carefully been taught it. But she is lovable, and a tough peasanty root is evident beneath the Chanel. "Once I bought a cocktail dress from Dior. How you say? Three thousand dollars!" She was flabbergastingly awed.

OCTOBER 21, 1963 Maria C rang from Monte Carlo—long outpouring: Everything is all right—don't believe newspapers—she's working hard—she will do the *Tosca* if everything is perfect[8]—she must see me—she would try to come for a day—should she come to America for the concerts? She seems in good spirits, but she does get down. "Twenty-six years . . . and they take away my confidence. . . ."

JOURNAL • JANUARY 5, 1964 • NEW YORK CITY At 8:45, I went out onto the steps and looking up at a wishing star thought of the extraordinary people—

7. Leo was writing this entry while sitting in the lobby of London's Ritz.
8. Zeffirelli's *Tosca* at Covent Garden in January 1964 would be one of Callas's great, and last, triumphs.

## Early Twelfth Night Party

| | |
|---|---|
| Marian Goodman | Robert Lescher |
| Ed Goodman | Kitty Hart |
| Sigrid De Lima | Nonnie and Tom Moore |
| Stephen Green | Doris and Leo Kepler |
| Jacqueline and Peter Basch | Viveca [Lindfors] Tabori |
| Grete Freund-Basch | George Tabori |
| Elaine and Arthur Cohen | Peter Lindamood |
| Diana and Lionel Trilling | Dolly and Al Hirschfeld |
| Mitzi and Sam Newhouse | Marcia Levant |
| Sue and Donald Newhouse | Leonard Bernstein |
| Si Newhouse | Joan Stanton |
| Victoria [de Ramel] | Milton Goldman |
| Dorothy Norman | Joan Sutherland |
| Sheldon Harnick | Richard Bonynge |
| Ruth Yorck | Jennie Tourel |
| Kenward Elmslie | Mr. and Mrs. [Herbert] Mayes |
| Anne and Bill Winkelman | Lennie Gerber |
| Iris and David Sawyer | Tracy and Bill Brigden |
| Barbara and Ernest Kafka | Leonard and Sylvia Lyons |
| Betty [Comden] Kyle | Ted Flicker |
| Steven Kyle | Betsy T. Blackwell |
| Lucia Collins | Constance and Theo Berliner |
| Norman Singer | Risë Stevens |
| Geoffrey Charlesworth | Walter [Szurovy] |
| Leontyne Price | Paula Laurence |
| Hubert Dilworth | Charles Bowden |
| Dorle and Dario Soria | Allene Talmey |
| Mimi Shapiro | Dick Plaut |
| Paul Brach | Helen Frankenthaler |
| Mary [Cantwell] Lescher | Robert Motherwell |

Eugenia and Eddie Halbmeier
Brigitta and Goddard Lieberson
Mina Curtiss
Rudolf Nureyev
Alice Ginsburg
Tom Ginsburg
Erik Bruhn
Gloria Steinem
Sybil Burton
Chris Allan
Tilly Losch

Herbert Kasper
Katie and Zero Mostel
Joanna and Dan Rose
Edith and Ralph Locke
Sono Osato
Victor Elmaleh
Isabel Eberstadt
Marion Levy
[Theodorus] Stamos
Audrey [Michaels]
The [Alexander] Libermans

women mostly—who had come up these steps and into 1453, and who were not to mount the steps this evening or, some of them, ever again. I blessed them and loved them that moment.

And so the [Twelfth Night] party began, and over two hundred poured in, and everything was magical; 1453 behaved marvelously, like a precocious child—glittering with charm, radiant. The wine flowed (forty-eight bottles in all) and Joan Sutherland said to Risë Stevens: "I've been in *Carmen*, too," and Risë said, "So I've heard."[9] And Alicia Markova and Nureyev and Erik [Bruhn][10] counted out *Petrouchka*. And Truman crouched in the corner of a sofa next to Mina. He seemed so old; she for the first time showed her real age. Parties burst and blossomed like exotic pods in every room. Newhouses and Mayeses trooped like tourists through Kronstadt. Lionel Trilling asked Joan Sutherland for an autograph (for [his son] James Lionel) and she asked him for his autograph for her son. This party had a definite rhythm to it, a real beat. All the pregnant girls looked like extras waiting for their cues in some modern-dress *Lysistrata*. I was touched to the deeps of my sentimental heart by Martha Graham suddenly appearing in a fur tippet, tiddly and fragrant with garlic. She fell upon Tilly Losch, crying, "She was one of my little ones," while Paula and Chucky [Bowden] and Betty Comden and others sat around the dining room table playing family. When Tilly looked at Pavlik [Tchelitchew]'s portrait of Alice, she stared coldly, appraisingly a long time, and did not say a word. A curious murmuring came out of her. So this was the end of her affair

9. Mezzo-soprano Risë Stevens (b. 1913) had been known by Leo as Rise Steenberg at Newtown High School. She had retired from the Met in 1961.
10. The outstanding Danish dancer, choreographer, and director Erik Bruhn (1928–86) was a frequent guest artist in New York.

with Raimund [von Hofmannsthal]?[11] [Painter Robert] Motherwell said he'd never seen a house so personal. [Broadway columnist] Lenny Lyons declared that it must become a national monument.

But I have not given the color of that party—a rich, dark—shot through with light like bubbles and glitter—winey color. It was deeply gay, with a kind of high-riding vivacity. I enjoyed every moment of it—only the dear dead making some moments unbearable. Thirteen years this month [since Eleonora died], and I still ache. We sat around the fire—Peter [Lindamood], [fashion designer Herbert] Kasper, Gray, and I—sipping coffee, munching stollen crumbs, and talking the whole long festivity over, until four a.m., and then off they went, down the desolate avenue where once Poppa had carried me, almost fifty years ago.

JANUARY 8, 1964   On Monday, I discovered myself presenting Barbra Streisand her *Mademoiselle* Merit Award at Ray Diffin's costume-executing emporium—a shop whose walls are composed of windows and wherein magic is created. This time blueprinted by Irene [Sharaff], who stood amid the brilliant mounds of finery like a determined, worldly Bo-Peep midst the meadows and sheep on a gala shearing day. Barbra was on a podium, done up in American Beauty [deep red] velvet, huge black hat, and pink-satin blouse, all very, very hobble skirt. When I came in, an owl-eyed hulk (male) was interviewing her, but getting nowhere. Then I stepped up and, since to me this was a game, we did splendidly. She is a plain, Jewish-looking girl, huge eyes, huge voice, huge zany smile, naturally offbeat, and conventionally out-of-bounds. She takes instant likes and dislikes. She will obviously be a star. She is very, very Jewish—almost with the spirit of a dancing Hasidic boy. I even looked to see whether she had payess.[12]

JANUARY 18, 1964   "Mr. Bing likes me to do it: He saves on the makeup," Leontyne when a Brazilian said something about her *Aïda*. Leontyne after a disastrous Pamina: "Well, that'll teach Mr. Bing I'm not an ingénue."

Brigitta: "I would like to be married to Balanchine again, if I didn't have Goddard and the family and all that. Balanchine is the most interesting man. . . ."

JANUARY 21, 1964   Carol Channing loves her audience so much that they find her irresistible and mass demonstrations of affection take place. To be part of this is overwhelming. She is old-time theater. Her "art" is based on that look

---

11. The Austrian journalist and writer Raimund von Hofmannsthal (1906–74) became Alice Astor's second husband in 1932. Vienna-born Tilly Losch (1904–75) turned from dancing to exotic film roles after a scandalous divorce from Edward James in 1934 London.

12. Leo timed this photo shoot with Streisand so it would appear in *Mademoiselle* three months later, when she opened in *Funny Girl*.

of apologetic, hopeful anguish seen on the face of a little girl who has just peed in her pants.[13]

"Singing's like sex. You never know whether you'll make it after fifty."
—Maria Callas

MAY 2, 1964 • NEW YORK CITY
**TO RICHARD HUNTER** • LONDON

I had a "boy and girl" date with Joan Sutherland. She met me at the Plaza (Oak Room) and then, for dessert, we went to the [hotel's] Palm Court. Joan Sutherland is a cross between Margaret Dumont and a high-school pageant. She has one wonderful little "act"—being a pouting baby girl—ugum-mugum—but she also has loads of humor about herself, is very candid about the tight fit of her husband [conductor Richard Bonynge]'s pants, and she loathes Bing and worships Maria C. It was a bright, hilarious, not too expensive evening.

Then there were my two encounters with Liz [Taylor] Burton. Have I written about those? She has nothing in her head save vanity. She is the most self-consumed narcissist I have seen, and I have seen the supreme examples of our time. You feel that if she sat staring into nothingness, that absence of anything at all becomes a looking glass. I also feel that he will leave her one day—and that she may well commit suicide.

JUNE 24, 1964 • NEW YORK CITY
**TO RICHARD HUNTER** • LONDON

The great surprise of the season is the Actors Studio *Three Sisters*, much the best one I have ever seen, and the glorious one in it is—Kim Stanley! Unforgivable!!![14] It is carefully directed to exhibit Chekhov, and since it does that, it is most satisfying. You hear him so clearly and so immediately. This is a new translation (or adaptation) by Randall Jarrell—unarchaic and good for contemporary actors. The diction, the voices, not all "classic," but of a piece, so one is never reminded by a "good" example of how bad the others are—like putting a new piece of furniture in this house and so showing how shabby it actually is. This *Three Sisters* lacks audible poetry, but is visually lovely. Most of all, here is this heartbreaking, shining play—a present, it seems. Oh, how rich it is and how influential it has been. V. Woolf comes out of it and even [Bergman's film] *Wild Strawberries*. Chekhov sees life as it trembles—here it is, now it isn't—all in the same moment. Miss Stanley is heavy, marmoreal, very funny, and full of pitiful snobbish pretensions and horrible wrenching anguish. This play is so deeply aware of "good" people playing by rules. They have to. But

13. She had triumphantly opened in *Hello, Dolly!* a few days before. Leo had been among the first to spot Channing (b. 1921), in the 1949 revue *Lend an Ear*, and suggested her to Anita Loos for Lorelei Lee in the musical *Gentlemen Prefer Blondes*, which really launched Channing's career later that same year.
14. An ironic remark, meaning it was "unforgivable" of Kim Stanley (1925–2001) to defy Leo's low appraisal of her talent. Chekhov's Masha would be the last role she played on Broadway.

"bad" people—awful, common people—do not play by rules, so they win out over the "good" people. Materially. The spirit, one hopes (and must believe), triumphs ultimately—but, oh dear, how lonely and frugal and woeful that the "bad" should enjoy material victory. How many of us are constituted to be saints?

JOURNAL • JULY 19, 1964 • SANDS POINT, NEW YORK It is not that I have lost my scribbling, but it seems to lie doggo, until such moments as these, the loosened moments, the unwound minutes. Part of me is in Alice's house at Rhinebeck, having read in yesterday's newspapers that Ivan [Obolensky, her son] has sold it to be used as a "home" for "fallen" women. How Alice must be smiling, and Ela roaring with laughter, each having "fallen" so many times. I wonder whether the new fallen will sleep in my bedroom?

The sound of a knife clattering against a porcelain dish, the sound I heard as a very small child in my grandmother's kitchen on 107th Street, almost fifty years ago, here this moment, past. When then, does it all go? Where? I go—it goes? Is it all really forever, needing only the right combination to make it clear, audible at any moment in time? Not the ship itself, but the wake of the ship . . . Not the tree itself, but the tree's shadow . . . Not the loved one himself, but the loved one's love—and there both the loved and his love are indivisible.

AUGUST 4, 1964 • NEW YORK CITY [Publisher] Roger Straus's party for Paul Horgan [novelist and historian] in that Westchester Tudor mansion: the wicker sideboard, the mixture of Westchester "gentry," pretty "girls" from the office, daughters of friends, literary gents and their ladies, literary ladies and other ladies' gents, literary ladies sans gents. Ruth Elizabeth [Ford] as loud and as raucous as a ballyhoo truck on a dim night and even harder. [Harpsichordist] Sylvia Marlowe, pale gold beside Ruth Elizabeth's blatant stridency. An ancient puss and a venerable spaniel. Anne Fremantle [writer and editor of *Commonweal*] in rusty, grimy black complete with shooting stick and any-which-way Ceres hair. Horgan was faculty-meeting dapper: "I've so many books, formal books planned out"—with a gesture like a nursery gardener demonstrating growing boxes—"waiting to be filled in. I don't have time to write an autobiography." He was well-acolyted.

NOTE: On September 29, 1964, Leo and Gray sailed for England. They leased an apartment in London from their friend Eileen Maremont. Leo conducted interviews and gathered research for his book, tentatively called *The Seismograph of Taste: Sotheby's, 1744–1964.*

He felt hampered from the start by the lack of business archives at Sotheby's. The auction house also did not intend that Leo write honestly about auctioneering practices, which involved a great deal of obituary watching and sharp dealing. The following October, disillusioned, he would write: "I must not trust people whose lives are centered in gain: They are different from me, totally different in intention."

For the months in London, however, Leo went at it hammer and tongs, interviewing employees, many long retired, and rummaging through the Bond Street offices in search of material.

The life in London at this time gratified both Leo and Gray. The combination of arduous research, memos home to *Mademoiselle* about upcoming articles, and many social pleasures resulted in fewer journal entries.

OCTOBER 3, 1964 • LONDON

**TO RICHARD HUNTER** • AUGUSTA, MAINE

Oh, Reezl, you must come. Because this is such a lovely place—central heating, burning hot water, and even more room than we were told. We live in a sort of wide-awake dream. How will we ever settle down again. Thus far everyone at Sotheby's is friendly and helpful.

OCTOBER 4

Yesterday went to lunch at Ken Tynan's and discovered that he was the man I've been watching across the road! The Osborne play [*Inadmissible Evidence*] is endless and dispiriting. The actor [Nicol Williamson]—a new man—gives a tour de force of memory and endurance. But again, who wants to sit through a nervous breakdown lasting almost three hours? The audience thought it all most comical and roared with laughter. I could not—save a bit of horrified choking. He's written a list-of-current-problems play—carefully checking them off and crowing, "Well, I got that one in!" Everything from perversions to politics—and that's the range of emotion from *p* to *p*.

**JOURNAL** • OCTOBER 3, 1964 • LONDON  Ken [Tynan] says he will demolish Truman's book. He feels that T could save the killers' lives, and wouldn't because he has to have them dead to finish his book.[15]

OCTOBER 13, 1964  When Hobson [head of the book department] talks to me about incunabula, very rare bindings, etc., I must say honestly that I know nothing about this and do not even understand him. But, of course, he probably knows this and he is snobbing me. The great spirit so instantly perceivable at Sotheby's—everyone deeply interested, mad about their work, which does not preclude jealousy, unrest, ambition, and anger.

NOVEMBER 18, 1964 • LONDON

**TO AMY GROSS**[16] • NEW YORK CITY

My arm becomes so very tired because of the endless note-taking. I do all the interviews "by hand," scrupulously taking down each implied punctuation

15. The killers portrayed in Capote's *In Cold Blood* would be hanged on April 14, 1965.
16. Amy Gross (b. 1942) began her career as Leo's assistant at *Mademoiselle* (1964–66), then worked with him at *Vogue* from 1978, and succeeded him as that magazine's features editor in 1983. Later she edited *Mirabella* and *O: The Oprah Magazine*.

mark. These last weeks I have been querying the local ancients, for fear that they will abruptly demise and so the past be obliterated. I have also been on the town (or in the country) nights and weekends and lunchtimes. I am starting this (at least) in Siberia—the name I have given my freezing office (although London is springlike today and was yesterday, a sort of warmth of death—ugh). This cell, with three enormous windows looking onto scenes from Dickens, is in a new part of Sotheby's and so still remote from all other human and inhuman elements.

I took yesterday afternoon off because Sylvia (Danny Kaye's wife and a childhood chum [at the Grossinger]) is here, and she took me to Margot Fonteyn's gala at Drury Lane. The whole dance world—English, French, even from *Mitteleuropa* and Scandinavia, also Freddie Ashton in a box with Princess Marina and everyone done up. . . . Fonteyn superb, as always these days; Nureyev very odd and lost—deeply introverted in *Paquita* (a dull piece, two circusy dancers from the French Opéra—superconfident, all flashing smiles and Gallic teeth, sort of like bad French jokes, and such leapings, cavortings, and one-hand lifts, rather like a nightclub act years, years ago, but everyone loved it).

Last night we were taken by some lads to see life in the East End and along the Thames docksides—pubs such as one only sees in well-documented fin-de-siècle movies. First we trooped through a series of houses lived in by English chums (houses which seemed to long for *The Madwoman of Chaillot*[17]) and then the pubs jammed with every sort of creature, raucous with music and singing and conviviality and strange life. This does not exist in New York anymore.

JOURNAL · JANUARY 22, 1965 This is the day of the Clive Bell valuation.[18] Met at Victoria [Station] for a train to Lewes. I didn't realize where I was going. I see a woman with heavy, open shopping bag or rucksack, so like Virginia Woolf. Thus the enchantment begins—a voyage into the past. When Jamie [Dugdale] meets me at Lewes, I discover this woman is [Angelica Bell]— V. Woolf's niece, Vanessa Bell's daughter, David Garnett's wife.[19] Here is a great living tradition, an Omega day—Vanessa Bell's decorations carefully preserved by Duncan Grant, who lives there; the books and letters and notes in

17. The title character in a satiric play by Jean Giraudoux, she dispatches greedy businessmen via the sewer under her cellar.
18. Sotheby's was valuing the estate of Clive Bell (1881–1964), the Bloomsbury author and art critic. Leo filled out this journal entry after his return.
19. Artist Angelica Bell (b. 1918) was married (1942–61) to novelist and editor David Garnett (1892–1981). He had previously been the lover of her father, Duncan Grant. Mina Curtiss also had an affair with David Garnett, during the thirties. Vanessa Bell (1879–1961), elder sister of Virginia Woolf, was a painter and designer. Charles James Dugdale (b. 1939), later Baron Crathorne, worked for the Sotheby's Impressionist department in the sixties.

them; Duncan Grant's studio; the lunch at the Omega table. The colors—greenery-yallery [Art Nouveau]. The designs were all so Roger Fry.[20] A bust of Virginia Woolf. I was deeply tempted to steal a scrap of Lytton Strachey manuscript that fell out of Clive Bell's [book] *Proust*. The moldiness of all this establishment. The good bread and bits of roast or ham. David Garnett, who had his eightieth the previous day, was sexless. [Ballets Russes dancer] Lydia Lopokova a brown bear in her window, the great paintings thick on her walls. The sun's beams, from behind clouds, spotlit the Woolfs' house. A thin, silver ribbon in the distance—here she [Virginia Woolf] wandered into the waters and was gone. When I was going away and saw Mrs. Garnett and Duncan Grant in the doorway, I thought: "She's his daughter." Later, as I was telling this all to Yvonne Hamilton [wife of publisher Jamie Hamilton], she said, "Of course! Everyone knows that. . . ."

JANUARY 25, 1965 • LONDON

**TO JERRY LERMAN** • NEW YORK CITY

I had a lovely, lively encounter with Princess Margaret last week at Cecil Beaton's party for Audrey Hepburn (who looked wonderful in a short, puffed-skirt, bright green, tightly bodiced dress from Givenchy). The princess came up to me, held out her hand, and said, "How are you, Mr. Lerman?" So I held out mine and told her. Then she went on for about half an hour about how awful *Maggie-May* (the musical) was—mostly because Rachel Roberts (Mrs. Rex Harrison) was bad in it. Mrs. Rex Harrison was standing within earshot! The princess also talked about piano playing (she does it well), did a few intimate impersonations (she does those well), and babbled on and on. So we were chums. She wore a long, rather full dress—pale silver-gilt embroidery on white gauze, fashioned from a sari. The bodice very tight and lovely. She has a beautiful complexion. Her diamonds were small flower clusters in ears and on her hands. She's kind of jazzy and looks like her father struck it good in the female-shoe business. That is the end of my society column today.[21]

NOTE: Winston Churchill died on January 24, 1965. He would be the only commoner in the twentieth century honored in Britain with a full state funeral.

JOURNAL • JANUARY 31, 1965 On Friday, before [the opera] *Arabella*, the Crathornes picked me up in Bond Street and, all squinched together, we went

20. Omega Workshops was a decorative arts company founded in 1913 by critic and painter Roger Fry (1866–1934). It closed in 1919. Painters Duncan Grant and Vanessa Bell had joined the endeavor. Grant was basically homosexual, but he lived happily with Vanessa Bell (and her husband, Clive) from 1916 and fathered Angelica Bell.
21. Leo later noted that Lady Juliet Duff remarked of Cecil Beaton's house, "Like a very successful Parisian madam had decided to give it all up, moved to the English countryside, and took all her bordello belongings with her."

off to the special entrance reserved for friends and important people (Lord Crathorne was very close to Churchill) and so into Westminster Hall. The soundlessness of that—thousands of people all moving slowly, sedately through the brown-velour light, past the amber candles and the Union Jack–draped coffin, with its guardians, their heads bowed over their swords. Great skeins of people—all ages, all kinds—and not a discordant sound—looking back. They came as Emma Lazarus envisioned the poor of Europe pouring into America— hordes—not a feeling of sensation-seeking or hysteria, but love, respect, loyalty, gratitude. Over all of these ceremonies and these days I have never been without the feeling that Churchill was watching and enjoying every moment.

Just random jottings on Churchill's funeral: We went early in the bleak morning to Trafalgar Square, where thousands were gathered beneath Nelson's Column and the glorious lions, not jammed upon the monument but orderly and still beneath it, some behind iron railings and some perched on those railings. The feeling was that of respect—prodigious respect and dignity. All ages—babies on shoulders, sometimes grown women on men's shoulders, and many women holding their compact looking glasses high aloft to see the procession. The clean sweep of pigeon-wing sound when the cannon saluted. The black tide in the Strand—busbies all moving toward St. Paul's. The sudden scarlet of coachmen's caped cloaks and tall hats on the first coach. The elegance everywhere throughout the procession. A work of pure art functioning miraculously, nothing left to chance, and even chance become part of the work of art: the sun suddenly making the lowering of the coffin from the gun carriage to the shoulders of the Grenadiers a triumph. The Grenadiers looked, as they carried the coffin, in love, as though they were listening. The funeral tread, but never for one moment sad. No sorrowing. A sense of Churchillian humor, for he had planned Operation No Hope for a decade. This was the nineteenth century departing, the afterpiece to Victoria's funeral, when the crowned heads packed into the special bound-for-Windsor train; the kaiser in his gold armor clinging on at the very end. (All dashed from the train into the conveniences at Windsor station.)

Watching the television at [Peter Wilson's secretary] Elizabeth [Chanler]'s: This is what television does best—events. Alexander the drum horse with his cascading mane and clop-clop steps—The cranes on the riverside bowing as the cortege passed—The great splurge of light on the untrafficked river—The bridges and the Thames as Canaletto could have seen it—Then the long, freshly painted line of dining cars and the baggage car and the coffin slowly, slowly, slowly into the special darkness (all baggage trains are dense with that darkness)—And the door inexorably closing—Suddenly a feeling of emptiness, of vacancy, the special life had gone out of that day and the usual Saturday feeling could not be summoned or even wooed into the emptiness—The sound of the piping, the shrill, thin sailor's piping—The bagpipes lamenting—a sad-happy tune, a loving tune—the "Battle Hymn of the Republic"—all of its verses, and how delighted Julia Ward Howe would have been. I remembered that old Mr. [Mark Antony De Wolfe] Howe of Boston told me that Mrs. Howe, who also lived to be very ancient, would disrupt dinner parties by announcing, "I am now going to sing my hymn . . ." and then she did—all verses and more— The feeling that Sir Winston himself was enjoying this celebration, which he had planned and was giving—The most marvelous party in the world.

**SOTHEBY'S** *I wanted the atmosphere of the book to be enchantment with auctioning, a great feeling for the migration of treasures. I had never considered the wear and tear of daily immersion in mortality—the 3,000 or more canvases stacked in the cellar at Sotheby's. I wanted not a dreary listing of sales, but the potency of lists—Sitwell lists—names like exotica, like lists of old roses or stage properties—a list of the panorama of living. . . . But an auction house demonstrates the permanence of impermanence. Mortality.*

*The very beginning—confusion, the lack of an archive—was also the very end. The final question, as I departed, from Fred Rose [their jewelry and silver manager]: "What has been the biggest surprise in these six months?" "That a firm which has made its fame and fortune from the past has no regard for the past." Long pause. "Well, we've had no time." (1971)*

**JOURNAL · APRIL 2, 1965 · SS** *QUEEN ELIZABETH* EN ROUTE TO NEW YORK CITY Deck chair—silver sheen, gunmetal gray (such a bogus color word), ruffling-in-the-breeze vastness beneath the watered blue, a rubbed gray-white glowing dome above. Very smooth. The calm before? I must confess that I have had deeply serious perturbation about this sea voyage and at one time said we would go by air. A woman just clutched at her hair as though (should this be if?) she were about to lose it to the breeze. The weather is changing—great clouds, sort of sleeping clouds, indolent like white tigers, a kind of watchfulness beneath lowered lids. All of the "characters" Ruth Draper would have realized are on board. She had the genius to bring fiction into life—or life into the fiction she created, meaning that what she saw became life. Henri [Cartier-Bresson, on board] discovered me. At first, he looked older, washed out of his perennial youth, a golden, fined-down, old-gold-leaf fragility. Then he was suddenly Henri again.

APRIL 3, 1965 On closed deck, in chair, during fantastic (in the accurate sense) storm—waves crashing against this fleeing ship, sunlight annihilating all to a Turner madness, the beauty of it, the beauty obliterates the danger, rather like the beauty of any powerful cat beast—and the oddity of dazzling sunlight and the slate-gray, foam-white storm. Poor Puss is queasy and frightened in his bed. And I sit scribbling here—not believing in it, save its glorious, howlingly frantic beauty. There must be a meaning to such beauty. It cannot be purposeless, which is why Greeks and other ancients personified it. Great blotches and patches of molten silver, such as those dropped by gigantic ladles in smelting works—and suddenly all the world unbearably radiant—while this enormous vessel shudders and shivers and trembles like a strong man swept away into passion—sublime intimacy.

NOTE: Financial pressures apparently had compelled Leo to return to New York. After six months, the British government would have required that he pay taxes. Also, Condé Nast may have grown discontent with paying Leo as a consultant to *Mademoiselle* while he resided in London working on his own book.

Gray had felt very reluctant to leave London, and then finding their home in New York deteriorating—stairs coming apart; plumbing pressure failing—did not improve his outlook. The house's many stairs had also become more arduous for Leo to climb. In the face of these realities and the renewed pressure of New York's social life, Gray's nerves broke. He stopped drawing. Although Leo hopefully notes Gray's sketching again in coming years, he never resumed an artistic career. Leo described the situation briefly in letters, but he did not diligently resume his journal until the early seventies.

JOURNAL • MAY 23, 1965 • NEW YORK CITY  In my bed, still on the fourth floor of 1453. Today is my birthday. It is my first "old" feeling birthday. I cannot write a list of resolutions, self-promises. I know what must be done. It is the doing of it I do not know. I do not believe in any God—in man's image. I cannot. This makes me solitary. Now I will read in the Bible Maggie Henning gave me so many years ago. That fat, fat hirsute face, those doubtful blue eyes. Maggie had a passion for sentiment, which expressed itself in tremulous but searing renditions of the Indian Love Lyrics ("Less Than the Dust" and "Pale Hands I Loved") and readings from the Great (Shakespeare, Milton, Tagore), but from her [a high school English teacher] I learned poetry and graceful living and Christianity. She opened the door—and I zoomed through it. She understood more than I knew. She understood and made it all right because, as she said, "God did it—so it must be right."

Fortitude, patience, deathlike love does not come until—but always there is the open door, which must be recognized and the threshold crossed, never let anyone know, and they will know if they do. The signals are unmistakable, explanations unnecessary, as are passports, when the moment is the moment not to be avoided—fear only the minor and unimportant—but love—a loving heart, that is the saving grace. Gray has a loving heart, so does Richard.

NOTE: Leo and Gray would visit Richard Hunter's house in Maine several times for summer or holiday visits, including twice with Gray's mother.

JOURNAL • JULY 13, 1965 • AUGUSTA, MAINE  The blissful, sun-soothed endless summertime of childhood. I am reading volume two of [George] Painter's *Proust.* All those enormous stirrings again, suddenly focused by clearly seeing

Cousin Frieda, with her enormous plait of dark-honey hair, twined with black, dull-surfaced, neatly ribbed ribbons, sitting under the gaslight, snipping royalties from the rotogravure.[22] I see the page—whole upon the table, then held with the gaslight wavering upon it. This was in 1917 or 1918. Now these royalties—their descendants, "high" society, the environments of these exalted—have all become available. The basic seesaw in all individual and social relationships: Ruth Ford a headwaitress at Ella Barbour's circa 1934, now "high" society. Little T unexalted. The personages in the rotogravure became, during Hitler's war, beleaguered grand remains in New York.

I am haunted by Frieda's snipping royalties and by my constant, lifelong snipping—opera stars, dancers, society *en fête*, art collections, oddities. In a rage, Grandpa Goldwasser flung all of my cuttings out into the driveway. He hated my snipping. But is this cut-paper world I have made not the real unreal world in which I exist? This pursuit of artificial glamour, the discovery of what it is—the emptiness, but the sounding board aspect, as the sea in a shell: The shell is insensitive, but within is the sound of the sea. Am I that sea-sound heard within the ravishing shell?

Elizabeth Chanler says she was looking at some antique jewelry in the [Sotheby's] showroom, and one of the porters said she shouldn't touch this Egyptian jewelry, because some fifteen or twenty years ago, a man brought in a mummy in a case. Then he didn't call for it for about five years. It was put on a top shelf. Finally, he wanted it. When the porter tried to get it down, it broke open, and a mess of "black" matter fell on the porter, who became sick immediately, went home, and died that evening. Ever since, the porters believe that "antiquities" are cursed. Elizabeth is marrying Bruce [Chatwin]. We couldn't be more astonished at this Sotheby romance.[23]

AUGUST 9, 1965 • BETHEL, CONNECTICUT At Mina's, in my bed waiting for [the maid] Nicole to bring breakfast, but not a sound in the house—stillness like dust sheets spread upon the rooms everywhere, and birdsong and bird chatter so loud that it almost makes my head ache.

Yesterday we lunched at Philip [Johnson]'s fantastic—what to call those structures, all born of pavilions and follies?—not seeming there at all—nonexistent, magical, capricious. The greenness of the lawns ($4,000 a year to keep them in that condition) on which Philip's "houses"—pavilions—seem set

---

22. Frieda (later Flo Grossinger) was the daughter of Leo's aunt Helen and uncle Benjamin Goldwasser (his mother's eldest brother), who were deaf, as were two of their children, Frieda and Louis ("Lew").
23. Leo had believed Bruce Chatwin (1940–89), later a novelist and travel writer, to be homosexual. Chatwin and the American-born Chanler, who also became a writer, had both been working at Sotheby's.

by a master wizard. The new museum, underground, which must be ready by November when Mrs. Whitney is "bringing Princess Margaret and Tony to lunch."

One tiny sentence said to me by Philip darts like a well-plied needle through all my thinking, feeling, and being: "He always locked the door of his room and wouldn't come out." I am amused at Philip thinking Gray knew me before he knew Philip. I have always thought that Gray made a choice between Philip and me. I found Philip attractive, as smoothed as Oriental sculpture of the best periods.

SEPTEMBER 5, 1965 Here I sit again in my bed at Mina's, weeks later, experiences later (not many). Mina knew many of the Proust legendage. She had a passionate affair with Antoine Bibesco, who wrote her letters. ("So dirty, I must destroy them.") These past two evenings she has been tearing and burning letters from Lewis Galantière and others. Some feel of social history, but she says she doesn't want anyone to read them. How very odd for a biographer to do this—and how selfish.[24]

JANUARY 4, 1966 • NEW YORK CITY
TO RICHARD HUNTER • CAIRO

This morning, when I went out on the steps in my Christmas robe, the traffic jam stretched as far north and as far south as I could see. A driver shouted: "Go back to bed, grandpa! You won't get anywhere!" And another driver inquired, "How many beds yuh got?" Everyone is very jolly, while business alone loses at least $40 million! I wish I could find even a little of it.[25]

Jane Imbs brought her family to visit this evening. The children are lovely, beautifully behaved and dressed, such a sweet family. They stayed and stayed. I think she thinks I am her family. When the bell rang, I thought: Oh, here are Valeska and Bravig [her parents]! I thought it most vividly, and I could see them there—but, of course, they weren't. Then while Jane was here I realized that Valeska would be sixty-five [*sic*, sixty] and Bravig probably as old—and this was a shock. I had not thought of them older. Ah, Reezl, perhaps their plight is that they see us older and older—sort of reverse. I always think of the girl in *Our Town* saying "Momma, look at me . . ." and my heart breaks.

JANUARY 21, 1966 • NEW YORK CITY
TO RICHARD HUNTER • CAIRO

Amy [Gross] ran up to me in the reception room at Condé Nast and said, "Rut Yorck just died. . . ." Oh Reezl, it would be far worse for me if you or Puss

24. The Romanian prince Antoine Bibesco (1878–1951) was a diplomat and a writer who had been a friend of Proust's. Lewis Galantière (1893–1977) worked for Radio Free Europe and then the Federal Reserve Bank, while also being a translator, playwright, and critic.
25. The municipal transit union in New York City was on strike January 1–12, 1966.

or Jerry died, but this is awful—really awful. Not like when Eleonora died (which was fifteen years ago today or yesterday), but awful. When I went to the Bellevue [hospital] morgue to identify Rut, it wasn't bad in any fearsome way—just antiseptic and awful. I was relieved to see her, because she looked so fierce and listening and intent. She was trying to understand something amazing, astonishing—something she almost could not believe. Astonishment had forced her mouth wide open—not in a scream or terror—but in utter amazement, incredulity. Yesterday I went to a funeral place with Werner, her brother [a cellist], and he wasn't much use—nice, but he has no money, so I arranged the cremation and hired a hearse to take her to it and a car for us to go with her as far as we can.

JOURNAL · JANUARY 23, 1966 · SANDS POINT, NEW YORK Here we are at Sono's—snow falling thickly, great tides sending waves all askew and shattering into metamorphic shapes. Only now do I see the solid sadness of that little funeral—Puss, Werner, Ellen [Stewart], and Hertha somebody (a friend of Rut's childhood) taking that simple pine coffin to Union City, New Jersey.[26] I had a huge bunch of violets on the coffin and there were some carnations— pink and bright, fresh-paint red, still in their wrappings. So it ended, a kind man reading the Twenty-third Psalm, and we went away. I think cremation's better than burial. I do not think of her loneliness, deep in the earth. There is that meager consolation. Ken [Elmslie] took the ashes to Vermont to scatter, and this seems right. I do not think that I shall know anything more about the whys of life.

**RUTH YORCK** *Some years ago, I wrote a weekly column for* Playbill. *It was due each Monday in the afternoon. And at 6:30 each Monday morning, I was at my typewriter, clacking away. At twelve noon, I pulled the final sheet of copy from my typewriter, dialed a telephone number, and read what I had written, each word of it, each punctuation mark, to Ruth. She was always there—at first in a cold-water flat whose basic ugliness she cozened into Reynolds Wrap dazzlement. Yards of gleaming silver foil papered the walls, ceilings, even patches of the floor. Her furniture was mostly fruit crates—but such fruit crates! She witched them into simulacra of eighteenth-century painted works of Venetian cabinetmakers' art. She was a sorceress, our Rut. She magicked poverty into makebelieve splendor, prosaic prose into strong, moving, unhackneyed writing—at least for the moment she prodded you into writing, really writing. If you had a spark, the merest glimmer, she bellowed it into a roaring fire. She did not suffer*

26. Hertha Steinhart had gone to school with Ruth Yorck in Berlin. Ellen Stewart (b. 1920), the founder of La MaMa Experimental Theatre Club in 1961 and one of the leading producers off-off Broadway, was with Yorck at *Marat/Sade* when she died.

*mediocrities: She endured geniuses. She had the power of making you greater than yourself.*

*Her legend preceded her. I remember hearing about her long before she appeared, superbly sunbrowned in a marvelous white swath of a dress someone rich had given her. (She had pulled it here, tucked it here until it became uniquely her own—her style was George Sand out of the* Victory of Samothrace.) *She strode into Eleonora von Mendelssohn's room and inquired with a kind of velvet sharpness, "Why do you laugh so much?" After which we disliked each other for a year and loved one another for almost thirty. How to tell you Ruth?*

*One evening, when she walked down the grand stairs of the Paris Opéra, Jean Cocteau beside her, her friend Léon Kochnitzky said, "An eagle in woman's dress." She was eagle-strong and fierce. If eagles are tender, Ruth was tender like an eagle. She was so strong that she wore Hitler-created poverty like a splendid decoration. When the men and women she loved died, she wrote them: They became poems, stories, plays. I do not think that I ever saw Ruth weep, but I read her tears many, many times. She was a wonderful laugher, a wonderful, very Jewish laugher, and Jewish laughter is deeply watered by tears.*

*During her last years, she lived in the Village, on Cornelia Street—a floor-through that looked like a permanent Dada exhibition. And she worked constantly against time. But no matter what work, what writing she was pounding away at, she always gave herself to anyone of talent who needed her loving wisdom. The vanguard came to her as if she were a trysting place. And indeed she was, for here they got cakes and coffee and sausage and petting and slapping (when needed) and glamour and wine and always the best advice—for work, heart, finances, politics. Everyone came—singly and to the parties she managed to give by lantern light (outdoors, in her neighbor's garden), indoors. . . . I say managed—she never, in her post-Berlin years, had much money. Sometimes she had none. But even when she had none, she gave to those who needed something. We always knew that if Ruth had 50 cents, a hard-up chum would get 60 cents of it. So she came to be the living, gallant, courageous expression of pre-Hitler vanguard Europe to generations of post-Hitler-war American boys and girls. And the miracle of it was that she never dated: She was always younger than the youngest rebel, speaking their language because she had already invented it years ago for them.* (1967)

JANUARY 30, 1966 • NEW YORK CITY

**TO MARLENE DIETRICH** • PARIS

This is the sort of day when the bell would ring, and there you would be—the most beautiful creature in the world, with snow thick on your fur—and then we would roar with laughter or racket with conjecture. Oh, what an ache all that makes. And where are you now? Working, I guess.

Last night, I sat at the opening of *Sweet Charity*. Gwen Verdon really a one-woman show, with a bone (picked bare) thrown occasionally to the other "performers," and staged by her husband, Bob Fosse, to make her an instant star. But only God can make a tree. It was full of the dustiest memorable moments. I sat there, in the Palace (now opened, with this musical, as a musical-comedy house), and I thought about you so much.

I really have no news—save sadness. Rut Yorck died suddenly, much as she would have wanted to die, at a matinee of *Marat/Sade.* I am so rebellious at what life does, and I do not seem to understand one thing about it, so I go right on trying to be merry and cope and love at least you and Gray and one or two others. I haven't laughed the way we used to laugh since the last time we laughed.

Oh yes—You must not miss *Madame X* with Lana Turner, produced by Ross Hunter, the funniest movie since *The Egyptian.* I do not think that Universal will let me into its screening room again, but it's worth being banned. She has forty-six changes of Jean Louis dress and David Webb jewels in the first twenty minutes. And when she is down in the gutter in Tijuana drinking absinthe from the bottle and says to Burgess Meredith, "I had a son—No, he was not a son—He was a prince—He was a squab—under glass. . . ." Darling—I laughed, I screamed for both of us and wept with joy, which is the only way I ever want to weep. Come soon and we will weep for joy together.

JOURNAL • FEBRUARY 12, 1966 • NEW YORK CITY   I am in pain, a little every day. I am in despair every day, sometimes overwhelmingly. Now, with Rut dead, to whom do I go with all sorts of puzzlements and problems and despairs and joys?

FEBRUARY 20, 1966 • NEW YORK CITY
TO RICHARD HUNTER • BEIRUT?

Yesterday I sat in Rut's flat and went through her effects. I found, carefully kept, between sheets of blue tissue paper, a large, fine photograph of you. I put this with all of her papers. They are being sent to Boston University. They asked for them. A long, melancholy day. I was given some nine boxes—three Russian Tula-work. She left them to me in a scribbled paper found in her desk. That note was dated 1954, and everyone else mentioned is dead. I also have Rut's bedstead—very good cast iron—just right for the little room where I sleep in Augusta. Also Eleonora's small table came to me, and some fireplace tools and some logs—melancholy, melancholy. I do not really feel fifty-one, almost fifty-two—only at certain times—and although I have not had days for a long time without pain or anguish, I feel full of life and positiveness. This must be God's gift to me, and for that I am truly grateful. I wish that I could give some of my optimism and vigor to those I love. Puss is making a beautiful drawing. Rut's death seems to have started him up, so that is the sort of good she would have wanted.

**TO RICHARD HUNTER • LONDON**

I went to a great specialist, the one who healed my knee years ago. And, at last, found what is wrong. I have a rare sickness (wouldn't you know!). It is named "march fracture."[27] Only about eight or ten cases a year are seen. Cause is usually unknown. Thirty years ago, it was considered a malignancy and the afflicted foot was instantly amputated, to save the rest of one. Now, thank heavens, the treatment consists of being in a cast from the top of toes to knee (which I am). Dr. Graham says that during the last war this strange sickness was finally determined because soldiers got it after enforced long marches (hence march fracture). He likened it to metal fatigue, the kind that makes a jet plane collapse. Something happens in the metal, inexplicable—so it happens in the bone. It is nothing to do with weight. Anyway, I am thinner. I don't really have any news, because I go nowhere, and just sit in this house and try not to move too much.

**TO RICHARD HUNTER • LONDON**

The Met gala was, curiously, not at all moving—save Elisabeth Rethberg quietly weeping when a trio started the *Don Carlo* that Pinza was wont to sing so beautifully—then a moment when the back-to-your-seats bell rang, and ladies in long, trailing gowns all jammed onto the stairs. I saw them from behind—a magical moment of total remembrance of things past. Leontyne sang superbly. She was best. But when all of the "former" stars sat on the stage, it was rather like the graveyard scene in *Our Town*. I think my own grief was at losing a place where you and I had gone when we were so poor and stood and sat upstairs— you paying.[28]

**JOURNAL • JUNE 4, 1966** This morning, I was to go to Sam's Barber Shop, and just as I was about to go away I saw the *Shabbes* morning congregation come out of the "French" synagogue, three houses away. I was overwhelmed by Saturday mornings long ago in Woodside [Queens, near Jackson Heights]. Nothing, save dress, has changed. These French-American Orthodox Jews were the relations and friends and acquaintances of my remote childhood. The same basic types, faces, gestures, groups. Older young couples, solitary grandmothers, men walking together, women together, children popping about, teasing, being "naughty," admiration for new outfits, talk of weddings and bar mitzvahs and houses and food. Some of them stood on the pavement

---

27. Now known as a stress fracture.
28. Leo is describing the gala closing of the old Metropolitan Opera House at Broadway and Thirty-ninth Street, after which the company moved to Lincoln Center. The soprano Elisabeth Rethberg (1894–1976) had retired in 1942.

before this house, and I stood eavesdropping and being long ago and right now indivisibly, not knowing where past became present. . . . Ultimately, *"Gud Shabbes,"* they said one to the other—the rabbi (a little, very trim white beard, a French-accented Yiddish-English, a red ribbon on his lapel), the *rebbitzin* (all straw and grosgrain ribboned bonnet), the Régine-Crespin-looking woman in her bright green, flary jacket, the two upstate New York Christian-seeming youngish women (very ardently girlish), white-gloved women, felt-hatted men, little girls and boys and grown-ups in their neat, special, *Shabbes,* gleaming clothes. . . . Long ago and dead legions, you, this morning: Good *Shabbes.* Good *Shabbes* to uncles and aunts and little cousins and the family "next door." Good *Shabbes,* good *Shabbes* to life and love and long ago and now. . . . I wish that I could re-create that long ago and show what it has become. . . . All the thick Yiddish soup . . . then the thinning out . . . now almost nothing. . . . Part I—Grandpa . . . Part II—Momma . . . Part III—Me . . .

JULY 1966 · BETHEL, CONNECTICUT

**TO MARLENE DIETRICH · PARIS**

This is the long, long hot summer when local tension intensifies, and we wonder if and when comes the explosion in Harlem, and will it, this time, spill south below Ninety-sixth Street. So it goes here—almost everyone gone, and days and nights seem utterly wasted to me, because you are not even nearby on the telephone. There is no one here who really speaks our language. Surrounded by civilians—will life be this now and forever? I cannot urge you to come back to New York. It is more a machine, almost totally a marketplace, and so utterly destructive, killing slowly the people who try to survive here. And the expense! There is nothing to nourish one here, and the city becomes increasingly frightening—terrifying.

I suddenly was asleep, waking only at 4:30 a.m. with terror, because of my still unfinished (and mostly unwritten) [Sotheby's] book. But I think I have found a form for it, a shape quite my own and one within which I can, at last, work. This is a journal form, a sort of very fluid diary of those six London months, but a journal so flexible that it leaps ahead or back into the past when necessary. I have been trying to write a sort of epic, a history of taste and culture, but I am not that kind of intellect, nor am I that kind of writer. I am very good at creating atmosphere, teaching, and rather blithe. I am best at short things. Therefore, this diary form—so open to gossip and all sorts of trivia—is good for me. If only I could sit day in and day out and never have to go near the magazine. But a boy has to live, and a boy's ma has to live, and his chums have to live. You know all about that.

Well, you were at Chanel, so I know, at least, that you are in Paris. How did you find Truman? He does not change—basically cornball, curiously provincial, and always intent on one goal—success.

**THE BLACK AND WHITE BALL** *Truman said, "Oh, you're back. In this heat! Well, come on up and we'll talk." I leapt into a taxi and sped down to the U.N. Plaza [apartments], where, high up, T had one of his residences.*

*"Bless your little heart!" His voice seemed both deeper and higher than when I had last seen him in that early spring of 1966. No more little-boy, corn-silk bangs—Truman's hair was thinning. But behind his heavy, horn-rimmed glasses his blue eyes sparkled. Everything in that reddish room sparkled: the heap of color-suffused glass paperweights ("Colette gave me those! . . . Well, she gave me one of them"); the Tiffany glass lamp with its shade patterned in cascades of blossoming wisteria ("Fabulous, n'est-ce pas?"). He grabbed my arm, swung me around—a wall of shimmering afternoon light, a vastness of light and sky and city and river. "Yes," I said, "you have it all. You're leading a life like a Cole Porter lyric." "Champagne?" he asked, as I settled into a deeply comfortable, flowery sofa. "Non?" He now sprinkled his talk with bric-a-brac of fractured French. He raised his glittery goblet. "Toujours gai, always a lady!" (We all loved Archy and Mehitabel.)[29] Then he downed the bubbly, perched himself in a sort of yoga position on a black, papier-mâché chair, intricately inlaid with mother-of-pearl ("I think I found it when I was staying with Juliet at Wilton"), and pulled a pile of notebooks to him. "Is this a new story?" "Yes. Except this one is not written. It will, my dear, be written about . . . but that is not why I'm giving it. That's only part of the fun of it. You know how hard I've worked all these years. . . . That musical and the play and six ball-breaking years working on* In Cold Blood *. . . and now I want a reward, a great, big, all-time spectacular present. I want to get all my lives together, all of the people I really love and some I just respect and some I want to show off to. . . . And it is going to be a work of reaaalll art." (* VOGUE, SEPTEMBER 1987)

JOURNAL • DECEMBER 1, 1966 The guest list was written in the sort of children's notebook in which Truman painstakingly handwrites his stories, articles, books—a 10-cent, black-and-white-mottled cover enclosing lined sheets of homework paper. On the front cover of this notebook, on the label, Truman had neatly written DANCE. He said, "Look inside and see. . . ." I did. Name and address, name and address . . . front to back of the notebook and then back again, on the reverse of each sheet. "What," I asked, "is this for? The new Four Hundred?" "A little party I'm giving . . . a ball . . . for Kay Graham . . ."[30]

The approaches to the Plaza seemed Hollywood Boulevard on the night of a glorious movie premiere at Grauman's Chinese. The ballroom, seen from the corridor and foyer, was a room glimpsed in the background of an eighteenth-

---

29. Characters in a column by Don Marquis of the *New York Sun*: Archy, a free-verse-writing cockroach and Mehitabel, a dancer reincarnated as an alley cat but "always a lady."
30. Capote had chosen Katharine "Kay" Meyer Graham (1917–2001), owner of the *Washington Post*, as his guest of honor to cheer her after the suicide of her husband.

century Venetian painting. In the foreground, beside a pillar, Truman and his guest of honor—a receiving line of two. T's absolute devotion to each of his guests: He made you feel that you are *the* one for whom this entire entertainment had been devised. Each one of some 540 guests was the only person in Truman's world, at least for as long as he shook hands, kissed (females and males, all were kissed), and wafted them into his ballroom.

He was, Truman, the least intrusive of hosts. For hours he was so assimilated by his chums that seeing him on the floor dancing with Mrs. Guinness or Mrs. Paley was a shock—an agreeable, soft shock of deep pleasure.[31] He was having the time of his life and so were we—all of us. There wasn't a person in that ballroom who wasn't enchanted to be there, somehow deeply fond of the host and even of one another. This good-sized party was intimate, delicious, and private—genuinely private despite being the most publicized social event in years. It had a single, loving, worldly-wise spirit at the heart of it—the same spirit that had written out the most fabulous guest list in years in a child's school notebook and thought out the conceit of black and white masks and dress. In every sense this was a real party—old chums, newer chums, those to see, and those to be seen (many more of the latter than the former). It had the black and white, clean tones of Beardsley's drawings, the corruption of his special line and massed detail. The prettiness of the party came not from the decorations, which were minimal—red tablecloths, candelabra, token floral decorations (smilax)—but from the guests—what they wore and how they wore it—their joyous energy and animation.

Two memorable moments: Jerome Robbins embellishing the Peter Duchin [band's] beat, with the special Robbins-syncopated beat while dancing Lauren Bacall across the floor, only to be cut in on by Arthur Schlesinger, Jr. [historian and social critic], who after a moment of staid Harvard hopping abruptly left Miss Bacall on the floor, rushed up apologizing to Mr. Robbins, explaining that he hadn't realized. The new Astaire-Rogers resumed the Robbins-Duchin beat. At 2:45 a.m., when I was leaving, the intelligentsia (*Partisan Review, Commentary*, Norman Mailer, Norman Podhoretz, etc., etc.) took over the dance floor, forming a folksy ring around the *Paris Review* (George Plimpton seated on a chair), and as they circled him, the Plaza ballroom became every high school gym in the U.S.A. There hasn't been anything like it since the Crash. Nevertheless, you didn't feel that the host had spent $200,000. Not one person didn't want to be there (or was scornful. Even Norman Mailer).

Many of the women looked embalmed—but by the most perfect morticians in the world. Mrs. Paley in five flat strands of rubies (which others thought fake, but I knew were real) sort of sewn on to the dress. She's not aging very well. She seemed laid out magnificently. A woman with the most extraordinary

31. Gloria Guinness (1912–80) and Barbara "Babe" Paley (1915–78) were among the dozen or so rich, stylish beauties whom Capote called his "swans." He ranked Paley first among them.

voice said hello—Tallulah Bankhead. It was the great world, it really was. Spectrum ranged from Alice Longworth in paillettes and the most extraordinary dignity[32] to Marianne Moore sans tricorn hat to Janet Flanner in perfect tailleur to Amanda Burden, really quite extraordinary,[33] to Jean Stein [writer and publisher], who looked like all the wicked women. The only badly behaved person was Frank Sinatra, cretinish stupidity—in the men's room, outposted Mafia abused the man. He's vulgar. Oh, he's so awful. Glutted with power. The youngest person there was not Mrs. Frank Sinatra [Mia Farrow] but Penelope Tree, seventeen years old, very intriguing because you wondered, is she a virgin? You suspect she isn't.[34] Princess Pignatelli in enormous leaves threaded through her hair.[35] The Barzini girl, in enormous ruffles, ate fifteen buns by actual count.[36] [*McCall's* literary editor] Barbara Lawrence walked her round. A most intimate, delicious (to use Allene's word) party. Nobody was being bitchy. Food was breakfast—chicken hash and scrambled eggs—bad.

The spectacular moment was just before midnight when the floor was dense with black and white plumes—a really great masked-ball moment conceived by a master designer and draftsman. Moments after midnight all of the tables were massed with flung-down headdresses and masks. This was like the terrace of a Stately after a long day of shooting, when all of the bags have been emptied—gorgeous panoplies of feathers everywhere.

Years ago we played "Celebrities." Truman would say, "She's a first-rate celebrity. . . ." Then we would all argue about the "she" or "he." T assembled more first-rate celebrities from varied worlds . . . social, literary, political . . . very few theater . . . no music, no ballet . . . spiked this with Kansas[37] . . . his old, old chums. As Diana Trilling said on the blower the morning after, "It was beautiful and extraordinary and fascinating, but basically it was a very nice dance for friends. . . ."

MARCH 11, 1967 • NEW YORK CITY

**TO RICHARD HUNTER** • ATHENS

A Saturday so warm that the garden door is open. A gentle ghost rain drops meagerly—not a full rain, but an intimation or an afterthought. Do you know what Onassis gave Maria for a present? A tanker! This amuses me muchly. This

---

32. Alice Longworth (1884–1980), daughter of Theodore Roosevelt, was a socialite and hostess known for her sharp wit.
33. Amanda Mortimer Burden (b. 1943), daughter of Babe Paley and her first husband, oilheir Stanley Mortimer, was wearing one of Cecil Beaton's black-and-white costumes from *My Fair Lady*.
34. Penelope Tree (b. 1949), daughter of society families, sister of the writer Frances Fitzgerald, appeared at this event in a risqué dress by Betsey Johnson that launched Tree as a hip fashion model.
35. The Italian fashion model and designer Princess Luciana Pignatelli (b. 1935) attached a sixty-carat diamond to her headdress for the ball.
36. Benedetta Barzini (b. 1943), daughter of writer Luigi Barzini, was a super-thin model.
37. Capote had befriended people in Kansas during the writing of *In Cold Blood*.

week I have worked so very hard on that magazine [*Mademoiselle*]—a wretched hundred-day calendar I had to make—many events each day, fitted into little squares—endlessly trying to do, especially when so many events are only probable. Last week I came out of my office late, in the hallway only workmen and a scruffy messenger boy, his back to me—dirty black leather, awful, messy, bleachy hair. I said to the back, "I am happy to find you here. I hope that you will take me down. I never go in the lifts alone." The back said, "Of course, I will take you down, Leo," turned and roared with laughter. It was Tony Armstrong-Jones—looking awful. So we had a long visit, driving about in a taxi. He said that the past year has been the strangest ever—what with his being off so much and life odd at "home" and how he could never finish anything. Then he said that he envied my being able to work so hard and seeming able to finish things (little does he know).[38]

**THE OSBORNE**   *In 1967, on the last Friday in March, 1453 was sullen. 1453 was apprehensive. A house, especially a much-loved and lived-in house, is like an animal who knows, not being told, what his people are thinking, and even more certainly are feeling. 1453 felt that something was happening, something that 1453 did not like. Gray and I, seated in the back parlor, the afternoon pewter light seeping in, dulling the pinks and greens of the 1870s carpet I had bought during the sale of the Grand Union Hotel's effects in Saratoga to a hazy remembrance of enchanted gardens. It did not help lift the feeling of alarm, almost the sense of depression, which seemed to drape every loved object. "Yes, I will call him," I said to Gray.*

*Then I got heavily up and moved reluctantly into the front parlor and to the long American Empire sofa, which stood next to the table upon which stood the Tiffany glass lamp with the long, honey-colored fringe of lusters bought years ago in Philadelphia. I dialed. A man's voice, a sort of middle European inflection, answered. I said, "This is Leo Lerman, your tenant. We have lived here now for some nineteen years. You know that this house is the center of our lives. We love it. And now the time has come for us to buy it. At last we can afford it, and we want it. . . . We want to own it. We cannot go on living here, no matter how much we love it, because it has become almost uninhabitable. The stairs seem to be hanging by a thread. The furnace needs to be renewed. . . . Well, you know how it is. . . . The whole house needs restoration, and we want to make it into the house it once was. . . . We have to buy it. . . . What do you mean we can't buy it? Why can't we? . . . What do you mean we can't move? I don't have any signed agreement with you about staying here. . . . Oh! You think we can't move because we have so many things! So many books! What's that got to do with it? . . . The roof has to be done over. The rain comes in the skylight! . . . Why can't we buy it?" A*

38. Antony Armstrong-Jones, Earl of Snowdon (b. 1930), a British photographer and designer, was married (1960–78) to Princess Margaret.

very long pause, while I listened with my mouth wide open like a face in some Sunday-paper comic strip. Then Gray says he heard me say, in a voice of complete shock: "What do you mean you don't like me! What's that got to do with it? I am offering you money to buy this house, where we have lived and been very good tenants for nineteen years. What do you mean you don't like me? . . . You want the house? For yourself? For your mother? For your family? . . . You don't want the house for yourself? . . . You want to make it into a social club! What do you mean a social club? . . . Well, if you don't want us to live in your house, we'll move. . . . Thank you, I will now look for another house!" Gray and I sat side by side on the long, hard, brown velvet seat of the sofa. We held each other's hands.

We sat, Gray and I, looking about at the bookcases and cabinets lining the two halls facing into that room and at the overstrung square piano at which Marc Blitzstein one early morning had played hits of the day while Eileen Herlie sang them. We looked down at the bosky carpet, at the old-fashioned, bittersweet-red, deep-walled children's sledge that Buford Chisholm [an antiques dealer] had fashioned and given us on a Christmas Day long ago: It held dozens and dozens of LPs—all Christmas music. Looking out at the sledge was a battered old record player, which Eleonora had given me years before. It had played endlessly Toscanini, Eleonora sitting in an orgasmic rapture as she sang loudly to the empyrean surge of the Maestro's Beethoven.

I heard what I always thought were the new sounds of Lexington Avenue outside. New, because they were not the sounds of my ever longer and longer ago childhood, when Momma and I had walked along the west side of the trolley tracks and looked at these, we thought, forever secure brownstone houses . . . forever secure. Then Gray said, "What do we do now?" The phone rang. I said, "Maybe it's the beast calling up. Maybe he's changed his mind!" Gray said, "He hasn't." I picked up the phone. It was Barbara Kafka. She said, "I can hear that something's happened. What's the matter?" I said, "He doesn't want to sell the house to us!" There was a low animal moan in the phone. Barbara said, "Come for dinner on Sunday night. There will be some other people, but maybe we can all help. We all know that you love that house, but there are other houses." I said, "Barbara, I have a deadline. Barbara Kerr [at Mademoiselle] will kill me if I don't get the copy in." Barbara said, "Let her kill you, it won't hurt as much as moving out of the house."[39]

Sunday evening, Gray and I went to dinner at Barbara's. I sat next to a woman with the most beautiful hands. That is all I remember about that woman—except she gave me the name of an agent and said I must call that agent up on the following morning. The following morning was April 1, April Fools' Day. What was there to lose? I rang the agent and the agent said, "Oh, Mr. Lerman, I know you very well, don't you remember that some years ago,

---

39. Leo had launched the culinary writer Barbara Poses Kafka (b. 1933) when he sent her to review restaurants for *Playbill* in the early sixties.

*when you thought you might move, we talked about a house?" I did not remember. "I think you had better get rid of the idea that you are going to live in a house. You won't be able to live in a house. You will not be able to afford a house now." I considered this idea, and I said, "If I can't live in a house, what am I going to live in?" She laughed. "Do you know the Osborne?" I said, "Of course I know the Osborne. I've known the Osborne since sometime in the mid-thirties. It's where Imogene Coca's mother-in-law lived, and my darling friend Frances Zoline [Wormser], formerly Frances Dewey of the Broadway theater, and Imogene's best friend, would go to see her, and I would go along. And then, of course, Lennie and Felicia Bernstein live there, and Paula Laurence lived there, and the Hirschfelds lived there, and Sidney Kaye—he's very important there.[40] . . . Do I know the Osborne!" She said, "Meet me in the Osborne and I'll show you an apartment if you think you might want to live there. . . ."*

*I said to Gray, "She wants to show us an apartment in the Osborne. I think a very large apartment." Gray said, "It's snowing on April Fools' Day." I said, "You can't fool me! I know it's April Fools' Day, but you can't fool me." I looked out of the window and it was snowing—great big, angel-wing white flakes. I said, "That is a good omen."*

*We went to the Osborne, and as we went into the lobby, which seemed as though it had been waiting not only for Sarah Bernhardt but for us, I had a feeling that Momma would like me to live in the Osborne. It is very odd still, even today, when I am almost eighty years old, how eventually I want to please Momma. We went up to the sixth floor with the agent, went into this apartment, and it was what my cousin Rosalie and her sister Norma would later call "Magnificent!" It has rooms of state on one level and, down eight stairs, very cottagey rooms. It has splendors and miseries. We looked at it. We bought it. We did not move into it until the July Fourth weekend that same year. Back home, 1453 did not once in those months regain its cheerfulness.[41] (1993)*

MAY 18, 1967 • NEW YORK CITY

**TO DIANA TRILLING**

I am scrawling this on my lap, perched on a window seat while carpenters make a hideous noise in our new house—and that is why you haven't heard these long months. We are in the earthquake stages of moving. Have you ever tried to pack a house such as ours, in which you have accumulated (never throwing anything away) for twenty years? Don't. I bought a large (ten rooms—now eight because of two walls removed) apartment in the Osborne. Do you

---

40. Sidney Kaye (1914?–67), owner of the Russian Tea Room, organized the conversion of the Osborne to a cooperative building.
41. Mina Curtiss gave Leo half of the $40,000 that he paid for the apartment. He wrote at the time: "I got $10,000 from Momma, agreeing to pay the interest she would have had from the savings bank. Almost at once she inquired had I figured up the interest." *Letter to RH, May 18, 1967.*

both know it? It is diagonally across from Carnegie. It is a year younger than the Dakota, sixteen-foot ceilings, in excellent repair, gloriously full of light, it faces Fifty-seventh south and the park north. It is an 1884 split-level, steps leading down to the three bedrooms. At last we can be civil again and feed you, etc., etc. Think of living on Fifty-seventh Street!!! I've never lived "in town" before and never in an apartment house.[42] How to cope? Ah well, I can always sell it (I have had one offer already!) or sublet it and we can live penuriously in London—where I wish I was right at this moment. Even my skin is tired. We now pack almost twenty-four hours a day!

AUGUST 12, 1967 • BETHEL, CONNECTICUT
**TO RICHARD HUNTER • LONDON?**

I came here [to Mina's] this time to be a listener. Lincoln went quite mad and almost did in some ancient people in a hotel in Cambridge. Thus far not a word in any paper, but Mina is in a state. Fidelma hasn't gone up to see Lincoln, because she feels she must stay with the cat! Lincoln ran amok—stark naked—in the Commander. Five policemen and four firemen had to quell him. How this has been kept from the public is inexplicable—but please, please don't tell Howard or anyone. L's play about Abraham Lincoln [*White House Happening*] opened the night after he went violently mad—not too good, I gather. (A. Lincoln has a bastard son in it, a Negro who is a butler in the White House!) So "charming" and "brilliant" was Lincoln K—having been locked up in a most expensive private institution—that he was able to prevail upon his doctors to permit him to attend a performance of his play at Loeb (the new theater at Harvard), where, it seems, he behaved so perfectly that he almost convinced them of his utter sanity. However, he is back in the sanatorium.

**JOURNAL • AUGUST 13, 1967 • BETHEL, CONNECTICUT** Over one year [without a journal entry]. I cannot believe this. But how wasteful. What sort of writer can I be? Here I am again at Mina's, having been scribbling letters—to Richard, to Penelope, to Marlene—in my bed, reading Edward Sackville-West's 1927 novel (Gothic he says) *The Ruin*, a book artistically constructed and fleshed—full of dark bodings, Jamesian inflections and innuendoes. I've read the "new" Agatha Christie—a diversion, most dependable, everything in its preordained gory place, business as usual, immaculately run. I've read Leonard Woolf's fourth volume—monumental but not inhuman. He is a sure, passionate, just judge—setting down truths, but recognizing all fallibilities— austerely hot against injustice.

Mina reads patches of the Strachey [biographical] volumes aloud, and I

---

42. Because relatives filled the tenement building where Leo lived during his early childhood, he didn't recall it as apartment living. By "town" he means midtown's crowds and high-rises.

find myself in Sybil Colefax's huge party room, at Argyll House on the King's Road, in Colefax's high time, and more recently a great furniture-and-things cluttered room owned by Penelope—no parties, no memories, save to one who knows what that room once was.[43] And that is how 1453 must now be. I wonder whether our carpets remain upon the floors. I would go there, stealing in (I have the key) once more . . . but I do not think that I should indulge in so upsetting an experiment—not even with the excuse of finding letters.

What a disheveling year this has been: We moved; Tiffany lamps (the dragonfly and the poinsettia) were heisted; Richard went abroad in October and has not returned; Sidney Kaye died; Truman gave his ball and thereby made detractors, even enemies, globally; I found that my Sotheby book was basically no good and so came to a form for it, but have not written it;[44] upheavals at Condé Nast and *Playbill.* . . . I am being rained on, must retreat into this house.

AUGUST 14, 1967  In the late morning, Mina came down, distraught. She had had a nightmare: Lincoln would be in the madhouse permanently; she could not live if he died; he is the center of her life and he had almost always been the center of her life. "I am a hysteric, you know. No one realizes that I am a hysteric. . . ." She moved abruptly about, puffing away, huge with tragedy, eyes black with anguish.

AUGUST 27, 1967 • NEW YORK CITY
**TO RICHARD HUNTER • LONDON**

My, that Bloomsbury world—the gentlemen in it—were incestuous. Tell Howard that Maynard Keynes [the economist] took Duncan Grant away from Lytton Strachey and there was anguish indeed. Did you know that most of them were queer? Everyone told everything to the authorized two-volume life of L. Strachey. I sit reading it, wondering whether all of this is necessary—I mean the intimacies, etc.—for an appreciation of their works. But Michael Holroyd has done a superb job of research and arrangement—and what spurts of brilliance and he was still under thirty!

JOURNAL • OCTOBER 17, 1967 • NEW YORK CITY  The radio spews identical gobbets of news—antiwar strikes nationwide, the strongest at Berkeley, singer Joan Baez among those arrested. The world destroys itself insistently . . . I meant to scribble about Marlene's naïve fury at being called by *Time* "the oldest girl in town." Her rage and livid lack of understanding at reviews that accolade her

43. Carol and Penelope Reed owned a portion of the house where British decorator Sybil Colefax (1874–1950) had famously entertained in the twenties and thirties.
44. Leo did make a pass at constructing a narrative of his days at Sotheby's. Ironically, he was hampered by not having kept a journal diligently when in London.

(really glorious reviews), but are also blithe about her longevity. Ego-mad, a pain to all who love her or work with her—save for musicians (Bacharach[45]).

OCTOBER 19, 1967  Arnold Weissberger took me to the Verdi *Requiem* at Carnegie, across the road (Von Karajan, La Scala [Orchestra], Leontyne, a marvelous contralto, etc.)—one of the stupendous performances, absolutely overwhelming. Von Karajan is probably the greatest conductor today, and his physical presence is stunning—his movements minimal, a sort of miniature gothic man almost imperceptibly magicking prodigious sound out of a concourse of musicians, each perfect, at least for the time they are under Von K's spell. I went back, and Leontyne was very blithe, very pretty, many larger-than-life *cara* motions and gestures, but still gay Negro girl withal. The divas crowded in to kiss the air either side of Lee's happy, achieved face: Tebaldi very erect, very mischievous schoolteacher. (When Lee introduced me, Tebaldi said, "Oh, Callas's friend . . ."[46]); [soprano Pilar] Lorengar, small, blond, pretty, neat, and shy-seeming—a delicious smile; [soprano Lucine] Amara: "Oh, Leontyne . . ." advancing on Lee, arms outstretched in commiseration, face all pity and compassion, "I felt for you when you tripped." No one else had seen L trip. "The bitch . . ." muttered Leontyne to chums. So it went.

Then I went away—and on Seventh Avenue found [set designer] Boris Aronson wandering in a cloud. He had experienced a great thing—this *Requiem*. He was in love with Von K. He was overcome by the tremendousness of Verdi's work and its execution. We sat in the Russian Tea Room talking the world away—how it is even past the Decline and now in the Fall. I said that when the theater died in its own place and took to the streets (as it has here—the theater in the streets is fantastic; the novels in the daily papers are extraordinary; no fiction writer can compete with the daily news), when this happened revolution and war are inevitable. Boris agreed—all the while pondering the Verdi. He had been to view the Picasso sculptures and found them surface things. Everything in arts today, Boris feels, is surface, since nothing is the outcome, as the *Requiem* is, of greatness—no religion or faith, no belief. Today is the decorator's time. Stella [Adler] and Mitchell [Wilson] sat with us.[47] They had been to [Stoppard's play] *Rosencrantz and Guildenstern*—cold, heartless, brilliant, and ultimately doodling with words. So, we all sat talking the world away. Stella beautiful as always. She and Mitchell being like actors in a suc-

45. Songwriter Burt Bacharach (b. 1928) hit the big time as conductor and musical director of Dietrich's world concert tour between 1958 and 1961.
46. Italian soprano Renata Tebaldi (1922–2004) was Callas's main rival and somewhat her vocal antithesis, with great tonal richness. She sang mostly the Italian repertoire.
47. The acclaimed actress and influential acting teacher Stella Adler (1901–92) married first the director Harold Clurman, then the science writer and novelist Mitchell Wilson (1913–73).

cessful play—a long run—tired after the evening's work and the audience's vampirism. Stella raged against her students' utter lack of any comprehension, total lack of feeling, no culture. They bring nothing. I left Boris at one a.m. on the wind-roiled corner.

NOVEMBER 5, 1967 · BETHEL, CONNECTICUT  Philip Johnson is "mad" about Israel—the war spirit, the military feeling. This is what made him so partisan to the Nazis and ultimately put him in jail. His deep girlishness does it, his feeling of being tumbled into blissful annihilation by the military, by brutality. He is one of the chained and beaten ones; he longs for chains and lashings. Is this what he hoped for from Puss? Mina says Philip suffered a dreadful nervous breakdown twenty years ago. He hid under tables. I know of other reasons than a nervous breakdown that sent him under tables.

NOVEMBER 6, 1967  Anne [Morrow] Lindbergh came to lunch [at Mina's]— tiny, fragile, very stylish (which she isn't) in bright scarlet shoes and black stockings (patterned) and black-and-white-checked wool skirt and red shirt, a white Tyrolean jacket, a red-floral patterned little carryall (given by one of her daughters) very sensibly stylish. She has a beautiful profile, and she is a delight—feminine without clinging, thoughtful without boring, no pretensions, a most delicate sensibility and humor, reflective. We walked in the woods. She picked and plucked ground pine for me and saw everything, loving Mrs. Nature and her floral tributes, her bird constituents. She loves to walk alone, with her two cairns, in the woods. She said that [her husband] Charles Lindbergh really believes that everything will end—but that he will survive. What a strange, patient life she leads. He has no sense of comforts, will not spend money (always fearful that he will have none). He is off on his wildlife-conservation interests endlessly. Anne almost never hears from him and never knows when he will turn up. She is always ready—waiting.

NOVEMBER 14, 1967 · NEW YORK CITY  Maria at 12:30—until 4:30—the new, very young girl, loving, funny Maria—her life centered on a man, not music. "I am a better man," she said, "than most of them you know." Then to *Hello, Dolly!*, the great joyous [African American] *Dolly!* with Pearl Bailey—the house roused to an enormous standing ovation . . .

And time tosses me like a ship in an arrogant sea. The radio tells "three o'clock in the morning." Sleepless in time, I sit here, on the side of my bed, in this alien flat where all of my dead loved ones have never been. . . . But soon Richard will come and perhaps this will locate me better.

An awful dinner at the [Alex] Libermans'. Bill Lieberman [the exhibition's organizer] had the Museum [of Modern Art] opened for us, and we viewed the Picasso sculptures. Marlene said: "He sculpts stupidity." He does.

TO RICHARD HUNTER • GUADELOUPE • WEST INDIES

Two days ago, I was going through an enormous box of photographs in a picture-renting agency, and suddenly I came upon a yellow photo of a group of little boys, sort of seven-and-eightish, circa 1920 or 1921, on roller skates in Central Park. One little boy, in his short pants, looked so familiar—smiling away—and that little boy was Label Lerman. I felt that I had passed over. It was very odd. I smell the park and that moment.

TO PENELOPE REED • LONDON

I've had to put "The Highest Bidder" [about Sotheby's] aside until after December 31, 1968, because the Metropolitan Museum asked Viking Press to ask me to do the museum's hundredth-anniversary book—a huge picture book. I am now somehow led out of a dungeon into the daylight.

We think that you will love our new refuge. We do get homesick—no trees, no birds, no squirrels on the window ledges—but also no ever-wearying stairs, and when the heat thumps in the pipes, I am joyous with not having to worry about the furnace. Fifty-seventh Street is curiously quiet this morning. Even when our radio said riots were on Fifty-eighth Street and Seventh Avenue, we saw nothing from our windows. You know, my dear, this [Martin Luther King, Jr.] assassination is worse for us than the [John] Kennedy assassination. I have always known this to be a violent country. I also know that this is still the beginning—just the beginning. I saw fear in our offices and lifts and streets yesterday—fear at little groups of people who obviously stood fearing those who feared them. I could smell the terror in our editors' meeting, when a girl rushed in crying out about riots. I heard me say, "First, find out whether these reports are true. . . ." Later, when our editor said that I had been so calm (I wasn't—my stomach ached), I said that I have been Jewish too long to be frightened. I suspect there is some logic in all this—but I'll not question it. Also it is easier for me: I have no children.

JOURNAL • NOVEMBER 4, 1968  On Saturday we made off to view Barbra Streisand in *Funny Girl*, an elaborately idiot movie alchemized into awesomeness by the star's performance. She wins with her absolute self-conviction, her ritualistics, the stylization through which she semaphores tokens of the deepest passion and pleasure, the way she builds to a personal tumult—deluges of emotion and sound (the virtuosity, so amazing in so young a person), the voice (enormous, robust, musical—but of the streets and alleys), her affectations and, most importantly, her Jewishness. Saturday's matinee audience was 99 percent Jewish. They made Barbra their family celebration. She is the sacred monster of the moment. Obviously awful as a girl, but fascinating, enriching as a performer. The only genuine young star in America.

NOVEMBER 28, 1968 · AUGUSTA, MAINE   A lovely, lovely Thanksgiving. Exactly what such a day should be. Cooking. A walk to the little cemetery in the snow. The War Between the States graves always the saddest. This one has several such graves—including a boy twenty-three years and a few months and another who was a standard-bearer. I think of them going off from this still remote place and my heart breaks there in that hillside graveyard. Then dinner at four. [Richard's friend] Helen Matts, who knew [the dancer] Todd Bolender when he was a boy and they all lived in Canton, Ohio, came. She is a mixture of Fania and Geraldine Page and Una Merkel. Later, we sat around the fire, and Eleanor Morgan, who was born down the road a piece, came in. She is straight out of Sarah Orne Jewett.[48] They would know one another immediately. She is dry and has humor, is honest and deliberate, and all of her yearning is controlled. She has life, and even if she is a virgin, she has lived. Such a clue to Emily Dickinson and the Brontës and all of those remote women who blazoned passionately beside hearths on moors in little villages.

JANUARY 6, 1969 · NEW YORK CITY   At dinner, Larry Kelly told a saga: Onassis rang Maria, asking for a date. Maria said no. Onassis said that after all they were in business together—the tankers. She said all right, come to dinner. After dinner, Onassis said that he had to pee. He disappeared into Maria's bedroom. Soon Bruna, Maria's maid, went into the bedroom—rushed out screaming that Onassis was in there starkers. Maria told him to dress immediately. Onassis refused. Maria's butler, Ferruccio, was too airy-fairy to do anything but scream and swoon. Maria sent for the police, who made Onassis dress and leave. Maria flung down the window and screeched, into the three or four a.m. Paris night: "Shame on you! And on the anniversary of your second wife's first husband's death!" This was on November 22, 1968.

Onassis likes to fuck women up their asses. Mrs. Kennedy won't do it. Also, she will not sit in El Morocco with him and his three or four cigar-smoking Greek chums with their lavish, blondined females, while the Greek men talk business. Mrs. K likes "intellectuals"—Galbraith, Schlesinger—but this is not why he married her. He wants to display her; she won't be displayed. Hence, the rented house in Peapack, New Jersey ["Red Gate Farm"]. Onassis is bored with Mrs. K. They never planned a single day past their wedding day on [his island] Skorpios. Onassis planted it with a rain forest, and rain flows incessantly. Maria studied her role as Onassis's love. She would go to [the Parisian strip club] Crazy Horse and watch, preparing this new role as meticulously as she always had prepared her opera roles. She said to Larry and Mary Reed when they were all in Cuernavaca that being fucked up the ass hurt and was

48. Novelist Sarah Orne Jewett (1849–1909) wrote *The Country of the Pointed Firs* and other subdued portraits of New England communities.

boring. Larry said, "After all, I should know. . . ." Then for two hours she discussed this. Maria has been in the hospital having the bags removed, unpacking the satchels under her eyes. She canceled San Francisco because [its director Kurt] Adler wanted her to do eight *Traviatas* over two months—too long. Bing would give her only two "gala" *Toscas*. Maria wanted ten *Medeas*. So, no New York.

JANUARY 7, 1969 • 1:15 A.M. Elsa [Snapper] came in this evening, before Puss and I went to Ken Elmslie's Twelfth Night party in his new house on Greenwich Avenue (diagonally opposite to the house in which, many, many years ago Eugenia [Halbmeier] said, "Ermine all day, fox all night." We thought that racy and hilarious). Elsa came with her twenty-three-year-old, very Jokanaan nephew. Elsa appalled me. What has happened to her? She was hit by an auto on Fifty-eighth Street, just before Thanksgiving. She has suffered a concussion. But she is changed. Her eyes focus fitfully and with great trouble. She was in the room—all radiant and luminous—but amputated—as though someone had stolen part of her away. Too awful.

There was Rut's young face and shoulders by Kokoschka, over Ken's mantel. Ken told us that Rut's whippet, Rossignol, seemed to go mad, and when Ken opened the auto door in Vermont, Rossignol raced away into the hills and has not been seen since. Rut's ashes are scattered in those Vermont hills. I spoke mostly with Edwin Denby, now two years A Widow of Lincoln Kirstein. How many of us are there?[49] Edwin told me that in the Osborne, not too long ago, was one of New York's most expensive male brothels.

I shall now fall into my bed, listen to the broadcast of *Don Giovanni*, and read [Harry] Wedeck's manuscript, "The Triumph of Satan."

FEBRUARY 2, 1969 • OYSTER BAY, NEW YORK With Horst and Nicholas Lawford.[50] I came here in the morning, yesterday. Actually I arrived, one-ish, in a downpour—most *Anna Karenina*, the Syosset station obliterated by densities of steam—but I adore any railway journey. Even the Long Island [Railroad] behaved brilliantly, depositing me one minute ahead of its scheduled time. I should sue, for this was unprecedented.

The house: meticulously arranged (Cesco's Picasso was sold to help build this house, with its triple, transecting allées[51]), an index to Horst's and Nicholas's lives, each detail cluing the stops upon their journeys to this place, this time—Russian silver cups, batiks, photos of Maestro and so many others out of our Ela-Rut-Lucien past, drawings by Nicholas of his grandparents—

49. Lincoln Kirstein had cut both Denby and Leo out of his life.
50. The British writer and painter George Nicholas "Valentine" Lawford (1911–91) quit the diplomatic service in 1950 to live with his lover, photographer Horst P. Horst (1906–99).
51. GF: "Cesco had a Picasso that he offered to Leo for $100. Leo refused, saying that it was so little and he couldn't do that to Cesco. Horst did take it, however."

these good and very English-German, sometimes a Juliet feeling here—very Bulbridge (especially in Horst's loo with a wall of Turner engravings),[52] much blue-and-white—Japanese, Meissen, Dutch porcelain, and exquisite jade (the greens of high summer).

This is a curious ménage à trois—Horst (very *alt*-Saxony), Nicholas (very county English), Hans (very son-of-Austrian-peasants). Hans, now twenty-eight, looking twenty, was brought here when he was eighteen. A child in a large family, a twin whose female counterpart remained in Austria, Hans was given to Nicholas and Horst by his father, and so came to America and an affluent situation. Hans cooks, drives, assists Horst, services both I am sure, and cats about on his own. He has considerable looks, the kind that run to fat later, and great charm. He is loving, amused, given to swift, cloud-fleeting depressions, and he is constantly in heat—a sort of abiding heat—perhaps he is centrally cold.

Ultimately it was decided that I must spend the night here, and I have, but virginally, in the coldest bedroom since my weekends in the Statelies those long-ago six months in England. I love being here, because it is having one foot in my lost world of Ela and Rut and Ilse [Bois].

FEBRUARY 16, 1969 · BETHEL, CONNECTICUT  I had a disaster with my [National] Theatre of the Deaf piece [for the *New York Times*]. "Wonderful atmosphere and enthusiasm," said [arts editor] Sy Peck, "but not enough content . . ." I think that Sy is right. Also, he stood on the exact area, in my work and life, which makes me tremble: I do not have the kind of "content" expected. I am not intellectual; I am emotional, intuitive. I do atmospheres and surfaces and lightness with sincere deep feeling and genuine darkness beneath it all. I am decoration, not great art. The graces of life, not the webbed philosophies, are my domain. I work hard—incredibly hard—grasping solid facts the way the falling and drowning grasp straws.

Last night we watched television for three hours. The color television discolors rather than colors. Most people on the screen were white-lipped with joy, and the colors were quite like those crude smears on Russian or Italian popular prints. Also very Lichtenstein and Rauschenberg, the effect. Nevertheless, an enjoyable evening because of *Laugh-In*, with its own special mordant satire and fragmented rhythms. On Bob Hope's show, Mr. Hope and Mr. Crosby brought theatrical chills when they cavorted together—very old tyme. The Jack Benny show was not as good as the others. I expected Eddie Cantor to appear, as always faintly repulsive. The screen shows the techniques so clearly—the remarkable vaudeville timing; the utterly pro milking; the deadpan precisely adjusted to the lid; the ego; the deep gratification always lurking in the corners

52. Bulbridge was the house of Lady Juliet Duff, near Wilton House, the renowned home of her relative Sydney Herbert, Earl of Pembroke.

of the mouth, the corners of the eyes—no matter how passive the face, the hands, the body; the curious effeminacy of both Hope and Benny. It is where all vaudeville went. Television is vaudeville's gold-paved, gold-walled, gold-roofed heaven.

Do I really want to fuck with others? Why? To the first—I seem to, but only to be "taken," not to take. And that answers the second question. Do I do it with others? Almost never. Why? Too much trouble to go through it all over again, especially when I have it so much more gloriously and with real love at home—but monogamy is not a "normal" condition.

MARCH 2, 1969 • NEW YORK CITY Last night, to Paula and Chucky [Bowden] to dine with the Lunts. What a wonderful evening, to be with Lynn ("Lynnie," as she is called) and Alfred after years of adoring (I don't exaggerate) her. She is very old, but still has her beautiful, highly individual figure—the chin held high, the broad lids artificially lashed, the nacreous skin (so like Sargent's *Madame X*). She came in tottering a bit, but she has made this into a sort of wandering calculated glide, a sort of swing through a room (rather like Ellen Terry's walk).[53] When she saw the Sargent drawing of Ruth Draper, she said that Sargent was a great portrait painter but this drawing was the worst Sargent portrait she'd ever seen. "Ruth wasn't a pretty girl. This is a pretty girl. . . ." She slides her voice, which is quite high—like a high-pitched pale color, a rich lavender—and then falls an octave or more. Her lower register was always ugly—really unattractive—but she managed. She said (several times) that when she was a very young actress, just beginning, she had no lower register, her voice being incredibly high. She tells wonderful stories and suddenly forgets what she's been telling. One has to help get her on the central track, but it is all done with incredible charm and staging. Lunt is a great, genuine gentleman full of Scandinavian chuckles. He was delighted with the success of his modestly blue-and-white striped shirt, a departure for him, this coming to dine in a colored shirt. Lynnie rang Paula up to ask whether the last time they lunched Lynnie was wearing a dress with white sleeves. Paula said no. Lynnie didn't want to repeat the dress, which she had sewed, every stitch of it, herself, and a beautiful dress it is. The choice of Lynn's words is so fantastic. She is so right about the visual things.

MARCH 22, 1969 On March 20, in came Hugh Laing. He says that he is sixty-nine! Small-sized, lined, not a gray hair, a body like someone who has been years on a ship, cat-footed, compact, tightly muscled—he's not too bright, but dear and sweet. Then came Antony [Tudor] on his way to Juilliard, with a

---

53. Several women performers would evoke the legendary British actress Ellen Terry (1847–1928) for Leo, although he could not have seen her in person. Terry had worked with the great actor-manager Henry Irving, and she was widely adored, famously by George Bernard Shaw.

clean-baby look, inextricably threaded with some curious malice, a sort of indigenous reversal in him of anything he hears: He makes you think that he doesn't really believe anything you say to him—an innate skepticism. But I love him dearly. Then Armina [Marshall, of the Theatre Guild] arrived, scarlet hatbox in hand, and in hatbox big white-and-green frosted cake for Fania [Van Vechten]'s eighty-second birthday. Fania, attended by [actress] Regina Wallace, arrived. Regina, a pretty woman in her late seventies or early eighties, is given to occasional song in German (perfect). Fania, almost blind (save miraculously clear-sighted when peering at our Russian silver), almost deaf (complete with the suspicions of the deaf), and shrieking (very Mrs. Siddons as heroines of high drama and low tragedy), was in a beautiful pleated tissuey silver dress made so long ago by her "little dressmaker" and still stylish. As always, style survives all fashions.

JULY 21, 1969 · BETHEL, CONNECTICUT  Rain, rain, rain, and thicknesses of opaque light. The world is, paradoxically, sealed in this morning after man's first "walk" on the moon. We watched it on Mina's color television. It was utterly unreal—almost amateurish seeming in visual technique after these years of science-fiction preparations. I wonder with what "help" and how long it took the astronaut to work up his first remarks. I like Little T's quoted remark in *Esquire:* "So far, so good."

At luncheon at Philip Johnson's, talk was about all of Teddy Kennedy's curious [Chappaquiddick Island] mishaps—a slight word for what could be a devastating chapter in the Kennedys' House of Atreus history. Philip has no notion of real comfort, and if he has an eye, it is so very different from mine that I find it almost nonexistent. How very strange that so thin a . . . no, this is wrong. I feel Philip's quintessential emptiness and his personal fascism. The part that insists on a very feminine woman agreeing to house herself in his totally unfeminine architecture.

OCTOBER 8, 1969 · BETHEL, CONNECTICUT  Last night Mina showed me her partial translation of letters Proust wrote, in 1893, to [Daniel] Halévy. He signed them, almost all of them, Pauline. They were homosexual letters, mostly about a passion Proust had for a young man. I cannot remember the various code names, but in these unpublished letters the seeds of *Remembrance* are deeply rooted. She has offered them to [publisher] George Weidenfeld for inclusion in the Proust hundredth-anniversary volume. Proust was twenty-three when he wrote them and they are so immediate. I felt seventeen again, enthralled by Proust for the first time—all of that "secret" sharing.[54]

---

54. Curtiss ultimately published eight of the letters in her memoir *Other People's Letters* (1978). Proust had written them to the French historian Daniel Halévy (1872–1962) while they were planning an unrealized epistolary novel.

NOTE: In late November 1969, Viking published Leo's *The Museum: 100 Years and the Metropolitan Museum of Art*, a large-format, heavily illustrated book.

While Gray visited his mother in California over that holiday season, Leo carried on an affair with a younger man, Eugene Fracchia, then a sales clerk, later a restaurateur. Leo and Gray had first met him through the retired dancer Alexandra Danilova, whom Fracchia sometimes escorted around town. When Gray returned from Los Angeles, Leo admitted the affair and ended it at once, but Gray was deeply hurt and angry, scarcely speaking to Leo for nearly a month. What particularly infuriated Gray was that Fracchia had stayed in their apartment from the day of departure until shortly before his return. In the journal for December and January, Leo later cut out pages and cross-hatched over some paragraphs.

JOURNAL • JANUARY 1, 1970 • BETHEL, CONNECTICUT I deeply, tenderly, irresistibly am and have been in love with Puss some twenty-one years. Our enmeshed lives have never been easy—now here is this twenty-eight-year-old. I do not love him. I must remember constantly what the twenty-four-year-old taxi driver said to me on Sunday last. I asked him where he taught. He said: "Elementary school, Brooklyn." He asked me: "Do you have a family?" "No," I said. "Do you miss one?" he asked. "No," I said, "I wouldn't know how to help a boy your age . . . how to raise a family today. What would you want out of a parent?" "I would want you," he said, "to lead a life I could admire."

FEBRUARY 16, 1970 • PHILADELPHIA I am sitting in a bakery and lunchroom just off Rittenhouse Square. I have been sitting in the station, then walking about these little streets, feeling again how living in these tall, slightly mortuary houses would be. As I crossed Rittenhouse Square, toward the Barclay, looking up at windows—behind which Gray and I once had been happy—the other side of the square, where Martha [Speiser] lived her last days—desolation, a heavy gray-black wing, a dense cloud the color of nothingness settled upon my very being. . . . But still this curiously anonymous morning is rich for me. I never am alone this way, and for many years I have not been in lunchrooms like this one, where everything is alien to the dressy life I now experience. I like it, and this place is one which Gray would dislike—pitiful. I see and feel him— so pitiful—helpless.

I cannot write about these last weeks. For the "good" of Gray the best way would be for me to vanish—but I do not want to. How to survive in this desert of ice, which explodes volcanically, frequently without warning? I love sitting here midst the morning bustle of customers who know the waitresses, greeting them with long-lived catchphrases, and the waitresses bearing trays of poison-pink and poison-green frosted cakes to and fro. I must go to my television show peddling my book [*The Museum*].

MARCH 8, 1970 • NEW YORK CITY We are so far out that this sea may never carry us back again. Gray rang at two a.m. to say that he would not return until morning. I understand this, but I find—or hear—awful little sounds of pain—

and I do not sleep save fitfully, with my lamp lighted the night through. This is now excessive payment. I think if we parted I would be even nearer extinction than I have been during these seven dreadful weeks. We moved out of our house. Are we now moving out of our "life"—that life we accreted so carefully? "I cannot bear it," my inner voice screams—but I can and I will.

MARCH 9, 1970  Gray arrived home at noon. "Are you angry?" "No," I said. But I am angry at the lack of any genuine affection—and his spurty temper and this veneer of living together—the waste—the awful waste—and I am jealous. Ah well, I must sublimate this in work.

MARCH 19, 1970  On Sunday, drinking tea with Dorothy Norman, I heard footsteps on the stair in her house—but these were creakings, not footsteps. However, I was instantly flung back, some thirty years, to a summer's evening when Dorothy said no one was staying in her house and I heard footsteps on the stair and they were Alfred Kazin's steps.[55] For a moment I thought: These years have all been a dream and now I shall have to live these decades. I would live them—even with the anguish—because then I was lovely and loved, even during the dreadful interims. Now I am in a limbo—loved but shut away from any love, hated and at all times exposed to this hatred. No one to reach out a loving hand I can take. What I mean is a loving body to hold—just for a recharging moment.

For me to die would be the best solution—for everyone save me—and I am no longer certain that this isn't the best solution for me. What is the future? Perhaps one or two books and pain and old age and poverty and nothing—or is this because I am at a low, low tide—actually no tide, for the tide is so far out that I am almost a desert.

NOTE: On April 21, Leo underwent long-delayed hernia surgery. During what became a ten-day hospital stay, his doctors investigated his evident neurological dysfunction (most apparent in his poor dexterity and reflexes). Whatever they concluded, he pursued no further treatment. In the weeks leading up to his hospitalization, Leo and Gray mended their relationship.

JOURNAL · APRIL 20, 1970  How odd that I will "fall asleep" in this room [at Beth Israel Hospital] and, if all goes well, wake in 1161, the room in which I almost died last time I was here. My little radio pours enormous tides and torrents of Wagner. The nurses are making their nightly rounds. . . . "Inhalation Therapist! Inhalation Therapist! Night Porter! Night Porter!" . . . So time passes, and the wonder to me is: Here I am—quite healthy, very much alive—then comes a chasm, a gigantic divide—then, here I hope to be again—where am I in-between?

55. Leo doesn't elaborate, but it seems unlikely that the literary critic Alfred Kazin (1915–98) and the wealthy columnist and political activist Dorothy Norman were more than friends.

Last Tony [Awards] night I was kissed by Julie Andrews, Barbra Streisand, Betty Bacall, Tammy Grimes, Cary Grant, Noël Coward, Brian Bedford— dozens of others. The Tony Awards party seemed my party—and here I am, awaiting oblivion, brief oblivion, I hope. So what does it all mean? Nothing? This living must mean—a little something. These last months of horror—they must mean . . . Puss and I love one another. I love Puss more than anyone or thing in the world. Still, I will be gone for a time. . . . "Dr. Sugar! Dr. Sugar!" . . . The meaning will be if I live to write my book, my one book that will open windows for others. George London is singing "Wotan's Farewell."

APRIL 27, 1970 One week later—Perhaps tomorrow I will be able to go "home." This morning, my stitches should come out. I feel well—and even though part of me retreats from the problems in the world outside this sickness, the stronger part of me jumps with delight at having survived this blight—the poised disaster from my vagus nerve. Young Dr. Gross told me that my last words as I went under were: "If only I could know how to write this . . ." Since I can never be given any painkillers, when the pain became too intense (and that went on for two days), I sang "rain" songs.[56] When nurse and doctors put tubes into my various orifices, I asked Richard [Hunter] to read aloud. He read from [Smollett's] *The Adventures of Roderick Random* (which he was reading), but that prose did not soothe. So I asked for *Our Mutual Friend*, and Richard swept into the opening on the Thames and that was better than any balm— marvelously soothing pain.

APRIL 29, 1970 Yesterday, Howard Rothschild told the story of Mrs. Visher, who was first a dressmaker for some Jewish women, then dressmaker for some rich Jewish German-extraction ladies, then up and up to a summit from which she deigned to work for very rich society women—Astors, etc. One day, Mrs. Rothschild went to her, being one of the very few Jewish customers Mme V allowed to call, and Mrs. R, hearing Mme V sneeze, asked if she had taken cold. "Ah yes," Mme V beamed, "I caught it from Mrs. Vanderbilt."

Marlene as a continuity—the symbol of artifice. From the moment she emerges from behind the furniture, in the early thirties, no longer the plump, carelessly arranged hoyden of *The Blue Angel*, she becomes the permanent symbol of beauty's decay. While seeming to survive miraculously, her beauty is at first a work of art, and ultimately a triumph of artifice and spirit. She returns, in private, to the appearance of a German *Frau*—plumpish again—but in a Chanel suit and in superb wigs. As some great fortress, left unmanned, untenanted, gives itself up to the elements, which then gradually breach it,

56. Leo was deathly allergic to some painkillers and anesthetics and was terrified by all of them.

destroy it more swiftly than any enemy attack has in the past, so this hitherto impregnable bulwark of passion and love and emotion now uninhabited by any loving one, empty of any living thing, is sundered by emptiness, gradually destroyed.

JULY 18, 1970 · BETHEL, CONNECTICUT

**TO RICHARD HUNTER · LONDON**

Mina lurks within. Last night, she told me about a visit that she and Lincoln made, when they were young (he was still at Harvard), to Mrs. "Happy" Chandler (the one who wrote such engaging memoirs)[57], and how there were pears on the table, as a centerpiece and for fruit at breakfast, and how, since Kirsteins never can peel fruit, they were sloppy eaters. (I should recognize that, since I am a pig eater.) When the Kirstein children took to peeling, the pears slid all over the immaculate lace breakfast tablecloth—leaving pear-snail paths glistening in the summer morning sunlight (all very Mary Cassatt). This prompted, or tumbled, Mrs. Chandler's memory into her past. She told how, spending a weekend in a country house with Henry James, she soon realized that "The Master," as he was nicknamed by that set, was not happy in his sojourn. After three days of observing this troubled massive, she dared to ask would he tell her what was wrong. "Yes, yes . . ." The Master responded lugubriously . . . "Could you, would you, indeed, will you, please, please, request from our hostess . . ." Here he apparently went into a whole enclave of his parentheses, ring within ring, sonorous and now unremembered Jamesian rotundities, "please request our hostess to supply me with my dessert, for my dessert, for the better—um—oh—comprehension of this dessert—supply me with a fork and a spoon?" Isn't that quintessentially H. James—so much a little peephole into that world, that past? I suspect the most we can do in writing or talking past or present is make little peepholes. But oh—to make Proust peepholes or James peepholes or Turgenev—as for Dickens peepholes—and Tolstoy—they did make enormous apertures. I would cheerfully settle for the ability to make Virginia Woolf peepholes. I never could achieve the genuine apertures.

Lincoln arrives soon. Philip Johnson came to dine yesterday, with his "friend" David Whitney, a goiter-eyed lad of perhaps twenty-nine, who, when I asked him something about a painter whose name I could not remember (David owns a SoHo gallery of note), a painter who hangs in the Museum of Modern Art, said, "If he's before 1960, I don't know anything about him." The degradation of it all . . . the lack of blood . . . ugh. Philip has the lean, maniacal, self-pampered look of something Jesuitical—nameless sins—and all of that incense—musty flummery.

---

57. Mildred "Mama" Watkins Chandler (1899–1995) was the wife and adviser of Kentucky governor and senator A. B. "Happy" Chandler.

After midnight. So this lovely, free-within visit comes to an end. The tips are in their little envelopes, complete with dainty, illegible notes. My little comfort of a radio is spewing late-night music. The country is alive with night sounds—the intense kind heralding rain. Lincoln was mild, funny, flirtatious. I wonder what he wants. He's huge, incredibly aged, and old-fashioned. He'd done himself up in whites, blue jacket, tie, and white shirt. I said, "You look like you're giving out diplomas—or getting them. . . ." I look very soigné in my uncle's white pants, my white Bloomy shoes, my classic Italian light-knit, body-fitting shirt, and white cap—"Yachting, anyone?" Lincoln is also deeply curious to know what Howard owns.[58] He says he's recently bought three hundred pieces of Diaghilev correspondence—fascinating letters. I must nip into my sack—tomorrow is today, but the lark's not yet in his heaven, and only the owl terr-wit-terr-woos. If only this up-from-the-depths feeling will continue for a little lovely while. It feels good to feel so very good, and I am making the most of it, because this is more the way I really am than that man drooping and amputated and frightened so bleakly in the Osborne. I like it [the apartment], but I never really think that it is mine, the way I thought about 1453. Maybe I will. I do think that life with Gray may be taking a turn for better (his?).

**JOURNAL** • OCTOBER 30, 1970 • NEW YORK CITY  It is not years that age one, but recurrence—the same coming into "fashion" over and over again.

NOVEMBER 8, 1970  Living is cycles of evil days and good days. That is the source of my optimism. I know that good days (moments actually) will come, if I survive the bad days. And sometimes, the good days can be years. But while I have my good day, I know that somewhere, even in the next room, perhaps even in the same room with me, someone else is having a bad day. I am a realistic optimist given to moments of exuberant optimism and moments of black hell. . . . But even in the black hells of my life, some spar of amusement, hilarity blazed—my native optimism preserving me. When I lay, almost annihilated by pain, on that operating table [in 1952], having woken too soon while the doctor was still cutting, I laughed deep within my being at the irony, at the ridiculousness of being helpless, in incredible pain, while far below on Fifty-seventh Street there were people who knew me, who would have helped me. The incongruity of this made me laugh. Also, I felt: This must be how to withstand pain in a concentration camp—at least for a brief moment.

NOVEMBER 12, 1970  Earlier in the evening talked to Caroline Kennedy about what is medieval and what is marvelous about the Middle Ages. She is thirteen-ish, laconic, and sort of tough-voiced. Doesn't sound like her ma and certainly

58. Howard Rothschild collected art and letters related to Diaghilev and the Ballets Russes.

not like her father. Peter [Beard] says she's very sharp, bright. She's to have an exam tomorrow, and could not go to the Cloisters [medieval collection].[59]

Shopping bags, in my grandfather's day, were necessities for the poor and lower-middle classes, or for the very eccentric. No lady or middle-class person would carry one. They were not of paper then, but of oilcloth or strong canvas. Grandfather Goldwasser carried two of them—oilcloth—to contain fish, greens, tea, coffee, cocoa. And this is where I first saw their virtue. Many years later, I carried shopping bags of cloth instead of briefcases or attaché cases. Then I wrapped Christmas presents in paper shopping bags. I believe that I was the first to do this. Now almost everyone, even the rich, carry shopping bags—paper, string, plastic, cloth. And the Metropolitan Museum of Art has an ever-growing collection of them. Shops give them away, since these bags advertise.

Grandpa Lerman was a small sour man with sore-rimmed rheumy eyes and always wracked by asthma. Grandma Lerman was a potato dumpling of a woman who always slept in her dirty diamond earrings and was embraced only by her seal stole. I never saw her without her *sheitel* [wig], save once, and then found her hair a beautiful white wavy crop. I was slapped by my father for exclaiming at the *sheitel*: "Look! Grandma's hair!" The old lady (she was probably in her fifties then, younger than I am now) was in her bath, in a tub in the kitchen.[60]

A sense of joy, élan, and vitality is incredibly attractive and even transfigures into beauty people who are actually quite plain. That is why it is almost impossible for one generation to understand certain beauties of the preceding generation. Rut was thought beautiful by so many who saw her in the twenties and thirties. She wasn't. She captured the vitality of that moment. Had she continued to convey that specific vitality during her later life in New York, she would have been a dated, ridiculous woman, but she matured it into a style suitable to those latter years.

NOVEMBER 15, 1970 Mimicry, in my world, is a social phenomenon. Those who climb in society, or seek to be assimilated on any level, attempt to take on or automatically take on the outward characteristics of the level sought. I automatically take on bastard accents. I instinctively talk with an English accent when speaking with an English person; I take on a *mittel*-European one when speaking to a Hungarian ("You go to Hutschnecker, no?"); I have even been heard taking on a ridiculous Chinese accent. When I try to speak French—rarely—I speak with a very midwestern American accent. Thus I auditioned for [acting school with] Lucy Feagin in a fancy, would-be English accent, and when she talked to me, I took on from her a fake Southern accent. I try to stop

59. Photographer Peter Beard (b. 1938), a friend of the Kennedys, lived in the Osborne Apartments.
60. Leo's paternal grandparents were Isaac (1854–1937) and Naomi "Jenny" Simon Lerman.

this, but almost never can, since my need to identify and so gain a measure of social security is apparently so deep. This is because no matter how assimilated I have become, I have never been certain that I am firmly entrenched. The rifts in the disguise, the deficiencies in the mimicry—these interest me. Unintentional mimicry is always more complete than the most carefully planned, for it comes from within in a flash.

There's a past within me, a link from Aunt Minnie to Mitzi [Newhouse], which I can never elude, nor do I want to elude it. The richness of being Jewish, the very specialness of being queer—these are two of my foundations, and, whether false foundations or not, I have erected quite a structure upon them.

Momma, when I told her that Mrs. Onassis came with her two children to see me today: "You should make time. Sometimes it's good to cultivate people like that, who are so prominent." Momma also asked did Mrs. Onassis invite me to visit her!

NOVEMBER 16, 1970    Mrs. Onassis seemed as concussed as ever, given to pretty-girl smiling and very much a girl in a funny-paper or out of Walt Disney—Snow White grown up and tended by the worldliest. She loved this flat, and in the spare room and Gray's room exclaimed, "Oh—if only I could have a room like this!" She could buy hundreds. Gray said, later, "You should have said everything's for sale."

Irony: Maria Callas was the first not-close relation to come to this flat. Maria, Gray, and I stood in the kitchen, eating ice cream out of its container. Mrs. Onassis lurked over the desk, where, unbeknownst to her, Maria's letters are. Maria hates Mrs. Onassis. Mrs. O was in Marlene color—sand—a beautifully cut dress and coat—no jewels.

Caroline Kennedy is a lump of an adolescent with a pretty profile, but sort of hockey-playerish. John [her brother] doesn't say much but picks everything up. Both children have good manners, carefully drilled in. I tried to help Caroline with her homework. She was confused at the information she had from Dalton [School] anent the differences between medieval and Renaissance art (what a way to teach!) as personified by four paintings—two frescoes, the Piero *St. Simon*, and the Bellini *St. Jerome*, the latter being truly Renaissance and the Piero (one of the panels) being a transitional painting. What she wanted were facts. I don't believe in these, save as a calcifying foundation. What I wanted to give her was a joy in these works of art, and what they really signaled—religious spirit, economic status.

What the visit was about: Mrs. O cast her legend to net two hours of help for her Caroline, while she, Mrs. O, was able to view not only a unique environment, but one in which her rival and predecessor, Maria, had been. Mrs. O wanted to see for herself Maria's closest American chum. This is conjecture, but not impossible. There were, unknown to us, three limousines and secret service men in front of the Osborne.

NOVEMBER 20, 1970  Why do I seriously jot things down? I have been jotting this way since my earliest youth. Because I collect. This is like wandering the margin of the sea and filling a sack with pebbles, shells, bits of glass, and wood—the detritus. Why? A deep need for security? Acquisition—but that is a result, not a cause. The passion for living—perhaps that is the reason. Has it all been a sort of breathing, a confirmation of living, a will to be permanent, to go on forever, one with not wanting to go to sleep, the longing for that one extra moment, one extra day, that one moment more pleaded for so poignantly and pitifully by Madame Du Barry. (I think it was she.)[61] All I ever wanted was one extra moment, and then another, and another . . . to read to the end of the chapter before the lights went out.

NOVEMBER 22, 1970  Oona O'Neill, rushing into Truman's mother's living room, cried out, "I'm rich! I'm rich!" her hands aloft, clenching into greedy fists and unclenching over and over. This is when she told Truman that she was to marry Chaplin.[62]

Chaplin told me at the Liebersons' about Marion Davies, at a Hearst dinner given by her, looking up into Einstein's face and asking, "Why don't you get a haircut?"

NOVEMBER 24, 1970  John Coveney [artists' representative at Angel Records] says Maria's practically signed to do master classes. Onassis is in bed, needing babying, and he is very much in her life. So she canceled lunch, wanted dinner, but I couldn't. She's attached to her telephone like Ela for Maestro. So, Maria is a *damnée*—possibly *déchéance*—a Madame Bovary. I wonder if Mrs. Onassis isn't a sort of innocent.

Sex, by itself, was a basic force in my life. I would and could do it with a great range of men, even when I was sincerely in love with one man. I have never lost my amazement at other people being the way I am—sometimes verging on inexplicable naïveté. Is this an unwillingness to face it—that I am not unique?

I figured out (a vulgar expression) while crossing Roosevelt Avenue [in Elmhurst], when I was about fifteen or sixteen, that everyone was both male and female, all went through a homosexual stage, and some stuck there. I knew that I had stuck there. I always loved girls and fucked boys. I had some adolescent probings, hands only, of girls: Sylvia's breasts, Mildred's breasts and canetta [privates], an anonymous girl in a rumble seat, while driving down from the Grossinger (I made her come by fucking her with a finger, awkwardly,

61. During the French Revolution, Marie Jeanne Bécu Du Barry (1743–93), mistress of the late Louis XV, was charged with treason and guillotined.
62. Oona O'Neill (1925–91), daughter of the playwright Eugene O'Neill, was eighteen and Chaplin thirty-seven years her senior when they married in 1943.

under her clothes, while I came just by rubbing myself against the tight surroundings of my clothes and the auto). I didn't know who this "guest" was and never saw her again, since I did not even see her face while I was doing this, rushing through the night. However, I remember the many times I jerked Bruce M while we were being driven to New York from the Grossinger. I remember how he looked, the shape of his cock, and my pleasure.

Boys I went to bed with almost indiscriminately, in a world of pickups I knew even when I was fifteen. But I did not coincide love with sex—fully—until that spring and summer when I was seventeen (circa 1931) and deeply in love with John K, who was the best actor in Newtown High School and glamorous (a real queen, but I didn't know this then), and whom I overwhelmed with my love—sitting on rocks in empty lots and reading *Cyrano* in French, while I tightly clutched him. When at last he did come to bed with me, I was outraged. Having fucked some boy almost every day from the time I was about five, I did not coincide sex and love and suffered the only *crise* of that kind in my life. The moment I threw him out of our house I was sorry, knowing instantly how very wrong I had been. But he was haughty with me and, with an implacable gift for vengeance, stuck pins into me when we played a scene together in our school play. I thought this the least punishing revenge he could take and adored him. Only after months of punishing me by being distant did we become chums (not lovers, but more like girlfriends).

The year before John K, I was in love with Kenneth S, but he didn't want to go to bed with me—out of moral scruples. He was both queer and strange, in retrospect a touching man. We began our nonaffair, after seeing Maggie Henning off on her first voyage to Europe. Maggie knew him through William See, Risa Steenberg (Risë Stevens)'s closest friend in school. Maggie made a midnight sailing, after which we walked in Central Park and finally fell to hugging and kissing on a park bench set on a green rise in a great wash of early July moonlight and shadow. That was what we know as an Art Deco world (1930), and in memory the moonlight and shadows have the sheen I now see on Art Deco decoration, that silver and that black, geometric, subdued in color. I didn't know what was happening to me, but I did know that I wanted to go on kissing and clutching—with a hard-on. As that summer unrolled its hot, heady self, I would meet Ken in Maggie's one-room flat, which she had let me have hoping I would write a book there (even then!), and I would agonize at him, even unbuttoning my fly and taking my pants down. He let me sit on his lap, and sometimes held my cock. He kissed me, but he never went any further. He liked me and loved to talk about books and theater. He seemed much older to me than he was. He'd toured with Walter Hampden and he had that glamour,[63] and he knew a famous male dancer and his queer father. He gave me

---

63. The actor and director Walter Hampden (1879–1955) starred in many New York productions of *Cyrano* and Shakespeare.

Virginia Woolf's *Orlando* and Mann's *Death in Venice*. I was hopelessly enamored of his stolid manliness, his knowledge, his theatrical (he'd only been a
walk-on) past. We walked miles along the Greenpoint, Long Island City, dock-
side at night, the great factories silent, unworked because of the Depression.
Occasionally someone would call out from a docked houseboat. We were loving friends more than lovers, but since I was (and am) so sexy, I wanted that—
not to consummate my love, but for the pleasure of sex.

John K, ridiculous Conrad G [another classmate], and I bonded by theater
love, being queer, a passion for reading (and all of the arts), perfume—all
small-town queenly interests and pursuits. Connie was the first shoplifter I
ever knew. He painted his bedroom black (with chocolate-brown woodwork
and touches, very elegant at that time) and drenched it and himself with Nar-
cisse Noir.

Into this little enclave wandered John L, my next passion, with whom I
necked, whose beautiful prick I manipulated, but with whom I never experienced an orgasm. I was poetry-writing madly in love with him. Connie had
him; I never did. I wrote a series of verses to him, kissed him passionately in
backyards during graduation parties, made wild, starstruck love to him in the
local Lover's Lane (now massed with apartment houses), and after graduation
lost him.

I can only think that my passion for John K was genuine love—young love,
and that is why when he finally wanted to go to bed with me I rebelled—still
considering sex a thing apart from love. Years later, we did go to bed, in Connie's room, but it was a disaster at which we both laughed. This happened
while John was visiting during one of his appearances at [the Club Richman,
bandleader] Harry Richman's drag club. John became, as "Roni Warren," a
popular drag queen entertainer—New York, Miami, Saratoga. He also worked
as a call "girl."

John introduced me to the drag world, the pickup world, the real under-
belly of homosexuality. He introduced me to queer speakeasies. These were
in flats on West Seventy-second Street, where males met, more to pick one
another up than drink. Some of these places had rooms in which quickies took
place. I did one, in the blackness with someone I never saw. The risks I took. I
was seventeen. All of this while living a studious, artistic life at home.[64]

**THE DRAG WORLD**    *Jean Harlow, Joan Crawford, Greta Garbo, Mae
West, Sophie Tucker, Gloria Swanson, and the newcomer, Marlene Dietrich, are
all sitting in a small, windowless, tired-brown room, somewhere in a tenement,*

---

64. "Those years I slept in the dining room, and Richard and Knox [Laing] came and went,
quite unknown to anyone else in the house—or so I thought." *Journal, February 18, 1971.*

"I wonder about my mother's reaction. Of course, I was very secret—but how curious.
Was Momma so self-absorbed, or did she instinctively know that the only way that she could
hold me was to let me go?" *Journal, July 4, 1986.*

old when the century was new, slightly north of Bloomingdale's. They are sitting on an assortment of battered kitchen chairs, crates, and feather-oozing cushions. It is impossible to tell which are the stuffing feathers of the seats and which are the feathers cascading from the sitters' arms and heads as they arrange them—off a bridling shoulder, lavishly around a preening neck. The floor is a litter of sequins, beads, straight pins, hooks, eyes, and snippets of fabric—satins, crepes, tulles—no autumn foliage gleamed so brightly on a high-noon, wind-wild New England day.

A small, dark-complected creature pushes aside a cretonne drapery, slithers into the room, raises a brilliantly manicured, crimson-nailed hand, points at Marlene Dietrich, and screeches, "Listen, Essie, you are no Marlene Dietrich! She is plump. . . . Maybe she is even fat. . . . Have you looked at those thighs?" She points histrionically at Marlene. "You better eat!" This scrawny Marlene Dietrich drops her feathers, looks up, and screeches, "Go play stoop tag in the asparagus patch!" All the other girls scream. Greta Garbo says, "Thaaat girl," pointing at the little dark one, "Jersey Lily, will never get anywhere. She just won't go anywhere." All the girls scream again.[65]

This is not so much birds caged in an aviary, but a band of intensely vivacious ladies now having a high time at a very special sewing circle. A very tall one, bearing no movie-star or stage-star name, who sits quietly, her sewing rumpled in her lap, speaks up in a deep, hauntingly masculine voice, in which lurks a throaty woman's voice—mysterious, elusive, dark—more sensed than heard, another presence within the visible presence. I know "her." She is, indeed, the only one I know in that room. I know both the visible him and the almost imperceptible "her." When I first met him I thought that he was all he. This was John K. It was toward the end of the summer after we were sophomores that he took me first into the iridescent circle in which I now found myself sitting, rather primly.

They moved sure-footed through the city along ways of their own devising, passing among people who did not suspect their secret business, or their stellar identities. They moved always on the verge of disaster, because what they were selling, or merely giving away, was illegal. To the eye of passersby, they were young men, sometimes noticeable because of their mincing ways, more frequently unnoticed because they bore themselves like anyone who served behind counters in the city's department stores or meat markets. They hoped for a grand passion, at least "a little something," or any passion they could give. Some were out "to make a buck or two." They had designated routes: on the west side of Fifth Avenue, starting north from the Public Library [at Forty-second Street] and trotting swiftly to the edge of the Plaza; on the west side of Riverside Drive starting at

65. Lillie Langtry (1853–1929), a British actress and beauty famous for her amorous conquests, including Edward VII, was known as "the Jersey Lily."

Seventy-second Street and venturing bravely as far as the Soldiers and Sailors Monument [at Eighty-ninth Street].

The cruisers wafting along Fifth, along Riverside, on lucky nights found themselves in Fifth Avenue apartments, in West Side brownstones converted into one-room apartments, in Gramercy Park mansions, in Riverside Drive apartments whose former luxury had been subdivided into acne-walled cubicles, the putrid green of disintegration in color. The take that most of these "ladies of the evening" expected, could range from 50 cents to five or ten dollars. There was, after all, a depression.

Sometimes, on a quiet summer evening, you would suddenly hear screaming from the upper deck of the Fifth Avenue bus, and looking up you would see Gloria Swanson, Greta Garbo, Jean Harlow, Mae West, and some of the girls screeching away. Tattered rags of talk would float down: "Essie, I covered myself with black lace, and I just lay down beside it and cried!" This was a sound of summer revelry. But of course, there was, inevitably, a deep sadness. For all of the giddiness, the empty-headedness, each "girl" knew that she was—unless oh so lucky—ill-fated.

Each star shone most resplendently on Halloween, on Thanksgiving. All through the autumn months, they sewed and snipped. Then, on gala nights— autumn, winter, early spring—they trooped into what seemed to me at that time an immense ballroom, somewhere in the Harlem in which I had been born and been cherished by myriads of aunts, uncles, cousins, family friends (the Harlem in which I almost never could run away because someone who knew me would call out, "Label, Little Label, come in, have a piece of the cake I just baked!"). Now here I was in that Harlem, hidden away, obscure in a seething ballroom where in the dim light it was impossible to tell sex from sex, beauty from grotesquerie, but where, as the evening wore on and spotlights illuminated a runway, the stars and the would-be stars became effulgently clear. This was where the girls became—at least for the long walk on tottering heels along the shiny runway— stars. They swept in the elaborate costumes they had sewn night after night, some moving majestically, some fluttering aimlessly from side to side, some jumping with falsetto merriment. There were all kinds of girls in all kinds of gowns, and all of them were dazzling for that moment, and all of them were sad. The floor, the chairs around little tables, the boxes that surrounded the dance hall were jammed with onlookers, and some of these were also in the artful garments they had wrought or extravagantly bought. Rumors were always on the wing: "See over there? That's Bea Lillie! Over there? That's Tallulah Bankhead! And over there—know who that is? Well I won't tell you!" There was a lot of very saucy behavior.

It was customary, after a drag, for some of the "girls" and some of the "johns" (girls always had johns who were their escorts) to hie themselves downtown, the destination being secret clubs on West Seventy-second Street. The one John K *took me to was perhaps on the third floor of an old brownstone. Up a dimly lit stair covered with time-eaten, brown-stained linoleum, then another stair, then another, then an unexpectedly heavy-looking door. John knocked on the door. A voice within whispered, "Who is it?" John muttered something. The door opened a crack, an eye peered through the crack, then the door halfway opened, and John yanked me inside. Inside was very dim, soft light—not diffused, but soft, coming from darkly shaded electric bulbs. All about were men, most of them in ties and jackets, very businesslike, very proper. But two of them, enormous in size, roaring with laughter, hauled about in the tightest of down-to-the-ground glittering sequined dresses, stuck all over with what seemed to me rhinestone brooches, their heads topped with frantic wigs, one red, one blond, their faces brazenly painted in some caricature of "Oh, You Great Big Beautiful Doll," their arms encased in long white gloves, upon their arms endless jeweled bracelets . . . "Who are they?" I asked John. John laughed his high tittering laugh, the one without any merriment in it. "You will not believe it," he said, "the redhead drives a truck. The other one is his lover." I think this was the first time I ever heard that one man was another man's lover. Lovers? That was Tristan and Isolde, Romeo and Juliet. . . . I was baffled.*

*There was a lot of drinking—illegal drinking, for this was Prohibition, in an illegal room, where each man in the room was illegal. I knew this because all of the queens had told horrifying sagas of being picked up by good-looking men who turned out to be "bait," and bait got you a harsh sentence on "that island in the river." John looked at me and said, "The way out, if anything happens, is through that window." "What do you mean, 'The way out . . .'?" "Well," he said, "If—you know—if we get raided . . ." "What's outside the window?" "A roof . . ." I pointed at a door at the far end of the room. "What's in there?" "That's the back room." "What for?" "If you want to find out that's up to you, but if you find out I don't think I'll ever bring you here again." It was later that year that I found out, after which I never went back again—at least to that place.* (1993)

NOVEMBER 26, 1970 When Mishima came to lunch, he was not the boy who would one day commit hara-kiri—or was he?[66] I saw him several times—lunch, dinner. He came to 1453. He was always direct, collected, extremely soft-spoken, and coldly concerned with sex—his own homosexuality, mine, anyone's—and writing. He ate little. All of his movements were sparse—depths of impenetrability at all times. Going to bed with him would have been a concentrated hotness—almost ice because of its intense heat—the narcotic that extra pain manufactures. He was scornfully curious.

I will have to leap out of this downy bed to do my Thanksgiving Day chores. The table is set beautifully by Gray. I think of my aunt Silly and uncle Maxl

---

66. Leo's lunch with Yukio Mishima (né Kimitake Hiraoke, 1925–70), the Japanese novelist and reactionary activist, probably happened in June 1964, when Mishima was in New York.

[Goldwasser], hand in hand at the Macy's Thanksgiving Day Parade.[67] They went year after year, like two old children—marzipan children. He was full of gold-tooth smiles, a swart, shrewd man, sexy like all Goldwassers. She was said to be the family beauty. When Gray saw her photo, he was amazed: "But she's a pudding!" She was—with beautiful skin, little, sharp, sapphire-blue eyes, a tightly wound swirl of hair—at one time blond, then silver. She was our *Tante* from Vienna, and she had obviously consumed tons of *Schlagobers* [cream puffs]. Her brother compulsively barked like a dog and was found dead in Central Park, clutching a cigar box filled with stock coupons. . . . Aunt Silly's formal dinners in the house on High Bridge Hill . . . Aunt Silly's parrot and poodle and the Long Branch [New Jersey] house, where we all gathered in the summer . . . Aunt Silly dictating loving postcards to a woman who really knew the English language. The cards began: "Dear Nice and Nempsies . . ." and ended "Lox, Tante Syril" . . . Aunt Silly and her children sliding down High Bridge Hill, part of which Uncle Maxl owned, on dustpans in the snow . . . Aunt Silly's cruelty to Cousin Sadie, her only daughter, born so hirsute that Aunt Silly never looked at her . . . Aunt Silly and her button shop . . . Aunt Silly and sacks of broken biscuits, bought in the Sunshine factory . . . Aunt Silly to Aunt Minnie: "Marium? I don't know any Marium. I know a Minnie." That ended, at least in our family, any attempt by Minnie to lift herself up by changing her name. . . . Aunt Silly inevitably greeting a stranger with: "How much money do you make? My husband's a very rich man."

NOVEMBER 27, 1970 Garbo, in the late April day when I went up the Gunthers' steps into their back parlor where, between an immense Chagall bouquet of violet-colored lilacs (which burst like LSD in the head) and great torrents of pewter-silver rain (a springtime downpour, through the trees, cascading down over the huge windowpanes), between these parallel luminosities—the lilacs, the rain—something moved: a wood-brown moth, a tremendous butterfly. From behind the lilacs, she came toward me, arms outstretched. For a moment her hands clutched mine, while she looked—her eyes as deeply lilac gazing through curtains of lilac, violet, black-purple, looking into my eyes and out through them. Her hands fluttered to her temples, beneath the symbolic, protective canopy of her hat. Silently she sped away—not a word, not a footfall sound . . . nothing. I was left with the lilacs, the rain.

NOVEMBER 29, 1970 Maria says Onassis was sleeping with Mrs. Onassis's sister [Lee Radziwill][68] before Mrs. O grabbed him. All very Greek classical. Maria wants the world to know how Onassis wronged her, but she doesn't want

67. Celia "Silly" (1874?–1960) and Maxl (1867–1948) Goldwasser were Leo's great-aunt and uncle.
68. Caroline Lee Bouvier Radziwill (b. 1933) married the Polish prince Stanislaw Radziwill. She was widely reported to have had an affair with Aristotle Onassis in 1963.

this *histoire* to come from her. She wants vengeance, but protests that she is at peace and calm and at last has learned to live with herself—that Mr. O is in constant torment—that Mrs. O has nothing save the name, the fortune, and his wrath—that she, Maria, and he are bound by blood—in the very bloodstream.

NOVEMBER 30, 1970  On the radio, "Für Elise." Immediately I recall a piano teacher—German, smelly, poor, frustrated. He made me arch my wrists, insuring curvature by placing long pins, sharp end up, under my wrist. He slept. When the exhausted wrists fell—instant, awful pain. I played with my fingertips and wrists like gothic arches. "Für Elise" poured from my fingertips, but who could tell what poured, I played so badly, on that delicious-smelling upright piano, which I chewed on when I was a very small child. I can smell the delicious varnish, paint, and wood as I chewed. What an unnatural act—or was it?

DECEMBER 5, 1970  The saga of William Haines and his self-knowledge:[69] "I was just white trash from the South" that came to New York and showbiz, then to Hollywood, by way of fucking everything—into flicks, stardom, and the Prince of Wales (three feathers emblazoned on his underpants). And left his career when the studio head told him that he couldn't live that way (with the boy he loved [Jimmie Shields]), declining invitations that did not include the boy, entertaining as a married couple. "I wasn't any good anyway. I knew that we'd be accepted if I were an interior decorator." Fanny Brice [comedian and singer] was his closest friend. All Hollywood vied for his decorating skills. He became rich, well known, and old, never losing his sense of self-humor nor his love. They have been together forty years.

DECEMBER 9, 1970  Marlene on the blower—desperate-gay en route to Los Angeles and Rudi [Sieber].[70] "I have no money, absolutely none. We will borrow from the bank. . . . I never have before . . . and I will, at last, use my credit cards. Everybody's dying. When De Gaulle died, not one woman in Paris—not one of the state wives, the diplomatic wives—had a black suit. So I went to Chanel and I said, "You must make me a black suit . . . everyone's dying. . . . Bill [Riva, son-in-law] and I are friends—a sudden friendship. . . . Maria [Riva] is thin and happy in Madrid. . . . I got a job, at last, in Miami . . . and I'll do that television with [producer Alexander] Cohen. . . . He'll send a car for me, to the theater. . . . Not one queen in town to go with me . . ." So, I knew that I would not have to spend the whole latter evening with her, and I didn't. We rode around and around. I dropped her at River House and rushed off to the

69. William Haines (1900–1973), a comic film actor of the twenties and thirties (*Show People*), later became an interior decorator.
70. Rudolf Sieber (1897–1976) was an assistant director and a film production manager when he married Dietrich in 1923. They had a daughter, Maria, the next year. By the seventies they had lived apart for decades, he in the San Fernando Valley of Los Angeles.

Russian Tea Room to sup with Lorca Massine and Remi [Saunder] and Gray.[71] Marlene in the car acting sickness, so she could leave me for Johnny Gielgud at the [Joshua] Logans, and both of us being pros at this. She looked thin, pinched, withered. She says her legs are all right—when she eats no salt.

DECEMBER 11, 1970  Gray says most husbands are better away from their wives and vice versa. "Have you ever seen a couple who enhance one another?" I think about this. The same is true of homosexual couples.

Gray: "I don't understand Emily Dickinson!" Me: "What's to understand?" She spurts truths—beautifully—like seeds popping from a sun-sprung pod—or suddenly bursting into pyrotechnical bloom.

DECEMBER 12, 1970  Maria's Tosca was one of her greatest achievements— Violetta, Medea, Norma, Tosca. All during *Tosca*'s second act, the assassination was implicit: the contrived artlessness, the almost finicky way she sat at table—perched, not sat. The urgency—she had no time, and she knew this even before her entrance. When Maria picked up her glass, she was full of how she was going to do it—with what?—then seeing the knife—her hands knew— then her whole body knew. She was drawn from the scene of the assassination by a sort of self-hypnosis; a sort of euphoria propelled her away. Maria's vocal flaw worked dramatically when she sang-acted Tosca, Lady Macbeth, Medea. The ugliness leavened (wrong word) the texture. I mean roughened it, made it more awful . . . awesome, like a rough, full-bodied black-red wine, while the full-blown tunes flowed endlessly. The curvaceous line these melodies take— Puccini's writing is very Art Nouveau. Maria's curtain calls were so like Gypsy Rose Lee's—so naughty, so I've-done-it happy. Maria's way of ending a telephone conversation—glissades and diminuendos of ciao . . .

The mortality of the fashion world is so similar to that indifference shown by the lions (Balzac) to fallen companions, and, as [novelist and playwright] Félicien Marceau notes, this indifference is identical to that shown by the military where a lost companion is forgotten almost immediately, save by his lover. Who thinks of Miss Peck at *Mademoiselle*, or Cyrilly [Abels], or Toddy [Sturgis] all so much a part of the race when they were part of it.[72] Who knows of Stark [Young] today? And who will think of me? No one. This fashion magazine world, this world of reviewing . . . and the world of entertainment—television,

71. The dancer and choreographer Lorca Massine (b. 1944) was the son of Léonide Massine of the Diaghilev's Ballets Russes. The Russian-born Remi Saunder (b. 1923) was an interpreter and a friend to many expatriate Russians, particularly Baryshnikov and Rostropovich. GF: "We were much beguiled by Remi, who was an excellent hostess on very little and a superb *raconteuse*. Crossing the street would cause a story."
72. All of these women had worked at *Mademoiselle*: Bernice Peck as health and beauty editor (ca. 1936–58); Cyrilly Abels as managing editor (ca. 1943–59), later a literary agent; Willena Todd "Toddy" Sturgis as executive assistant (ca. 1952–62) to Betsy Blackwell.

LP—all even faster mortality. The Peppermint Lounge—gone—with its long lines, the furor, and the false, generated gaiety. But, of course, this mortality isn't only native to the fashion world. All business is permeated with it. The mighty for a moment.

Gray said that I am becoming a dirty old man, that I am always poking, touching, etc., and that others have commented on this. I think that this (not others commenting but the accusation) must, in some measure, be true. I know that I have been affectionate. Yes, Gray is right. But he is wrong when he says, "If I don't satisfy you enough . . ." That really has nothing to do (in this case) with the behavior of a sexy, aging man. The behavior is not simply born of physical need: Emotional needs also induce it.

DECEMBER 17, 1970 I walked through a sudden swirl of fine, glittery snow, feeling frumpy and non-Christmassy. Huge crocodiles of tagged and home-addressed children in Fifth Avenue all looked aimlessly, not at Christmas, but more impressed with being out on Fifth Avenue, part of the scene—the Bottom-headed, eighteenth-century automaton in Saks's windows, the bells, lights, fine snow, smell of roasting chestnuts and aging pine. I turned from a long look at the Radio City tree (a pyramid of black-green and white-silver, boughs, and balls of light), and abruptly I saw two very old people, man and woman, dressed in provincial clothing, painstakingly neat—ear muffs, scarves, heavy cloth, no fur—and eyes enormously aglow and smiles radiant as they looked at Christmas, holding Christmas and one another by mittened hands. My eyes filled and I felt my Scrooginess slip away, so that when I unexpectedly found Edith [Bel Geddes], I was all pleasure. She had just been to get a visa: "I'm going to Colombia to see him there . . . to see if I really want to marry him. . . ." Edith, born in Brussels, married her cousin [Archibald] Lutyens, then up and away, a sort of minor Colette figure, a direct line to Laci. And [her second husband Taylor] Moseley's death: He jumped from Edith's bedroom window. "Moseley, what are you doing down there?" Edith asked. The two ancient maiden ladies below in hysterics, not because a man had plummeted down onto their roof, but because he was naked. Edith visited Moseley in the hospital constantly and, so, terrified him to death. . . . Now she's a real estate agent.[73]

NOTE: Leo and Gray took Maebelle to spend the Christmas holiday with Richard Hunter at his house in Maine.

JOURNAL • DECEMBER 23, 1970 • AUGUSTA, MAINE When she grew old, congealed in her beauty, not the beauty of her greatest years, but that replica

---

73. Until the mid-sixties, Edith Lutyens Bel Geddes (1907–2002) designed and fabricated costumes for Broadway (*The Grass Harp, The Crucible*). Her last marriage was to the designer Norman Bel Geddes, which made her the stepmother of the actress Barbara Bel Geddes.

she had fixed as herself in the memories of those who saw her triumphal return upon return to the stages of the world . . . he [Leo] would still play her game—waiting upon her actressy whims, sitting in foyers, lurking before doors, running her needless errands, making believe that he was the adoring nobody she had known long ago. In keeping the proportion she had established in those earlier days, he kept her belief in herself, in her inviolability, sacrosanct. "I don't do it for myself . . . but for those who love me." And since so many of those were gone, dead, scattered, she was doing it, as she had always done it, for herself. For her selfless life of painstaking devotion had always been one of self-devotion. The face, the body in the glass had indeed been marveled at by millions, but never so devotedly as by the girl, then the woman, who had looked into that glass. She had been in love all of her life—with herself. The intensity of this passion had created such a hot climate that everyone who came within it was energized in some measure. (Basically Marlene.)

Richard has a list—everyone he knows, the oldest at the top, with boxes in which letters sent and received are checked off. You are dropped from this list if you don't answer Richard's missives. Richard and Howard know old ladies everywhere. Richard's thoroughness is a form of obstinacy. Once he starts something, he must finish it. I always think that this obstinacy will do him in one day.

DECEMBER 24, 1970  I have always had a sense of rootlessness, and I have always been in love with the America of my childhood, the America I first knew as seen through the windows of the books I read (*Pioneers and Patriots of America, Little Women*), the America of saluting the flag and singing national songs ("Old Black Joe," "Tramp, Tramp, the Boys Are Marching," "Tonight on the Old Camp Ground," "Juanita," "After the Ball," "Yankee Doodle Dandy," "Swanee"), the America fantasized by my father, the America of Stephen Foster and Irving Berlin and Francis Scott Key, the immigrants' dream America and the palaces along Fifth Avenue, the America that died with the year of my birth, 1914.

The life I found in Jackson Heights and Elmhurst, especially the schoolteachers, was that of an older America, where the flat ruler was still used as an instrument of justice or vengeance. That ruler was the visible symbol of might, autocracy. My deaf-mute uncle Benny [Goldwasser] plied the cat-o'-nine-tails, my father a wide leather belt, my grandfather his heavy walking stick, his hand, even his feet. I have seen teachers hit out with a blackboard pointer, a switch, a knotted rope, and a length of rubber hose (twice in Hebrew school).

DECEMBER 26, 1970  The year rushes to its end. At its close, we have shattered remains. Some of these are rich shards, whole designs intact. And it is from these complete fragments that we reconstruct our life. As in all archaeological reconstruction, we cannot actually re-create, we can only approximate.

So, we must use our findings not to try to build what we once knew, but to erect slowly, painstakingly, a fresh structure, hoping that it proves more durable than the previous one. Future Schliemanns [archaeologists], reading this document, will find clues to our previous lives.

The difference is between those who laugh at "tragedies" and those who cry. I mean domestic mishaps, minor catastrophes. A really great soul laughs rather than cries at all reversals. This does not mean that tragedy should be diminished by laughter—but laughter is positive in a way tears can never be. Worry is a destroyer, like all pollutants. Worry is not even a sincere emotion. It is a poison. I abhor worrying because of my long life with Momma, a calamity-howler.

DECEMBER 27, 1970    People who minutely analyze their own lives to one another, this is destructive. Some part of oneself must remain secret—for self-nourishment and for the nourishment of the relationship. There must be informed blindness in any close relationship.

DECEMBER 29, 1970    Personality—that is what I want to pin down, no matter how fleetingly, for personality of a man is component to personality of his era. A single personality contains the residue of all that has gone before (like certain wonderful rooms) much of what is going on, and seeds of the future, incipiency. . . .

I do not write in these notebooks: I scribble. My energy is almost inexhaustible, my energy filled by a kind of gay despair, which opens my eyes to the ridiculous and to the allusive. And my curiosity, a form of energy—these are the foundation. I am not intellectual, but I am intelligent. I have a passion for nature, but not for all things natural. I adore gossip of all kinds, trying to disguise the Jewish Puritan in me by animation. But I gossip less and less, save to myself. Of course, these notebooks are extreme narcissism. This is a search to find myself and my times in my own looking glass, and in looking glasses held up by others. In finding myself, I must find everyone, every place, and everything that has been part of me, my own voice and the resonances in my voice of all those others—people I knew, wanted to know. When [William Dean] Howells reflected, "I wonder why you hate the past so?" Mark Twain said, "It's so damned humiliating." I am little humiliated by my past, much by the world's.

I have been on an eating binge. Just like an alcoholic, I am in great danger again. *I must taper off.* I do not eat chocolate, ice cream, butter—but I have been stuffing everything else. *I will stop.* This has been a constant war. Eating to excess and alcoholism are identical. I am eating now because of the strain—constant goading, bickering, tension, and no sex. But I must not eat my way into annihilation.

DECEMBER 30, 1970    I want one extra day to spend with those I love, have loved. Who would I be with that extra day? My mother and father when they are young—perhaps that night when Poppa pulls me, on my Flexible Flyer, given by Uncle Herman, who is here—tall, so good-looking and sexy, wavy white hair of his latter days thatching his younger-days face. This is in the kitchen of our runaway, hideaway flat on the Boston Post Road, where the last firehorses still roar around their corner, Momma still has one leg in the air, pulling up a stocking, and I have, forever, lost a mitten somewhere on the trolley-car tracks, which gleam in the snow like ribbons, tautly binding this gift of memories together.

Availability—so rare today. Perhaps this has been one of my attractions. I have been so available. Perhaps I am sought because I am there.

"*Le grand goût, le goût veritable*" ["Fine taste, true taste"] (Leopardi). Ela had that for her friends. She was their seeing-eye dog. Rut was better at advice and criticism than she, but Ela was a life-giving force, and, oh, how I felt after being with her. (Unless another jealously consumed, dragonlike, the comfort she would give. We were all fiendishly jealous of one another.) Like all such deep friends, she gave solace: She was the perfect looking glass, lying if you wished that, but showing you your true face if that is what you wished, and ultimately she was a magician's looking glass, enlarging you, magnifying the best you. It is this oversize image of oneself that sustained us, nourished us, made us try to be that size rather than the puny creature bleeding from life who had crept up her threadbare stair and into her room. Her smelly room (cooking, expensive scent left over from decades of topsy-turvy high-low life), always overheated, always teeming with personalities, but somehow with a chasm of love and quiet and understanding for you alone.

DECEMBER 31, 1970   My devotion to Grand Central—How I love railroad stations, lobbies of hotels, centers of intense energy. I find them nourishing. I love watching. Some part of life must be vicarious, especially if one loves being alive.

# OPENING NIGHT EVERY DAY

**JOURNAL • JANUARY 1, 1971** Apartment 6C makes me feel that I am merely a visitor there. 1453 was permanent, mine forever; I was non-transient there. Perhaps in a single lifetime we have only one permanent, forever habitation. What we lived in previously was on the way to that permanent home, that only home, and what we dwell in after is only a wayside stopover. The fortunate live forever in the one permanence. The most fortunate carry this permanence within.

**JANUARY 2, 1971** The little radio cheers away—Perry Como: "Just wrap your troubles in dreams. . . . And dream your troubles away. . . . Just remember that sunshine always follows the rain. . . . So dream your troubles away. . . ." Those all-night dress rehearsals at the Grossinger—the orchestra boys—Eddie, who was a smooth trumpet, had a wife—I had him. (Later, after Maria's *Il Pirata*, and I had taken Blixen to a party and home to the Coz Club[1], when Nora, Puss, and I were going to meet Maria and Larry [Kelly] and others, the taxi driver was Eddie.) Affairs while working in a show are the result of the magnetic field set up by the common, intense endeavor. The tangle of their lives: Henriette Kay [thirties actress] became a well-to-do matron—Grand Concourse or Westchester, I don't know; [actress] Lee Brody is dead, jumping fourteen floors to her death; [comedian] Sylvia Sims vanished into burlesque as a straight woman; Al Parker vanished into drag shows in Florida and other resorts; [skit writer] Richard Mack died; Hank Henry had a Vegas career, last seen in the Liz Taylor–Warren Beatty movie [*The Only Game in Town*]; [bandleader] Dave Schooler dead; Jennie [Grossinger] herself, senile, last seen, unexpectedly, tottering through hospital corridors. She knew me.

**JANUARY 4, 1971** We have exchanges again about detesting little birds, squab, Cornish hen for eating. Maebelle "just loves them." Maebelle's currency, in talk, is exaggerated positives. That is her small change; she has no larger denominations. Sinclair Lewis could have, and did, write this character many times, and Tennessee did her his way. She tells about house parties, when she

1. The Cosmopolitan Club is a private women's club in Manhattan.

was sixteen, in Texas, where the darkies sang as they picked cotton and came up to the big house, in the forever evenings, plunking their banjos and singing ragtime. Bad novelists make fortunes this way. Hers is a constant effort to belong to what she considers "the best" while mooting that she's real old-time American. Maebelle doesn't like the candies in the little Christmas bag—gumdrops, etc. She doesn't like anything that she thinks beneath her. In this way she has helped ruin her child. But some tougher fiber, or younger generation, has alienated his appreciation of her idea of Southern Womanhood. Maebelle went to a plantation party as the Princess from Dallas. She requires attentions from her "Bud"[2]—glasses of water, forgotten necessities. He is very Southern gentleman courteous with her. Anyone watching would be impressed, taken.

JANUARY 6, 1971 · NEW YORK CITY  I did not recognize Betsey Johnson yesterday. When she came to *Mademoiselle*, she was plump, cheerful, with a knowing desperation—fizzing like overloaded apple juice—a sort of sixties-vintage American champagne.[3] Now, not even five years later, the fizz is deep down. She is emaciated. She looks like the best of the remains of the sixties. She is sort of put away within herself. But her talent deepens all of the time, while her life leaps from pinnacle to pinnacle of intensity, despair, and she seeks herself in India and Indianapolis, a typical child of these times. I gave her the hard, Federal sofa, which I bought from the Kochs when we were friends. Now she has lost it. How can anyone, save someone on a trip, lose a six-foot and more sofa, weighing over a hundred pounds? Betsey looks as though she's been on dozens of trips, but survived for future safaris.

JANUARY 9, 1971  Dinner with Mina in the Stanhope [hotel] dining room with Lincoln and Fidelma. Lincoln's lies: "Goosey exaggerates," says Mina. My surprise when Fido [Fidelma] talks cohesively about anything save cats ("pussums" as the Kirstein family always calls them). Lincoln so frequently seems on the verge of tears. This is alarming in a giant of a man. Mina now talks of moving into one large studio room and kitchenette at the Stanhope. She is still a millionaire, but poorer. I do not think that this is why she thinks of moving. She uses her flat rarely, never entertains in it, has her ample establishment near Bethel, and both age and her predilection for moving (and building houses, redoing apartments) dictate this move. She is almost incapable of social insincerity, and although her age, size, accomplishment (both intellectually—her books—and disciplining her character), family, and money cloak her in an awesome dignity, she can be as graceless as a forthright, brilliant

---

2. Gray was nicknamed "Bud" by his family.
3. One of the first Americans to design innovative clothes in the sixties, Betsey Johnson (b. 1942) started as a guest editor at *Mademoiselle*, where she made sweaters for the staff.

young girl. Typical: "I don't want to stay for the reception," so off she bounds, heedless of whether her guest wishes to stay or not.

An actress with small eyes cannot be great.

JANUARY 10, 1971  Robert Davison has great distinction, dark good looks, a slightly abstract bearing (this comes from his deafness), volatile spirit, and a genuine buoyancy. He is essentially a solitary. His hauteur, also partly because of his deafness, but even more from the characterization he has built. His deep sense of humor, which includes a deep sense of the ridiculous. His compassion. His reflex scorn at shams. His largely individual taste. He loved me—but we never slept together. He always has treated me like a wise, worldly, old man. He arrived at my bedside to be interviewed for "Before Bandwagons," and immediately became part of my life. Through Robert I entered the ballet world, heard the Anthologie Sonore [early music] for the first time, moved into 1453, and met Gray. Now he goes to and fro between Paris where he paints, New York where he makes money, or other parts of the U.S.A. (Los Angeles) and Europe working for [decorator] Valérian Rybar. Robert's Russophilia— White, of course. He and Gray both have this. Robert's obsession with Gray— I moved in on it and broke it up. I willfully did this and have been reaping the rewards for over two decades.

JANUARY 11, 1971  A party at Arnold Weissberger and Milton Goldman's—like a benefit for English actors. The whole party a pother of personal politics. The exaggerated personality of Van Johnson—his red socks. "I'll only come if your house is crowded. Tell me that it's crowded." The curious, off-beat, his-very-own-rhythm personality of Ralph Richardson—an unfocused tremulousness, but a most precise mind. "Like the weaving of a Persian carpet," he said of [David Storey's play] *Home*. "The design is there. . . . Oh, pardon me, I must go and make a grand obeisance." Richardson's manner—the feeling that this well-dressed hawk-eyed old man, a person of quiet distinction, at any moment could burst into tears of recrimination—at you, at the party, at self—the feeling that he is on the verge of an unpleasant situation—but all of the time, his mind quests—realistically, solidly. Johnny Gielgud always promises much, but nothing much comes out.

Dorothy Norman told me that one of her doctors adores Chinese food: "I sent him to Pearl's [restaurant], and he took Danny Kaye and the Duke and Duchess of Windsor. When I asked him how he liked it, he said, 'Forget it! She's impossible! She wouldn't accept my credit card, and she wouldn't take my check. She said her accountant told her not to take any more checks, and I didn't have any cash. It was embarrassing.' " The doctor finally had to ask the duke to lend him the cash. In my version the duke doesn't have it, so finally Danny pays for all of them—the Jewish boy from Brooklyn paying for the ex-King of England and the ex-Baltimore girl who cost him his throne, in a Chinese restaurant run by an ex-vaudeville acrobatic dancer, an Oriental from San Francisco.

JANUARY 12, 1971 I am really lost right now. No confidence this morning that this is worth the effort and the hurt it is inflicting. . . . But I will not be wrecked again. I am stronger. I am also whistling in an almost freezing limbo. It had to be said, and I understand it deeply, but the sadness and the pity of it. The pull of two people on one another. The giving of life and the giving of death. Is this the Grand Surprise: that old saw, "Each man kills the thing he loves"? Is that an inexorable law?

JANUARY 14, 1971 Alex held Tatiana's hand and she, suddenly, looked exactly like Francine, making possible a prevision of Francine, her daughter, as an older woman.[4] "The book (I cannot write her accent) about Mayakovski, by the Pole, it is horrible. What he says about me (she speaks a mixture of French, English, sometimes turning on the Russians a spate of that tongue), it is lies, all lies—and so vulgar. I am not like that. He says I married du Plessix because I was awed by his title. He was a nice, agreeable man, who loved me. I had no way to get back to Mayakovski. . . ."[5]

Marlene rang Alex to arrange for her to fly from Los Angeles to Paris for Chanel's funeral. She was at de Gaulle's, Colette's, Cocteau's—now Chanel's. She did not go to Von Sternberg's and not to Hemingway's.[6]

Maria Kalogeropoulos [Callas] born in Flower Hospital [Manhattan] and Jacqueline Bouvier Kennedy born in Southampton, Long Island. These intersect because I persuaded Maria to be an Egyptian empress at a charity gala, and there she met Elsa Maxwell, who fell in love with her.[7]

JANUARY 22, 1971 Shared experience—When this is impossible, death does do us apart. I am rebellious, when friendship abruptly ceases. That is why I grow broody when Richard goes off and away, and this whole year passed with a minimum of shared experience in this flat. Shared experience is a towering mountain in the range that Ivy Compton-Burnett conjured up (for she was a

4. Francine du Plessix Gray (b. 1930), novelist and biographer, is the daughter of Tatiana Iacovleva by her first husband, Bertrand du Plessix, hence the stepdaughter of Alexander Liberman.
5. A celebrated poet of the early Soviet Union, and the lover of Tatiana Iacovleva in the twenties, Vladimir Mayakovski (1893–1930) committed suicide soon after Tatiana's marriage to Count Bertrand du Plessix.
6. Josef von Sternberg (1894–1969), the Austrian-born film director, had been Dietrich's mentor and lover.
7. Elsa Maxwell (1883–1963) had been a devotee of rival soprano Renata Tebaldi. Callas, after her October 1956 New York debut in *Norma*, encountered Maxwell and swiftly resolved to enchant this powerful columnist. The arrival by Callas at a costume ball (January 11, 1957) dressed as Hatshepsut and wearing $3 million in emeralds apparently clinched it. Maxwell introduced Callas to Aristotle Onassis in the summer of 1957.

wizard!) when she said [to Wyndham Lewis at tea] that the most important aspect of friendship is "availability."

The net in which each of us must pass his adult days is that identical net in which we have passed our younger years, but then it was invisible—or, at most, only discernible in flashes—and defied or not believed: We knew, in those flashes, that we could leap out of that net. When we were children, anything was possible. Now aging, old, only the spirit contends, sometimes destroying the net—but only in flashes.

JANUARY 29, 1971 Suddenly Gertie Lawrence singing "Getting to Know You," and I am deeply moved at the youth of this thin, dying woman and the gaiety and trust (knowing that it was all part truth, part make-believe).[8] I got out of bed and danced into Gray's room, and we held hands while he said, "Don't be sad," and I said, "But life is sad," (and I was also glad), "maybe we should give a party next week. Maria will be here . . . and Marlene. . . ." And Gray said, "All I need is a great big party. We'll see. . . ." I said, "It's so light outside, I hate to go to bed. It's so useless going to sleep." I danced off to bed. That is the Grand Surprise you also discover—how gay and sad life is simultaneously.

Alvin Ailey has good dancers but what they dance is showbiz, not concert, and the audience behaves as if they have just been part of an outpouring by the Nijinsky-Karsavina–led Ballets Russes. *Revelations* is theatrically crafty, mannered to bring audience reaction—just as the "Hello, Dolly" number was in Act II of that musical. It works every time, overwhelmingly, and nostalgia is as much an ingredient as the vigorous beat of the music and the dancing bodies in its immense success—a success which requires encores—makes the audience clap in rhythm to the music of each of these (*Dolly* and *Revelations*) theatrical peaks. Pinchbeck can be gold under the proper lights. But Alvin Ailey (now a huge black man with a dark-honey-colored smile in a tremendous thick-piled, black-gray coat, and a forest-green scarf) has dipped into Weidman and Humphrey and Katherine Dunham and Pearl Primus, coming up with this audience-whacker, *Revelations*.[9] The other items programmed are trash— the sort of thing that brought revue audiences of the late twenties and the thirties out of the theater feeling that they had seen life and art. Last night's audience felt precisely that way. So we have been standing in one place for almost half a century—as not only demonstrated by Ailey's company, but the Australian [Ballet] and Béjart. Meanwhile Balanchine, Robbins, Tudor, even Freddie [Ashton] have all moved dance on—so has Martha. I suddenly thought, watching Ailey's company: Martha Graham is the Mae West of the dance.

8. "Getting to Know You" had been written for Lawrence in *The King and I*. She died of cancer in 1952, during its Broadway run.
9. Charles Weidman, Doris Humphrey, Katherine Dunham, and Pearl Primus were all seminal dancers, choreographers, and teachers in modern American dance.

JANUARY 31, 1971  Andy Warhol more wraith than ever—the badly complected boy who never grew up, but became craftier and craftier, filling with a slow-seeming cunning and a positive destruction—lighting up like a tallow candle whose flame burns dimly within the candle rather than atop it. He lights shallow, surface places hitherto hidden.

I do not believe, as Proust did, that all self is successively different. The core is permanent, or should be—the matrix. We extend—as a coral reef—accretions transforming the contours. We are not actually changed within—the kernel. We are each a metamorphosis—but the central, central being, that does not change. Image: those Russian dolls-within-dolls almost endlessly.

When I lectured in biography at New York University [in 1945] and came into the lecture room, finding upon the blackboard, "Give the direct causes of the Italian Renaissance," I laughed and erased this, because only one who has no understanding of the flow of life whatsoever could pose such a question. But Proust's intuition of himself as an absolute entity, that is the verity. The knowledge one must acquire that nothing is forever save the central truth. No love is forever but the idea of love is eternal. "The distortion of the self is a continuous death." There is no greater reference than to self. All vanishes, but everything is here. That is my deepest conviction. We are obliterated, but we are not gone. I knew it when I saw the plum-and-gold dust [of the butterfly] on my hands, I knew this instinctively and I never forgot it. When I saw the wintered trees one afternoon, as I stood on the railroad bridge near the synagogue in Woodside when I was eleven, and, even then, Rembrandt's trees in my eyes—and now Pollock's *Autumn Rhythm*—confirming my continuity and the continuity of being. I know this is the essential truth—the Grand Surprise—and only by becoming art (through life the crucible) do we survive. What is the important motive in my life? Is it recollection or the allusive—a constant linking, thus forging a chain of continuity? I suspect that that is the important motive—recognizing the elements of continuity, re-creating them.

NOTE: In January 1971, Leo told publisher Holt, Rinehart, and Winston that he would not complete his Sotheby's book, agreeing to repay a portion of his $9,000 advance. The project eventually went to the writer and publisher Frank Hermann, whose thorough history of the firm would appear in 1980.

JOURNAL · FEBRUARY 2, 1971  [Jim] Bailey, the female impersonator, appeared on the telly, a family show (albeit from ten to eleven)—Carol Burnett, that paragon mother. Has it really come out of the closet? A return to transvestitism as family entertainment? Julian Eltinge was one of the town's toasts.[10] Poppa took me to see vaudeville in which female impersonators shone, also those acts that were half-man and half-woman, the sexes carefully defined

10. The actor Julian Eltinge (1881–1941) had huge success early in the twentieth century as a convincing female impersonator.

by a decisive line vertically down the middle. We were always amazed to be presented, by the man side, suddenly with the woman side—a swift turn to the left or to the right and the creature was man, was woman. Even then I knew life was not quite like that. But I was years away from discovering that in each of us exists man and woman, and I continue to discover and explore the degrees of masculinity in women, the converse in men.

Maria, her voice deep mezzo, on the blower—the voice she has on the day before the performance: "To be warm in a house in the country in snow is fine."

Anaïs on the blower—the shadow quality of her voice, like a French country house built from a mill—a Cézanne house, complete with its shadow, late in the day, slightly worn.

FEBRUARY 3, 1971   Remi Saunder's Russian colony is not White but off-White. Not the royals or the aristocrats but the Jewish middle class risen to wealth by artful deals while still in Russia (in the twenties or thirties). Some of them come from the lower classes. Now they mix with grand dukes or the posterity of the royals at charity balls, sometimes in private places—at the Gregorys. But this is symptomatic. The colony includes Angela and Marcel [Clairmont], Rumanian, and kindred very rich Slavs. Some of it comes from Russian bohemia: Tatiana Liberman (whose sister is a Duchess of France now, but common[11]) who was [Alexandre] Iacovleff's niece and was traded for thirty of his paintings and who then married du Plessix, having been Mayakovski's lover.[12] Lydia [Gregory] moved in bohemia. Grischa [Gregory] was very middle-class. Some came from Bessarabia, Latvia—the movable places on the continental chessboard. Some are Jews from Poland, which was Russia in those days. To all of these, mostly Jews, the Revolution had been a godsend, tossing them from their never-secure tree and blowing them across dissolving borders into richer lands. Some of the first generation born in America, having been absorbed into this colony, made much of a Russian heritage which did not exist, save in the bloody Cossack assaults on their forebears in the various ghettos and Pales. Some of these firstborn were here only through the accidents of grandparents being at the bottom heap of murdered dead, and so surviving. Didn't Grischa [Gregory]'s fortune come from a button deal?[13]

Mina made a list of her lovers, by categories.

11. Tatiana Liberman's sister, Ludmila Iacovleva, and brother-in-law claimed to be the Duke and Duchess de Caylus.

12. Alexandre Iacovleff (1890?–1938), a favorite portrait artist of the Parisian beau monde in the twenties, had a three-year-long affair with Henriette Pascar, Alex Liberman's mother. Alex Liberman met Tatiana through Iacovleff, her uncle. Leo's remark about Iacovleff trading thirty paintings is mysterious.

13. George "Grischa" Gregory (1896–1983) once had the button concession for the USSR. By this time he was a real estate investor. He and his wife Lydia were a central point in New York's Russian community.

Maria, in her gray dress (very Colette schoolgirl, her work clothes) and hair down, was delightful, absolutely in command, treated the large audience [at Juilliard for her answers to questions] as a single, quite intimate friend *tête-à-tête*. She has a great gift for intimacy. Her public is her friend . . . and she has the assurance of being the greatest. Mary Garden had this superb authority. Maria said that she didn't like Puccini; thought *Turandot* an operetta; loved *Traviata* and *Norma* best; *solfeggio* music was the basis of all opera education; ornamentation was not merely that but always expressed emotion. At the reception, she was surrounded by worshipping young people. I was somewhat heartbroken to hear them exhort, "Come back to the stage. We are too young to have seen you and heard you. . . ." Maria seemed almost as young as they: I felt old. In the lift going up to the reception, I accidentally touched her bosom and she murmured, "Oh, oh, you're exciting me. . . ."

FEBRUARY 4, 1971 Gray says that, basically all that Maria told the questioners was, "You must work hard, practice always, learn music first." I think that she gave them many insights, but, most of all, a glimpse of the starriness and the truth that, beneath the glamour is an indefatigable musical-theatrical intelligence working constantly. She also showed them that she has humor and a louche sense of the ridiculous. When a big black man in a flaming-blue jumpsuit asked, "Miss Callas, why are there no longer roles for countertenors and castrati?" Maria promptly answered, "Thank God! Do you know what castrati means?" The audience was wild with hilarity at her look of horror—not entirely feigned.

FEBRUARY 5, 1971 I did not realize that so many of those who sat beneath the gaslit chandelier (a shimmering circle of blazing lilies aglow over rapt heads) listening to Paquita Anderson playing her piano and singing her songs, listening to Yul play his Russian instrument and singing his exotic songs, listening to Touche and his supper-club songs—I did not realize that so many of them were on some sort of dope. Only when Ela came home to her flat above the carpenter shop after she had been in the Gladstone, staying there while [Max] Reinhardt died. He died, directly, because Ela opened his windows, letting in a wind, she having been warned that he could not survive this and having the strength to do it for him because she had loved him so intensely. Also, now he would be hers entirely. So she gave him his death—or his rebirth.

Reinhardt had gotten her with child when she was nineteen, in Vienna, and because he did not want that child, she had had an abortion. That abortion had been so badly done that she had gone raving mad with fear and pain and had been given dope (heroin? morphine?) and so had become hooked. Sometimes her ass festered from badly executed injections of her dope. When she hoped to capture the object of her passion, she would go off to a sanitarium, ostensibly for help with her poisoned ass, but really for a cure. She would return worn but radiant, and the cycle began again. But this late morning when she sent for me, she was rigid with terror in her bed, torment and lack of dope making her into a raving, lost maenad or a gigantically grieving mother-earth woman. Her essence was her deep womanliness. She had lost, beautiful, tear-washed eyes sometimes made ugly from drink or dope or from the intensity of her living. Only when Ela came home and sat wild-eyed and distracted, kneading her hands, and I saw these beautifully shaped hands transformed into clutching claws, talons, did I at last know that she was an addict.[14] I loved her so very much that I was not horrified but enraged. Soon after, I went to Dr. [Arnold] Hutschnecker (then Ela's doctor, later Nixon's adviser) and demanded that he stop giving her this dope. He has always hated me since, and I loathe him.

FEBRUARY 6, 1971 Howard Rothschild, the great-grandson of a German Jewish peddler, helps support Kchessinska, the morganatic wife of a Russian grand duke. She is almost one hundred. He also helps support Karsavina and other remnants of the Diaghilev Ballets Russes, also Ray Papineau (the son of a drunk and a madwoman) and Lolotte [Lowenstein, Howard's cousin], relatives of very *haute bourgeoisie* French Jews, and he pays for many of Richard's outings (Richard the son of a farm-boy, printer's-devil Methodist minister and the grandson of a Scottish miner who became wealthy in Canadian lumber and upstate New York real estate).

FEBRUARY 7, 1971 Lennie Bernstein, standing in the middle of his sitting room, encased in a dark blue, lavishly embroidered in off-white, Hungarian shepherd's coat. He stood there, clasping Adolph [Green] and repeating, loudly, "I've had affairs with every man in this room, well at least mentally, but not Adolph. . . ." Adolph had prompted this outburst by sadly saying, "I'm the only one who never gets kissed"—by the boys, he meant. And, of course, this was true about both Lennie and Adolph. Lennie to his littlest daughter: "Isn't Mr. Lerman sexier? Isn't he? He's the sexiest man." The child—not even ten—looked bewildered and then agreed, while Lennie pinched my ass a lot.

Larry Kelly rang from the Plaza on Friday. While I was at Lennie's, he was dining Maria, who was in dreadful humor because she had just fought with Onassis. She is now using witchcraft—of her own devising—to get him back. Mrs. Onassis had best not accept any present of hot pants, no matter how enchanting, those could be the hot pants of Nessus.[15] And she'd best not take or buy anything from endearing crones lurking next to her door.

---

14. "Now I remember how she disappeared into a 'clinic' after that. Her bed was filthy, her nightdress torn, her face was a screaming darkness under hair as wild as Medea's." *Journal, December 12, 1989.*
15. In Greek mythology, Heracles is burned to death by a robe that his wife has been persuaded to smear with the vengeful centaur Nessus's blood as a love potion.

Maria on the blower: "A great love affair is baloney. That sounds common . . . but it's all baloney. . . . I can't have sex with anyone unless I love with both my head and my heart. . . . That's a sad thing, but that's how I am. . . . I want to give what I know to young people. On the good side is . . . I haven't sung in five, six years but look how they come. . . ." Peter Mennin will see Maria today and ask her to take over the dramatic department—opera acting.[16]

FEBRUARY 13, 1971 Strangers stop in the streets to look at Gray. The bolder ones, or those who must express their sudden infatuations, tell him how astonishing or beautiful he looks. This is the equivalent of people standing on their chairs to see the Edwardian beauties pass.

FEBRUARY 14, 1971 A long, hilarious evening and early morning at Remi Saunder's. The saga of Natasha de Wolfe (née Grischa Gregory's sister [Fanya]) as related with amazement and amusement by Remi:

Grischa and Lydia Gregory were sorry for Natasha ("Fanya" she never liked—"common"). They lent her their East Hampton house for two weeks, in season, and went off. When they returned, the driveway was filled with Rolls-Royces and Cadillacs. Natasha had become a princess who had been forced to take to the stage in the old country. All of the WASP Long Island old-guard society was thronging to meet her. She was the delight of the Meadowbrook Club, from which her very rich brother and sister-in-law had been barred. She fed her new friends blintzes and hot chocolate—a combination none of them had ever before experienced. Not one of them knew a blintz from a crepe. Princess Natasha dazzled them. Lydia's sweet little dog, hated by Lydia, had been "rescued" by the princess, and was part of her decor. This dog ate only the juicy ends of carrots, and Lydia's only reaction to the princess's high place in society was that the dog was ruining her house—liberally strewn with chewed carrot ends.

The princess told Grischa that he really must not push his connection with her and that he really must not try to get into her set. Soon she married de Wolfe, who was, most everyone knew, virtually of the French blood royal—at least 350 years ago—and so the princess became the connection by marriage of one of America's "royal" families. Even Julia Ward Howe, were she alive, could be called cousin by this Jewish, lowborn woman. Mrs. de Wolfe and husband moved to Paris where she reigns in the midst of the remains of Proust's Faubourg Saint-Germain, she having, according to Mr. de Wolfe, bravely renounced her Russian title for his not uncommon, not far from royal, but definitely American name. When the Gregorys come to Paris, they are not invited to Mrs. de Wolfe's soigné dinners and teas, but she does see them—sort of

16. Callas did not join the faculty of the Juilliard School. Leo soon suspected, however, that she and Peter Mennin (1923–83), its president, were carrying on an affair.

boudoir, side-door visitations—and her house is always strewn with the chewed carrot ends of the sweet little dog.[17]

Ultimately, levels of society are teeter-totters, and the bottom can become, at least in the public eye and finally in the eyes of the young, borne into the upper level. Finally, people like Natasha-Fanya can be seen as the pinnacle of society—irrefutably leaders. That happened with Madame Verdurin [in Proust] who became the Princess-Duchess Guermantes, calling [Baron de] Charlus cousin, and he became nothing, a leftover anonymity. Increasingly, people I have never met believe me to have been part of a world in which they were supreme and to which I aspired—sometimes moving on its fringes. If I am here long enough, I will be looked on as a former ornament of that world. Yet, in the current sense, I have never "made it," although I have been in and around it. The Grand Surprise is, partly, that none of this matters.

FEBRUARY 18, 1971    Maria, in a pale dress, confronted by Mina in her blue cut-velvet. Mina, "We have a dear friend in common. . . ." Maria, "That makes two of us." "My," said Mina, "she's tough. I remembered my rule with celebrities: lay it on thick. And I did—with a trowel, but I couldn't give her enough. I never saw Mac Lowry [of the Ford Foundation] and Goosey make over someone that much, and Walter [the chauffeur] was beside himself when he saw her going in. . . ."

Lincoln called to ask me would I ask Maria to do *La Voix Humaine* at the New York State Theater next season. I will ask her.

FEBRUARY 19, 1971    Talk with Lincoln on the phone, first time [on the phone] in almost ten years. He very Lincoln—sort of torn up. Maria, when asked would she do *La Voix Humaine:* "No, no, no . . ."

Maria: "I am going to Juilliard to do a little research on my own. . . . You have your police everywhere." Me: "Like Scarpia." Maria: "But you are kind and good and sweet." Me: "That's the worst kind of Scarpia."

FEBRUARY 20, 1971    Maria: "I'm studying . . . *Traviata*. . . . There's always more to learn." I suspect more to this than meets my ear.

She was at the first *Werther*—a boring, badly done work, at which Maria had the heaviest applause. She looked young, beautiful, and determined, in floating emerald-green chiffon, on Bing's arm. The recognition of Maria began first as a stirring box to box, then an acceleration of heads toward her box (thirteen, Bing's), then a rustling on the parterre, like those little winds which herald a storm, then the winds louder and the turning and standing up and the

17. Natasha (previously Fanya) Fliegern married a very rich man who claimed the title "baron" and lived out her last years at the Paris Ritz as the Baroness de Wolfe. Leo was fond of saying, "Anyone who lives long enough becomes a White Russian."

applause and shouts of "Brava, Callas!" This started from the top of the house. The rush into the aisles—the logjam of admirers, detractors, thrill-seekers—the cascades of adulation, which torrent ever more fiercely and finally sweep everything before them as she advances to the front of the box and waves, bows, smiles, and almost weeps. Everyone played his part very well indeed. Then the repetition of this during the interval, as she glides on Bing's arm to the refreshment room. He hangs his head—smirking, sheepish, not willing to show his capitulation. There isn't any in him. He has the least generous of natures. But Maria is, of course, graciously triumphant—only the corners of her mouth betray, to those few who know her well, her deep triumph over this monster who terminated her career on the Met Opera stage but, obviously, served only as a minor factor in making her legend, and who, or so last night made it seem, will be known only because of her glory.

The demonstration is remarkable in that she has not sung for six years, but she has been an evolving legend, greatly accelerated in these years, and is considered by the public a wronged woman, splendid in her dignity. Mrs. Onassis is, paradoxically, thought of as "the other woman," a part tradition would have assigned, in this farce, to Maria. All of which is an indication of the morality of these times: The mistress is the wronged one, and the loyal wife the villainess.

NOTE: After thirty-five years in charge of *Vogue's* features, Allene Talmey abruptly left the magazine in February 1971, citing health problems. Although some said that Talmey left because she found the mercurial Diana Vreeland a headache, she had been coping with Vreeland there for nine years. Leo believed Alex Liberman forced her retirement.

FEBRUARY 26, 1971 • NEW YORK CITY
**TO RICHARD HUNTER** • JOHANNESBURG, SOUTH AFRICA

I must tell you the tragicomedy of Allene Talmey. Mitzi told me, in strict secrecy, that Allene's blood pressure was so high that her doctors had forbidden her to work ever again: She had to retire immediately. Then she, Mitzi, said that when Alex had heard this, he cried. Also the head of Condé Nast, Perry Ruston, had cried! Then I encountered Alex, the weeper, and he said, "Have you heard from Allene? Has she had her operation?" solemnly. So I said how sad that she had to retire because of her high blood pressure, went home, called up Allene, and there she was—her voice quite as healthy as we have always known it: "I wanted to call you right away and tell you everything," she said. Then, after ten minutes of cheerful talk, she remembered how sick she is and her voice faded! Think how elaborate a cover-up!!! Very 39 *Steps* since the man with the missing part to his finger is the weeper, Alex, who several weeks ago told me that she was going to have to go soon.[18] That is the saga of

18. In Hitchcock's *The 39 Steps* (1935), the villain is identified by a missing finger.

A. Talmey. Please tell no one, even Howard, because I could find myself without a job if this secret ever came back.

JOURNAL • FEBRUARY 26, 1971   How amazing that this genuinely shrewd, seemingly hard-boiled woman would cover so stupidly. Telling that when she told Alex, he cried. Ye gods! The Little Funny Face indeed.[19] Who, as she would put it, does she think she's kidding? So, almost the last of a certain breed departs, screaming all the way. I couldn't be more surprised at Allene's erecting this facade. The epitome of magazine career women and how they refuse to give up.

FEBRUARY 27, 1971   Talk with Julie Harris on the blower. She wasn't sanguine about her play [*And Miss Reardon Drinks a Little*], saying that she was sure that it is doomed. The quality of her voice—sudden sunlight through miasmas of cloud. Her discretion, her strength. She reminds me of my grandmother. When I say grandmother, I always mean my Goldwasser grandmother. We called on my Lerman grandparents. They were forbidding, formal, disdainful, selfish, and lived in a small, dreadful flat that had oilcloth on the floor. Nevertheless, the tall looking glass in my bedroom, the first piece of furniture I bought, is a memory of those visits. They had a similar one, the top chopped off: I adored it. They owned a smelly, dark paint shop on Second Avenue [near 100th Street] and lived in the tenement over it, with the "El" clattering by. I can smell the châteaux stations and see the crotchety men in the change booths. I smell kerosene, urine, old food, dirt, sweat, and coal. Each one had a thriving pot-bellied stove. The cheerful clatter on the rails and wires . . . the stations shook and swayed. That was a very early science lesson: An uncle had told us that they had to sway in order to stick together.

FEBRUARY 28, 1971   The boys at [playwright] Jerry Lawrence's, most of them twenty-five and under, were actors, ad-agency men, account executives, teachers on all levels, playwrights, composers, dancers. ("But I'm leaving it—there's no future. I'm going into modeling and acting. When I was in Toronto doing a television series, I found out I had a New York face.") There were too few older men, thus the tension sagged, and the [social] "affair" was over-narcissistic. Few seemed vicious; most had the look of being out on the beach (Fire Island) or in the sun all day and dancing and fucking all night; all were slim to emaciation; almost all were dull, wore skintight pants; some shirts were open down to the pubic hair. There was not so much a feeling of goods for sale as there was an atmosphere remarkably similar to that in a Ziegfeld Follies showgirl dress-

19. *Vogue* editor Kate Lloyd had referred to Talmey thus, a reference to the 1956 film *Funny Face*, which was about a fashion editor and photographer.

ing room. Few were drunk; many were stoned (Gray says). They were not on the make sexually, but in honest New York style were on the make for whatever gains (career) they could achieve. These young men are exactly what they are. They do not seem to pretend. Some of the in-between ones are hostile.

MARCH 2, 1971 Édouard Roditi at lunch. He is larger, more sedate in an out-of-register way—cleaner looking, more pulled together—and he is becoming a mysterious-seeming old man. He is loyal, and the long ties are still tight. Édouard owns a house in Tunis. Paul [Bowles], he says, is sunk into fat, lethargy, and remorse and masochism over Jane—now, mostly a vegetable in a Málaga nunnery.[20] When Paul went to visit her some months ago, she came alive and begged him to get her out of there. Then he returned and she was a vegetable again. Meanwhile Paul sells the writings he forces out of his untalented Arab-boy lovers and dopes himself. He is frightened, as is [painter and poet] Brion Gysin. Édouard, this scion of Sephardic Jews, lives in a market in Paris, in a flat he owns and occupies with two Arab-boy lovers, who work in garages and adore him but have numerous affairs with other boys. Édouard is always off to exotic places, translating, teaching, lecturing. He also sells a few art works. He has seven languages. He knows the queer bars of North Africa, the new African republics, South American cities (remote ones), Soviet Russia. Édouard goes to Sunday tea—one of New York's last—in a Gramercy Park flat. He wore a little handkerchief pulled through a ring—most discreetly with-it—and on his fingers, many unusual, quite large rings—one a black skull. Some of Édouard's rings are African, silver, barbaric, and splendid.

MARCH 3, 1971 [Richard] Fletcher came up from Washington to talk with me about [a biography of] Mary Garden. Fletcher has a mouth that furls and unfurls like a banner in a high wind. He described her last five years. She spent them in the public insane asylum—but, since she had plenty of money in the Morgan Guaranty Trust, Paris, she had whatever she needed. And she felt no pain—at least known to those who saw her. This was because she believed herself in her prime, her heyday when she was a glorious, tempestuous star—a glamour girl. All the attendants, she believed, were her dressers, her servants, and secretaries. Those who came to call were journalists, writers, composers seeking her. "I cannot see you this afternoon," she would say. "We are rehearsing *Aphrodite*. We are putting it on in a month, and it takes all of my time."[21]

She told Fletcher that she had never known Proust but that he was "a gay boy," and she meant, of course, queer. Also, that Proust was always trying to

20. In 1967, ten years after a severe stroke, deteriorating health had required that Jane Bowles be committed to a clinic.
21. *Aphrodite* is an opera (1906) by Camille Erlanger, in which Garden had given an acclaimed performance as Chrysis.

give parties for Debussy, but that Debussy never permitted that, since he thought Proust and his chums very queer and frivolous. Of Debussy, she said that she had never slept with him, but, said Fletcher, "What she knew of his sexual technique could only have come from someone who had slept with him. She said he wasn't very good in bed." So we sat in the Tratt [Trattoria restaurant], while a storm roared in Forty-fifth Street and were sometimes in Mary Garden's fin-de-siècle Paris, sometimes in her loony bin in Aberdeen, sometimes in her wicked sister Helen's villa. M.G. was actually ninety-three when she died. She had lied about her age.

MARCH 4, 1971 All sorts of people, even comparative strangers, feel that they can criticize my whiskers, can tell me how to cut them, even that I should not have them. This latter advice has lessened over the years. When I first had a beard, in 1943, demands to cut it off were universal, save for Rut and Ela. The beard itself seemed to threaten people. Whole busloads would cackle with laughter and exhort derisively, "Git a haircut!" People act threatened by my whiskers—now by the shape and abundance. There are many who praise this shape, but almost every near-and-dear detests the shape—vociferously. Maria: "You are so nice looking, with a neat beard." Mina: "You look like a bad *Mikado* actor."

Example of how facts are heard the way the hearer hears: Siobhan [McKenna] told me that what she remembers most of all of the sagas I've told her is the one about Poppa not coming home all night, me finally finding him a bleeding mess in the dawn, then swiftly making back to my bed, leaping in, pulling the covers over my head, saying to myself, "I didn't see it! It didn't happen!" She says that this last helps her through life. Every time something is too much, she thinks, "It didn't happen!" The truth is that I told her about my finding Poppa and my telling Momma, who screamed, "Sam, what have you done to me!" Yet, Siobhan is honest and believes that I told her the version she told me. (That is also true of Anaïs and what she has written in her diaries about me.) I did not tell her that saga: She heard it or remembers it that way.[22]

MARCH 14, 1971 I woke poor Gray twice in the night with my howlings and screamings. These are mandrake clamors torn out of my innermost terrors. Sometimes I feel a time when I am the only one left. I shake with horror and flee from that moment, annihilated. I loathe the idea of going, leaving, but to remain alone with no one to comfort me in the night, no one who has been part of my going toward this awful moment. I cannot think of this, but I must teach myself to look at it and to face it with equanimity and with dignity.

22. When Nin's novel *Ladders of Fire* (1946) appeared Leo told her to "lie low." "Because she was all set *épater* [to shock] *le bourgeois* . . . to send out dykish photographs of herself." *Journal, April 23,* 1982. Her journals called it a betrayal.

MARCH 18, 1971 Howard Gilman[23] on dinner at Leonard Sillman's house. (This is Leonard seeking backing for his project of *New Faces of 1952* revival.) He took Howard and mother on a house tour—loads of [drawings by René] Bouché, since he lived in the two top floors. A brace of good, but in bad condition, Adams [Staffordshire pottery] pieces. A wall of pornographic drawings by Frank Loesser: "Mother didn't seem surprised or flinch. I think she thought that she was looking at mushrooms! They're all of these huge, crossed cocks with inscriptions like, 'Jews should stick together.' "

This curious convolution by which a gossip columnist [Leonard Lyons], with a somewhat liberal reputation and kudos for never dealing dirty, brings rich Jews to Leonard Sillman. And this gently nurtured (*sic*) Jewish matron [Sylvia Gilman] peering at male organs, limned by a leading American popular composer, and thinking them mushrooms—grotesque manipulation—while her homosexual son lives with the son of an Italian short-order joint and is beloved to frenzy by the daughter of the Czar's dentist [Remi Saunder]—all in the home of a former hoofer and vaudevillian who produces only disasters.

MARCH 22, 1971 Lydia [Gregory] on Mayakovski and Tatiana: "He was in love with her. He was. I saw him every day in Moscow, and he told me." (All of Lydia's *o*'s are long, drawn out; her *r*'s go on forever—har-r-rd—and she sort of does a trill on them.) "Mostly he loved her because she was so beeeg. The day before he keeled heemself I saw heem. He want I should come in café, but I was just goink my father with foood to jail, so I tooold heeem, leave me alone. . . ."[24]

NOTE: Betsy Blackwell retired as editor in chief of *Mademoiselle* at the end of March 1971. In the following months Leo considered other employment. He did a pilot tape for a radio talk show, met with several publishers to discuss a memoir, and reviewed books for *Vogue*—his first work for them in two decades. After Allene Talmey's departure from *Vogue*, editor Kate Lloyd oversaw its features, but Alex Liberman often consulted Leo about matters at the magazine. Liberman was particularly concerned over Truman Capote, who had sold to *Vogue* the right to publish his next fiction but showed no sign of delivering.

JOURNAL • APRIL 2, 1971 The Ike and Tina Turner Revue—ugh—the stench of pot, the hysteria, the scene in Carnegie Hall—legs thrown over box fronts, the bright cigarette ends, the elaborate undress and dress undress, the constant migrations of the audience. "They have the attention spans of two-year-olds," said Puss. The hustlers constantly active. The contrast between my early visits

23. Heir to a paper-manufacturing fortune and an arts philanthropist, Howard Gilman (1924–98) also amassed an important photography collection.
24. Elizabeth "Lydia" Gregory (1898–1973?) had also been a lover of the poet Mayakovski. Her father was a prominent Russian lawyer imprisoned by the Soviets.

to Carnegie—*To a Wild Rose, A Victory Ball*, Walter Damrosch, Ernest Schelling,[25] Maestro. Then, the glitter of rhinestones on women; now jewels on slim-hipped, breathlessly tight-pantsed boys showing everything they've got, prominently bunched and displayed. The elaborate rags today—Fats Domino in red velvet and satin and immense rings . . . slow, dim . . . "Get off! We want Tina!" some screamed. Tina and Ike are primitive, outdoor water-closet, behind-the-barn pornography. She has great energy, seems old, lacks any variation, and turns them on with stupid smut. My father would have found her provocative. These very young people find her a dirty joke, which they share vociferously. She received a standing ovation. In second-rate burlesque and at stag parties this went on when I was young. What was really depressing about Tina Turner's audience: They were turned on by her non-sexuality, her whore's manipulations. She gave facsimile service, laughing at her well paying audience-trade all the time she was giving them emptiness.[26]

APRIL 6, 1971 Great gales, snow, slush, thunder, lightning—portents and alarums. Stravinsky died this morning, here in town. An anti-sympathetic man, with a curious, clutching handshake (an avaricious clasp). A selfish, ungiving man, but he did write *Petrouchka* and *Firebird* and *Les Noces* and *Sacre du Printemps* and the haunting repeated theme of *The Cage* score. Nevertheless, I remember his penetrating owl stare, which made me feel a mouse being inspected for my nutritive values. He was always the eater, not the eaten. Mrs. Stravinsky was a lush, vigorous garden.

NOTE: For some months, Gray had been feeling constant pain in his right ankle. Diagnosis, a long time coming, was a degenerative ailment of the ligaments, for which little could be done.

JOURNAL • APRIL 9, 1971 I got through this week—solidly—and even finished a feature. Puss hasn't cancer—but a permanent, painful sickness of the ankle muscle. He will have to learn to live with this—and so will I.

APRIL 19, 1971 My people were among the 2,650,000 Jews who came from Eastern Europe between 1881 and 1925. We came in the 1880s and were here before the Great Blizzard of 1888. My grandfather Goldwasser and his brothers surely saw the Metropolitan Museum of Art being built on the deer park, and they could have stood, on that rain-drowned March day, watching the quality

25. Ernest Schelling (1876–1939), pianist and composer of the popular symphonic poem *A Victory Ball*, was also conductor of the Young People's Concerts of the New York Philharmonic. As a boy, Leo won awards for his musical knowledge from the organization in 1928 and 1929.
26. The rhythm-and-blues artists Ike and Tina Turner recorded their album *What You Hear Is What You Get* at this concert.

arrive for the museum's grand-opening ceremonies. My people believed that America was the "Land of Golden Promise." They believed that all were equal here, and that this was a democracy in which anyone could become rich, famous. In America, no one was persecuted for his faith. They did not know about race. The Statue of Liberty was reality to them—not promises, not symbol, but portent and prophet. When did the disillusionment set in? When they had to make their living? When they found that they had to break the Sabbath laws, the dietary laws? Did the sweatshop do it? The life in the public schools? My father saluted the flag, with conviction. Saluting was one of the earliest things he taught me. He loved the U.S.A.

The *Forverts* started in 1897.[27] Grandpa read it, interminably arguing with such male chums as came in to drink a *glasel thé* with him, as he sat in his heavy black knitted cardigan (but he did not know that it was a cardigan), smoking the endless cigarettes he rolled, taking snuff . . . there in a tie, but collarless, a gold stud in the buttonhole . . . with his yarmulke firmly on his head . . . spitting and hawking and blowing his nose between his fingers. He was bad tempered, irascible, suspicious, autocratic—and he had to know everything! He was in complete, despotic control—a violent man given to dreadful, hurting practical jokes. When he got himself up for *shul* or, on Saturday nights, Lodzer True Brothers, or for out-of-his-house card playing, he was neat and even smart-looking.[28] When I knew Grandpa, he was living on what his children made.

APRIL 22, 1971 Alex Liberman spread across *Time*. Am I pleased that I started his public career in art? I must analyze this awful relationship.[29]

NOTE: On April 25, Leo and Gray joined a large march in Washington, D.C., to protest the war in Vietnam.

JOURNAL · APRIL 25, 1971 I will brekkie [breakfast] and down and away to march for peace. This will do little general good, but I will be benefited hugely [by the exercise].

The people on the Metroliner to Washington were Jewish middle class and intelligentsia—such good humor. The march was really a friendly rabble, vast multitudes, blue-jeaned hordes. I think of Emma Lazarus. It was not disorganized; it was not organized. The hand-clapping. The occasional crying out for

27. The *Jewish Daily Forward*, a Yiddish-language daily newspaper.
28. Many Jewish immigrant men in America joined *Landsmannschaften*, lodges of men from the same place and culture. Jacob Goldwasser's was named for Lodz, in central Poland.
29. Around the end of April 1954, Leo urged James Johnson Sweeney, director of the Guggenheim Museum, to see the work of Liberman. Sweeney did so, and put a painting in the museum's "Younger American Painters" show. It became Liberman's breakthrough.

LEFT: Hedda Sterne's 1947 portrait of Leo captured, Gray has said, "the essence of him— mystical and mischievous." BELOW: Milton Avery portrayed Leo in the studio of sculptor Mitzi Solomon, 1948.

By Richard Hunter, probably painted in the early forties

*Interior: Leo Lerman,* by John Koch, 1953

*Cocktail Party*, by John Koch, 1956. Leo, in the foreground, converses with pianist Ania Dorfmann. The other guests, *left to right*, are artist Roger Baker, artist and critic Maurice Grosser, the Dr. Leonard Smileys, the painter John Koch (mixing drinks), Mrs. Edgar Feder, an unidentified woman, composer Virgil Thomson, music critic Noel Straus, Dora Koch (*standing*), an unknown seated woman, artist Felicia Meyer Marsh, an unknown man, artist Aaron Shikler, art dealer Roy Davis, butler Leroy Lowry, artist Raphael Soyer, and biographer Frances Winwar.

Leo's bedroom at the Osborne apartment.
All the paintings depict dogs.

In the Fifty-seventh Street apartment's foyer, surrounded by
nineteenth-century paintings of Vesuvius, 1993

LEFT: The editorial adviser
to Condé Nast Publications
in his office, 1990
BELOW: The features editor
of *Vogue*, 1979

"Peace Now!" The feeling of being photographed for FBI files. The babies carried or toted papoose-style. Deeply touching when handmade signs said Woods Hole, Massachusetts, or any other remote place and, carrying these signs, bright-eyed young people—or a covey of middle-aged ones. The black man, oldish, carrying a huge pole, atop which was, "My son died in Vietnam. Stop the war." The kindness of strangers. The bright, spring day petaled by cherry blossoms. The two streams of humanity converging from Pennsylvania and Constitution Avenues. The truck from which little ladders made of wood were being sold for seating and elevators, the proceeds to go to some war-stopping organization. The proper Hadassah-looking woman, blue bands—"End the War"—across her correct, ample bosoms.

APRIL 26, 1971 Norman [Singer] went to Trenton to a reunion with four people he hasn't seen in twenty years. They went to Cornell with him.[30] The husband of one of the girls was out of the room, but in telling about our going to protest, Norman mentioned my name. The girl, a Mrs. Robinson, wife of a pediatrician, said, "Oh, my husband knew him years ago in Lakewood." When Dr. Robinson returned, he told Norman that I had been a glamorous, tall, good-looking boy from the big city, and that I had wanted to go to bed with him, and that he'd liked me a lot, but he was frightened. He remembered that I had a sensuous mouth, that he had read one book by Galsworthy but that I had read all of them, that I had given him a long lecture on the value of Galsworthy, and that I had been brilliant and made no secret of my homosexuality. (This was during the time I was finding out and then being sure. I was sure by 1931.) Dr. Robinson said that I rang him and asked him to come to a movie and said that was what I wanted. I remember a tall, thin, aquiline-nosed boy, with a shock of black hair. We lolled on green hillsides, talked literature, and I wanted him desperately and poetically. Dr. Robinson now turns out to be that boy, Irving Rubinovitch. He's a white-haired man and husband, about whom I have not thought in forty years and who was the only charmer I ever found in Lakewood, when I was sixteen and seventeen. That was a time when excessive sexual energy led me to experimental necking with Helen T in the backseat of the auto and to nightly, and sometimes daily, sexual pleasures with [cousin] Martin (which we both enjoyed, like puppies, and never talked about, and which neither one of us connected with homosexuality).[31]

In those Lakewood days, I never knew that I was good-looking, tall, brilliant. I knew that I lusted mightily and that I read and wrote and fantasized all of the time—and was terrified, ecstatic, and loved beauty of all kinds and literature

30. Leo's friend Norman Singer (1921–2001) directed New York's City Center, then the Chamber Music Society.
31. Martin Goldwasser (1915–85) was the son of Leo's uncle Harry and aunt Ida. He became an air force colonel in the Strategic Air Command, a husband, and a father.

and music and theater and writing—others' and my own. I wrote odd, bad verse and gloried in it. I feared the full moon, but became breathless with its beauty when it drenched the lonely streets and yards. . . . The library, the movie house . . . reading, reading, reading, and writing—endless scribbling—and being romantically ill and taking long, afternoon baths, eating chocolate bars and reading in the bath through endless empty summer days.

APRIL 28, 1971 This is marriage, save no divorce. A most tenuous arrangement seemingly as free as the trust itself, but fraught with dangers. Definitely for better or worse, but, as in most such arrangements, no holds barred. I've come a long way from butterflies, but the Grand Surprise is, indeed, beginning and end. I am a married, Jewish, middle-aged man. I see that I am typical in so many ways, especially of my generation. In trying to avoid life's problems, I took them in heavily. "Now life ends and survival begins."—Bertolucci.

MAY 3, 1971 Off to the "Y" with Felicia Bernstein ("Not steen, stein—like a beer mug.")[32] to hear Steve Sondheim's talk on being the most successful lyricist we have. There was an outpouring of famous chums—almost all sitting together in a Roman fighting square, as in my *Gallic Wars* years ago. He was disarmingly confident of his genius, disarmingly confident of his amateur platform technique, and so, taking his audience into his confidence, or lack of it, he made instant chumship. They adored him and his highly organized, now professional technique. Steve did not mention Lennie as an influence. Indeed, he mentioned no musical influences, but gave glorious due to Arthur Laurents, Oscar Hammerstein, Cole Porter, Frank Loesser—not to Larry [Lorenz] Hart. What the audience got was a genuine view of how Steve works. And they heard songs not available to them. The evening was very long and hot. I dozed occasionally. The audience adored every moment because it felt that it was in on creativity, being part of this desirable process, this vivid world.

MAY 7, 1971 Maria: "I'm finished . . . last March was too much. He [Onassis] almost had me again—but he's such a pig. And what for? . . . I'm doing Juilliard for nothing. I have enough. Not as much as before. They can't pay much—so I do it for nothing."

Marlene in a good, oldish, *Hausfrau* mood—tired, gentle, worn by life: "My hands are so old. And Rudi is suddenly very old. The earthquake . . .[33] He's a displaced person. His last friend, a rich man he loves, said we should make a bank loan and rebuild the house, but Rudi doesn't do anything. He doesn't

32. The actress and pianist Felicia Montealegre (1922?–78) had married Leonard Bernstein in 1951.
33. The San Fernando (Sylmar) earthquake had occurred in Los Angeles on February 9, 1971.

move. He's rootless. I must work in July—and I'm so tired. . . ." The voice low, slow, sweet, womanly, with the young golden girl always peeping from under the womanliness—all very Berma.[34]

**MARLENE AND RUDI**  *Men wanted desperately to marry Marlene, but she always had a wonderful excuse, the one that extricated her from the possibility of marrying any of them: "But darling, I am mawied. I am a mawied woman. I am always mawied to Rudi. I love Rudi." And indeed she loved the Rudi she had married, when she was a very young girl. But hers was an astoundingly free life in which Rudi and her daughter Maria were constants. She paid for his life and his mistress, Tamara, who was a deeply neurotic woman, but who was fond of Marlene and of whom Marlene was very fond.[35] Marlene would disappear suddenly, calling from Rudi's San Fernando Valley chicken farm, which she had bought for him, and enunciating in her forever Berlin-accented English, said, "I am here at Rudi cleaning up the place. You should see how much it needs cleaning. I have been here three days scrubbing everything."*

*Rudi and Marlene were bound together by some intangible cord. She was a responsible woman, and he was her responsibility. Perhaps he was her way of making peace with the life she so arrogantly led. It is difficult to think of Marlene as a guilty woman, but in her excessive efforts to please her husband, in her inexhaustible giving to her daughter, there must be some seed of guilt, some scrap of remote Lutheran ethic? I think that Marlene and Rudi, through all the years of glitter and glamour and chicken farming and even misery, always saw one another as those two beautiful young people in Berlin who had first met and fallen in love in some strange, golden time before Hitler.* (1993)

JOURNAL · MAY 9, 1971  I rang Marlene's bell, and soon she opened her door—cautiously—a small, not awake, very, very old person—so old that the creature was sexless—bleary blue eyes, a straight line for a mouth. "Oh, who? What? . . ." She had obviously forgotten that she'd asked me to lunch. She was plastered—ancient and plastered and very small. I gathered her in my arms. She, fragile, relaxed gratefully. I saw that her hair was thin to baldness on top. And when I held her at arm's length and saw her legs—they were ugly, veins knotted. But somehow, deep within this wreck where not one glimmer of her beauty was visible, the young girl peeped out. I was reminded of Laurette Taylor in *Outward Bound*.[36] She finally pulled herself together and swiftly cooked

---

34. In Proust, Berma is a grand actress of the older generation.
35. Tamara Matul (1909–65), a Russian-born former dancer, lived with Rudolf Sieber for forty years while he was married to Dietrich.
36. After Broadway success in the teens and twenties, the actress Laurette Taylor (1884–1946) entered a long alcoholic seclusion, then returned to the stage late in life to deliver landmark performances in *Outward Bound* (revival, 1938) and *The Glass Menagerie* (1945).

a hamburger, made a salad, peas, mashed potatoes—all with careful attention to what I could and could not eat. Thinking of Marlene exhausts me. . . . We ate in the kitchen, where a wig block, with Marlene's hair upon it, led an active life of its own. "They go their way," she said, poking at the tight blond curls. I could see the future thousands, viewing this *Blonde Venus* apparition, "Isn't she marvelous!" She is. Her restorative powers are tremendous.

MAY 11, 1971  Marlene came to the Russian Tea Room. She talked about her forthcoming engagements:[37] "What should I wear? Which dress? That is the question. . . . The gold, the feather coat? That is too much, too theatrical. The pear-shaped diamonds, the coat, and the dress gray-pavé? The Danes love it and call it the Electric Eel. . . ." That one, I advised, will look wonderful against the penguin orchestra. Then she told about her various encounters with Prince Philip. "She [Queen Elizabeth] doesn't like me. She has a be-oo-tee-fool laugh" (Marlene says "beautiful" like no one else, almost crooning it, making it an adornment, a warm cover for herself. She makes it into a precious, cozy word). "When I was at the Café de Paris, the first time [in June 1954], she wanted to hear me and it couldn't be in a theater, so they showed me all the private houses, and I picked Astor's. They all came, and Philip danced with me, dance after dance, and finally I told him he must stop, and he was like a child. Then one time he made jokes and she told him to behave himself. And years ago, when I made a picture with Gabin, there was a big reception at Joinville, in the pouring rain. Philip was attached to the embassy. They were always trying to find jobs for him. We went, Gabin and I, and he was the star, but it was pouring rain . . . those French journalists and critics, always so poor and so hungry . . . all the way to Joinville, in the pouring rain . . . and Gabin wouldn't even come in. So, Gabin was sitting in the car, and I went into the reception. There was Philip, and I said, 'What are you doing here in all this rain and everything?' I was be-oo-tee-fool in a gray dress by Grès . . . all tucks and . . . you know . . . be-oo-tee-fool . . . with a big hat. . . ." She gestured the hat into being—a huge, soft swirl haloing her head. "And Philip said, 'I came to see you. . . .' He was so nice. . . . But he is naughty, very naughty. . . . No she doesn't like me. . . . But she has such a be-oo-tee-fool laugh. . . ."

MAY 17, 1971  We brunched, really lunched, with Howard [Gilman], Luigi [Gasparinetti],[38] and Remi. Quite splendid, all done by Ouj in a bright red apron, hair slicked back under a huge chef's hat, heavy black-rimmed specta-

37. Dietrich would soon be performing at Copenhagen's Tivoli, and later giving a command performance for Queen Elizabeth at Covent Garden.
38. Luigi "Ouj" Gasparinetti (1942–2002) was a chorus boy who became an actor and the lover of Howard Gilman. Later he directed Gilman's philanthropic foundation.

cles. He was marvelously handsome and excessively right. We talked about my gala birthday: Seventy-five have accepted.[39] We lingered laughing and listening to [music-hall singer] Mistinguett (a rather big mouse being eaten by a cat) and various golden throats, with Joan [Sutherland] sumptuous and clear—even her diction—in the aria from *Attila*. Ouj: "She must have been in a rage that morning with Ricky [Bonynge, her conductor-husband]."

Remember Maria's one a.m. call—strong, gay, serious (but this is always through a sort of grand-opera scrim), roaring with laughter over Onassis pursuing her and her rejection of him. "Let him have his two whores. I'll never forgive him for humiliating me in public and taking me away from my music. 'What d'ya wanna work for?' he asks me. . . . So adolescent." Then she went on about how she has told Onassis that only with a married man would she have an affair—safest.

MAY 18, 1971   Reezl returned [from Africa via Europe]. I found him just arrived when I came home in the late afternoon. He is full of "giraffes like showgirls," "flights of zebras," Kilimanjaro in snowy remoteness, Victoria Falls zigzagging, myriads of petrol-slick-colored butterflies, cascades of bright birds, and decay of the world everywhere.

We went to see Freddie [Ashton]'s *Beatrix Potter*, which is lovely: The dancers as beasties enchantingly like their originals and [dancer] Alex Grant spectacular. Fascinating how original styles of dancing come through, and how the work, as a whole, is a genuine and practical stage piece. Thinking of how Alice would have loved it, my eyes teared.

Mike [Bessie, editor and publisher]'s tales about Tallulah: When he came to dine and to take away her proofs of the autobiography with which he had gotten [her press agent] Richard Maney to help, she said: "It's an honest book, isn't it? Of course . . . there was lesbianism, love among girls, but . . ." and she gradually, getting drunker and drunker, enumerated all the well-known underground of her life—the dope, the drink—reiterating, "But it's an honest book, isn't it?" Do omissions make autobiography dishonest if everything in the book is honest?

NOTE: After months of losses in circulation and advertising at *Vogue*, its publishing director, S. I. Newhouse, Jr., resolved in May 1971 to replace Editor in Chief Diana Vreeland. She was abruptly made a consulting editor, essentially a sinecure. Vreeland was replaced by her associate and frequent deputy Grace Mirabella.

JOURNAL · MAY 23, 1971   A talk with Allene: "What's going on at *Vogue*?" she quavered, "I haven't been able to talk to anyone." Irony. I was sad for her.

---

39. Within the week, Gilman would throw a party in his penthouse for Leo's fifty-seventh birthday.

Rachel [Crespin, fashion stylist] on Alex Liberman: "He's the villain. At last he's the czar of the fashion magazine world. He's power-crazy," she says. "God gave him his worst attack of ulcers."

JUNE 23, 1971  Dolly Haas Hirschfeld screening, at MoMA, of her *Broken Blossoms* with Emlyn Williams.[40] "Very interesting," said Puss, anent my fling with E.W., some years ago. "I went steady," as Ouj would say, meaning one brief tumble, late in the night. The cries of "Daddy! Daddy! Fuck me. . . ." which I did, and the terror of his perfect murderer acting after.[41]

JUNE 26, 1971  Lotte Lenya singing Weill is the epitome of that world—as Rut was. The perverted innocence of Lotte's voice. I can see Ela's smile in it. Their perversity was deep, so *raffiniert*, that it was pure. Ruth Gordon has some of this—a common willfulness, a willful perversity beyond perversity, so that she has innocence, no matter how sinister (meaning left-handed).

Lotte Lenya . . . That little hall bedroom between Ela and Ilse [Bois] (she had the grandest) in East Seventy-fifth Street, where Lotte had her threesomes, always young queer "poets," while in the great house, up river near Nyack, little, thick-lens-bespectacled Kurt, a sort of minor functionary or servant in appearance, worked away at his minor-major masterpieces (the masterpieces had been done before he came to *Amerika*—now he made money). Music—always music before money—and Lotte supreme, the daughter of a coachman and a laundress, born in a Viennese slum, who at four walked the tightrope in a little circus.

The gallantry of these Weill songs—the fling of them, the optimism—and Lotte's voice has that. The music assimilates the jazz idiom, the Yiddish idiom, the German idiom, and the result is an original language, Weill's own—the music of the twenties and early thirties, gone by the mid-thirties, and not exportable. The source—Weill. He, himself, as a creative (how I hesitate to use that word) didn't travel well. Lotte did. Lotte sings. She has a little girl quality—Lucrezia Borgia and Marilyn Monroe and Mitzi Newhouse in one. Lotte has such a sense of rhythm—or Kurt Weill had a sense of *her* rhythm. The tango was twenties—Valentino and Novarro—and Kurt's.

JULY 3, 1971 • HARBOURTON, NEW JERSEY  On this bed [at the Samuel Newhouses'] , reclining in the long twilight, pop tunes softly on my little radio, and all of me in love this Fourth of July—not with anyone or anything save the long

---

40. This 1936 *Broken Blossoms* was a remake of the great D. W. Griffith–Lillian Gish silent film.

41. Emlyn Williams performed in his own psychological thrillers. In *Night Must Fall*, he created the part of a homicidal young man. In the fall of 1936 Leo went to see the play after he and Williams had had their roll and was terrified retrospectively.

years behind me—the boys and girls and places and happenings . . . in love with that long life. Is this, then, the most hopeless love or the most fulfilling? Jagged shadows on the window screens of this quiet, chintz-hung, country-house room, so far removed in time and place and being from those years ago when I was a little boy in Grandpa's house or Aunt Silly's or Uncle Harry's or Aunt Annie's or even in Momma and Poppa's. How difficult being alive must be for Momma, with her even longer burden of years. Was she ever in love with that past? What does she remember? The aches, pains, sicknesses, slights—and how she *gave* herself.

JULY 12, 1971 · NEW YORK CITY Women in hot pursuit of homosexual men are doomed before they start, for they seek to make over the objects of their pursuits, to make them into men, while not desiring this transformation at all. It is the inadequacy that they "love"—the feminine, nonheterosexual qualities. Are these women then a form of lesbian? I know that they are sick women, who are terrified of preponderantly heterosexual men. They are the real moms—the son-fucking moms—for they want to consume the male-female. Women like Ela—or even Marlene (to a degree)—who pursue great men (Toscanini, Reinhardt) are also doomed, but this is a different species. The homosexual-loving women pursue death through negatives; the Elas pursue doom through positives—seeking what seems life at its most intense, seeking that one extra day this route.[42] There is no Northwest Passage. Both are pitiful (as we all are), but the Elas are alive, interesting, the others are ridiculously pitiful—well, not quite: Anyone who is sincerely sick is, basically, not ridiculous.

JULY 14, 1971 Mina came into town, in "The Glory,"[43] toting a brown paper sack. First, she went to the Morgan Library and sent for Charles Ryskamp [the director], who grabbed at the sack. "No," she told him, "it's not all for you." Then she gave him Manet's letters written during the 1870 war. After which she made off, sack in hand, to the New York Public Library and the Berg Collection, to which Mina gave the rest of the sack's contents—even David Garnett's love letters to her. "Forty years of letters from Rosamond [Lehmann, novelist] and David and all those, and I had such a nice conversation with the woman who heads the collection—I can't remember her name, but she was nice.[44] I did enjoy snubbing Charles."

42. This expression, "one extra day," recurs in Leo's journal, meaning some transcendence of life's limits, especially time. He fantasized briefly escaping time, as characters had in Thornton Wilder's *Our Town*. Writing about his past and experiencing great art were two ways in which Leo thought he had found that "day" for himself.
43. Mina Curtiss had an oversize Rolls-Royce nicknamed "The Glory."
44. The curator of the Berg Collection of English and American Literature was Lola Szladits (1923–90).

JULY 18, 1971 Robert Davison said, "I always thought I was the one that got away, but when I thought tonight, I wondered whether they got away. Not that I left them, but they left me?" (When I told Puss, he said, "How sad. That's one of the saddest things I ever heard." He looked on the verge of tears. Since our troubles—early in 1970, Puss is very secret.) Robert enjoyed his birthday, two days ago, but it made him think, and being Robert he will think positively. He is a remarkable creature. "The word is escaped, not left," says Robert on the blower. "I hate entanglement. It's so graceless. I always wonder now, if I've missed anything. I don't have any entanglements. All this identity seeking. I abhor that. But I can't help thinking about it now." Robert is genuinely elegant. Robert always had style, even [with Gray] in Los Angeles City College.

JULY 21, 1971 Margot Fonteyn's performance of the Scriabin *Extase*, a work that could have been devised (basically) for Ida Rubinstein's debut with Diaghilev's Ballets Russes—but which she could not have danced.[45] A gaudy, gorgeously corny, transition-into-maturity John Cranko [choreographed] opus redeemed into extraordinary art and spirit, not so much pure dance, by Margot. Her technique is assimilated to such a degree that it is almost invisible. Cranko (in pale gold, muchly jeweled kaftan out in the house) protects her vulnerabilities, covers her with soaring hands, frantic, leaping male bodies— five glorious dancers, and exquisite costumes. The decor is Klimt. Swirling hundred-foot-long curtains drop from the flies. But it is Margot—her femininity, her technique, her spirit—that triumphs. She makes the acrobatics (difficult lifts, turns while upheld by the males, Maxfield Parrish poses, the whole apparatus of Cranko's vulgarities and virtues) define the human condition. She enlarges us, as we marvel and are then lost beyond marvels at the miracle of this fifty-two-year-old woman revealing the perfect beauty of her art and beauty (inner and outer).

Backstage, as she went to and from her tumultuous ovations (fifteen minutes?) she was lined, corded, wet from the prodigious exertion—but still her great inner and outer beauty—her goodness—prevailed over age and its erosions. A high moral quality shines from her playful eyes—her radiance. I do not mean that she is good. I mean that she conveys goodness, belief in life, continuity of spirit, reassurance of immortality—although we know how fragile she is— and we are—all of our culture. I see us all, *en masse*, moving through to extinction . . . yet while I watch Margot I see death but I do not believe in death.

JULY 24, 1971 E. M. Forster told Gore about his hidden novel, *Maurice*.
Gore: What happens in it? F: Well—two boys are in bed together. . . . G: What do they do? F: . . . Talk—

---

45. For Diaghilev, Russian ballet dancer Ida Rubinstein (1885–1960) had created *Cléopâtre* and *Scheherazade*, in which her striking appearance carried more than her technique.

Reading *Maurice* suddenly made my eyes tear. It is such a young book—sometimes a patch of purple, but so young. Those poor boys. It is the way I felt—so very much—but I was deep in practices only not coinciding my [sexual] actions with the miseries and splendors of falling and being in love. Like [Maurice] Hall, I waited for letters and carried them about with me, never letting them off my person.

How could any young person understand *Maurice* today? This book has been hidden, secreted my entire lifetime! Can a homosexual man wake up from a physical sickness (flu) and declare, "I am no longer homosexual!" as Clive does in *Maurice*? I doubt this—at least I doubt the simplification. But I know that Maurice's subsequent hell is written with agonizing accuracy. Did this happen in Forster's life—this being rejected, after several years of mutual love—even passion—by his lover? *Maurice* is sometimes a queen's dream, but at all times a deep look into the past, when "the passion that knows no name" was just that. I still see [British actor] Oliver Reed as Maurice. There is considerable art in it.

NOTE: Leo went to London (with Gray) to research a feature for *Mademoiselle* about Ken Russell, the British film director. Russell's flamboyant film *The Devils*, about apparent demoniacal possession in a nunnery, which starred Oliver Reed and Vanessa Redgrave, had just been released.

JOURNAL · JULY 28, 1971 · EN ROUTE FROM NEW YORK TO LONDON In plane en route to my interview with Ken Russell. Oliver Reed came in to see me. He is mad on Art Nouveau, and is even more what I thought he was. He talks marvelously—mostly, this time, about Ken Russell. The basics of his talk: Russell destroys actors to remake themselves into the creatures of his own sickness. Rather like Michelangelo annihilating the layers of marble in order to make a work of art. He works by a creative destruction. Oliver believes that Russell is growing quite mad. He has been known to fling an actor against the wall. "He makes us bleed. . . ." Russell wanted to do a film of Nijinsky, in which Oliver was to play Diaghilev. So, Oliver studied Diaghilev and feels that, having talked to dancers who danced with Nijinsky, Russell is showing some of the early signs of Nijinsky's madness—the signs after *Le Dieu Bleu*. (When Russell talked to Nureyev about playing Nijinsky, Nureyev said, "Why should I play an inferior dancer?") Oliver's talk is rich in nighttime imagery, although he says, "I'm illiterate." But he isn't. His eyes are incredibly fixed, fathomless blue. His bottom is ample. He's a great toucher. He knows the intensity of his sexuality and he knows how to use it—on male, female. He feels that New York has betrayed him in not understanding *The Devils*. "The one thing that woman will never forgive man is that he is the penetrator. Ken is trying to find the penetrator. He finds that in me, a little bit in me. I'm only a weapon in his tearful story. I'll only continue when he feels that he needs a penetrator again."

AUGUST 7, 1971 • LONDON  Yesterday morning, a lovely talk with Glenda Jackson, high up in 52 Mount Street—the architecture so intensely Betjeman, now I see it drawn or painted by Osbert Lancaster.[46] She is thin to scrawniness, her tallish, slight, no-waist figure, in a faded brown-and-white foliage print, nondescript-length dress, illuminated, really lighted, by her somewhat Halloween-pumpkin smile. There is an intelligent ruefulness in her. And she makes a sound case for her acting being gone at through her intelligence, sieved through the decision she must make of how to project what she feels about that character, the person, that situation, this involvement. Vanessa [Redgrave], Glenda says, is able to make her decision without intellectualizing. Vanessa has immediate response to her emotional reaction to the person she is being. Glenda is immensely intelligent, well-read. "The Russians should make Proust. They'd have ten hours. . . . I couldn't play anyone in Proust. . . ." She has a teacher in her. "Yes . . . but I would want to teach five-year-olds. . . . No, I can't write anything: There's too much time between my thought and my pen. . . ." This was the most rewarding interview. She has no side. She agreed that Elizabeth I (having just played her to Vanessa's Mary Queen of Scots) was an hysteric. She tried to get under history's embalming, and so found Edith's [*Fanfare for*] *Elizabeth* the greatest stimulus. "She was a poet. That helped the most. This historian says one thing about Elizabeth, and about that identical thing another historian says the opposite. Edith Sitwell's intuitions—that gave me the clues I needed." Now she's off to Spain to play Isabella: "She's not as dull as you think."

NOTE: Through the twenty-two years since Robert had moved out of 1453 Lexington, Leo and Gray had seen him only during his trips to New York on assignment for the Parisian decorator Valérian Stux-Rybar. In 1971, however, they stayed with him for ten days, on their first return to Paris in nearly sixteen years.

JOURNAL • AUGUST 11, 1971 • PARIS  The evening and early morning at [decorator] Jean-François Diagre's. He in carefully torn blue denims, with his father's medals—a solid block of virtues and courage's rewards—over his heart. He is a somewhat lost boy, who adores his mother—but healthily. I like him, knowing exactly how treacherous he could be. He is the one who designed the Baron de Redé's party, and is doing the Rothschilds' Proust party near the Guermantes château in December.

Puss and Robert vanished, and Puss told Robert that he was sorry for these years, etc. This happened in the kitchen. They were gone a long time. And Robert said over and over, "Could he have said it fifteen years ago, when it

46. The British poet laureate John Betjeman (1906–84) became a champion of preserving the Victorian scale and style of London. Osbert Lancaster (1906–86), British cartoonist, theatrical designer, and painter, had satirized architectural excess.

would have mattered?" But, of course, it did matter. I don't know quite what Puss said. They were both drunk.

AUGUST 12, 1971  Gray to Robert: "Richard [Hunter] is eccentric in every respect. In fact, he is one of the oddest people I've ever known. You would have to have him to stay with you to know." Robert: "For seven months! You have excessive kindness." Gray: "I don't. Leo does. He's the kind one."

AUGUST 13, 1971  Gray's temper is just beneath the skin—almost showing at all times—scorn and temper and contemptuousness. There must be a French phrase for this condition—just barely covered by skin. The American expression thin-skinned covers (pun intended) all sorts of acerbating conditions. Sometimes I cannot bear this. Most of the time, I cannot but I do. Will this ever blow up? It must not. Too much would pour out too late.

AUGUST 14, 1971  Marlene's flat and her preparations for tomorrow's party—Orson [Welles], Tony Perkins, and [director Claude] Chabrol. Marlene leaning on the balustrade of her minuscule, bright-red-geranium-lined terrace, just a ledge upon which to stand, looking down in the Avenue Montaigne, into the trees and out at the lighted church, the motors fleeing down the avenue—great rushes of autos—saying, "I was too dumb when I was young—too shut away. All I knew was nightclubs and hotels." She has just come from her Copenhagen triumph ("Better than ever") by way of Switzerland, where she had Neiman's injections. She looks better than she did in New York: The famous beauty—the bones, the smile—is apparent again beneath the erosions, the scratches and scourges of time, which, like the prehistoric glacier, has moved across her face.

AUGUST 16, 1971  A happy evening with Marlene—such laughter and talk and reminiscences, the kind we used to have years ago in New York. "If only somebody had told me that it was only glands . . . years ago . . . not love . . . only glands. All of that misery and that waiting and that meaning—Did he mean that? Did he turn his face this way or that? Now it's better—to bed with Rex Stout. No worrying."[47]

Marlene on Garbo: "That blankness, that beautiful blankness behind that face . . . that was it. . . . So touching. She was no actress. . . . I was in the hospital with a strep throat, and she was in a room above me . . . with the clap. She got it from [director Rouben] Mamoulian. And Mercedes [de Acosta] was running between us with food. The hospital food was so bad. . . . Mercedes said Garbo used everybody. She wrecked [Mauritz] Stiller and she killed [John]

47. Dietrich was reading, not sleeping with, the mystery novelist Rex Stout.

Gilbert. . . . She was a monster.[48] When Stiller was dead, she thought she became Stiller—and she raped men. That is why she had queer men. She unzipped her fly and jumped on them. . . . I was making crayfish . . . which I had flown in from the Midwest . . . with dill, the way I learned in Hamburg. . . . You were never in Hamburg? I don't remember. . . . Mercedes was running with them to Garbo, saying she had made them. She couldn't cook anything. . . . Garbo was so stingy. She made Mercedes pay for the littlest thing. When they were together, she made Mercedes count the sugar lumps every morning. 'You have to know how much your breakfast costs,' she said. And she put things in certain ways on the little tables to see if the maid cleaned. . . . She was awful. . . . I never knew her. We met at parties. But when she went away with Mamoulian into the mountains on a camping trip, they bought cheap things in the Army & Navy store. . . . Oh, she was stingy. . . . He paid for everything. . . . That was when they were making *Queen Christina* and the police ran after them at the border, because they drove through it, not wanting it to be known that they were together. There was going to be a scandal, and nobody wanted that—not Garbo, not Mamoulian, not Mercedes, not MGM. I offered to go to where they were and to get into the car and Garbo could get away and I would return quite openly with Mamoulian, and she would be saved . . . but she said no and they all had a field day—Louella Parsons and all of them. . . .

"Oh, I was a pretty girl, but I never knew it. I didn't believe it. . . . In those days, when I first came to Hollywood, and I had a big waist, and I was with Von Sternberg, we all wore dressing gowns—long, trailing dressing gowns with all sorts of frou-frou on the sleeves and the bottoms. Irene made them for me.[49] And Von Sternberg always had to be playing golf in the early morning, and [daughter] Maria had always to open the door so she could see that he was coming from playing golf, and he would say, 'Did you have a good night?' and I would answer, 'Oooh yes. I dreamt of Greta Garbo—oooh, yes. . . .' " Von Sternberg had been sleeping with her all night during those years.

"When I was at the Reinhardt school, we all adored Garbo—and Bergner. I remember Garbo as Anna Karenina, the silent one [*Love* (1927)], when she sat by the side of her son's bed and she swallowed—oh—that was beautiful. And when Bergner stood on the landing, at the top of the stair, in a white coat with a big stand-up collar. She always wore dark makeup, and the makeup was on the collar. I was in the play—an English play—and I was one of the girls who sat with my back to the audience—only the back of my dress was embroidered. 'You don't turn around, so you don't need an embroidered front.' And I said, 'I

---

48. The poet, playwright, and author Mercedes de Acosta (1896–1968) is reputed to have been the lover of Greta Garbo, Marlene Dietrich, Eva Le Gallienne, and Ona Munson, among others. Mauritz Stiller (1883–1928), one of the greatest directors in Swedish silent movies, is remembered as the first to use Garbo.
49. Irene Lentz (1900–62), credited simply as "Irene," designed costumes for several movie studios.

pass.' That was my part . . . but I was where I could see Bergner and that—oh, that was everything."

The woman who follows Marlene everywhere—Margit, the speechless one ("She's not a lesbian")—and the Canadian, who gave her a diamond necklace. Marlene is so funny and human about them. Women who follow stars: "Tallulah always had them, but she made them into useful creatures—secretaries. I can't do that. I'm too well brought-up. I always have to do everything myself. I can't have a secretary because I don't lead that kind of life. What if I told her to come at eleven, and Maria called? Or I wanted to do something else? So, I type my own letters" on a bogus fourteenth-century enormous table complete with machine and all sorts of writing materials, neatly arranged. The podge of the flat, which I find touching and that Gray says is so unlike her New York controlled elegance. I like both and find both very much the way she is.

AUGUST 19, 1971   Marlene—mostly on her maid, who seems to be having a change of life, and for whom she prepares three meals a day and serves them to her. She went on about how stupid this maid is. This is boring, but it was all told with the greatest, marveling joy. She talked about her first maid, Rezi, who had been her dresser for *The Blue Angel*, a woman of about fifty who came to America with her, and during the voyage on the German ship, Rezi lost her uppers down the drain and into the Atlantic. Rezi refused to emerge from her cabin. "In those days, maids were always seasick. Everyone was sitting together in first class and worrying about their maids. But Rezi was not only seasick, she lost her teeth—and was the reason I was late for the first interview. It was all men—not a woman. Paramount arranged it that way, and when the man came aboard from one of those little things—chug choo choo . . . a tug boat—he took one look at me and said, "Oh, no . . . I can't let America see you like that. They'll think you're a lesbian." I had on what any German wore when traveling—a gray flannel suit and a slouch hat, very manly, and gloves. All the Americans had black dresses and pearls and mink coats and the orchids, ropes of orchids, they had been saving in the icebox all through the voyage. So my trunk had to be brought up again, and I had to get dressed all over. But Rezi, she wouldn't come out from her cabin until I promised to take her to a dentist immediately. So, we went to the Ambassador [hotel], where they put me, and I found a dentist, and Rezi said she would stay there all day or two or three days until she had teeth. I left her and went to the interview and was an hour late. I am never late."

AUGUST 21, 1971   Cabourg-Balbec, the Grand Hotel:[50] It was precisely as I expected it to be—large, cozy-stately, empty, rain-swept, deferential—the same

---

50. Every summer from 1907 through 1914, Marcel Proust visited the Grand Hotel in Cabourg on the sea in Normandy, where he had first gone in his teens. For *Remembrance of Things Past* he reinvented its population and setting as a resort called Balbec.

youths—a high, white dining room—but all of that life gone out of it. I could feel Proust there. I could see the frieze of girls (a gaggle of schoolchildren, in my today's view, in scarlet and blue and green macs) and the long, rain-fractured front. Which had been his room? I wondered, looking up at the 1880s or '90s baroque facade. But, oh, the feeling was there, precisely as I knew it must be. And coming up in the Channel mists and fogs . . . the occasional tall steeples punctuating the fog . . . that was very Proustian. What a marvelous day. How just and generous, this day.

Now, the last day. And always the gone feeling which [Alphonse] Daudet has in his story "The Last Day of School." I read it first when I was in school and very young. I have in me, even stronger, the Alain-Fournier feeling of yesterday:[51] That lost world in the mists and rain. That desolation—a happy regret. And, typically, when we finally arrived at the Grand Hotel, Cabourg, Robert came, but Gray did not.[52] Perhaps he was desperately tired by then, but he had been doing his usual destruction for some time—a sort of sneering—a kind of contempt—charmless, infuriating—the sort of thing he does when he's not getting his way. I must develop this from its beginnings in my life, when I fully realized that I must not get caught by it, through being caught by it, to not feeling much, save anger against the negativism in it, and the horrible continuity of his self-destruction. This does not kill love, but it does draw me in upon myself. Love must be outgoing and out-giving. From each of these pouting rages, I go on—growing ever more isolated, but somehow keeping alive my affection—albeit feeling less and less about anything save my scribbling and beauty. I admire industry in people and courage and quiet and devotion and humor and a sense of irony and laughter and a loving heart and optimism and genuine *douleur* and style and panache. I detest negativism and destructiveness and niggardly-stingy ways. Energy exults me.

I must not forget the description of my tone of voice with Gray, which Robert said is quite dead and like a patient mother, i.e., when I finally asked, "Why didn't you go into the Grand Hotel?" or "Is something wrong? Are you sick?" A dead, irritating patience. "Don't hover," Robert said to me.

AUGUST 30, 1971 • NEW YORK CITY  Maria to dinner [at the Plaza] and hearing her recording.[53] (Tennessee at the next table—older, but seems better, more in control—dazzled by Maria.) Her voice is better, more together, rounder. There is no vengeance in it. Later, listening to her early recordings confirms that the 1970ish voice is glorious—more sustained and intact.

---

51. *Le Grand Meulnes*, the one novel by Henri-Alban Fournier (1886–1914, pseudonym Alain-Fournier), tells of a young man who discovers love in an enchanted, ephemeral land, then searches his life long for that lost happiness.
52. GF: "I was exhausted, thought the hotel would be sad, and didn't want to face it."
53. Callas very likely played for him the Verdi arias that she had recorded for EMI in 1969. They were not then commercially released.

Maria was girlish, but not coy, amiable and funny about "Aristo" and the "sisters." She has Lee Radziwill's letters to use in case Mrs. O tries to declare Aristo mentally undone and tries to put him away. "She's a gold digger. . . . His servants and family—they love me." Olympic Airways still flies her errands. There are close ties, but: "I finished with him in Nassau. He's sick, destructive. He brainwashed me. 'You with that whistle in your throat, on your high horse.' But when I played him the record, he was astonished. He knows nothing about it—but he, too, said there is no vengeance in it. . . . If I had stayed with him, he would have killed me or I would have killed him: 'You can't break me,' I told him. 'You can kill me, but you can't break me.' . . . Oh, those Orientals! He's Greek, but born in Turkey. They can't let anything out. It's in the head, and they can't let it out. They can't go to a doctor and say, 'Help me. I can't sleep. I have anxiety. I am nervous.' I am born in America, so I know these things. You have something wrong in the head, you go to a doctor, and he helps you—like with a broken toe. The first duty is to cure the brain. . . . I have the hernia, in my diaphragm, but I don't do anything, since the doctor told me that if I had an operation, I couldn't sing. I will sing. I must show myself that I can do it—and I will do it. . . ." The determination is fantastic.

SEPTEMBER 9, 1971 • WASHINGTON, D.C. How ironic that this evening I am taking Helen Hayes to the opening of the Kennedy Center's Concert Hall.[54] She will have to be presented to the president during the intermission. No, I didn't want to go up with her, which was just as well: "Maybe that is something you would want to forgo . . . ," she wisely said.

SEPTEMBER 10, 1971 "There are two things I don't like about Mr. Nixon: Vietnam and his personality," said Miss Hayes. Later, when she was going up the stairs to be received by Mr. Nixon, she said, "I don't believe in being snotty to the president. . . ." Sometimes the tempo and pitch and the color of her voice is very Ruth Gordon—the slant of it. Is this a common period thing? People reach out automatically to touch her—obviously to touch magic, vitality, life. Mamie Eisenhower looked drugged. Mr. Nixon looked clothing-store-dummy bright. Mrs. Nixon was pretty.

NOTE: Leo returned briefly to New York, then flew south with Howard Gilman for a stay with him in Georgia.

JOURNAL • OCTOBER 1, 1971 • SAINT MARYS, GEORGIA Momma [younger] was full of hospitality. That is, she aggrandized herself, another view of realiz-

---

54. The irony is partially that Leo, a failure in theater, is escorting the "First Lady of the American Stage," actress Helen Hayes (1900–1993), but also because her husband, playwright Charles Macarthur, had pursued Eleonora von Mendelssohn while he was married to Hayes.

ing herself, with perpetual hospitality. This was her sphere of creativity—her hold on family and friends, her active life and her future legend. Her reputation for common sense came straight from her diligence and, indeed, excellence, with pots, pans, *volgar holz* [rolling pin], stove (wood-burning, then gas) . . . from her way with cakes. She was a household goddess, and all because she knew her proportion, confining it to cooking, housekeeping, and a vivacious way of family life—within her home and any other home open to her. Her sisters-in-law detested her, while admiring her jealously. Her brothers adored her with a kind of underskin of loathing. She was a laughing bully, given to excesses of self-pity, hypochondria. Her weapons were health and sickness. She was the most vigorous sick woman I ever knew—plunging into the kitchen or the hospital with equal vigor. Momma was what in the Argentine is known as a "knife." I mean that she killed almost anyone who crossed her path—not physically, but spiritually or mentally, and this ultimately meant physically. The body inevitably is shaped or misshapen by what goes on within itself.

Truman in red shirt, orange tie, and leather, at lunch at the Colony [Club], yesterday. Truman: "Jack's having dinner with Todd [Bolender] tonight!" Traces of the young T come through this fat, blubbery, middle-aged, hanging-on man. Talk of his film script of *The Great Gatsby* and his upcoming television show. ("I'll just talk.") T: "Garbo has been married for seven years—to Cécile de Rothschild—the best of them.[55] She even has a ring. Cécile is very rich, which Garbo loves. . . ." On Mrs. O: "There's nothing devious about her. That's not the way she thinks. She has curiosity. She heard that you had a beautiful apartment and that's why she wanted to see it."

OCTOBER 12, 1971 • NEW YORK CITY  Maria's first class: "Don't call me a teacher. I hate that!" M [Mennin]: "You illuminate. . . ." She: "Eh!" (She says this like a peasant woman) "Yes—anything—not a teacher. I don't teach. I advise." She was extraordinary. Her patience and consideration and smiling encouragement of the young. Her knowledge. She reminded me of Maestro—some vague resemblance—perhaps the degree of consecratedness and dedication.[56]

OCTOBER 13, 1971  The Bernstein party for [art authority] Peggy Bernier. She in silver-thread, flowered, sulphur-yellow Saint Laurent. "My name is really

---

55. Baroness Cécile de Rothschild (1913–95) was a wealthy socialite: "Drooping, almost sagging, expensive fabric and glitter, an effect of jewels and bountiful mouse hair, guttural voice, raspy, an atmosphere of calculated eccentricity, withdrawn almost to deafness, two shrewd wizard eyes, peering. Obviously Cécile de Rothschild was a privileged being. She gave that off as a palpable odor, a kind of disdain, which her closest [friends] probably explain as shyness." *Journal, March 25, 1973.*
56. Callas gave twenty-four master classes at the Juilliard School (October 11, 1971–March 16, 1972).

Rosamond," she explained to me, who knew this about thirty years ago. I sat on a beaded gros-point stool, talking (too much) to Diana Vreeland through the evening—mostly about Ken Russell, [actress-model] Twiggy, *Jesus Christ Superstar* (D.V.: "I loathed it. I was really shocked. I've seen everything, but I was really shocked at the blasphemy. I thought *Trash* was marvelous, *Hair* turned the page, but this . . . I'm very square. Everything in its right place.") She told me that Truman had rung her up and come to see her one night last May and sprawled on a sofa and he'd talked and talked—telling her that he'd lost his Amagansett house with all of his manuscripts. A storm had eaten away the dune, and the house had broken and fallen into the bay: "I just couldn't wait to get to the phone to ask my daughter-in-law why she hadn't told me of this unbelievable catastrophe. I couldn't understand it. We never have violent storms like that at that time of year. Finally, after about four hours, Truman left. I rushed to the phone. . . . None of it was true. . . . I suppose he was trying to end something, to close out something . . . and this was his way."

Puss: "I'm full of anger. I wake up angry left over from the day before. It's all right when I'm on my feet, but when I open my eyes, I'm angry."

NOVEMBER 12, 1971 Maria talking more to the class—even involving me. I was funny. She told them I was her most loyal admirer. When a soprano really got brilliantly pyrotechnical, she said to her, "What was that all about?" but said it so darkly amazed that the comment was kind, constructive. She then explained all about how excessive fireworks were tasteless in that place, also redundant. The soprano had done it all earlier in the [*Barber of Seville*] aria "Una voce poco fa . . ." Maria's lessons are always lessons in taste, proportion, balance, in the architecture and climate of singing. She wore a rich red, longish tunic, belted broadly in patent leather, over flaring black pants. She talked to the soprano about her excessively short skirt: "Remember, the audience always sees more. . . ."

NOVEMBER 13, 1971 At night to Newark, with Howard [Gilman] and Ouj [Gasparinetti], to *Fedora* with Magda Olivero—at sixty-one or sixty-two amazing, pretty, restrained but not stylized, the fragments of a tour-de-force voice.[57] A huge claque of faggots and local Italian society. (Note a specific homosexual anguish: One's chum not being invited, whereas if he were my wife, he would have been.)

[Soprano Maria] Jeritza in white satin, white fox, ropes of real pearls, diamonds, white hair heavily waved (precisely as her blond hair had been), makeup identical with her makeup in 1932, when she was the subject of the first interview I ever did (for the *X-Ray* at Newtown High School) and a figure

57. Magda Olivero (b. 1910), an Italian soprano, did not make her Metropolitan Opera debut until four years later, at the age of sixty-five.

of incredible glamour—now the queen of this opera gala in Newark (where she lives, as did Von Sternberg). Passing me in the Mosque [Theatre] corridors (now Symphony Hall) she could, of course, not recognize that boy in this graybeard. Laci told me tales about her. (Jeritza always sewed a wedding ring in her white satin gowns where her navel is.) Always these women have ladies-in-waiting. She had them.

NOVEMBER 21, 1971    Waiting for our Callas festivity to begin [at home], thinking of 1956, when we gave our first gala ("Attire mystical") for Maria. We had food arranged by Pearl's [Cantonese restaurant] then, and pink tablecloths and napkins (and rice puddings galore that I made on the Monday following), and roses, and hysterics. We still have hysterics and food arranged by Pearl, but almost everything else has changed.

NOVEMBER 22, 1971    The Liberman party for Andrei Voznesensky—a small, very compact, dark, pale, potato-nosed man in very fine French clothes, a round, trim head, a sort of cadet atmosphere. He has a firm, somewhat friendly voice and a little, warm hand.[58] Tatiana—a huge bonfire, so much scarlet satin. Her eyebrows go higher and higher to affirm her face lift—two thick black, slightly cartouche lines, painted high on her blond face—permanently aghast.

   Around eight, Tatiana finally bellowed everyone into silence. When everyone sat on the floors, on the stair rail, on the steps, on the chairs and sofas and arms of same, jammed into the two rooms and the landing, the poet—chinless, but rife with vitality—rose in his chic Parisian leather outfit and announced that his translators would read first in English, his poems, and then he would say them in Russian ("to let hear the sound of the Russian"). This was frequently interrupted by shouts from Tatiana, who was stationed volcanically at the far end of the back parlor. When the translator, a gray-haired man of nineteenth-century dignity, rose and uttered, he was immediately exhorted by Tatiana, "Lowdah! Lowdah! Cannot hear yuh . . ." The translator went desperately on through these frequent assaults. When the poet spoke, this was sounded in English and Russian, "Lowdah!" Finally, he said that if his hostess would permit, he would recite—and at that moment, Tatiana's chum (actually Alex's—I feel Tatiana detests her) [painter] Helen Frankenthaler, exclaimed quietly but audibly through all of the rooms, "If you'd shut up, Tatiana, we could hear." Tatiana, somewhat quelled, continued to make sounds like a flock of cawing rooks. And so this Lucia-like event proceeded desperately to its end.[59] If Tatiana wished to hold a poetry recital, she should not have given a

---

58. The modernist poet Andrei Voznesensky (b. 1933) gave readings internationally but continued to live in the USSR.
59. Lucia is the pretentious central character in novels by E. F. Benson about the melodramas of small-town life in England.

party. "It will be only one or two people," she told those invited, meanwhile sending out dozens of telegrams summoning her faithful.

DECEMBER 9, 1971  Yesterday was momentous. Alex rang, and I went in to see him. We both laughed at the oddity of life. He practically told me that I might become the *Vogue* features editor, and then he suggested that "we go along quietly."[60] I asked for $15,000, including one piece a month, after which anything I write is paid at the going *Vogue* rate. He said that he might have trouble with the money. Alex is so bloodless. He would do much to benefit *Vogue* and even more to keep his art-life going. He and Tatiana seem to have grown closer— more in alliance. He has a huge, painstakingly neat, black table—an enlarged Parsons table kept at grand-piano polish—and on one of his walls a poster of one of his exhibits. So we parted—he a severe, thin, dark-suited figure, in his brilliantly white office, an office like a burst of light, standing behind his black table. "Good day, Eminence," I said. I have that strange calm which, coming from somewhere, isolates me when I am pushing through danger.

In Kessler:[61] "July 9, 1929—Max Reinhardt's new production of *Die Fledermaus* at the Deutsche Theater. Press and gala performance, by invitation only. *Tout* Berlin . . ." Laci did the costumes. I read this book knowing the awful end [brought by Hitler], and that makes for a kind of greatness bestowed on Kessler's document by history. Reading Kessler, I understand much better that in all of Ela's deepest relationships—Reinhardt, Rathenau, Toscanini—she was only an episode, but she, believing each to be the whole world, worshiped them throughout her life. I envy Kessler his succinct pinpointing ability. I haven't read the unedited version—however, I miss the personal. His diary, in this form, is externalized. Where is the passionate man? Such an ability to catch personages, so many specimens, but Kessler describes more than interprets. He is a chronicler, but does he also create?

DECEMBER 18, 1971  Morning with Marlene. Yesterday the beat of a sob— fright—in her voice—constant. The scene between Rudi and Marlene in the farmhouse, in the [San Fernando] Valley, when he told her that she had alienated everyone, and so had no friends—only those because she had been Dietrich, and she said almost everyone had died. "I went into my room and lay down without undressing, and in the morning, very early, I went away without saying good-bye. . . . He is sick . . . I see it in his eyes . . . You can always tell by the eyes . . . I have a crying jag . . . I never had that . . . I don't give in." She is frightened for the first time in her life—nothing more to sell.

Mrs. Pat Campbell, viewing the Gielgud *Hamlet* [in 1936], asked why

60. Liberman was intimating that Leo could have Allene Talmey's former job.
61. Leo was reading the recently translated diaries of Count Harry Kessler (1868–1937), an Anglo-German writer and patron of modern art.

Judith Anderson, the queen, sat on her bed during the closet scene. "Only housemaids sit on the bed," said Mrs. P. C. A little anecdote that summarizes a whole way of life.

DECEMBER 26, 1971 · BETHEL, CONNECTICUT An organ playing jazz is an elephant doing a soft-shoe.

Talking last night [here] to Mina, I said, "The American Revolution was not a revolution: It was a rebellion. All revolutions, starting with Cromwell's, destroy or deteriorate all levels of society, making an upheaval during which new social levels rise. The motion is inevitable—up from below and down from above. Rebellions can fail. Revolutions cannot. They are triumphant failures."

I have long wanted to write a book about Pauline Viardot-García. Berlioz adored her. She was Turgenev's mistress, the prototype of the woman in *A Month in the Country*. If Ela had been a good actress, she would have been perfect in that role. Ruth Gordon [in 1950] was amazingly good—rather Garboesque. (Garbo would have been too shut-in—too surface right.) Viardot was sister of Malibran, daughter of García.[62] She seemed to live forever—actually spanning the nineteenth century. Pianist, actress, great voice (both soprano and mezzo), intellectual, no beauty, but of great fascination, an enchantress— Dickens, Tolstoy, Tchaikovsky, Berlioz all were captivated by her. Her grand-nephew and pupil died in London, 1946. Viardot composed songs, taught, and at a great age sang exquisitely in a drawing room. She sang the premiere of Berlioz's *La Captive* and, I think, Meyerbeer's *Le Prophète* (the blind woman). She sang both Orpheus and Alceste (Gluck) with Berlioz and sang Cassandra in the only public performance of [the Berlioz opera] *Les Troyens*. She was also a painter and linguist. She's in the Pasta-Callas line—a great monument.[63] But her correspondence is held by nieces who won't release it.

DECEMBER 28, 1971 Maria on blower: "Someone's been in town. I've been seeing him. He's awful ... sad ... in a bad time. And who wasn't even touched? Me! He needs a shoulder to cry on, so he came to me. He's not so young anymore." (a note of triumph) "But I know what I'm after—my voice, *Tosca*'s not what it was—but I'm getting there. . . . The skunk!"

DECEMBER 29, 1971 Sam Green[64] about Garbo: "When I spent the weekend with her and Cécile [de Rothschild] and Cecil [Beaton], I hadn't even seen a

62. Pauline Viardot-García (1821–1910) was daughter of Manuel García (1775–1832), a Spanish tenor, teacher, and the composer of nearly a hundred operas, and sister of Maria Malibran (1808–36), a celebrated and volatile mezzo-contralto.
63. Italian soprano Giuditta Pasta (1798–1865) had, as did Callas, a wide, if uneven, vocal range and a gift for poignant dramatic interpretation.
64. The private art broker Samuel Adams Green (b. 1940) later became director of the monument-preserving Landmarks Foundation.

Garbo movie. . . . I'm beglamoured. . . . I was so embarrassed by Cecil.[65] Why did he do it? He says he's never coming to America again." Sometimes Sam seems so Yiddish. "Well," he said, "most of my friends are Jewish."

Sam is an inheritor of my search for the Grand Surprise. He carries on the continuity into the twenty-first century.

JANUARY 1, 1972  Having just finished (for the eighth or ninth time) the "Overture" to [Proust's] *A la Récherche*, I am overwhelmed by the beauty, the profundity, the limpid mind, the eyes, in that morsel of the grand whole, that scrap of miraculous terrain—especially the final pages, from the duchess's entrance at the wedding in the church, to the last word, "day."

Meanwhile, another miracle continues its torrential outpouring by my side—*Das Rheingold*. Those Spanish rhythms, so sharply accented in this recording. These voices, women's, which shoot up out of the dark earth like flowers, flowers now born in my ears, never before born anywhere in time, in space . . . I can hear their radiant, pale colors (how wrong most of the descriptives are in these last scribblings). There is such a madness in this music, such a tenderness. Wagner made audible the caress. Yet his tensions, even when small by design, are monumental. Listening to Wagner is always like traveling through ranges of mountains, each more overwhelming, through size or beauty or sheer being, than those traversed—the sudden, sweeping vast forests—the shimmer, the sheen, all sunlight fluttering—a vastness of soaring, wings in motion—running, that happens in Wagner constantly—the sound of a single bee enlarged to a magnificent thunder—sense of alarums. In Proust's opening pages, night—hurrying through the night. Certain pages of Proust, Beethoven, and Wagner are linked by this sense of distant hurrying, by carriage, by horse, through night. And in Wagner such a sense of covert evil, snide evil, the evil beneath the winking eye, the grimace that is mistaken by the unwary for an open smile.

JANUARY 2, 1972  [The painter] Ellen Oppenheim said: "We stopped fighting, my mother (Stella Adler) and I, when she bought a house one mile down the road. You can fight with your mother, but you can't fight with your neighbors."

JANUARY 5, 1972  The rituals practiced by my family, and everyone we knew in Jewish [East] Harlem, in Flatbush, Brooklyn, the Bronx Grand Concourse, Washington Heights: No one went to visit anyone without "taking a little something." No one went anywhere unless "their" underwear was clean.

---

65. A month earlier, *Newsweek* had revealed that Cecil Beaton's forthcoming volume of diaries would contain explicit accounts of his affair with Garbo in 1947–48.

"What if you fall down in the street? What if something happens?" "It's a *shanda* and sport for the neighbors!" Always, everything "for the neighbors," meaning you lived up to their dicta.

No one bought from the hokey-pokey man.[66] No one played with matches, hitched rides on ice wagons or anything else, "ate Chinese" or anything else not kosher. Of course, many children did the first two (even some tomboys), and my father most certainly did the last. (He sucked clams, eggs.) When you saw nuns from the church ("cathedral") down the street, you made the sign against the evil eye and chanted "7, 6, 5, 4, 3, 2, 1." Nuns were seen to become terrified before our eyes, and the more timid fled like crows along 106th Street, flying east to their nests. The significance of *goyim:* "Such a nice man . . ." the voice filled with amazement that a *goy* could be a nice man, a voice brimming with distrust.

The *mishpoche* [clan]—they were all the world, no one else mattered, and the *mishpoche* included kissing cousins, honorary uncles, and even aunts—*machetunim* [extended in-laws]. A range of personalities in which individuality was necessary for survival, and honor thy father and mother and grandparents and all uncles was the rock upon which the system was solidly built: "My son—what he's gonna do for me." "Mrs. Levi's son, the dentist, he makes his mother a paradise!" "A golden girl, she does everything for her mother—everything. She doesn't make a move, without her mother's say-so."

The week was systematized. Each day's eating followed week after week, identical food on its night—a basic, solid, ritualistic system. The family weekly cycle—washing on Monday, baths on Friday (in the daytime) or Saturday (at night), etc., fitted into larger, seasonal cycles—spring cleaning, covers on furniture for the summer, October moving day, straw hats on telegraph poles on Labor Day, June walks with maypoles. These larger cycles were common to middle-class families—both *yiddim* and *goyim.*

JANUARY 11, 1972 A friend took me to the only pornographic movie I have ever seen. Intensely heterosexual and unbelievably sexless and repetitiously dull. I was titillated only at seeing large cocks, but not for long (no pun), and once at a cock being rubbed on a cunt . . . too dreary. . . . Yet the actors, almost all present, seemed usual, rather nice, young people. That interested me. The boys get $50, the girls $100. There are more boys available. Stars get $100. It all resembles early movie days.

JANUARY 17, 1972 Puss on his return [from California] came to sleep here again, and how lovely this is.[67]

66. Hokey-pokey was cheap ice cream sold by street vendors.
67. From 1956, when Gray and Leo took over 1453 Lexington entirely, they had kept separate bedrooms but slept together in Leo's room, excepting when they had an overnight guest, one of them was ill, or an argument stood unresolved.

JANUARY 31, 1972 Robert Phelps on Glenway: "Not until he was thirty-five did he face what he really liked and wanted. One day, at Stone-blossom [their home in New Jersey], he came downstairs and, through a slightly open door, he saw Monroe and George Platt Lynes making love. He watched, fascinated, and then ran off into the woods and was sick and masturbated and realized that this is what he wanted most—voyeurism. So, thereafter he lived in triangles. Then Dr. Kinsey came along and laughed Glenway into complete realization." Did Glenway think I would be part of a triangle with Robert Davison? Is that the explanation? Will Robert Phelps find the explanation while preparing his Glenway book?[68]

FEBRUARY 4, 1972 Jerry [Robbins's] new work [*Watermill*]—genius.[69] He is the only first-rate creative force now working at full strength in that world. This is a total departure, and so only time will make it comprehensible. I was utterly absorbed, so much and so deeply that I ached—actually ached all over. Some brutish dowds booed this work that leads to a new world. I must see it again. The long Balanchine discipline gave Jerry the [New York City Ballet] dancers, but only Jerry's genius made them into this superb creation.

Then to Lincoln [Kirstein], after these years of silences. Fido more distraught than ever. No change in Lincoln, save he seems more fragmented (not the right word—disjointed? agitated?) and more ruefully smiling. Impossible to know whether he is drunk or pilled. The cupboards jammed with pussums [cats], where once his mother's pink china had gloried—now all broken. Lincoln is an overwhelming presence—his bulk and the knowledge that he is unpredictable. Puss says of Lincoln: "Such a strong man. Very childlike, like you and your mother, and so petulant and crazy—a child ogre."

FEBRUARY 5, 1972 A lovely evening. Maria, after dinner: "Let's face it. I'm not gonna hit the road again!" In her new teeth, Maria really confirms *The Makropulos Affair*.[70] She looks younger than she did fifteen years ago. And: "I hate opera—so old-fashioned. I detest it—but it is what I do—what I can do— what I'm good at." Later: "I'm a very literal woman."

Jennie Tourel: "Look, you know Maria's voice. You know she can't do it.

68. Leo is seeking the explanation for Wescott's brief flirtation with him in January 1948. Biographer Robert Phelps was editing the journals of Glenway Wescott. This story as retold by Leo is incredible, as Wescott's companion Monroe Wheeler had brought the photographer George Platt Lynes (1907–55) into their relationship a decade earlier. Wescott and Wheeler did know Dr. Alfred Kinsey, even assisting in his research by setting up homosexual orgies for observation.
69. Influenced by Noh theater and set to music by Teijo Ito, the ballet *Watermill* had premiered the evening before.
70. Janáček opera of 1926, in which a famous singer, revealed to be three hundred years old (the result of an experiment), is now bored and burdened by life's pleasures.

Actually, I was instrumental in her coming to Juilliard. I don't expect her grat-itude. We're not friends. She isn't a voice teacher. She should have told them how to be an artist, not how to open the throat."[71]

FEBRUARY 17, 1972  Peter Lindamood's death—alone, fallen over a tele-phone, in a squalid room in an even more squalid hotel, the Henry Hudson.[72] He was found after four days of being dead, alone. All the life—once so central to New York—the parties and gaieties and jealousies, pride lifted and pride fallen—that whole world almost gone.

FEBRUARY 18, 1972  Peter's funeral was delightful—from the detail of [restau-rateur] Johnny Nicholson putting a vase of daisies on the floor near the coffin, immediately provoking a quiet man into picking this up and surreptitiously placing a saucer under it to save the carpet. Peter would have loved this little stealthy irony and constructed a baroque fantasy out of it, all a comment on manners and mannerisms. Puss said that Peter told him that he wanted his epi-taph to be: "I was never bored."

Puss said: "I've lost every single illusion I've ever had. I want to get out of this place! I want to go so far away. . . ." But how can he go so far away, or even a little distance, from himself? He says: "Why must I take everything, even things that don't concern me, so personally, so seriously? I know, you'll say it is Calvinism, but it isn't. The world is rotten. . . . What we need is a Beaumar-chais crossed with Genet. . . . I'm not wise enough to know how to live sans illusions."[73]

FEBRUARY 20, 1972  I said that how lovely if I could stay here and write my book. Puss said, from his bath, "Which book?" This immediately set up guilt and such. "The one I'm working on . . ." "Like everything else," he said, "it gets away from you. Do you even know where you would start?" I thought: Nobody needs the truth all of the time. I have known for a very long time where to start. This scribbling is temporizing. I must start. I get very tired—but only at sudden low moments do I doubt. I have not ever lost faith in my writing this book.

FEBRUARY 24, 1972  Beverly Sills's art, and it is considerable, when viewed in the context of opera today, it is almost on a level with Maria's. I am talking of

---

71. Mezzo-soprano Tourel (1900?–1973) had been on Juilliard's faculty since 1963 and given master classes at Carnegie Hall.
72. Lindamood underwent several major intestinal surgeries and had been convalescing in a hospital's housing for outpatients.
73. The French dramatist Beaumarchais (1732–99) wrote *The Barber of Seville* and *The Mar-riage of Figaro*. Jean Genet (1910–86) was a French novelist and dramatist whose works (such as *The Maids*) defied both popular and radical moralities.

her acting—ritualistic, as Elizabeth I, very Oriental—underlined by her white makeup, her mask.[74] Maria's comes from within, strained through deep wells of suffering—harsh, torn-out sufferings. Beverly's comes from a lighter temperament. Beverly is more known; I can read it easily. Maria is mysterious. I feel that Beverly's vocalistics are in the Patti-Lind tradition—with some coloring from the Pasta tradition, this having come to her through Maria.[75] Beverly in her being is a great artist. Joan Sutherland isn't an artist: She is a Trilby.[76] God gave her the crystal, Ricky [Bonynge] filled it—all quite natural, but limited— no real musical intelligence or dramatic sensibility—a phenomenon. Beverly and Maria each represent a tradition that ultimately joins in Beverly, as great rivers pour into a bay and so into the vast seas. Both are works of art. Maria has a natural dignity—all of her art pours from this. Beverly hasn't this dignity, naturally. She has gaiety and joy and determination—and she can assume dignity. She can act it. But what about such vulgarities as her waddle in *Roberto Devereux*? And her table rapping—assumed stage business not assimilated into the seeming life being created before your eyes? Compare Maria's actions in *Tosca*, Act II: Maria unexpectedly touches the knife, and the whole bloody consequence flows from this accidental touch. You see it happening. You are glued to life happening in a room—across a gulf, but a real room pulsing with real life. Watching Beverly, you are always conscious of Beverly acting—isn't she wonderful at this—as you are conscious of her brilliant technique, her range. Maria makes you feel that she is. Beverly makes you feel that Beverly is being.

MARCH 17, 1972  Puss told me about her, Maria's, last class—how radiant she was; how she apologized for her behavior the last times; how a line stretched around the block to get tickets; how people sat on the floor; how Elizabeth Schwarzkopf flew in to hear it and how Howard [Gilman] thought that she was Maria's cook; how Maria made a spontaneous speech about the delights of the class, the virtues of the students, praising each individually; how she said that she didn't know whether she would come back, and she didn't know whether she would ever sing again, but that didn't matter—whether she ever sang again or not—the young mattered, these future voices.

Maria's life at a crossroad: It went in a straight line until Onassis—then the hiatus—then Juilliard and a new life. I asked her did she ever want a child: "More than anything."

---

74. Soprano Beverly Sills (b. 1929) had performed on the previous evening as Elizabeth I in Donizetti's *Roberto Devereux*. Leo claimed cousinage (through his Lerman grandmother) to Sills, who was born in Brooklyn.

75. The sopranos Adelina Patti (1843–1919) and Jenny Lind (1820–87) were both songbirds, famous for the range, purity, and control of their voices, rather than for their dramatic technique.

76. The singer hypnotically enslaved by the musician-mesmerist Svengali in George du Maurier's novel *Trilby* (1894).

NOTE: On March 25, Leo was master of ceremonies for a tribute to Richard Rodgers at Broadway's Imperial Theatre. There were songs and reminiscences from most of Rodgers's musical scores, with Mary Martin, Celeste Holm, Leonard Bernstein, and Agnes de Mille among the performers.

MARCH 28, 1972 • NEW YORK CITY
**TO RICHARD HUNTER • MADRID**

Well, I did it. I co-starred with Mary Martin and the others, at the Imperial Theatre. I was onstage over two hours, and I never felt more at home, and I made people laugh and cry, and I had the loveliest time being a Wampas [rising star]! You would have had stage fright for me, and you would have been proud, as would have Miz Feagin. Now that I've been a musical comedy favorite, I can retire—as I did from my movie career. I'm down to everyday life again, although I've even had an offer from the Stratford company (in Connecticut) to come play any of the Bard's clowns I would. I laughed merrily and suggested that they mount the all-male *Macbeth* for me—I to be Lady Macbeth, and Zero Mostel to be Lady Macduff. They didn't think much of this notion, so I guess I've retired in reality. Here we have the longest winter and the shortest money in years. I haven't even paid my taxes. Somehow my little success has given me some courage: I've even made a date to ask for a raise at Condé Nast. I've started reviewing books for *Vogue*. They pay $300 for 600 words. That is a lavish fee. So it goes, and I with it.[77]

**JOURNAL • APRIL 4, 1972** Liv Ullmann—excellent English, accented charmingly, a wide, genuine, smiling nature. She should play comedy, but no one gives her comedy. "Bergman is always saying: You will play comedy. Then the script comes and I am sad and ugly." She is not pretty but beautiful. She believes in the Pope Joan saga. "Oh—you are the first in America who even knows about it," she said, the delight welling up into her honest eyes.[78] She is entirely womanly. Her gestures are as you see them in Degas. Colette would have instinctively been in accord with her movements, her feeling. Everything Liv Ullmann does composes—the way a cat composes—instinctively. She has found Proust. "Swann," she said, "Swann loving . . . I love it. . . . I cannot get out of Proust now." She is deeply literate.

**MAY 19, 1972** Television came to our house.[79] I find something, at least one presentation of deep interest, daily. Several nights past, I saw *Stage Door*

77. Two months later he wrote, "concluded the *Vogue* business—$10,000 only [for consulting] plus writing fees as the writing goes." *Journal*, May 20, 1972.
78. In 1972, the Norwegian actress Liv Ullman (b. 1938) starred in the British film *Pope Joan*, based on medieval chronicles reporting that a woman disguised as a man was elected pope in A.D. 855. Ullmann often starred in films directed by her lover, Ingmar Bergman.
79. Dietrich had given them a set during the fifties, to watch her appearances, but it had not come to the Osborne apartment.

[1937], which made me teary. It is incredibly real—as I knew theater in those days—harsh, glamorous, optimistic, despairing, but with a future—wise-cracking, good-looking, highly individual, and young—amazingly, gloriously young—so much the way we were at Feagin's, but even more one year later, spread out in rooming houses (Mrs. Cornish's on West Fifty-fourth and West Fifty-second, Anni Oakley's [sic] on West Fifty-fourth), at the Footlights Club, in the Penn Astor drugstore (oblivion now—gimcrackery on the site of the Astor) . . . that world gone—but roaring away somewhere in time-space and in *Stage Door*.

Five-hour dinner at Le Pavillon with George Balanchine. Barbara Horgan [his assistant] also present. George pyrotechnical, the way Pavlik [Tche-litchew] was. When George told about Diaghilev, his voice grew higher, bro-ken, had a kind of feminine curve and register. This was obviously Diaghilev being heard by George: "I knew nothing—He took me to museums, churches—He say—Perugino—I look—I see nothing—He goes away— I look—still nothing—nothing—a blob orange—a piece blue—He comes back—'So, tell me. So, you see?' 'No,' I tell him, 'nothing. I see nothing.' 'So, stay here until you see. We go lunch. You no lunch. You stay. . . .' He go— I stay—Later—much later—I see—beautiful—beautiful . . . And always, I look, everywhere for Perugino. Perugino is the only one I know, so I look for him. We came to the Sistine—everyone—Diaghilev, Nijinsky, Stravinsky—look and look. . . . I say, 'See, up there, high—Perugino—small, but Perugino.' 'What Perugino!' they all say. 'No—Raphael, Michelangelo—no Perugino here.' Diaghilev opens Baedecker, which he always carried, and there says—Peru-gino. Later, I saw Michelangelo, Raphael, everyone—but always Perugino first." His talk was nonstop—garlands of words, fantasias of words, floods of thought—all linked by ribbing as delineated as rib constructions of butterflies, darning needles [dragonflies]. George's talk was hoarfrost upon the window-pane. "You must write about art," I said. Sometimes we engaged in duets, but mostly he was solo—and tremendous. "I can't write," he said. "But out of this jungle," I told him, ". . . patches of this jungle are gardens." The gestures— modified wizard gestures—nothing baroque about his gestures, more etched on air. But his talk—a sort of neoclassical base, pure—the thought and words meshed—not padded with images—but pure constructions—imagined facts . . . Five hours of this.

MAY 23, 1972  My birthday—fifty-eight—a beautiful morning. I am waiting for celebration to begin. Yesterday, T came to lunch at the Lafayette. He was properly dressed. "I'm very proper," he said. "I'm the most proper person you know. . . ." He is heavy, even more wise and ageless—to say froglike is not exact—rather, in his face, the way his mouth shapes when within him a smile or laughter grows is ancient frog-elder wisdom. His laugh is still absolutely untrammeled when he loosens it—a rare upward cascade of burnished, disk-shaped joyful noises—pure as it was thirty years ago. I sat looking at this middle-aged, watchful man, and I tried to find Little T. When he laughed he was Little T. When he suddenly hotted up with nostalgia and love he was Little T. We talked about his "affair." "I know it was all wrong," he said. "Everything about it. But it came out of nostalgia—out of longing. I'd known hot, loving, sexy boys when I was young. . . . That kind of memory . . . I can hypnotize myself. I met him at the Spa, that place in Palm Springs—you know . . ." (His voice has a frequent question mark in it, requiring no answer.) "He was everything those boys had been, and irresistibly I was in it—consumed by it, exhausted, exhilarated by it. I could stop. . . . I didn't love Jack less. . . . What? . . . Yes, I think someone told him, but we've never talked about it. Never. I think he tried to approach it several times, but I never let him. . . . No, he's never had anything like that. He has his French. He's wonderful at French. . . . But that affair put me in the hospital. . . . That was two years ago. Last year . . ." His voice was full of self-raillery, recollected emotion, and a little despair. He told me about his young cousin and Steve McQueen, who came every day and ultimately took the twenty-nine-year-old off into a canyon and blew him against a tree. T says he loves living in "our little enclave in Bridgehampton most." He loves his dog, Maggie. "You know, I think female dogs—Maggie (a big English bull) is the first female I've ever had—female dogs are smarter, more intelligent." About his novel: "It's a big book. It grew and grew. Every section—it's all in sections—is novella length. I'm doing the links now—and in one place sixty-seven pages to come—that sort of thing. I don't know if I want it published at all before it comes out. I don't know if it diminishes the surprise. Writing it is like riding a high wire all the time. It's going to shock and blow everything sky-high." He looked highly pleased, amazed, delighted. "I had it read by the lawyers. . . . When [editor Joe] Fox read it, he took to his bed for two days. . . . There's a section called 'Côte Basque,' a two-way dialogue. . . . I don't know what the moral consideration is . . . the legal. . . . I'll talk in confidence first, and then we'll talk all about it. . . ." (For *Vogue*, with whom he has an agreement, which I have now seen—$25,000 given him in 1964, $25,000 to come upon delivery.)

NOTE: During the seventies, Leo and Gray were occasionally invited to the Connecticut home of Alex and Tatiana Liberman or to that of Cleve and Francine Gray, whose property adjoined the Libermans'. Cleve Gray, an abstract painter, had married Francine du Plessix in 1957, and both he and Alex had studios there.

JOURNAL • MAY 26, 1972 • CORNWALL BRIDGE, CONNECTICUT Francine on her eight hours in jail:[80] Felicia Bernstein, standing at the bars of her cell in Washington, chain-smoking, her eyes hot with rage; her thin, frail body quiver-

---

80. Several friends had been arrested recently during an antiwar protest in Washington, D.C.

ing with rage all night long. That is how Francine told this to me, she trembling, slicing her homegrown asparagus smoothly but violently. Her control is superb. Larry Rivers was a shit, taking pictures. Women were treated more harshly than men, but no one was treated badly. One painter said to another, behind bars, "Do you know what Helen [Frankenthaler] would say if she were here?" "Yes," said the other, "I'm here because of my paintings."

The countryside teems with New York horror. Three more "darlinks" will be coming to lunch. [Then] today's dinner—Grace Mirabella and "man." Tomorrow's dinner: Claudette Colbert and "man." Tatiana said to Puss, "You garden in that?" (white duck, etc.). "that Deauville—save for Claudette . . ." Tatiana spent the summer of 1926 with Colette. This visit is more like novels I've read than even Juliet [Duff]'s weekends at Wilton. Rut would be deeply amused. Alex calls Tatiana "Babooosh" (all o's are forever here). Tatiana shows her young legs and thighs. "What would the New Englanders think?" asks Puss. "It's a long way from *Desire Under the Elms*," I say.

MAY 28, 1972 Alex's workshop—I could not believe the Stonehenge quality of his work, the religiosity of his work. He is an important sculptor. How horrible to be tied to his Condé Nast job. Alex's sculpture is the memorial to contemporary decay, obsolescence. He makes it out of gigantic mechanical (technological) parts, components found when huge, overland vehicles die in the nearby highroads, when ships collapse. His sculpture transforms the planned obsolescence into memorials. The most tremendous one is an authentic monument to junkyards, scrap heaps, auto garages.

MAY 29, 1972 Claudette Colbert is a nice woman: practical, a little maidenly raunchy in her talk, well-read, well-lived (a flat in Paris, a flat in New York, a house in Barbados). "She recently looose her girlfriend," says Tatiana. Talk last evening about theater, Claudette and I contributing anecdotes. Claudette always wanted to play Joan of Arc, but had to do *Three-Cornered Moon* instead. She talked about Mary Boland, who, reeling down a corridor while on location, said to Claudette, "Do you know what's wrong with me?" ("I knew," said she, "so did everyone else.") "My body is too big for my feet." Claudette Colbert has a gamine warmth and easy, responsive laughter.

The [Francine and Cleve] Gray party is going to lunch at Philip Roth's. "Are you going to have liver for lunch?" Puss sweetly asked. Tatiana: "Yeah, he fooked the liver all night before—full of vitamins.[81] Dis was Rasputin's sickness. It could never go down. Could do it with everyone—and all women of Petrograd think it personal compliment—even my mother. It never go down. I know." Later she said: "Green—chief psychiatrist of Roosevelt Hospital— I said to Francine—the rich people never knows. Let's have him for friend—for

81. In Philip Roth's novel *Portnoy's Complaint* (1969), a teenager masturbates with raw liver.

godfather. So he come every day for tea—drinks—at five o'clock—and we no need psychiatrist. We have it."

JUNE 24, 1972 • NEW YORK CITY  George Balanchine is interested in staging ballets for people now—not in the future. "I'm absolutely not concerned. There will be different people then. I don't want my ballets preserved for people to laugh at what used to be. . . ." George Balanchine's ballets have not been recorded. What about the film of *Midsummer Night's Dream?*

JUNE 26, 1972  Nicolas Nabokov on Stravinsky:[82] "This non-melodic man, later, never got away from basic, vulgar, corny Russian melody." Nicky about Balanchine: "The fun is how musical he is—making the piano reduction himself. He goes into every room of the music, into every bed, every cupboard. Jerry [Robbins] listens and listens to tapes and makes movement." "Yes," said Lennie. "We were in Jamaica a few months ago, working on our project (*The Dybbuk,* a ballet) and I worked in one part of the house, as Jerry was working on *Canticles* (Stravinsky), in another part, from a cassette, listening over and over and over. Then he would run in and say, 'I've got such a movement!' and show it to me." Nicky: "But George works from inside the music. He is the music."

JUNE 30, 1972  [Publicist and biographer] Patrick O'Higgins on Somerset Maugham. His plans for a book—really a novel. Douglas Cooper told Patrick that he called on Maugham at the Villa Mauresque and found Maugham rising from behind a sofa, where he had been shitting in the drawing room. When he saw Cooper, he scooped up the shit and handed it to him—a fair exchange.[83] The key to Maugham is that he was excessively middle-class, always making the proprieties. He was also a nasty, mean man, part of that backbiting world in which friends were more vituperative than enemies. Someone describing a man said, "He is second-rate Glenway Wescott." Maugham, a friend of Glenway's, said, "How can that be? Glenway is himself second-rate." Apocryphal? I doubt it. Maugham was, of course, a sacred monster.

JULY 14, 1972 • SARATOGA SPRINGS  Balanchine went on quietly (he is always quiet-spoken) about how he does not think, talk, live the past: "Karinska—she has good ideas. She makes beautiful things. She works hard—but she lives in the past. Always she is remembering—living past—what happened

---

82. The composer Nicolas Nabokov (1903–78), cousin of Vladimir Nabokov, had written the score for Balanchine's *Don Quixote* in 1962.
83. Douglas Cooper (1911–84) was a British art historian and collector.

thirty years ago, forty years ago—this little thing—that little thing. I live now. I am not interested in the past."

JULY 22, 1972  Eddie Villella at three a.m. on the pavement:[84] "This is where it is right now. This is where I want to be—lucky to be. Ballet's here with the New York City Ballet—the center—the living center—Balanchine—George's given us glory—the glorious opportunity." Millie [Hayden] said it. Violette [Verdy] said it. Everyone said it. Richard Tanner: "Balanchine's said it all. There's nothing left for me. . . . I've come too late. . . ."[85]

JULY 23, 1972 · NEW YORK CITY  Villella, driving me home, said, "Tonight I had a real trip [*Watermill*]. . . . I went in so deep. When I came off Jerry grabbed me and shook me. He said, 'I want that trip. I want that trip.' " Eddie has Italian humor, deep funniness, and sadness. So many ballet people are Renaissance in looks—from early to high Renaissance.

JULY 28, 1972  Jed Harris—very quiet, carefully enunciated immense erudition, spilling cigarette ash, a constant ebb and flow of marvelous stories, color washed out by his long age.[86] He wore no tie, but his pale lemon-yogurt-colored shirt, silky, was buttoned up under his chin. Harris:

"When I was at Yale, I always wanted a shore dinner at Lenox's (?), but I couldn't afford it. Then years later I had money and I was seeing a lot of Ruth [Gordon]—but I didn't really like her. I told her that I had always wanted a shore dinner at Lenox's. She said, 'Why not?' So we went up there in a car. It was an enormous menu. I am a very abstemious man. I eat very little. Shrimps came in. . . . Ruth ate every one. Lobster . . . soup . . . vegetables . . . steak . . . fresh corn . . . enormous dessert. . . . The more she ate, the more I loathed her. Finally I couldn't stand her. I got up to pay the bill. She stood, leaning against a post—so small, nothing she'd eaten affecting her—so tiny, picking her teeth with a toothpick. I hated her. I wanted to get away from her as fast as possible. Suddenly she shouted 'Wow!' All delight, happiness, triumph was in that 'Wow' and I fell in love with her that minute.[87]

"John and Lionel Barrymore hated the theater. Lionel was in Paris, learning art, and John was living in a furnished room, over a nightclub on Forty-second Street—Leonard's?—with [journalist] Herbert Bayard Swope. John was an

84. Edward Villella (b. 1936) was one of the first American-born male ballet stars. He danced at New York City Ballet from 1957 to 1975.
85. Violette Verdy, Melissa Hayden, and Richard Tanner were all dancers with New York City Ballet.
86. Jed Harris (1900–1979) directed and produced many plays for Broadway (*The Front Page, Our Town, The Crucible*).
87. Ruth Gordon and he had a son, Jones Harris, in 1929.

assistant cartoonist. Ethel [his sister] wanted him to go into the theater. Finally he said all right, and she gave him a small part in a play she was touring. By the time they reached Philadelphia, he was leading her on for curtain calls. He dominated the stage. So when they came back to New York, he went to see his father, Maurice, who was living at The Lambs.[88] Maurice always stayed in bed. He slept only in a pajama top. John said, 'Father, should I be an actor?' Maurice hopped out of bed. 'He had the biggest balls I've ever seen,' John told me. He walked up and down scratching his scrotum. Finally he said, 'Son, if you want to be an artist—you'll be an artist and pick, pick, scratch, scratch. If you want to be an actor—you'll act and you'll fuck. There's nothing better,' then scratching his balls and hopping back into bed. . . .

"Lillian [Gish] never knew that she was inaudible on stage, rehearsing *Uncle Vanya*. She never, never knew. And I didn't tell her. . . ." He provided her with a silent entrance and everyone thought that was genius. "She was no actress. She got by on character."

Jed Harris also told me about how meticulous [drama critic] George Jean Nathan was—and how his rooms in the Royalton [hotel] looked like a college boy's, with a pennant pinned to one wall. "Everything was laid out carefully. Such aridity. I'd read a story in [Nathan's magazine] *Smart Set*, which I worshiped. I believed this story. In it the man had a rain machine attached to his window, so when a girl said she had to go home, he pressed a button and rain poured down and she stayed and . . . well, when I went to see George Jean Nathan, I looked for that rain machine. Of course, he didn't have it. . . ."

He talks excellent Yiddish, quotes Hebrew beautifully, loved Leonard Woolf's books, smokes incessantly, wants Maria C (with whom he's obsessed as a comedian and character) to make a movie of *Dark Eyes* with him. She would be the Russian diva. He says so many of his best effects were accidents. He works on a play even years after it's closed. Ten years after *The Front Page* closed, he suddenly thought that Hildy should have been sniffing a boutonnière gardenia while all the murder excitement and suicide, etc., were going on.

Paula Laurence is having her teeth redone. I said to her, "At last your bite will be worse than your bark."

Did Toscanini or Beecham say to the female cellist: "Madam, you have between your legs one of the greatest instruments devised for the pleasure of man. Can you do nothing but scratch it?" Probably Beecham.

AUGUST 13, 1972 · WASHINGTON, D.C.   I sit, naked, scribbling away on a rickety faux Louis Quinze table, looking out at the redbrick-pathed park at the White House (so cardboard). "Is it a short story," Gray asks, never knowing how thin-skinned I am about scribbling . . . as he inevitably misjudges my wanting him to enjoy things I have seen without him. Yesterday, when I was sad at not

---

88. A prominent theatrical club in New York.

being able to show him the interesting iron stair and vista at the Renwick (it shut off on Saturday), he said, "Never enough. You never have enough." I had seen it. I didn't want it for myself.

AUGUST 22, 1972  Today Alex made a concrete offer (even in the gangster sense), lunching me at the Century Club, in the library. He wants me to become features editor of *Vogue*. In a sense, I've been waiting for that for years.

AUGUST 25, 1972  I told Alex I would come to *Vogue* if the money, etc., could be arranged.

NOTE: In 1972, the Swiss art historian Manuel Gasser, editor in chief of the art magazine *DU*, had the Osborne apartment photographed. Leo wrote the following letter at the time to describe Gray and his decorative style.

AUGUST 28, 1972 • NEW YORK CITY
**TO MANUEL GASSER** • SWITZERLAND?

Two decades ago, these objects (furniture, bibelots, lamps, fabrics, books . . . everything that could, in a sense, reproduce the past, from about the 1840s until the 1914 war) were quite inexpensive, actually to be found in junk shops, in cellars and attics. Many visitors to the house, a typical 1870ish New York brownstone on upper, then unfashionable, Lexington Avenue, found the contents funny. Some even thought the Tiffany glass lamps ugly. Nothing in the collection cost much—the kinds of things one generation adores, the next scorns, and some succeeding covets.

The collections range from horn cups to Staffordshire cottage ornaments to depictions of firework displays to a series of Russian views to Tiffany and other Art Nouveau lamps and glass and furniture to majolica to bucolic and "forest" beast wood carvings to Neapolitan gouaches of Vesuvius to toys (especially dolls) to over 15,000 books. There are, literally, hundreds and hundreds of objects, mostly European or American: (glass [bells over]) waxed fruits and flowers and paper construction arrangements, walking sticks, beadwork cushions, Russian lacquer boxes, dozens of paintings of dogs . . . And all collected out of love for the solid past they represent, collected to return the life in these objects to the times in which we live.

NOTE: Their friend Eileen Maremont enlisted Gray's help to decorate her home in Barbados. Leo and Gray had known her first as Eileen Adler in 1955 London, wife of the harmonica artist Larry Adler, years before her marriage to the wealthy businessman Arnold Maremont. Gray would travel to Barbados five times in the next year. On August 31, 1972, Leo flew down to join them for a week, his only visit.

**JOURNAL** • AUGUST 31, 1972 • BARBADOS  The fisherman, who has been out in the sea ever since—last night?—is near the spearheaded jut of the beach, standing in his low-lying rowboat. I can hear his oars in their locks. His shirt, raspberry-and-cream color, hangs halfway to his knees. His ancient shorts are sawed-off, Italian blue—the color with which they paint their rafters. On his head, a tall peak of straw, which weather has twisted into elegance. This man, I could see through my opera glasses, works exceedingly hard, never stopping. The long-breaking, ever-changing in color and form tides and the sound of them—smoothing, unwrinkling, flashing and flashing and tumbling on the pale, silver-tan beaches . . .

The fisherman is onshore, met by a woman in a black-striped, brief frock—tight to her ample body—her head is turbaned in a smear (at this distance) of scarlet. (I would add coin dots of pumpkin yellow, but that is the fiction of her dress—Strachey's half inch.) Also a male, whose gestures are regal (the inherent regal quality of movement here) and whose dress is pale, much-washed lemon. The three stand examining—the catch?—all akimbo, all animated, busy with onshore matters. The fisherman's hat, now seen closely, is suddenly a flat squash of straw, almost two-dimensional upon the black, cropped head. This, again, makes me wonder: What does one actually see? How much is there and how much do we think is there?

From the house come Eileen and Puss's voices, incessant in "doing" the house. Somewhere shovels scrape against the coral-stone . . . hammering . . . anonymous voices, shreds of them . . . the constant inhalation and exhalation of the tide upon the shore. . . . This house, these gardens and terraces and beaches—a Riviera I have never really known save from a distance. Colette described them. I love overcast days by the sea. These are kind to my eyes. This is the most rewarding place to scribble, on a jutting terrace, overhanging the sea . . . sufficiently divorced from immediate living, but within earshot and eyesight of it.

NOTE: Leo was reading *Before the Deluge,* Otto Friedrich's history of Berlin in the twenties.

JOURNAL · SEPTEMBER 5, 1972 I built cities and eras out of what I heard and what I read. So the Berlin of the twenties, this *Hochzeit* [golden era] was alive in me, fed by endless tales from the brilliant people who had been—those were the key words—had been Berlin's glory and now were New York's refugees—more scorned than venerated, in buses, in taxicabs, on the streets, and in the shops—who drove or fed or waited upon us . . . but to me the refugees were my friends and, indeed, my lovers. They were the living history, in which their past was to be heard constantly—and which inevitably, inexorably, became my past—a past I knew only from their mouths, their gestures and movements, their ways of living, the beautiful princely things they did or no longer knew they did, their embraces and lovemaking. Their Berlin of the twenties, their Viennas and Budapests, became the Berlins, the Viennas, the Budapests of my mind and heart. I absorbed their movements and appearances and became part of them—a *mittel*-European echo in my mustache, my black homburg.[89]

OCTOBER 7, 1972 · NEW YORK CITY [Alexis] Léger showed Mina two letters he'd written to her—one in 1958 and one in 1959. These would have saved her anguish. But he never sent them. "Why?" she asked. "I forgot," he said. They would have made all of the difference in her life. She says: "Maybe he wrote them recently, just to fill in. . . ." She will never know. They will appear in the Pléiade edition of his works. He clung to her. "Such a small, frail, clinging man now," she said, of this man who had been the last giant in her life.[90] Dot [his wife] cannot leave him alone—he's so infirm, but his mind is unimpaired, and "he talked incessantly—so many tales of his childhood and youth. Old people do that. I almost died after an hour—so exhausting. Also my hearing aid couldn't take more. . . ." The spectacle of these two *grands amoureux* in this plight.

Then, in Yorkshire, Lincoln confessed [to Mina], "I don't know how you'll take this, but many times I've been taken for your husband." "Oh," said Mina, "that's so flattering—you being ten years younger." So that came to this pass, that incestuous passion.

OCTOBER 10, 1972 I went to the Sachs [gallery] on Fifty-seventh Street to see Betty Parsons's paintings,[91] and there I found an assortment of elderly women who greeted me with joy. Only when I somehow unfocused these seamed, other-shaped faces, so confidently presenting themselves for friendly kisses, did I perceive within each quite unfamiliar visage the face of some other person I had once known well. Here were women I had seen or chatted with daily— a *danse macabre*—even Buffie Johnson, looking quite as she did thirty years ago running down Fifty-seventh Street. Meanwhile, making all of this even more macabre, Ruth Stephan (née Walgreen, now Franklin) queened—or princessed, that is it—in a sort of Valois topcoat and hat, looking quite unchanged. Only she survives this chaos of time, continuing to inhabit her fairy tale, while all others have become those anonymous old women and men who make up lamenting choruses in verse plays. Then Rita Petersen came up

89. "Frequently I did not understand a word uttered amongst them, but I could read the turn of a head, the tilt of eyes during listening or silences. I had known these in my infancy. I had had to perfect my instinctive knowledge, and now, because of my long-ago great-aunts and -uncles, I was not a foreigner to these foreigners." *Journal*, July 27, 1981.

90. Alexis Saint-Léger Léger (pseudonym Saint-John Perse, 1887–1975) was a Nobel Prize–winning French poet, diplomat, and consultant (1940–57) to the Library of Congress. "Mina and Alexi were lovers some seventeen years. The evidence, a shred of it, is the sign-board on Alexi's house [in Giens] on the Riviera. Mina gave him that house." *Journal*, February 2, 1980.

91. Betty Parsons (1900–1982), a watercolorist, was most influential as an art dealer who nurtured Abstract Expressionists.

and told me that Cesco [von Mendelssohn] had died three weeks ago, suddenly, of heart failure, and he had left her a legacy. Cesco dead . . . His quiet, lobotomized years spent doing crossword puzzles. I wondered whether Rut immediately took him in tow and is looking after him. I must believe that they will all be there to make that life as remarkable as this has been. They help, by being there—even if I only believe this in my last moments. Cesco dead . . . and these weird, Bohemian sisters survive—all of them out in daylight for Betty's vernissage.

**TO RICHARD HUNTER • LONDON**

Bless you for insisting that I see Dr. Berliner [the ophthalmologist]. Now, you must promise, on our forty years friendship and love, not to tell anyone what I am going to tell you. Only Gray and [brother] Jerry will know, because if anyone I work for finds out, they will think that I will no longer be able to handle my jobs.

I am fast losing the sight in my right eye, because the cataract there is ripening. This, in itself, would not be that important, since the usual operation could fix it into usefulness, but, apparently, because of the eye sickness I had years ago,[92] an operation could lead to pretty awful results—such as blindness in that eye. The left eye is going, but more slowly. Berliner thinks I could last until spring. I could even last, miraculously, for a longer time, but he does say that an operation—a drastic one—will be necessary. For some reason I feel relieved and, curiously, optimistic. I can use my eyes, until the crucial time, as much as possible. I am having a variety of new glasses made. I will wear glasses on the street as frequently as possible.

My beautiful teeth, my eyes, etc. Ah well, I grow into an ever-more fascinating monster. Also, I am even thinner and can wear more of my glamorous togs. Be of cheer—I am. And Puss seems to be. He is always better when I have an emergency—which is all this is.

**JOURNAL • OCTOBER 27, 1972** The curious sense of finding the photograph taken of me in 1937 (onstage at the Mansfield Theater, in my blue twin-sweater set, me trim beneath a good, herringbone Uncle Irving suit—gray, I think) in an envelope with a letter from Jerrie Maxwell's husband sent from Ireland, telling me that she had [recently] discovered this among her things, having kept it all of these years.[93] I looked at that twenty-three-year-old boy and thought, "He's nice looking!" The taxi carrying me to Condé Nast crept for-

---

92. The conjunctivitis that had temporarily blinded him in November 1953.
93. Mary Jane "Jerrie" Maxwell, a friend from Leo's high-school theater group, had then been killed in an auto accident soon after finding that photograph. It had been taken when he was stage-managing *Behind Red Lights*, in which he got her a part.

ward, while I crept backward in time. Written on the reverse side of the photograph, in Jerrie's meticulous, early-this-century-taught hand, the pencil curves bright: "My . . . nice looking and so sweet . . ." My being filled with regret at the loss, at not having been told that I was nice looking. I never knew. I feel this nostalgia at not knowing, at believing that I wasn't a looker at all. . . .

Last night, I got me up in my black velvet corduroy $83 plushy suit from Barney's, put on a shirt from Turnbull Asser, took out the homburg I bought in London from Locke in 1951 (now put on for the first time), the Cardin black evening-tie from Bonwit, and the Cardin bronze dancing pumps, over my one-dollar purple socks. I got my Lennie-style stick and went off to the Miró opening at the Guggenheim, where I was a sensation. I knew it, because I had costumed the part brilliantly, and in that huge motley I stood out—distinguished, not freakish. That was for Jerrie Maxwell and for me. I enjoyed it all immensely—and I hope that that boy did too.

A long blower talk with Little T—He, just returned from preparing a documentary at San Quentin, was wild with his life—a criminal stabbed to death and dead in his arms: "I was drenched in his blood—drenched in it!" Then: "Saint[-Subber] and I were having dinner in Orsini's two nights ago, and suddenly his face went white and a whole side of it fell in. . . . It was awful. . . . I rushed him to Roosevelt. . . . He's all right now. . . . And I had Lee Radziwill, hysterical over Peter Beard, on the Coast. She's gone to England to arrange a divorce. He's bad news, isn't he? Maybe she won't marry him, but she thinks she will. . . . And Amanda [Burden] in that [divorce] mess . . ." I said, "You've arranged it all—an end for your book. All of your 'Answered Prayers' getting their answers."[94] We chatted away as we did years go. "I always wish," he said: "Don't let anyone doing a piece on me go near Leo Lerman. . . ."

OCTOBER 28, 1972  A Mrs. Levy I had met at the Hirschfelds, on the blower saying she was publicizing the wildest happening today. From noon to midnight, Charlotte [Moorman] would be in a tank underwater, playing her cello—and other such Dada, dated, hit-the-bourgeoisie-in-the-eye highjinks—the Christo curtain—all of that. I told her that she should earn her money, since she needs it, but that this had all been assaulted and it was unnecessary now. Presently, I thought that, like the "revolution" in fashion, now subsided into squareness again, the Dada antics of recent years were dead—almost dead. We are in the ground swell of a return to all sorts of squareness. Mrs. Levy said she'd been working for [Senator George] McGovern, and the people in his office were just as disorganized as those putting on today's happening. We are, indeed, in amateur times and the evil men are the pros. Is evil always well organized? Satan was organized.

94. "Answered Prayers" was to be the title of Capote's magnum opus about New York society, toward which he had begun making notes as early as 1958.

NOVEMBER 14, 1972  Jean Stafford[95] told me about coming away from an American Academy of Arts and Letters meeting today with [historian] Henry Steele Commager, who put upon his head the strangest covering she had ever seen. She felt that they had become such instant friends that she could tell him how strange his headgear was. "Yes," he said, "it's a breadwrapper. I fancied hats when I was young and always lost them. So I hit upon breadwrappers. Of course, I have to travel far to find round ones large enough, but the money I save on hats more than makes up for it." Jean loved him: "Such a small, twinkly, pop-up of a man . . ." Her talk is in jolts—as though she were puffing on a cigarette—long deep puffs—or jerky and jolty with booze . . . but she did come through with her "On My Mind" [copy for *Vogue*].

NOVEMBER 18, 1972  An important day: I became consulting feature editor of *Vogue*, and remained contributing editor of *Mademoiselle* and senior editor of *Playbill*. I saw Diana Vreeland's red hell, which suite I am to occupy—also was rung up for "the story" by *Women's Wear Daily*—and all sorts crowded in— some weeping because they thought *Mademoiselle* would suffer.

NOVEMBER 19, 1972  Federico Pallavicini—as light, beautifully mannered, and full of gaiety and observation and graces as ever—a bit plumper— a delight.[96] He found that the eight chairs I bought in Barbados are Thonet, from Vienna, marked. We are deeply pleased—from Vienna, by way of Bar- bados and the De Acosta family [furniture manufactory]! Federico's stories are the best. The Cavalli saga: How [Cavalli's mother-in-law], a Russian princess, was so fat that her private train, which took her from St. Petersburg to Florence, was a boxcar that she fitted up with Gobelins and palms and rare carpets, which stopped in goods yards and sidings en route—Warsaw, Berlin, everywhere. Local royalties came out to greet her—bowering her in blooms and being wined and dined by her—caviar, all of it—a royal progress in a freight car through the sidings of Europe. Later, her daughter who married Cavalli lived in a palazzo in Venice, with [photographer] Baron de Meyer's furniture, and was a great friend of Rut's. Federico frequently slept in Réjane's bed.[97]

Federico has layers and layers of mannerisms derived from great ladies,

---

95. Jean Stafford (1915–79) was a novelist and short-story writer. She married poet Robert Lowell, then journalist A. J. Liebling.

96. Baron Federico von Berzeviczy-Pallavicini (1909–89), a Swiss-born set designer and magazine art director (*Flair*), started out in the twenties dressing windows at the luxurious Viennese confectionery Demel. During the thirties, he made a *mariage blanc* with the niece of Demel's Jewish owners, which allowed her to enter a convent under his name and survive the war. She died in 1965, leaving Demel to Pallavicini.

97. Gabrielle Réjane (née Gabrielle-Charlotte Réju, 1857–1920) was the leading player of light comedy in Paris at her time.

whole female families he knew when he was a child—a history of *Die Elegante Welt*—the continental world of luxe—Vienna, Rome, Paris, Budapest, Berlin, St. Petersburg—the gestures of that female world preserved in Federico's body language—and he born in Switzerland, *par hazard*, of a mother there from Vienna. Beneath the genuine rare lace of his movement and talk: a collected, ever-shrewd man, as capable as any man of those women was of a good stroke of business—or passion. He is a loving, wise-eyed, worldly, be-and-let-be man.

NOVEMBER 27, 1972    How to write Federico? How his little noises—so expressive, communicative, allusive—make a tree he describes come to life—trunk, boughs, twigs, flights of leaves. He paints, with these noises, on air. How layers of Austro-Hungarian high life flash before us, while he unreels sagas such as Ouida never dreamed upon her purple pages. The history of his uncle Wy und Wy (that is how the name sounds), an archbishop more girl than boy: When in the Lido, a rich woman showed him her vanity case, and he immediately powdered his nose from it. And his sister—very *hochgeboren* [highborn]—more man than girl—ran off and married a girl in [Venice's] San Marco, and the emperor, out of his own purse, paid to keep the scandal quiet. This lady-man ruled Viennese society using a scandal sheet she edited and wrote. No one could afford to omit her from the lists. And the history of [society portraitist] Boldini (a dwarf who pounced on his sitters—and assaulted them sexually) and his two wives, the last Madame Boldini still alive in Paris . . . Such heady chronicles pour out of Federico—a whole fantastic world now lost.

DECEMBER 3, 1972    Dr. Berliner says the eye operation will be absolutely necessary. I can, he mentions, wait until spring. Meanwhile, a third pair of spectacles—trifocal. The immediate danger is loss of depth perception, which caused me to spill a cup of coffee recently. I must not only build up a bank account but must build up a reserve of courage and health—physical and mental—and some method of writing to immediately replace the way I do it now, in case I am blinded, even partially. But having had so much luck in my life, I cannot believe luck will desert me forever. It will seem to go, but it will not go—and I have been so much loved—actually loved.

The Coward [revue *Oh, Coward!*]—I did not realize how brilliant, feeling, and sentimentally romantic Noël is—a practical romantic. I heard, constantly, Ela's voice and Noël's and Gertie's and Bea [Lillie]'s and, scoffingly, Marlene's. I was feeling: Ela a suicide-murder, walking to that destiny—really running—all of her life, Bea mad, Gertie dead of cancer, and Noël—really an invalid. Marlene goes on, a marvelous wreckage upon whom the moon never sets.

DECEMBER 17, 1972  Alex Liberman told [art critic] Barbara Rose that after Barney Newman died, he closed off all human relationships.[98]

DECEMBER 18, 1972  Marlene to dine with us at Pearl's. She was infinitely touching, even more touching than boring, in her long, long tirade against her television show.[99] "I'm so pretty," she said, "I could throw up." When I asked about the children, she ignored the question. She is not going to Christmas with Noël. She told the *Times* that she was, to get away from papers. "He's a dying man," she said—looking lost, alone, sturdy, but fragile. To have nothing is sad, but to have had everything, including great beauty, is sadder.

DECEMBER 20, 1972  The tucked-in, slightly bewildered, feel-of-bitter-knowledge look on Marlene's face. "It seems that I did everything wrong—to people. I didn't know that." Her silence when asked about the children. Not a word—a chasm opened, icy. Then on to something else. But about Rudi—sweetness and Mother Earth feelings. "The evening . . . around six . . . that's the bad time for him. . . . No one to talk to . . . everyone is dead. . . . The animals are taken care of . . . only the television . . ."[100]

DECEMBER 19, 1972 • SAINT MARYS, GEORGIA
TO RICHARD HUNTER • MEXICO CITY

*Vogue* goes apace. I haven't worked so hard since I was stage manager at the Grossinger. I love it. I write this instinctively—like a bird flying. Yesterday was the most difficult seeing because there is so very much bright light here [at Howard Gilman's]—beautiful, clean-shining, radiant—but making seeing for me almost impossible. I was deeply depressed, but I am out of the slough now.

I had two sessions with George Cukor—very like a somewhat prettier Edna Ferber and full of good anecdotes. I liked him, but always the feeling that I put my nickel in and the Pianola played the tunes it had played many times before.

JOURNAL • DECEMBER 22, 1972  Marlene told me that she was going to spend the holidays with Rudi. No one else wants her. That is why she could not even talk about Maria and the children.

---

98. Barnett Newman (1905–70) had been one of the initiators of Color Field painting. He and Alex Liberman became friends in the early sixties, when Newman's work inspired Liberman to instill a spiritual element into his own minimalist paintings.
99. Dietrich's show *I Wish You Love* had been filmed in London for television. It appeared first in America.
100. Rudi Sieber's longtime lover, Tamara Matul, had died in 1965.

DECEMBER 29, 1972 The comedy of Robert MacBride's research into Diana Vreeland's life. She wanted an "autobiography" written, so T procured MacBride to do it. MacBride diligently unearthed all sorts of concealed-behind-the-arras facts—such as D.V. is Jewish, both sides.[101]

JANUARY 6, 1973 Watching [the revived musical] *Irene*, I suddenly realized that working with Alex at *Vogue* was like having an opening night every day.

 I am reading Cecil [Beaton]'s forties diaries—a tremendous ramble fraught with historical and semi-historical chichis (this period argot applies) . . . rather like a semi-official sightseeing tour along a back road of history, which road sometimes has to join the main highway. The Garbo sections are the most vital—sometimes silly. Like over-embroidery on a fine fabric, his sissiness threads the sincere fabric of his emotion. I cannot doubt the sincerity of his emotions over Garbo. I can only continue to feel the basic insecurity of his life—or is it a kind of prodigious triviality?—chichi is the word. But surely any person exterior to my life would feel this about me. "How do you maintain your standards, standing as a real lover of literature—all that—a real being—and the life you have elected—*Vogue, Mademoiselle?*" the woman married to the museum man asked me. There it is. But my truth is so deep in me. Perhaps Cecil's truth is equivalent. When he was agonizing over that dreary, tall, American boy, seven years ago, Cecil's agonizing was sincere, his tramping over mountains, camping out in sleeping bags, although seemingly so ridiculous, was sincere. Cecil thinking himself in love is in love.[102] Nevertheless—here and there he strikes authentic, revealing notes. He makes people live. But these diaries are deficient in humor, and only the Garbo sections seem unleashed out into a life of their own.

JANUARY 8, 1973 So Cord Meyer, Jr., the World Federalist leader, is a CIA chief.[103] How the world topsy-turvies. Those years ago, when he and Mary [Pinchot Meyer] were our neighbors, and he was all for glorious freedom—a rich boy married happily to a pretty, rich girl whose sister (Rosamund Pinchot) had tragically killed herself in a pact with Cesco Mendelssohn, who didn't keep his part of the agreement (!). Then the Cord Meyers moved to Washington.[104]

 Mary was Scotty Fitzgerald Lanahan's closest friend. They wheeled their babies in carriages side by side: Mary pretty, in an old-fashioned rose-in-bloom

101. The freelance writer Robert MacBride collaborated with Capote on several unrealized television projects in the early seventies.
102. Cecil Beaton's decade-long romance with a San Francisco high-school teacher (identified in his diaries simply as "Kin") began in 1963.
103. The previous day the *New York Times* had published an account of the CIA involvement of Cord Meyers (1920–2001), begun in 1951.
104. Mary Pinchot Meyer (1920–64) was an artist, her sister Rosamund Pinchot (1904–38) an actress.

way; Scotty a worn, good-looking girl—rather like her father [F. Scott Fitzgerald], and a bit like her mother [Zelda]. Then Mary was murdered in Washington, Scotty became a Washington social force, and Cord [already was] a CIA man. Curiouser and curiouser.[105]

And now [journalist] Merle Miller wiring the Cord Meyer revelations with a photo of Cord and Mary—he a very young, very vulnerable boy, eyes on an everyone-loving-one-another-and-mankind future. I never suspected that Merle was queer, in that long-ago worldly innocence of the Lanahans' annual garden party and Mary's stop-bys—and all the world lilacs and promises at 1453.

JANUARY 14, 1973 Marlene's television broadcast, at last. Not as bad as she said it would be. Actually, quite touching and fascinating, although too static, demonstrating that what is electric in a theater is not on the television screen. The serious songs came across better. She looked extraordinary—quite beautiful, and sometimes the essence is joyful, precious beauty. After, on the blower, she seemed calmer to have it over.

JANUARY 16, 1973 Noël's gala [*Oh, Coward!*]. The photo in the morning's *Times* told it all: Marlene and Noël tight together, two very old, very worn people—worn by their talent, their beauty, their wit—exhausted by time and horror at what time did to them. I have rarely seen two so vulnerable. And last night midst their near-peers—two old troupers, she all Wendy-love and he all of the Lost Boys in one very sick old, old man. Valentina came in Garbo's curls and clutched me intermittently.[106] I took Anita [Loos] who was the youngest person there. "Thank you for getting me out of my rut," she said.

JANUARY 31, 1973 Quick look-in at Horst and Hansl [assisting] who were photographing Truman's menagerie for me, in Little T's U.N. Plaza flat, while Truman is in Palm Springs. The flat was in an appalling condition. Obviously T got away at some last minute—ties, underwear, manuscript pages, trash, shirts helter-skelter in his bedroom—a chaos. Hats everywhere, one tossed onto the famous Tiffany wisteria lamp. Dog shit on the pretty late Victorian carpet. I thought it a practical joke, but Horst warned, "It's real. . . ." The menagerie ranged from tacky to splendid, Woolworth to fine eighteenth-century Japanese

---

105. "Mary was killed while strolling along the banks of the canal near Georgetown, where she lived. Her diary, which possibly contained revelations of an intimacy with John Kennedy and of his murder, was never found, Ben [Bradlee] being suspected of having taken it." *Journal, June 21, 1986.* Bradlee, *Washington Post* executive editor from 1968 to 1991, confirmed in his autobiography that the diary had been found by another and later burned by Bradlee's wife, Mary Meyer's sister Antoinette.

106. Fashion and costume designer Valentina Schlee (1894–1989) and Garbo had been friends until Schlee's husband, George, became Garbo's constant companion. After his 1964 death, Schlee and Garbo didn't speak.

ivory. A wall-covering painting of fish is the aquarium section of this zoo. No taste, not even an eye, but a sense of old-child fun and sensitivity to curious and colorful objects—a dim stirring of souk—and anything he could capture from his self-made past.

"Bring me your old beauties," cried Diana Vreeland. "I hate the modern. But everyone said, 'What's the old girl doing in the museum—dead things. She loves the alive!' . . . Well, this is where the action is. . . . Look at all of these young people. . . . When someone breaks a date with me, for luncheon, and says she has to be in Washington, and I find out she's been seen lunching in New York—that's nothing—that's arranging your life. But when she sits opposite and lies—lies about business—that's lying. . . ." Diana in the museum—her silhouette—her aura. The technology of that place. "It's immaculate—surgical." Diana: "I've thought about it, and there's no reason why, after a long life dedicated to fashion and beauty and fantasy . . ." (She went on elaborating—Salzburg baroque isn't in it!) ". . . no reason why I should not be photographed moving down the corridors of history . . ."

FEBRUARY 6, 1973  Norman Mailer's fiftieth birthday party at the Four Seasons. Everyone there, but a bust—pay as you celebrate. A rabble of intellects, sycophants, Mailer groupies, politicals, Warhols—a paprika of hysterics—a bust. The chief ingredient—ego, in each and every performance and would-be performance.

FEBRUARY 21, 1973  This afternoon to look over Mrs. Onassis's "new" library, shuffled by [decorator] Harrison Coultra and his partner. Nothing much, as interior decoration, but interesting because it is hers. John [Kennedy, Jr.] actually rules this "family" room now. But Mrs. O did say what she wanted: Indian fabrics on the visible walls, the bookshelves crammed with red leather bound books, the desk quite good early nineteenth-century English (the one on which the first Nuclear Test Ban Treaty was signed, now used and ink-stained by John doing his "studying"), nothing too fragile, because he is always throwing pillows cased in old Liberty silk scarves and hiding behind the curtains. A reddish-brownish rectangular room looking out over the frozen reservoir—conversation-piece paintings on the walls—but somehow verging on impersonality. The "living" room quite pretty—all cream and rose, color splattered, masses of enchanting watercolors and drawings. Good Greek heads and a fine Egyptian figure. "I couldn't go into this room for two years. I hated it. . . ." The year after the death [of Kennedy] she bought things—many. Now she's stopped—only clothes, jewels. "Onassis, who [otherwise] wasn't much in this flat, couldn't be pried from the library to work after his son's death."[107]

107. Aristotle Onassis's son Alexander died in a plane crash on January 22, 1973.

FEBRUARY 27, 1973  Mitchell Wilson dead. Poor Stella [Adler]. I think that he was the love of her latter years, the solace of her unacknowledged old age. Now she will be old—this miracle of youth, whose increasingly rare entrances into the "social" scene amazed all beholders. "How can she look so beautiful?" People stood in awe, gaping at her. Together, Mitchell and Stella looked like star actors "resting"—not because no one wanted them, but because they were wary about the play in which they would finally triumphantly make their appearances. They never made comebacks, since no one ever thought of them as away. They were always lights in this midnight of despair.

MARCH 5, 1973  Just to note that I saw Maestro's house and grounds on the front page of the real-estate section and read that the grounds were being "devastated" by a modern school building (Jewish). Those long, long ago, during-the-war nights when Ela and I crouched under the mulberry tree. She trembling when Maestro cleared his throat or coughed in that late-night-shielded way. Ela thinking herself disguised in cap, pants, and tough's jersey—all trembling, giggling, and rapture . . . and madness—Caroline Lamb again and again.[108]

NOTE: Gray was in Barbados for much of the spring of 1973.

JOURNAL • MARCH 10, 1973 • BETHEL, CONNECTICUT  I cannot yet decide whether the day is smeary or whether my eyes see it that way. But, oh, the joy of not having to have that operation now. Later always seems never. That is why death is never until death is now. Surely we know, if only for one horrible moment of pathetic regret—or one exulting moment of relief?

MARCH 12, 1973 • NEW YORK CITY  I fall in love with Puss over and over again. Should describe my pangs about marriage and thoughts of doing it, in some state in which this is possible—because of love and taxes and after life comes financial desolation. I write love letters to Puss, incessantly, in my head—a tempest of love letters in my head. . . .

MARCH 13, 1973  Mrs. Paley about T: "He's getting waspish lately."

MARCH 15, 1973 • NEW YORK CITY
**TO RICHARD HUNTER** • VIENNA
You cannot believe under what terror we [at Condé Nast] work in this Graybar Building [near Grand Central Station]. The bank was robbed. Men with knives appeared and chased through the floors here and there until chased

108. Lady Caroline Lamb (1785–1828), young wife of the prime minister Melbourne, became notorious for her affair and romantic obsession with Lord Byron.

from the premises. On the seventeenth floor a whole office was locked up and the crooks took everything from them save their hysteria. The J. Walter Thompson office cashiers were robbed. So we now have private police—all so totteringly ancient that they couldn't do anything preventative, so they lock essential doors, thereby making escape in case of fire impossible, also causing me to walk almost all around the block because the door next to my door is locked. Very eighteenth century. Where is Hogarth?[109]

NOTE: In July 1972, Diana Vreeland had become special consultant to the Metropolitan Museum of Art's Costume Institute. The first major exhibit that she curated there was a celebration of couturier Cristóbal Balenciaga. Soon, the Institute's annual autumn opening would be the gala centerpiece of New York's social and fashion schedule.

JOURNAL • MARCH 29, 1973  The Balenciaga opening was the most elegant event Manhattan's experienced in years and all Diana Vreeland's doing. She rang up, late in the day (anxious about her Balenciaga photos, her "piece" [in Vogue]), unexpectedly revealing the truth about Truman and Robert MacBride. "How can he do that to a friend? Twenty years of friendship—sending that man to work with me—such a middle-class man—not anywhere in the limits of Truman's world—so dull—the father of five children—and Truman taking him away—in love with him!"

How others, thinking you must know, because of your social ramifications, tell you what you have been (idly) curious to know, how they fill in your gaps.

APRIL 10, 1973 • NEW YORK CITY
**TO RICHARD HUNTER • PARIS**

We went to see Joan Crawford, in person at Town Hall. Her film clips were monotonous (not near as fascinating as Bette Davis's), but she was very homey, very funny, and looked remarkable—very cultivated in a discreet, pretty, black dress—pale, neatly piled blond hair—making no bones about age—talking salty. Her humor always comes out of her strong, realistic view of life. She said, "I worked for Joan Crawford for years; now Joan Crawford is working for me and Pepsi-Cola." The jammed house pelted her with tawny roses. She picked up each and every one and trotted along the apron of the stage, shaking hands and beaming and tearing up. It was like a Jewish wedding. We couldn't help but admire this extraordinary creation: "I was born in front of a camera. Hollywood invented me. All I was—all I have—comes from Hollywood."

JOURNAL • APRIL 15, 1973 • BOSTON  I must write down my rules of conduct between two people who have lived together for years. A basis: Never say any-

---

109. British painter and engraver William Hogarth (1697–1764) is known for his engravings satirizing contemporary politics and morality (A Rake's Progress).

thing recriminatory—never. Recriminations are best left unsaid, like unopened letters.

APRIL 23, 1973 · NEW YORK CITY  I must now grow a swift skin against the sadisms of Alex [Liberman]. He is as monstrous as I knew instinctively he would be. Curious to feel used-up in these few months, but from this moment I reassume the shell that helped me until I fell ill last week. I need to make this money, and I will, but I must not be sucked into the making of it. Alex is hard, hollow, cold, shrewd, and the enemy. I must not forget this—not for one moment. My anguish is that I cannot see easily. If I could be sure that my eyes would function as they did, I would have this operation during the week Alex is on the seas (on or about June 15). But for the time, now, I must put on my armor again.

NOTE: At this time an ophthalmologist told Leo that the easiest color on troubled eyes was purple. Leo promptly began writing everything in that color and brought all hues of purple into his wardrobe and decoration. The color's royal associations—and its eccentricity—added to his pleasure in it.

JOURNAL · APRIL 27, 1973  Anita's eightieth yesterday. Ruth Dubonnet invited us to a party at which we knew no one actually, save our date, Anita, and she knew no one.[110] They seemed some horsey set. Anita told us about the time she and Paulette Goddard were in a railroad station somewhere, and they wanted to call someone up: "Paulette was trying to find a nickel in her purse— that is what it cost in those days," ruefully said A.L., "and this old bum just stood there gaping at Paulette. Finally he took out a nickel and offered it to her—and she took it! I said, as we went away, 'You shouldn't have taken that poor man's nickel, Paulette!' And she said, 'But that's all he had.' Paulette's gotten more loot than anyone I've known. And you know how? Positive thinking—not Norman Vincent Peale's kind—but her kind."[111]

APRIL 29, 1973  I never worry about the percentage of feminine in me, the percentage of masculine. I am grateful for whatever percentages I have and try to use these. I am watchful only in outward manifestations. I am protective of the woman in me, and don't permit her to show in my walk or in my hand movements or in my voice—because she is vulnerable in our world. Less than she was several years ago—but still I must be vigilant and try to keep her within myself, where she nourishes me—imbuing my masculinity with all sorts of wisdoms.

110. Wealthy Ruth Obre Dubonnet (d. 1992) was friend to many in New York's theatrical community.
111. The film actress Paulette Goddard (1905–90) married Charles Chaplin, Burgess Meredith, and Erich Maria Remarque.

APRIL 30, 1973 Mina called—Lincoln's gone around the bend· again. This means brilliance unbelievable, so no one believes him bonkers—save the few who really know the signs and how dangerous he is to self and others.

MAY 1, 1973 Jean Stafford on the blower—I can never decide whether she is drunk: "My father loved Job best. Whenever he was really down, he read Job and roared with laughter and slapped his thighs and shouted: 'Give it to him again, God! There goes God giving him another boil!' So when I met Cal Lowell, in Boulder when he was in the army, and he said, 'Don't you think Milton is the funniest poet in the English language?' I knew I had to marry Cal Lowell." Her two blue beacon eyes beam. Her talk is metered with cackles and shouts of laughter, and afloat on tides of topless waves and troughs of gutturals.

MAY 11, 1973 Alex said, "Bob Hughes [art critic for *Time*] was writing a piece on me, and he said: 'He is a Fabergé box, which you open and find Boris Godunov inside.' " That sums Alex up—to that stone wall—but leap over the wall and you find deep morasses and swamps in which even more bizarre monsters flourish more wildly than ever Boris Godunov did in that Fabergé box.

    *The Women* at [*Playbill* Spelvin] lunch.[112] The little-girl attentiveness—no, the blond-cat attentiveness of Alexis [Smith]; the prettiness and deep quiet voice of Rhonda Fleming—a surprise—such pretty, pale autumn coloring; Myrna Loy (Morgan le Fay) and her quiet humor. "We never did know Asta. He was a professional dog. A nice dog, but he did his job [in *The Thin Man*] the way his master told him and didn't pay any attention to us. . . ." So a myth drifts away. I told Puss and he was sad.

MAY 30, 1973 • NEW YORK CITY

TO W. H. AUDEN • PÖLTEN, BEI NEULENGBACH, AUSTRIA

I became features editor of *Vogue* last January, and I've been longing to publish you in these pages. I started a department here titled "On My Mind." These are short pieces, from 500 to 600 words, and they can be about anything at all—anything you feel deeply about or anything you feel nostalgic about. Rebecca West wrote about the Virginia Woolf and [travel writer] Rose Macaulay she knew but did not quite find in recent lives of these ladies. Anthony Burgess wrote about how he cannot cash a check in New York despite the fact that his name is on theater marquees. Anne Fremantle wrote on dowries: how girls must be given them. Graham Greene wrote about the virtue

---

112. Beginning in November 1970 and for the next twenty years, Leo chaired a monthly luncheon that he christened "The Friends of George Spelvin." (George Spelvin is the name traditionally used when a playwright wishes to disguise the fact that one actor is playing two roles.) Leo would invite the cast and creators of a current play to lunch with some of *Playbill*'s advertisers.

of disloyalty. Jean Stafford wrote about the horror of being visited in the hospital. I am also trying to publish verse. Do, please, keep me in mind for that.

And I have been publishing fiction: E. M. Forster, Vladimir Nabokov, the Flaubert Egyptian Journal, and coming out in a month or so will be a piece by Kurt Vonnegut, Jr. Also, fiction by Iris Murdoch, Angus Wilson, Willa Cather—I found an unpublished manuscript! I am publishing a piece on bird-watching by John McPhee and a piece on flower-watching by May Sarton. Would you want to do anything about music-listening, or even more specifically, Mozart-listening?[113]

JOURNAL • JUNE 1, 1973 Jane Bowles dead in this morning's *Times* (on May 4, in Màlaga). It was in 1943 that I wrote my review of [her novel] *Two Serious Ladies* for Irita [van Doren], and that was the stone upon which I stood to enter the carriage that has carried me to this far place, thirty years later. Jane—loving and lost—even then, long ago, in those early moments of her glory.

AN IMBS EVENING, 1943 *We are packed together around Bravig and Valeska's dining table, an outsize, white-painted, curlicue cast-iron, glass-topped garden table. Here were the remnants of the Imbs's Paris life now intermingled with Americans, mostly new, save known at times in translation or by reputation, to both the refugee American expatriates and native Europeans. We were in a reverse Henry James situation: Europeans being Americanized. Valeska was a superb cook, the kind who even with wartime restrictions set a bountiful table.*

*Mary Reynolds (Duchamp's friend, who had worked in the French Underground [until summer 1942] and walked her way to safety),[114] Nicolas Calas,[115] Brion Gysin, Janet Flanner, Virgil Thomson, Maurice Grosser,[116] Richard, and I were at the dessert (mousse au chocolat, new to some of us and always clamored for), when the door to the apartment was abruptly flung open. Two people almost ran into the room. He was tallish, seemed to be brushed by the reflection of a jumping flame, there was an artful dishevelment about him, an air of danger. I have felt this danger in an intricately incised eighteenth-century sword blade. Admire but do not touch! She advanced, hitching herself along quickly. She was dark, crop-headed curly, huge-eyed—later I saw the fun and compassion in their dark depths. She was steadfastly awry. She was very young and very old: Precocious children are like that.*

113. Auden sent an unpublished poem ("Thank You, Fog") and then wrote a piece for *Vogue* about his opposition to recent revisions to the Bible and the Book of Common Prayer ("I Have a Precious Bee in My Bonnet"). Leo published both.
114. Mary Reynolds (1891–1950), an artisanal bookbinder, lived in Greenwich Village with Duchamp during the war.
115. Nicolas Calas (1907–88), a Greek-born art critic and Surrealist poet, fled Paris for New York in 1940.
116. The painter Maurice Grosser (1903–86) wrote art criticism for *The Nation*. He was also the longtime lover of Virgil Thomson.

*"Jane! Paul!" Everyone was excited. Paul Bowles I knew as a composer, and I had heard, years before, when I was casting* Behind Red Lights, *from Florence Auer (who came to audition for Madam of the Whorehouse) about her little niece, Janey. Jane wedged herself beside me. She spooned some of my mousse into her widely grinning mouth. She pulled out of a bag a book. She waved it. "I just got it!" Pandemonium! The next morning I called Irita van Doren, editor of the* New York Herald Tribune Weekly Book Review *and asked, "May I please review* Two Serious Ladies *for you?"*[117] (1993)

JOURNAL • JUNE 8, 1973 Josephine Baker opened at Carnegie Hall. I have never seen as many black women in white-blond curly wigs—really platinum blond. Josephine Baker, at around sixty-eight, looks forty. Her figure, completely revealed in a body stocking (flowers here and there in sequins, the color of her skin), is slender to emaciation. "I'm so hungry," she murmured, patting her razor-thin thigh, as she moved into the footlights, four feet and more of orange-red ostrich blooms on her head, like an imperial Russian escaping across the wintered steppes—fleeing from the last imperial ball before the Bolshevik hordes! Singers in the aisles like from *My Fair Lady*. The last of Carlo's *Nigger Heaven* was in Carnegie Hall that night.[118] Diana Vreeland about Josephine Baker: "She was my you-th. . . ." How wrong Andy Warhol is when he thinks Josephine Baker and Marlene are the same thing.

JUNE 11, 1973 Bill Inge dead by carbon monoxide—after trying at an earlier time, having committed himself, and having signed himself out. His deep depression—long, long depression—took him into his garage, into his car, and so out of this world. He had been walking toward this death for years. I am saddened. A small hand momentarily blots out the huge sun. . . . And I sit upon my tidy, summer bed and scribble . . . scribble. . . .

Today's [*Vogue* photo] sitting with Carol Channing: "You are the only one who saw through that fat—saw me," she said. She *was* fat, frightened, and funny when I first saw her, but she knew what she wanted—to be thought beautiful (or to think herself beautiful) and to be a star. She is the latter and she believes the former. "Everything," she said, "must come from the character. You must believe in her and then you are free. Nothing can happen to you—only to her."

JUNE 17, 1973 • WESTHAMPTON, NEW YORK A drear morning, following on a Sag Harbor graveyard picnic in a vast downpour. I felt that those lost at sea,

---

117. He wrote, in part: "She is as honest and lucid as children and just sufficiently intoxicated, and like them she speaks the truth with an astonishing, amusing, and innocent clairvoyance quite regardless of consequence." The *New York Herald Tribune Weekly Book Review*, April 25, 1943.
118. Van Vechten's novel *Nigger Heaven* (1926) was a sympathetic, realistic depiction of various strata of Harlem life.

done in by the "behemoths of the deep" (from an inscription on a monument there) were one with us, as we crouched over the excellent tarragon chicken, the brioche, the good butter, and bread-and-butter pickle. Charlie [Addams, the cartoonist] was a lamb—which girlish expression suits precisely his behavior. This six-foot-one dark-complected sixty-one-year-old from Westfield, New Jersey, is so essentially American—with his voice sometimes going very Fred Allen,[119] his look of having been carved from good American oak, of having been weathered by time and across-continent peering, the preoccupation with horror (death) and his laughter in it. The mischief in him. I con him into laughter if I throw what I say just a little askew—into the impossible-possible. His barefoot-boy charm. His sexiness—I feel this and women adore him. "Doesn't he look like John Wayne?" one asked in the graveyard. Now, this long-famous man who's given a certain kind of house his name (many know immediately what's meant by an "Addams house" or "perfect Charles Addams") seems to want this story. I don't think that he has, in his time, been garlanded with public praises the way [cartoonist] Saul Steinberg has.[120]

JUNE 23, 1973 · NEW YORK CITY I rang up Puss [in Barbados at the Maremonts] and said, "I've been trying to put off ringing so as to have the anticipation all day, but I couldn't. I love you so much." That is in my bones, in my being. If Bill [Inge] had someone he loved that way, or vice versa, would he have killed himself? I am haunted by Bill's death. My feeling of well-being, after talking to Richard—knowing that he was there in Augusta, and that Puss is there in Barbados, but will be here. Suddenly I don't feel lonely—just alone—which is different.

JUNE 27, 1973 Just before we left *Vogue* today: "There's a strange man on the phone. . . ." His voice was reptilian, and his message was to the point: "We've been watching you, and even people in your own circle—movie circles—think you're very far out—Red. Even those who are Left, think you are too far Left. . . . We're watching you. . . ." This about my *State of Siege* review and my saying [film director] Costa-Gavras is on the side of humankind. "You're pushing the Soviet line," this reptile said. Not pleasant and actually rather frightening.

JUNE 30, 1973 The Bernsteins—all of them—were received by the pope. Did Lennie kiss the pope on his mouth? On his toe? On his ring? Felicia, of course, knew how to behave.

---

119. A hugely popular comic on radio and television, Fred Allen (1894–1956) used a deadpan, nasal delivery.
120. Dona Guimaraes (1926?–89), then executive editor of *Mademoiselle,* had arranged the meeting in order for Leo to propose a *Mademoiselle* feature to Charles Addams.

JULY 2, 1973 I read Colette and Sainte-Beuve, both tonic: the former one of my deep passions, the latter remarkable even in English translation.[121] The balanced flow of these Sainte-Beuve portraits—a sort of blush of irony mantling the clerical contours of Sainte-Beuve's prose and his shafts of delicate wit and shrewd observation, comparison illuminating here this feature, there that feature—the perfections and the blemishes. He casts a sort of gentle, but persistent, revolving light upon his subject—so clear a light that the distant recesses are brought out into sharp, succinct view—but calmly, dispassionately. There is a serenity here, the unruffled serenity of a sea on a calm, brilliantly sunlighted day, but one is always aware that this is the sea and that the calm is a practiced, calculated deception.

JULY 4, 1973 Our family came, in one generation, from golden hope and faith to despair and disbelief. Each Fourth of July in that long-ago was rich. Always rain fell, thunder added the cannons' boom to the firecrackers' blast, and the beauty fizzled into acrid smoke as the rain triumphed. "So much racket gets into the clouds and so it rains." That was the explanation for us kids. We believed this—maybe it is true. Oh, how American we were, sincerely believing all of the truths and all of the myths. It was so important to be part of this glorious promise the U.S.A. That is one reason we became deeply involved in celebrating July Fourth, Thanksgiving, the [presidential] birthday month of February, Arbor Day, Election Day, and Flag Day (in white flannels—very heavy, very hot, quick to stain if any hanky-panky occurred). We vied to be included in American celebrations. We were even more American in intent than "real" Americans—despite being sheenies and kikes and dagos. The discriminations were endless and hurting—scarifying—the reparations almost equally. (I must fix this last. It's not quite true.)

JULY 7, 1973 · BETHEL, CONNECTICUT Why I read anything but Proust, I can't understand. Oriane (the Princesse des Laumes) on furniture and decoration is superb. The musical evening at Mme de Saint-Euverte's, with his microscope on minor, minor people—endless—and the humor, the irony. Oriane's "remarks"—to use Guermantes's quotation marks, which is how Proust communicates inflections of speech, these semaphoring a whole "set's" flavor, the nuance of their talk—this is miraculous—not God created the world, but Proust re-creating certain worlds—as infinite in its variety as Mrs. Nature's own. I know how these people sound, move, smell, think. I know their darkest and their most luminous deeps. I know more about them than they know about themselves and, definitely, about one another. I do not know this the way Dickens's people or even Dostoyevsky's or Tolstoy's know one another and each

121. The essays of Charles-Augustin Sainte-Beuve (1804–69), a French poet and critic, were a foundation of modern literary journalism.

himself, but in a new way—a twentieth-century way—Proust's way. In Proust, character is felt metamorphosing into psychology. Proust sees through and beyond. I have the feeling he sees not only into the past, but into the future.

And so I return to Proust and Mme de Saint-Euverte's musical evening, and poor Swann meandering through Vinteuil's precious little [musical] phrase to that awful "sell" Odette . . . whilst seeing (Proust, and I through Proust) Oriane for the "sell" she is—the social sell; seeing the grease of affectation, even on the highest social pinnacle, which makes society function, the grease of social lies and subterfuges—all a deception, but a necessary deception. What a true satire the garden party is in *Alice*. On one level, the Rev. Dodgson [Lewis Carroll] is annihilating shams as clearly as Don Quixote attempts to annihilate, the Reverend and Cervantes each tilting against social shibboleths.

The rapture, the pure rapture of sitting here [at Mina's], in this benediction of summer heat, this blessing of brilliant sun, scribbling—the joy of scribbling. . . . The end of *Swann in Love*—the brilliant truth of that end: "To think that I have wasted years of my life, that I have longed for death, that the greatest love that I have ever known has been for a woman who did not please me, who was not in my style!"

JULY 8, 1973   Why autobiography? Mina says she can't write her autobiography and wonders why. I say I write this because I love to scribble. I am so curious about people, things. I know that the conclusions, either set down or inferred, will tell not one new thing—but the affirmation, my belief in people, in character (what we meant by a person having character), in beauty, in truth (Keatsian), in the glorious and in the terrible—as demonstrated in the extraordinary creatures I have been privileged to reflect, in my very deepest self—all of this is valuable, is a beacon in this world which needs constant confirmation of its miracle of existence. How or why we are all still here, I do not know, nor understand.

I dipped into the pretty Orion edition of Da Ponte's *Memoirs*—finding this proximity to Mozart irresistible. Da Ponte and his "celestial" Mozart—by a flick of my wrist and a twiddle of my fingers I had Mozart by his hand.[122] Oh, the reassurance. If only I could give this reassurance to some future graybeard or beardless creature. If I could put into that future anonymous hand my hand, and so the hand of Ela and of Mozart. . . . If I could by my fingertips bridge time and so assure this future friend that the continuity is forever, even as myth—perhaps only as myth—and that even if we are time's junk shop, this is worth our little while. Nothing ends; we survive. This morning I held Mozart's hand and my heart leapt up with his. The fountains of the world spring into the air—not a single, infinitesimal, glittering sequin of water is lost. I have

---

122. Lorenzo Da Ponte (1749–1838) was the Italian librettist who wrote *The Marriage of Figaro*, *Don Giovanni*, and *Così Fan Tutte*. He lived from 1805 in New York City.

been tortured inadvertently—as when I woke during that operation—and irony, bone-deep irony, and beauty and hope (the fountains springing forever) saved me.

JULY 17, 1973 · NEW YORK CITY  Momma into the Florence Nightingale nursing home today—a nightmare, thronged with ancient medieval faces as viewed by Goya—or Ken Russell. The faces with hair skimped, gone, or tousled; the constantly fluttering hands; the mumbling and crying out. And she lamenting all of the time. Momma is, actually, more *compos mentis* than most of the others. We will keep her in her own house until we can't. I deposited $650 for two weeks and arranged for a phone to be installed at her bedside, where, I hope, she will not be all of the time.[123]

JULY 26, 1973  Howard Rothschild had a letter, from some ancient Diaghilev ballerina, in which she wrote: "Diaghilev was interested onlie in his homoskschul mistrisies [*sic*] and in having them always in the most expensive hotels."

JULY 29, 1973 · WASHINGTON, D.C.  The long look Momma gave me as I sat there on the side of that Florence Nightingale bed, on the edge of those yellow covers. She sat stolidly in her chair. What was going on in that head so fuddled by self-pity, hysteria, conviction, craftiness? I suddenly thought: Maybe she's about to tell me that I am not my father's son. Curious how this persists—even now, when I am almost sixty. Whose son? Uncle Herman's? I must trace the influence of Uncle Herman in my life. Is my absolute passion and love for Puss an Uncle Herman result?

I have finished Lillian [Hellman]'s book. She is one of the most self-exposing writers—and, finally, thus permitting herself to show, to emerge bone clean, her inabilities and abilities shredded. She is a considerable being—the secret anatomy of her fears, triumphs, ruses, resorts, joys, sorrows a chart easy to read. Reading this *Pentimento*, the vulnerable, tough, intensely girl-woman Lillian is plain to see, to feel. That battleground face, which seems to be disintegrating as one looks at it, is a solid, revealing mask: It, unlike so many other phizzes [*sic*], does not lie.[124]

I remember taking tea in her living room, Lil unable to say [Dashiell] Hammett's name, as he lay above us. Whenever she came to his name, she pointed her index finger abruptly ceilingward, giving her a sort of theological cast, as she sat there in a lilac crepe house gown. Her eyes are troubled, sort of veiled

---

123. Ida Lerman was convalescing after some medical treatment. She soon returned home, and Leo arranged for her to have daily assistance.
124. A section of *Pentimento*, published as a memoir, in which Hellman claimed to have smuggled money to antifascists in Nazi Germany, subsequently proved to be a fabrication.

angry, large, and watery. Her face is that of a dowager politico—either domestic or state, but women with such faces are both domestic and state—and even in midlife the difficulty is to decide whether this is a man's or a woman's face. I think these faces must be bisexual faces.[125]

Then, reading [Alexander] Herzen, I remember the old creature who came to Momma's, that ancient sidler who "gave" change on the elevated. He sidled in. First an ear would appear in the thin crack of the opening kitchen door— a listening ear, rather dirty and hirsute, the hair gushing like a gray moss from a cracked garden stepping-stone. Then, to the delight of the children, gradually the rest of the creature oozed through the crack—his head materializing in his time-greasy peaked cap, his rheumy eyes, his knobby red nose (somehow as pointed as Pinocchio's, despite the encrustations of red and purple upon it— a baroque organ it was), and his emaciated body in the longest overcoat—tightly buttoned up under his snaggly chin whiskers, even in hot summer. His eyes pleaded, and his whole being quivered toward the food on our table. Momma always asked him in, always calling him "Mister." I never knew who he really was. A relative? A leftover from her [downtown] Second Avenue days? I am sure that his eyes were blue and he was sweet natured, with a kind of tremulous cheerfulness—more like a dog slightly unsure of his welcome, but using all of his dogginess to bridge the possible chasm. We, the children, were embarrassed, but bubbled with secret delight and a feeling of superiority as we sat sure before our heaped plates, Momma saying, "Eat!" He always preceded all of his tissuey scraps of talk with a little flurry of greeting, in Yiddish all of it: "Hearty, happy appetite," to which we all shouted, "Ask with eating . . ." He never sat down, and his rivulets of talk rose into an incessant soprano—as shrill as flutes— and he ate and ate and ate—anything—standing there with his grotesque coat, this emaciated creature, putting away more than our entire family of five.

AUGUST 7, 1973 · NEW YORK CITY  Long talk on the blower with Kay Graham, she protesting that she doesn't want any publicity. "Please, please, let me off. It was a team. We all did it. It had to be done, so we did it."[126] She has a low, good, somewhat rich voice—a sort of light-velvet voice—full of sheen—a voice that feels good in the ear. I like the sound of her: "*Vogue*'s been so kind to me— but please, please let me off. . . ."

AUGUST 8, 1973  Cathleen Nesbitt came to dine in the Russian Tea Room. She remembered so many parties at 1453. "The very first one I ever came to, there were three men sitting together on a sofa, and I asked who they were— they were all so odd looking—and you said, 'Truman Capote, Tennessee

---

125. "Lillian Hellman has lesbian charm, which she uses on weak males, not, I believe, on females." *Journal*, April 12, 1961.
126. In May 1973, owner and publisher Kay Graham's *Washington Post* had won a Pulitzer Prize for its reporting of the Watergate affair.

Williams, and Saint-Subber,' and I thought: These are the great men. . . ." She remembered Rudi Nureyev coming up the stairs and peering at her as she lay on my bed. Cathleen's eyes are glittery, dark, deep-set Irish eyes, seeing-into-the-future eyes. She remains a beauty—an old beauty now. Her air of witty appreciation. She uses her pained claws of hands, with virtuosity—making the pain and deformity of these arthritic hands into a kind of symbol of her long courageous life. I took her home, she protesting that she could go alone—a truly remarkable creature, who looks at her long, hard life as an adventure and as good fortune.[127]

AUGUST 14, 1973  Mrs. Graham's New York office is utterly unadorned save by a lean, green-leafed, somewhat tropical plant. Her walls are pale. Her table is almost bare, save for a stack of the *Washington Post*. Her talk—thoughtful but girlish into womanly and suddenly flooded with laughter—a sort of tide of self-hilarity, under which the agile aquatic life of her mind is very busy (that's an image—inflated!). She is a plain, sallow, disheveled-hair woman, her features brought to sudden prettinesses by her inner life. I think that she is a nice woman, likable but deeply troubled—about nation, world, family. She could be a passionate woman—and perhaps she is—but guilt eats at her. She does not want to hurt. She is the kind of woman who would rather be hurt than hurt?

AUGUST 15, 1973  Sono [Osato] and I talked about Felicia [Bernstein]. Sono said: "She's always so busy. Those little feet pit-pat, pit-pat. On a very thin edge. Even in the middle of a long conversation, she suddenly looks off into some far, far distance. . . ." So this is what happens when you make up your mind, as Felicia did [for Leonard Bernstein], to get someone, no matter what—the most insecure security. For some twenty-three years she's been walking the high wire she knew she would have to walk. Lennie is like pages with glorious geniusy stuff on them—all loose. Felicia's the binding (and most handsome) that keeps the Lennie pages together. Without Felicia he would have been a public mess years ago.

AUGUST 16, 1973  Nixon's speech [on the Watergate break-in] was precisely what we expected. He looked badly embalmed; his speech was as fat as synthetic grease. But many will believe it all—its message of "Let's get on with the business of our future and leave Watergate, which is unimportant, to the proper authorities." If Nixon gets away with this, the basic principle (ironic word), so prevalent, so endemic in these United States, of "getting away" with something, will be forever enshrined as a positive moral value.

127. The British stage actress Cathleen Nesbitt (1889–1982) had a career spanning seventy years (*The Cocktail Party, Gigi, My Fair Lady*). As a young woman she had been the love of poet Rupert Brooke (d. 1915).

AUGUST 19, 1973 · SANDS POINT, NEW YORK  [With Sono and Victor Elmaleh] at Sands Point—literally East Egg [of *The Great Gatsby*], but I could not see any green light across the Sound last night. Garbo's *The Temptress* late on the telly, was visually superb, beautifully directed, and Antonio Moreno was—the only word is that old girlie-kitsch—stunning. Garbo was beauty. She looked as if she had just been struck fresh from a transfixed crystal wave—her skin was lucent—absolutely lucent. She moved more dancer than any other human, her figure thin to emaciation. She did little or nothing save token gestures. Then suddenly, from some icy deep—overwhelming emotion. After exhaustion, or in the throes, she tapped the universal well. She was all plastique brought to intense life by her feeling. Sometimes she was faintly bemused, almost withdrawn in her bemusement—and this fortified her mystery. Above all she was (and is) mysterious. Fascinating how Moreno and Garbo seemed precisely right for another's wanting. An unexpected joy, *The Temptress*, its direction amazing, especially in the earlier sequences, which owe much to German films. The dinner at which the millionaire kills himself, denounces Garbo—the table unrolling to immensity—did Lubitsch learn this from Niblo or did Niblo learn from Lubitsch?[128] But most of all, the glory of *The Temptress* is Garbo—her economy, her overwhelming beauty, which transcends period, her indifference—ice upon the volcano and the volcano suddenly erupts—soundlessly. Her suffering—Garbo's suffering was always a natural force, like rain or flood. Garbo should have played Tosca—a perfect part for her. Sometimes in *The Temptress*, she seems about to sing.

AUGUST 20, 1973  I must try to be more understanding of Momma. She's terrified, but I cannot bear to hear her terror.

AUGUST 24, 1973 · NEW YORK CITY  Two days ago, an early telephone call from Sandra [McElwaine] telling that Rogers had resigned [as Secretary of State], Kissinger nominated—no, designated. A call from [photographer] Harry Benson from the San Clemente White House: Did we want to photograph A Final Importance? A call from Bea [Miller]: Princess Anne in white fox and feathers, by [Norman] Parkinson, is on her way. . . . That sort of thing goes on daily.[129] All so serious—and always I feel how intensely of-this-moment it all is, even when it involves "major" figures. I cannot see this as the giant sort of history. Is it that wars and Toscaninis and such make this moment less epic?

---

128. Fred Niblo (1874–1948), who took over directing *The Temptress* (1926) from Mauritz Stiller, made many costume spectacles in the silent era (*The Three Musketeers*, *Ben-Hur*).
129. Leo had hired reporter Sandra McElwaine as *Vogue*'s Washington correspondent. Beatrix Miller was editor of London *Vogue* (1964–86).

SEPTEMBER 19, 1973 Maria canceled her first concert, saying her physician said that she couldn't do it because of her eyes. I know that the cause was nerves—and who cannot forgive her those? How horrendous to "come back," especially if you cannot be sure that you have what you had before you went away. I cabled: "Courage, trust your heart . . ." etc.

SEPTEMBER 30, 1973 Here is W. H. Auden's hound-dog face on the front page of the *Times*—dead at sixty-six in a Viennese hotel, cause unspecified, although yesterday's single wireless flash news said "heart attack." I rang up Mina to tell her so that she could tell Lincoln, and found that Wystan was to come to stay with Goosey, and that he was dreading this advent. Why? Wystan had been complaining how old he felt. Mina said, "So he was as old physically as he said he felt." I must quickly publish the beautiful poem he sent some months ago.

I remember Wystan "playing" butler at the birthday party we had for Osbert [Sitwell], when we introduced Marlene to Edith and they sat together on Mary Rose,[130] holding hands, and finally Wystan said angrily, "I didn't come to be butler!" but he had insisted on opening the champagne. I remember Wystan in carpet slippers, trudging about his classroom at Bennington, when Carmel sent me there to do a story [for *Junior Bazaar*] in 1945. I remember Wystan's blubbery kisses and the horror of that worn and smelly face. I remember Lincoln turning over the table, at lunch in the Plaza dining room, when I said that I wished Wystan would wash, and then Goosey didn't talk to me for many years, after he rushed out into Central Park South. I remember Wystan, quiet and quirky at Anne Fremantle's—he was in carpet slippers again. And then those annual birthday fêtes in that shambles of a flat on East Eighth Street in the East Village—a heady rabble of fine literary folk and street scum, of the upper reaches (Nin Ryan and the Kronenbergers and the Trillings and the ballet and the literary establishment) and boys he and Chester [Kallman] had picked up in baths, in the streets—all of this among bookshelves which stood about like the ruins of a lost, or losing, culture—askew, aslant. Then I remember Wystan's kindness when I wrote to him and asked for a poem and a short piece. They came in immediately. His poetry justifying his being, his perfections monumentally overwhelming any dross: Who am I to enumerate his imperfections?

OCTOBER 23, 1973 · EN ROUTE TO SYRACUSE, NEW YORK Mindy [Wager]'s party for Felicia—during which she confided that she's to have her face lifted on November 11 ("Just a little lift"), and Lennie, across the room, confided that he was having the best time of his life because "I've had more cocks in all of my holes! Such cocks! . . ."

130. A sofa that had come from the set of a production of J. M. Barrie's play *Mary Rose.*

**TO RICHARD HUNTER** • EDINBURGH

I guess that our Christmas plans have been decided for us. On Thursday, my navel burst. It was awful. It happened early in the morning while I was dressing—the navel got huge and stuck out like a doorknob and was lurid purple. The pain was dreadful. I didn't want Puss to know. I took my bath and put on my clean underwear, in case I had to be whisked to Beth Israel, but Puss was suspicious because I was unearthly quiet. So he burst in, and I fainted. It was all more awful for Puss than for me.

The next day we went to Dr. Freund, the surgeon who did the last two operations. He said, yes, the navel was completely open (and still is) and showed us how to push it in again, because he won't operate unless it strangles—which it could at any moment. This is a mess. I now have three possible operations: the navel, the eyes, my left leg which is in a bad way. Nevertheless, I feel fine and look that way, and I am losing weight fast and will be a sylph again—and everyone will say how sick I look.

**JOURNAL** • OCTOBER 28, 1973 Ruth Prawer Jhabvala came to lunch (as did James Ivory) with us in the Rose Room of the Algonquin. She was one of the few writers I have been curious to be with. I was not disappointed.[131] She is more Indian than Polish—although the Polish Jew is there—a sort of allusive atmosphere. Ruth P.J. is very small (or small seeming), very quiet—her special quiet, running smoothly over submerged pebbles and rocks and shards of laughter. She said she went nowhere, did nothing save be at home, take care of the family, and write. When I said that we thought of her always at parties gathering material for her comedies of manners, she answered: "One party goes a long way!" She did say that years ago she had gone out a lot. We liked her deeply.

Twyla Tharp—"It's a Mormon name," she said. Small, become a cult figure, pleasant with a residue of reserve, a sediment of caution, pale—sort of faded coffee skin (perhaps the last of summer), a suggestion of intense vigor—or is it evidence of bone-deep commitment? Her new work is transitional, incredibly professional, having assimilated Jerry [Robbins]'s and George [Balanchine]'s idiom, making a shrewd, lovingly comic comment on it.[132]

NOVEMBER 24, 1973 Jennie Tourel died near midnight, slipping away. All of that effort, ego, hard work, all of that being Jennie Tourel . . . gone. Those hundreds of thousands of times Jennie looked into her glass. . . . She was a great

131. The screenwriter and novelist Ruth Prawer Jhabvala (b. 1927), the director James Ivory, and the producer Ismail Merchant were the creative principals of Merchant-Ivory films. Jhabvala was born in Germany. Her father was a Polish Jew.
132. *Deuce Coupe*, set to The Beach Boys by choreographer Twyla Tharp (b. 1941), had recently marked her turn to the mainstream.

musician, a great singer, triumphing over her lack of a great voice by the strength, the fineness of her musicianship, and her technique. Her surroundings were vulgar, her eye was perhaps vulgar, but her ear was impeccable, although sometimes, in these later years, betrayed by her monstrous ego. She was intensely Jewish, and loyal, and had her own sense of humor—although she was humorless about herself. She thought of herself as an *amoureuse*, and indeed she had many lovers and several husbands and scores of admirers. She also attracted a certain variety of *yenta*, which we always could spot immediately as "Jennies"—no matter what born religion or race, these were Jennie *yachnas* [busybodies]—rich, full of low animal cunning, overdone, and each a princess.

I first saw Jennie singing with Maestro. She wore a white "gown" (all of her dresses were "gowns") and she sang superbly. This was her first New York concert appearance, and I stood, having come to hear Maestro, in the back of Carnegie Hall, overwhelmed. Later she told me that the gown cost $90 at Bonwit Teller's. She was dark, intense, passionate—with the technique—a triumph, rather like Nora [Kaye]'s, over the Grand Concourses of this world. I know that she is at peace, if she is somewhere singing away, her voice more glorious than all others in some heavenly choir, in which she is, of course, the soloist.

DECEMBER 4, 1973 [Comedians] Peter Cook and Dudley Moore came to lunch—most likable. The civility of Peter Cook. When I asked Peter what he really felt like, he said, promptly, "Secretariat . . . I would like to feel like [the racehorse] Secretariat—all that money and then being put out to stud!" Dudley said that he felt "like a libidinous possum."

DECEMBER 28, 1973 Gloria Emerson to lunch at the Algonquin. She loves Frankie Fitzgerald—or rather admires her—but feels more comfortable with Marietta [Tree, Fitzgerald's mother] and is deeply fond of Penelope [Tree, the sister]. "Frankie insists that you have to earn everything. You have to walk a mile to earn a taxi ride. You must ride in subways. She's rich in her own right. We're the ones that hire cars and do extravagant things, but she's the historian of our generation."[133] About Gloria's return from Vietnam: "I went immediately to Dior (Paris) and sat in the *cabane* and cried, and then I went into the loo and sat there and cried. I was weepy to be alive and there." Gloria is splendid to look at—very tall ("I'm rangy"), huge dark eyes with well-depths of speculative compassion in them, immaculately, elegantly dressed—a pole of a forty-three-year-old woman, who's been twice married. Gloria's eyes are like those delicious prunes that come from Farmers Market [in Los Angeles].

133. Gloria Emerson (1929–2004) was a correspondent for the *New York Times* in Vietnam (1965–72). Frances Fitzgerald (b. 1940) had won the Pulitzer Prize and the National Book Award in 1972 for her book on Vietnam, *Fire in the Lake*.

Yesterday, climbing a stair at a party, my right leg weakened into absolute uselessness, and I fell as I reached the upper landing—but painlessly, not even spilling the food upon my plate. My leg, literally, gave out.

DECEMBER 30, 1973  Tatiana rang from Cornwall Bridge to ask me to ring Marlene (who crept into town last night to arrange for an operation upon her wounded leg).[134] My heart told me not to ring, but I did, and Annie welcomed me, went off to tell Marlene, whom I could hear in the background: "Say I stepped out a minute." Then Annie returned, abashed, and told me this. I said, loudly, "Tell Miss Dietrich I'm at home. . . ." So be that. She will ring if she wants a service, etc. She is old, spoiled, stupid, and quite frequently drunk. Such a topple from tipple—a result not a cause. She's to be pitied, for she lived by and from her beauty—not her true beauty, of which she had much, but the artifice which her fans saw, applauded, and paid for. As Momma's center was her open door, mistaken for an open heart, so Marlene's center was her insatiable narcissism—her "beauty"—and this is now gone, this center, although she can counterfeit it for huge audiences. I am almost always sad for one who has lost his kingdom—his domain. Neither Momma nor Marlene has made the necessary transition. The possibility: Nothing exists save one's self.[135]

NOTE: On January 23, 1974, Leo entered the hospital in New York for extensive nerve tests and surgeries to repair his abdominal hernia and remedy the weakness in his right leg.

JOURNAL • JANUARY 23, 1974  Sitting on the edge of my bed in Room 1162, the Lensky Pavilion [at Beth Israel Hospital]. Three years since I was last here, in that room 1161, next to this one, where I almost died, and where David Webster came to see me (or was that the time before, on the floor below?), and where Maria C came, carrying great gifts of fruit. Now I feel well and know that tomorrow I will be sick. Odd, that—but Puss finding the little photo of Ela, on the pantry floor, seems so good a sign, meaning that they who have gone on ahead are all watching over me. So now I must say good night and rest in the love that nourishes me and in the hope that my "time" has not come. I love being alive. It was my own Gray most of anything or anyone ever in all my life. I did do something extra: I lived. I will live. . . .

134. On November 7, 1973, on her final bow at a theater in Maryland, Dietrich had fallen into the orchestra pit, reinjuring an already badly damaged leg.
135. After the television broadcast of Dietrich's show, Leo ran an article about it by Jim Sirmans in the February 1973 issue of *Vogue*. Although flattering about the performance, Sirmans led with Dietrich's reluctance to discuss her age, then went on to describe the large sums she was earning and how difficult her producer Alexander Cohen had found her. It's not difficult to imagine that Dietrich had been irritated.

6:30 A.M.  A shiny-eyed black woman—really delicious chocolate brown—
came in, gave me a thermometer, marveled at my farmyard and quilt,[136] said,
"You sure travel heavy. . . . All these things. I would sure hate to clean your
place. What a mess. . . ." All most friendly, with a great show of magnificent
white teeth and gleaming of the whites of her eyes. Then she told me about the
curative weeds and sea grasses of Jamaica. Many of these, she said lovingly,
could be bought in the 116th Street Market, where I went, sometimes twice
weekly, when I was a very small boy, with Grandpa Goldwasser. The black
woman told me about fever grass (brew it fresh in the morning for tea) and
breadfruit and something for cancer and nutmeg for a stroke and about fishing—the trout leaping under Niagara Falls and caves. She spoke pure poetry,
matrix poetry, with deep, calm, loving laughter. Then a little nurse came, took
my pulse and pressure, and soon she will return, bind up my legs, give me "my
needle" and so to oblivion—or wherever—and out again I hope. Night. I wish
that I could see dawn. I love dawn, perhaps best of any time. On my little
radio—Debussy—*The Sea*. And if I can't see, hear the sea . . . this Debussy is
the most sea-satisfying. I could add up the signs again, but I won't. . . . The best
sign was Puss finding Ela's picture on the pantry floor. Now I will read, *Theater
Left*, or maybe my Shakespeare, until I fall asleep and wake again. I need
splendor in my heart and glory in my eyes and a great music of words in my
eyes and ears.

FEBRUARY 5, 1974  Still in Beth Israel (Alvin Colt reminds, in a letter, that
there was a stripper yclept Beth Israel). I haven't written in this notebook—days
on end—because so much and so little happened and that made a wall. But I
have learned so much and I've been trying to sort it out. Now I will wear a
brace, do therapeutic exercises, carry my stick, and cope.

FEBRUARY 18, 1974  Last night we went across (my first outing) to Carnegie,
to find Maria's concert canceled. The behavior of the public was odd:[137] I like
best [actress, later producer] Valentina Fratti, gaping from her window high
over Fifty-sixth Street with a perfect view of Carnegie's stage door. Valentina
announcing the arrival of each floral tribute. "Such roses—at least six dozen
long-stemmed red roses! Going in!" Then after an hour of this—deep silence,
speculative silence, from Valentina—followed by: "The roses are coming out!"
So, the tide flowed and ebbed, and Maria was fast away in the Stanhope. I
think that Maria is sick—physically—and also she is terrified.[138]

So much more to write about these last weeks—the agony and the terror

---

136. *GF:* "We were sentimental always and brought along comforting things, a variety of
miniature animals and small toys, to make hospital or hotel rooms more familiar."
137. Mounted police had to be called to quiet some irate ticket holders.
138. Callas had overmedicated herself with sleeping pills the previous evening and was
unable to sing.

(I had little of that) and the amusement (sometimes the pain was funny) and those earliest nights when I crept, in mind—almost physically—through the night, from square to square on my patchwork quilt. That is how I got from pain to pain to pain and so to the other side of pain. But the needles and electrodes—only interest in hearing the sounds in my muscles and seeing their action—jumping geometric green, gold lines on the little monitor screens—muscles making sounds of forest fires or spring ponds alive with peepers or motorboats chugging across bays—always preceded by the sharp click-click-click. The Small Adventures, which mean so much—fishing up the telephone when it fell, the vast winter skies and their armadas, the light on the windows, the petals of the masses of flowers falling with sound of snowflakes. Also the goodness of Nurse [Toby] Jensky. All of it—this strong, wonderful month.

FEBRUARY 26, 1974 • NEW YORK CITY
**TO RICHARD HUNTER • BERMUDA**

The brace is no good. It rubs my knee skin off, slips almost instantly, is cumbersome; I can't put it on or take it off by myself; I can't get into taxis or out by myself; it will make me into a cripple! So, that's that. Good news is the exercises I have. I do them twice a day, and they do seem to help. I also play with Silly Putty. I go to my office and get tired.

**JOURNAL • MARCH 6, 1974** Tonight's Maria concert was appalling—wholly awful. She and [tenor Giuseppe] di Stefano seemed like two pitiful people auditioning unsuccessfully at some provincial Italian opera house. She looked wonderful—eagle, heroic, young—and her dress was a miracle of subtle diminishing—celadon green and great trailing sleeves—all very luna moth. She used her hands exquisitely. But when she opened her mouth—[139]

MARCH 7, 1974 Maria on the blower: "Oh, we want to see you,[140] but don't bother you because you were sick. I want to tell you: I know I looked good, but I can sing better. That wasn't good, as good as I can do. . . ." She knows. And she knows that I know.

APRIL 2, 1974 Kirk [Askew] died. Ironically, [his wife] Constance lives, she having been an unapproachable invalid these many years. The last time I saw

---

139. Callas blamed her performance on distress caused by the sudden death that afternoon of her longtime tour manager Sol Hurok. "Maria's last recital here—the great magnificent blossom fell apart—like wax roses—all crumbled . . . So different from Maria's classes, she then distilling her art in phials of elixir for the young, for the future." *Journal, April 11, 1979.* GF: "Maria was the last great heroine of the theater that Leo had. Her voice always had a flaw—gorgeous, but in the top register a bit scratchy. The flaw grew—like a crack in the sidewalk—and by the time she was that age she just couldn't step over it any longer."
140. The "we" refers to her and Giuseppe di Stefano. The concert tour had begun with a romance between them but would end in acrimony.

them, she stood on one of Peter [Lindamood]'s gorgeously flowered [Grand Union Hotel] Saratoga carpets, muffled in white marabou, only her head free—that Hogarthian visage cracked and shattered with laughter. So, Constance emerges. Kirk having been the prisoner of her sickness, she now appears to be the prisoner of his black endeavor these last years. He made the prison and she made the prisoner—or each was the other's prisoner. The Askew daughters are now three middle-aged women. The artworks still marvelous, but everything else worn and unglamorous—including all of those formerly powerful people. If you laid us end to end, you could hear the pterodactyls scream. Constance was upholstered in a brownish tweed and bosomed in efficiency, her hearing-aid battery prominent, like a large industrial part on her ample bosoms. Puss and I walked, in memoriam, past the Durlacher [gallery's] doors.

APRIL 20, 1974 · NEW YORK CITY

**TO RICHARD HUNTER · PARIS**

Constance seemed to rally for this event, which was semi-thronged with survivors, most of whom had known one another well years ago and now took moments—into minutes—to recognize one another. Awful. Janet Flanner, Lillian Hellman, and Louise Crane [patron and poet] stood together, and I said, "I wouldn't know to which one of you lovelies to give the apple." And Janet, in her eighties, said promptly, "Don't bother, I ate it years ago."

JOURNAL · APRIL 28, 1974 This week I spent most of an afternoon with Nancy [Mrs. Henry] Kissinger, having Avedon photograph her, and I have now interviewed her. I liked her for her reasonableness, her consideration, her good looks, especially the outline of her face (V. Woolf cheekbones), her niceness, and her candor. This was a neighborly visit rather than an interview.

This morning Marguerite Young rang up to tell me that Ruth Stephan had hired a car, driven off into the woods on the vastness she had bought, on which her house was to start building on May 1, and there in the wood, on the cold April ground, had lain down, swallowed sleeping pills, and so died. I do not believe this, unless she was driven to it by that dreadful Mr. F [Franklin, her last husband] or cancer, but she, always optimistic, would not have killed herself over sickness. When I last saw her, several months ago, she was full of life and hope. She did this on April 9. I rang Richard up in London and he was flabbergasted—but then complained, as usual, about expense, a pain in his side, etc.

I wonder what Ruth wore. Did she run back to get a scarf, a sweater to warm her in the cold April day? I see her as I first saw her, so many years ago, in blue velvet—almost crushed pansy blue—her blond hair loose and long—a sort of fairy-tale atmosphere. "I am a poetess like a bird sings," she said. Then all those times we met in a tea saloon and consumed enormous sundaes, parfaits, rich sweets, mountainous ice creams. Then she sent me that $1,000 I needed to buy the lease of 1453. There the check was, early on the last morning, a present which solidified my future.

MAY 1, 1974 I have now "formally" left *Mademoiselle*, after twenty-six years. Most fortunately, I have (I am so aware of precisely how completely risky this is) *Vogue* and the remnants of *Playbill*. So ends twenty-six years. I will see them through August.[141]

MAY 9, 1974 I must be resolute now and rid myself of—first most of the books. I can no longer hold out. I must conserve such strength as I have for any work that I wish to do. I cannot waste myself on any of these matters. I must be solid within. I sell the books to buy, I hope, some domestic peace. I do not for one little moment believe that selling the books will buy that, because my experience shows me that when this is done, something other instantly will take its place. This has nothing to do with love: That does not change. This has to do with my being: I can be without the externals. If I can manage, as I have, my sight impaired, my muscles withering, I can manage about the externals. I must not say one word about any of this. I must do it, knowing that what I do will do no good save for me. . . . Most of my friends are dead, far off, or alienated. I must cut myself from things and since these books are of the first importance, I must begin with them. *I have had* them. What a comfort, the sweet, spring rain. If I cannot go into the country, I will go there in my mind, in my heart. There is so little discontent in me, almost no envy. I have had more than my share of love, joy, admiration, opportunity.

MAY 29, 1974 Wanda told me that Volodya [Horowitz] plays only one hour a day, walks thirty blocks each day. All food must be sent on to each concert place—gray sole, etc.—special foods.[142] The funniness of Wanda. She stands like her mother, has her father's eyes, and still wonders whether he ever slept with Ela—which he did—and she describes Ela taking the Guardi drawing from the wall of Kammerschloss—"a fake" says Wanda—and giving it to Maestro.[143] This was a real *rencontre* at Alex and Tatiana's.

JUNE 3, 1974 · WASHINGTON, D.C. Yesterday afternoon with Mrs. [Gerald] Ford in the little house in Alexandria in a sloping meadow.[144] She has an Amer-

141. Leo had continued to be a consulting editor for *Mademoiselle*, supplementing his income, after he started at *Vogue*.
142. Vladimir "Volodya" Horowitz (1903–89), the supreme Russian-born pianist, was married to Toscanini's daughter Wanda (1907–98).
143. Upon their first meeting, in August 1935, Mendelssohn had presented Toscanini with a small painting by Guardi. Of course, she may have given him others.
144. At the time, Betty Ford's husband was vice president. She would become first lady on August 9, 1974.

ican midwestern gentility and sadness and optimism and aspiration and reverence for "beautiful." Easy to make fun of and hard to explain to Manhattan
and Europe. She is good, kind, dreamy, sedated, boring—a family woman who
said, "Well, I was going into a business—dyeing fabrics—when all of this happened and . . ." The facial and hand gestures (very graceful) articulated the
rest—dreams flown away, annihilated. . . . She talks a lot and always quietly—
smiles coming and going like clouds with sun behind them. Everything she
says comes after a silence, while—through the sedation—she thinks out what
you have said. Then she talks in quiet, very quiet "takes"—leaving spaces during which I had to make myself not talk and somehow gauge when to talk. I
would have to count slowly.

The deep disorder in the upstairs bedrooms, with her many, many dresses
hanging in closets, on their doors. A house much too small for the family
and its situation. "I gave up on furniture . . . because I decided that the children should feel they could come and go . . . and bring their friends . . . and
cats and dogs. . . ." Mrs. Ford has made many compromises. Her family and
husband always come first. "I never see him . . . at night. . . ." Mats—his
name on one, hers on another—either side of the huge bed. I felt that she
has some vision of the house as "decorated," some sense of a color scheme,
obscure to any eye save hers. She is a most lovable woman. I wanted to protect and help her. She hugged and kissed me and stood waving a long time
when I went away. Her hulking, nice daughter and the good relationship
between them. The Secret Service in isolation booths and "They know all
about us, so we like to know all about them . . . specially the good-looking
ones. . . ."

The sense of this family: his Siamese cat, Chan ("Momma got the name
when they went to China"), [Michael] the son who will be a minister and his
wife-to-be Gayle [Brumbaugh] (who will be interested in his "work"). All of
this is a typical American family, perfectly cast, even Mrs. Ford as the bright
wife who is deprived of her husband because of his "business." She loves to
dance—social—and reveres Martha Graham. (She had two years of Martha.)
"When I saw Mr. Ford—his way, his inspiration. I thought of Martha. . . . She
was my inspiration. . . . I went to her when I was twenty. . . . That's when you
get inspiration. . . ." She loves to tango, foxtrot, and polka. ("Mr. Ford's a marvelous dancer.") Her high time was when she returned to Grand Rapids and
taught "colored children to dance . . . the way Martha taught me. . . . She
would put a knee in my back. . . ." This all ended (dancing, skiing) because of
a pinched nerve. Mrs. Ford said, "I love art . . . paintings, sculpture, and,
strange enough, I like modern art—Gottlieb, Rothko—but I don't get the time
to go to museums the way I would like. . . . So, I get art books and I look at
them and look at them. . . ." In this woman Carol Kennicott [of *Main Street*]
always lurks.

JUNE 8, 1974 · NEW YORK CITY  Dr. Wiseman said, yesterday, that this is a "progressive" sickness—and going, now, at a very slow pace. That behooves me to consider some, I hope, remote future—when I can't use my leg even as I do now—and this, I suppose, will include my hands. The only way I can confront this unimaginable (meaning my own reluctance to look squarely) future is to teach myself that this also is an adventure and, as with all adventures, must be taken as it comes, the only preparation being courage, and the basis of this is patience and faith—absolute faith, the will to see life through. Curiosity will help me. The future can be downhill, but I will try to make this seem so gradual that we will seem to be on a solid plateau. I worry only about how to make financial security. Now we will have a sort of whistling in the dark. An adventure.

AUGUST 1, 1974  Mikhail Baryshnikov yesterday morning. He came to be photographed by Avedon, who came from Fire Island and his illness to do this. He could be any boy on a street corner—pale, stockyish, blond, retiring, but friendly, slight [presence]. If he were in a room with other people, he would not be noticed save for his deep-set, heavily shadowed, sad, somewhat doomed blue eyes—eyes curiously related to Marlene's now that she is old and lost, her world gone quite awry. His dancing strength comes from his feet—beautifully shaped feet of enormous strength and flexibility. You feel that he could write with his feet. (Rudi's dancing strength comes from his buttocks, Eddie Villella's from his thighs.) When this boy stands on the floor, peering into a long glass, warming up, he becomes noble romantic—a tremendous presence, not flashy but magical. Then suddenly he is airborne: There is no visible preparation. He is so masculine that there is a sort of feminine quality that flavors his dancing. He could be a marvelous Spectre de la Rose or Harlequin or Petrouchka—all of the Nijinsky roles—but with a different sensibility. Baryshnikov has humor, a sense of fun. Also, he has a sense of atmosphere in stage works.

AUGUST 5, 1974  A day in the country at [dermatologist] Alvin Friedman-Kien's. Louise Nevelson talked about her early days in Maine, how I took her home from a party thirty-five years ago, how she wondered did her life have a design, how she knows that it did, and how she and Diana [MacKown, her assistant] find oddments of wood from which she makes her sculptures. "We look like two gypsies," Louise said. "Two gypsy women." She is aware, at all times, of the effect she is making, always calculated, even when an accident of art or malice or appearance. Her orderly disorder: "There must be order," she said firmly. "My kind of order."

OCTOBER 27, 1974  The decline of Momma—She sounds like a motorboat setting out to sea, and frequently she makes noises like a long-distance runner on his last lap. Mary [Callabras, her aide] is mysterious because she seems so good.

I have just realized that some fifty-five years ago, in 106th Street, there was a black Mary—the "fire-goya," a unique thing[145]—a mammy-kind, in turban and print dress and white apron, survivor of antebellum days. She always led the annual June Walk, which I believe came in late May, a sort of spring ritual that sent costumed children marching through Harlem's streets and into the vast (so they seemed) meadows of the park, there to dance around maypoles and throw up with excitement.

NOTE: Leo found the pressure of working under Alexander Liberman's direction frustrating. In his journal, he mentioned being double-crossed, fully growing distrust, and worrying that the job would grow even tougher as his eyesight worsened, but he provided few details. He seldom recounted office events at length in these notebooks.

JOURNAL · NOVEMBER 30, 1974  This has been, in the office, a horror. I now know that Alex is evil—a dreadful being, a wretched, murderous Russian of the blackest blood. As Diana [Vreeland] says, "A yellow rat." Since I need to hold on to this job, I must try to build a fortress about my being. I have played hypocrite these many months: I must intensify this. "Use him," Diana advises. I must. But he must suffer some horrible payment. And I must find some path out of this horror. I love doing the work, but I will not be able to do the work with his machinations depleting me. I have inevitably managed to survive: I must manage now. Such a waste.

DECEMBER 9, 1974  I must stop complaining. I must stop eating. I must try to hear what I do say—if I say bad things. I cannot believe that I do—but I must stop complaining. I wasn't aware that I did to excess—but if I do, I must hear this and stop doing it. I am full of grief.

DECEMBER 24, 1974  These have been bad times for me at Vogue. I felt that I could no longer go on there, that the price is too high for me, that I have sold myself to the devil. But, of course, how can I give that moneymaking up? So much more is needed now. And this morning, I feel almost better.

Last night, at the Hirschfelds, [photographer] Peter Basch's mother[146] told how Freud was their house doctor and came weekly on Friday: "A nice quiet man. He wasn't yet a psychiatrist, but he knew everything about the whole family, so he was a psychiatrist—but we didn't know about any of that." She also explained why *Hänsel und Gretel* and *Rosenkavalier* (1893 and 1911) are so

145. To perform chores on the Sabbath (such as lighting the furnace), some Orthodox Jewish households employed a gentile, more often called a "*Shabbes goy.*"
146. Grete Freund-Basch (1885–1982), an Austrian-born actress and singer, had opened a Viennese restaurant in New York during the Second World War.

similar in musical ideas, atmosphere, and color: "They were always together in Vienna—in cafés all day long. They grew, Humperdinck and Strauss, together. They breathed the same air—like Haydn and Mozart." An amazing old lady, once notable on the *Mitteleuropa* opera stage, now living in her own flats in Munich and Vienna—climbing mountains in the spring—with rich high humor, spirits, and awareness. She knows all of the young voices in Europe.

MARCH 31, 1975    The [Russian soprano] Vishnevskaya's *Tosca* at the Metropolitan—incredibly provincial and awful. She emoted—intensely 1917 silent movies. She was (is) mean-faced. She planted herself stage-center, folded her little hands, and sang "Vissi d'arte" as if in recital. And her voice was, at all times, shrill and never on key. She was horrible during rehearsal—wanting sets repainted and constantly demanding new costumes—seven from Karinska, and not one pleased her. A part of the audience cheered: I am tired of political demonstrations instead of reactions to works of performing art.

Yesterday, Momma said to me, "Can I make a request? When I pass over, promise me you'll bury me with your book (*The Museum*—a large, heavy tome). In case there's anybody around I'll be able to show it to them." We were all flabbergasted and ruefully amused. Apparently, she hopes for an afterlife.

# A GLORIOUS SOJOURN

JOURNAL · APRIL 5, 1975 In bed part of the day. Talk on the blower to Herbie Ross, and later Nora [Kaye, his wife], about the Sherlock Holmes movie [*The Seven-Per-Cent Solution*].[1] I said absolutely no on Marlene, but definitely yes on Lotte Lenya, and will give them her number and address. . . . But part of the day—the tide out—actually since yesterday at Avedon's. I begin to loathe some photographers and their phony "star" ways. I have watched carefully. Irving Penn comes close, and Penn's really an artist. But Avedon—no. I saw suddenly and with utter clarity the emptiness, the waste of that [magazine features] part of my life. I've done it: I am the best there is at it. I want to be the best at writing this book—but I have obligations—always more and more.

APRIL 8, 1975 Beverly [Sills]'s Metropolitan Opera debut [in Rossini's *The Siege of Corinth*]—the mid-act tidal ovation was the most unusual ovation I have ever heard in any theater. (Remembering the one which greeted Vivien Leigh on her entrance in *The Duel of Angels*, the one which accoladed Margot at the end of her first *Sleeping Beauty* in New York, and ovations for Gielgud's *Hamlet* and Bergner's *Escape Me Never* and Maria's first *Norma* at the Met.) The ovation for Beverly, mid–second act, after she sang most beautifully, reclining, and, after the third part of the aria, stood with back to the audience— a slender, blue-cloaked, bright-haired figure—quite mortal. This ovation was unique, not so much for the length as for the shape. Its form was that of the ocean's waves before, during, and after a violent storm. It swept down and out, down and out. It was tremendous in its intensity; it was a whisper. It was the reward of virtue, goodness, survival.

APRIL 29, 1975 The perfect *Giselle* by the Bolshoi, the antithesis of their awful *Spartacus*. This *Giselle* immaculate in every detail. No one burst it at its fragile seams with "star" antics. All in a fine proportion—all lyrical, dream-like—an incident observed at any time in history, these last hundreds and hun-

---

1. The dancer, choreographer, film director (*The Turning Point*, *The Goodbye Girl*), and producer Herbert Ross (1926–2001) was married to the dancer Nora Kaye from 1959 until her death in 1987. He was later married (1988–99) to Lee Radziwill.

dreds of years, not period and not especially now but eternal—all dancing of such lyrical, romantic excellence, such a high level. This was the greatest of ballet, making our domestic troupes and stars seem puny and shabby and showbiz. This *Giselle* a rapture. I wonder if Wagner knew the structure of this [Adolphe] Adam score, which the orchestra played marvelously. Here is a whole scheme of leitmotifs—a fabric so deftly woven. This *Giselle* a complete expression of the Romantic period, the romantic heart. I expected Lincoln Center's plaza to be fragrant and shadowy with enormous, flowery lilac trees.

NOTE: Gray went to California for several weeks to assist with his mother's move from Burbank to an apartment in a retirement community in Laguna Hills, fifty miles to the south.

JOURNAL • MAY 2, 1975 • BETHEL, CONNECTICUT Yesterday, after Richard had gone [from Mina's], Mina said, "He's a different man when he's not with that awful friend of his [Howard Rothschild]. What could the attraction be?" I have wondered that for almost three decades. Mina talked of love, and almost all of her loves now seemed not love at all—only passion and curiosity. Only three—Alexi (Saint-John Perse), Harry Curtiss, and Henrietta [Bingham] were truly "love," not [John] Houseman, none of those.[2] I said that my whole life seems not to have been at all—only this moment, and all else—save Puss—had happened to someone else, all of it an experience remembered, as in a book— the miserable, now incredible, wallowings in strange rooms with odd men, the devastating passions—scarifying—I thought forever—now the traces are like those left by the passage of Ice Age tumults in Central Park boulders. . . . All of it happened, but to whom? To me and to those other me's, who preceded and formed this moment's man.

Later: I am not frightened of dying. Death is an adventure—a rebirth. But I am terrified of not being. I want my being—with Puss. I want that. I do not have the prop of religion—formal, organized, predigested religion. I am always fearful in the dark, but somehow the dark is blessed. I love, however, light—

2. "Mina talks about how she was deeply in love with Henrietta Bingham, and how she could not think of writing about that [affair], which evaporated: 'I thought that I could do something for her—take her to [the Freudian analyst] Ernest Jones—but she became vicious. Her father became an ambassador, and she took against me.' " *Journal*, October 13, 1973. In 1922, Mina Curtiss took a leave from teaching at Smith College to travel to London with Henrietta Bingham (1900–68), then recently her student. In London, Bingham would have many other affairs (said to include John Houseman, Lytton Strachey, and Dora Carrington). Mina Curtiss returned to America in 1923 and resumed teaching at Smith. In 1926 she married Henry "Harry" Tomlinson Curtiss (1888–1928), head of the golf-ball division at Spalding & Bros., where his father was company president. He died a year and a half later.

John Houseman (1902–88), best known today for his creation of Dr. Kingsfield in *The Paper Chase*, had a long career as a producer and director, including cofounding the Mercury Theatre with Orson Welles. He and Curtiss were friends and lovers through many years, beginning in the mid-thirties.

and sitting in the same place at table, no matter whose table. I feel sickish if I cannot face the room, if only by peering into a looking glass. But there does come that curious moment when I give up, slip into oblivion. . . . Is that how death will be? When Poppa died, holding his hand I saw him pass—shadowily—along his way. . . . He was gone. He was elsewhere.

MAY 4, 1975  Mina said, when Lincoln was in the hospital, having had his heart attacks, "If anything happens to Goosey, I'll kill myself." Then, some days later, she said, "There are so many letters—so much to do. I will have to do that first." I was wryly amused. Her emotionalism is as precipitous as a burst water pipe—sometimes a pipe of water-main size, sometimes a tiny ancillary pipe.

MAY 5, 1975  Ulanova[3] told George Balanchine that no longer are "all the little steps, the pearls, taught at the Bolshoi or the Kirov." Now only mass action, leaps, other athleticism are the mode, so that all of the "pearls" will be lost. She was fascinated with *Donizetti Variations*—"so full of pearls." That is what she calls all of the little steps, the *vrai* vocabulary. "We no longer can do these." So this is how fascism erodes the truth, the beauty. . . .

I am bone-lonely for my Puss. . . . Now, this little wireless plays "Chambres Separées"—too much. . . . I will count over my feastings: crepes with loganberries; cheese soufflé and Canadian bacon; shrimp in a white dill sauce; turkey stuffed with a purée of chestnuts and sausage; hot asparagus cream soup; cold oxtail soup; strawberry meringues; rhubarb pie; breasts of chicken in a white-wine tarragon cream; a kidney stew. . . . I still miss my Puss, bone-deep I miss my Puss.

MAY 6, 1975  Mina is semi-solitary, after a long life peopled with remarkables. "Why," she asks, "should it be that at 9:30 on June 1, 1926, a justice of the peace should have made my life what it is?" She has [her late husband] Harry Curtiss's nameplate on the door, so that if he comes this way, he will know that this is his house. "But he would know anyway. . . . He knew exactly how to handle me. Every day he gave me a list of what to do."

MAY 27, 1975 • NEW YORK CITY  A wedding in Philip [Johnson]'s glass house, with Aaron Copland giving Peggy Bernier away to John Russell [art historian], and Stephen Spender [poet and critic] (huge and Auden-untidy—shirttails out and an air of a wilting lily) standing up for John. Virgil Thomson senile and baby-lumbering. [Duo-pianists] Fizdale and Gold ushering. Then everyone, about 125, dotted and clotted in frazzled garden-party dress over the lawn, and so to the sculpture structure, which was all slats, levels, and shadows—like

3. The Russian ballerina Galina Ulanova (1910–98) had danced with the Bolshoi from 1944 to 1962.

being inside a marvelous phantasmagoria of superbly delineated linears—utterly insubstantial, fashioned of light. Very like Norman Bel Geddes's modern-dress *Hamlet* but of blazing white.[4] Here we played at *Midsummer Night's Dream*, with the bridal party throned on high, while the organ furiously jollied Bach. Trumpets clarioned. [Actress] Irene Worth read Shakespeare sonnets and the Millamant-Mirabell proposal scene [from *The Way of the World*] (surely the finest single comedy scene in all our literature), but the acoustics, fine for organ and trumpets, lifted only the awful timbre of Irene's clamor into the air. And the heat was devastating on this sudden summer day. Almost all elements of my life continued to echo during this curious wedding party, above the pond that Puss helped to excavate while he was deciding between Philip and me. The Proust touch was really in Minnie and Jamie Fosburgh: She so eager to be kissed and so to recapture a past that she fondly remembered; he smiling benignly at another past, of which she possibly knew nothing.[5]

JUNE 16, 1975 My plunge through Virginia Woolf's letters left no scribbling in me. I finished this volume and felt both uplifted and desolate. I lived so intensely in that world: I now was beached in my world. And, like the thin, bitter, subcutaneous underskin of an orange lay the knowledge that I should have had a life of letters, not journalism. But the most prodigious emotion was exultation at having shared with such intensity and detail V. Woolf's day-to-day living. I felt nourished, able to carry on more elegantly and eloquently. I had had an immersion in literature, in the true literary life, and I was delighted, amused, edified, confirmed, and for that moment complete.

JUNE 24, 1975 Martha Graham gala on Thursday last: Mrs. Ford's embraces and small-town neighborly ways. Margot [Fonteyn] wearily taking off her makeup and, onstage, her air of a "lady"—sweet tempered and beautifully mannered, visiting some milieu in which she knew that she did not belong. Martha whispered to me, "Thank you for Halston."[6] Nancy Wilson Ross Young[7] told me that when she went backstage she found Margot and Rudi

4. The architect and scenic designer Norman Bel Geddes (1893–1958) designed the General Motors "Futurama" pavilion at the 1939 World's Fair. Leo and Richard assisted in painting its scenery, Leo often napping under it.

5. James Whitney Fosburgh (1910–78) was a painter and a teacher who had been openly homosexual and then married Minnie Cushing (1906–78), previously the wife of Vincent Astor.

6. When Martha Graham (1894–1991) had been invited to the White House earlier in 1975 to receive the Presidential Medal of Freedom, she called Leo for advice on how to dress. He recommended the designer Halston. Graham was so thrilled with the result that she asked Halston to design costumes for her company. That gala's *Lucifer* would be the first of their many collaborations.

7. Nancy Wilson Ross (1901–86), a novelist and an authority on Eastern religions, was married to the playwright Stanley Preston Young.

[Nureyev]'s rooms empty save for great crowds of floral tributes. Then she opened a door and there were Martha and seven men all toking up. *Lucifer* looked like a fabric promotion: It is a bad work in which Martha permitted her "gorgeousness" to get out of hand—her hand.

NOTE: Leo and Gray went to Europe for a summer holiday, which would include their first return to Venice since 1953. During a gathering at Penelope and Carol Reed's home in London, Leo had some sort of seizure, which was taken for a heart attack, although later tests revealed no cause. Gray believes in retrospect that it may have been an anxiety attack. Penelope Reed had called in Dr. Patrick Woodcock, a physician to many in the London theatrical community, to care for Leo, and the men became friends. After a week's recovery, Leo and Gray went on to Paris.

JOURNAL • JULY 13, 1975 • LONDON   I have done with *Pride and Prejudice*, which helped sustain me during this bloody seizure. I found *P & P* even more exhilarating than ever before—such sustained complacency. I think Miss Austen the most superior student of manners in the world, but this is because she so obviously invented them.

The most terrifying moments of my sickness were the fainting and then the iron band, which sought to bind my chest in the relentless vise—that was awful.

JULY 14, 1975   Patrick [Woodcock] told of Noël—alone at night in the Savoy, shaking and rigid with vigor and chattering, "Oh, Patrick, do put my cock in my hand, so I can at least toss myself off." He need not have died since nothing was wrong save his way of life—stopping in bed all day, eating chocolate incessantly.

JULY 19, 1975 • PARIS   I have just finished *The Vagabond* (Colette), not having read it in years. What a master, but no man could have written any of Colette. This, today, is a feminist document. They will (have they already?) made it into an edict. But it is a sensuous, sentient book—more poem than prose—no—it is prose of deep, but cool intensity—a nectarine or peach in hot summer, its juices unexpectedly cool beneath its sun-hot skin.

Yesterday, Federico [Pallavicini] came and off we went to the Petit Palais—there to feast on Fuseli. Superb—his craftsmanship, his color, and his fantasy—the torment, the tension—the horror, the vigor, the force. And how clear the seeds of David and the Pre-Raphaelites, the kinship with Blake and Romney (whom Fuseli befriended). It was a huge exhibit, which I drank in deeply in measured, slow drafts. I like the wit of Madame Fuseli, having the last laugh. She ends this exhibit, alone in a panel, smiling. What a curious home life they surely had. And how neurasthenic he was. Great depressions ooze like megrims [the blues] from these almost overartful drawings so fraught with phallicism. Then we saw the Vuillards—the marvelous panels—and the awful Cézanne "seasons," which confirms me in my dislike of much Cézanne.

JULY 21, 1975  Versailles looked like a Frith painting of a holidaymaking—Bank Holiday on Hampstead Heath. Enormous blue buses passing with tourists, dozens of buses like a logjam in the Kennebec. Africans, all sorts, selling heaps of goods laid out on clothes over the cobbles. Anthills broken open—what word descriptive?—of people—all agawk, agape. Horrid. We sped away through the quiet streets of Versailles (so secret a village) having circled paths in the park.

JULY 22, 1975  We went away to the Alcazar theater, so close to that described by Colette, so a part of that English music-hall life I knew in 1937 and in those vaudeville days in New York, and at one with my Grossinger years. But this was witty, lavish, ribald, talented—sometimes to genius—and above all joyous. The cancan in its Lautrec number made me drop a tear for my long-ago youth; the opening with the waiters made me drop a tear. Between tears I roared with laughter, was wide eyed and open mouthed at the exuberance, the gaiety—especially of the mad-mad waiters taking off the "artistes"; the Viennese waltzing—yards of tulle and lifts and swiveling; a soprano who elongated in her crinolines when she soared her scales; the capsule past of the musical with a black drag queen doing a superlative "Bill" while two male waiters wailed, fell sobbing upon one another; the grand finale (in a very long show of many finales) in which the whole company went Latin American and all sorts of other rhythmic wild, while cascades of rose petals, confetti, colored streamers, and huge balloons snowed into the audience; and—oh—the great snowstorm which descended upon one huge, mincing transvestite, who then kicked mountains of it into the audience, which sat there feathered thickly and roaring with laughter. There were even doggies.

The necropolis feeling of Paris comes because so many of the beautiful buildings are no longer used for their original purpose. There is no real life, no living in them. Where once huge families rose up in the mornings, lay down in the nights, ate, voided, loved, hated, did accounts, talked servant problems and steel blades, jewels and fans and foolishness and shared eternity—now commerce, a life for which these buildings were not made, from which they stand apart. Will the [high-rise] Défense quarter become this too? It will have a shorter life. When architecture became flat-topped boxes, our world was ended, this new world came into being, a debased world of machines and heartlessness. Therefore the Alcazar show and the necropolis beauty of this city are so wrenchingly poignant.

JULY 23, 1975  At the intersection of the rue St. Honoré and the rue Cambon—suddenly Federico trotting along, neat in blue, but plain and a little wan. He was carrying a wild plaid carrier bag:

"Where have you been, Federico?"

"My bank."

"What do you have in that bag, Federico?"

"Eggies."

We were astonished to hear that he had, obviously, found eggies in his bank—nest-eggies? Then he drew, from this quite ordinary sack, life-size eggs of [solid] sapphire, ruby matrix ("Ugly," he said, "but . . .")—Fabergé. He has two hundred of these "eggies."

JULY 24, 1975   Across Paris in the burnished gold of evening—the Corot light—to Susan [Sontag] and Nicole [Stéphane],[8] who live in what Denyse [Dreyfus Harari] calls "such a dull, bourgeois neighborhood. How could they!" But the difference: They live with a great personal style—free; Denyse lives luxuriously, guilty of her money and privilege. Nicole (James-Henri de Rothschild's daughter) seems to have none of this. Her sister Margot is disturbed—but by what? "It's very typical, very French, this best-friend-being-your-sister," said Susan, and her under-voice was tired and tinged by a little sediment of resentment and worn patience.

Nicole is plumply beautiful; Susan, lean and wildly beautiful with writing her book (*On Photography*), which warms her like a constant fever. She has that fever-worn, bony beauty. "Nicole is the most loving, patient, kind woman. She gives everything, but sometimes she can't help just turning the screw, pressing in the needle," said Susan, when at dinner Nicole urged her to take a week to make a movie about Portugal. The former garden pavilion of Bébé Goldschmidt-Rothschild now houses Nicole—her floor with mullioned, trompe l'oeiled cupboards and some pretty Dutch paintings, Cocteau's drawing of her, a small Louise Abbéma portrait of Sarah Bernhardt with lust in it,[9] comfy furniture, distinguished odd chairs "from a gondola. They were my grandmother's." A pretty dining room. A large living room, looking out into a curtain of green. Up a ladderlike stair is Susan's floor, workmanlike, many books, piles of papers on the floor. "Each pile is a photographer. I really don't look at them, but they give me confidence."

JULY 29, 1975 · VENICE   The moment we walked along the quai to the Gritti [hotel]'s launch we felt as if we had been here always. We sit on the terrace, under the blue-and-white striped awning off the bar. The terrace life grows thicker. If we sit long enough, we will see everyone.

After our long day's enchanting rest, yesterday we went down and found Gore [Vidal]—big, complacent, pompous, assured that his every platitude is an apothegm, a witty wisdom. But despite this lifelong dry rot, he has charm

8. Nicole Stéphane (b. 1923), the French film actress (*Les Enfants Terribles*) and producer, was then the lover of essayist and novelist Susan Sontag (1933–2004).

9. Louise Abbéma's 1876 portrait of Bernhardt, who was rumored to be her lover, launched the painter's career.

and a certain attractiveness. He said that he didn't eat much, but drank a lot. "I'm an alcoholic. . . ." Later, when [*New York Review of Books* editor] Barbara Epstein joined him (they are motoring to Salzburg together), he said, "The reason alcoholics are so boring is that they are always thinking of the next drink." Of course, he ultimately asked about T and said, "Truman hasn't written anything in years, and what's more, he hasn't read anything in years."

At a certain moment, Puss passed me a note on a paper coaster: "C. P. Snow behind you." So, I animated the flow and finally turned to [his wife] Pamela Hansford Johnson.[10] After introductions, I said: "But you have written such scenes on terraces, and that handicaps you, since your scenes are so much more witty than our moment here." She sat gimlet eyed, sallow, dark browed, plump cheeked beneath implacable hair—a woman of spare—almost no—words (never a one between them), with the look of a bone from which all sustenance has been gnawed. Actually, she seems more moorscape than any other image. Her lord (his face Edna May Oliver's blown into a balloon[11]) rose with instant affability—a courteous man. We made the civilities and off they went, with hopes (the lord's and mine) that we would talk again and assurances that we all loved the Trillings, "Such good friends . . ." Meanwhile, Caroline Kennedy (rather pretty now that she has unlumped) and a traveling chum ran in and out like demented animals. Later, in the night, they ran (the chum barefooted) out into the gondola end of the pavement that side of the Gritti—their long American hair streaming behind—but a Secret Service man and plainclothes police drove them back into the hotel. Puss, going up to bed, talked to Caroline, who he says is just like all girls that age—vernacular, chewing-gummy, overflowing with adolescent energy and certain uncertainty.

JULY 30, 1975 • VENICE

**TO RICHARD HUNTER** • AUGUSTA, MAINE

Venice has been radiant. A glorious sojourn—with weather such as one has in childhood quite without even noticing it, but which as one grows older becomes a gift. We hired a car and spent most of a day at the Villa Maser. La Contessa was away (she and her sister), but preparations had been made for us, and we were given the "house" to lurk in and around by ourselves with the doggies. Well, it is the most beautiful Palladio house and church, and best of all is the quality of life which the Lulings (She's a Volpi) live in it—so many wonderful collections—and, on a richer more enormous scale, so much of what I've accumulated.

10. Baron C. P. Snow (1905–80), a British scientist, novelist, and biographer, was married to Pamela Hansford Johnson (1912–81), also a novelist.
11. Edna May Oliver (1883–1942) often played amusing spinsters onscreen (*Little Women, David Copperfield*).

JOURNAL • AUGUST 3, 1975 • MONTE CARLO Last night, the town, especially the Hotel de Paris and the crowd filling the opera house (a riot of decoration) was intensely carpetbagger. I think of Maria and her life here—her joys and her miseries and how her career really ended when Elsa Maxwell (that round, sick, archly painted clown's face, the face of a procuress) came into her life—with her party, her perverse smile, and her passion—black steel rods from her dark eyes. That moment [in 1956] was the end of the Callas glory.

AUGUST 4, 1975 Yesterday's almost daylong visit with Lesley [Blanch], in that villa above the tracks [in Menton]. Lesley's made her little house into a Turkish corner—it is hidden in vines, creepers, crushing green growths, and flowering shrubberies—heavy with jasmine, jacaranda, scented geraniums, and that fragrance peculiar to Mediterranean places—a mixture of olive oil, sun heat, vegetable growth, and salt sea. "The most polluted bit of sea on the entire coast, my dears," Lesley cries. She is unchanged—her head swathed in muslins, her body robed in mysterious garments from Afghanistan and Egypt and Persia and Tuareg countries, and her cupboards bulging with splendors from the Near East—robes given by sheikhs after passion, robes bought from the backs of workers in kitchens and fields and palaces, robes scrounged in souks. "Oh, my dears, I don't know why I'm alive—the life I've led. Why aren't I riddled with dread diseases?" Lesley cries, her retrospective raptures those of an intrepid English *amoureuse* who has achieved repeated exotic triumphs. All so Lesley—and her constant stream of talk—complaints, conjectures, gossip, thought, romances . . . now the fill is Pierre Loti—her work in progress.[12]

In her "extra" kitchen a huge fridge gleams, *un cadeau* from [French banker] Pierre David-Weill: "With whom I had a little do in New York. You know Nicole was mad about him, they were lovers for years, and he gave her everything—that fortune and that house and that grotto and that impeccable green lawn . . . everything. She adored him. My do was while she was ill in New York. I was there . . . and I knew that this was just a little . . . Well, when I was going away, and it was at an end, he said, 'You are a very impractical woman, and instead of a brooch, I am going to give you a refrigerator—the biggest and the best.' At that time, they were impossible to get in France—and the duty! So it was arranged to send it diplomatic—and that all went wrong. One day a small child rushed up, from the *poste* in Roquebrune, crying that the *douane* [customs officer] in Marseilles wanted me. So off I went, and they said an enormous shipment had arrived for me from America, and the duty was $600. I didn't have that money, and how to explain to Romain?[13] Oh—my

12. Lesley Blanch was writing a biography of Pierre Loti (1850–1923), a French author of novels set in exotic locales.
13. Blanch was then married to French diplomat and novelist Romain Gary (1914–80).

dears . . . So, I went away and thought and thought, and finally I went back to the *douane* and wept and told him, through my tears, that it was a *cadeau pour l'amour,* and he smiled and said '*Mais non . . .*' and understood. So, there was 100 francs to pay—and then the trauma, my dears, of getting it up the mountains and into the house, where it stood, dead center in the kitchen—for months—and when Romain came, all he said was that he needed ice—and never even noticed it!" The most contemporary Maupassant I have ever heard.

AUGUST 18, 1975 • NEW YORK CITY  Last night in the Magic Pan [restaurant] we found Martha [Graham] and her dark amanuensis, Ron Protas. Martha looks frail—a flame burning to death-thin brightness—but she is overflowing with that intensity peculiar to herself. She has projects to outlast another lifetime. "History is the garment of God," she said to me: "That's Blake, I think. . . . 'A seed must dissolve in the earth, fall apart before it begins to give life again.' You know who said that to me? You mustn't tell—that's Doris Duke [the reclusive heiress]. She takes class sometimes. She's been doing it for years. . . ." She enveloped me in her radiance, her blazing self shutting out the world, while keeping it all within our luminous pavilion. When we came out, there she was, looking up at the moon from the filthy Manhattan pavement.

AUGUST 26, 1975  T called yesterday to regale me with his future movie-star career. "I'll be dressed [for *Murder by Death*] by Dunhill—three outfits, and I'm going to Canada for a week to get in place. There's a marvelous place there. I'm a real star. How's my sweet, darling Gray?" Also he told me that *Esquire* will publish the section of "Answered Prayers" we turned down. T was being adorable.[14]

SEPTEMBER 11, 1975  Avedon's opening [at the Marlborough Gallery]— Hundreds of marginal persons and many looking like stars but anonymous. Avedon's entrance, with mother and *naches-schleppers* [hangers-on], then comes from Avedon, "Where's Louise Dahl-Wolfe?" as through the Red Sea of wide eyes he cut (followed by [photographer] Milton Green) bellowing, "I was her assistant!"[15] When Avedon got to Louise, at the far end of the main room, he clutched her to his bosom, deftly hiding her face there, while cameras clicked and other lens "stars," now safely entombed in books, looked sourly on. This was a "star" performance—the *vedette* on the crest, seeking, vociferously, the

14. *Esquire* had published one section of "Answered Prayers," titled "Mojave," in its June 1975 issue. *Vogue*'s letter of agreement and advance payment had given it a right of first refusal. Leo noted later that Capote had to return $25,000 advanced to him by Diana Vreeland.
15. Louise Dahl-Wolfe (1895–1989) had been *Bazaar*'s fashion photographer for eight years before Avedon came to the magazine in 1944. He immediately became editor Carmel Snow's favorite, but Dahl-Wolfe stayed until 1958, often doing *Bazaar*'s covers. She regarded Avedon as a usurper, not as an apprentice.

nearest, safe, living legend, and tailed by a fallen star, one not on the crest. The exhibit (really the "show") tells that Avedon hasn't a shred of humanity in him. I mean each person photographed is maimed, sick, ugly. There is no warmth here, certainly no nobility. Again the camera lies—or at best tells a smidgen of the truth.

SEPTEMBER 17, 1975 Visit to Tilly Losch on Saturday afternoon. Tilly dying. Does she know? She says that she is, but she then says, "I'm regressing, not improving. . . ." She laughs a lot, is very Tilly. I think of Rut, and how when Tilly was mentioned, Rut softened, as if the color of delight was tingeing her entire being. Tilly talked about how Richard Strauss had discovered her, a small child at the barre in Vienna, and how she had progressed from helping to carry on the veils (*Salome*) to Reinhardt's Deutsches Theater and so to Cochran.[16]

So the echoes of Rut and Ela went on, and Tilly sipped a little borscht that Puss had made for her, and we went away leaving her all alone. I was so deeply overcome—beyond depression—that I did not go to [publicist Earl] Black-well's party for Liza [Minnelli]. I could not. Here was the past, the smell of it, the feel of it, in those huge cat eyes of Tilly's so world famous years ago.

OCTOBER 18, 1975 • NEW YORK CITY
**TO RICHARD HUNTER • PARIS**

Marlene is here in the hospital and asked would I call. Her choices are: an operation during which she could die (plastic hips) or three months in traction and remain crippled the rest of her days.[17] Meanwhile Rudi [Sieber, after a stroke] is paralyzed in California. He can speak a few German words and cannot move at all! Awesome. When I rang Marlene in the hospital, she had her little-girl voice and tried to act "well" and sounded deathly bright.

JOURNAL • OCTOBER 31, 1975 My telephone "chat" with C. Z. Guest [socialite garden columnist]: "Those girls were fools to tell Truman everything. He told me everything they told him. What did they expect? I've traveled with him over the country—I've never told him anything. . . ."[18]

NOVEMBER 3, 1975 [*New York Times* writer] Charlotte Curtis lunched with Alex and me at La Côte Basque. She knew Jackie Onassis at Vassar, and two of

16. The British impresario of revues C. B. Cochran (1872–1951) had Tilly Losch choreograph and dance numbers in his show *Wake Up and Sing* (1928). She also starred in Balanchine's *Les Ballets 1933*.
17. Dietrich had again collapsed, this time with a broken femur at a performance in Sydney, Australia. The leg would be put into traction for some four months.
18. Capote's "La Côte Basque" appeared in the November 1975 *Esquire*. The thinly fictionalized society figures in his story were humiliated and outraged by it. Ann Woodward, whose real-life shotgunning of her blueblood husband had been recycled by Capote, committed suicide. Worse for the author, many society friends (including his idol, Babe Paley) cut him off afterward.

Charlotte's roommates knew her very well. Charlotte's summing up of J.O.: "Rapacious."

I fell, crossing Forty-fifth Street, walking with Alex. Me: "Did I tear my suit? It's my favorite suit!" Alex: "Don't do this to me. It's bad for my heart. . . . It's been so wonderful working with you. . . ."

NOVEMBER 11, 1975   Lionel Trilling's funeral in an academically filled Columbia chapel. A smiling grad student led us through a secret passage into the old campus and so by an American medieval stair into the chapel. The penetrating stench of dying flowers—chrysanthemums . . . the plain coffin under the pale blue, white-bordered, and crown-blazoned pall of Columbia— a last royal vestige . . . the assembly of Trilling friends, relatives, colleagues, and the discreet, the educated air of this assembling. Only those who knew the individual rancors and rigors could see the visible signs on faces, in movements. Much of the service in Hebrew, a cantor singing beautifully settings I have never heard. Later, Diana said, "Li and I wrote that service out a year ago. He found the texts: I wrote it. Then he shrugged. . . ." She said this sitting in their bedroom at the foot of the "fantasy" bed they had both occupied so many years. In the crematorium, a moment when Diana took the pall from the coffin, folded it neatly, and gave it to James Lionel. This was, I felt, the silent commemoration of a Victor in Academic Wars. Then Diana and James Lionel walked swiftly up the brief aisle and out of the little room—very like Adam and Eve going from Eden in the Masaccio in Florence.

NOVEMBER 12, 1975   James Lionel on the blower: "She's organizing everything. She's so busy organizing—and me most." His air of exasperated amusement at Diana. I suggested that she be given New York City to organize.

NOVEMBER 16, 1975   At Momma's. How sharp she is: As I peered covertly to see which cheese-and-onion sandwich had the most filling, Momma said, "That one." We had the same deeply interested look.

DECEMBER 1, 1975   When Laurence Olivier told Alfred Lunt, over the blower, that he (Olivier) was seventy, Alfred responded, "Well, now it's time to take up Spanish dancing." When Alfred told Noël Coward that he was going blind and asked Noël what, if he were going blind, he would do first, Noël said, "I'll have to sleep on it." The next morning he came down to breakfast and said, "Alfred, the first thing to do is not to have whitebait on a white plate." The savagery of this joshing and the relentless chin-up.

## To Welcome the New Year

Wanda [Toscanini] Horowitz

Wally [Toscanini] Castelbarco

Sally Horwitz

Lennie Bernstein

Felicia Bernstein

Jamie Bernstein

Harold Reed

Marjorie Reed

Steven Kyle

Betty [Comden] Kyle

Herbert Kasper

Dolly Haas

Al Hirschfeld

Marion Field

Woody Allen

Dorothy Hammerstein

Marina Schiano

Richard Rodgers

Dorothy Rodgers

Charlotte Curtis

Leontyne Price

Hubert Dilworth

Eileen Herlie

Paula Landesman

Fred Landesman

William Cahan

Grace Mirabella

Gerry Stutz Gibbs

David Gibbs

Dorothea Straus

Roger Straus

Alex Liberman

Tatiana Liberman

Arthur Cohen

Elaine Cohen

Paula Laurence Bowden

Chuck Bowden

Beverly Sills Greenough

Peter Greenough

Joel Grey

Jo Grey

Sandra Feigen

Richard Feigen

Estée Lauder

Joe Lauder

Leonard Lauder

Evelyn Lauder

Ann Gaussen

Gerard Gaussen

Milton Goldman

Arnold Weissberger

John Lindsay

Mary Lindsay

Mindy Wager

Bea Renfield

Deda Blair

Mary Lasker

Anita Loos

Enid Haupt

Morton Gottlieb

Diana Vreeland

Gwen Verdon

Maureen Stapleton
Bobby Fosse
Irene Worth
Julie Harris
Geraldine Page
Rip Torn
Lynn Redgrave
Donald Sinden
Mrs. Donald [Diana] Sinden
Celeste Holm
Wesley Addy
Schuyler Chapin
Mrs. Schuyler [Elizabeth] Chapin
Aileen Mehle ["Suzy"]
Peter Glenville
Bill Smith
Tammy Grimes
Cynthia O'Neal
Patrick O'Neal
Lloyd Williams
Anne Peerce
Joel Kaye
Gene Hovis
Hans Tietz
Christopher Plummer
Mrs. C. [Elaine Taylor] Plummer
Arthur Laurents
Tom Hatcher
Martha Graham
Ron Protas
Françoise de la Renta
Oscar de la Renta
Ismail Merchant
James Ivory
Peter Shaffer
Alexis Smith
Hal Prince
Judy Prince
Constance Hope Berliner
Theo Berliner
Carole Shelley

Mitzi Newhouse
Scott McKay
Samuel Adams Green
John Wood
Si Newhouse
Victoria Newhouse
Joan [Micklin] Silver
Eleanor Perry
Frank Perry
Clive Barnes
[Patricia] Tish Barnes
Lydia Gregory
[George] Grischa Gregory
André Gregory
Chiquita Gregory
Alex Gregory
Tamara Guilden
Prince [Alexander] Romanov
Mimi di Niscemi
Ruth Gordon
Garson Kanin
Joan Sutherland
Richard Bonynge
Pavarotti (plus two)
Chesbrough Rayner
William Rayner
Halston
Elsa Peretti
Victor Elmaleh
Sono Osato Elmaleh
Nicolas Nabokov
Dominique Nabokov
Candice Bergen
Charles Ludlum
Barbara Walters
Richard Avedon
Nancy Kissinger
Henry Kissinger
Louise Nevelson
André Emmerich
Sybil Burton

| | |
|---|---|
| Jordan Christopher | Evelyn Lambert |
| Jean Stralem | Marisa Berenson |
| Jack Frizzelle | Berry Berenson |
| Melanie Kahane Grauer | Tony Perkins |
| Ben Grauer | Federico Pallavicini |
| Rex Reed | Natacha Stewart |
| Joe Heller | Donna McKechnie |
| June Weir | Jay Castle |
| Mala Rubinstein | Estelle Parsons |
| Pauline Trigère | Norman Singer |
| Lee Radziwill | Goddard Lieberson |
| Shirley Lord Anderson | Brigitta Lieberson |
| David Anderson | Horst & Co. |
| Joanne Cummings | Lillian Hellman |
| Nat Cummings | Sylvia Lyons |
| Bobby Short | Alain Coblence |
| Arthur Gold | Faye Dunaway |
| Robert Fizdale | Persian Ambassador |
| Rosamond [Bernier] Russell | Ernest and Barbara Kafka |
| John Russell | Jule Styne |
| Rita Moreno | Mikhail Baryshnikov |
| Andrew Anspach | Gelsey Kirkland |
| Kenny Lane | Rudolf Nureyev |
| The Guidi [Gioia and Marcello] | Erik Bruhn |
| George Balanchine | Margot Fonteyn |
| Emlyn Williams | |

DECEMBER 31, 1975 When next I write, that will be in 1976. I have had a long silence. I do not know why, but now I must continue. Remember— December 24—the unexpected dizzy spell. This week—the clot. So I must continue. Tilly died the day before Christmas. She was the last of the really *vie de scandale* ladies. I sit on the side of my bed listening to *The Gypsy Baron* and the finale of *Fledermaus* and now will make the list of flowers for Christmas, and telephones [calls] for New Year's—so pitifully small. Marlene's being chums again. Jerry Lerman hasn't rung in two months. Little T mentioned me on "national" television. I have Miss Mapp suspicions about that.[19] So life goes—but I must complete my book before I go with life. So off to [the ballets]

19. Miss Elizabeth Mapp is a small-town busybody in E. F. Benson's Lucia novels.

*Lilac Garden* and *Spectre de la Rose* and Woody [Allen]'s party and the Motherthalers' [Robert Motherwell and Helen Frankenthaler] and so into 1976.

I said to Paula Laurence: "If you don't write a book, I'll put on your tombstone, 'Guess Who's Here!' " Merriment.

FEBRUARY 9, 1976  I must do something about this prison [*Vogue*]. It is becoming airless. I enjoy the writing—such as it is—when I am writing—and even planning, but I am stultifying. The deepest places are becoming arid, parched. What can I do? I knew that I was selling myself into some sort of servitude, but I did not know the price. I now begin to know the price. I can pay it still, but not for long. What can I do?

MARCH 1, 1976  Marlene yesterday—a hank of hair, swollen legs, walking with a walker from which hangs a Saint Laurent bag. Too awful. "You never know anything," she said, "about anyone. . . ." This is the total of all that glamour, that experience?

MAY 14, 1976  Paul Bonner [director of Condé Nast Books] recalled today that Alec Woollcott had once told his mother that she had to go and see Ela, who was "desolate" in a hospital. His mother didn't like Ela "much," but she went—and returned wrathful: "Desolate! Einstein was sitting there. Casals had just left. Toscanini was on his way in. . . ."

NOTE: After five years of delay, Leo underwent cataract surgery on his right eye in July 1976. The procedure dramatically improved his perception of color and distance.

JOURNAL • JULY 10, 1976  The semi-stillness of this hospital night—my little radio delicately diffusing quiet eighteenth-century music—the nearby low chatter of nurses and aides—early morning shufflings and scufflings—four a.m., the dying hour. The tide goes out, carrying with it. A golden, puffy biscuit of a moon in the southern sky. A nurse, with the friendly ghastliness of a skeletal head, came in. "No sleep," she stated. She had little English, but she was full of grisly, amiable smiles. [Private-duty] Nurse Coles, having never read Henry James, plunged into my little paper-covered copy of *The American* and devoured it. She said, "I never get to meet this class of people on a case."

7:50 A.M.  All quiet. Stockinged and socked, my legs are still good-looking—such is vanity! But all of my "good" features have been walloped—mouth, teeth, eyes—even nose dented. So a little vanity about legs—although varicosed and blood-clotted—that little vanity *is* permitted!

JULY 12, 1976  I know the operation happened to me, but it is as if it had not happened to me. I can hear the remarkable characters talking as they snipped and stitched—and I lie here bandaged—but, as in so much of my life, it partook of me. I know it. I was "in being" through it—and in some state of extension. Perhaps paper is a good image: I write upon this paper; that experience wrote upon me.

AUGUST 5, 1976 Meeting Francis Robinson, last night—he seemed tight (and was). He's lost (temporarily) his fiendish laughter. He said, "I can't write a truthful book. Why, if I wrote the truth about Bing—the publisher's lawyers wouldn't let them publish. Of all the people I've known, he was the most evil. He was pure evil." Francis said this with a detachment born of experiencing this evil, a detachment that was horror frozen into a semblance of detachment. But I knew this the first time I saw Bing. I came home and told Puss, "I have just seen a truly dreadful man."[20]

AUGUST 23, 1976 "Rudolf, this is where we throw the baby to the wolves." Martha Graham while the photograph was being taken for "What Becomes a Legend Most?"[21]

NOVEMBER 1, 1976 Saturday lunch at Jane Gunther's. All summer joy in an autumn afternoon swept clean of clouds by great gusts—and tumbles and seesaws of laughter. Then the doorbell rang and in came an unidentifiable woman. "Valentina [Schlee] seems changed," Puss and I thought. She had changed: She was Garbo—the only (?) authentic legend left. Garbo is beautiful (or we thought her beautiful) when she laughs—throwing her head back and becoming, suddenly, the essence of laughter, golden laughter, pure joy before any of us knew of pollution, contamination. She has abrupt shifts— almost like an actor who has been directed to speak thoughts in a character submerged until this moment. She murmured to herself: "I don't talk to anybody. . . . I don't talk over anything. . . . So I am forgetting. . . . I forget the past." She is full of wide-eyed incredulities and amazements. She is sometimes so similar to Marlene, in a kind of German down-to-earth impregnable confidence. And she is permeated by self-raillery. She seems almost always poised for flight—solitary—so solitary. She was dressed in men's clothes, very good, tans and browns, outdoor clothes made for walking. She walks everywhere. She is startled at things we all know. Example: The Trade Center. She had instant visions of Indians trading their pelts and baskets.

**GLIMPSES OF GARBO** *If I can manage to say something that amuses this Swede, she will become the Garbo we have all loved. She is addicted to asking what I think are foolish questions. She says that she walks an enormous*

20. Francis A. Robinson (1910–80), assistant manager (1952–76) of the Metropolitan Opera, was writing a book on the company, as was its retired general manager Rudolf Bing.
21. Graham was speaking to Nureyev, with whom she and Margot Fonteyn were being photographed in furs for an advertisement.

amount, and how long would it take her to walk from her place, East Fifty-second Street, to those new buildings down in the harbor. I do not think for a moment that she does not know how long. She asks questions about places, and I'm sure she knows what those places are. The voice is lovely, quiet, Swedish-inflected—a voice with reservation in it. But when she laughs, everything is there. By and by, it is three or four hours later, and she gets up, goes to the door. We all follow to see her go down the street. She walks off swiftly, a single straight line slightly veering to the left as she fades into the distance. It was laughter that revivified her, that nourished her into being Greta Garbo. It was audiences that nourished Marlene into being the Marlene of legend.

.   .   .

I am crossing Madison Avenue with Eudora Welty, who has just lunched with me in the Carlyle. We are talking animatedly about some photographs she's taken of the circus, and about what she has written, and as we step into the gutter, for the traffic is stopped, Eudora clutches my arm. She is breathless, incredulous, a little girl opening a Christmas surprise: "Look!" she whispers. I look, but I do not see anything, and suddenly the lights change, the traffic rushes, and so does Eudora. She is gone, sprinting up the avenue after some invisible figure. Later that day I ring up the Algonquin. "Eudora, where in hell did you go?" She says, "I followed her!" I say, "Who in hell's name did you follow?" A silence. Eudora says, "Didn't you see her? Garbo!" I laugh. "Did you meet her? Did you talk to her? You would have scared the devil out of her!" Eudora says, "I followed her up Madison Avenue and she went into Jensen's and she looked at things and picked them up, but she didn't buy anything, and she went up the avenue and looked into most of the windows, and I looked at her and her reflection—didn't dare talk to her, and—oh—what a wonderful afternoon."

.   .   .

I am going up the Gunthers's stair, this is in the late evening after a Broadway opening. I am in my black tie and my old black suit. As I go up the stair, toward sounds of revelry, I see on the landing, where I know there is a sofa, two beautiful, very large, black satin evening shoes. The shoes are on legs that swing. I can only see the ankles, rather heavyish ankles, utilitarian ankles, but they swing in a girl-ish way, under endless minute ruffles of black lace. As I get higher, there are more and more ruffles of black lace. I get to the midriff where the black lace ends tightly and where a stalwart bodice rises to a face surrounded by Camille-like blondish ringlets. I see Miss Garbo, whose hands are folded neatly in her lap. As I get to the landing, I see that behind Miss Garbo is, posed impassively, disguised as a handmaiden, arms folded like Ftatateeta [Cleopatra's nurse], cloaked in a voluminous flux of beige, head to foot, Valentina. . . . As I stand there about to extend a hand, two girls rush by, clutching one another's hands, obviously Mäd-chen from some provincial German finishing school, giggling away. These girls drag me between them, rush me into a back parlor, and sit me down on a small *sofa where three people could hardly sit. The girls are Marlene Dietrich and Vera Zorina. We sit there clutching one another, and I laugh. The girls look up, then I look up, and in the corner is a solid bank of backs in black evening suits, impenetrable men standing in a semicircle, and as one of them goes away the circle parts, and we can see clearly, in the corner, a young woman, a rather smoky blonde in a somewhat worn-seeming white evening dress. She is Grace Kelly. None of the men look at Dietrich, Zorina, or Garbo.*

. . .

*I am lunching again in the old dining room of the Plaza. Suddenly a great quiet. All talk and clatter ceases and all eyes are looking at two women who walk swiftly, almost stealthily, between the tables. One has a great big hat clamped down over her face and a great big coat covering herself and a very determined stride. The other is Jane Gunther, who is very pretty. She does not even give me a glance, and I have known her since she was sixteen. They both go to the far end of the room. The room resumes its chatter-clatter. Suddenly, there is an enormous rush from the far end of the room, and Miss Garbo runs the full length of the room and is gone. Later in the day I ring up Jane, who says, "She didn't really like all that attention." I say, "Well, if she didn't like all that attention, she certainly managed to get it, didn't she?"* (1993)

JOURNAL · DECEMBER 11, 1976 · BETHEL, CONNECTICUT  Having showered, breakfasted, gaped at the wooded vistas and the rolling hills and the windswept skies [at Mina's], having eaten them hungrily—oh—how I crave trees and skies and nature's own voices—winds, silences . . . I am so happy to have my eyes again. The fogs of these last years—are they vanishing? Will this help me to put the horrors of Liberman's *Vogue* in true proportion? I must alleviate them. I coped with this last operation—physical and mental pain. Surely I can cope with this. I must.

DECEMBER 27, 1976  [Senator] Eugene McCarthy at a Christmas party: "I don't like Jimmy Carter; he uses too many adverbs. I didn't like McGovern; he used too many adjectives. And I don't like any of the senators; they're all fools."

JANUARY 2, 1977  Anita [Loos] says Vivien Leigh came to her just a few months before she died and said, "Anita, can't you think of a play for me? Can't you? They don't write plays for pretty women anymore." Larry [Olivier] brought Vivien to see Anita when they first came to Hollywood and Vivien told Anita: "You know how I managed the press? I told them everything Larry and I did and in such four-letter words—four times an hour I told them—that they didn't dare print a word of it!"

Stella Adler, when Ned Rorem[22] told her that he had been introduced to her

---

22. Ned Rorem (b. 1923), an American composer of art songs and choral music, gained some notoriety in the sixties and seventies by publishing his frank journals.

five times and she still did not recognize him: "To me all *goyim* look alike." Stella was stopped by a man who said, "I knew your mother when you were born. I know her age then, so how can you be forty-five now?" Stella: "My mother had her age, and I had mine."

JANUARY 15, 1977 • WASHINGTON, D.C. Kay Graham and [political columnist] Joe Alsop's dinner for the Kissingers and Rockefellers in Kay's house, a coldish seeming (at least in the rooms I saw) largish house, set behind a circular drive—sheets of ice. I think this would all be more *gemütlich* in spring and summer. The dinner—a "family affair" for sixty or seventy. Many I. P. s (International People)—Rockefellers, Guinnesses, [William] Paley (she is too ill?), Harrimans, Agnellis—that chic—all in *grand tenue*—the hostess distrait in purple chiffon—and magazine guests as pawns. Evangeline [Bruce] in lion's mane hair and masses of gold coin;[23] Marietta [Tree] always a bit bimbo; Mary Alsop in Alix Grès—masses of folds and pleats;[24] [Mrs. Nelson] Happy Rockefeller in burgundy chiffon—and so much assurance everywhere. Mrs. Laurence Rockefeller talked to me about plane versus train travel. She hadn't been on a train in years, since "We have our planes," but she is a kindly faced older woman, in discreet diamonds and well-brushed black velvet. I wish I knew where everyone's from and why they came. Sally Quinn knows, and there she was with her American-girl atmosphere—a real campus-date flavor—very hug-bunny.[25] Also Meg Greenfield—small, smooth as a sea-smoothed pebble—in a harlequin-patterned and colored tight-skin dress.[26] Kissinger very late-German-Empire and asking couldn't I persuade Nancy to stop smoking. "Only," I said, "by appealing to her concern for others . . . telling her that it was bad for those around her." "What a diplomat you are," he said, laughing. Nancy in white shirt with deep neck ruffles and black full skirt and tossing fifties American-girl hair—always an immediate good-girl chum. It was a scattered evening with spot exchanges, "witty" speeches, family badinage, and everyone sure of everyone else—a sort of Whig establishment (Holland House in the late 1790s, early 1810s). Washington has, indeed, been taken by the South. So they have, dear Margaret Mitchell, won the war at last. Scarlett's day has come—but a little on the trashy side.

---

23. Leo's friend the socialite and writer Evangeline Bell Bruce (1914–95) was married to David Bruce, who had been U.S. ambassador to France, West Germany, and the United Kingdom.
24. Susan Mary Alsop (1918?–2004), considered the grande dame of Washington, D.C., society, was also a historian who had been married (1961–73) to columnist Joseph Alsop.
25. Sally Quinn, a journalist, became the second wife of *Washington Post* executive editor Ben Bradlee in 1978. "Hug-bunny" was Leo's term for an amiable, informal eatery, typically with a collegiate atmosphere.
26. Mary Ellen "Meg" Greenfield (1930–99) was editor of the *Washington Post's* editorial page.

MAY 10, 1977 · NEW YORK CITY  The *va-et-vient* of our Liberman weekend [in Connecticut]. Marella Agnelli—the young girl still shining through the wear of time—something flowerlike in her. She said: "So we fly to the skiing and then the helicopter takes us to the yacht for the swimming—and from the ice to the warm sea—all in a few hours—horrible. I did it three times and I told Gianni, 'Never again'—too boring."[27]

MAY 11, 1977  Joan Crawford is dead, the first of "those" ladies to go— Marlene, Garbo left. Marlene crippled, bitter in Paris; Greta Garbo wandering, and, when made to laugh, a luminous glimpse of her old self. But Joan Crawford made us all laugh. She never quite knew how much hilarity she gave, with her huger-than-life self, her belief in her Movie Queen infallibility. She never knew why, when Mitzi [Newhouse] introduced us at a gala years ago (a gala in which J.C. was one of the threesome who chaired [the Mayor's Committee for Free] Shakespeare, the antithesis of what she represented) why I laughed and laughed out of delight at my memory of what she had been to us. I roared, as I shook her strong hand, "Oh—you've given me so much pleasure. . . ." and she took this as her due, her eyes shining narcissistically, all glowing with self-pleasure. Her enormous eyes always semaphored a Morse code of good-humored mockery and "I know what pleasure is all about." Light danced in her eyes. Early in her career she was a good actress and, of course, she was a beauty, who projected her self-knowledge of this. She also projected the vulnerability of a strange creature—always touching. And in her was a strong element of transvestitism: She was a model for female impersonators. Do not forget how she summarized her era—the twenties and thirties. She was one of the authentic Screen Stars in our world of movie make-believe.

MAY 30, 1977  Yesterday, during lunch at the Cahans,[28] Bill suddenly said, while talking about how tired he and Grace [Mirabella] were, "Goddard died at two a.m." The shock was knife-jab sudden—a sharp slice of hot-cold unexpected pain from an unpremeditated knife. I suspect that he had been wondering how to tell us—but perhaps he told us this way because he can have no idea of the place Goddard and Brigitta had in our lives, in the earlier years of our life together.

I came home, rang Brigitta—no answer—and no answer into the night. At ten, I suddenly knew that Brigitta must be at Felicia's. I rang, Lennie answered. (How curious if Goddard's death returns Lennie to Felicia.) He said that Brigitta was indeed there, in the bath. How extraordinary (and how only Proust

---

27. The Agnellis owned Fiat. Giovanni ("Gianni") Agnelli (1921–2003) and his wife Princess Marella Caracciolo di Castagneto (b. 1927) were for years the personification of jet-set industrialists.

28. In 1974, Grace Mirabella had married Dr. William Cahan (1914–2001), a thoracic surgeon who would later oversee Leo's medical treatment.

could have anticipated this convolution)—the envy, even hatred of Goddard & Brigitta for Felicia & Lennie twists their relationship. Brigitta detested Felicia and raged about her because Felicia had usurped Brigitta's role, sailing on Lennie's reputation onto concert stages, delivering the [performance] works Brigitta had made her own. . . . That moment in Brigitta's room at Lenox Hill [hospital] when Felicia rang to tell her that she was doing *Jeanne d'Arc au Bûcher* and to ask her advice on dress—and Brigitta's explosion of rage and hatred after she rang off.[29] . . . Goddard sitting in the Columbia box, at Carnegie Hall, following the score Lennie was conducting—following it sardonically. (How Goddard envied Lennie's success as conductor and composer.) . . . Felicia saying to Goddard, in the Plaza dining room, while lunching: "God-dard—look—at—me!" because he had wandering eyes, and never could, until recently, content himself with being with the person he was with[30] . . . all of this . . . and the birthday dinners. Somehow we were inevitably involved—on both sides. The Liebersons were the enviers—no matter what they achieved—until recent years, when not only did the envy seem to diminish, but the competitiveness between Brigitta and Goddard seemed to cease. Did Brigitta's religion help? Or was this age?

Brigitta rang me and was worn, quiet, affectionate. She said that the evening had been quiet, that he had gone to sleep at about midnight, that Peter [their son] had woken her at about one—all quiet, Goddard breathing quietly—then about 1:40 Goddard stopped breathing. . . . She hugged him and he started breathing again. At two he stopped breathing as she held his hand, and he was gone. "Peter opened the window, for the first time in weeks, and a great cold wind came up, roaring away in the night," she said. Now here she was stopping with Felicia, and Lennie answering the telephone, and their lives even more deeply entwined. . . . Rain fell all night long, last night.

The last thing Goddard said to me, a week ago, when I told him that I had seen his television show and how good it was, "When I wake up . . . if I wake up . . . they put me to sleep so much . . . we'll see one another. . . ." He did not wake up, and will we see one another? That is the great adventure.

JUNE 5, 1977 The end first: A deep, as deep as chasms in the sea, nightmare. I remember only my screaming, howling—a far-off monstrous noise—and Puss rushing into this room. "Thank you for rescuing me," I told him, without even surfacing from this deep deep. Was it the result of suddenly suspecting a conspiracy of women—a conspiracy that they do not plan, but is part of the

29. *Jeanne d'Arc au Bûcher* [ *Joan of Arc at the Stake*] is a dramatic oratorio by Arthur Honegger and Paul Claudel. Much of Brigitta Lieberson's later career had been narrating such works.

30. What Leo had never heard, until the ensuing days, was that while Leonard Bernstein had pursued extramarital homosexual pleasures, his wife Felicia at one point had an affair with Goddard Lieberson.

fabric of their being? At [interior designer] Melanie Kahane's to pay our "obligations," I suddenly, looking about at table, realized that we are now surrounded by widows. Why? Why do women survive their men? At Goddard's memorial, we sat with Diana [Trilling]—a widow, Sylvia Marlowe—a widow, Marion Field, Sylvia Lyons—widows. Did I scream in the night because I felt hunted? (Image here: Jerry Robbins's *The Cage*.) I see Eileen Maremont, a widow to be.[31] Will Tatiana survive Alex? In homosexual relationships which partner survives? Momma survives—but here I pause. Poppa slept his life away.

The little circle of friends quite obliterated as a circle in the larger manifestation of Goddard's "formal" obsequies in the Beth El chapel of Temple Emanu-El. Some 350 invited "guests"—all chosen by Brigitta, who had started these arrangements a week before Goddard died. So Goddard had, at last, the party he had always wanted. Diana Trilling said, on the blower, "Truman had his party while alive, but Goddard had to die to have his." The composition of both parties was similar—indeed overlapping—but this time we sat with Diana, who had asked us to sit with her. When I settled in, Diana whispered, "Lillian [Hellman]—five rows directly in front of me . . ." Indeed, the blondined head beneath a fierce hat was there. Row on row: Mrs. Onassis, Princess Lee [Radziwill], Charlie Addams, the Richard Rodgers (all three), Mai-mai [Sze] and Irene [Sharaff], the little circle, everyone . . . and all quite cold . . . not a party of genuine convives, but "guests." This was the place to be at 10:45 a.m. on Friday morning, June 3. These were "party" people, on view to other "party" people. I felt that the lights would dim, the overture strike up, and the "piece"—a play with music, would get under way. A quartet filed in, the "speakers" came on—Lennie, Bill Schuman,[32] [Walter] Cronkite, two temple men. One came to the lectern, opened his mouth, and out came a sure, sweet, simple song. I couldn't have been more surprised. . . . Then followed the usual tributes (oh, yes—Betty [Comden] was the only woman onstage, a visibly nervous Betty—so unsure). The acoustics—awful. The atmosphere not hottened up even by Betty's sincerity, Lennie's Hebrew sallies . . . nothing dispelled the chill. Then we stood, endlessly, in line to kiss the widow, who stood pale, exhausted, and determined to do her duty, as Mrs. O had done.

The next morning I rang Brigitta, and Felicia's housekeeper told me that she had gone to Europe. When I told Puss, he said, "She's swimming to the next raft." And that is what she's done all of her life: All survivors do that.[33]

---

31. A prophetic remark, as Arnold Maremont would die suddenly of a heart attack the next year, with only his wife and Gray present. Marion Field was the widow of a Hollywood producer and Sylvia Lyons of Broadway columnist Leonard Lyons.
32. Composer William Schuman (1910–92) had been head of Juilliard and Lincoln Center.
33. Gray is alluding to the young Brigitta's chance meeting of Serge Lifar in Venice, which launched her ballet career.

JUNE 8, 1977 The Anita Bryant "outcry": When I read that she "even danced a little jig," I saw Hitler dancing his little jigs of "victory."[34] This country is full of latent and dramatized hysteria. Jews, blacks, Indians no longer can be kicked about to release these hysterias, so homosexuals are "fair game." What if we stopped paying income taxes: no civil rights, no income-tax payments?

JUNE 10, 1977 Irving Penn photographed me for an hour today. It was intercourse on the highest level of being. He nourishes, unlike Dick Avedon, who consumes, who psychs himself. Irving brings out the finest in his subject. This was like a two-man meditation.

NOTE: In 1977, Leo and Gray traveled abroad for the first time in two years. The summer was particularly memorable. They attended a gala weekend party, at the end of June, to mark the closing and death-duty sale of Crathorne Hall, the largest country house built in Edwardian England. Then from London they went to Paris, where they stayed until the Bastille Day holiday, visiting both Callas and Dietrich on July 6. Zurich, then Venice followed, with some days in the Veneto at the palatial villa of Evelyn Lambert. Through Lambert, and their friend the glass designer Charles Lin Tissot, a new level of Venetian society now opened to Leo. For the next ten years, each summer brought an extended trip to Europe, always including three to four weeks in Venice and its environs. Although these stays seldom had a specific business purpose, they often paid dividends in story ideas, leads, or connections, and Condé Nast reimbursed Leo's expenses.

**A PERSPECTIVE OF SACRED MONSTERS**[35] *July in Paris. We all know that everyone is gone, but this July Maria was there in her apartment and Marlene was there in her apartment.*

*In an afternoon, Gray and I went to spend some hours with Maria. We went into her very proper residence in the Avenue Georges Mendel, and her very proper servant let us into a very large apartment full of things and emptiness. It was one of the least occupied places I have ever been.*

*Maria came in. She was in an ample, bottle-green dressing gown. Her hair sleek, her eyes large and questioning. Her smile loving. She was fragile—something was missing. I think it was her spirit. I could no longer hear the sound of applause. From the first moment I had seen Maria, all those long years before in Venice, I had always heard the sound of applause. She settled into her sofa. We settled down beside her. She took out her eye drops and dashed them into her eyes. Maria smiled at us, and, for a moment, she was the old Maria. This was the wide, uninhibited, trusting smile of a very young girl. It was the Maria smile that had always managed to obliterate any anguish, any uncertainty, any intuition*

---

34. Anita Bryant (b. 1940), pop singer and onetime Miss Oklahoma, promoted the anti-homosexual "Save Our Children" campaign in Dade County, Florida, which led to repeal of an ordinance prohibiting discrimination on the basis of sexual orientation.
35. Leo later gave this title to the events.

*that all was not radiant, in which she could, for at least some moments soar beyond time. "Tell me all about everything," she said.*

*We fell to talking about who was singing what where. Maria said that she had heard this and that, and she'd been asked to do this and that, but she said, "Why should I? I've done it all." She walked us over every inch of that apartment proudly and displayed it to us. It was all very luxurious, and it was of the emptiness of waiting—all expecting gone, dead. There was only one photograph in her bedroom. It was Meneghini, on her mantelpiece. She said, "I never disliked Jackie, but I hate Lee. I hate her. I have a dream all the time. I dream about him, Onassis, all the time. I want to help him, but I can't." Her voice had that twang in it, a metallic sheen—almost brassiness. When Maria felt something deeply her talking voice was more in the brass section of the orchestra than in the strings or the woodwinds.*[36]

. . .

*In the evening of the afternoon we spent with Maria, we went to be with Marlene. She lived in a sterile apartment block facing the Plaza Athenée. Before the door of her apartment opened, we heard, "I'm coming! I'm coming! I'm here!" The door was flung open, and she was indeed there, her arms flung about us hugging as only she could, putting everything, all of her strength, into her delight at seeing us. The foyer, the living room beyond, the kitchen back of us boiled with life, with the heady, almost palpable smell of feasting to come.*

*Marlene in constant motion—putting hats here, tugging chairs there, pushing us this way, pushing us that way, shouting, "Here, here, sit here. . . ." We were almost immediately at table in the foyer, a table loaded with caviar and toast. She stood for a moment, arms akimbo. She was wrapped in a sort of smock tied around her waist. It came to just below her knees and she stood as so many thousands had seen her standing, her left foot jutting out, one arm on the left hip, the other arm waving in the air, sometimes brushing back her hair, which was helter-skelter all over her head.*

*She never stopped talking. The talk was in Marlene English and sometimes in Marlene French and sometimes in Marlene German. It was a fine mix, and every single syllable of it understandable. It was a constant, all-persuasive aria. It was about what we were to eat, what was happening to her family, what was happening to all sorts of friends, what was not happening that should be happening to everyone. "Could have all been different . . . Could have come out the right*

---

36. "Maria's dream: She and Onassis were in a hotel suite, and they were putting many things into suitcases. They looked out the window, and it was absolutely desolate. As far as they could see, it was just a landscape of mud. They were deeply affected by it and depressed. Then the telephone rang, either a voice on the end of the telephone said it was 'a call from Churchill' or it was a call from Churchill himself. The whole atmosphere was pervaded with despair. Maria felt acute desolation, and then she woke. She had the same dream, or variations, many times. She thought it an ill omen. She told us this quietly, measured out, and seemed so serene." *Journal, August 5, 1980.*

way . . . If only they'd listened. Nobody ever listens. Carole Lombard didn't listen!"[37] And as she talked, she ran back and forth into the kitchen and out came more and more things to eat. "I've been cooking for hours for you. I know how you love to eat. Eat!" It was her special schnitzel dinner with those extraordinary fried potatoes so packed with onion—very German, endless green vegetables ("So wery good for you!"), and endless huge goblets of the best red wine—endless. It was salad after salad and at least three ripe cheeses with a different wine. And then came one of Marlene's great specialties, a sweet dessert omelette, all puffed up and oozing apricot jam. All powdery with sugar. We ate and we ate, and she never sat down, never ate a thing, and never stopped swigging Scotch from a bottle, which she thought she kept a secret from us in the kitchen. But the talk was very, very good.

Then we waddled into the living room, Gray collapsed into a chair, and I collapsed into a sofa. Marlene leaned against the piano. Then the aria went on, and this time it was about Marlene bereft of her theater, and how she would give anything to be back on the stage. "Not the movies! I never want to make a movie again! Never! But if only I could be on the stage again! Look, look, under this piano, look, everything is there. Everything is packed. All the rags are there ready to go, but nobody asks me. If only I could be on the stage again!" I sat there looking at this creature so radiant still, so battered, so desirous of being excavated. . . .

At about two o'clock in the morning, when Gray and I were sitting stuffed with her feast, she nipped into the kitchen for her swig of Scotch, nipped out and up to a card table piled high with manuscripts, and grasping a thick sheaf, nipped back to the piano, propped herself, proclaimed, "I will read you what I have written of my book! My life! Don't expect any revelations—there ain't any. There won't be any. Not that kind of book!"

She had been at this book for years: Marlene's Life According to Marlene. I had read a sixty-page beginning years ago, one long night, in her suite atop the Dorchester, while she was dazzling mobs at the Café de Paris. "It's like Colette," I had told Gray, "It's beautiful and so touching." Now Marlene plunged in. . . .

I fastened to each word the way a drowning man clings to a repeatedly tossed lifesaving rope. Where was the magic? Where was the atmosphere? Where were the Marlene words, her Berlin wit, her self-mockery and mockery of others, her . . . I fell asleep, my eyes seemingly shuttered in appreciation, my left leg flung over my right knee swinging metronomically. Gray knew that I was asleep. Marlene only knew the Marlene she was disinterring, chapter after chapter. I woke suddenly and cried out, "But, darling, how much you've done! That's all there is? No more—even a little more?" . . . Out in the still, dawn-cool Avenue Montaigne I said to Gray, "That wasn't the book I read years ago. How was what you heard?" Gray gave me a look. (1993)

---

37. GF: "Marlene's psychic told her to tell Carole Lombard not to go on that plane trip. Marlene did tell her; Lombard did go, and died when it crashed."

**TO RICHARD HUNTER** • VASSALBORO, MAINE

What is this rich fat life which I am delighting in? Last evening I sat in the Palazzo Polignac with Peggy Guggenheim on the left (she is very ill, but mellowed by it) and Miss Curtis (the Palazzo Barbaro inheritor) to the right,[38] midst a throng of folk at a party so Jamesian that time stopped. We are thick in the center of Venetian life. I don't know whether I see it or I see the novels I've read, but it is all there to be sorted out. We are being kidnapped to weekend near Vicenza and to take various meals (along with the rest of a house party) at some of the villas I know only from books and movies. This is a high life—and so corny.

During the Redentore, a bridge was flung up in one day—just the way I saw it described by Leonardo in his notebooks.[39] Then the following night: the most glorious fireworks we have ever seen. Only in eighteenth-century engravings have I seen such. In the early hours after the Redentore fireworks, a terrifying storm over Venice—but so luridly beautiful—like gigantic boxes of violet fire bursting asunder. We trudge enormously and my leg feels better than it has in years. I think exercise is the great therapy. But we *are* fatter!

**TO RICHARD HUNTER** • AUGUSTA, MAINE

We had the most glorious weekend in a remarkable villa near Vicenza. It's owned by Evelyn Lambert, a woman I knew in Dallas years ago, and it is perfection, set in a large English park created by an Italian poet in the eighteenth century and added to in the early nineteenth. One part has a Louisiana bayou and a sequoia (the poet went to America circa 1770). The park has incredible vistas to the Dolomites and—set like precious stones—distant, needle-thin campaniles. The villa has two Veronese-inspired rooms: one is distinctly inspired by the Villa [Barbaro] Maser's frescoes. We were, it seems, "on the Contessa circuit." We lunched high above Asolo in the Villa de Galero, owned by the Count de Lord Rinaldi. Oh Reezl—the exquisite life in these villas— much-loved beautiful objects and such careful, loving attention; enchanting pale green, pink, lavender, and yellow rooms; the most delicate plasterwork; birds, cartoucherie, mythological heads; small, jewel rooms—much more beautiful than the Longhi remains in the Ca' Rezzonico; the food and service delicious; white-gloved footmen, maids; real silver conch-shell washbasins in the bathroom—and with all this: "Our most beautiful things are hidden away" because of the crooks. An elegant world tottering on the precipice of catastro-

---

38. The family of the textile businesswoman Patricia Curtis Vignano acquired the Palazzo Barbaro in Venice in 1885.
39. On the third weekend of July in Venice, for the Feast of the Redeemer, a wooden pontoon bridge is rapidly thrown across the lagoon to the Church of the Redeemer (*Il Redentore*) on the Giudecca.

phe: Russia in 1917, the old South just before Sumter. But the cultivation of these people—centuries of it.

The party last night in [the Venetian] Palazzo Barbaro—just to be in those Henry James rooms, those *Wings of the Dove* chambers, to see a moon over the garden of the Palazzo Polignac opposite . . . The current Miss Curtis casually said, "I will be here for some days, if I do not go to Singapore—but maybe I stay for two weeks while they make the movie." The Curtises have no money, so they are permitting a movie company to film there. "Never again," said Mrs. C in trailing, faintly patterned white silk.

The "taxis" in Venice are striking—so much hardship [getting around]—but the canal waters are still and at night deepest black. I think this purgatory— with great crowds being shipped off to various Heavens and Hells.

I sat next to Freya Stark at [an Evelyn Lambert] lunch—a hope realized!!![40]

AUGUST 22, 1977 • NEW YORK CITY While [Herbert] Kasper, [his wife] Sandra, Puss, and I ate in the Raga [Indian restaurant], all of our bags were stolen from Sandra's borrowed station wagon, which stood in front. That manuscript and all of my European notes—the first draft for my hoped-for book—gone. Also: my far eyes, my near eyes; my second set of teeth; my best buttonhooks; my beautiful silver soap box; my Penelope brass box; my new Italian blue-striped shirt; my new London cashmere pullover; all of my office papers . . . so much. Puss lost his traveling beasts and his moonstone ring and his keys. . . . Is this, then, a fitting end for my book . . . the epilogue? I feel hit over the head. Oh—I lost the Christmas presents bought for Puss . . . lost . . . gone . . . not my optimism . . . but almost that too. . . . Six weeks in Europe with nothing stolen, nothing lost, but here in this jungle—the immediate, written-down facts lost— this stroke—I must start over now.

NOTE: In Venice, Leo had written a memoir that interwove daily experience with memories of his childhood. As he later said, it was "my life caught up in the envelope of a summer journey." Leo soon made some notes recalling their visits with Callas and Dietrich (and dictated that story during the early nineties for his memoir), but he never re-created the rest. Traumatized, he did not resume keeping a regular journal until late the following spring.

JOURNAL • AUGUST 24, 1977 I put ads in the "Lost & Found" in the *Times* and *News*. This could lead to recovery of my notebook and it could also bring me danger—so many criminal minds. We're not allowed to say "stolen" or even

---

40. British writer Freya Stark (1893–1993) was a heroine of Leo's for her intrepid travels (often solo, still riding horseback in her eighties) and for her productivity (dozens of travel books, autobiographies, and eight volumes of letters).

"taken." "Lost" is the word. Also: not allowed to say "reward" or "no questions asked." That would be an accusation. Said Puss, "Everything for the criminal!"

SEPTEMBER 6, 1977 The twilight of Madame Stravinsky, who goes on an annual visit to Monsieur Stravinsky [in a Venetian cemetery]. Mean tongues say that she has her money secreted at his grave. The fact: Stravinsky is her money and her legend.

SEPTEMBER 16, 1977 Maria did something unexpected last night: She died.

NOTE: Leo did not write again about Callas for three months.

NOVEMBER 13, 1977 • NEW YORK CITY
**TO RICHARD HUNTER** • EDINBURGH

Do you remember a black woman, Alberta Hunter, who was a glorious blues singer in the Georgette Harvey days?[41] Well—at eighty-three she has emerged from retirement and is jamming the Cookery (a University Place hug-bunny) nightly—twicely and thricely. She is astonishing. Years ago, there were at least a dozen more of such remarkable voices—rhythm and feeling and enunciation—all beating out their joy and despair and hard-bitten humor. Now she is the only one. She's not affected—as Josephine Baker and [calypso singer] Josephine Premice and even Ethel Waters were. She's solid and hearty and honest and full of wisdom.

**JOURNAL** • DECEMBER 9, 1977 Franco Zeffirelli about Maria dead: "So beautiful, so beautiful . . . like *Traviata*." He told me how she died: She called out to Bruna [her maid] and told her to put her on the bed. Her last words: "Put me on the bed."[42] The butler and Bruna moved her. This made the blood clot move, and she was dead when she was placed on the bed. If she had not asked to be picked up from the floor and moved, she, possibly, would not have died. Franco and Maria were planning a *Merry Widow* and *Coronation of Poppea* for Rome, 1979 season. Franco said Maria had no culture, but "created it."

JANUARY 9, 1978 The complaints about my job have taken the place formerly occupied by the complaints about the house [1453 Lexington]. I got us out of the house—at great emotional cost—but I cannot get us out of my job. The reasons are obvious.

41. The singer and actress Georgette Harvey (1882–1952) and Leo met during the run of *Behind Red Lights*, in which she had a small part. Harvey then enlisted Leo to write a book about the adventures of female African American performers in czarist Russia. Around 1937 they produced a manuscript, but it has vanished.
42. Callas had collapsed after arising from bed in the morning.

This morning with Miss Piggy, Irving Penn, and Frank Oz. A most extraordinary session, during a great blizzard.[43] Oz looks—thin, upper-framed spectacles, svelte, intelligent, soft-voiced, generous eared, and mustached. Oz sublimates his transvestitism in Miss Piggy, and Miss Piggy has taken over Oz—almost 75 percent. Oz: "She started on the show the first year. We never really planned. She was an extra pig character, kind of a nondescript pig. Then I had some time with her, and I began to see something in her. It was about a six-week process. The first thing that happened, she hit Kermit with a karate shot. She can't hold on to her appropriateness. She goes over the edge. She has this facade of femininity, which women are fighting against. Women feel the dimensionality behind all that. To me, Miss Piggy has been tremendously hurt in her life—a lot of swine, a lot of pigs, and a lot of butchers." Question: Miss Piggy can't stand the fact that she's dependent on Frank Oz?

MISS PIGGY: "I'm not mean. Life is cruel. I just have to survive. We girls know this."

GRAY: "Isn't it extraordinary how beautiful things become when they are isolated."

MISS PIGGY: "Thank you. I know how to please a man. . . . Are you getting the eyes, Irving?"

PENN: "Yes. That's good."

MISS PIGGY: "I know. . . . Don't you ever try to look prettier than me. . . . I know coy."

She knows the whole gamut of expressions—human and inhuman. She's really a pig after your own heart.

FEBRUARY 22, 1978 Diane Keaton came to Penn for a [*Vogue*] cover-try in black-and-white. This could be a little revolution if realized. Atmosphere of studio: tentative, since Penn does not believe that a black-and-white cover could ever happen. Call midway in sitting from Alex: "Since she was so cooperative, couldn't we do a color cover after we finish the black-and-white?" Typical of him, an arrangement having been made, by letter—strict, taking over a year to manage. He sees no reason why this would be chicanery. Couldn't be done, anyway, because it took over two and one-half hours to make up D.K. for the black-and-white. She behaved wonderfully—the antithesis of Faye Dunaway. Diane Keaton is unexpectedly small, has enormous eyes, a Regency delicacy and willfulness—when made up, a great and grave curiosity. Her speech is common—or, rather, regional. She knows this. When I asked, "Wouldn't you ever play *The Way of the World*?" she said, "But could I handle the lan-

43. Leo had Jim Henson's puppet Miss Piggy and Frank Oz, who voiced her, photographed by Irving Penn for *Vogue*. He then suggested that she be put on the cover. Liberman's response is not recorded.

guage?" When handed a slip of paper on which was written "You've just been nominated for the Academy Award [for *Annie Hall*]," she said, "Oh, I won't get it. Vanessa should have it [for *Julia*]." She thinks Vanessa is the "greatest" actress.

MARCH 6, 1978   The Elizabeth Taylor birthday party: supplicating figures on the pavement kneeling, begging to come in. The Studio 54 rings of Hell. Beardsley out of Moreau.[44] The emptiness behind Elizabeth's beautiful staring eyes. Diana Vreeland on the floor gyrating and swaying and shaking. A red, green, gold, glittering blackness.

MAY 14, 1978   Yesterday morning's talk over the blower with Diana Trilling, and she vehement about and against Alfred Kazin and his [memoir] *New York Jew* (the title gives all). Diana says: "I can't write about this, and his book will be history. Nobody will know the truth. This book will become the truth. I can't tell how at a *Partisan Review* party—in the fifties, not the early sixties— I came up to Alfred and Lionel and heard Alfred say: 'Why don't you get rid of that wife?' I can't say that the real truth—I know this must be the real truth—is that Alfred had deep homosexual feelings for Lionel. Anybody who reads the book should be able to feel that, but who will?" So she went on, unhysterically, with plateaus of laughter, scaling successfully whole ranges of emotions. The truth is that Alfred has no grace and has never even been able to recognize grace in others. He is the *bulvon* (such a good Yiddish word [for "oaf"]) of American letters.

Diana also told me that Lionel was attractive to both men and women—or that should be reversed. I do not think that Lionel was homosexual. He was intellectual, understanding, a gent, and an ardent friend—but that is inadequate. As an example of Lionel's charisma (I used that word) Diana told me the saga of Mary McCarthy's Lionel pursuit. Mary, returning to Manhattan from several years of living with her false meringue of a husband, Bowden Broadwater, in Newport, felt that she had lost the New York intelligentsia world. She felt that she had to make a comeback.[45] Lionel being the lion of that moment, she set out to capture him. (Even to draw that thorn Diana from his foot? Surely Mary thought of Diana as a thorn.) So Mary invited the Trillings to dine.

Looking about her flat, in the East Nineties, Mary decided that it was not a sufficiently splendid place in which to receive literary Royals, so she borrowed

44. The French Symbolist Gustave Moreau (1826–98) painted mythological subjects in a hallucinatory style.
45. The writer Mary McCarthy (1912–89) became notorious for her sharp judgments and public skirmishes with Lillian Hellman, Philip Rahv, and Diana Trilling. Bowden Broadwater, writer and school administrator, had been McCarthy's third husband. They divorced in 1961.

paintings from [art dealer] Valentine Dudensing, insuring them for this one gala evening. Then she telephoned her "girlfriends" (Sylvia Marlowe, et al.) to discuss the menu. She invited one guest—Virgil [Thomson]. Then, on the special evening she made one mistake. ("Oh," Diana said, "you know how Lionel almost never knew what was on the walls of a room. He was interested in the people, not the things.") Mary's mistake: She never addressed one word to Diana. Diana, meeting Virgil for the first time, became great chums with him, and Mary was never invited back. "Lionel wouldn't let her into the house," says Diana. "He loathed her because she had been so rude to me."[46]

*The Greek Tycoon* [film about Onassis]—a drear, not even funny. Only one moment: when Jacqueline Bisset (Jackie Onassis) tumblesaults in the ocean, and Anthony Quinn (Onassis) takes one delighted, cock-rising look at her widespread ass in its scarlet cloth. But who will know why this is amusing? Onassis adored asses. He loved to bugger. This is the "it" the Greeks had a word for. I knew so many involved—Maria, Onassis (met once), [his first wife] Tina Livanos, Jackie Onassis, Lee Radziwill . . . but most of what I know came from Maria.

I finished Alfred's book. How curiously parallel our lives and how wonderfully different—the lives of two housepainters' sons. The difference wells from who my father married and who Alfred's father married.

Irony as a vertebra in the Jewish skeleton. A sense of irony has sustained Jews throughout their entire history?

MAY 17, 1978   Teatime with Vera Stravinsky (sans tea). This ninety-year-old woman seems, in a white, simple, curiously flowing, "short" dress, a girl. Her incredibly beautiful smile brimming with a sad, but triumphant (too big a word) wisdom. She has been kind to time. Her apartment is again a playhouse. She has the innocence of wisdom—or has she the reverse?

MAY 28, 1978 · WESTON, CONNECTICUT   In my bed in Mina's "new" house. Here, in Weston, Mina sits on four or five acres, undeniably suburban, with a privacy that is suburban in all of America, and now even in England or France. The privacy of a little land—roadways visible and audible through gaps in "plantings," neighbors' voices heard, off-island sounds polluting the privacy. This is a step, not even giant, into the ordinary. Bethel was hundreds of acres— real privacy. Ashfield [Chapelbrook Farm] was of an even grander privacy. How did Mina get here? By a mixture of goodness and fantasy. The goodness: largesse to friends, pensioners, "artists." The fantasy: born rich, raised richer, married rich, she lived rich. "Oh," she says now, wryly, "I do miss being rich. . . ." Then: "But I have enough. . . ." And indeed she does, at this moment

---

46. "Of course, Mary McCarthy didn't know Elsie Mendl's dictum: 'Dear, never ignore the wives.' Advice to climbers in any milieu." *Journal, December 10, 1989.*

a sufficiency to keep this very pretty house, a tumble of in-and-out helpers, and, at last, the kind of success for which she longed: [her memoir] *Other People's Letters*, the result of her true being, her real character—this a mixture of retailing blood, young American woman, dollar-princess dreams, hard work, and romantic imagination. Her face and person altered by age (eighty-two), her circumstances reduced from intense privacy to near-privacy, from elegance to prettiness—but she always craved acknowledgment, at least from her peers, seeing her peers as very few.

Goosey and Fido lunched and visited. He sitting folded into his huge self on the sofa next to Mina, Fido straight up on a stiff chair. Both looked like peasant creatures plainly dressed to go to town. They had the atmosphere of those hideous people badly carved from wood—browns, greens, urine colors. After they left, Mina said: "Well, the three of us sitting there certainly looked like three normal people!" She said this in faint exasperation, a sort of depressed voice—Lincoln having been put away for violence, Fido having been put away for paranoia. (She thought Lincoln and [her brother] Paul Cadmus were trying to kill her—were they? I doubt it.) Now Fido is on nine pills a day. So, one footnote to the decline and fall.

Here is another: Sometime in this past week, Depy [Messinesi, *Vogue* travel editor] told me that she'd received a telephone call from Kitty Miller, who is in Roosevelt Hospital, eleventh floor, corner room, the biggest, but still . . . "Kitty asked me to stop in and dine with her. I went. The door was opened by her butler. Inside, Kitty sat in her own linens, Bache pictures on the walls, her maid and a footman unloading hampers full of her own beautiful table linens, silver, china, exquisite, for each of five courses, a superb meal cooked by her own chef. When this was finished, Kitty said, 'Well, now, Depy, run along home. You've seen how the rich do it.' "[47]

I think of Bea Lillie (now in an institution) leaning down to say an ostensible "good night" at one of the Millers' New Year's parties and suddenly biting Kitty (who was always a beast) on her naked shoulder, then twinkling and clattering with laughter, swiftly exiting—while Kitty fainted.

How different writing is from thinking, even from planning what one is to write. This is a small microcosm of each enormous life. . . . I should be able to say this succinctly. I balloon with words. I grow lardy with words. I am fat—hideously fat—with words.

MAY 29, 1978  Mina told me last night about Dot Léger's courage. Dot was told, in 1967, that [her husband] Alexi was mortally cancerous. She immediately swore the doctor to secrecy, never told a soul ("You know what a tyrant he was," said Mina. "He insisted on seeing every letter that came into that

47. Kitty Miller (1900–79), the daughter of banker and painting collector Jules Bache, married the theatrical producer Gilbert Miller.

house!"), and for eight years she pretended [to him] that he suffered only from the ills of aging. Dot said that he'd changed completely in those years. From being fanatically private, wanting no réclame, he hungered for it—tributes, celebrations of his importance. (Mina: "What if I'd married him!") Now, an English scholar researching Alexi has discovered what Dot, Mina, and I knew: Alexi made up letters, changed those he'd written years ago, making the ones from China prescient of future politics. He invented the letters to Mina, now published in the Pléiade edition. Mina has the real letters here and will leave them to the Morgan Library. Alexi had a hypnotic charm, the charm of an authentic tale-teller. Blixen had it. They mesmerized you. You believed anything that came from their lips. Being with them was being in a dragon's cave, Moreau mysterious—jewels, loot, mysteries, unfathomable, sinister but addictive, voluptuous, scary the way rooms in gaslight were.

I realize how shadows have changed. In electric-lighted rooms they have lost their richness, their possibilities of beauty and terror. Robert Louis Stevenson would not recognize today's interior shadows, nor would Peter Pan. Peter Pan has almost literally lost his shadow.

JUNE 17, 1978 · NEW YORK CITY  Felicia's death [yesterday]—I had a dream at five a.m.: Me shaving (improbable), a door opened, and I saw Felicia in a beautiful dress, swathed, pseudo-Grecian in striated grays. Then I learned later that morning she had died at about the time of my dream. Did she visit on the way?

Yesterday, we went to the Dakota to visit Lennie and the children. Glorious flowers, food, and many chums, the whole apartment reeking of Felicia. It is hers. She haunts it—as she must.[48] Lennie distraught. The chums wearing cheerfulness like fancy dress. Mindy [Wager] hysterical, that is, more hysterical than usual. When Marit [Gentele] was told that "it had been for the best," she asked sharply, "What is the second best?"[49] Brigitta, in a foulard—I saw that with her from-the-land face, her hard-worked face, which now has a certain aspect of nobility and ballet-girl fused, she could play Ouspenskaya roles.

The irony: Felicia and Goddard gone; Brigitta and Lennie left.

JUNE 26, 1978 · LONDON  Reading *The Awkward Age* and bewitched by Henry James's penetration, his indirection, in which always is a direction—like peering for signposts in a dense, high-summer garden, signposts almost totally obliterated by the thickset boskage. I read it with Cortès excitement at the inference, the submerged evil, the wit and social observation, the worldliness, the profound Puritan sense of frivolity. The most Edwardian of novels.

48. GF: "It was Felicia who persuaded Lennie to move to the Dakota, leaving the East Side, and she made an exhausting effort to create what she hoped would be a sort of Chekhovian atmosphere. Everything was worn, not necessarily pretty, but 'meaningful.' "
49. Her husband, Göran Gentele, had died in an automobile accident in 1972, three weeks after succeeding Rudolf Bing as general manager of the Metropolitan Opera.

JUNE 27, 1978  To Penelope [Reed]'s enchanting garden. There is always the first moment of relief that time has not ravaged excessively. Such a beautiful "wild" garden, all blue and silvery green, sudden spurts of golden-flower yellow, and white roses. Penelope, unadorned. Her mole job for [the photo agency] Blau allows her to see the world through the photographs that pour in: "I pass on the porn and the violence." This little girl, who, on her seventh birthday, said the only thing she wanted was to go to the Embassy Club, where her mother had danced with the Prince of Wales. So Freda took her child, and when Penelope saw the daytime desolation she sat down on the floor and wept bitter tears of disappointment.

JUNE 30, 1978  *Evita* was a surprise: words banal, music *Jesus Christ Superstar* in form and sometimes content, but everything in the performance redeemed by Hal [Prince]'s superb, flawless direction. Tremendously agitprop, very thirties and WPA and Living Newspaper[50] and Theatre Guild, it could have been found in *Theatre Arts* [magazine] of that day, but so remarkable now. Hal again the best Broadway musical director. The musical is more about showbiz than politics—but all stops out. The Evita a very ordinary girl [Elaine Paige], but ordinariness is what's wanted.

JULY 3, 1978  Diana Vreeland in the [hotel] dining-room door with Bianca Jagger and child. Diana intact: Her voice is ripe, not metallic, a little aged, but as in fine wood: "I've had a setback this morning. . . . Call me, darling, tomorrow morning." The child sweetly polite. Bianca Jagger, insolent or uninterested, very much Old Hollywood's idea of a half-caste woman transformed into a "lady," but the original, marketplace Central American showing through the good dress, refined shoes, placed hair, and makeup.

JULY 6, 1978 · PARIS  Daniel Salem [director of Condé Nast in Europe]: "But you always know that we want you here. You can have anything you want." But I cannot make a move because of parents—Puss's and mine.

JULY 7, 1978  Gray: "It's like an endurance test—every day." The flight too brief to eat the cold lunch, which was Pussy's pieces [scraps] of charcuterie, with huge, whiskered strawberries, a blue-tinfoiled wedge of Camembert-chalk, and champagne as bitter as tears of departure. And there, on the curb at the Ritz, was Robert [Davison], all delight and "Thank God you're here!" His morale has been low. We are in the [Ritz] hotel's rue Cambon mansard, somewhere in Chanel's nest. The bedroom—with its brass beds; deep embrasure of oeil-de-boeufs [circular windows]; ivory-painted, typically Ritz furniture; a pink, shiny bathroom—all breathes "illicit." This whole "apartment" is more in

50. Living Newspaper was a program of the Depression-era Federal Theater Project to create theatrical documentaries.

someone's imagination than in any other region of reality. We love it. It would be bliss and passion in winter. It is, of course, bliss and (will be) passion now. Very secretly.

JULY 8, 1978   To Paloma Picasso's flat, next to the American Church, high up, vast, and very much fin-de-siècle.[51] Grand vistas of Paris from a little terrace, the Seine nearby, stillness and amplitude of *haute bourgeoisie* wealth. Rollicking, skidding, never still, sausage-fat Martha, a nine-month-old English bull. And Paloma herself: slight, elegant—enormous dark eyes, mellow skin, generous reddish lips, marvelous slender, strong worker hands—very elegant, a great lady in the making, but most of her already there—wit, observation, purposeful in a relaxed way. She showed us all her costume sketches for *Success*, explaining the entire "spectacle" as she showed, all with humor and detail.[52] The sketches owe much to her early copying of funny papers. Her voice is quiet always, sedimented with laughter, always reasonable, deep—like good, very heavy silk, this voice, darkish and rich. High up in her workroom, Picasso's little swift watercolor of her. Then another, in the bedroom—all distinctly his, distinctly loving.

Nicole [Stéphane] and Susan Sontag and David [Rieff, Sontag's son, a writer] and we had dinner in the most exquisite restaurant dining room I have ever seen, at Beauvilliers. The tan lacquer ceiling and the "horsehair" black walls; the flowers set about in tremendously full vases on the floors—paling purple heath, pink peonies, yellow roses. [Restaurateur] Édouard Carlier is a genius.

JULY 9, 1978   The presentation at Beauvilliers: ice cream (rhubarb, cinnamon) brought in tight silver cylinders, the lids removed at table and the ice cream spooned into the plates; the sugar—seven varieties, each in its small, doily-lined basket, all on a silver tray, a bouquet of sugars. My dish of sweetbreads (which I usually abhor) a miracle of seasoning, cooked (but how?) delicately, five different veggies, each *primeur*, two cheeses, one the inevitable chèvre, a dazzling chilled light red wine. The tables, each individual, scattered, very at-home, but the flowers as glorious as the cuisine. Vuillard could have created this exquisite room (there are two others). In the color-geometrical loo the sconces are *pappagallos* [urinals]. The proprietor is rotund, a linking of broad ovals—head, body, even legs—has the sure smile of success and the ability to overthrow any preconceived notions of what one wishes to eat, substituting his ideas of what one should eat in his restaurant. Comfort, luxe, and glorious *gastronomie* served with perfect detail (at least five breads)

---

51. The artist's daughter, Paloma Picasso (b. 1949) became a businesswoman and designer of jewelry and leather.
52. *Success* was a theatrical production coauthored by Paloma Picasso's then husband, the Argentine playwright Rafael López-Sanchez.

and discretion. At dinner Susan suddenly announced that Roger [Straus, the publisher] and she found Puss "sexually attractive." And Nicole said: "It was very hard to be *lesbienne* in the fifties."

JULY 20, 1978 · VENICE   One morning at about four, the [Gritti's concierge] desk had a call from Valentina [Schlee]: Someone must come up immediately. Someone did, to find her cutting up her sheets: "I will do this," she told him, "until you give me pure linen . . . pure." How patient people here are with Valentina. Every night she goes to say good night to San Marco. The gondoliers kiss her hand.

JULY 21, 1978   So here is Little T in the newspaper again: drunk, pills, not able to finish a television appearance, saying he "would probably end up killing himself accidentally." Adding, "nothing has ever jelled" in his life. What does he really mean? What is this about? The result of having tried for something he could not achieve? His gift was anecdotal, atmospheres, nuances of terror and mystification. He was a remarkable storyteller with a sensitive heart. He was (is, I believe still) an intuitive. The extent was journalism, which made him believe *(In Cold Blood)* that he was a "great" writer, one of the greatest. In his genre (and it was always genre fiction or reporting), he was very good, sometimes first-rate ("Children on Their Birthdays," "Christmas Memory"), but to become this American Proust—I think impossible for him. He has broken himself upon this wheel. He has come undone. And only yesterday John Malcolm [Brinnin] asked me, as we sat in a trattoria on the [island of] Murano, if I thought that T would kill himself.[53] Is this clipping then the answer? T believed the legend that he made, which the American way of publicity aggrandized. Publicity—media—identical. In a sense, he is Marilyn Monroe. The Strasbergs [Actors Studio] tried to educate her into something she could not be. T could be the Marilyn Monroe of literature.

JULY 29, 1978 · THE VENETO   For a long time, I was unable to find a key, peculiarly my own, to my past. I was frustrated by Proust's madeleine, by Virginia Woolf's river of time. But now, here in the Palladian villas of the Veneto, here in Villa Lambert, remote in place and time from the Manhattan thick Jewish soup in which I was born, here in Venice, in its palazzos, on the Gritti's terraces, in its *campos* and *calles* and Jewish quarter, I have found my key—not in an odor, nor a texture, but in voices and gestures, in the angle of a cheekbone, the slant of an eye, the curve of a smile. Here, in beings who never knew the lost creatures of my past, the dead, the disappeared, are echoes that reverberate into being my long-lost life. Echoes, then, are the key.

---

53. The poet and biographer John Malcolm Brinnin (1916–98) had been at Yaddo with Leo and Truman Capote in the summer of 1946.

AUGUST 1, 1978 · NICE   Hotel Negresco, overlooking the gray [Mediter-ranean], tinged with a blur of blue, a memory of blue. The flags, the stone balustrade, wind-frayed palms, the *plage*-attired summer people—all intensely Dufy. Dufy conditions the eye here, since I saw him before Matisse. Matisse sees with an agile, swift humor, a tinge of malice in his sensuality; Dufy views with a fat sensuality, a passion. The difference: Matisse is intellectual; Dufy is elemental.

This hotel with its costumed retainers looks like a misplaced Mississippi steamboat. The enormous oval hall with its huge copies of portraits of Louis Quatorze luminaries and the bust of Louis as one enters: What would Saint-Simon have written about it all?[54] The imitation of Belle Epoque in the grill, with the waitresses done up as a fin-de-siècle notion of bucolic eighteenth century. The vitrines, with full-sized eighteenth-century-attired [mannequin] pages proffering the vend of Givenchy's boutique. The Vasarely-inspired [Op art] carpeting of the endless corridors. But the "help" is good-humored. We are spoiled by the petting of the Gritti and chums in the Veneto. That was the real world. This is the unreal real world—everything rooted in the material.

SEPTEMBER 23, 1978 · NEW YORK CITY   Felicia Bernstein's memorial [on September 18]—Maria's voice as Felicia acted "Vissi d'arte," that was the eerie moment.[55]

In Mexico, Felicia had sparkled, and Lennie had never seen her like that. She went to a doctor to be sure that she got pregnant. "I'm gonna keep him down there until I get pregnant."

Lennie married Felicia because he needed a wife when he became conduc-tor of the New York Philharmonic; Felicia married him on the rebound after the death of Richard Hart, an actor ([the play] *Dark of the Moon*) whom she had loved. Their marriage was a business arrangement: He got the Philhar-monic; she got his charge plate. But with all the money and the analysis, she couldn't handle it. The age when everything unfolds.

JANUARY 5, 1979   An important factor in the greatness of *Middlemarch* is that we have no assurance of happy endings. We do not know that Dorothea will marry Ladislaw, that Lydgate will emerge triumphantly from his troubles. So *Middlemarch* is life itself, the world as we live it—knowing no "end" to any life—not even the condemned life. Indeed, knowing that we are, each of us, condemned or, depending on religious or superstitious belief, elevated ulti-mately into the great light after life. I almost put the last in quotation marks.

54. Louis de Rouvroy, duc de Saint-Simon (1675–1755), was one of the great diarists, vividly recording the court at Versailles.
55. In 1961, Stephen Sondheim had made a home-movie version of the second act of *Tosca*, with Felicia Bernstein in the title role and Leonard Bernstein playing Scarpia.

MARCH 17, 1979  Maria wanted to be a movie star ([via Twentieth Century–Fox's head] Spyros Skouras), an international society star (Onassis), even though she knew that what she had done on the opera stage was forever. She had gone as far as possible with it. Floria Tosca claimed that she lived for art and love. This sums up Maria—with one difference: Maria lived for art; she died for love.

Was she ever any other than Maria Callas? No. Not onstage or in life apart from the stage. Yet, upon the armature of her self, she layered the imaginary substance until you saw these victims of operatic passion, realized fully in all of their tragic being, while perceptible within them was, visibly, Maria Callas herself. In no wise did this Maria diminish the creatures of her creation, nor did they diminish her, since they were, while in her being, their own alive beings, as corporeal to the eye, to the ear, as she herself was. At no moment were we unaware of this tremendous woman or of those other, more enduring creatures to whose reality she gave herself. This was like looking into an enfilade of facing looking glasses and seeing there an infinity of Marias, Normas, Violettas, Medeas, Toscas—seeing an eternity of past anguished, ecstatic women, until in the remotest glass, the future, Maria and her beauty became a single incandescence.

APRIL 11, 1979  Tebaldi: "I don't know about any feud. There's room for all sorts of singers in opera." Then she smiled sweetly.

Stage light strengthened Maria's features. Her myopia gave her movement a little mystery, even majesty. In opera—with its implied larger-than-even-the-largest life—this objectifying of movement, this ritualization of movement is even in domestic tragedy necessary. Maria's great art was that she could, as an actress, take this grandeur, this nobility of movement (as abstract a regality and beauty as seen in the maidens on the portico of the Erectheum) and make it as intimate as one's own tears and despairs. Maria onstage was the conduit between epic passion and despairs, ironies and everyday personal upheavals. She immortalized them for her beholders. She made beholders participants in the gigantic tumults she endured on stage. No one ever wanted to "protect" Maria. She exuded the strength of certainty, of intense and positive passion. There was nothing negative about her. She was definite in her likes, dislikes, and, most deeply, in what she felt about herself.

Maria had no great or profound intellect. She was intelligent—even shrewd—but none of this mattered, since she was a genius, and a genius is deep, in touch with the basic laws which govern our nature. A genius of the theater reveals those laws to us—the dynamics of passion and hilarity. A genius powerfully illuminates the mysteries of our being—while reminding us of our transience. This is why ballet (dance) is more touching than theater, why some song is more persistently touching than acted, non-operatic performance. The singer's career, the dancer's (which is the most poignant) are, by their very nature, more devastating than the actor's.

APRIL 17, 1979   When I was about seventeen, I fell in love with Elinor Wylie's verses. So much so that later I copied out her *Collected Poems*, since I could not afford to buy the book. I decided to write a "life" of E.W. and, because I knew nothing about either writing such a book or getting it published, I plunged into the Forty-second Street library and set to work all summer long to discover and write down everything I could find about E.W. This led me to the Gotham Book Mart, where I saw, on the left wall, a framed photograph of my divinity. After several worshipful visits (I bought nothing, since I had not money), I courageously asked the tousle-haired, small demon of a woman in this bookshop whether I could buy the photograph. "Yes," she said, "for five dollars." So off I went to earn the money, which I did in Best [department store] or Sarnoff-Nederlander. When I returned to the Gotham Book Mart, the woman squawked with laughter and said, "I wouldn't sell that to you. . . . Maybe for $15 or $25 . . . maybe never." That woman was the literary doyenne Frances Steloff. I loathed her.

Over time I went into the Gotham Book Mart rarely. She represented Cruelty to the Young. Several times Richard tried to buy the E.W. photograph for me as a birthday or Christmas present, but always F.S. scorned him. Then, last week, I needed a copy of Praz's *The Romantic Agony* (since I am trying to get together my Maria Callas [article]). So, I rang Andreas Brown [now owner], and during our talk he said something like why didn't I come in, and I told him about my E.W. picture. That afternoon I found the E.W. photograph waiting for me here. She is now on my worktable—all mine.

NOTE: Journal entries become sparse until Leo and Gray's annual arrival in Venice.

JOURNAL • JUNE 25, 1979 • VENICE   My father in later life was, in outline, a testimony to my mother's rich, Jewish cooking and baking, but at the time of my birth Sam was, apparently, a sensual man given to sudden spurts of unexpected energy, as revealed by family snapshots and by Rita Glasberg:[56] "Sam was a nice-looking young man with a good figure and happy way with life. Sam loved to laugh, to dance, to sing, to drink, to eat. And he certainly went on a tear the night you were born!"

My father (whose father had opened a small paint-supply shop on Second Avenue), having been summoned from a house-painting job in Long Branch, stood drunk and waiting at the foot of the stair, the main spine of this house, to hear news of my birth, and when at last, on this quiet Saturday evening, he did

56. Rita Glasberg (1890–1985) had been a neighbor on 107th Street during Leo's first years, and she remained a lifelong friend to the Lermans.

hear a great bustle and a silence, his wife's desperate screams stilled, suddenly, he tore off his overalls, rushed to a parlor window, and stood naked for all to behold, shouting wildly into 107th Street, "I have a son! I have a son!"

Grandpa Goldwasser, on the way to his Saturday evening lodge meeting, ignored his naked, exulting son-in-law in the parlor window and, accompanied by his two eldest sons (one a deaf-mute), made off into the night. Nothing interfered with his Saturday Lodzer True Brothers weekly meetings and their subsequent pinochle games.

JULY 5, 1979  The departure [from the Gritti] of Valentina Cortese: The Actress.[57] She [appearing] as the most old-fashioned, silent-movie star, based on *les grandes vedettes* of the nineteenth century, a real Lubitsch departure. Endless pages and porters and retainers bearing Vuitton bags of more sizes and shapes than ever existed before they were born for this moment; a (fake) leopard skin enormous pillow; a heavily furred coat; capes and shawls of dun and brilliance; armloads of flowers; a dog—shaggy, mysterious, his eyes under deep bangs, but determinedly independent; the two retainers—a vulgar frizzy blonde, very Bronx but heavy around the throat with an enormous golden and ponderous version of a charm bracelet, and then a quiet, severely (gray) coiffed woman in a white-dotted blue silk dress and a modified toque; the *cicisbeo* [gallant]—or lover—the man whose shoulders and back V.C. so expertly and persistently massaged at lunch, dapper in a pale suit, spruce handkerchief in breast pocket, portfolio under left arm . . . The blonde, the gray, and the lover all built up tension by running into the hotel and out. Finally, somehow he giving the impression that he was in full anticipatory movement while standing in one point-of-vantage place. So everyone, including a great part of the Gritti staff, waited, eyes on the main entrance.

The *vedette* then swept upon us—not from the expected exit, but from the bar door, this route giving her a complete cross, in full view of not only the Gritti, but the opposite shore of the Grand Canal and so a considerable section of Venice. She swooped—lavishing smiles of concern and shyness and gratitude—her whole panoply of "don't please notice me I can't bear it, this adoration, but"—very Miss Piggy—"if you don't I can't bear it even more." She was swathed in bright yellow draperies, patterned in scarlet and green, garments sweeping on the boards of the terraces, shawls deeply fringed, wisps of this and that, heavy gold and turquoise jewelry, a heavy scarf holding her together, tied under her chin, the edge just above her eyes forming a bandeau and lending a silent-screen siren touch—and all of this topped by a *souvenir de Venise* straw boater (the typical *gondolieri* hat, the scarlet band stamped in gold "Venezia"). She did not exactly wave, but she somehow gave illusion that she

57. The Italian film actress Valentina Cortese (b. 1925) is best remembered as the fading film star in Truffaut's *Day for Night*.

was waving a sweet, somewhat despairing good-bye, pervaded with a promise of bright return, and then loped—broken-winged—off to be literally borne into the boat, now stacked with her luggage, and so disappeared from view into the little cabin—her dark eyes self-deprecating, while her lips parted to display a radiant triumph of dental art. We, of course, literally and heartily applauded this wonderful show and felt vacant when it ended. She must be a perfect Madame Ranevskaya in *The Cherry Orchard.*

JULY 8, 1979  A heated discussion, at the Albrizzi, about "bluestockings." Susan [Sontag] crying out that this is always pejorative. Susan jumps onto the back of an idea, a point, a passing remark—breaking the back, and then stamping the broken bones and flesh into shards and scraps. Susan is all reason, lined with a sort of self-passion, as certain tough fabrics are backed with other fabrics, perhaps of a more tender substance. Puss says that Susan is obsessed with me. I see that she is starstruck in an old-fashioned movie magazine way. She went on worrying this—as she does—crying out in deep, even profound, rage against abuse of women writers. "I've been intelligent since I was a child," she said last night, "so I don't need anyone to tell people that I'm a bluestocking. . . . It can't mean anything else but that I'm being classed as a woman and because of being a woman, a freak . . . to be called a bluestocking because women aren't supposed to be intelligent . . . so it's freakish to be and so you're a bluestocking. . . . That's shit." When I asked about "a maiden lady," Susan was equally scornful about that. She carries herself away to the point of pedantry, while Nicole sits or moves quietly—a silvery, pale gold presence wrapped in a kind of lunar sadness. . . . Susan reveres Sarah Bernhardt. Susan doesn't even greet anyone, but comes right into a room and makes for an object and touches it. Susan's obsession to touch—even she comments on it.

SEPTEMBER 4, 1979 · NEW YORK CITY  The Kissingers' dinner for the Sinatras—Frank Sinatra's face puffed as though he's been taking cortisone. Those famous, shock-blue eyes now pig-points, and the sexy, boyish, clean-cut, jagged features obliterated, save in what memory restores (memory, the great restorer) in a shiny, artificially healthy roundness. Mrs. [Barbara Ann] Sinatra—big, blond, controlled blustery. At least ten ambassadors. To Nancy's right, Frank Sinatra, and to her left the Israeli ambassador. At Henry's table— [Robert] Strauss.[58] Henry's diligently coy, constant self-commendations. The usual Henry speeches and toasts—welcoming to Frank Sinatra, an exegesis about Strauss—were cut short by Nancy shouting across the room: "Henry, do we want coffee served here or in the living room?" Everybody immediately crowded out of the dining room.

58. Robert Strauss (b. 1918), a Democratic Party fund-raiser, was then President Carter's personal representative to the Middle East peace negotiations.

SEPTEMBER 9, 1979 Momma and Maebelle's birthdays [today]—Momma clutching the [customary age-plus-one] $91 I gave, became almost totally rational! Money in the hand seems to do this to the senile and deranged. I want to know more about this curious manifestation. How the blistering black hates pour from Momma's aged lips—so much lava exploding from her hidden, formerly protected deeps—all the sludge and long-buried monsters. Death is not the enemy; the enemy is senility.

Truman on the blower, this past week—his voice, beneath his laughter . . . his laughter is like a continual high-strung bridge over a vast, bottomless morass. He rings to report progress: "I'm writing you the most beautiful . . ." That sort of progress-promise. He said: "I'm putting my whole life on the line." All of this makes me intensely nervous for him.

**LITTLE T RETURNS** *An old man shuffled into my office at* Vogue. . . . *A scourged old man. Emaciated. His good clothes had gone bad on him. But his huge straw hat sat blithely on his head, a remembrance of Southern big-house life he, as a small unwanted boy, had never known. His blue eyes darted this way, that way: They never came to rest. . . . An after-midnight face. Life had had this man. He had also had life. And the fight wasn't finished—not yet.*

*"Little darling . . . my own little darling . . ." His voice came from some far and arid place. "I want Irving Penn to photograph me, and I want you to publish the picture in* Vogue. *I want this veeeeerrrry, veeeeeerrrry much." This was Truman in a frenzy, his voice high and squeaking with anxiety. "And I'll write a piece to go with it, and, yes, little dear, I'll be interviewed." The hysterical old man vanished. Little T materialized. "Yes, Myrt, Marge always knows what's going on in your little ole connivin' head. Now, if you will please excuse me, I will just have to leave this room for a minute. Which way is it?" Exit Little T doing a time step. During the hour he was with me, he exited some twelve times.* (VOGUE, SEPTEMBER 1987)

**JOURNAL** · SEPTEMBER 13, 1979 Truman yesterday afternoon taping. He looks as if he had been in a dreadful fire and come out of it scorched within himself and without, his face a wonderfully reproduced facsimile of Little T as a young man, but scarred—only the eyes blazingly alive. He is a walking death inhabited by a coruscating, willful spirit determined to remain vividly, even violently alive until it has fulfilled its destiny of being a great, even the greatest master of fictional-reality of our time. "Since I was seventeen I feel as if I lived in an electric light"—a blazing electric lightbulb, of course. He said, "I really have very little ego, but a great deal of pride." His visit was tumultuous and deeply upsetting.

**TRUMAN'S GIFT** *So Irving Penn took his picture . . . and his piece came in. I read it. I called T. "It is wonderful. It's the best thing you've written in years.*

*You made me cry. And you made me feel hopelessly full of hope." "I know. The end. That sure enough made you cry. Wham! The beginning: 'When God hands you a gift, he also hands you a whip; and the whip is intended solely for self-flagellation.' Then that end . . . yes siree: 'I'm here alone in my dark madness, all by myself with my deck of cards and, of course, the whip God gave me.' " (No one, absolutely no one, ever read Truman's prose better than he did himself, excepting Geraldine Page, and she was acting in* A Christmas Memory.)

*"How much do you want for this marvelous piece?"*

*"Nothing. Not one penny. It's a present to you. I will not take a penny."*

*So I sat there, feeling guilty, hearing that flirty-skirty voice in the all-night cafeteria so many fraught years ago. . . .* (VOGUE, SEPTEMBER 1987)[59]

JOURNAL · DECEMBER 8, 1979  The torture of not writing is worse than the rigors of writing.

The "Fashions of the Hapsburgs" [Costume Institute] gala, on Monday last at the Metropolitan Museum—A perfect moment came when the whole lavish crowd was traipsing the long, narrow, grenadier-scarlet carpet away from the wretched dinner, a quarter-mile path between black-tied musicians, who stood on either side effusing waltzes. So potent was this magic, that the diners swirled from the carpet, waltzing among the Greek, Roman, and Etruscan sarcophagi, broken-nosed statues, and dead dancers now immobilized in marble, in terra-cotta—a dazzling, unexpected moment. The most beautiful party of the year, with memories of long-ago parties. The reopening of the museum after the war, with ranks of royals standing beneath their remote ancestors in the medieval and Renaissance halls, when suddenly the lights blew—blackout—and when they suddenly blazed again, a moment of terror clearly frozen in time on every royal face. Then relief composed those history-worn faces into sureness—not yet—not yet. You could smell the terror. You could hear the exhalation of relief.

DECEMBER 24, 1979  "I have known White Russians. I have known Red Russians. But I have never before known a Yellow Russian." Diana Vreeland about Alex Liberman.

FEBRUARY 2, 1980  Irving Penn about Susan Sontag: "She can't see. She has no eye. She sees flat." Her book on photography: "She is not visual," says Irving, in his quiet, slightly inflected voice, a voice of hill country—no, a country swelling into calm roundlings. . . . There are no heights to scale in Irving's voice . . . sometimes little hillocks of exasperation, with not even a hint of defunct volcanoes.

59. The piece refers to "Truman Capote by Truman Capote," the story of his evolution as a writer, which appeared in the December 1979 *Vogue*. Random House reprinted it as the preface to his *Music for Chameleons* in 1980.

My life conceived as drama—since I have always existed in a theater of my imagination—so each person in my life has been a character. Indeed, entrances and exits of each of the important persons in my life have been theatrical experiences. Ela (her entrance having been built up, as we say in the theater, by Laci) throwing open the door to Laci's room and catapulting me into all of my later days, instantly plunging me into the nonstop fantastic drama of her life . . . Mina, in gray chiffon, seated on a sofa in Lincoln's Nineteenth Street house, asking could we drop her at the Ambassador . . . Marlene in Ela's upstairs East Seventy-third Street flat, on the bed in her khaki army fatigues . . . Rut, Hellmut, and Fritz crying out: "Ela! Ela! We are here!" and leaping over someone on the floor . . . Richard, in brown suede shoes, in the greenroom at Feagin's . . . Puss, in blazer, by Robert's drawing table . . . Maggie Henning, fat, rosy—in bobby socks?—very enormous Shirley Temple, striding along the corridor of Public School 89, Newtown Annex . . . Eugenia Halbmeier in the Jackson Heights movie house at *Dracula* . . . Alice . . . Evangeline . . . Robert all making entrances . . . and some making exits—or disappearing: The crimson rose in the gutter after the hearse bore Ela away . . . So, my life as theater.

MARCH 12, 1980   I loathe Alex, at times actually hate him, although we have a deep sibling tie—a knotted cord binds us. He bares his lack of understanding of essential American ways and his dirty-man feral instincts, our "friend."[60] Grace Mirabella [now editor in chief of *Vogue*] has less culture than Alex does; he has almost too much—and most of it French, in the traditional Russian style.

MARCH 27, 1980   I rang up Anita [Loos] to make her laugh over the account in the appalling Errol Flynn "life" of how that jolly joker loosed a raccoon in the Brown Derby [restaurant] and how that raccoon ran up [actress] Kay Francis's leg. What became of the beast is not told. Then I told Anita how relentlessly flaccid Tennessee's Fitzgeralds play [*Clothes for a Summer Hotel*] was. She said, "But the Fitzgeralds were so boring. Oh, they were boring—and so narcissistic. They thought they'd invented it. And that Zelda—she was always taking off her clothes—and you know—she didn't have a thing to show—not a thing. . . ."

NOTE: As their summertime European holiday approached, Gray contracted chicken pox. They canceled the first leg of their trip and flew directly to Venice at the beginning of July, then after three weeks went to London.

JOURNAL • JUNE 26, 1980   Poor Puss—just now beginning to come out of his tunnel of chicken pox misery. Horrid, devastating, useless agonies. Two weeks

60. "My friend" was an expression often used by Alex Liberman.

lost from our holidays, and the only rewards (but such a bounty!) being together (even in agony this is the most glorious delight) and I reading aloud [Robert K.] Massie's to-be-published life of Peter the Great—a book written like a silent movie, but with such gusto, such devotion, and out of such prodigious research and awareness of what a reader should get that it is irresistible. Peter the Great is so much like Lincoln Kirstein.

JUNE 30, 1980  This morning I looked at the great cliff of the Gulf & Western building to see the sunrise reflected on it. I must make the most of what I have: a tower of an office block in place of cliffs and mountains, a single ailanthus stripling rooted on the edge of an apartment-house terrace in place of a copse of trees, a little piping city bird in place of the flocks we fed at 1453. I must make my own nature. The green that springs to life on the roof of the theater below our windows, a green which nobody has planned or planted.

JULY 5, 1980 · VENICE  Here we are in our room at the Gritti, after lunching on the terrace with the majestic chords of Basilica Santa Maria della Salute opposite. "I could look at it forever," said tired Gray—invitations, floral tributes, fruit offerings, and genteel hullabaloo. My "good" leg seems to give out now. I did not make a noble entrance. I had to creep like a monster onto the dock. But we are safe in our beds, going to no parties, and I am relieved. Venice preserved—and that means unchanged.

JULY 7, 1980  Mary McCarthy's *Venice Observed* [1956] preserves in the cookery sense, in a vinegar that she exudes in place of perspiration. Despite her cleverness, even brilliance, this book has no heart, and ultimately reveals Mary, while she opens steely eyes on Venice. Such an ungenerous, chiding book. Mary is a self-afflicted scourge: "Venice is not made to be seen in the round. Venetian architecture, indeed, is stage architecture." But very few of the sets have been struck.

JULY 12, 1980  Puss says: "Isn't it unlikely that we should be photographed with the sister (Jean Smith) of an assassinated president in a back alley in Venice, along with Adolph Green ("The Prince of Showbiz"), and by his son, Adam?" and then that upon hearing that Maestro's house was "behind there," Jean Smith should say, "Oh, my cook will be pleased. Did you ever hear of Herva Nelli?" I could not believe my ears: Maestro's favorite (she gave Ela such pain) is Jean Kennedy Smith's cook![61]

JULY 20, 1980  Venice is a truly sexy city. During the fireworks, my terror at the cannonading diminished from fingers in my ears to absolutely unterrified

---

61. Toscanini used the soprano Herva Nelli (1909–94) for several opera recordings, and she was one of his last mistresses.

enjoyment. The fireworks dyed the canal a flux of lost Victorian colors—those strange-to-our-eyes changeable colors—brazen, burnished, unhealthy colors, which led to greenery-yallery [Art Nouveau] depravities and gaslit sins. (All so much more pleasurable for being "secret," in the closet.) The new firework color was mauve. Is this a lavender, purple, mauve time again?

All day long the footsteps on the [wooden Redentore] bridge make our room a new setting from the opening of A *Tale of Two Cities*. After the fireworks, late last night, with Prince Enrico Esterházy and the Paloma Picassos, all of us standing on the [Gritti] terrace (so like a ship's deck) and looking at the great gush and glut of lantern-festooned boats streaming back, we were so like the group of *ancien régime* personages that, in Pola Negri's *Madame DuBarry* ([a silent film] seen at the Garlic Opera when I was perhaps six), stood peering out and commenting on the peasantry at their games—cut to the Conciergerie and the guillotine. Why do I remember this so clearly? And the dark woman in the vertically striped, perfectly cut, 1792(?) dress, complete with hat, reading a little book calmly as she was called, turning the page for one last look and then serenely proceeding to her death.

JULY 22, 1980   To Patricia Curtis Vignano and the Barbaro: Almonds and grapefruit juice and so much to see—from the great staircase (up which I crept) to the glorious rooms, specially the Henry James, with the eighteenth-century green lacquer chinoiserie desk on which he wrote *The Wings of the Dove*; the dim looking glasses; Patricia's grandmother [Mrs. Ralph Curtis] by Sargent, such esprit, never loaned out; the ballroom fantastic under sheets; their Tintoretto is a sweet-faced Madonna and child.

JULY 29, 1980 · LONDON   Lord George Weidenfeld, alone, in his library—sprawled, pale, a sort of blancmange, well-cut clothes—but that is only outward. Inward—force, power, wit, anecdotage, self-made, as an *ébéniste* makes Fine French Furniture, a certain charm, and a cultivated *grand seigneur* played by a gifted German actor. He talked about his memories, his social life, the secret language by which society signal to one another, his political life, his mother (she is still alive), about his "debt" to me: "You were so kind, always, to me when I was very young. You introduced me to Callas." He was tired geniality itself. He talked about his life with the Payson woman,[62] and the awful Christmases in Manhasset "with mountains of Cartier and Hammacher Schlemmer," and a Vanderbilt or Whitney cold blue eye or lock of blond hair gleaming through a crevice in the mountains, as they unwrapped presents. . . . No heart, no love. "But we remained great friends."

. The Vienna-born British publisher Baron Weidenfeld (b. 1919) had been married (1966–76) to Sandra Payson, a New York society figure.

AUGUST 2, 1980   David [Hockney] lives in Pembroke Studios, lost in a private place of gardens and studios. His high-ceilinged (actually two or three stories high) rooms are rowdy with light and color (his free, child-eyed colors), crammed with the detritus of his frenetic life. And since he is working on the three pieces for the Met [Opera] *(Parade, Les Mamelles de Tiresias,* and *L'Enfant et les sortilèges)* his big studio is like a brilliant genius child's imagination—huge canvases of ideas for these three.

David is a master showman. He has the music play and he tells his ideas of his production, meanwhile moving the results of his idea about a toy theater, which he has constructed, with a tiny lighting system and all—the envy of any young person mad on the theater. David is soft-spoken, Yorkshire accented, dry humored, twinkle eyed. He moves with a certain precision. He has nanny qualities with his ideas. He talked about his trials with Nureyev (the Russian arrogance and the vulgarity: "He wanted to build a whole set, a nightclub set with a huge stair!"). David intends to have Colette typing away in *Parade* as an overture—but Cocteau wrote it and Colette, I believe, did not type.

AUGUST 3, 1980   Penelope [Reed] is very decided, very aloud, nowadays, about likes and dislikes: "I hate Proust. Oh, how boring." This is what worries others, but this is her aging and evolving character, the emotional topography emerging as those unexpected islands propelled from sea or land depths by unseen cataclysms. Penelope—now sixty-seven and a widow of the man she so desperately wanted to marry.

AUGUST 4, 1980   A birthday visit to Rebecca West. She is almost blind, quite deaf, and altogether witty, in a vastness of Laura Ashley, surrounded by tea, scones, and white-frosted little cakes. Rebecca seemed improved over last year, but very brimming and sparkling with gossip, observation, history, personal anecdotage. Her talk is being aboard a speeding coaster, which flashes in and out of tunnels and sometimes leaps a loop and lands you in an unexpected terrain, from which it flies through the air to some cloud-plateau and then off again to a mire, from which it extracts itself and rushes full speed into safety and the station, all wheels revolving triumphantly. Rebecca West bears comparison to Mrs. Tiggy-Winkle and *The Wind in the Willows.* She talked vindictively about Jane Gunther and Greta ("Greeta") Garbo. (How Greeta was fascinated with Egyptian things, and Henry [Andrews] said he would show her the special objects she fancied (from photographs) in the British Museum.[63] Garbo said she would walk down the street and he would pick her up, and he said firmly, "I will be waiting here at Claridge's." So it happened.) Rebecca talked about having to evacuate when the [Irish Republican Army] bombings happened. She talked about how desperate life is here and everywhere and about politics—a real Rebecca splurge.

63. Henry Maxwell Andrews (1894–1968), a British banker, married Rebecca West in 1930.

AUGUST 11, 1980 · NEW YORK CITY  A call from Diana Trilling, on Martha's Vineyard and much provoked by Jacques Barzun's marriage to a Texas professor (English) of fifty and about the inequality of women: how older men find younger women to marry—indeed, how women seek out older men. How an older woman can have a lively social life—but marriage or a sex life!!! So on . . . Diana is rampageous about this.[64]

**MOMMA GOING**  *Two weeks after her ninety-second birthday, and after eight years of tormenting senility, at six o'clock one Indian summer evening my mother told Mary [Callabras], her angelic housekeeper, to take her to "my kitchen." There she sat in her wheelchair, peering into the whiteness of what had once been a source of her power over her relations and friends—her superb, abundant, and typical cooking. Then she said, "Take me back." Six hours later, having made up her mind (for even in these last years of mindlessness we suspected her of having a mind), she shut her blue eyes and died. And that, save for my tenuous hold, was the end of the family as a family. Our center had gone. We were no longer a family—merely relations who soon grew to be strangers. (1981)*

JOURNAL · OCTOBER 24, 1980  Long silence, in which Momma died. "Going," she said, and she went. Every evening at about six, I start for the telephone. This is habit, but she seems to be there, in her flat in Jackson Heights, where the autumn smells as it did when I ambled to and from school, to and from the library, seething with curiosity, plans, and passion. I loved the world. I still love the world. I made Momma's eulogy, and I made everyone laugh and tear, and Momma would have had that look: mingled pride at her achievement and baffled understanding at my achievement. Then she would have said, "That's my Label!"

NOVEMBER 15, 1980  Discussion about why Puss doesn't work: "Because we are headed for complete annihilation," he says. "Don't you understand about annihilation? I don't want to contribute to the debris. That's my choice." Me: "Then why put drops in my eyes, if we're all doomed?" Puss: "Because I want you to see it."

DECEMBER 1, 1980  Lillian Hellman, expensively grotesque, seen at lunch in the Grill Room of the Four Seasons. She, as her elderly escort led her away, was Pique Dame—malign, a terrible face.

Maria Callas is the only Violetta I have seen who died with her eyes open.

---

64. Jacques Barzun (b. 1907), a cultural historian, was on the faculty of Columbia University. GF: "Diana wanted an affair with Barzun, or was hot and heavy after him. She told me that Berlioz was her and Barzun's sexual music."

DECEMBER 12, 1980 Ultimately all of this life must be a comedy. It is to avoid the realization that all life is a black comedy that most people take to religion. How much a creator realizes the black comedy of life is the measure of greatness: Shakespeare, Michelangelo, Beethoven, Mozart, Proust, Goethe, and then the poets—in a single explosion of verse (Shelley, Keats). I suspect there can be no "masterpiece" without this realization of life as black comedy. The final irony: Death. I think of Spain and the Spanish temperament, the distillation of this bitter knowledge (which breeds Spanish elegance).

FEBRUARY 2, 1981 Alex, in secrecy, told me that Si [Newhouse] plans to revive *Vanity Fair*. "Who to be editor?" he asked. "Me!" I blurted. . . . I felt a surge of youth, vitality . . . but isn't this too late for me?

NOTE: Leo and Gray went to the White House with Grace Mirabella and Horst to photograph new First Lady Nancy Reagan.

JOURNAL • FEBRUARY 5, 1981 • WASHINGTON, D.C. Off we went into the brilliant white light of noon to the White House and Mrs. Reagan, the state rooms looking better than they did when the Fords were there (I never went while the Carters were in residence). The buildup to Mrs. Reagan's entrance. "She'll feel the chill." So, a roaring fire in the Red Room. "She loves red. That's her color." Extravagant preparations for Mr. Reagan's "surprise" birthday party. We hear careful planning to meet the early-morning editions.

Mrs. Reagan—everything save her shoes wrong. The Galanos [dress], really cruel, exposing her sixty-year-old flabbiness. (The White House rang to tell us that she has "an upper-arm problem" and she does—also sags under the chin, no figure, no bosom.) Mrs. Reagan widens her eyes into hypnotic hugeness the way she was taught in Hollywood. She takes direction the way a novice star does. She said to Horst: "I'm depending on you to erase the last six months of my life." When Horst said, asking her to sit on an arm of a chair, "Now you look as though you are at home," she instantly answered, "That's what I am supposed to be." She has a useless, vacant laugh—mirthless. "Tomorrow I'm wearing a very old, long, white-beaded dress because Ronny loves it. It's so old I don't even know who made it. " Everything is according to script. She gave expected smiles and words of pleasure. She said to Horst, "I'm such a great fan of yours," and somehow implied that she was entirely and trustingly in his hands. She seems an empty vessel—but not one easily filled. She is a poor actress in a four-year starring role. She needs help—scheduled surprise, planned spontaneity. The basic image is moviemaking, and the movie from the start is strictly Grade B.

FEBRUARY 7, 1981 President Reagan is an actor who can work best (perhaps only) from a carefully prepared script, with artfully disposed props, crafty staging. Proof: his "impromptus" for press or a television show—bad. His scripted, staged "economics" message to the nation—superb, his "finest" hour. And this morning, the president and the first lady on the front page of the *Washington Post*, a gleam and a smile at his four-tier birthday cake, another episode in the Grade B movie, in which we are now all involved. But Ronald Reagan does radiate confidence and agreeableness and gentlemanliness. Mrs. Reagan does glitter with American-woman charm and wide eyes—ever-widening, sherry-colored eyes, ingenuous and appealing for understanding, while promising understanding with her "nice-woman" smile.

FEBRUARY 15, 1981 · NEW YORK CITY   Marlene [on the telephone]—old, sick, drinking, penniless, and full of her peculiar Berlin humor. "So, I sold my piano, and I took a $75,000 mortgage on this place, and there's nobody here with whom to rehearse, so I don't get out of bed to walk. . . . If I could rehearse walking . . ." Marlene's young-girl voice, slurred by drink, but, suddenly ballooning into a marvelous exhilaration and splintering into roulades and trills—a baroque display—of laughter, all the more joyful because of the darkness beneath it. "Sometimes I think: Why do I hang on? Promise me that when it happens, you'll see that I'm taken down the back way—right into the cellar. I don't want anybody to see me." Then the voice shrugs. I can see her shoulders shrugging off despair, lifting gloom into a brighter air. No more *coq* feather disguises, no filmy veils—just her naked will to linger a little longer. . . .

FEBRUARY 28, 1981   Never noted that Mrs. Onassis came to lunch on Wednesday last. Tall, slender as a girl playing a boy in the school play, her dark hair flying in calculated disarray, she suited in perfectly cut narrow pants, a windbreaker-looking jacket—all woodsy-in-winter colors (no, late, late autumn, just before the countryside goes winter white and black). She raced through the Grill Room, swooped down, kissed me. . . . Not a fork, spoon, what have you, moved in the room (only Bubbles [Sills] caused this silence and suspended animation) as Mrs. O made her swift, apologetic passage. Then she fell into immediate talk. She was interested to hear about Mrs. Reagan and was the White House shabby. But mostly she loved hearing about Lesley Blanch, about books, music, actresses. In the middle of my flow, she asked didn't I really want to write a book about it all. I said yes—but not really for Doubleday.[65] She has Vivien Leigh's ability, by looking intently at you (but is Mrs. O nearsighted?), by never wavering as she looks, to make you believe that you are the only one in the world, you are the most glorious dramatizer of life. Anaïs had this, too—but her look also contained a pinch of skepticism and a long dose of amusement. Mrs. O is the girl with the fairy tale absolutely transporting her out of the real world.

65. Jacqueline Onassis was an editor at Doubleday.

NOTE: Leo again went to Los Angeles with Gray, this time to supervise the shooting of a *Vogue* feature on Jo Ann and Julian Ganz, collectors of nineteenth-century American art. They also scouted several other homes for the magazine.

JOURNAL · MARCH 2, 1981 · LOS ANGELES The last time I ever saw Lady Mendl [Elsie de Wolfe], she held a porcelain cabbage gently in her lap as her companion (were they all called Edie?) wheeled her along Fifty-seventh Street and into the doorway of 11 East, going on to Kirk Askew's gallery. She royally inclined her head, as she peered at me from beneath hooded eyes—a small, slender, upright, toqued figure on her last foray into the marketplace.

Herbie Ross—so queenly. Herbie and Nora [Kaye] (who has a robust humor) check each other. They live a rich, working-together marriage. Nora on her very early days: How, at five, she got diabetes because her mother was a Tolstoy follower and fed Nora on fruits and nuts. How Nora was taken to Fokine and got a scholarship—but arrived weekly with huge tins of caviar, her father working at that time for a caviar supplier.[66] Now, Herbie can scoff: "Scholarship! It was the caviar!" Nora: "He had that little room at the top of the huge mansion and he didn't like to give barre. That didn't interest him. . . . So he'd say, 'Go up—do exercises—come down—I teach!' And he did—his complete repertoire. . . . But even at five I knew that I had to know steps to dance the repertoire, so I told my mother, and she took me to the Met. That was the best place for steps."

So when I, with Mrs. Svedrofsky, saw [Respighi's opera] *The Sunken Bell*, I saw Nora—one of five little girls. She was an elf. They all peered into the well, as Elisabeth Rethberg emerged like some huge, very odd creature—garlanded, festooned, and a quivery mountain of rosy flesh.[67]

MARCH 11, 1981 · NEW YORK CITY Return, yesterday, to the [Plaza's] Edwardian Room—thronged with the past. This (and the [hotel's] Oak Room) is the public place where I first felt "known." Here I knew Cary Grant and [film actress] Jean Seberg and had my annual birthday parties—only women—and lunched with Schiaparelli after Carmel's funeral and lunched after Ela's funeral. . . . So much in this now shabby—no—worn, a kinder word—room, where yesterday I was still "known," greeted by Tonio, who long ago was a busboy there.

66. When Nora Kaye was five, the Ballets Russes dancer and choreographer Mikhail Fokine (1880–1942) was working in the United States with his own company.
67. This was probably in 1928. Ernestine Svedrofsky was the wife of Michael Svedrofsky, concertmaster of the Metropolitan Opera orchestra. Neighbors to the Lermans in Queens, they had musical evenings that enchanted young Leo: "How I waited desperately for the Svedrofskys to ask me to the opera. I arrived to sit in the Morgenthau box, the center one, in Uncle Irving's cast-off 'white tie,' my stiff shirt projecting from my fly, unbuttoned. All were not gods, not creatures of the netherworld, just earthlings, but I sat in an effulgence which, so long as the old Met stood, never dimmed for me." *Journal, December 8, 1984.*

APRIL 4, 1981 A scrap of a phrase, a wisp: "The gardens were filled with violets. I thought of Eleonora," writes Richard on a postcard of Aranjuez, and this swift, almost indistinguishable, little string of words becomes an enormous net, in which my whole life wiggles. I am a fish, an enormous Biblical monster, caught in a fragile net of simple words.

APRIL 16, 1981 "I know what I know by experience; you know it by imagination." Henry James in *The Bostonians*. In the beginning I knew everything "by imagination," and now, having lived about seventy years, I know less by experience.

NOTE: On April 26, Easter morning, Leo suffered a rectal hemorrhage. Although the rupture was nothing ordinarily serious, he bled profusely and stanching it required paramedical aid.

JOURNAL · APRIL 28, 1981 At last I feel well this morning. After a night threaded with worriments—"raveling up the sleeve of care." I was "the sleeve." That horror on the floor of the bathroom, when I knew that I was almost gone . . . I was so aware, even when fading in and out. . . . I saw sharply, and I felt (not reasoned) with a sharp irony—the tense, fraught attempt to save me— four men working furiously fast, concentrated, murmuring. All sound was a murmur or a sudden intensification of a murmur. I felt my life coming and going . . . tidal . . . ebb and flow . . . became that ebb and flow, somewhere deep within me knowing that I could go out with the ebb, and so somehow clinging to being as a tide-tossed man clings to a spar.

I can, I see, still scribble a bit. Such excesses of floral tributes, the most unexpected from Mrs. Reagan—a conventional centerpiece arrangement of pink and white—carnations, dogwood, and quince twigs. Carol Channing's note, with a splendor of Spanish yellow and scarlet-striped tulips: "Don't worry—Mary Baker Eddy will take care of everything." If we had waited for M.B.E., I would now be dead. [Dr.] Bill Cahan took care of everything, and that is why I am now alive.

The muck that poured out of me lay like a thick impasto—rich, scarlet, fluttery edges—almost pinking-shears edges—like carnations—almost too right-angle scarlet edges, a smooth surface of rich, rich brown black—very Rothko.

MAY 9, 1981 *The Little Foxes* opening—The play creaks like Sardou [nineteenth-century melodrama]. Elizabeth Taylor performing is not an actress. Like Marlene, she is a larger-than-life old-time star. Elizabeth is very beautiful, with a kind of fatal doom in her dark face. When she is onstage, her beauty, her legend usurp all other theater elements: We watch her. Why not go to see Elizabeth Taylor not to see her act, but to see Elizabeth? She does not shortchange you, the would-be actress does. When she is offstage, the real actors are very good, coming into their legitimate own. This Regina and this Birdie are more like the "real" prototypes than any of their predecessors—Tallulah (who acted), Geraldine Page, Pat Collinge,[68] Felicia [Bernstein]. Altogether the most glamorous Broadway opening in a decade.

Evangeline Bruce (very "The Italian Lesson"[69]) on the Reagan dinner for Prince Charles: "Everyone wondered what the Mellons and I were doing in that *galère*. But it *was* fascinating. . . . I talked with the prince about Lady Diana's sweet expression. . . . She's had it since she was a little girl of three, and he was delighted that I mentioned it. . . . He doesn't have a touch of sentiment about her, but he went away muttering 'sweet expression.' . . ."

MAY 10, 1981  That Harlem of my childhood, now totally obliterated, save in my mind—that teeming Jewish place, a set map invisible to any eyes save mine. (Aunts at every window—who could run far with the aunts so watchful?) At the center of my map—Grandpa, the uncles, Momma, Poppa, the cousinage. The long, late-spring, early-summer twilights—how I awaited them then, for we were permitted to stay up longer to hop from square to square of the chalked pavement in front of our house. And in the sunset sky, over the park, flagrantly green with approaching summer, great torrents of pink light (years later suddenly alive again on Venetian ceilings). The sounds of that now invisible Harlem . . . The Irish girl in her flyaway pinafore dress, her waist-length plaits swinging wildly, as she danced to the raucous, tin-pan sound of the merry-go-round. Then, one day, a fat, serious round of pale roses, from which depended broad purple and black ribbons, hung on the wooden door of the house—and she emerged, her plaits severe, her dress frowns in black, sculptured folds—all her brightness quenched beneath a pall of black veiling.

MAY 13, 1981  Last night, the Niagara energy of Lena Horne [*The Lady and Her Music*, on Broadway] proving that at sixty-four (in June) she is still emerging. But now she is no longer an entertainer, she is a concert-platform artist—of a splendor. I wired, saying she was up there with Gielgud and Callas. I meant that wonderful [1959] season when Gielgud brought his evening of Shakespeare, Maria did her concert *Il Pirata* in Carnegie Hall, and Karen [Blixen] told stories at the Y. Lena last night fitted into that season: She is the event. She has overwhelming passion, wit, judgment—all disciplined. The cabin on her shoulder has fallen off.[70] She now looks at life, but is not hardened by it. She is a most worldly black artiste. Lena's wise-girl eyes, her long,

---

68. The Irish actress Patricia Collinge (1892–1974) played Birdie in the original production of *The Little Foxes* in 1939.
69. "The Italian Lesson" was a Ruth Draper monologue in which a society lady's life was encapsulated by a fruitless session with her Italian tutor.
70. The singer Lena Horne (b. 1917) had starred in Vincente Minnelli's 1943 film *Cabin in the Sky*.

thin neck and that antique head, alert for any of life's tornadoes, any of life's rich handouts; the little girl-child-smarts; the Cotton Club adolescent, all of the Lenas preserved, apparent—like ancient leaves preserved as fossils in a rock. It is a going off the edge, reaching beyond the point of no return that gets the crowd out of its expensive seats and stands them cheering. It is the danger made visible, the madness that is hidden [made] suddenly visible that gets the crowd. Constant standing ovations. Lena made a *coup de théâtre*, each song a wholly dramatic event. The audience was the kind, not seen in years, found in a Carlo [Van Vechten] novel. This was really black elegance, chic. This evening returns me to the Harlem of my childhood.

MAY 21, 1981  This morning in the *Times*, Elizabeth Otis was dead at eighty. I didn't feel anything when Puss told me, then about an hour later, I burst into tears. What a long, intense life we shared, for some years. And did she ever know that, briefly, I shared Larry [Kiser], her muddled husband? I found out that even married men were queer. (I would exclaim, "But he's married!") The importance of Elizabeth, Mavis, and Annie Laurie during those formative years is in the all-night jaws, the sharing, the hours of laughter, and the doors they opened. John Steinbeck and Howard Fast and Rachel Field—all in and out. I read eighteen manuscripts a week and got $18 (such riches!), met everyone, and so became part of that "literary" world.[71]

MAY 30, 1981  Yesterday morning—Jan Morris (formerly James) came to talk about the piece that she will be writing for *Vogue* about Monte Carlo.[72] After some years of telephone chumminess, in which she seemed all gush and girlish flutter and laughter, here she was in a blue-and-white horizontally striped sailor shirt and white button earrings, her attractive, careful, calm, very English ("I am Welsh!"), more male than female voice embroidered with bright laughter, appreciative chuckles, knowing inflections—mirth always just under the surface.

I got my genders mixed, sometimes referring to Jan as she, then he. "Forgive my slips of gender," I said. When she stepped into the lift, she said sweetly, "Don't mind about the gender. You'll get used to it." She laughed and was whisked away. An altogether pleasant person—agreeable at all times, but with a toughness, a fiber. "Are you sure I'm the person to do this article? I'm not the least interested in fancy society and all that sort of thing. I couldn't be farther

71. Leo began his literary career in the late thirties reading for Elizabeth Otis and Mavis McIntosh Riordan's agency, McIntosh & Otis, where Annie Laurie Williams was then an associate. Later Otis was Leo's literary agent (until 1977). Howard Fast (1914–2003) was a leftist journalist, novelist, and screenwriter. Rachel Field (1894–1942) was a novelist (*All This and Heaven Too*), poet, and author of children's fiction.
72. First published as James Morris, the travel writer and historian Jan Morris (b. 1926) had had a sex-change operation in 1972.

away from it. I'm interested in power." She became, as she said that, a moment of power, very strong, a complete affirmation of the idea and of her chosen self. She has the air of a good-sport girl, a shoulder-bag girl, a girl who will pitch in and help, a girl who could be a sublimated dyke. And she has a certain blondish, blue-eyed prettiness—unspoiled somehow. I liked her. She referred to the time she was a man as "my disability."

MAY 31, 1981  The look in the eyes of Grandpa and Grandma's generation (they were probably in their forties when I first knew them!) when they listened to music—Caruso or [soprano] Alma Gluck, or [cantor] Yossele Rosenblatt, or any opera chorus, or *The Masked Ball* with Caruso, or violinists (Elman, Heifitz) or pianists . . . that look of hearing angels or even God . . . a special veiled sparkle in which the soul was visible looking out at wonders, splendors, the promised land . . . the stillest listening, the heart standing still between throbs. This look was also apparent at the performances of children. Every child could become, indeed was, a prodigy, an adorable, impossible prodigy, dressed in white satin and Little Lord Fauntleroy rig. Inconceivable to become president of the U.S.A. at that time, but a great musician—a player of world renown and immense fortune—that was a golden possibility. Look at [the pianists] Hofmann, de Pachmann, and that newcomer Horowitz.

One early morning, Aunt Sara [Lerman] called to my mother. We found her sitting at the top of the backstairs which connected her second-floor apartment. (The Jackson Heights house was divided between two brothers—my uncle Max and my father Sam. In a year Poppa was to buy his brother out.) Her knees were spread wide apart. I saw, with flesh-creeping alarm, that between her legs was a large dark vacant place—a chasm—where on me and on the bodies of the cousins with whom I had played show-me-yours-and-I'll-show-you-mine was a reassuring, handy appendage, something I could hold on to— a fact, not a nothingness. Did this first glimpse of a woman's sexual area help determine my future sexuality? I was a very hot little boy. I needed a lot of sexual warmth, reassurance, and I got it from my little boy chums, not from the girls. . . . So many taboos instilled by adults: They did not forbid boys (probably they thought about the dangers). So it was natural to seek pleasures, before the possibility of orgasm, from boys. Dire results could happen from tampering with girls. Who said anything bad could result from "playing" with boys?

JUNE 2, 1981  Last night the Daniel Roses [he a real-estate investor] gave Francine [Gray] a dinner at the Century (not the Harmony!) honoring her [novel] *World Without End* and commemorating the long friendship between Francine and Joanna [Semel Rose]. I had the feeling of an engagement party. Francine I knew when Alex and Tatiana first came. I saw eleven-year-old Francine at Henriette [Pascar, Alex Liberman's mother]'s—a stiff child, very secretive, a child in one of Julian Green's enclosed gardens—pretty when she smiled, beautifully dressed by her beautiful and terrifyingly arrogant mother. Alex, in gray flannel, had a Middle Eastern look—Turkish? He could have been a boy in a Michael Arlen saga—no, more Konrad Bercovici. All three were tremendously Continental.[73] Henriette was one of the centers of the Russo-Franco émigré colony. The grown-ups seemed to suffer intense pain and shame over her. Later I discovered that this was rage and indeed shame.[74] Francine and Joanna came to work with me at *Mademoiselle* as June girls, long ago (both came from Bryn Mawr). Francine was by then a beauty—tall, slender, beautiful bones—a sort of late-medieval sculpture on a French cathedral facade, and they were so literary, so intellectual.

JUNE 6, 1981  Richard Locke to be editor of *Vanity Fair*. My hopes dashed, but I don't mind since this book is the only interest and *Vanity Fair* is too late for me—also I've had almost a decade of its remains.[75] "Can you work with him," Alex asked eagerly. No free rides.

Locke came to lunch—a guarded man, squarish, a burrow beast—some culture, but no international scope. He will last for a time—even longer. "He'll have me," says Alex, who, obviously, intends to edit *Vanity Fair*. I see *Vogue* will become a fashion magazine, ultimately losing what I bring to it—but by then I hope to be away from it and hopefully "booked." Locke seems to appreciate humor. He must have connections because of his twelve years with the [*New York*] *Times Book Review* (a dreary sheet).

JUNE 7, 1981  I think, reading the beginning of *Swann in Love* (how witty is the fine blade of caricature) of John and Dora Koch and their "circle"—Virgil [Thomson], Ania [Dorfmann], the Reginald Marshes [both painters], us, some worn music critics, eager young piano students who were then in the "slave" state (larvae—the parallel should be bees). The pretentiousness of the Kochs and the vulgarity of Dora . . . Her voice was more a scream—a hawking scream, the voice of a woman peddling newspapers from a pavement booth or one of those kiosks found in the lobbies of public buildings. Dora's voice had matured in just such circumstances. Her father kept a newsstand in a downtown office building, and there Dora, with beautiful skin and an echo of Judy Garland in her face, dispensed the views of the day for a nickel a throw—

---

73. The French-American novelist and memoirist Julian Green (1900–1998) wrote somber stories of psychological struggle. The Romanian-American writer Konrad Bercovici (1881–1961) depicted life in the Balkans and among the Gypsies.
74. Henriette Pascar embarrassed her son Alex by tarting herself up and flirting with men well into her old age.
75. *Vanity Fair* closed in 1936. Allene Talmey was moved to *Vogue* and given a few feature pages to fill monthly. Until 1983 *Vogue* bore a line reading "Incorporating *Vanity Fair*."

shrieking her wares, raking in the take—between lessons on the pianoforte, lessons which were not to make her the great concert artist which was her father's dream, but which were to fashion her into one of the world's great teachers. She determined to marry John, and after he was beaten up in a doorway, where he had been "doing one of his pickups" (the latter almost killed), Dora was able to catch him. She made him the extraordinary success he became in their life with very rich out-of-New-York (Detroit, etc.) "society"—also Roosevelt ladies. John became the master of flashy, obviously sensual, rich portraiture. His portrait of me—black and pink—hangs in Kansas City.[76]

Their feasts were first in a brownstone walk-up, one-plate gumbo dinner on laps, and later elaborate "banquets" in a huge, Central Park West double co-op, very Art Deco, where Dora would scream: "This is just like old St. Petersburg!" She shouted affluence—at her sit-down dinners for seventy-five, at her collection of Guardis and Bouchers and El Grecos ("Aren't they a dream!" she would shriek. "All real!"). When she ran out of self-praise for her possessions, for her enormous person, she would glare wildly about—her eyes those of a carousel horse—and howl, "And this is my table!" as John's pink tongue darted avidly between his full lips, and his hands surreptitiously felt the limbs of any young male seated deliberately nearby at table. At the heart of this circle was John's homosexuality. He told all by his body and his facial movements (remnants of his former flirtatious girlishness), and, of course, I was astonished to find that he was a practicing homosexual. I think that Dora knew.

This world had its "little nucleus," as all such worlds must have to exist—a core of devotees—the charities and benevolences done so quietly that you cannot fail to hear them. They had a box at the old Metropolitan Opera. They went everywhere except into the higher reaches of New York "society." They were the Verdurins or the Veneerings [parvenus] of the moment, starting to climb in the forties, reaching their apogee in the late fifties and sixties, declining in the seventies with John's drawn-out death.

JUNE 12, 1981  Miltie [Goldman] is carrying on with young men. Each time when he is fucked, [the late] Arnold's photograph bounds off his bureau. "I have a poltergeist in my bedroom," says Miltie, who somehow combines being a new kind of Merry Widow and an old-fashioned relict—sad, tearful, huddling in the dead spouse's jacket—and, withal, Miltie is appealing. He is so honest in his behavior and laughs at himself. He is basically nice. Why doesn't anyone write about the Miltie-Arnold kind of relationship or ours—the good, sound, long-lived relations. What's written about are the one-night stands, the broken homes after two years playing the field, the unattractive sex arrangements.

---

76. John Koch's 1953 painting *Interior: Leo Lerman* is now at New York's National Academy of Design. Leo also appears as a guest in Koch's *The Cocktail Party* (1956).

JUNE 14, 1981 The [Metropolitan] museum distrusts, probably even dislikes, Diana Vreeland—the peacock among the domestic fowl—but this exotic brings golden eggs (money). Her legend and sure glamour attract funds, so the museum, so greedy, must "put up" with D.V., her much publicized eccentricities, her prized (in the outside world) originality. D.V. and Stephen [Jamail, her assistant] appear an eighteenth-century painting of a "Royal" and her— what is the word?—man-of-all-work, the one who gets the menu, watches the servants, spies, even arranges assassinations and intrigues and seductions— could be even earlier, painted by Van Dyck. Diana is the antithesis of the museum world. Curators and librarians usually feel that their "charges" belong to them. They frequently resent any public use, forgetting that they are public servants, and behave like proprietors.

# RATHER LIKE BEING JILTED

JOURNAL • JUNE 29, 1981 • PARIS  A week ago we had the *Vogue* car (the first day after Mitterand was definitely in office and had appointed his four Communist cabinet officers), picked up Stephen Jamail (here as Diana Vreeland's emissary), and were off to Versailles to arrange the loan of the replica of the Oris diamond necklace and some "important" portraits for D.V.'s eighteenth-century woman exhibit. Stephen regaled us with the decline "international society" had fallen into on learning that Cappy Badrutt was dying of cancer.

Cappy actually is the best example of what is now known as "society." She was born Caprice Capron in Hollywood, was a "dancer" in a low joint, the Florentine Gardens, in Hollywood, became notorious when she was seventeen, having been lured—according to her mother—into the Hollywood Hills and there raped by an army pilot (this during World War II). The mother sued. The case was splashed in the headlines. Caprice was off and away, climbing through studio execs (her best chums were two strippers—Jet Black, a pale beauty, and Beverly Hills) and through a rich Chinese connection to Saint-Moritz and Badrutt, who owns the Palace Hotel there. This is where she became "international society" (actually *Women's Wear* [*Daily*] riffraff). So she passed on, accumulating jewels and wealth, her hoarse voice, her foul mouth, her "good heart," and her "stinginess."

This day also included the Peter Brook [directed] *Cherry Orchard*—the most glorious I have ever seen. So, I saw two worlds already ended: Versailles like flowers pressed between the pages of a book; *The Cherry Orchard* like life observed through a glass that renders the large view microcosmic and so even more potent. This Chekhov is the central play of modern times. Each of us had a *Cherry Orchard*—or even several—and the whole world is the result of a *Cherry Orchard*. The orchard has become an airway terminal or a parking lot.

JULY 12, 1981 • VENICE  Was my family, then, what set me apart, made me different from all the other boys and girls I knew—whose families didn't walk so proudly ("Why do they walk like princes?" Puss asked when he first saw them, en masse in Seventy-fourth Street [Jackson Heights]), whose families weren't so much a clan, a single everyday force? (By family, I mean Momma's people.) When I see a Venetian family, coming away from Sunday lunch, I see that family in our sense still exists, and that past comes into being—the way stage scenery materializes in a transformation scene [is how] that Manhattan past returns in a sunstruck Venetian *calle*.

Here, in Venice, I recapture the family I thought lost after Momma died, while feeling no ties to that America in which we were saved, in which I was born and grew—corporeally—while living my life of the imagination here, in Paris of the Revolution, in Russia of the 1870s, in a Belle Epoque world wherever it was rich and high and effulgent.

JULY 13, 1981 When Hester Sporer gave me those first volumes of Proust, and I sat reading them at the kitchen table—in a state of intense excitement, filling with surmise—the world I wanted became diamond-solid.[1] It was more available then, since this was late 1932 or 1933, but it was available to me only in fantasy—in books, music, magazines—so I organized a gang. I became a young Fagin, and sent them foraging for magazines in the cellars of the apartment houses now beginning to surround us.

I walked the new streets and longed at the skyline, seen clearly across the meadows, now become empty lots, and knew that New Ilium, those giddy, topless towers must one day be mine. I wished to be a sort of Trojan horse in this world—to penetrate the surface glitter, to get behind the dazzle, and there to experience its reality. I wanted, although I did not then know this, to collect it. For sitting here in my wing chair in this room overlooking the Grand Canal, I understand that I am basically that little boy, who went very early on certain workdays with his hated grandfather, carrying bags to collect such loot as he could find—a cut-glass bowl, a battered silver serving dish, a porcelain or even paste dancing figure—slightly chipped in the nose but *en pointe*—oh ecstasy— poised to fly into some richer air where a world of grandeur glittered and tinkled, and the only sound heard was a joyful applause. I hated my grandfather, but because of him I became a collector—my collecting being a sesame to my dream world. The Jewishness of the Harlem market and Orchard Street— more lost worlds. So the Proustian world became a lost one as much as the immigrant world of my grandfather—both lost save in my memory, revived here in Venice, when a family came out into a *calle* after Sunday lunch.

One evening, I found at the door of a huge apartment in which I had been invited to dine, Alice [Astor]'s old butler, who immediately whispered, as he took my coat, "What, Mr. Leo, are you doing here?" And what, indeed, was I doing here, in rooms upon which more money than taste or heart had been lavished, where all was for show that told of the host's riches, where little I pon-

---

1. "I remember Hester taking me to lunch when I was still in high school. I thought Hester the most worldly of women. She worked at Random House, and she was the first woman I had ever heard talk about sex and even homosexuality. My, I thought her the bee's knees, and now I don't even know where or what she is." *Letter to RH, March 17, 1954.*

dered could be understood—but where my "legend" was still appreciated, where I was thought to be worldly and learned and clever and "in the know," and where when my usefulness diminished I would no longer be welcome. This new world lacked all sense of continuity—that continuity which I was to find in Venice—long tentacles, veins, reaching back into the remotest past, a past as alive as the future—a world in which that past and the possible future made an almost imperceptible present.

The importance of the hemorrhage is what was decided for me as I lay upon the tiled bathroom floor: "I've always been late for deadlines, but this is the latest I've ever been." For the first time, I was frightened at a sickness. Death was in that room. I could have gone with him, but I resisted because I wanted to stop a while longer with Puss and I wanted to make a memorial to all the lost worlds that I have known and all of the people who made up those worlds. I want to add to continuity. Continuity is the only reassurance, the only immortality: Ela lives, Alice lives, Laci lives, my family lives—in me, in these pages. . . .

JULY 16, 1981  My "return" to Europeanization, I learned much from Laci, not recovered until I found it again in Venice.

About Laci: I was hungry for his past. I needed that past, that Europe, that glamour, the people of that past—some of what the papers called the "best people, the best minds, the greatest creators" now beleaguered in my Manhattan. So, instinctively I became, even before I knew what I had become, part of this past, his present—even outreaching him, in the years ahead going beyond him. As he needed my youth, my Manhattan *savoir* (as he called it), as he marveled at my broad knowledge of European theater and dance and opera and design and literature, so his (now my) Europeans appreciated me for these very "qualities" with a greater understanding. They were "deeper" than he was, neurotic in different ways; they were not mad. And it was only years later, when I was quite detached from the sensual, the voluptuous part of Laci and my affair— when I was no longer in love with him, but felt for him as one feels for a relative—a kind of blood love and hate—that I realized how intellectually shallow he was, how his heart was incapable of any but (for me) surface feelings, how he was interested in me for services—sexual and physical—how he was actually a man. But by that time none of this mattered. And when, one day, I read in the morning paper that he had killed himself (sitting in his bathtub, pills, a knife), I was sad for him and a little furious that I, who had worked so hard to help make him a success, to give him the triumphs his talent and his art deserved, did not inherit a thing. Not a trifle, let alone any of the $80,000 he left to the crippled boy who had replaced me. Laci had told me how much I meant to him, how I was the "love" of his "life," how he could not go on without me— even as I lay in his arms, did the things he loved and which I grew to need. I had fallen in love with a bias-cut white dress and ended up with a European education, a glory of great Europeans as my true friends, and upon my upper lip a black mustache. His father had sported a black mustache; he was excited by a black mustache; for him I grew a black mustache. Even when we were "mad" about one another, we could not be physically monogamous. But he did open the world of his past, which became my future, a world of exultation and sundry pain, a confirmation that for each shard of knowledge received, each bead of ecstasy received over years (how I would finger, count this rosary in the future) payment was not only expected but exacted. I knew, when all the furor had ended, that I would always have to pay as I went—not one tittle of experience was free. An education in the high finance of experience.

JULY 21, 1981  When one is writing, painting, composing, one is like a person in love—undependable as a social being, irresponsible in the daily concourse of time. Firm dates are broken, excuses made. A person in creation—whether love or any other creative work—is so dedicated to that work that he cannot give himself to social obligations. So when Maria was married to Meneghini she was a worker—they worked together. They were creating Maria—*prima donna del mondo*—La Superba—the glorious legend. But when she fell in love with Onassis—with his power, his world—she had to do that work. She had to abdicate her own throne, and because of the nature of her attachment had to become his vassal, his creature. That was part of their wager: Who was to be on top? Her center moved. She was no longer the vassal of music—the vestal—but the petitioner of heart—his heart. She had no pride—not about this. The fire and fury and pride of her opera days had turned to a pliant silken rope with which she was slowly strangling herself.

JULY 22, 1981  At Lin [Tissot]'s party,[2] "the Vendramina,"[3] a pale-complexioned woman looking as if she wears no makeup—the face of a Roman consul—chiseled, intense—but suddenly alive with interest—a small, spare woman of power. The power burned low. She had been the social arbiter of Venice—now fading into oblivion, but still the center of the oldest Venetian society. She was the leading Fascist woman in Italy. When the war ended, she was told that the partisans would kill her and to get out. She sent her family away; she went to her *castello*. In her garden with a grandchild when the partisans came, when they told her that they had come to kill her, she said, "But surely not before the child . . ." She sent him away. Then, "But before you kill me, surely, some wine . . ." She dispensed wine, and the parti-

2. In his later years, the glass designer Charles Lin Tissot (1904–94), who lived six months each year in Venice's Palazzo Polignac, introduced Leo to many in Venetian society.
3. The Venetian aristocrat Vendramina Brandolini d'Adda Marcello del Majno (1902–91) was, understandably, known more simply as "the Vendramina."

sans drank her wine until they finally decided that they could not kill this kind lady. So they went away—and she remained to rule Venetian society.

Marlene rang last night, but I was too "exhausted" to ring back. This morning I rang. At first she made believe that she was an old French maid. "*Qui parle?*" she croaked into the phone, in various rising, cracked voices. When she understood that this was her own Leo she became herself. Drunk or old, that voice?—which sometimes even now is the free sound, the buoyant sound of a confident and sure future for the most beautiful girl in the world. "I'm the same," she said this morning, "in bed, with a book and a bottle."

JULY 31, 1981 · LONDON  At Evangeline Bruce's in Albany [apartments], in those cozy, pretty rooms, full of very personal choices, Vangy dispensing tea, looking large, lean, and a Fuseli beauty. Evangeline dispensing vodka to "Coop" (Lady Diana Cooper[4]), who, cuddling the smallest Chihuahua in the world (Puss: "So dangerous to have around. He's transparent!"), from under her very broad-brimmed straw dispensed wit and anecdote: "I never expect to live through the night. . . ." She has traces of her beauty—or rather her beauty is there beneath a veil of age (She is eighty-eight: "Now that I am very old . . ."), much like the beauty of a face just before the sculptor chisels away the final layer of marble. She always had a marmoreal beauty. She talked about Hemingway, who came to see her in Paris while she was in bed, and who drank and drank: "I wasn't really frightened. I was bored. I'd heard what a lady-killer he was, but I never was alarmed—just bored in my bed." She was full of interest, interested, then by-and-by tottered off, leaving a feeling of historic occasion in Lord Melbourne's old rooms, as she beetled away in a tiny brown auto.

AUGUST 2, 1981  The V. S. Pritchetts came to lunch. Victor has just written his Proust piece. He said: "You know, it's a group of short stories, connected by sermons." Dorothy said that "when I typed his manuscript the second time, and it was still all about the joy of reading Proust and not a word about [the translator] Kilmartin, I asked him, didn't he think that he should say something about this edition? After all, that's why he was writing the piece. '. . . Oh,' he said." Dorothy's very loving. The Pritchetts are the genial Captain Andy and Parthy Ann of the literary *Show Boat.*

AUGUST 6, 1981  Rebecca West, a highly disciplined renegade with the best manners in the world: "Ken Tynan was the worst—no, Malcolm Muggeridge[5]—no,

---

4. Many considered Lady Diana Cooper (1892–1986) the great aristocratic beauty of her generation in Britain. She made some appearances onstage (Max Reinhardt's *The Miracle*) and screen, married Alfred Duff Cooper, Viscount Norwich, and wrote engaging memoirs.
5. Malcolm Muggeridge (1903–90) was a British writer, broadcaster, and journalist.

Evelyn Waugh—yes—he was the worst man I ever knew!" She came to the door, peering out: "I just must look at you one more time."

The odd realization that the time since Ela died is now longer than all of the time I spent with her.

AUGUST 8, 1981 • NEW YORK CITY  I am overwhelmed by the "things," the possessions that I have accumulated. This is new to me.

AUGUST 19, 1981  Yesterday Anita [Loos] died—a woman very small in stature, but immense in every other aspect—hilarity, interest, heart, catholicity, envy. Friend of Huxley and Colette and . . . to gangsters? She worked almost until the day she died. "No moroses," she said, "at my funeral." *Gentlemen Prefer Blondes* is the laughing, knowing, worldly, spirit of the mid-twenties. It could only have been written in America and only by a woman so intensely feminine that she laughed compassionately at other "girls." Hardworking (at 4:30 a.m. at ninety-three in April) and planning for the fall this year. She is the only old person who is missed as if her death had been untimely—as if a young person full of future had died. She was full of future. "Whadya know?" she'd ask, and sometimes you made it up just to hear her wicked, worldly, girlish laughter. When she dedicated a book to me, I felt as though I had been awarded the Nobel Prize.

SEPTEMBER 1, 1981  Carol [Channing] about Anita: "Anita and I traveled in Europe together, and I didn't know what a bidet was. 'What do you do with it, Anita? What's it for?' 'Well, dear, the French are known to be the dirtiest people in the world, but they are clean—in only one place. . . .' "

SEPTEMBER 5, 1981 • PALM BEACH, FLORIDA  Mar-a-Lago, the Marjorie Post house, another American manifestation—plus the *Cherry Orchard* touch of the jets zooming overhead, the sound of the trees being chopped down. The house (its entire interior designed by Joseph Urban, who brought Viennese artisans to help execute his decoration[6]) is the link between movie palaces of the twenties and fantasies of how the rich lived. The whole place is such an act of vulgar, extravagant imagination. Dina [Merrill]'s room is consciously the chamber of Princess Aurora, Sleeping Beauty—with its silver canopied bed, its "posts" little beasts and thorns—the bed of a princess asleep until kissed into mortality by her prince.[7] This vast "palace"—with its dining room and drawing room amalgams of Venetian and Roman palazzos and Strawberry Hill, with its nineteenth-century reproductions of Fine French Furniture—is the American

6. The Austrian architect and designer Joseph Urban (1872–1933) created sets for the Ziegfeld Follies from 1915 to 1931.
7. Actress Dina Merrill (b. 1925) was the daughter of Marjorie Merriweather Post and E. F. Hutton.

dream in full frenzy. Now here it is on the edge of dissolution. Fourteen servants still "keep it up." Even the vistas from the windows are movie-splendor American dreams. It all is what America imagined romantic and rich to be in Los Angeles and in Palm Beach—the greatest example of domestic architecture created in the fantasy theatrical idiom of the early twenties.

SEPTEMBER 9, 1981 · NEW YORK CITY Last night, while watching *Chariots of Fire*, a film which is a work of art (meaning a film composed on clearly defined aesthetic principles, disciplining the chaos of life, presenting certain moral considerations, permitting its characters to be people making moral decisions—a humane film in which the eye, the mind, the heart are all nourished), watching this gem, I suddenly, at the departure of the running team on a Channel steamer for France, was overcome by wrenching pangs of some deep and, for the moment, elusive memory—almost an anguish. What was this? Then I knew: I was experiencing again, after all of those years, ship sailings. My whole being was suffused with that ecstasy of departure, that reality, so unbelievable, of going—no, getting away—on a great ship, out into the unknown vastness of the sea, into a thick "extra" life, an intensification and liberation of life, a genuine adventure, with "new" people to meet, all sorts of experiences—maybe even perils. All of one's family to be left behind screaming or weeping on the dock. That moment when the plank went up and the ship finally pulled away, gliding into the river—the band blaring, the crowds cheering, tugs as full throated as a pack of hounds baying their quarry, confetti, streamers, a delicious frenzy, a delectable release, with Europe five—or even eleven—days in the future. Europe. We would, we all knew, return from "Europe" transformed.

SEPTEMBER 15, 1981 Marlene on the blower—"Probably she [Maria Riva] is writing 'Dearest Mommy.'" I hadn't the heart to tell her that Maria, indeed, had already collected a half-a-million-dollar advance. "She doesn't talk to me anymore," said Marlene—not complaining, but stating a fact of her desolate life. "But the boys [her grandsons] all write."

SEPTEMBER 22, 1981 Diana Trilling, at dinner last night at Maurice, talked about something she's noticed for the last few years now: "So many of the men I know, who have been married for thirty-seven or so years, have come out as homosexuals. What does this mean? What have they been doing about their sexuality all of these years? What does this mean about our culture?"

Even twenty years ago, those men could not have "come out" so easily, in the social, artistic, literary (even political) world in which they and their families lived. Also, twenty years ago Diana and Puss and I couldn't have been discussing this so freely and so "generously." I belong to the generation who screamed, "But he's married!" Diana says it's much more difficult for single women of advanced or even middle years—"alone" women. She went on about how insulting not being even flirted with was for these women. "So much easier for men," she said, "because a man, no matter how grotesque, is always desired by some woman." About lesbians: She said she didn't know of any women who, late in life, came out like men do today.

She also reminded me of Katherine Anne Porter and Dylan Thomas, the latter picking K.A.P. up, holding her, in his drunken state, aloft as if she were a totem . . . how "gracious" she was, how generous, how easy she made it for Dylan to put her down . . . smiling, masking it all into a sort of sexual triumph for herself, and she was, at that time, in her fifties, middle-aged: couldn't have been easy for her. Diana: "I never liked her until that moment. Years later she told me that as Dylan set her down she saw my face and it was full of horror!"[8]

SEPTEMBER 24, 1981 Didn't go to Paloma Picasso's party. After I decided to go and even arranged with Fernando [Sanchez, loungewear designer] to take me, Puss's outburst about "how very interesting" that I would go to [Studio] 54. I knew that I wouldn't hear the end of it, so the most expedient thing was not to go. I am in an inner tunnel, because I wanted to see this "event" in what I consider a Manhattan Hell. This would have been an important episode in my book. I am also depressed because I see that, in some way, we have, each of us, while adding to each other's lives, harmed one another. I have wrecked his, and permitted him, to some small extent, to impair mine. Is this lost time? Perhaps not. There are episodes important to a work in progress (I see now that my life has been a work in progress), and tonight was one of them. We have been wonderful for one another, and we couldn't have been worse for one another, and I wouldn't have not had this love for anything else in the world. . . . I will rebound again.

NOTE: Leo's unstable right leg increasingly gave way without warning, and he was sometimes unable to raise himself after a fall. He no longer went out unescorted.

JOURNAL · SEPTEMBER 28, 1981 Dinner at [journalist and novelist] Joan [Buck] and [drama critic] John [Heilpern]'s for John and Helen Osborne. He, this former angry young man, is now fifty-one, portly, gray-bearded, with two prominent front teeth, which give him a Bugs Bunny geniality, a sort of laughing inquisitivity (would Thackeray have enjoyed that word?). Helen is a surprise after Pamela [Lane] (whom I never knew), Penelope Gilliat, Mary Ure, Jill Bennett.[9] Helen is a caretaker with sarcastic humor, a cutting edge. A good

---

8. Leo later recalled: "Katherine Anne said to me as the first-act curtain fell on *Dylan*: 'They can distort it, a little, but they can't exaggerate it,' after a scene during which he carried her off the stage over his shoulder." *Journal, January 18, 1964.*

9. Lane, Gilliat, Ure, and Bennett had all been married to John Osborne (1929–94). His play *Look Back in Anger* (1956) is cited as the start of a new wave in postwar British theater, whose playwrights were often dubbed "angry young men."

sport spiked with knowingness, "wifey"—plain and snappy-eyed, she would be perfect in an 1840ish bonnet, and Jane Carlyle would have understood—even liked—her.[10] I surprised John by being "the man with Marlene" when she wrote him, in Sardi's, a note: "You are wonderful—Please call me—where? when?"—etc. "I sat by my telephone for four days," this middle-aged man said, remembering those [1958] days of *The Entertainer*.

Actresses are so much more interesting than actors—except those with a double sexuality—Olivier, Gielgud.

OCTOBER 3, 1981 • WASHINGTON, D.C. At the White House, in Muffie [Brandon]'s office the great question to me: "Will this thing about China blow over? Will it haunt us for the next four years?" I thought: "China! What do I know about China!" So I temporized . . . and finally realized I was being asked about their extravagant dishes.[11] "It won't blow over," said I. "It will haunt you. Just go on and ignore it. The timing was dreadful." "If only we'd announced last July," Muffie moaned, meaning before Reagan began to do in the poor. "Well," she said, "no more big extravagances—just little dinners—private and only state dinners which are a necessity—but an all-out program of helping the arts and culture—all-out. You're being invited for lunch on the fourteenth. That's when the program will be announced. We're having Ella Fitzgerald, the king and queen of Spain, and I hope to get Benny Goodman for King Hussein [of Jordan]. . . ." Then her face hardened. "Why, oh why, is the *Washington Post* being so mean to Mrs. Reagan?"

OCTOBER 11, 1981 • NEW YORK CITY On Yom Kippur, a visit to Katharine Hepburn[12]—not a tremor, not a quiver (is she now controlled medically?)— seemingly younger than I. She said, "But, you know, I'm not an actress. I've never been an actress. People think that I'm different in each part. I've always been myself, only the writers are different . . . and I've been so lucky there, and so I sound different. . . . I have doubts about my whole life. . . . What have I done? Have I done anything? I don't think that I have."

OCTOBER 17, 1981 Visit to Mina for her eighty-fifth birthday. "I don't know what my life means. I feel as if it all happened to someone else. Nothing much

10. The British journalist Helen Dawson Osborne (1939–2004) later became arts editor of the *Observer*.

11. Mabel "Muffie" Brandon Cabot, then Nancy Reagan's social secretary, was worried because the first lady had acquired for the White House a four-thousand-piece set of china valued at $200,000, even as the Reagan administration was calling for cuts in domestic programs.

12. Leo had commissioned two articles and a photograph of Hepburn to run in *Vogue* that November, when her film *On Golden Pond* opened.

is close to me. For a moment, when Fido asked me last Sunday—she's madder and madder—whether I ever got up for breakfast at [the Chapelbrook Farm on] Ashfield, and I said that from the day Harry [Curtiss] died, I never got up for breakfast again—and then I realized that I did for [John] Houseman—Ashfield was close, touched me, it was part of me for that moment. Of course, I've tried to cut myself off from being close to Goosey. I've always lived entirely in the present."

OCTOBER 21, 1981 The unexpected importance of Clare Luce in my life—Poppa painted her penthouse. Her silver-paper dining room and white drawing room were High Life glimpsed. Poppa saying to her, "This is my son. . . ." She was the first woman I ever saw in a Chanel suit. Years later, a dinner Margaret Case gave to "bring together" the Luces and the senior Newhouses, when Sam was being "considered" for a *Time* cover story.[13] The Luces and the Newhouses together—"old" dynasty, new "empire," and the "old" not at all understanding the "new." "But how, Mr. Newhouse," asked Claire de Luce [*sic*], "can you have all of these papers and magazines and not inject your own opinions, your own politics in them?" I could see that neither Luce believed Sam when he explained that he liked having them, that he believed each one should remain itself regardless of Sam's own politics. He lusted for possessions—specifically "media." He was a collector of media. That was his power. Si [his son] influences, originates; Sam shepherded.

OCTOBER 30, 1981 Nora on the blower: "Hugh [Laing] and Tudor cooked dinner for us, and in only a few minutes they were bickering over some minor thing—just the way they always have. Nothing ever changes." Me: "Out of that bickering came your career and a whole revolution in dance." She roared with laughter. In her laughter you can hear bells of pure enjoyment, amusement clanging.

NOVEMBER 8, 1981 A vision of ballerinas: Some rich, in splendid nests: Eugenia (Delarova) Doll, Tamara Geva,[14] Sono (Osato) Elmaleh, Vera Zorina, Nora (Kaye) Ross (in Hollywood, a producer). Some moulting in little, memorabilia-littered flats, furnished rooms, or "institutions"—and who of their neighbors

---

13. Henry Luce (1898–1967), the politically conservative founder and chairman of *Time, Fortune,* and *Life* magazines, married Clare Boothe Luce (1903–87). She had been managing editor at *Vanity Fair,* as well as a playwright (*The Women*), a politician, and an ambassador to Italy. Margaret Case Harriman (1891–1971) was the society editor of *Vogue* for nearly fifty years.
14. Eugenia Delarova Doll (1911?–90) danced with de Basil's Ballets Russes while married (1927–38) to its choreographer Léonide Massine. Later, she married industrialist Henri G. Doll and became a dance patron. The Russian-born ballerina and actress Tamara Geva (1906–97) was the first wife of George Balanchine.

suspects their former effulgent glory, their litheness, their tributes of jewels? (the futures of flowers, the mutations of dreams) Then those who still teach or even drag themselves from "star" engagement to "star" engagement. And those who preside—Margot [Fonteyn], Margrethe [Schanne], Alicia [Markova], Irina Baronova,[15] Choura Danilova . . .

Thoughts of Marlene—the model for a whole generation of Germans today—in bed in Paris, with her bottle and her book and her extravagance. ("My only extravagance is the telephone.") Maria [Riva] saying: "If only she would do the deals I arranged . . . hundreds of thousands of dollars for a voice-over . . . She doesn't have to be seen . . . not even seen . . . but no. . . . It suits her madness to say I'm no daughter, [that] I hate her."

Recalling Tallulah at T's [Black and White] party—the public face had become the private woman. Conversely, the private woman had become the public face. She was nothing but the ruin of this notorious facade. . . . The vigor of her legend—the maintenance of it had eroded all else. This wreck of her public facade clear to see, even in the darkened crystal ballroom of the Plaza.

NOVEMBER 11, 1981 After a certain age, meaning an age of self-knowledge, it is a sin not to know and even a greater sin to forget who one really is. Yesterday, after a walk with Alex, I forgot who I am—I mean the essential me, the mansion I have constructed of myself, for myself. The punishment for forgetting is depression, even death.

This morning Alex really struck at a vulnerable place: "You have enough vitality," he said, "to make these scoops." He was talking about *Architectural Digest* getting the Reagan "private" rooms in the White House, giving them eighteen pages. This is trivial and trashy, but more than ever I want to go from that place. I don't want to have anything to do with him and those debased, sadistic creatures. He is an extraordinary man—crippled within and a minor monster, but destructive, a causer of pain.

NOVEMBER 17, 1981 A whole world of new young people in [Sondheim's musical] *Merrily We Roll Along*, and this touched me. I saw, at the end, which was the touching part, all of those long-ago girls: Joan McCracken, Diana Adams, young Sono, young Nora, even Maya [Deren] and [dancer-choreographer] Valerie Bettis . . . a great garland of girls—all with starry futures, all destined to glitter and to shine and to sink into oblivion. Then at Hal [Prince]'s party in the Plaza, a tide of *Merrily* young people swept around my chair, obliterating me. I knew none of them. I was not part of their future, as I had been so many years ago.

15. Irina Baronova (b. 1919) began as a "baby ballerina" of the Ballets Russes, eventually marrying the theatrical impresario and aristocrat Cecil Tennant.

NOVEMBER 20, 1981  Claudette Colbert at lunch. I asked, "Who was the sexiest?" Claudette: "Clark Gable. Even my mother—who wasn't a pushover and never came on set, came when I was making *It Happened One Night*, and she swooooned." (acting out swooned) "But for me—oh, Ray Milland! Oh, Ray Milland!" She murmured, as she sat down: "Don't ask me a question. I'm no good at that sort of thing. I won't say a thing." I thought: "I must charm and keep afloat." It did work.

NOVEMBER 22, 1981  The privileged exist in each world, no matter what social level, even beggars, *clochards*. Each world is a microcosm of the great world. Poppa's people broke Momma's people's windows when Poppa married Momma. This was reverse snobbism. Poppa's people thought Momma's too rich and too advanced—too American.

NOVEMBER 24, 1981  Tilly Losch's advice to Nora, when Tilly joined Ballet Theatre: "Always have a good little black dress, pearls, and stay in the best hotel, even if you can have only the worst room."

NOVEMBER 26, 1981  Heard from Morty [Janklow, literary agent] how valuable I am to Condé Nast, Morty having heard this from Si. This helps. I never believe in my true value, knowing how that can topple without even a warning crack.

NOVEMBER 28, 1981 • LAGUNA HILLS, CALIFORNIA  Philip Ziegler's [biography of Diana Cooper] *Diana* is all about privilege—its uses, abuses. Ziegler succeeds at the amazing task of making Diana Cooper not only a full-blooded creation, but a "real" person of fictional size, complete with eccentricities, awfulness, even hatefulness—and vulnerabilities—a sacred monster. Finally she is a total expression of a class, a series of moments in history, vanished eras. Rut had some of Diana Cooper's privileged ways. Rut said: "I am the aristocracy of originality."

Maebelle at dinner tonight to Missy [Cockrell, her great-niece]: "Tell me, has any of your little friends had anything unpleasant happen—like rape?"

DECEMBER 1, 1981  Diana Vreeland's visual sense is that of the most sophisticated child in the world. She understands combinations of quality, and she can see quality in everything from the most everyday street life thing to the most exotic and most exclusive. Visually, she looks to the vibrancy of the moment. She adores to laugh; it starts from her intellect and descends to her belly button. She also has the ability to make people feel witty and worldly. Vreeland said stoically, "Don't you know that *Vogue* is the myth of the next reality?"

DECEMBER 6, 1981 • NEW YORK CITY  Momma's "unveiling" in an almost vacant, gale-swept, sun-washed Mt. Zion cemetery, the tombstones so dense as to almost obliterate all else. In the distance, the city skyline seemingly more tombstones. All the world, as far as we could see, a necropolis. There we huddled, all the remnants of our huge cousinage and friend circle. The rabbi never arrived. I took over, asked Rosalie [Goldwasser] to read the Twenty-third Psalm, said a few bits, making everyone laugh (Momma always wanted, on a cold day, everyone to hurry, because she wanted to get to the bathroom), and then asked each person present to say one thing that came instantly to mind about Momma. Mary [Callabras, the nurse] said, "She was strong!" Puss said, "She took me into the family and made me feel welcome."

DECEMBER 7, 1981  The cemetery stretched out like a floorcloth, pinned down by the three huge smokestacks, by the far towers of Manhattan, by the old, now delicate iron fence—rolling here, level there—and the dense graves energetic with dreams and hopes and despairs and plannings and such energy even in death and with death. I had such a feeling of pinned-down energy. Now I feel that cemetery out there as a constant—being there in all sorts of light and weather—immutable, unchanged, a densely populated unpopular place. So the family were again reunited! Those above ground and those in their vociferous, but empty graves.

DECEMBER 15, 1981  Even circa 1931 or 32 we heard news that the famous triumvirate—Anne Morgan, Elsie de Wolfe, and Elisabeth "Bessie" Marbury—were "Sapphic."[16] We also heard that as sacrosanct as the Morgan name was, walled behind wealth and immured in High Society, Miss Anne Morgan's "sumptuous" apartment was "watched" by the police. Such gossip sent frissons of surmise. Then there were Alice Toklas and Gertrude Stein. But did we know of "men" as redoubtable as any of these female "leaders"? Whispers about Carl Van Vechten, Guthrie [McClintic, Broadway producer] (Katherine Cornell [his wife] was!), and Stark [Young]. Then George Jean Nathan's essay on lesbians in the theater that named names. The Eva Le Gallienne and Josephine Hutchinson scandal[17] . . . [Radclyffe Hall's novel] *The Well of Lone-liness* . . . All of this was heady evidence and, in a sense, not only confirmation

---

16. The suffragist Anne Morgan (1873–1952) was the daughter of financier J. P. Morgan. Elisabeth Marbury (1856–1933), a theatrical and literary agent, shared a house near Gramercy Park with the decorator Elsie de Wolfe.
17. Eva Le Gallienne (1899–1991), actress, director, and producer, is said to have had many affairs with women, including Nazimova and Mercedes de Acosta, and her relationship with the actress Josephine Hutchinson was a public sensation in 1927, when it was revealed in Hutchinson's divorce proceedings.

but approval. Here we touched, and seemed one, with—if not greatness—glamour.

DECEMBER 25, 1981  Mina: "I never liked [Proust's] Albertine and the 'little band.' They're too Monet for me. I'm a Manet girl."

Ela, living in German and Austrian palaces, always, even in Kammerschloss, never had more than one room in her life. I—having no room of my own until I had a little room in a rooming house on East Seventy-first Street, then railroad flats—always lived in a great number of rooms. Even when I had a house (1453 Lex) and then this "apartment," I lived as if I had a huge palace. We always lived "big." That's why my uncles walked like princes.

DECEMBER 26, 1981  I said to Toni Morrison, "I don't believe in any life hereafter, but I do believe in ghosts." She looked at me, laughed, and said, "Honey, you sure are in trouble."

Marlene no longer permits flowers to be delivered. "No one is allowed to ring her bell to deliver flowers," the concierge told the messenger. Flowers are too close to death.

JANUARY 10, 1982  I gulped down whatever I found in print. I began this on 106th Street and read voraciously even before I could talk coherently. For years the aunts (Minnie and Rose) scornfully chided Momma: "Always, his head buried in a book he can't even understand! What'll he be, some kind of sissy?" Momma paid them no mind (as we later said at the Feagin School, in mimicking emulation of our southern cicerones). But Poppa sometimes would flower into his impotent, curiously quiet rages: "Be a man!" he would say in a strangled roar that never got higher than two steps. "Be a man!" I went on reading away, snipping magazines and papers, scribbling. No bats for me and the only balls I ever handled were my own or some of my male chums and relations. Not "to be a man," not to hit a ball with a stick (kicking it came later and at this time still seemed foreign) was to be un-American in this young immigrant world of my father and my older uncles. To be American was to be on the way up—hence, passion for prize (I thought "price") fights, Masonry, even ragtime and jazz.

JANUARY 16, 1982  My first Violetta [in *La Traviata*] was [Lucrezia] Bori. Cousin Dave [Goldwasser], the furrier, took me. We sat almost in the last row of the top balcony and were ecstatic. Part of the ecstasy came from being part of that world—if only for a Saturday matinee. We could read the names of the box holders in the program, and over the proscenium the gold oblongs deified Gluck, Mozart, Beethoven, Verdi, Wagner, and Gounod. Bori in white flounces with six camellias off-center down the front. I think we could see this costume at other times in the window of the costumer Brooks, high up on Broadway.

JANUARY 21, 1982  Yesterday Penelope died. That last time—watching the [Charles and Diana] wedding fireworks on the telly, she held my hand all through the long viewing—a last, long, heart-in-hand good-bye. All those years ago, in the Plaza, the center of her life was "getting" Carol to be in New York, to marry her. I think that after Carol died, after those years of living with her suitcase packed and on the ready, she was as diligent in pursuit of him as she had been long ago. Everyone says how wonderfully [her mother] Freda is "taking" this. But people of Freda's age feel differently about outside heights and depths. They have used up so much. They have little or no room for tragedy—their own old age being tragedy that they cannot bear.

Penelope died on the same date on which Ela died. I think of the red rose in the gutter, after the hearse had gone from the Little Church Around the Corner [on Twenty-ninth Street]. What will be there in the gutter after the hearse has gone at midday on Monday, from the Old Chelsea Church [in London], Henry James's church?

JANUARY 24, 1982  Watching a telecast of *La Bohème*, I realized that none of these young people would ever become anything. They would all be failures in what they set out to become. Franco [Zeffirelli]'s *Bohème* is closer to the original than any other: Mimi a realistic flowermaker of that day, Musetta an aging coquette, never to be a courtesan. (Clare Boothe Luce told me, some days ago, that the thirty-year-olds of *Harper's* thought a courtesan was "someone who hung out with famous men.") The young men (Franco's onstage "kids") would never be great creators. Theirs is the charm of so many groups of young people who came to "the big city," an ageless true story.

JANUARY 26, 1982  Faye Dunaway—very Okie—albino in atmosphere. She has determination. Her technique shows like some girls' slips or brassiere straps. Related, in a way, to Meryl Streep. Dunaway counterfeits larger than life—specially when handled by [Roman] Polanski (*Chinatown*) or when impersonating (*Mommie Dearest*). But she is not larger than life in the Crawford sense, or an abstract—and so a symbol, a quintessential—in the Louise Brooks sense.[18]

JANUARY 30, 1982  Lillian Gish on the Scott Fitzgeralds: "You never saw people so young, so beautiful—young, blue-eyed, blond people . . . but you knew that she was crazy. You knew that she had to do what she was doing. . . . And Tallulah was always trying to copy her." Lillian—so young herself today at lunch, talking with great spirit and total recall and strong convictions. Lillian,

18. Late in life, the silent-film actress Louise Brooks (1906–85) had been recognized as one of the first to master screen performance (*Pandora's Box*). Her memoir *Lulu in Hollywood* had then just appeared.

the most remarkable elder I know, exclaiming that [Blake Edwards's film] *S.O.B.* was the closest to Hollywood, that the death on the beach was based on Griffith, "who wandered from place to place, willing to work for $50 and no one would give him a job!"

FEBRUARY 28, 1982  Betty Parsons burst into tears when I came away [from her gallery] not "seeing" (was it [painter] Clyff Still?), weeping passionately as we waited for the lift: "You won't understand! You won't see. All you want is Rembrandt!" Poppa's a great influence on me here: This master of the brush, my father the housepainter, revered art. He took me to museums. Did he see the beauty? Or was the beauty the money value of the work of art, the social meaning—kings, queens, tycoons—its "worldly" and "prestige" connotations? The coruscating visions of the power and the glory, the splendor—was that what got Poppa? That is what got me. Also, I got a sense of desolation, of all-gone, of anguish and inspiration.

Is Alex Liberman a nihilist? He has a very low opinion of people and their motives. He extols the word "noble," but he sees almost everyone as base. Schadenfreude—this joy of destruction.

MARCH 6, 1982  Henry James to a young acquaintance who had just met Edith Wharton: "Ah my dear man, you have made friends with Edith Wharton. I congratulate you. You may find her difficult, but you will never find her stupid, and you will never find her mean." This is so like Mina, whom I just rang up, finding her in a ferment of delight, surmise, and wondering where to publish an essay she would write based on a book just come from Paris—a book very long and chockablock with new material about Proust's family (his ancestry) and an essay by Suzy Mante[-Proust, his niece]: "So full of lies—as we could expect . . ." But the energy that came from eighty-five-year-old Mina . . . the vigor had interest. She had to ring off because Lincoln surprised her by suddenly appearing. "Who's that?" I heard her murmur. "Oh—it's Goosey!" she exclaimed, the delight suddenly shining in her voice like the glow of a freshly polished apple. Lincoln came to talk to her about their parents. Since he is also writing his memoirs. "It's so strange. We don't know anything about our parents' childhoods. I don't know anything about my father until he's about sixteen." What do we know about parents' early days?

Walking with my uncles and cousins, or riding on the upper deck of the bus with my aunts, I would marvel at those "palaces" lining the east side of Fifth Avenue, sometimes glimpsing an interior brightness through an open door, where a uniformed "man" stood for a moment waiting some arrival, or—bliss—finding an unshuttered window, its curtains and draperies agape, espied from my lofty but fleeting perch—splendor, dazzlement, gleaming surfaces adrift on tides of light, like telltale wreckage on a placid sea. I was instantly immersed in conjecture, visions of rooms thronged with treasures more gorgeously incredible than any I had seen, and even tried to touch, in the museum to which my father had taken me frequently. I even saw *elegantes* being helped into carriages (for in those days some New Yorkers still went out on their social rounds in their own carriages) and men and women in heavy furs climbing up and down steps to and from the pleasures, vanishing into the "palaces" or into highly polished motors, doors held ajar by liveried footmen, while at the wheel sat a visored and uniformed chauffeur. This was life secure, untroubled by screaming scenes, not undone by subterfuges. ("Don't let your grandpa know you had an egg this morning.") For me in these early years, the glimpses into the mansions then lining the avenue, the works of art in the museum, symbolized the high romance of monarchy and court life. I had entered this world through the movies. I saw it existing. I was to pursue it all my life, this glitter of power, of lavish dress and house. This life larger than any I knew seemed the best of all the world's possibilities. I never wanted to be president. I wanted to be king—a star-crossed monarch in full panoply—divinely rightful, even doomed—but rescued, of course, just in time, as the "mob" (people) was about to tear me apart, rescued by the most stalwart, the most ravishing of men, just like in the movies I saw at the Garlic Opera or the Starlight The-a-ter.

MARCH 13, 1982   There is no love between Lady Macbeth and her lord. There is adolescent exuberance between Romeo and Juliet. Ophelia is "mad" about Hamlet: He is actually indifferent to her, seeing only himself, aggrieved, in all eyes. Desdemona loves, to excess, her Moor, while he is in a complicated passion about her: She is a symbol of his emancipation, the brightest jewel in his conquest of a world in which he will never really be accepted—only used. Viola loves Orsino: This is pure love. I think all of the women in the comedies love the men of their choice; only in the tragedies are the loves complicated from within the people themselves. Difficult to assess Cleopatra—she is such an ornament, such a conscientious superstar in the Liz Taylor mode. Her passions are possibly sincere, but art-size—grand gestures. The others are human in size and intensity.

APRIL 3, 1982   Last night, walking home from *I Lombardi*, we came upon Jack Dunphy. Gray had not seen him in over thirty years. I saw him several years ago (when I was still able—or allowed—to go about alone). Here, then, was Jack, waiting to cross Fifty-ninth Street and Columbus Circle. "Isn't that Jack Dunphy?" Puss whispered. "Jack?" I quavered. He turned, smiled hugely, presenting at arms a mouth of large, well-polished, obviously fake, gleaming dining-room furniture.[19] He is an old man—very neat, civil, pulled together, his atmosphere still actually clinging to him like a perfume—an eternal, per-

---

19. Leo is quoting Carmel Snow, who had once flashed her new dentures and said, "Look, my new dining-room furniture."

durable fragrance. He has a seaman feeling, a man who had been long at sea now having become—unwillingly, patiently—a landlubber . . . and Irishness. All very cordial; he very deaf. A pleasant encounter—not one word of Little T. But there with us was that dark winter night when he left Todd [Bolender] for Truman.

APRIL 16, 1982   John Simon's consuming passion for Alexandra Isles. He's almost given up. Eating his heart out over the blower: "I must make up my mind that she doesn't love me. If I had ten million dollars, she would love me. She can't take me to her society friends, but she doesn't have anyone. She's an outsider, and what she wants most is to be inside, to be invited by society and be a hostess. She doesn't want me. Von Bülow was Alexandra's dream prince. He seemed to have everything I didn't have. She really hasn't decided that he killed [his wife], but from what she's told me, how can she doubt it?"[20] John went on and on—quite pitifully—this man, considered so relentless, such a monster—now bleeding for a woman quite unworthy of his brilliance, even of his strange charm.

Middle-aged male crisis: So many marriages end because they have become "a duty" and someone is found who is untrammeled, even undisciplined, who is "fun" and returns one to youth and not caring in the sense of not caring for anything save the passion of this released moment. Wise women sit this out and find a renewed husband—repentant, somewhat worn, and, for a time, obligated.

APRIL 23, 1982   Is what I feel real lust, or the memory of past desire?

First view of Anaïs Nin: dancing with Lucia Cristofanetti[21] (so full of the future, full of narcissistic self-love, even self-lust). Everything Anaïs did, her every concern was, according to Anaïs, high drama, sometimes tinged with charming comedy. That is how she saw her life. I saw it as a perpetual silent movie as exaggerated as any performance Pola Negri or Theda Bara ever bestowed upon her anguished fans. That first view of Anaïs dancing showed me the diarist in movement, self-absorbed, almost lost to her vigilance, her constant role as observer, The Keeper of the Diary almost engulfed by her own formal movements in this improvised parlor performance. Later—much later—she told me that her "refuges were writing and movement." And we had between us a chain which bound us as tightly as ship to shore.

20. Danish-born socialite Claus von Bülow (b. 1926) was prosecuted for attempting to murder his wife, heiress Martha "Sunny" Crawford von Bülow. A guilty verdict was overturned on appeal. Von Bülow had been involved with the actress and filmmaker Alexandra Isles (b. 1947) overlapping the time that she was seeing critic John Simon (b. 1925), then reviewing theater for *New York* magazine.
21. Lucia Cristofanetti (1902–74) was a designer, jewelry maker, and painter.

MAY 14, 1982

AGE

This morning, I dropped Syke's *Evelyn Waugh*, the book slipping out of my hand onto my bedroom floor. I lowered myself to pick up the book: I could not right myself. I went down on one knee. Even more impossible to right myself. Pushing Waugh before me, I tried to lift myself by leaning on Mr. Bear [the coat stand]. He wobbled. What to do? On both knees, pushing Waugh ahead, trying to make no sound (I didn't want Puss to hear me), I crept, an ancient child, out of my bedroom, across two thresholds, onto the tile floor of the bathroom, where by clutching the bathtub rim I was able, using not the impoverished muscles of my body, but the determination of my spirit, to raise myself and, seating myself on the loo, retrieve Waugh from the floor. At which moment I breathed faintness away, breathed a thin vigor in, and saw clearly the grim face of age staring back from the looking glass on the basin wall. Resilience . . . is that what sees one through? Suddenly I am bone tired—from coping with neurotics.

THE NIGHT SIDE OF THE GODS

Volodya [Vladimir Horowitz] so much resembles Petrouchka. The two very tall, bearded young men—slender, moody-alert, obviously "guardians"—being followed by Volodya moving automaton-like, jerked along on invisible strings, his features set in a semblance of a smile, his eyes very large and staring ahead save for a slight twitch, which could have been a side-glance. Wanda [Horowitz] following—a moving dark force, put-out, permanently furious, scornful, as suspicious as a Greek or a deaf-mute, a Royal not receiving the Royal Treatment she deems her due. This little, mad world moved out of Mortimer's [restaurant]—a blackness on a brightness.

On the blower, Nicholas Lawford: "I am in a state of shock. I rang up Lincoln Kirstein and asked him to tell me anything about Horst, and he replied— so sweetly and gently and nicely—that he couldn't tell me anything about Horst because Horst was a psychotic liar and he, Lincoln, had tried to kill him once. I feel absolutely sick—is Lincoln mad?" I had to tell Nicholas that Lincoln is mad. Lincoln has done good and been celebrated and has been mad— sometimes violently—for years—even put away. When I talked to Nancy Lassalle this morning and said that I'd heard that Lincoln had come back much "improved" from London, she said, "Yes, but he's still not really well."[22] Nicholas, without realizing, told me that Lincoln is definitely unwell. I could not tell Nicholas that the *Times* had canceled a piece on Lincoln because he had "assaulted" (the word Mina used) their reporter or photographer.

How can I find a way to write about all of this sans hurting everyone? I must

---

22. As an executive and later board member of the School of American Ballet, Nancy Lassalle, the daughter of Dorothy Norman, worked closely with Lincoln Kirstein.

find the deeper significance. Lincoln is a powerful example of a man who benefits society while being a monster.

MAY 22, 1982 I began my travels in America (meaning outside of New York, New England, Philadelphia) in the war years, when I went lecturing.[23] Long train rides into places with names heard later in [Latouche's cantata] *Ballad for Americans* and read, early in my life, in history books: Zanesville—I pictured the little girl running to the well and so saving her settlement from a fiery, Indian death. Altoona—I thought, and even said, how necessary a little bombing (as London was being bombed) was for us in our fat lives. We would never feel the necessity for everlasting peace unless we experienced true devastation, brutality. This view was not a popular view in Dayton, Ohio, where my lecture was delayed while a decision was made about whether colored (not black in those war-for-freedom days) were to be permitted to sit in the hall along with the whites. During these years, I went to museums, department stores, bookshops, people's houses, and I learned about hotel living and train travel, which I loved. I was not only exploring America, I was exploring Christian America.

MAY 23, 1982 Mina told me that her cook, going to market [in Connecticut] at about 6:30 a.m., found Lincoln wandering near his parked car in an obscure country road. Lincoln explained that the car had broken down while he was going to early mass. Lincoln told Cook that this was a secret and that he frequently went to mass. Years ago, during a breakdown, Lincoln talked of converting. Mina expostulated, telling him how awful for a Jew to do this and, until Cook told her, never heard of this again. He is, of course, in his "high" state again.

NOTE: Leo and Gray left for Europe on June 20, this time for seven weeks, beginning in London, finishing in Paris, with nearly a month in Venice between.

JOURNAL · JUNE 29, 1982 · LONDON Yesterday, through wrath-of-God storms and peaceable kingdoms (the Chatsworth approach) to lunch with the Devonshires—Debo and Andrew.[24] She leads; he is childlike and nervously sweet. Her voice, her personality, is deeper, more positive, more earthborn than Andrew's. Among highborns, the female is frequently more "manly" than the male. Andrew is wispy, very "dear," very "boy." She is Mitford fun. And here is the key to Lesley [Blanch] and [her friend the painter] Eden [Box]'s manner of talking: "He's brill!" "Darling Self" "Pass the butts [butter]." The Mitfords—

23. In most of these lectures, Leo spoke about reading and the state of writing in America.
24. Chatsworth, home to the Cavendishes, dukes of Devonshire, is one of the greatest stately homes of England. The then-duke, Andrew Robert Buxton Cavendish (1920–2004), had married Deborah "Debo" Mitford (b. 1920), the youngest of the celebrated Mitford sisters.

their talk, their mean wit, their exuberance, their deprecations. When [the duchess's sister] Diana Mosley saw the Yellow Room she said: "Rather like a railway waiting room." The Sargent [of Lady Evelyn Cavendish] splendid—a daytime perpendicular rather than the grand evening Wyndham girls. The duke shows his toys—and such toys!—and is humorous about glorious possession. "What is the difference between envy and jealousy?" Such talk of Turgenev and Tolstoy and Powell. The duke has a shelf of disasters: *Titanic*, *Lusitania*, Black Hole of Calcutta. ("Is there a good book about the San Francisco earthquake?") He stutters with deference and self-protectiveness. She, when asked what she does all day, produces on a blue sheet a schedule for one day that looks (but more orderly) like my engagement book for a Manhattan week. Then while at table she gets Puss to sing popular songs, Cole Porter, etc., she joining in. Last summer Puss went cabaret with the Duc de Valmarana; this summer with the Duchess of Devonshire. Next summer . . .

JULY 1, 1982   Pammy Harlech with Judy (Brittain) to tea—Judy's profuse, heavy-with-waves, Edwardian blond hair down, making her a beauty of serious and noble vintage. Pammy now early middle-aged, hilarious, shrewd, and her voice, accent, and laugh so like Allene and Georgia that, if I were in another room, I would think her aunt or mother here.[25]

Pammy found, tucked behind a photo of herself that she gave Harlech when first married, a photo of Mrs. Onassis, cut from a newspaper. He'd had a heavily publicized go-around with Mrs. O. "I told him that I didn't care," chortled Pam. "She's so stupid!" Then she did a fine-lined takeoff on concussed Jackie, murmuring almost inaudibly and gaping with huge invitational eyes into one's eyes—all application and devotion. A lovely, joyful, sharp-edged tea.

JULY 5, 1982 • VENICE   Venice is more home than New York or London because I here feel closer to my Ela, Rut, Maestro, etc., past. Here I have no holes. My dead died elsewhere, leaving their long-ago youths alive here. And my living still live here. In Manhattan, my dead are restless dead, and now in London Penelope has joined that ever-increasing horde. Also, Venice is for me a distilled Proustian world, microcosmic—titled, a foundation of servants long in service, everyone knowing everything about everyone.

JULY 8, 1982   Wanda's jealousy of Wally [Castelbarco] makes her the "black-hearted" sister. Wally is always the beauty, the happy one, the one men adored, who married brilliantly, whom their father (Maestro) loved. Wanda married Horowitz and was detested by her father for it. Also Horowitz didn't love her, since he wanted men.

25. Pamela, Lady Harlech (b. 1934), was the daughter of Allene Talmey's sister Georgia Talmey Colin. Both Lady Harlech and Judy Brittain were editors for British *Vogue*.

JULY 13, 1982  When very young, we were made to leave our families, leave "the company," and go to bed early, leaving behind a "bath" of jollity, gaiety, banter, or argument, "fun," possibilities, as we went to bed. Now I find that I am slowly retracing that painful terrain. Last night, when the others went to the piazza to watch the [soccer World Cup] victory celebrations, I went with Puss up to my room, the cries and cheers and clappings and music left behind. I could, as when I was a child, hear the gaiety off in the distance . . . and once again I felt deprived, a little desolation. So, we inevitably circle and circle and circle until we come, seemingly, full circle. And is it in that moment, in that place, when the true, the great adventure begins? I think we experience two great adventures, two births—into life, into death.

JULY 15, 1982 • VENICE
**TO RICHARD HUNTER** • VASSALBORO, MAINE

Today the Redentore bridge is being built—with a regular Manhattan hub-bub, but more operatic—under our windows. Tonight is the Fenice's first *Don Quichotte* (Massenet). Wally (Toscanini) and Emanuela [her daughter], the Duchess d'Acquarone, are in residence. Wally's enchanting house is hidden behind a wall, bowered in wisteria, jasmine, gardenia bushes, trumpet vines— a garden, a pergola, a little orchard, a low-lying, lovely, very operetta house, beautiful northern-Italian early Victorian furniture—a surcease. And Wally, at eighty-four, lovely to look at—a sweet, sweet smile, quiet unlike that Turandot, Wanda. Wally always says, "Oh, Leo, Eleonora's friend . . ."

I guess one reason I like Venice is that I can't go anywhere without encountering Venetian chums. This is such a family place—very like when I was very young in Harlem—and I couldn't go anywhere without a relation or family friend stopping me. Now that I am old I appreciate that. Also, yesterday—as I was being hoisted by helping hands onto a vaporetto, I was so reminded of my mother never venturing out without the protection of relatives. I have become, in that respect, so like her—and so like my horrible grandfather (but, of course, I am a dear) with bevies of creatures always surrounding me to get advice or talk things over. . . . Such self-revelations!

**JOURNAL** • JULY 21, 1982  If I were writing a novel, I could say it all candidly, disguising the names, the places . . . but in an autobiography? How much of the deep truth, how much of the darkest, most luminous secret places of my heart, my very being, can I reveal?

JULY 26, 1982  I find that I must try to put myself in the position of other men. In this, I am similar to [male] writers who write women. When I write a man, I wonder if I really know how he feels. I know how my kind of man feels, as much as it is possible for one person to know about another's feelings, to fish up from the common well similarities, consanguinities. I think that, in writing letters, my kind of man is at his most feminine, he most takes on the qualities of women he admires in life and in fiction.

AUGUST 3, 1982 · PARIS   Elie de Rothschild really looks like a baron.[26] The Rothschild Jewish nose has become, with time and breeding, aquiline, a mark of *racé* [distinction]—not race.

AUGUST 4, 1982   The world closes in: In this morning's *International Herald Tribune*, Cathleen Nesbitt is dead. All that early beauty, mature wit, laughing drama, that delight she gave to so very many, that pillar of fortitude which comforted, that symbol of survival . . . gone—now, indeed, legend. I see her in flashes, as one does, sudden illuminations: pink bed jacket in the bamboo bed in our "spare" room . . . coping with her poor arthritic, burned hand in a little, perfect, Central Park West flat . . . making a smiling entrance at the Van Vechtens', when she was triumphing in *Gigi*, in *The Cocktail Party* . . . clutching my hand as we left May Seymour's funeral,[27] and she said, "You know, darling, I wake up in the morning and look around and I say, 'Still here, Cathleen?' " . . . and Cathleen is, and Cathleen isn't . . . but, of course, I hear her sniffing away with Lynnie [Fontanne] in Genesee [Depot, Wisconsin], as they redo *There Shall Be No Night*.

AUGUST 5, 1982   Certain mothers do not want their sons to be interested in girls: These mothers, wanting their sons for themselves, wanting to hear their friends extol: "He does everything for his mother! He thinks only of his mother!" will, consciously or subconsciously, condone any relationship with a male. I know of one who came to America to place her son "somewhere where he will be homosexual"! The sequel: I think that my mother (and Maebelle) were and are more pleased at how we are than if we were married.

AUGUST 6, 1982   I have such a strong sense of the allée Proust—the darkening under the trees before the lamps go on, a sort of icing of lingering gray daylight. I can feel little Marcel there—hungry for Gilberte, as I can see him looking for Madame Swann in the Bois. All of Proust seems so close—and is, of course: Proust encountering Madame de Greffulhe in the [rue] Boissy d'Anglas . . .

So I come to Lucien Vogel in the rue Saint-Florentin, and how he kept Rut's letters in the right side of his desk with plans for their house in Marrakech, and how she was lost—utterly lost—when he died. What became of those letters?

So to Ela, on her last swift voyage, before the Nazis entered Paris. She

---

26. The French banker Baron Elie de Rothschild (b. 1917) managed the Château Lafite vineyards.
27. May Davenport Seymour (1884?–1967) directed the theater and music collections at the Museum of the City of New York.

rushed to the Invalides to say good-bye to Napoleon, and to Lanvin for the brown, changeable taffeta *robe-de-style*, paid for by Noël, who still had the flat on Place Vendôme, which Denyse [Harari] (who is coming to a farewell dinner tonight) has now. The circle again.

AUGUST 21, 1982 • EAST HAMPTON, NEW YORK  I wonder if one can suffer "little" breakdowns, similar to "little" strokes, almost or actually invisible to those who surround us, even those who are with us most intimately? I feel that I have sometimes suffered such little nervous breakdowns, perhaps even as recently as yesterday, when I suddenly questioned: Have I ever really belonged to any world or group? This feeling of alienation. Recognizing it, I can control it.

AUGUST 22, 1982  I want to write my resentment at having to inch myself precariously off toilet seats, my anger at having to scheme my way or be helped off simple steps, my fury at even trying to stand or walk easily across a small surface. . . . I hate not being free to go walk by myself. I am grateful to have the loving help of Puss, but I do miss my own unaided locomotion. My knees have betrayed me.

SEPTEMBER 10, 1982 • NEW YORK CITY  The first day of ridding out books. A man came from Strand [bookseller].

I found a photo of Marlene, embedded in trunks and fur, embarking on the *Liberté,* and later I was told, confidentially, that she had cabled Alex [Liberman], asking for money—desperate. He sent some. This is heartbreaking . . . even if she did live as though millions would go on for forever. She was prodigally generous.

SEPTEMBER 11, 1982  Parting with things—how one clutches while trying to let go. Mina said, "I never expected to be eighty-six." Improbable. I am sixty-eight and I resent my physical restraints, restraints of age and health. I have returned to childhood when my not being able to button or tie brought reproaches, screams of rage, sometimes slaps. I sat endlessly trying. No avail. I could not, until I was about nine or ten. Could this present infirmity—my deteriorating muscles—even then have conditioned my abilities? I wonder whether this is rooted in my awesome [very difficult] birth? But the baby in snapshots seems cheerful, healthy. That little child has a look to the future. He is suffused with cheerfulness in his carriage, in his mother's arms. A mystery.

SEPTEMBER 18, 1982  *La Nuit de Varennes* [Ettore Scola's film] is an extraordinary invention, superbly cast, with Hanna Schygulla the unforgettable presence, somehow gathering regret for the departed loveliness of a way of life sacrificed to the "new" world of brutishness and consumerism. "There is a new show, with the audience on the stage." A movie about departed glory and politesse and gentility and dignity—a beautiful world [now] peopled by airport populations. Hanna should play the Marschallin [in *Der Rosenkavalier*].

Judy Krantz, a *yenta* who has made good in today's world. "What color should the next heroine's hair be? My next one's set in New York City. I'm going back to my classic formula: *Scruples*."[28] Judy tries to direct everything. The *yentas* and *yachnas* and carpetbaggers inherit the Earth. Where recently hairdressers reigned, dressmakers queen it. We must always remember that Leonard, Marie Antoinette's hairdresser, helped to hinder the royal escape.

As we left Tiffany yesterday, after looking at Puss's table ("A Pre-Hibernation Tea for Bears—Grizzly Delights"),[29] we encountered Dorle Soria, and I asked her had she read Meneghini's book. "Yes—in Italian. It was amusing . . . and sad." I said, "I found a letter in which she was so bitter against him." Dorle: "She hated him—but then Maria turned against everybody." Me: "But never against us." D: "We surrounded her with love. We never preferred another soprano. If you had ever praised another soprano . . ."

SEPTEMBER 27, 1982  Deep in the treasure of Sylvia Townsend Warner's letters.[30] Cornucopia is cliché. The image is a purse, but a purse of iridescent sheen and indefinable size, not vast but deep, such direct talk from her to me, or any other reader. "I can tell you for your comfort that the only house I can never be dislodged from was our lovely Frankfort Manor, where we lived for two years and then were forced to be sensible about. I can still turn its door-handles and remember where the squeak came in the passages." That is how I feel about 1453. I have never left it. I trudge up the slightly swaying, yelping stairs. I sit in the chair next to the long parlor's fireplace, in the comforting dark, the full weight of the house above me, comforting me while the Lexington Avenue subway clatters and rumbles under the house.

OCTOBER 13, 1982  An advantage: I never had to talk to my mother or father about being in love. I never had to get them to agree to my marriage.

NOVEMBER 2, 1982  [Writer Harold] Brodkey came to Diana Trilling bringing [his] forty-page manuscript written in "defense" of her, against critics of her *Mrs. Harris*.[31] He insisted she read this; she retaliated with the first chapter of her memoir. Harold then told Diana that she had no taste, she lived with

28. Romance novelist Judith Krantz's 1978 book, *Scruples*, had been a huge seller.
29. Tiffany & Co. annually invited guests to style tabletops displaying its wares. Gray had done one that year.
30. Sylvia Townsend Warner (1893–1978) was a British novelist, poet, and short-story writer.
31. Diana Trilling's book *Mrs. Harris: The Death of the Scarsdale Diet Doctor* (1981) depicted the trial and conviction of headmistress Jean Harris for the murder of Dr. Herman Tarnover.

"mail-order" furniture, and a collection of "cheap" third-rate drawings and Japanese woodcuts typical of academe house furnishings. He ended, as he left, saying out of nowhere, "Give my love to Leo Lerman!"

NOVEMBER 19, 1982  The visit, in a vast dark-glassed limousine, to a restaurant on Mulberry Street [in Little Italy], and the "natives" standing agape, their activities suspended, precisely as we did sixty years ago when "someone" descended on 106th Street in a highly polished carriage or touring car. Here at this moment time was transfixed: 1919 and 1982 fixed precisely together, a single identity emerging from their merging. Even the sounds became a single moment, all senses fused. This was, then, a moment where the tracks do meet. Here I was in infinity.

NOVEMBER 22, 1982  I have been reading Proust's letters in the early morning, thinking about how much of the recipient is reflected in the writing of the letter. I feel each letter mirrors the person to whom it is addressed, each letter is colored by that person, since the writer of the letter must automatically, if he is a sensitive person, a feeling being, must in his letter accommodate the future recipient. We always try to please, and in trying put on some little semblance of the one we are trying to please.

DECEMBER 23, 1982  Diana [Stainforth], Rebecca's secretary, said: "Dame Rebecca is very quiet, very quiet. On her [ninetieth] birthday she only woke when her favorite nephew came down. Then she seemed so sad when he went away." I said, "She knows that she is saying good-bye." I can almost feel what must be happening in her head and heart. I know that she knows. It is Ela leaning against me, in that brocade dress, after I took her to see *Twentieth Century* and was dropping her off as I was off to London in January 1951.[32] It is Penelope holding my hand, so quietly all the long while we sat watching the wedding-of-Diana-and-Charles fireworks on the television and then insisting that she see us to a cab on the King's Road. All instinctively saying good-bye—but forever?

DECEMBER 31, 1982  Mina asked Antoine Bibesco: "Did you really love Proust?" And he said, "No—my brother and I just knew that he was a great man."

JANUARY 14, 1983  Yesterday I asked Gore (he in Ravello, I in 350 Madison [Condé Nast]) to write a piece about drag. He, in a fat, cushiony, wine-manipulated (as a breeze manipulates a weathervane or a mobile) voice, his measured, elder-statesman voice: "But I know nothing about drag." "Boosh-

---

32. "She leaned forlornly and quite hopelessly, as though to warm herself, against me in the cab. She was very, very sad—not like her at all." *Letter to RH, October 24, 1955.*

wah!" I wanted to say to him, *"Myra Breckenridge!"*[33] Then, he soon came to "What about little Troosey? You know, I don't know why, but I am sorry about him . . . his life. . . ." Gore went on about how sorry he was and about how he didn't know why he should be; how Gore had the lead article in *Vanity Fair's* first issue; how "they" had had to get rid of "little Troosey" because his first column was unpublishable: "So dated . . . the Duchess of Windsor . . . all that . . . so obsolete . . . so sad." Then Gore extolled his Ravello life: "After dinner—and it's so good—and vino, Howard and I just go down into the little village and sit with our bottle of wine in the square, where we know everybody. We just sit in the quiet. I can't take New York anymore . . . the backbiting, the filth, the noise. . . . Why don't you and Gray come for a month, anytime . . . anytime you want." Gore said that maybe his feeling for "little Troosey" was because "we all started out together," an old-school-tie sort of feeling, and all in his fruitiest, late-night voice, spliced by wine. I had a feeling of endless bottles of red wine and nights so late that splendid dawns gorgeously streaked Mediterranean skies—purple prose nights, sentiment oozing like red juice from pomegranates.

JANUARY 15, 1983   Mina: "I'm so old! I don't understand about heartbreak anymore. I don't remember what heartbreak is. Don't they know that it passes?"

JANUARY 23, 1983 • KENT, CONNECTICUT   At Brigitta Lieberson's, reading Ian Hamilton's *Robert Lowell*, untangling when I first knew Cal [Lowell] (his terrible, raging, black-black beauty) and Jean Stafford (her battered-wife life as plain to read on her face as any clear-set type on a printed page; her temples scarred by Cal's violence). But I must not forget Jean's sense of the ridiculous, irony eating at her misery, in the mid-forties at Ruth and John Stephan's Westport property. Cal Lowell and [editor] Albert Erskine sunned and lolled in a walled garden (shards of glass encrusted the garden walls, glittering and gleaming like dragon teeth), while Jean and Rut [Yorck] and Marguerite Young and Ruth dressed up in Ruth's extravagant evening dresses. Richard and I lurked in the enormous attic library–guest room (Pareto and Spengler, Veblen and James in first editions), peering down at Cal and Albert.

During the thirties I had a horror of being involved in causes. I was committed to poetry, actually to the word. I was muddled over the Spanish Civil War, hating Communism but also knowing that Franco was not "my side." I was rabid against Nazis. When that ruination first stuck its head out of its Wagnerian cave, about 1932, I was still in high school, "having an affair" with a man I met in one of "those" speakeasy, upstairs places on West Seventy-second Street. Hans Anselm he called himself. He lived in the Village, in some rooms

---

33. Vidal's 1968 satiric novel about the adventures of a transsexual.

with Turkish latticework covering the walls, and he claimed to be the Duc de Rhône. His head was skull-like, and he sat strumming some vibrant guitarlike instrument, and sang, in a soft southern German, his high, very pretty voice fraught with longing, "Rose of the World" and other songs from Viennese-Berliner operettas. One early morning, he said, "I must back to the Germany, to the *Schwarzwald* where are my people, and I must do something about those murderers." And he vanished. Then I read every word I could find about what was happening in Germany. When I could I tried to help: first the few, then the trickle, then the flood of refugees. I was not committed to a Cause. I was committed to Living, to Art. I was committed to devouring the High Life—this instinct having started in my grandfather's house, before I could talk. Causes came much later—marching against the Vietnam War, against nuclear testing. I followed the road. I don't think that I set the direction. And I continue to follow it, as one who wanders along, never knowing save by instinct, what is around the bend. This is predestination, but to me this is the adventure, with—always—the possibility of the Grand Surprise.

JANUARY 28, 1983 • NEW YORK CITY  I gave a dinner at Hubert's [restaurant] on Wednesday night for four widows, all over sixty-five: Diana Trilling, Jane Gunther, Betty [Comden] Kyle, Brigitta Lieberson. Diana says on the blower: "So special—I don't know if you realize how special that evening was—four women so respectful of one another, so courteous and generous with one another." "It was like chamber music," Puss said. Individual talk is always strung upon threads. Some thread what they have to say on perpetual nervous laughter (not real laughter, but a simulacrum which occasionally bursts the thread and splatters all over the place). Some thread their talk on silence.

JANUARY 29, 1983  "I became disenchanted with Hollywood when I discovered that the greatest movie star in the world was a mouse!" Lillian Gish to Lily Tomlin.

FEBRUARY 4, 1983  This morning at Memorial Hospital, Bill Cahan told Dr. Brya: "It's congenital." Meaning this goiter that descends into my upper ribs. So, Momma is trying to have the last word. What a strong woman! "Why must you always have something so complicated?" Bill asked, echoing Puss's "Why must you always be so different? I wish you would stop having friends who 'do' things!" The last word of this book should be "congenital." Aren't we all congenital?

FEBRUARY 23, 1983  I must write about falling apart. But should this not be a time of approaching wholeness? All of the tests are, basically, endurance tests. My claustrophobia is becoming much more acute. [During a scan,] Puss read Iris Murdoch aloud for over an hour. He stood in a lead apron weighing forty pounds. The kindness of the technicians, doctors, and *yentas* in the waiting room. You can become more and more innocent, as life goes on, and ultimate innocence is senility.

FEBRUARY 25, 1983  I have more of a sense of foolishness than of humor.

Paula Laurence on the blower to tell me—her voice minimal, cut clean of sarcasm, innuendo—that Tennessee had been found dead in his room at the [Hotel] Elysée, presumably having died in the night of a heart attack. This, we both agreed, was sad and glad. He always feared a long painful illness; his career had ended—seemingly. He had (I learned from Miltie [Goldman], whom I reached at the Four Seasons, where he was lunching) just finished a short story (so hope had surely not died). Paula most feared that Maureen [Stapleton] would suffer ("flip out"), but Miltie said that she was, at that moment, probably getting off a train in Florida, where "She's going to a fat farm, and she'll be all right."[34] Miltie has been all morning there, at the hotel, "and the police won't let the body be moved, or anything touched. He had a lot of money in his wallet. His 'new' boyfriend had been there in the night. His brother [Dakin], to whom he hasn't talked in a long time, is on the way. I talked to him. He wants a big funeral. I think that he should be cremated, and a big memorial service should be held in a theater." Paula: "You know, Chucky [Bowden] produced his last hit [*Night of the Iguana*]. Chucky must be on the stage at that memorial. . . . I was up and out today at dawn to audition for a commercial—a grand dowager. There was a woman all done up in twenty-button gloves, a tiara. . . . I'm sure she's got it. . . ." So life ends, or transmutes, and life goes on and on.

FEBRUARY 26, 1983  When Tatiana (an ancient Russian woman who takes care of Rose [Williams]) went to Rose and told her that Tennessee was dead, Rose said: "But I really love bacon." Paula thinks that Rose—lobotomized—is, in her "condition," crafty, and said "Dakin," realizing that now she would have to look to him for her keep.[35] "Tennessee," said Paula, "would have been a bum, these last years, if it hadn't been for Rose. He had two fears: that he wouldn't have enough money to keep Rose and that he would die of a heart attack. Well, he always had enough to keep Rose; he drove himself to make the money. And he did die of a heart attack."

I remember coming away from *Streetcar*, to which I had taken [photographer] Harold Halma. We left the theater in some sort of fierce weather, and I was in a state. This was during the time when Richard was leaving me for

34. The actress Maureen Stapleton (1925–2006) had starred in several Williams plays on Broadway, including a legendary performance in *The Rose Tattoo* (1951).
35. Tennessee Williams's older sister Rose (1909–96) had been placed in an asylum in 1937, declared schizophrenic, and lobotomized. After Tennessee Williams's death, Paula Laurence and Charles Bowden managed her personal care.

Howard and I was having those Sunday nights of mass affection [January 1948], and I said to Harold, "I cannot bear any more. I cannot bear any more," weeping uncontrollably and leaning, what surely looked drunkenly, against a storefront. Harold said, "You'll bear it, and you'll be all right. You will come out triumphantly." And, of course, I did.

We now discover that Tennessee died from choking. He inadvertently swallowed a bottle top, possibly from a nose spray. Odd, very odd. I see one of his bedrooms, years ago, with his few neckties flung over the supports to his bureau looking glass, very hall bedroom. He had a hall-bedroom personality.[36]

MARCH 5, 1983  Chucky [Bowden] told me how Tennessee, returning from the baths on West Sixtieth or Sixty-first saw an attractive Oriental: "I always was curious how an Oriental would be," Tennessee told Chucky, "so I cruised this one and finally, looking into a shop window on Broadway, I realized he was actually cruising me. He caught my eye and I caught his. I took him home and it was fine, and then he told me who he was and I told him who I was. He was Mishima, and he hadn't even known who I was!"

Tennessee was a deliberate mischief maker. Carson [McCullers] was that, but different, sort of spiteful. I don't think that Tennessee was spiteful.

Tennessee was all the women he ever wrote, and the men he wrote were his wet dreams. He did get a bit Big Daddy. Also Rose was Blanche and Laura. She is so many of his women. His mother, who signed a male name the last eight years of her life, is the mother in *The Glass Menagerie*, of course. Tennessee is buried in her grave—or that was Dakin's plan.

MARCH 19, 1983  Rebecca died during this past week, after her three-month decline and decay. A mercy. I am tired of saying that. How do we know what goes on in the deeps of an "unconscious" body? Other than feeling that I have lost someone I loved very much, someone I valued for her glorious mind and wit, and her legend, I somehow felt that I have lost a sort of mother. Very odd that.

What undid me were her last weeks—Diana, Rebecca's secretary, telling me, each Monday, that the apartment had become unbearably filled with Rebecca's weeping in her terror at dying. ("You couldn't get away from it.") "She's so frightened. . . . She never stops crying unless we put her to sleep." If this great, flashing mind was terrified at death, who am I not to be horrified? I am scared—not of after death, but of that death itself—then I have terrors at the claustrophobia of being shut in. Now this grows more acute—in lifts, during tests in machines, even in small rooms with doors closed. The terror is sudden, self-enlarging, and self-perpetuating.

I had a strenuous nightmare the night before Rebecca died. I could hear

36. The hall bedrooms Leo is recalling were in boardinghouses.

Puss crying out "Wake up! Label, wake up!" I could feel him shaking me, but all of that became part of the nightmare, part of the tug-of-war. Would I make it out of the evil that was invading me from some heretofore friendly "person" now dying on the floor wherever I was . . . or would that evil take over, annihilate me. I could see the transformation of the "person" into something awful, and I could feel me becoming even more awful . . . changing . . . but Puss saved me just in time.

Then, after Diana rang, I went to my office, where later in the day I began to have the most awesome pains in my lower right side. These were sundering, intermittent, awful. I did not tell Puss, because I did not want to upset him, which actually upsets me. Out of love, he becomes explosive. I told no one until they became unbearable late in the evening. So then Puss rang up the doctor, who told him to do this and that, and finally I fell asleep, waking at about three a.m. feeling healed. Oh, the bliss engendered by the cessation of pain. I believe all of this was one manifestation, nightmare and pains—Rebecca's death.

MARCH 26, 1983 Lillian Gish told me today, when she rang to ask me what *Heat and Dust* was really about, that when Eugene and Carlotta O'Neill returned from India, Gene said: "Don't ever go, Lillian. Everywhere, everywhere it smells, it reeks of death. Death is the atmosphere of India." But Lillian went twice, and each time found that Gene had been "Oh, so right, dear!"

NOTE: The much-publicized relaunch of Condé Nast's *Vanity Fair* magazine occurred in March 1983. Reaction was swift and negative; advertising pages plummeted immediately.

APRIL 16, 1983 · NEW YORK CITY
TO RICHARD HUNTER · LONDON

We had a lovely visit from Elie de Rothschild and his amour, Ariane Dandois.[37] Marvelous diamonds on her, superb tailoring on him—all very Odette and Swann, except Swann was not on the top of that heap, and Ariane is one of the great Orientalists (fantastic objects in her gallery). He is very gallant with her and she very *Casque d'Or* with him.[38] Meanwhile his baroness lives in Rothschild splendor in London, and he jaunts from wife to mistress. . . . All very old time and somehow pleasing—the way reading Proust is pleasing.

I have had an "interesting" proposition from Alex Liberman and S. I. Newhouse, Jr., anent *Vanity Fair*, and when I see a definite commitment I will tell you. A.L. said: "A marriage has been arranged." To which I answered: "When you get married, rings are exchanged and presents start pouring in. . . ." We will see what we will see.

37. The antiques dealer Ariane Dandois was the longtime mistress of Elie de Rothschild. They had a daughter, Ondine, in 1979.
38. *Casque d'Or* is a Jacques Becker film set in Belle Epoque Paris.

JOURNAL · APRIL 16, 1983 Tina Brown says she could not work with the Groke (Richard Locke), but she would take on the job if I did it. I will now wait for Alex and Si's next move.[39]

APRIL 21, 1983 Today Alex offered me *Vanity Fair*. I wanted that more than anything.... Too late? I would [also] have to "uncle" *Vogue* and write my book. Si, he says, opposed because this could harm *Vogue*. I should feel good, since they think that I am the only one who can edit *Vogue*—my part of it—and I am obviously the only one who could edit *Vanity Fair*.

APRIL 23, 1983 Today Alex and Si definitely gave me the job of editing *Vanity Fair*. So I got what I wanted. Now what do I do with what I got?

NOTE: On April 27 S. I. Newhouse, Jr., announced Leo's appointment as *Vanity Fair's* editor in chief. He began there five days later. Whatever his initial agreement, Leo did not keep his hand in at *Vogue*.

JOURNAL · MAY 27, 1983 I went to *Vanity Fair* at last, fulfilling some fifty-five years of wanting this job. So much happened these last weeks that I haven't been able to write or read a word, other than for this job. I even seem to have lost my fear of death. One morning, when I was on the fourteenth floor, alone, the lift doors opened and—surprise to me—I went into that lift, descending fourteen floors—alone! I could not do that, all of these years, with my terror of lifts. But suddenly, having got what I wanted (all but finishing my book), I lost my fear. I see death as an adventure. What an unexpected result of realizing a lifelong dream!

NOTE: At *Vanity Fair*, intense and long workdays ensued. Leo essentially kept the staff Richard Locke had hired, augmented by a few of his own. Alex Liberman visited daily, often conferred with Leo or the art directors, and telephoned continually with suggestions.

Leo struggled to create a magazine evoking the spirit of its Jazz Age predecessor. He encouraged the editors to have fun with it, to search for talent rather than pander to celebrity, and to commission sharp essays on social issues. "Our platform would promise an astonishing thought in every head, an irreverent song in every heart," said his letter in the September 1983 issue.

Invigorating *Vanity Fair*, as circulation and morale continued to fall, demanded speed, organization, and indeed ruthlessness of a sort Leo may never have possessed. Certainly it proved beyond his reach as he approached his seventieth birthday. Years of working autonomously for *Mademoiselle* and *Vogue* had not equipped him to manage

---

39. Journalist and editor Tina Brown (b. 1953) had resigned on January 1, 1983, as editor in chief of the British monthly *The Tatler*. She had reinvigorated that moribund society publication in three and a half years, with Condé Nast acquiring it in 1982. In the spring of 1983, rumor had her a contender to replace Richard Locke at *Vanity Fair*. Instead, when Leo took over the magazine, she signed on as an editorial consultant.

**TRUMAN CAPOTE**
LEFT: At Yaddo, in the
room Leo described as
"a Renaissance eyrie," 1946
BELOW: With Charlie T.
Fatburger, mid-fifties
BOTTOM: With Leo and
Lee Radziwill, 1975

ABOVE: Alice Astor Pleydell-Bouverie, late forties
BELOW: Carson McCullers in Nyack,
New York, 1946

ABOVE: Penelope Dudley Ward Reed, 1947
BELOW: Mina Curtiss at her farm near
Northampton, Massachusetts, 1946

**MARIA CALLAS**
ABOVE LEFT: With Giuseppe
di Stefano taking bows for
*La Traviata*, Mexico, 1952
ABOVE RIGHT: Tellingly
caught between Aristotle
Onassis, *left*, and her husband,
Battista Meneghini, London,
1959
LEFT: Fired by Rudolf Bing:
in her dressing room, holding
his infamous telegram; Leo
stands left and Meneghini
center, Dallas, 1959.

**MARLENE DIETRICH**
LEFT: Relaxing in Alex
and Tatiana Liberman's
apartment, ca. 1962
BELOW: Recording her
show *I Wish You Love*
for television, 1973
BOTTOM: With Leo and
Leah Luboshutz, at the
Philadelphia Fashion
Group's tribute to
Dietrich, 1957

ABOVE LEFT: Betsy
Blackwell, editor in
chief of *Mademoiselle*,
1957
ABOVE RIGHT: *Vogue*'s
features editor Allene
Talmey, some time in
the forties
LEFT: Carmel Snow
with, on floor, *Harper's
Bazaar* art director
Alexey Brodovitch and,
standing, managing
editor Bob Gerdy, 1952

LEFT: Leo in the art department
with Grace Mirabella,
then *Vogue*'s editor in chief, and
Alex Liberman, ca. 1976
ABOVE RIGHT: Diana Vreeland
at *Harper's Bazaar* on the day of
the announcement that she would
become editor in chief of *Vogue*, 1962
BELOW: Working at *Vogue*, 1981.
To the left behind him, photos of
Capote, top; Mia Farrow, bottom
right; and Maria Callas, bottom left

ABOVE: Leonard Bernstein and Felicia Montealegre,
three years before their marriage, 1947
BELOW: Brigitta (Vera Zorina) and Goddard Lieberson,
*left*, with Igor Stravinsky, some time in the sixties

ABOVE: Nora Kaye and Antony Tudor
during rehearsal, Tokyo, 1954
BELOW: Kaye arriving at the opening of the film *Pennies
from Heaven* with its director, her husband,
Herbert Ross, 1981

LEFT: Congratulating
Martha Graham, 1974
BELOW: With Gray and
Sono Osato Elmaleh after
the thirty-fifth anniversary
gala of American Ballet
Theatre, 1975

RIGHT: With Rudolf Nureyev, at a gala dinner thrown by Sol Hurok for Nureyev and Margot Fonteyn, 1973
BELOW: With Margot Fonteyn during Hurok's party. *Left*, the former dancer Robert Helpmann; *right*, Fonteyn's husband, Roberto "Tito" Arias.

ABOVE LEFT: Rebecca West, 1957
ABOVE RIGHT: Edith Sitwell and her brother Osbert, 1962
BELOW LEFT: Lionel and Diana Trilling, early forties
BELOW RIGHT: Isak Dinesen (Baroness Karen Blixen), 1959

ABOVE: Bravig Imbs showing off his virginal, *left*, and his wife, Valeska, *right*, dressed for one of their parties in the early forties. Their gatherings were central to the émigré world that Leo first encountered in the late thirties.

BELOW: Art dealer Kirk Askew, *left*, and his wife, Constance, *right*. Many artists and musicians first met at their cocktail parties in New York or London from the thirties through the fifties.

ABOVE: Anita Loos, *left*, and Helen Hayes, *right*, celebrate with Leo
the publication of their book about New York, *Twice over Lightly*, 1972.
BELOW: Leo had invited Maureen Stapleton, *left*, and Julie Harris, *right*, to one of his
monthly "Friends of George Spelvin" *Playbill* lunches at the Algonquin Hotel, 1971.

ABOVE LEFT: With soprano Jennie Tourel, ca. 1953
ABOVE RIGHT: Painter Stella Reichman kicking
up her heels between Leo and Gray, 1991
BELOW: With another of his favorite sopranos,
Beverly Sills, late seventies

With Gypsy Rose Lee on fashion designer Bonnie Cashin's terrace, 1957

such an unwieldy project. It had been a long-held dream, however, and he went at the task bravely.

Leo made very few notes unrelated to work during the next six months.

**JOURNAL · JULY 31, 1983** Eyesight failing. I can hardly see what I am scribbling, but I am optimistic. I am almost always optimistic.

Chucky [Bowden] rang, early yesterday, to tell that Lynnie [Fontanne] had quietly died. So glamour is almost all gone, fades away early in a summer morning. This affected me deeply. I cried. (Why does wept sound so melodramatic?) I think of Lynnie's forever mature, womanly being, her quintessential style, her presence, a deep, laughing humor, humane and worldly . . . all gone, this world of make-believe, this miracle of "class."

NOTE: Leo and Gray went to London in mid-November 1983. Their return was delayed by a kidney-stone attack that hospitalized Leo. During this crisis, he realized that the *Vanity Fair* assignment was overtaxing. He had tired of contending with the magazine's fractious editors, although he was fond of many of them individually. Liberman's constant watch and counsel, to which Leo customarily deferred, was not making leadership easier.

**JOURNAL · NOVEMBER 17, 1983 · LONDON** I wind up my mind: I will "stand" as much as I can, and then I will go. I've done what I wanted to do. I need prove myself no longer to myself. I must plan my own graceful exit. I cannot take much more of Liberman, and I know of no reason for taking him. I see fully that he is bad in his heart: I want none of it. I have done what I wanted to do. No life for either of us, this one with Alex.

DECEMBER 7, 1983 · NEW YORK CITY A choice on Tuesday between dining with the Donald Newhouses or the king and queen of Spain. Having promised the Newhouses months ago, I regretted the royals. A vengeance on the Inquisition.[40]

The Vreeland Saint Laurent evening [at the Costume Institute]—*grand tenue*—and all the grand French ladies, thinking themselves grand duchesses, seemed more Grand Horizontals [courtesans] aping grand duchesses—a right hand to a place above the left breast and head held "regally" but graciously, almost enquiringly, to the right and all pivoting from the solar plexus. The fashion groupies shouted "Jacqueline!" "Jasmine!" "Catrine!" Almost every woman wore black, and the silhouettes looked superb as they moved about the museum's great halls and along the red carpet through the defiles of white lilac, white orchids, great white screens after dinner toward the waiting mobs— very Scenes from the French Revolution. Dancing in the Temple of Dendur room was very decadent.

---

40. Donald Newhouse (b. 1930), the chief executive and co-owner (with his older brother, S. I. Newhouse, Jr.) of Advance Publications, married Susan Marley.

NOTE: Leo was not alone in feeling that *Vanity Fair* was not jelling. Over the New Year holiday, S. I. Newhouse, Jr., told Leo that Tina Brown would replace him as the editor in chief at the magazine. At the week's end, Leo departed its offices.

His new assignment would be Condé Nast editorial adviser, a corporate position created for him. Alex Liberman's title was editorial director. There was never any question of Leo competing with Liberman's authority at the magazines, but in the next ten years, the company's editors in chief came often to ask Leo's guidance on features and to seek his help in securing some personality, house, or artwork for their magazines.

JOURNAL · JANUARY 6, 1984 Now I can begin my notebooks and my book again. On this day my brief, but consuming, *Vanity Fair* life ended. I feel regret, some residue of anger, but most of all relief: A gigantic burden has been lifted from me, and another adventure begins.

The glorious farewell party the *Vanity Fair* staff literally threw—great torrents of confetti as thick as heaviest snow—and the love, which I never suspected, that filled my room; the remarkable "book" that the staff made. No other departure—not from *Vogue*, not from *Mademoiselle*, was so rich, so loving, so riotous an "affair." But, of course, this departure was an unwilling going-out and that helped make these (I thought cold) people love me.

JANUARY 8, 1984 Rather like being jilted, or having a lover run off with someone else . . . not the same pain, but a similar anguish . . . all too short a time . . . why not a chance to have developed . . . that sort of irritation . . . and much mulling over what the new "one," the supplanter, will do . . . deep wishes that she not survive, that she go down in ignominy, while at all times (save when with intimates) one maintains an "I-don't-care" surface. My guardian angels have been calling, all seemingly relieved.

JANUARY 15, 1984 We lived as if we were privileged in Grandpa's house. We never equated being Jewish with poverty. We were upwardly mobile (awful designation), and heaven-bent on having a good time—a rich time on the way to the top. Grandpa wanted his sons to get to that top, but he also wanted them to remain in the Pale—strictly Orthodox—and this, I now see, made him a monster. For years I saw only the monster, but in writing this I discover the tragic figure, the figure in which the old and the new warred, with the winning side predestined even before the war began.

JANUARY 21, 1984 At last I see the shape of my life as a parabola: the level, seemingly forever, of my earliest years, burgeoning into the curve, more fully, and then, when the swell, the breast-shape, seemed most full, leveling to the last great plain. Time alters the view. Time bends straight lines and straightens bent ones.

JANUARY 24, 1984  Lunch with Prince Michael [of Greece, historical novelist] and Dan Harvey [book publicist], the latter butternut and coonskin-hat America, the former *ancien régime* touched by *modernisme*—liquid, deep, Vienna blond's eyes, fluid hands and wrists, all absorbed interest, very private. So much to note: The fisherman who told Prince Michael's father: "I saw a vision—the madonna, all in white in a long white boat sailing swiftly off of Corfu." "Not the madonna, the Empress Elizabeth [of Austria]," said Michael's father; the tale of his great-aunt who saw a gardener slash off the head of a rose with such delight that she fired him: "There is a murderer!" she told someone. And later he murdered the Empress Elizabeth. Prince Michael touched me in so many moments of my life: "I had a relative, so evil I could never go near her. She bought the house in Venice with thirteen windows on each floor." Aspasia, whose daughter wanders mad in Venice.[41] Prince Michael is in constant communication with a psychic in Paris. He dotes on historical mysteries, and she "feels" solutions to these mysteries, tells them, almost enacts them: Lincoln and Booth, Jeanne d'Arc and the fake Jeanne, Anastasia, the death of Ludwig [II of Bavaria]. He suddenly extends his whole arm, stretching it from shoulder to fingertip, imperiously. Royal gestures in everyday life.

FEBRUARY 4, 1984  Norman [Singer] (now closer to the shape of his father) talking about the gathering Inevitability murmured: "I guess the only thing to do is to gather poison. You know, Geoffrey and I think: Well, we're two hours away. . . ."[42] "There's no away," I said. "So . . . poison . . ." he murmured even more quietly. As we talked, another scene unreeled in my head. . . .

Rebecca West, years ago, 1964, when I was staying with Henry and her in the country, pausing for a moment in the corridor, before we went into lunch, peering at a large, blue and saffron-yellow patterned ancient majolica dish, and murmuring, "We all knew that we were on Hitler's list, and we'd be the first to be taken, so we all had pellets of poison in readiness." Autumn smoldered outside in the Chilterns Woods, and there was a feeling of secret gypsy fires. I wondered: Would I believe so strongly in my mortality—I mean immortality—that I would refuse to take poison? I always feel that I will have another chance. I suspect that mad Virginia Woolf felt that all of her chances were gone. She was utterly without hope.

For a moment, just now, I smelled Czettel's smoky, cologney room. At any moment, one's entire life is there, more impatient than objects (how very patient they are), waiting to be lived again. The sorrow of things, their histories so mortal; the mortality of memory, entirely dependent on longevity, dead

---

41. Princess Aspasia of Greece (1896–1972) married Greece's King Alexander shortly before his death but never claimed the title of queen. Her daughter was Princess Alexandra.
42. Geoffrey Charlesworth, a gardening expert, was Singer's long-term lover.

when all receptacles have vanished, transmuted to some other state, even when recorded.

FEBRUARY 11, 1984  Yesterday, starting with a walk from Twenty-second [Street] and First Avenue along Second Avenue, where all is now sordid and the few "little" old shops linger hopelessly midst enormous apartment blocks. Not poor and optimistic and an adventure, as it was, but vulgar and inhuman and depersonalized, the pavements filthy and graffiti on even the newest surfaces.

Starting here, as we walked in the cold wind, I knew that I had to face a future in which I must choose between my eyes and my kidneys. To control the glaucoma, I will have to take pills that help "manufacture" kidney stones. As simple as that, with as little possibility. Perhaps some manipulation of drops can avoid such a choice, perhaps a "not too dependable laser" can help. But all grim.

Also, I am trying to adjust to my new office life. Perhaps, if I am patient, this can be fulfilling. It doesn't use much of what I do best (and I wonder how to fill [assistants] Stephen [Pascal] and David [Holland]'s energies and hours).[43] I have, I must face it, been "kicked upstairs" with all that implies. I am trying to make the best of that. I must be patient. I must take it all as a sickness to be lived through. But how hard this is, all of it, on Puss, who has, partly because of my perils and my recent life (*Vanity Fair*), more of his own health troubles.

FEBRUARY 22, 1984  Mrs. Onassis came to lunch, and we verged on intimacy for the first time. As I sat waiting for her a few minutes, Philip Johnson came up and suddenly kissed me—after all these years! Mrs. O talked of death. "Men think more of death," she said, "than women do. . . . Perhaps it has to do with potency," she ruminated. So our long, quiet lunch.

FEBRUARY 25, 1984  Lee Radziwill rang Tina Brown, saying, "I can't be on a magazine that has Taki on its staff." Alex Liberman instantly concluded that I had told Jackie the news of Taki [Theodoracopulos, society columnist] in *Vanity Fair*, which has been told in newspapers, even on television. A sudden realization that what caused our wretchedness at Condé Nast was Alex Liberman's increasing paranoia. The sickness is that of all Russian "leaders," which leads to the destruction of multitudes. In these last years, this sickness has spread to some American "leaders."

FEBRUARY 26, 1984  Dinner at Diana Vreeland's—she has a passion for quality and an appreciation of vulgarity. She hates teasing: "I believe in reality. I'm too real for teasing."

43. David Holland worked in Leo's Condé Nast office from 1983 to 1986. He later became a jewelry artist.

MARCH 3, 1984 Have I kept myself a child, a Peter Pan, by my life with Puss? Grandpa the monster is equaled by Alex the monster. (Alex: "Well, I'm off for two weeks, now it's all yours!") As a child, I had not to cope with money, except knowing that it bought goodies. I pay the bills, but that is, in a sense, a fantasy. When the accountant talks about taxes, my mind shuts clam-fast.

MARCH 18, 1984 Dinner at Diana Trilling's—Ned [Rorem] came back from the loo and solemnly declared: "There's a cello back there!" This led to the fascinating saga of James Lionel Trilling and the cello, which, although he was tone deaf, he did play so adroitly that he could have had a brilliant musical career, not as a soloist, but as a member of a quartet. This never happened because he could not tune his instrument. Diana, with her perfect pitch, tuned it for him—sans piano. He found this unbearable and stopped playing the cello, but will not permit Di to give it away: "I tried to get him to tune it by listening to his teacher over the telephone. That never worked. Jim didn't know how to go down or go up. He simply couldn't bear for me to tune his cello." So the instrument remains—a permanent monument to this son's hatred of his mother. "There's something in me he really loathes," Di told me months ago. "We're friends, but he hates me."

NOTE: *Gourmet* had been acquired by Condé Nast in the autumn of 1983. Leo regularly advised its editor in chief, Jane Montant, how to tailor the magazine to the company line. Leo began writing cookbook reviews for her magazine. He also wrote for *House & Garden*, particularly on houses in Los Angeles, where business trips could always combine with a visit to Gray's mother in Laguna Hills.

JOURNAL · APRIL 25, 1984 · LOS ANGELES How to write the way lives have crisscrossed without our knowing it? For instance: If Lewis Galantière hadn't asked Jack Houseman to go with him to one of the Askews' Sunday afternoons, Jack wouldn't have met Virgil Thomson and so would not have been involved in the Hartford production of *Four Saints in Three Acts*, and so would never have come into the world which became "our world." Here, then, we also have people of importance, the Askews, the center of a world, whose members and additions become more important than the center. Today, Houseman is world famous, the Askews utterly unknown.

APRIL 26, 1984 A real tea with Carol and Walter Matthau—a little girl's dream come true—little chicken sandwiches, little watercress sandwiches, little lemon-meringue pies. She was one of three competitive friends: Carol, Gloria [Vanderbilt], and Oona [O'Neill]. "Oona . . . she's bad now. You know that O'Neill blood." Carol was Gloria's bridesmaid.

She's like a woman in a Restoration comedy: Plenty beyond plenty. She explains the enormous, almost empty bedroom: "I like to see Walter coming toward me." The house is more cushions on more sofas, all roses, all frills, all lace—all illusion. Those glass fruit and flowers lighted from within that host-esses once used for centerpieces on West End Avenue, Carol started collecting, Gloria followed, and America now collects. She did some sort of secret work against the Nazis. She has a whole closet given over to boots; a room the size of a normal Manhattan living room for her clothes; the bathroom stocked like a drugstore. The help, mammies, love her. She's so [face-powdered] white. "This is why it's good to be rich!" says Carol blithely. She has humor about it all.[44]

APRIL 28, 1984 Nobody here is building anything under the cost of a major Broadway musical. So much building and decoration, because money is com-ing out of hiding (see Spengler, *Decline of the West*). Each new house is built on a site that was occupied by a previous house. During Hitler's War we heard: "He was . . . She was . . ." In Los Angeles we hear: "That was the so-and-so house." They live for the moment but, like the Egyptians in death, have life's trappings in excess and richness to see them through the journey. A world of replaced and displaced persons. The Reagans are the perfect expression of this world. I feel that maybe all of this is illusion and we are on the other side of the screen. The quality of the light here is part of the illusion—the knobs are all turned to a different angle. And living rich, as we do here, is all part of behind-the-screen. [Critic] Nora Sayre says Edmund Wilson was a man of the twen-ties. Am I a man of the thirties?

MAY 3, 1984 · NEW YORK CITY Mina: "I have no pain. I just wish I could go to sleep soon. I feel cast up on an island of indifference."

MAY 8, 1984 Norman Mailer at lunch at the Four Seasons: "Women are essentially cold—killers." He intends this marriage, "unless Norris runs off with a younger man," to last. He says that he has ten years left in which to write novels. "So now I must be careful about what I choose. I want to write two more of *Ancient Evenings*; a book about Russia; a book about the Nazis." He talked about us ("We must be related—fifth cousins, maybe"); about his chil-dren, lovingly; about how he has nothing in common with Norris's family, and when they come he doesn't know how to talk with or to them; about Christians—he feels that they are cold people, alien to him. "But I've never felt," he said, "that I'm American. I feel European. I've never felt that I belonged here." He told about Voltaire visiting the male brothel. I told him about Joseph Hergesheimer enjoying the experience, but not liking the view.[45] He gets restless, even in this marriage sometimes, but he's "too tired" to do any-

<hr>

44. Carol Marcus Matthau (1925–2003) had been an actress and had twice married the play-wright William Saroyan before marrying Walter Matthau. Known as a madcap, she had been one of Capote's models for Holly Golightly in *Breakfast at Tiffany's*.
45. Novelist and biographer Joseph Hergesheimer (1880–1954) told Richard Hunter that he had that response to trying homosexuality.

thing about it. He talked about his way of writing—exhausting himself, always writing in longhand. "Writing poisons me, it poisons my system." Right now he's signing single pages for the Franklin Mint. For this he's paid two dollars per. ("Pays the rent.") This horrifies me. He feels that Updike could write a great novel and will. "Oh, his prose, that beautiful prose . . . only Truman's early things . . . I suppose they'll bracket Updike's book and mine." We lunched for almost three hours. He said: "I know you're saying all these witty things, but I'm getting deaf—move closer." I said: "You want me to make a scandal?" He loved that.

MAY 9, 1984  The first anniversary of [the musical] *My One and Only*—all the true words: enchanting, charming, wonderful. Twiggy older, visibly, by a hard year, but adorable; Tommy Tune [dancer and choreographer] now a superb performer, breaking (I can see him as through a paper hoop he springs) into being an artist. I took Puss onto the St. James stage, and as we peered into the empty theater, a special magic particular and peculiar to this theater—so defenseless—specially in this city—so open-armed and eager, almost doglike. And then all those glorious ghosts thronging that stage—such optimisms and hopes fulfilled and hopes dashed, such instant splendors. . . . My heart broke and unleashed torrents. I thought of Joan McCracken and Diana Adams [both in *Oklahoma!*]; Gertie [in *The King and I*] waltzing with Yul and teaching the little Siamese children; me delivering Marlene's New Year's Eve doughnuts to Yul; Johnny Gielgud haunted as Hamlet; Maurice Evans superimposed as Richard II, then as John of Gaunt—oh, so many ghosts. And I wept. Then Tommy and everyone hailed me as the godfather of the show.[46]

MAY 13, 1984 • WASHINGTON, D.C.  Bess Myerson [New York City comissioner of consumer affairs] today said that when Jackie married Onassis she said that she did it not so much for the money, but because she thought that the money would bring her the privacy she craved and the protection for herself and her children. Indeed, the money brought, as we all know, the notoriety she did not want. I am haunted by her intense, almost-to-herself cry, when we last lunched: "If only I had made the most of the years in Washington. There were so many brilliant people. I could have learned so much more. But it all went so fast . . . so fast. . . ."

MAY 19, 1984 • NEW YORK CITY  Reading a proof of Bill Weaver's *Duse: A Biography*, I hear Ela's voice as I read Duse's fraught letters—so like Ela's. And hear Duse's voice in her goddaughter Ela's. I feel that Duse influenced Ruth Draper's voice and "delivery," and that Evangeline [Bruce]'s voice was influ-

46. Leo had attended rehearsals and given *My One and Only* an enthusiastic feature spread in *Vogue*.

enced by Ruth Draper. I saw Duse. I remember her atmosphere, her stillness, her sorrowing pervading the huge theater, not her sound but her *being* took that theater and imprisoned it. I spent an afternoon with Ruth Draper (having seen her many times onstage) and I felt that Duse hush, that perfume of grief, distilled, in that memento-filled flat overlooking the Society Library. Now the echo of Duse in Evangeline's voice.[47]

MAY 20, 1984  I recall watching Maria at four a.m. in the Ambassador Hotel, while she sat, bespectacled, in her bed. Meneghini tapped away, bookkeeper insect, in a corner. Maria, deep in the score of *Lucrezia Borgia*, flicked her pencil at this red morocco-bound volume that I had given her, a first edition from the Mendelssohn library.

**MARIA AND LUCREZIA BORGIA**  *She hopped into bed, took up a pencil, opened the score, and she was gone, completely immersed in the score. Occasionally, she looked at me and she smiled, but she didn't see me. This went on for a very long time, and I was enthralled. Mr. Meneghini's typewriting stopped. He seemed to be dozing over his typewriter, and I was sitting there absolutely fixed. Maria took off her glasses, closed the book, put down the pencil, looked at me, and said, "It's wonderful. It's really wonderful." And I said, "Do you know it all now?" And she said, "Well, you know, you have to know it all, so that when you go out on the stage for the first rehearsal, you know who you are. Then I am free," she told me, "to breathe onstage. You know who that girl Lucrezia Borgia is. You know that what people say about her is either lies or not lies, but you know that you are Lucrezia Borgia. You also know that you are Maria Callas." . . . "You know who everyone else is?" I asked. (1993)*

JOURNAL • JUNE 2, 1984  Why have I spent a great part of my life working for and with fashion magazines and all of their ramifications? I no longer believe in what they offer: I have not believed for a long time. *Vanity Fair* gave me an opportunity, I thought, to elevate, illuminate, confirm those splendors of intellect, taste, grace . . . the charm of living. I thought *Vanity Fair* could signal: "Look, there are others like you. . . . Don't despair. Here is a signal fire, a home fire in the dark night." When I was very young and came upon *Vanity Fair*, *Vogue*, *Theatre Arts*, *Theater*, the Civic Rep, certain people—they were the signal fires. Even in the features pages of *Vogue* I felt that I was doing this—but I wasn't always pure or "impractical." I lived by the rule of: "Give one, or even two, get one, or even two." That is, partially, how I coped with Liberman. I felt like Robin Hood, one of my basic heroes. But, of course, my fashion magazine job (not work but job, a distinction) has given me that rich bourgeois life, or

---

47. In 1956 Leo had arranged for Ruth Draper to be photographed by Mark Shaw shortly before her sudden death.

the trappings of it, so seemingly necessary to my well-being, that life which my mother and father would have wanted for me—able-to-boast-about-it success. Even the most "bent" life is "straight," at least in the married world in which we live. I did not, as a child, want to be the myselfs I saw about me. I wanted to be those others out there, up there. I became one of those others, but I remained the myself I did not want to be.

JUNE 7, 1984 "Do you realize how Proustian movies are?" said Puss. "You see a whole life. We saw Alain Delon years ago as a juvenile and last night, as an aging creature."[48] That is why I find Los Angeles so fascinating: the closest to hereafter—immortality in the mortal world. That's the illusion we seek, and the illusion which makes living bearable.

JULY 1, 1984 · VENICE Here in the Gritti, in our room, now redecorated beautifully—pale yellow, pale gray. Puss exhausted, unpacking. *Falstaff* on the radio. So strange, here we feel most at home, most having-come-home. I said to the waiter, "At last, here in Venice, I feel that I can feel tired."

*Falstaff* is Verdi's most glorious. What inspiration—his having composed this marvel so late, late, late. . . . I breathe hope from it—from its variety, its "newness," its lyricism, its flow proliferating as branches and foliage from an ancient tree, the tree of life itself. Here's *Falstaff* in which Verdi is as pure and as perfect as Mozart: They share laughter—every variety save the cynical.

JULY 5, 1984 What other people consider unreality is my reality. Venice is my reality. Here all seems fantasy, but here all is realistic. Time is in constant flux: in the water's wash, the bells, the people herding, the buildings crumbling forever. Everything is immortally mortal.

JULY 19, 1984 After Herbert Ross elucidated the Bettelheim [psychoanalytic] interpretation of Cinderella, Nora said matter-of-factly: "No, Herbert. Cinderella is just a girl with a broom, and she sweeps," making a firm, horizontal sweeping gesture.

JULY 20, 1984 We children did not know the word "anti-Semitism," but we knew that Miss Lyons, a local schoolteacher (a "mick"), hated us. I found this out during the flu epidemic of 1919, after a fight between Miss Lyons and Momma in the street, while kettles of boiling water were constantly being emptied onto the slate pavements in attempt to fight the contagion. She called us "sheenies." Sometime later, during the high holidays, as I stood on the steps of the *shul* house in my holiday blue serge suit and hat, some wild Irish boys

48. They had just seen Delon (b. 1935) playing the Baron de Charlus in Volker Schlöndorff's 1984 film *Swann in Love*.

tried to choke me, yelling: "Get the sheenie!" I did not experience this as anti-Semitism, but as the micks not liking the Jews. We didn't like them either.

**MISS GRIGGS** *She was a tall, dithering, spectacled, old-maidish body, who sported long, long skirts (even in 1925) and held even longer-nosed views. One day [in Jackson Heights] she twanged, "Leo Lerman, stand up!" I did. Miss Griggs had never been unfriendly. I liked her because each Friday afternoon she gave out library books and I was allowed to choose which I wanted. On this morning, Miss Griggs brightly smiled. "Now I want you all to look at Leo Lerman. Jews are very different from the rest of you." I was deeply interested. Nobody had ever told me this before. "Jews smell different." There was a lot of laughter. Even I laughed. So she went on in this wise for quite some time, about how Jews dressed differently and ate different foods and thought differently. I was really, really interested. This was most instructive. I didn't feel that she was talking about me. So, I went home and told my mother. This produced an entirely different effect than I had intended. My mother marched off to school the next day. "I want Miss Griggs out of this school. I want my son transferred to another class. . . . Or . . ." Somehow, peace was made, and I remained in Miss Griggs's class. And Miss Griggs never again said another word about Jews.*[49] (1993)

**JOURNAL · JULY 21, 1984** This morning, as we stood on the vaporetto going to the [palazzo] Ca d'Oro, I realized that the Goldwassers, and to some extent the Lermans, never felt that we didn't belong. We were the center of that little world of immigrant Russian, Polish, Hungarian Jews. Others came to ask Grandpa's advice. The women of our family set a sort of pace, specially in matters of the table, cooking bountifully, even prodigally. We spoke Yiddish, lived in a kosher world, but already we had at least one foot in America. We belonged, because this was our world: the Miss Lyons, the Irish roughnecks, the Italians were the outsiders, the oddities. Only later did I discover that I did not belong, that there was, alas, a world from which I was excluded. We were not exotic like some foreigners, but we were undesirable.[50] Jesters got in everywhere. Here we find why, perhaps, from a very early age I was entranced with "stars." Even in high society, in the world aborning in the kaiser's war: Society breaking down—Elisabeth Marbury and Elsie de Wolfe opening the doors; [hostess] Mrs. Stuyvesant Fish mixing classes and cultures; Duse, Bernhardt, the Diaghilev Ballet all "got in"; Otto Kahn and other Jews began to infiltrate,

49. When the Lermans moved to Jackson Heights in the early twenties, the corporation that was building most of the neighborhood excluded Jews, Catholics, and African Americans from its model housing. Jewish Jackson Heights grew on the lots surrounding it.
50. "On a Sunday morning walk, Grandpa Goldwasser said to his brothers and sons while I stared longingly at the great house [of Otto Kahn]: 'This little *mamser* [bastard] will never know the *maedlin* [girls] who live in there. Mr. Kahn's *tuchters* [daughters] he will never know.' " *Journal*, July 18, 1982.

and we in our 106th Street congeries knew this. Grandpa and his brothers didn't believe it could happen, but Aunt Minnie didn't doubt it for a moment. She was the American aunt, working in some shirtwaist place as the bookkeeper; her sister working in an auction house. They believed—even that German Jews would one day "receive" Russian Jews. The improbable was always probable to Minnie. And the magic wand of theatricality always somehow touched us in our little, intact, tempestuous, tears-and-laughter world.

JULY 25, 1984 Maria was essentially middle class in her view of living; even her seeming to break out (Onassis, etc.) of the middle class was middle class. Meneghini was definitely middle class, Italian middle class, and it was this Maria was fleeing.

JULY 26, 1984 There was Jan Morris, winsome, in Harry's Bar. [Opera coach] Randy Michaelson at the next table thought her flirtatious, even a little naughty, but wanting not sex but the dress and the brassieres—the drag. He said all the drag queens he knew in the fifties wanted to be Mother or Nanny. The drag queens I knew in the thirties all wanted to be movie stars. James Morris may have wanted other men sexually, but I think he wanted womanliness more—the freedom of femaleness, of being just another girl. When I said that we had been here a month, Jan, aghast, said: "But I'd go mad!" What's put *her* off Venice, when *he* wrote the best book about it—a loving, cherishing book?

JULY 31, 1984 · MUNICH I am most at peace in the countryside. At Ettal [outside Munich], for example, the protective skin is dissolved, and I sit or stand enraptured. But I am now more baffled than ever: I cannot understand that mass madness. How could it have happened in this Bavaria? I see mean faces. I hear *"Grüss Gott"* constantly. I see this gleaming, abundant, beautiful land. I stand in a sort of exultation in the Baroque and Rococo German churches, amazed at the ecstasy, at one with the worldliness—specially in the figures. (In Ettal, the practicing organist thundering and pealing—what passion in that church.) The sameness of words in Bavarian German and Yiddish—I expected this, but not as much. And the sameness of the cooking—so much of it I knew at home when I was young. So seductive. I feel no homecoming here as I do in Venice, yet I will long to come back when I am away. . . . The violet stockings on our waitress, and the perfection of the food, on onionskin-patterned dishes (made in East Berlin) . . . How could the madness infect *these* people in these sublime surroundings? This must be the basis of my bafflement in Bavaria. Glorious churches and monasteries in vast meadows—at Ettal were chickens and the green fragrance of haymaking, the lowing of cattle, and a steady concourse of visitors—but always I find someone in me calculating how fast I could get across the border to some assumed safety. This does not leave me. And always I am accompanied by Ela and Alice and Rut and even Tilly. A sign on the way to *Vogue:* "Dachau"—in yellow! What did this mean to me after days of gradual seduction? Can anyone believe in "reasonableness" after 1934?

AUGUST 10, 1984 • NEW YORK CITY  I am a burden. I will become slowly, if fortunate, more and more a burden. I must face this. I must not become an oppressive burden. Ralph Colin[51] and I talked about this at lunch, and whether we would have the courage to make a "graceful" exit. Neither of us could face the positive answer. Yet, I know that there is only one solution.

MY LIABILITIES — PHYSICAL:
- unstable legs
- knees that cave in
- three sicknesses in my left eye, impaired vision
- two sicknesses in my right eye, impaired vision
- a cyst on my right lid
- a goiter, which has hemorrhaged internally
- an odd "connection" from my heart
- kidney stones—left and right
- vascular problems
- something wrong with my sense of touch and some reflexes
- unable to button and tie (I can manage neckties and apron bows, but I cannot button or unbutton my shirts; I cannot tie my shoelaces; I have difficulty cutting meat)
- sometimes peeing frequently, with loos surprisingly up or down stairs, which are very difficult for me
- [allergies to] Demerol and iodides, which make for an impossible medical situation

MY ASSETS:
- I still think in my muddled logical way
- my memory is good
- I can, with my operated-upon eye, see distances, and I can read!
- my hearing is good
- my sense of smell is good
- pulse, heart, etc. all seem normal
- my spirits are usually good (but when I know that I am a burden, the slough of despond opens, I fall in; if I am courageous, I will one day—when being a burden becomes intolerable—open that little narrow exit in the bottom of the slough)

---

51. Ralph Colin (1900–1985), a lawyer and trustee to arts organizations, was Allene Talmey's brother-in-law.

AUGUST 11, 1984  Anxiety like a distant ship, very far off. What is it? It rises like a miasma from my deep feeling that I am not working enough to earn my pay. All those years of unceasing work, and now—shreds. Diana Vreeland said: "Listen, buster, you must get used to leisure!"

AUGUST 17, 1984  Last night's play, *Hurlyburly* [by David Rabe], loathsome. I didn't care (in the most acute sense of this word) for anyone in it. All worthless. The play padded into three acts—and filthy! I do not remember being shocked in the theater until I saw Sigourney Weaver and William Hurt in their first scene together. His head under her dress, then she starkers with him straddling her. I do not understand how these good actors can do it. The audience, specially the women, roared with laughter throughout. This is genuine decadence: Hurt hopelessly asking Weaver to "suck my cock," the audience roaring. When are the rest of the Roman games?

AUGUST 18, 1984  At the Frick, I sat looking across the room at Bellini's *Saint Francis in Ecstasy.* I sat marveling at the solidity of this work, wondering at its color, amazed again at its detail—both physical and spiritual. No heavenly messengers in this lucid work, only low-lying light and the almost passive acceptance by St. Francis of the state of ecstasy. No celestial hocus-pocus here, exquisitely winged angels visibly bear tidings from the Lord. No—each stone, blade of grass, cloud, ray of light is a messenger, an instrument, and the saint himself becomes an instrument. A fraught tree in the upper-left—tormented by the Divine Spirit? Has this painting been cut down? I could sit for hours bathing in this painting, becoming one with it.

I can no longer go from painting to painting, as I can no longer sit in a concert hall through a program of diverse works by different hands. I want one or two works or an exhibit or program by one creator, or connected works (e.g., Ferrarese paintings or a musical program of Weber and early Wagner). But even the orderly jumble of a museum or a concert—no. A theme—yes. Showing how paint has been applied to a surface, e.g., Hals, Manet, Kline, but this a viewer should invent as an approach when a gallery hasn't devised it.

AUGUST 22, 1984  *Faux marbre* is becoming the *boeuf* Wellington of the decorating world. Emptiness casts a heavy shadow, because of the passion for faux marbling everything, and this signals a need to seem rich, but artificially. Another evidence of the decline of reality. With what consequences? Not even to eyes accustomed to disaster on the television screen is disaster real. Inhumanity creeps over us like the Ice Age creeping down from the North, a hardening of the sensibilities.

AUGUST 26, 1984 · PALM BEACH, FLORIDA  Si [Newhouse] came back to the dinner table [yesterday] in the fake Belle Epoque restaurant (an epidemic of this now) and said bluntly: "Truman died today." He'd heard this from some-one. "How?" I asked, automatically. "Why do you ask that?" he asked. "Do you think he killed himself?" "He could have. He could have died of an auto acci-dent, dope and drink, cancer. He said he had cancer." All the while I tried to hide that I was in deep shock, feeling our first meeting at Mary Lou [Aswell]'s. This close friendship lapsed about three years ago. I believe that he could not bear to see his old friends. The Black and White Ball was his last genuine work of art.

News now: He died in Bel-Air. He was with Johnny Carson's ex-wife [Joanne]. She went into his bedroom and found that he had died in his sleep. There were drugs in his room, but this is not thought to have caused his death (what stilted words). What a *déchéance*, Little T's life. That doomed genera-tion: Tennessee, Little T, Harold Halma. Little T was his own victim: Even if he died a natural death, he killed himself.

AUGUST 26, 1984 · NEW YORK CITY  Home [from visiting the Newhouses in Palm Beach]. Told Si about Truman as we drove into the city, where Little T wanted to be emperor-empress, and was, for a very little time. I think of Jack [Dunphy]—What is he doing?—and of that winter night when Jack and Todd [Bolender] came to visit us in the darkish back parlor, and T drifted in, unex-pectedly, trailing a mile-long scarf, and then we all five went to see T's first apartment—one room, fading photographs, a little rocking chair. T tapped and put on a vaudeville show, rocked away to Bessie Smith on the record player, and we all went out into the awful cold at two a.m. "Doesn't anyone want anything to eat?" Very little boy. No one wanted anything, so he went. And at the corner, Jack looked back, and we saw that Little T was standing at the far corner looking at us. The next morning, very early, Todd rang up—rage and tears: "He's gone. He left me for Truman!" Jack never, never went back, and no matter what T did, Little T came back to Jack. T strayed, but Jack was his, and he was Jack's.

AUGUST 28, 1984  I think, underlying all my visible actions, of Truman con-stantly, and those earliest days: evenings at Harold Halma's, before *Other Voices*, and how we planned that photo which made him, almost instantly, a media event;[52] times with Mary Lou or our then family at the Russian Tea Room; Yaddo and hearing through the wall, when he was having his affair with Howard Doughty, "Can you do it laying down?" (the ungrammatical question making the sexual part even more hilarious coming from T, who was so worldly as to be naïve); late-night games of Murder, when I was the murderer and I murdered him, who went hiding about with me because he thought I

---

52. The controversial jacket photo, of a louche young Capote sprawled on a Victorian sofa, was taken by Harold Halma (1920–1968).

was his safest protection; parties in East Eighty-eighth Street at my place (with Richard and after); the morning at about four a.m. when he rushed up my stairs, threw dozens of envelopes on my bed, T twitching, exhausted: "Nina's drunken mad. She threw all of Newton's letters out of the window on to Park Avenue!"; the nights we sat in the cafeteria on Madison between Eighty-fifth and Eighty-sixth Streets, and the lunches in the Eighty-eighth Street Schrafft's, roaring with laughter at the *yentas* and their bobbed-nose daughters; that time when a woman came up to us and said to T: "I know who you are. I have a son who's a writer, too," and that son turned out to be J. D. Salinger! So many moments, so many intimacies.

His dissolution began with the success of *In Cold Blood,* or rather with his falling in love with one of the murderers. But the real blow was the day Babe Paley refused to see him anymore. He could not bear that. He could accept more easily Gloria Vanderbilt and Carol Matthau shutting him out—all others—but Paley was his duchess and he never could understand her reaction to what he had written about Bill Paley in "Answered Prayers." All those chums knew that he was a writer. They made him their confidant, their pet, their jester, their vitality, their escape, because writing, and a certain freakishness, sexuality, and ability to be news had brought him celebrity and brought him to them. How did they not expect to be in his work?

This is a closed, shut-in city. I almost never see any life in the great block of modern flats opposite my bedroom windows or in the old building opposite our drawing room on Fifty-seventh Street. I tell the weather, see the sunrise, reflected on the sky-tall flank of the building over on the north side of Columbus Circle. I see oblongs of lighted windows, sometimes beaming all night long, a sort of code signaling vacant rooms, but I almost never see people, domestic animals, in any of the rooms or on any of the terraces of the roofs surrounding me. These cliffs are filled with secret lives. I go out into Fifty-seventh Street—cars, buses, carriages, trucks of all sizes, taxis with fantastic company names, and raucous annihilating noise. People like lava from a sudden volcanic explosion—but almost never anything personal. Misery, yes, rending arguments even, sometimes a jangle of laughter, but always the impersonal brush and trudge, more purposeful than desultory. I wonder: is this inhuman, or is the inhumanity in me? I laugh a lot at what I see. I am horrified. But still these are detached reactions, so much the opposite of what I feel in Venice, Munich, even London. I feel personal in what I continue to feel is my neighborhood—that area on the East Side, especially above Eighty-sixth Street, ceasing about Ninety-sixth on Madison, Park, or Lex, and continuing up to 106th on Fifth. Streets haunted by my childhood. I see Momma climbing up the iron steps, in her bright yellow coat and hat (dyed black after Grandma died). Momma, me in hand, crossing 106th Street to Grandma and safety from whistles blowing in celebration of what we later knew was the False

Armistice. I was terrified, because I had overheard grown-ups talking about those German dirigibles dropping bombs on us: "Okay! Okay!" Momma told me, "Grandma will take you down to the cellar. . . ."

AUGUST 28, 1984  Choura Danilova to lunch with Holly Brubach at the Café des Artistes. Choura punctual, punctilious, meticulously neat and mannered, in a good white suit, her hair tinted quietly brown and blond, round agate-brown eyes sometimes speaking more than her mouth, hands folded—the ballerina severe, but the Russian smiling—everything suited to her age, in the eighties. The mischief, the comic is still here. Everyone always said she had the wittiest legs in the world ("dainty, jocund, and sure"), but that was a misunderstanding, the wit was in her head and her legs expressed that wit. "Nora hated Alicia [Markova]," she said, "You know when [choreographer Léonide] Massine asked me to do *Beau Danube*, Eugenia Delarova said, 'But the costumes are awful! We must have new costumes.' 'Let me see,' I said." Her look held all the old shrewdness of ballerina versus ballerina: "I sew . . . I give a little lift to the skirt . . . a little puff . . . I like." That is how that insouciant movement was born, which the world adored. Choura's skirt worked [to embody] the whole of the Ballet Russe de Monte Carlo, as Nina Novak's teeth did.[53] "Massine . . . he hated me," Choura said. What a wonderful, sapient, great lady she is. The fun bubbling as quietly as boiling water. Holly "secretly" scribbled it all down.[54]

AUGUST 31, 1984  Little T came home to Bridgehampton, in a golden Tiffany-made book labeled *Truman Capote*. This book containing his remains will be, Jack hopes, buried in the cemetery there. But the real remains will be "Answered Prayers." For surely we will now have some book, some accumulation titled "Answered Prayers," and some of it will be brilliant, wrought with his special malice and poetry.

SEPTEMBER 6, 1984  A little, girlishly playful voice on the blower: "Do you know who this is? Can you recognize the voice? You don't remember a little Italian girl—a wop?" This went on for a time. Finally, sweetly: "It's Wanda. . . . I've been in hell for the last years. I couldn't go out. I was like somebody living in a boardinghouse." She seemed to think that I knew of some awfulness in her life. This could only be Volodya—the Petrouchka Horowitz himself. "Now I'm beginning to look out again, and I think of you so much, so much of the old times. I hear you were in Venice—Venice! I rang Tatiana [Liberman] one time. Not happy. She got so old. She always said, 'You're so

53. Nina Novak (b. 1927?) was also a ballerina with Ballet Russe de Monte Carlo. *GF:* "A strong dancer with a horsey smile that looked as though painted on."
54. Holly Brubach, fashion journalist, consultant, and editor, worked with Danilova on her memoirs.

much older than me.' Older!" Wanda laughed, but all of this had a kind of sad, slow, low tone, a faraway sweetness to it. "Wasn't very interesting, Tatiana. She smiles a lot. She never was very intelligent. . . . Wally [Castelbarco] goes out every night in Milan—beautiful, she looks so beautiful. If you sit on a sofa and talk about forty or sixty years ago, she's wonderful, talks and talks, as if it's now . . . but talk about now and she's gone. . . ." So she went on reestablishing old ties. This is what's become of the Toscanini girls.

I am reading Hilary Spurling's life of Ivy Compton-Burnett, so filled with cat's-cradle connections to us. . . . In 1955, when Gray and I were in London, we sat one day in the "lunch" room of the Victoria & Albert, and there, at a table two removed from us sat A Brooding Presence—dark, out of some turn-of-the-century print with touches of the twenties. She should have sported amber beads, but she did not. A sort of modest chamber-pot hat fitted closely over her mousy fringe (or perhaps that was a hairnet?). She sat, permeating aloneness, intent. Years before, I had seen Georgia O'Keeffe so intent, watching the antics of Kiki Imbs [youngest daughter of Bravig and Valeska], a child inhabited by some mischievous spirit, which carried her—no one knew how—to the tops of inaccessible armoires, where she sat like a gargoyle, and set to mouthing curious lines like: "There's a yink in the tizzie!" . . . Now, here, in London, in the unexpected quiet of the V & A commissary, sat this seemingly malign presence, more alone than anyone I had ever seen, but inside concentrated on the dark side of the moon, on the black side of human nature, on the freakishness of people. And this Presence, Puss and I knew immediately, was Ivy Compton-Burnett.

SEPTEMBER 16, 1984  My night was peopled by my Lerman grandparents. He: small, ungenerous, rheumy-eyed, bearded, very meager. She: raisin-eyed, plumpish, *sheiteled* [in a wig], and smiling—in that little flat on Second Avenue, between 99th and 100th Streets, where the convenience (one to a floor) was in the public hallway, a sort of earth-closet, and the tub was in the kitchen. She made tough poppy-seed cookies. I liked that. And she had, on the oilcloth-covered, round table a dish of bubs and a plate of buck. Oh, yes—they lived over the store: a dark, greasy shop that sold paint, wallpaper, and products for the painting of places, and was redolent of resinous smells—turpentine, kerosene. Something in me liked the shop, and when that Grandpa was in it (white bearded, rimless glasses on pale blue eyes, a woolly vest hanging over his tieless shirt), he seemed some strong and even magical creature. I adored color cards—solid little rectangles of pure color. I craved them the way I craved chocolate, and I lusted after the wallpaper sample books. I still do.

SEPTEMBER 23, 1984  I woke thinking of Little T and of [gossip columnist] Liz Smith's distorted view of his feelings for Lee Radziwill. The heart of the matter isn't quite where Liz places it. Little T's heart did not have Lee or Babe on it. More likely Newton, or perhaps Jack, or one of those men—fathers of four or five—whom he picked up and made part of his private (almost, at least semipublic) life. He was loyal. He never let anyone really go. But Truman was a great mythomaniac, and his myth now enlarges.

SEPTEMBER 25, 1984 The memorial was very much Little T's triumph. The irony was unnoted, but at last he had a success, and a nearly full house in a Broadway theater. But it didn't answer any of his prayers. . . . As I toddled across the Shubert stage from the wings stage right to the lectern, I felt deeply, helplessly old for the first time.

**OTHER VOICES, OTHER ROOMS** *Last night I took off the shelf the copy that T gave to me of* Other Voices, Other Rooms. *The dust jacket, with the photograph of the boy with the invitational face, has vanished, but the yarn inside is intact. And here, on the flyleaf, is what T wrote, in his best hand: "For Leo—and what does the following bring to mind? Piggyback, snakes, The Cow, grapefruit, the all-night café, a bunch of love letters, Nantucket, Poor Butterfly. Ah Hilary" (I am Hilary in Truman's* Local Color; *I am not Turner Boatwright in "Answered Prayers," although his brownstone does house some of my tatty furniture and a gaggle of my chums), "when the time comes to go, should we simply laugh? Mille tenderesses [sic] (which is after all another landmark)*[55]*—T"* (VOGUE, SEPTEMBER 1987)

---

55. "The Cow" was Leo and Capote's nickname for writer Marguerite Young. Because Leo often dieted, many of his meals with Capote at Schrafft's in the forties consisted of grapefruit. "Poor Butterfly" was the theme song of their favorite thirties radio drama, *Myrt & Marge. Local Color* (1950) was an anthology of Capote's sketches of life in different places, which included his story "Tea with Hilary." In their friendship's early years, many of Capote's notes closed, in ungrammatical French, with *"mille tenderesses"* (a thousand caresses).

# WHO DO THEY THINK I AM?

JOURNAL · SEPTEMBER 30, 1984 I rang Mina. She is in a hard-to-breathe bad way. Her mind is cluttered with trivial, irrelevant details: "I've never been that way," she said. "I can't even sit up to read. Dying is so boring. I must get up to be given a bath. I must do that!" She talks of Howard Adams's Proust album [*A Proust Souvenir*], and how much better Ngaio Marsh is than Agatha Christie, and how marvelous Virginia Woolf's [diary] volume five is, and how kind she is to Angelica [Bell] and Bunny [David Garnett]. (He was Mina's lover. That is how I met this bone-selfish, talented man.) "Good night, dear, I wish I could work. Tell me things."

OCTOBER 5, 1984 Arthur Miller's *After the Fall:* The most wonderful thing that happens in one's life is also the most awful. This great play is perhaps the greatest American play since the best O'Neill. (*Our Town* is the quintessential American play.) *Fall* is so close to the facts of Arthur and Marilyn's life. She said to me: "I can't even remember words!" He echoes this. These two wreck one another's natural lives, but he, in a sense, triumphs. Arthur's great play reveals its author's agonies, while confirming and elevating its audience's. Do all lovers kill and exalt simultaneously? Is this what Shakespeare and Wagner and Proust tell us is the essence of love? Only in Mozart is there clear, steady radiance? A very tired, young person inside, exalted by Arthur's play and the acting of it, suddenly caught a glimpse, in the looking glass above the basin in the bathroom, of a distinguished, white-bearded old man exterior, with inquiring eyes.

Mina's throaty voice is thickened but fast, a husky tumult, as if racing against fear, as if this rush of talk could hold back her night of pain and exhaustion and sleeplessness. . . . She throbs on about books and Proust and Philip Johnson ("That Fascist Nazi in the morning paper leaning over Jackie Onassis. That's what I think when I see him—now so respectable.") I could not say: "But Lincoln helped make him respectable." She said: "Oh, dear—you looked like a rabbi in the morning paper." She laughed sweetly. "The painkiller lasts only fifteen minutes, then the exhaustion. Such a bore. I cling by reading. I find the only way to go on is reading."

OCTOBER 7, 1984   Diana Trilling on D.H. Lawrence, about whose early novels she is writing 2,500 words for the *Times* . . . She went on about the revelation she'd had: Frieda Lawrence unfaithful to D.H. from the very beginning. She loved to bed down in the hay (literally) in a barn, with Bunny Garnett, some friend of his (Middleton Murry[1]) nearby listening, and she would pound away. (Or was F.L. doing it with Murry?) She made sure that D.H. knew about every one of her infidelities, and he always accepted them. She made dreadful scenes in front of people, jeering at D.H.'s sexual impotence or inadequacies. I was surprised that Diana hadn't known this. When I was about seventeen or eighteen, Hester Sporer told me all about this. Wasn't it Hester who described Frieda Lawrence raging at D.H. in Taos, screaming: "Show them! Show them what you don't have! Open your fly!"

OCTOBER 8, 1984   When I was a little boy, Momma would say to me: "Don't be a Leopold and Loeb!"

Why do I fight the happiness of writing? Reluctance to give birth, to part with—yet, I never have been reluctant to give myself. I have always been ardent—actually a pushover—for charm, for sex, for influence, for certain kinds of looks, for lovingness, for wit, for gaiety . . . even for certain smells or colors.

Since Friday late we have been here [three days at home] with—miraculously—almost no scratched or rubbed-wrong places. I have written very sparsely about our personal and private lives, the loving life we live here together, the life we have shared (and the parts we could not share without capsizing the boat). What of this rich, loving together life? Surely, if this is an honest book, our life (singular in every aspect, save the parts unshared) must suffuse it. Our life is the deep well that nourishes us. We have been married—what other way to look at our state?—for some thirty-four years, with all of the ups, downs, a midlife crisis (mine) any "normal" marriage engenders. How can this not be part of this book, if only to show the young that such a life is possible? Is this scribbling "doing it for the children"? I think of Stephen [Pascal] and all the family relations. I have one life, one center, and that is Puss. It seems impossible to be entirely truthful. Not so much about "big things"—never the pleasures, the joys—as about the little irksomes. Here, we seem to get into the Good Manners of Love, which make for calm and proportion. Knots, which, if I fumble persistently and long enough, I manage to untie. But sometimes my patience trickles away.

1. The British critic and novelist John Middleton Murry (1889–1957) was married to Katherine Mansfield. Their relationships with the Lawrences are reflected in D. H. Lawrence's *Women in Love.*

OCTOBER 14, 1984  We went out to the Kern gala in the refurbished Town Hall—a maniac taxi driver, a stinking Forty-third Street, Manhattan at its pestilential nadir. Then—Town Hall reborn and pristine, righting all. The gala enchanting, with laughter and tears, so much well-trained talent—especially the boys. Paula [Laurence] sang Kern's "Blue Danube Blues" from *Hello Dearie* (1921) with great delicacy, tenderness, wit, and charm.

Kitty Carlisle Hart came up to us. Always groomed, she looks good at all times. Paula was Moss Hart's [lover, before Kitty]. Kitty said to Paula: "Your dress, darling—probably very effective onstage." At the reception, Paula, seeing Kitty with Lara Teeter (Kitty played in [the 1983] *On Your Toes* with this youth), said to Kitty, "Oh, darling, how nice that you've continued your summer-stock romance." I like these *The Women* exchanges—"jungle red" exciting. Kitty: "You know, I worked with Kern in Hollywood at the Bowl. He was so irascible—with the accent on the *rascible*." Kitty still has the New Orleans touch. She said to me: "My mother brought me to Town Hall. What did your mother bring you to hear?" "My mother," I said, "didn't bring me. I brought her."

OCTOBER 16, 1984  Lee Radziwill (understated, lean, face cheekbony, large dark eyes and wide-lipped smile) hosted a party for "The Adorables" (Fizdale and Gold) in John and Tug's old house on Seventy-fourth Street, now hers.[2] So odd—shadows of parties for Margot and of Lili Darvas being launched as a cateress: She catered and came as a guest, her black cook having learned all of Lili's mother's recipes, marvelous Hungarian dishes (Laci and I dined there at least once a week). There I sat in Lee's drawing room, a deep mango-colored room, that past and me at this party.

OCTOBER 19, 1984  At dinner with [composer] Lukas and [painter] Cornelia Foss, Prince Romanov's sister-in-law told how her sister, the prince's wife, Mimi di Niscemi, sat on her chest and banged her head against the floor when they were children.[3] Mimi beat her little sister [Maita]—now big in size, not tall like Mimi, but all huge curves like an Oriental view of a eunuch. Once, when Mimi bit her sister deeply on her arm, their nanny asked Mimi, "Did you enjoy it?" Mimi said, "Yes!" The nanny bit her deeply. Mimi never bit her sister again—but she beat the hell out of her with a hockey stick. "Island people suffer from inferiority no matter how exalted their position," she said.

At the Fosses I suddenly played fiction, telling Mimi's sister and Earl [McGrath, art dealer] a version of my second try at running away when young:

2. As Gray Foy recalls, John McHugh and Trumbel "Tug" Bartan, a male couple, were wealthy balletomanes.
3. Great-grandson of Czar Alexander III, Prince Alexander Romanov (1929–2002) was married to the jewelry designer Maria Valguarnera di Niscemi (b. 1931), who was descended from a noble Sicilian family.

going off to London, at eighteen (!), with four trunks—based on solid blocks of truth, but decorated fantastically. This was elaborate and utterly believable, even by me—an experiment, which sprang full-blown.

OCTOBER 20, 1984 Because of painting the kitchen of our apartment, I have been forced into the "real" world. Yesterday, trying to flag a cab, having already to-and-fro-ed for breakfast, I was so undone. I felt salt-eyed and filthy and deaf-ened and distraught. I, at last, fully realized what a sheltered life I have been living during these last years: taken down, put into a car (Stephen usually wait-ing), driven to the office (David usually waiting if Stephen isn't with me), taken up to the office, protected by Stephen and David, taken down to the car, driven to lunch at the Four Seasons or Hubert's, someone always helping, taken away again. . . . So I go—almost never alone, almost, literally, never touching earth. If I had not had years of earth—deep in earth—this would be unhealthy, this protected life.

OCTOBER 26, 1984 A human infant is being kept alive by a baboon's heart. How Edith Sitwell would flame that into a sun-gold poem.

Little startles, in the night . . . at suspended moments in the day . . . a little tremor, like a knuckle rapping the heart . . . a sudden knife in a muscle . . . breath rhythms altered . . . death nibbling away silently, unseen—but what a terrifying clamor, within . . . a tocsin perpetually warning . . . and after seventy the noise of oblivion is deafening. The blackness always lurking at the bottom is not frightening, in a sense, comforting and inviting obliteration. . . .

NOTE: During these months, Leo devoted many weekends to organizing papers and sorting through his books for sale to a secondhand dealer. In the following, he reflects on several photographs he had come across, some of them from his childhood.

JOURNAL · NOVEMBER 17, 1984 Who then, am I, have I become? All of them, those boys and men: the one in Uncle Irving's camel-hair coat and green fedora, yellow wool scarf, very thirties, very young, very romantic leading man? The sweet-faced, big-eared stage manager in the twin-sweater set—blue and woolly—backstage at the greasepaint-fragrant Mansfield—the girls clatter-ing down the iron steps in their mules, ready for Act I, heavily beaded eye-lashes, satin kimonos, my hand raised to signal lights down in the house or footlights up—was I that stage-managing, theater boy? And what of the one who hungrily strolled the avenues or Riverside Drive in the late spring, early summer evenings, hungry for experiences, that lucky high school boy who never—God knows why—got into trouble, even in the upstairs speakeasies, in shadowy, sometimes totally black rooms on West Seventy-second Street? What of that boy—who somehow, no matter what he did, remained somewhere within innocent? Who then is this somewhat staid, sometimes priggish, always correct on the surface man? Who is this gray-bearded, gimpy-legged man? This public figure of a private man? Who was the man involved in setting this house to rights today, who ate pizza and pumpkin pie, who was petted and excoriated by the person he loves best, fell into blackness, climbed up into the light, who hears Lotte Lehmann, *Die Frau ohne Schatten*, at the moment—but the moment is already gone, the voice still. And what of the future intimations of creatures in him? And mortality—this man trying to evaluate how much time is left and—surprise—how much time there was before? All those years— were they really a long time, a moment, or moments strung like beads? No, inextricably mixed—always—forming and transforming simultaneously. And I suspect so is personality: the sum total is a character? Another question: What attracts so many people? Who do they think I am? Death is the pin that fixes the moment. This I know. And I know this also: Any one life is one moment. Some lives are bigger, more intensely lasting—Shakespeare, Leonardo, Michelangelo, Mozart . . . these are the fullest moments.

I tire more easily. I fall into sudden sleep—a brief, intense, dream world glimpsed through a slatted fence, shards of some familiar world gone unfamiliar in sleep. The stair creaks and I wake, prop my book up—a protection. All life long books have been my protection, but have I ever fooled anyone with this ruse?

I have no great gift for sharing, despite my apparent talent for almost immediate intimacy. I write to breathe.

NOVEMBER 22, 1984 Yesterday to Dorothy Norman's. I hadn't been for years. I hadn't seen Dorothy for years. Ascending in the little seat that glides up the handrail, very *deus ex machina* in classical drama, I saw, as in a faded photograph taken sixty years ago, Dorothy and the remains of her "circle"—a photo from which I had to blow the heavy, oily dust, some of the must of time never vanishing.

In this room I made Mary McCarthy cry. I saw [Arthur] Koestler pass across the far end, rather like [Albert] Bassermann in a film about Nazi Germany. I met La Pasionaria[4] and the mayor of New York, Indira Gandhi and Nehru, [political theorist] Hannah Arendt and [artist] John Marin. I heard Edward [Norman] and Dorothy rage at one another and saw the adding-machine mind of Dorothy at telegraphic speed. Someone said: "Dorothy, all your lives, who knows them? Yours was the place the Europeans came, the one place we all gathered. Who knows your two books about Nehru, your anti-Fascist life?" Dorothy replied: "When I look back and see the shy girl I was, the innocent girl . . ." The turning point came early for Dorothy when, after her idealistic honeymoon at Harvard, she was disillusioned in [her husband] Edward's ideal-

---

4. A Communist heroine of the Spanish Civil War, Dolores Ibárruri (1895–1989) was known as "La Pasionaria."

ism. Then she found Stieglitz, Art, International Politics, causes, and herself.[5] She found herself repeatedly. Dorothy's caviar's gone quite red with age, but the refreshments, the decor, and the cast haven't changed.

NOVEMBER 24, 1984 Thanksgiving at Diana Trilling's—the hard bone of the conversation was Diana's admiration for Lillian [Hellman]'s strength of character, in going out in public, when she was visibly and horrifyingly old, ugly, sick: "No one wants the old, ugly, and sick to show themselves. No one wants to be reminded." Yet when Lillian died [on June 30], Diana said, "I've lost my most hated enemy."

DECEMBER 2, 1984 Alex Liberman: "To be truly creative, to create anything, you must demolish first." Trapped in the demolition, that was my life for a decade.

DECEMBER 8, 1984 Carl Bernstein brought Matthew Tynan, who is heart-breakingly his father, in the face and pallor and the way he holds his head and smiles—Ken's shy smile, before importance and self-certitude fixed that smile into a permanent skepticism and gloss on his own wit. Kathleen [Tynan, Matthew's mother] was born too late for what she is, and could have been any time pre-1939. Her abundant, flowing mane is her beauty. Her air of sexual languor, all the references are from eighteenth- and nineteenth-century hightum layabouts. She would have had dukes, a brilliant playwright, and assorted frogs and wogs. I see her by Gainsborough teeming through St. James Park in one of those glorious hats. Edward VII would have had a go, between Daisy Warwick and Mrs. Keppel. Surely Kathleen would have been a triple duchess. Now she, discreetly, has a French lover (moviemaker) and stacks up men lustily, even has got Mr. *Heartburn* to play nanny-tutor to Matthew.[6] She peers at one with those laughing, wide eyes, beneath that gorgeous tumult of Gainsborough hair. She is rather like marvelous poetry: I hear the sound, so beautiful that I forget to make sense of the words.

DECEMBER 9, 1984 I plunged into Virginia Woolf's final volume of letters, but not as rewarding to me as the diary. The bones are the same, but the letters

5. Dorothy Norman (1905–97), a wealthy advocate for causes of civil rights and India, had a long affair with the photographer Alfred Stieglitz, while he was married to Georgia O'Keeffe. "Dorothy said: 'Georgia O'Keeffe always hated me. There were always young girls around him—except I became *the* girl. But she was all over in 1929. She went to the Southwest—that was inevitable. She wanted adulation. She wanted to be the only one.'" *Journal*, March 28, 1982.
6. Critic Kenneth Tynan's second marriage was to Kathleen Halton (1937–95), early on a journalist and later her husband's biographer. Matthew was their son. Carl Bernstein (b. 1944) had won the *Washington Post* a Pulitzer Prize for his investigative reporting of the Watergate break-in. His ex-wife, Nora Ephron, based the plot of her novel *Heartburn* on their marriage.

are flashy. The diary, even though she seems aware that it will be read, one day, by others, is to and about the darling self. I am writing to be read, one day—I don't care when—but I am really writing to talk to myself. I am talking to my best friend, and I forget anyone else, forget future readers, am only concerned to question myself, interpret myself, re-create myself, my worlds and the denizens, monsters, angels (and combinations in each) in my jungles, to collect, save, and cherish, to confirm our being at least for a little moment longer . . . narcissistic, of course.

[Ballet critic] Dickie Buckle's been after Brigitta all week, filling in his Balanchine book. He remarks in the first eight chapters, which he gave her to read, something about Balanchine's "idiosyncratic sexual behavior." Brigitta: "I asked him, 'What do you mean?' 'Impotent,' Buckle said. Oh, Lucia Davidova, she always is such an intriguante. 'Who was married to him?' I asked."[7] Buckle went on about the evils of Bernard Taper and how he said Balanchine stood, unseen in the night, looking up at Brigitta's window. Brigitta: "I asked him, 'What are your sources? I don't believe that.' It's all those old Russian women. I asked George what he thought of Bernard Taper's book [*Balanchine: A Biography*]. He said, 'I never read that trash.' " Gossip and rumor become fact and history. She went on about Jamie Bernstein's mis-organized wedding and [her father] Lennie's speech and tears: "Everyone trembled at what he might say next. Adolph [Green] made a speech all about himself." That's that world—always all about themselves. They were singular, but they've lost their singularity—all except Betty [Comden].

DECEMBER 10, 1984 André and Chiquita [Gregory][8] gave a dinner for Nora and Herbert [Ross], which was historic because Steve Sondheim and Jerry Robbins talked to one another, the first time in years, and because Betty Bacall did not use one four-letter word all evening long and behaved softly and sweetly, not her usual imitation of a pistol-packing mama.[9] Steve on early influences: movies of the thirties and forties colored his whole life. Betty on wanting to "show" Hollywood, hoping to do so when she returned there in [the musical] *Applause*: "I was more frightened than at opening night in New York, and you know what? Nobody cared. No one even came." The desperate life of stars. Steve's ecstatic over his recently bought house and acres in Roxbury, things left him by [librettist] Burt Shevelove, and all of the things from his

7. Lucia Davidova, a Russian actress who came to New York with the Parisian vaudeville troupe Le Chauve-Souris, was a great friend of Balanchine's. Brigitta Lieberson had been married to him from 1938 to 1946.
8. André Gregory (b. 1934), an actor *(My Dinner with André)* and avant-garde director, was married to the filmmaker and experimental theater producer Mercedes "Chiquita" Gregory (1935?–92).
9. "The new Betty Bacall, inexplicable—a modulated voice and a kindliness that strikes terror in those of us who have known her for years." *Journal, December 30, 1984.*

mother Foxy's apartment: "She's in a nursing home." He intends to lead a very private life. The Gregorys put on the dawg: two maids in caps, aprons, and black uniforms.

Tanny LeClercq came to the Gregorys, brought by Jerry [Robbins] who wheeled her in and out.[10] She is now somewhat carved in a curious stone, all of her features elongated (mouth, eyes, hands) by age and suffering—no glimpse of the fragile, whimsical, droopy-handed ballerina (*La Valse, L'Après-midi d'un Faune*)—still her long flowing, straight, dark honey hair, but lusterless—that's it: She's lusterless. Jerry silver-bearded, jolly, full of giggles and chuckles, much more a chum. Nora gave no hint of America's greatest dramatic ballerina (Jerry did *The Cage* for her)—not a hint—but warm, lovable, and laughter all the way.

DECEMBER 15, 1984 *New York* magazine tells me that I'm too famous to be identified, which I don't believe. You become a part of the other end of the street, even when you find that the end you saw when very young isn't there anymore, its palaces gone, only echoes of its glamour heard. Still, even in that shoddy street which replaced it (was it always shoddy?), I am as insecure as any historic monument marked for preservation. I can, and doubtless am, being demolished without even knowing it. Perhaps that perpetual Manhattan roar is the bulldozer. Writing this has made me somewhat cheerful. I will read *Persuasion*.

DECEMBER 16, 1984 I was scribbling when Norman Mailer arrived. "Finish the sentence," he said. I did. "I love to write," I said. "I can see by the way you wrote that." Norman is as familiar to me as boys with whom I slept or, more accurately, fucked around with when I was young. It is his Jewishness—his constant self-examination, his humor—that I find so appealing, it immediately lends a genuine family-feeling between us. I carry on as if I have written a great mass of superb books.

Norman: "The apparatus is still as good as ever, but . . ." We were talking about desire. He had seen a girl—very blond, tall, slim. "I would have wanted to jump on her and fuck her," he said. "You know what it is with me?" I said. "It is my absence of regret that I regret. I am so surprised by that—that I feel no regret at not wanting to jump on anybody." We talked about being "over the hill," and about male exchanges I heard when I was young. "Oh, like being a 'comfortably married man,' " said Norman, ruefully, but smiling, as though he had never expected that state, with its implied obligations and restrictions, but taking a quiet pleasure in it all. Then, as always, Norman talked money. How hard he must work to pay everything he is obligated to pay. "We'll be at home with all the children," he said about the holidays. So, here we have Norman,

10. The ballerina Tanaquil LeClercq (1929–2000) had been married (1952–69) to Balan-chine, who created roles for her in two dozen ballets before polio crippled her in 1956.

the former wild boy of letters, a paterfamilias, a benign older man, a responsible citizen doing good works.

DECEMBER 24, 1984  What a fortunate man I am. What a strange, disturbing year this has been. The Condé Nast part of what I am doing isn't, of course, satisfying. I am no longer doing what I alone do—or did (I must grow accustomed to the past tense)—superbly. I was uniquely an editor and a specialized *Vogue* (a symbol) writer. Now I am selling what I used to give away (Mae West): advice, certain catalytic tasks, booking this and that, and I am getting more money for this—ironic.

DECEMBER 26, 1984  What a circle of odious people surround Anne, our heroine in *Persuasion*. How they serve Miss Austen, who sitting at her dining-room table was visibly, I am sure, A Living Reproach. As I read, I see our Judith Martin, [etiquette columnist] "Miss Manners." Is she, then, our Jane Austen? She is more Jane Austen than Emily Post. How Miss Austen strikes flint on stone, and how sparks fly, sometimes igniting small, astonishing fires, sometimes bursting into conflagration. "He had an affectionate heart. He must love someone." "Of course, they had fallen in love over poetry." Just random examples. The amusement and shock of joy comes from how she views commonsensically, from some sharp eminence. She startles realistically—there's the link with Judith. The view from the same sharp eminence. The comedy comes from Miss Austen's microscopic scrutiny of vanities, prides, aggrandizements, pretensions.

DECEMBER 30, 1984  At lunch on Friday we played "Who are Proust's characters today?" That's how we discovered that Jeremy [Irons] had never read Proust. "I never had time," he pleaded, this Swann of a different color, this bird that really never went.[11] Then Marisa Berenson [actress and model] at Joan Buck's (and memories of that long-ago lunch I gave her grandmother Schiaparelli, after Carmel died). Marisa: "I begged to play Odette, but he insisted on the Duchess de Guermantes, so I said no." Anna [Wintour], behind her hair and perhaps shy, but certainly withdrawn and not deep, but dark.[12]

DECEMBER 31, 1984  A grand champagne wallow, the house intensely alive, and memories of bygone New Year's Eves: at Ruth [Ford] and Zachary Scott's in the Dakota (Cecil [Beaton] and [actor] Laurence Harvey coupling in the courtyard, and Rex Harrison making spaghetti); at the Strasbergs'; at the

11. The actor Jeremy Irons had recently played Proust's character Charles Swann in the film *Swann in Love.*
12. Anna Wintour was creative director at *Vogue* (1983–86) while Grace Mirabella was editor in chief.

Hirschfelds'; at Woody Allen's; at Kate and Zero Mostel's in London (so still, only the clangor of bells); with Marlene at Maria and Bill Riva's (jumping off chairs, pouring hot lead [to foretell fortunes], eating the raised, apricot-filled doughnuts Marlene made); at the Van Vechtens'; at Sol Hurok's (the most glamorous, on the St. Regis Roof—star-splattered, frost-laced, mysterious and luxurious. How beautiful and elegant you always felt in that pink room). We did the rounds. Has New Year's Day calling gone too? On New Year's Day we would hold open house: To the last one Betsy Thurman brought the entire cast and crew, twenty-one, of the Chekhov Theatre. The rituals depart. There seem to be no new rituals to replace the vanished. I was delighted to hear people blowing horns in the street.

JANUARY 1, 1985  Lily Tomlin acts out a thought, not completing a sentence, but acting it out, trying it out as one of her characters, looking at one for corroboration. Her silken darkness and appealing, coltish legginess has a kinship to Rut.[13]

I dipped into [Byron's] *Don Juan*, who immediately leaped off the page and socked me straight between the eyes: "Dead scandals form good subjects for dissection" (*Canto I, XXXI*). I dipped into V. Woolf's letters and she waved sodden hankies, [her nephew] Julian Bell having been killed in Spain. All of this life and lifelessness in that 1937 July when Richard and I were in London. I dipped into her *Moment of Being* and was told of the impossibility of capturing her mother—her gestures, her wit—on the page. I know this feeling. I think of Diana [Trilling] saying yesterday, "I sit here and think: Why should I write this book, why?" I dipped into Vita Sackville-West's love letters to Virginia Woolf and V.W.'s letters to Vita and somehow this glimmers, glows, bursts into sparks, intimations of flame. The forest will burn. Schoolgirlish. Little cat feet. But the courtship, courtliness, and courtesy is there. Life is there to reassure us.

JANUARY 5, 1985  Dorothy Norman called: "They want me to do a book of Indira [Gandhi]'s letters." I tell her she must do it, because how else will anyone know that Indira was human? Dorothy read one or two of her annotations: "But I can't do the introduction, because people will think I'm prejudiced." I think of Indira, smiling while the Pandit girls giggled, sitting on the floor of the back parlor in our old house. Dorothy goes on confirming to herself that only she can make the world know Indira, the individual behind the public figure. Finally she gets me to say that I will be her "sounding board."[14]

---

13. Leo had become friendly with comic actress Lily Tomlin (b. 1939) after an introduction in the early eighties by her producers Paula and Charles Bowden.
14. Norman's book was published later in 1985 as *Indira Gandhi: Letters to an American Friend, 1950–1984*.

JANUARY 6, 1985 I am plunging through, with immense pleasure, Victor Hugo's *Things Seen*, his journalism. I plucked this book from the shelf because Balzac was too high for me to reach. Such verve and gusto of observation, so detailed, such a joy in telling, hot steam rises from the pages. Talleyrand's brain thrown down the sewer of the rue Saint-Florentin; Napoleon's great, golden-bee strewn catafalque moving through the hard sunlight; Louis XVI in his white garments mounting the guillotine. . . . Oh—the irony, the wit, the observation, the breadth of the mind behind this seeing!

JANUARY 10, 1985 In today's *Times*, a photograph of youngsters guiding sheep along 104th Street in an annual Three Kings Day parade. There, when I was a little boy, I saw the rabbis and congregation joyfully dancing the Torahs to their holy ark on Simchas Torah. So for some Puerto Rican youngster today is the beginning of his street, at whose end I am. I wonder if this little boy has the same vision I had: a vision of a golden world, a world of miracle lights, of gorgeousness. My dream world is a lost one, but his dream world is to come. I know that mine, for all its "real" glitter and glamour, was false as his.

I am reminded of [photographer] Bill Caskey, Christopher Isherwood's chum, when he was stopping at Mary Lou and T's in Siasconset. They came every day to us at the Hagerdorn house, outside of Quidnit. Hadn't Caskey been in jail? He, in a tattered white shirt, was standing on the edge of our cliff, peering out over the sands, out across the tumbling Atlantic. "You can really see Portugal!" I thought, standing next to him in my heavy, blue linen pants. And he murmured: "Honey, my sables are dyed in shit."

Yesterday, Bill Maxwell came to lunch at the Four Seasons.[15] "You know everything about me," he said. "I've written it all." "Almost all," I said. "There are one or two things . . . but I don't really care. . . . " We have laughing, loving, mutually nourishing times, each of us making the other feel whole and rich in experience and exceptional. Bill said, "I wanted to bring you a present, so I typed out this early poem of Louise Bogan's. I am reading the biography in proof. It's always (what was his word?) to find out things you didn't know about someone you know very well. She had a love affair."

We talked of death (always) and sickness and aging and books and writing and one another and love and just being. . . . We are the best mutual appreciation society in the world. Bill has a passion for naps: "I jump into my pajamas," he says. He is so very young—a young man—seems so vulnerable and spiritual. And he has sensuality. Is this the wick of the lamp? He gives such a pure light. Actually, he has the purity of the good-worldly, by which I mean that of goodness beyond cynicism, indeed having assimilated cynicism.

After lunch [today] at Mortimer's, a moment of pure love and sweet-sad

15. The novelist and short-story writer William Maxwell (1908–2000) edited fiction at *The New Yorker* for forty years.

pleasure. The tape played "Time on My Hands"; my guests had gone; I sat at table, having paid the bill; Puss stood by—just a moment, as pure and uncomplicated as a drop of honey. "What is it?" Puss asked. "Nothing," I murmured.

JANUARY 22, 1985  The Reagans cannot fail. They embody every element of the American drama: a supposed idealism tempered by the traditional. I am sure the Reagans feel that they are broadminded. They are intolerantly broadminded, the middle-American way. Visually, they are everything America wants—dancing a few steps together, she in her visibly expensive garb, he slicked up—the perfect couple. The boy and girl whom the yearbook foretold would definitely be the most likely to succeed. "If you can get away with it, okay."

Alex and I had lunch today at the Four Seasons. Alex's ennui is a result of his having used up so much. He canceled his exhibit. "I don't need all that fuss and having at me. I am always aimed at. Why should I expose myself? I don't need the money. . . . I'm tied in. I would love to go somewhere, but Tatiana gets exhausted."

JANUARY 28, 1985  Last night Puss at last told me that Martin [Goldwasser] has an incurable brain tumor. I rang [his wife] Electa ("Lucky"), and she calmly told me that he has three months to a year. He is my favorite cousin. I have always loved him. Of all the cousinage, he is the one with whom, when we were young, I was most, in every sense, intimate.

FEBRUARY 7, 1985  Newtown High School was a remarkable incubator, how remarkable none of us realized until later. We lived by Untermeyer [*Modern American Poetry*] and Dickinson and poets. The center of our lives was literature and drama and high life and passions requited and unrequited. Our little coterie lived exciting times—the twenties American literary scene. Everything from [Edgar Lee Masters's] *Domesday Book* and Amy Lowell to Lady Murasaki. All of the poets—Sappho to Edna Saint Vincent Millay and Elinor Wylie, our great passion. And fiction—the Russians, the Germans, Gide— everything—even Pandit Istrati, Symonds and Symons,[16] [John Livingston Lowes's] *Convention and Revolt in Poetry*, Burckhardt, Pater, Taine, Maurois . . . and Proust.

Each day was packed with discoveries. We all wrote verse. We lived for it, writing in strict forms, with a passion for sonnets. We fought to set verse free, not yet realizing that it had already been freed by Amy Lowell. We wrote and

---

16. The British critic John Addington Symonds (1840–93) was among the first to write historical studies of homosexuality, but Leo and his friends were undoubtedly reading his *Renaissance in Italy* and his biographies of Whitman and Shelley. Arthur Symons (1865–1945) was a British poet and essayist who wrote on Baudelaire and Rossetti, among others.

wrote and talked and talked and laughed a lot and were superb in our electiveness. We felt we led "romantic" lives—so many Byrons and Shelleys, longing for Europe, thinking we were the crème de la crème and would always be that. And of course we developed Passions and held Riots and made fun of one another.[17] We had no money, but we had everything else, including the future. Books showed us that there were others like us. From the women poets we learned self-mockery and irony. We grew in a time when anything was possible, anything comprehensible—not like today when the world has gone beyond possibility and comprehension.

FEBRUARY 9, 1985 Sauk Center, Minnesota, celebrates Sinclair Lewis in precisely the ways he derided in *Main Street*. The television cameras brush his gravestone clean of snow: "To get a clearer picture." I remember my long—well, he was long, I didn't dare intrude—telephone session with Red Lewis. He was kind, soft-voiced, incessant, asked questions about me and the young, talked about B [Brion Gysin] (his "amanuensis") and said that although he could not write a book for my series ("Highways of the World"), he was interested.[18] He called frequently to give advice, egg on. He seemed lonely, a man with endless unfilled time.

FEBRUARY 11, 1985 Our Philco radio, the Gothic box through which poured The A & P Gypsies [studio orchestra], *Myrt & Marge, Lux Radio Theater*, Bing Crosby, Morton Downey, Kate Smith (her voice as rotund as her person, and as farm-fresh as the eggs sent in silver-ridged containers by Uncle Harry and Aunt Ida [Goldwasser] from Lakewood, New Jersey), the Boswell Sisters, *Amos and Andy* . . . At seven from each house on the block the dulcet tones of [*Amos and Andy's*] Madame Queen poured under the sound of wind in the trees . . . [Metropolitan Opera] concertmaster Svedrofsky had, in season, already left his pale lavender simulated-brocade panels. Oh, their walls were rich in make-believe (sconces—we called them wall brackets), and they flew high, the Svedrofskys and the Curiels, and crashed with the Crash. Sadie Curiel was made of disproportionate parts of choler, rage, and sweet neighborliness. She sued me when I was fourteen.[19] . . . So back to the Gothic box . . . on to [bandleader] Vincent Lopez and all those bands, Cab Calloway with "Minnie, the Moocher"—did we know this was about dope? No! And then there was Saturday afternoon and "This is Milton Cross from the Metropolitan Opera House in New York." Oh Life! Oh Art! Oh Glamour!

17. Leo had put the name "The Rioters" on this group of high school friends.
18. In the early forties, Leo had signed with the publishers Reynal & Hitchcock to edit a series of books on different highways and their regional histories. When Curtice Hitchcock died in 1946, the project apparently ended.
19. Sadie Curiel, a friend of Leo's mother in Jackson Heights, was a cellist and sister of the Met's concertmaster, Michael Svedrofsky. No one in the family recalls why she sued Leo.

FEBRUARY 13, 1985 The *Times* tells why Si is so interested in talk at *The New Yorker:* He's offered $26 million [for it]. Natacha Stewart [a staff writer] reports gloom there. I remember when Condé Nast bought Street & Smith [in 1959], and Mrs. Blackwell said: "Can't you please say something funny, Leo, to cheer us?"

Long on the blower with Kennedy [Fraser, fashion writer]—everyone is frightened and uneasy at *The New Yorker.* Si came to ask what I had heard. I told him. He had a "What will be, will be" attitude.

Eleanor [Lambert, fashion publicist] rang to say that I am on the International Best Dressed List again. This is the best joke ever! I have been worse dressed this year than ever before in my life.

FEBRUARY 15, 1985 Last night to New York City Ballet to see Jerry [Robbins]'s new work. Clumsy programming, but a packed house delighted. Brahms's "Liebeslieder Waltzes" (Balanchine [1960]) were abstractions of sensuality, intimacy—distillations—exquisite mimicry of passions, youth, and gentility—all very beautiful, plus Karinska's magical dresses. Then Jerry's new, but so dated, work [*Eight Lines*]—frenetic, itchy. I liked how he transfixed the [Steve] Reich rhythms. I liked the primary colors. I liked it very much—until I saw the Balanchine-Stravinsky that came after. That made Jerry's opus look makeshift, too influenced both by George and by Jerry himself—a not-too-good, serious ballet in a lavish Broadway musical, the kind so breathtaking, so evolutionary—in the late twenties and the thirties.

FEBRUARY 16, 1985 Last night at the opening of the films of the Weimar Republic festival at the Museum of Modern Art, Dolly [Haas Hirschfeld]'s *Scampolo, ein Kind der Strasse.* An early Billy Wilder script [1932] and slight. Dolly enchanting, because of her perky face, her beautiful skin, her smile, her innocence, and her naturalness. That girl not far removed: "I was never as young as I looked," she told the enthralled audience. Today's Dolly had a greater success than her movie's. She played straight from her heart, sometimes reminding me of Jessie Matthews.[20]

No film made in Germany before Hitler took over can be a completely joyous experience. We look at that Berlin, at those people, and sometimes we know their awful individual fates; always we are obsessed with their horrible futures. Dolly wore a protective, wide-brimmed hat, her beautiful furled and knotted red hair, a black velvet suit, a blouse of delicately patterned lace, high-necked, the whole somehow *echt alte* [true old-time] German. She talked wonderfully in that clear, resounding, almost unnuanced voice, the most important sound in our lives while she spoke, the voice and the personality obliterated MoMA, this time, this place.

---

20. The actress, dancer, and singer Jessie Matthews (1907–81) was a major star of London musical revues and prewar British films.

She was funny: "When Billy Wilder was in a Hollywood success, he thought his mother still in Vienna would realize this was her son's name on the screen [and not be pleased], so he wrote to her: 'Momma, I have to change my name, here in America. Now when you see Thornton Wilder on the screen, that's me.' " She was deeply touching: "Share with me a moment of silence in memory of those colleagues." She carried the jammed house with her, nothing mawkish, as pure as her [screen] performance—straight from the heart. The audience held the remnants of the refugee community and spooky movie-obsessed creatures looking for "stars."

Dolly told about the glorious theater, movie, and culturally thriving life of Berlin, about the first night of *The Blue Angel* [in 1930] and the actress who said it had been written for her by Heinrich Mann and then never said another word after it began. Then, the most important: "A year after, Max Hansen, the greatest operetta star in German, beloved by millions, and I stood on a stage in Berlin, bowing to tremendous applause. Suddenly there were shouts and loud, dreadful words, things thrown. I looked down and there were rotten vegetables and fruit. I looked at that audience and I thought: 'I have lost my respect for my audience. I must leave.' And I did."[21] This was the most significant statement. I thought: I have lost my respect for the people of this country, who elected that man [Reagan] and his scum to power. Where should we go? I who have been in love with America as only a first-generation Jew can be?

I feel that, in a sense, Dolly's life has been wasted. She had so much to give and our theater did not permit her to give it. She has had a difficult life, although good, I think with Al [Hirschfeld], and she has been a wonderful wife. But there is something implacable, forceful about Dolly, like a room already prepared—permanently clean in its most hidden places. I see no shadows.

Last night, helping to dry supper dishes, I tripped and fell down. I did not hurt myself, but frightened Gray, who has too much to bear with my ills and falls—and then I could not be got up. So I slid across the kitchen floor on my bottom, as I had when a small child, saying, "I haven't felt this way since I was five." Gray was too concerned to be amused: "So we return to childhood. Is this, then, second childhood?" We tried to get me up by my clinging to the teacher's chair in the pantry, but that didn't work. Finally, Gray called [neighbor] Jerry Berger, and he, with one giant heave, raised me. None of this was funny, but I tried, unsuccessfully, to lighten the gloom. Gray said, "I don't know how to cope anymore."

I now know that the necessary is letting go, in the sense of letting things, people, places, even works of art or nature go. Those can all be there, in house so to

21. After performing, in 1933, a cabaret act portraying Hitler as homosexual, Max Hansen (1897–1961) fled to Scandinavia, eventually settling in Denmark, where he continued to be a popular singer and movie actor.

speak, and already let go. I do not mean to give up, but to let go—always retaining in one's skin the quintessential beauty, terror, irony, form, discipline of the let-go. I am sad about the necessity of let-go, but I recognize that age must, in order to be a fulfillment, bring wisdom, and let-go is a particle of wisdom.

FEBRUARY 18, 1985   I have made myths to make myself interesting. I made up all sorts of life: moving my family onto Fifth Avenue; inventing a maid being burned to death and Grandpa making us look at the charred remains, saying, "She played with matches." All sorts of myths—Estelle [Klein, a cousin] coming home from tea dance in the Palm Court, crying, "Children! Children! Promise me you won't do that. You will have lived too soon!" and Grandpa punishing her by locking her in her room and taking all of her clothes away, leaving her stark naked. This was actually one of his punishments, when Momma and the uncles were little.

My mythmaking entranced Anaïs and Rut and Ela. All of my myths were grounded in some scrap of fact, some scrap that had happened or that I had heard as I hid under tables eavesdropping on grown-ups. Mostly Yiddish was spoken, only Yiddish by Grandpa and most of his generation (also some Russian, Polish, Romanian, Hungarian), but the younger generation and the great-uncles (Grandpa's brothers) all spoke various kinds of English with heavy Yiddish accents. The young, of course, were slangy and tried not to speak Yiddish, but had to with Grandpa and his chums. I spoke a mixture, and finally, at a public school on 103rd Street, won a purple pencil box for writing a "perfect" sentence, in Miss Cohen's class. (I cleaned her shoes with the costumes from the Victory Pageant. That was an honor.) I was always scribbling, even before I could write. I did not, consciously, want to be a writer: I just wrote. Not wanting to be, but being. And I have worked on this all my life, even when I seemed to be diverted into other forays and byways, writing has always been the highway.

Poppa and his "mistress." Is any of this myth? Maybe that Poppa slept with her. He probably *slept*, really snoring sleep. He went to see her in the afternoon. Momma did explain about a fur coat: "You father's friend gave it to me—a lovely woman." Momma was, I could see and hear, relieved. "And, anyway, she's Catholic," said Momma in a voice which meant: So it doesn't count.

FEBRUARY 22, 1985   I recall dinner on a bridge table at Fania [Van Vechten]'s when Judith Anderson came, gone quite blond from being Damed. Fania brought out a box and said, "Here are all my letters from Gene [O'Neill]." Then she read some long passages. She read in a tone that clearly was telling "Judy" that Gene had had a passion for Fania. So sucks to Judy, who—I gathered—had had "something" with Gene. After which I took Judy to the San Remo, where she stayed in [photographer] Gjon Mili's apartment. ("Raw meat!" she said to Puss, after her *Medea*, as she stood in a bloodstained apron in that little kitchen.) But on the way, I asked her if she didn't want to come to Lincoln's, where he was celebrating the Sitwells. Judy said yes. So I took her, and there in Lincoln's back parlor, surrounded by Manhattan crème de la crème, catamites, and dancers, was Edith—turbaned, Byzantine-jeweled, an icon in black "glasses"—enthroned. Osbert on a low stool beside her. I took Dame Judy up to Dame Doctor Sitwell (Edith was most particular about Dame *and* Doctor). Dame Judy, in *her* black glasses, made a deep court reverence, and as she came up, I clearly saw Dame Edith reflected in Dame Judy's glasses and Dame Judy in Dame Doctor Edith's. They never said one word to each other all evening, but Dame Judy was surrounded by the young until we left.[22]

FEBRUARY 23, 1985  The Arnold Glimchers [he an art dealer] gave a party for Louise Nevelson on her eighty-fifth in the Rauschenberg room of the Four Seasons. The difference between a dinner at the Guggenheim for Helen [Frankenthaler] and Louise's: Helen's was a museum-corporate sponsored "public" event, in the well of Frank Lloyd Wright's revenge on art. Louise's was a private party, a genuine celebration of an amazing, original, incredibly individual woman. Helen—minor, all narcissism. Louise has made her ego into important, if perhaps minor, art. Helen is a follower; Louise leads. Louise imposes order on chaos; her work is a portrait of my "interior." At Louise's I saw no critics, save [architecture's] Paul Goldberger. I saw friends, collectors who seem friends. This was in every sense a private party, with loving tributes, very pretty with calla lilies, tuberoses, black and white settings, at most seventy-five "intimates," not black-tie (like Helen's), nothing phony, no corporate and museum self-tributes, no Louise self-praise and aggrandizements.

And surprise: This was not the flamboyant Louise—no heavy, fake eyelashes (no eyelashes at all—constant application of those have done away with Louise's own over the years), but eyeliner, no makeup. Her skin was soft as chamois when I kissed her. She wore an old black rabbit-fur pointy hat, a Ralph Lauren–looking little figured faded China-red blouse, gray wool jacket and skirt, long of course, and her unimportant fur coat throughout the evening. She was her basic self. Not that the Louise in gorgeous and outré drag, the Marchesa Casati Louise, isn't herself, but this was the Louise out of Maine, who has worked inexhaustibly for decades. At eighty-five, she, without trappings, is more monumental than her sculptures, more playful. Her huge eyes are undimmed: She sees everything. Her tongue is as dry and as tart as a northern apple.

---

22. Leo's memory may have made Judith Anderson a dame prematurely. These events probably occurred in the fifties, but she was made a Dame Commander of the British Empire in 1960.

FEBRUARY 25, 1985   Saturday night we went to dine with George and Jennifer Lang [restaurateurs and writers], and my wish was granted—[soprano] Eva Marton and her husband Zoltán, a surgeon, sat there. I think her the greatest of today's divas. She is commanding in figure, not fat, but imposing. In dress, diva taste—a pink angora "evening" sweater, beaded somewhat and touched by marabou but somehow suitable, unnoticeable jewels, dark hair, not a beauty but beautiful, her skin the texture of a damask rose, and large, lustrous eyes. Her atmosphere very Hungarian. She is forty; Zoltán is forty-six, but in appearance is older. She talks with a profuse Hungarian accent, slipping into Hungarian and German, in and out of English rapidly with porpoise fluidity (recalled my years with Hungarians).

Eva Marton is the most intellectual diva I have met. We spent the evening almost *à deux.* I felt encased with her. My having no peripheral vision helped. She is so enmeshed in her work. She prepares by reading everything. I have never known any diva to do this. She has been working on the "Four Last Songs" [of Richard Strauss], reading Hesse, finding her own vision of them: "They are about death, but everyone thinks them negative. I find them positive. They are about acceptance." She told me about them in enormous detail, singing softly. Then she talked to me about *Salome,* citing dates of Wilde's productions, and about the significance of it: "Salome was never loved by anybody—anybody. She is not sensual. She is a virgin. She is unloved. She wants purity from Jokanaan." Eva Marton's movements are all serene. She knows who she is, where she is going. She is filled with grace, love, and reflectiveness. She knows what she can do: "I will never sing the Marschallin—not for me." But she will do Lady Macbeth at the Met. "Make your voice ugly—like Verdi wanted it." "Yes . . ." she said. All placid, deeply felt. She has lovely humor. She said: "I never felt I was a star until *Die Frau ohne Schatten,* Act II, at the Metropolitan Opera. Here there's generosity. We have everything in Hamburg: a beautiful house, a swimming pool, I sing my parts—but if you are not German in Germany you are not really important. Here in America you are a STAR."

FEBRUARY 26, 1985   I remembered that [cardiologist] Dr. Freiman is Valentina [Schlee]'s doctor, so I asked him whether he knew how oddly she was behaving.[23] He said, "Oh—I had to put her away to keep her from harming herself. I put her up in Westchester. It was pretty bad. She didn't want to go, we had a straitjacket there. Finally she went, and as she walked out of her apartment, she said, 'I want to die in my bed.' " One night she had opened her great cupboard and taken all of her beautiful clothes out, piled them in the center of

---

23. Ten days before, Leo's friend Lin Tissot had told of going to dine at Valentina's and finding her apartment helter-skelter and Valentina virtually "in rags." She spoke directly to Tissot only once, when their desolate dinner was finished, saying, "I don't care."

the room, on the floor, and looked in her big looking glass and said, "Who is that?" I rang Lin [Tissot], and he said that she always did this stealthily at night, tearing everything apart.

I thought of Valentina in her glory, proudly striding down the aisle at the Shubert in a huge envelopment of heavy, silver-gray faille, only her eyes peering through eyeholes, the night of the Lunts' opening in *Amphytrion 38*. . . . And Valentina at the Gunthers' standing guard over Garbo, reclining on a sofa, one satin-shod foot tapping the air, dangling from masses of tiny black lace ruffles. . . . And Valentina in Venice . . . in her Fifth Avenue shop . . . in her Sixty-ninth Street building . . . in her own beautiful apartment . . . so many memories. Valentina climbed by her trade, as a Russian refugee who came with the Chauve-Souris and her exotic fled-the-revolution background, and could have been a duchess—who knew? Now, here she is at the other end of her street.

MARCH 2, 1985  I rang, my weekly call, to [Cousin] Marty. He answered, having difficulty completing thoughts with the appropriate words. "I want you!" he said. "You can have me," I said, three thousand miles away, and we both laughed, both very young.

Now, sitting here, on the edge of my bed, in this deep red and pale violet room that I try not to love (I know the danger of loving rooms and houses— even more dangerous than loving people). . . . I see the graveyard and the family plot (Molke's grave is covered with poison ivy!), and, at last, I feel what I did not feel as I stood there, shutting my eyes against harsh sunlight.[24]

MARCH 8, 1985  Brigitta on the blower around eightish. "You're the only one I know I can talk to so early in the morning." She's been in tears, unexpected floods, as she sits writing. She feels keenly that the fascinating life she had with Goddard no longer exists: "But surely it exists somewhere." I assured her that it doesn't. Brigitta is weeping at the low time in which we find ourselves, the airport and *Dynasty* world with costly emptiness at the top and attrition everywhere.

The Old Order Changes Department: Si rang at 3:45 p.m. "Hear anything about *The New Yorker*?" he asked. I knew before he said, since he sounded like a gleeful twelve-year-old: "The Board voted unanimously to sell it to us." "Should I congratulate you?" "I don't know," he said. "Well, mazeltov," I said. We laughed a lot.

MARCH 9, 1985  If the *Times* is accurate, [editor William] Shawn has behaved badly, specially to the staff he cherishes. Why hasn't he gracefully made this

---

24. Leo and Gray had attended the unveiling of the gravestone of Leo's sister-in-law, Ellen Greenfield (1925–84). Molke Goldwasser was Leo's great-aunt.

inevitable transition easier for his staff? [Board chairman] Peter Fleischmann, dying of cancer, must want to make his family secure. The only possibility: a huge sum of money and sign this. Shawn, seventy-seven or seventy-eight, holds his chair in a vise. I understand this, but surely he could not expect the board of *The New Yorker* to withhold this prodigious sale, to permit him to—what? How could he match $142 million? Si has got himself some of America's glories, but also a nest of seething neurotics, making fantastical demands. I do not think that Si plans to touch *The New Yorker* editorially. He reveres it. But surely he will seek to improve business. The magazine has become increasingly dull. Shawn rousing up his staff is a wretched, stupid business. Natacha [Stewart] told tales of weeping in the corridors of the magazine, of mourning, gloom, apprehension.

Si acquired Random, Knopf, *The New Yorker*, and doesn't have to use any of it to climb. He is where he and Victoria want to be.[25] Si is no Taubman, Trump, Helmsley, or Gutfreund. Si and Victoria are the least vulgar of today's rich people, as are Donald and Sue [Newhouse]. No flamboyance here—art, books, music, movies, and power, but a different power than the *Dynasty* ilk. Sam Newhouse bought for the joy of buying, building an empire. This, I feel, is part of Si's drive, the passion to own symbols of culture.

MARCH 18, 1985    John Simon's homophobic review of *The Octette Bridge Club* and his remark [leaving the theater] after *Anatol* (about his hoping that AIDS kills off all homosexuals) produces a powerful column in Sunday's *Daily News* from Liz Smith. I liked John Simon, but I would cut him now.[26] If I had had a neighbor I liked and discovered that that neighbor was a Nazi, would I go on liking him? I did enjoy John; he is the most brilliant of the [theater] critics. (Stanley Kauffmann is less; Brendan Gill is not educated as broadly and deeply as John.) But John has in him the rage of certain leaders of the French Revolution. He has interested me: his tears over [Alexandra] Isles, who came and went in his life; his attacks on physical appearances (going too far, but these were on individuals—Liza Minnelli's face, Zoe Caldwell's breasts). Now he has become, or at last he has emerged, mad with homophobia, and I will not be a friend to anyone who says, in effect: "Some of my best friends are queens."

MARCH 30, 1985    I never had a conversation with my father. We never talked about anything, not even sex, but he has become more a person since his death, many years ago, than he was while alive in my life.

Now I look at Puss and my heart faints and is fearful and I hold him as

---

25. Victoria Benedict de Ramel Newhouse (b. 1938), architectural critic and historian, had married S. I. Newhouse, Jr., in 1973.
26. In *New York* magazine, critic Simon had called *The Octette Bridge Club* "faggot nonsense."

tightly as possible, even when I do not do this physically. I look at him and he is the total, he is the pure self that is my being.

APRIL 12, 1985  My stockings are now lavender, to lure spring hopefully. I should write about support hose and what they mean—and what trusses meant. Age, when I was very young, was symbolized by the truss (now obsolete?). The truss could be, when inverted, a headdress for An Invader from the North.

Yesterday, late in the day, I felt that I had been Struck a Mortal Blow. (How the books I loved when I was young—and still love—cling. *Robin Hood* and the saga of the Round Table.) We were told that, indeed, Saint Thomas [church] is going to build its choir school back of us, where a theater now stands, and that the structure will be twelve stories high. After that, Puss burst into such rage— a devastating, destructive, fruitless rage. The following hours I felt poleaxed, bludgeoned. What to do? Where could we go—not only during the blasting, but if we were entombed—the school at our windows, all light and sky and sun gone?

Part of me considers: Have all of these years been worth all of the anguish? I know that the answer is yes, but I also know that the price of my weakness is Puss stopping his unique, beautiful work. That is what he had to give, but instead he has thrown it away and put me in its place. Kirk [Askew] knew that this would happen. ("If you stay together, Gray will eventually not draw a stroke.") Question: Has Puss been a happier person this way, or would he have been happier, more fulfilled, if he had been true to his genius? I think the latter. This is the bitterness.

APRIL 13, 1985  Long discussion with Stephen, Puss, Lloyd [Williams], and Joel [Kaye][27] about AIDS and how this will bring (and is bringing) social changes. In the homosexual world: celibacy, courtship, limited sexual encounters and practices, terror . . . In the heterosexual world: bewilderment, terror. I said, "When AIDS hits the heterosexual world that will be the time of devastating backlash at the homosexual world." The signs are already visible: The selfish, I-don't-care fringe of the homosexual world and the already infected who want to revenge themselves by taking with them "sacrifices" are identical with their long-ago forebears in the Black Death. Thus far we have, to the best of my knowledge, no Poe ["Masque of the Red Death"]. We have would-be Wildes, Cowards, even Sheridans and Neil Simons. This plague, if it is a plague—draws closer and closer. Theater pieces try to show it; fiction, television, movies lag. I heard of the roommate [lover] who, at the service for his dead chum, thanked those who had come to see him and specially those who had touched him.

27. The fashion designer Lloyd Williams and his lover Joel Kaye, son of the Russian Tea Room founder Sidney Kaye, were frequent companions of Leo and Gray from the early seventies. Kaye became co-executor of Leo's estate.

APRIL 14, 1985 Van Johnson—huge, extrovert, full of asides ("I'm not circumcised!"), campy ("I was married and have three children, two adopted. I really want to marry George Hearn!"[28]), taking the uneaten fish for his cats—seems to ENJOY! He is an unceasing flow of anecdotes. "I hate nostalgia!" he said, but when asked by one of the guests what "was the most glamorous," he answers before she finishes the question: "Carole Lombard and Clark Gable coming into the commissary at MGM for lunch. That was when we all wore suits and ties to work. They glowed. She was so beautiful and he was so—oh—electric. He came up to us kids at our table and we all nearly died." Van is a molting, enormous tassel flower at that sun-dazzling moment when the corn is higher than houses and winds sweep the sky pristine blue. Everything he does or says is on tippy-toes. I think that he must be compulsively neat.

Miltie Goldman told me that [British comedian] Hermione Gingold, thinking that she is dying, asked for a rabbi to come. He did, and she seemed to be consoled or resigned. When she talked to Miltie, he mentioned that *Gigi* was being done in London. Suddenly, the old warrior Hermione was there—breathing fury: "*Gigi!* And they didn't ask me! Why didn't they ask me!?" This spirit never dies first. Does it after the body dies?

NOTE: Leo and Gray went to Los Angeles to do a feature on the house that had been George Cukor's and to scout other houses for possible stories in *House & Garden.*

JOURNAL • APRIL 22, 1985 • LOS ANGELES The DeMille house—the shock of its plain ugliness; the contrast between his grandiose, opulent, epic films and this almost colorless austerity. "Mrs. DeMille liked only pink flowers in the house," said the eighty-five-year-old housekeeper. "She didn't like to see them being cut or carried in. She just liked them to be here." A *Cherry Orchard* feeling in the dusty velour and endless memorabilia. Which were the movie props and which the real furniture?

Then George Cukor's house, still intact (flowers in vases), but haunted—specially in his office, beginning in the passage where all of the photos are huge—so sad—tears—such mementos of Cecil [Beaton] and everyone in their glory—a sad photo of Marilyn Monroe. George's bedroom, so unloved. A house with no center.

APRIL 26, 1985 In Los Angeles artworks are purchased according to reputation and sized according to income. The rooms are like hotel rooms waiting for visitors to stop a day or two.

Gray: "The tendency now is to have a gallery, not just to have things hanging around. [Talent agent Michael] Ovitz has one; [television producer] Doug Cramer will. They all have their little collections of primitive art, authenticity

28. Johnson was playing opposite Hearn in the musical *La Cage aux Folles.*

depending on the people who are buying it for them. They all have their little collections of classics, 'Old Masters'—like Jack Youngerman and [James] Rosenquist, and all the tiny Rothkos! I didn't know that Rothko painted such tiny paintings—like bathroom windows. Then there's always an Agnes Martin. She doesn't interfere with the decor or the upholstery—a decorator's dream. They always have the painter on the wall that they have just walked into a gallery and discovered—usually local—and 'just bought,' and he just happened to turn out to be worth a fortune, usually touted to fame by a dealer. They can't believe their luck, 'getting in on the ground floor.' Occasionally there's a Monet, some hope for a Léger. 'Well, if I found a Mondrian I wouldn't turn that down,' a collector who'd plunged in four years ago said. They say: 'This is an old [Frank] Stella,' which means it's got to be two or three years old, and add apologetically, with a tone of I-don't-really-care-I'm-courageous, 'Not his latest.' Sitting around on coffee tables, the latest art books. Then—this has been forever—the painting that covers the movie screen. I haven't see any profoundly felt eccentricity, anything that isn't safe or negotiable—only at Nora and Herbie's."

The closest thing to Old Masters I've seen on this trip are [producer] Ray Stark's sculptures (genuinely knowledgeable, he invited us to stroke them); Edie Goetz's superb collection (second- or third-generation Hollywood—thirties prime), and of course the Ganzes.[29]

APRIL 28, 1985   We're on the way to Palos Verdes and Elin Vanderlip's [Friends of French Art] "do" for the French Nobility, when Eleanore [Phillips], one of the most worldly people I have ever known, in lilac, pale mauve, and white said, "You never know what you'll find at Elin's—horror or comedy."[30] About to go up from the highway to Elin's cloud-cuckoo-land, Evelyn Lambert (the reason for our entrapment), flashed by: "I'm just going to little Mrs. Miller's. She's so nice and she's a $4,000 member." Here was the full Evelyn: in bright yellow eyelet dress, shocking-pink scarf and stockings, red shoes, huge shocking-pink scarfed hat. She looked like an emerging nation's flag. We drove into the courtyard, to find the gate festooned in red, white, and blue balloons and buntings. We sat roaring with laughter at the cries of the peacocks, now grown so numerous, since the original six Grandpa Vanderlip brought. They are a menace—maniacal with screams of "Hooray! Hooray!" (most patriotic, these birds) as they lunged at the guests and proprietors. "You know," said Eleanore, "they jab you in the most frightful places!" This then was to be titled "Wanna See Where the Peacock Bit Me?" So, we sat and roared

29. Edith Mayer Goetz (1905–88), the daughter of Louis B. Mayer, was the wife of movie producer William Goetz. In 1981 Leo had featured the home of nineteenth-century American art collectors Jo Ann and Julian Ganz in *Vogue*.
30. Eleanore Phillips Colt (1910–99) was the longtime Los Angeles editor for Condé Nast Publications. She was married to Ethel Barrymore's son, Samuel Colt.

and were mean tongues to arriving guests. "What's that?" startled "ladies" screamed. "Oh—the peacocks. They just love human hair," I told them. [Philanthropist] Mary Lasker's stepdaughter asked, "Did anyone ever tell you that you look like Matisse?" "Everyone," I told her, although more think Monet. The local gentry, in going-to-church attitudes, fled in. We followed, into Natacha Rambova's idea of Tivoli-cum-Alhambra.

The French Nobility finally drove up in a yellow bus, labeled "The Tiffany Line." The sounds of pistol fire were balloons exploding. Somehow, Evelyn and we became the receiving line as the Nobility sashayed past: the Prince and Princess Napoleon, the Princess de Ligne, the Count and Countess de Boisgelin, Count Charles André Walewski. I finally ending up in the throne of honor. Here were ancient French names, Napoleonic nobility, *aristos* . . . all on the huge terrace, under giddy umbrellas, facing the sea, at a promotion to save their châteaux, manipulated by a former secretary [Vanderlip], her lover [assistant film director Lee] Katz, and Evelyn Lambert—the senior heroine. All filmed by NBC. The spirit of Margaret Dumont is not dead!

APRIL 29, 1985 • LAGUNA HILLS, CALIFORNIA    The Ritz-Carlton in Laguna—another American dream of a French château (like Newport and Palm Beach). Splendors of marble, Chinese carpet, nouvelle cuisine in a mediocre California way, Pacific vastnesses, and flora galora. It is all Hollywood Movie Millionaire fin-de-siècle whorehouse. What could this throwback decoration signify? Social levels are all mixed up, but a caste system remains. The cultural possibilities are vaster. What *Main Street's* Carol Kennicott thought she wanted is so abundantly available that we could, like the Duchess of Malfi, die of a surfeit. What is *Main Street* today, when all the world is *Main Street*, and boosterism is equated with morality? Here in Orange County, the developer is God, and culture is the Social Ladder, as it is in Manhattan and everywhere else. I am chicken-soup aristocracy—with noodles, of course, even with matzo balls.

MAY 7, 1985 • NEW YORK CITY    This afternoon [Allene Talmey's sister] Georgia Colin rang: "Allene is fading fast. . . . Would you write her obituary for the *Times*? You are the only one who could do it." I said "Of course." I thought of our long years together: that first meeting, when Mrs. Chase sent for her, and we became chums . . . how she said one day, "Now I'm going to put this copy in the typewriter and comb all the raspberry jam out of it" . . . the evening she said, "I know the kind of mind you've got—full of spaghetti with a lot of good chunks of meat in it" . . . all of those walks through the city, from theaters and concerts, stopping at Schrafft's for sodas . . . the night I sat in her cabbage-rose-wallpapered living room, and she cautiously asked me about Noël's sex life . . . the night she first had Alex and Tatiana to dinner. . . . All of this was during the war. I could go on and on and on, but this is not an obituary, more a love letter, to a small, sharp-eyed, plumpish, lethal woman, fascinated by the show, a woman who always knew when the show was perfection and that it was always passing. Some girls went away in hysterics, some in glory. No one forgot her who had ever felt her editorial pen—or, as some felt, her editorial sword . . . much more—as she would write—"tk."[31]

This request was immediately followed by Paula Laurence asking would I be on the committee to honor Yul. I laughed, telling her about the early, early morning when he had tried to kill me, because, as he reminded me eight years ago, I said, "No." Yul, flung back in Touche's bed, Narcissus naked, murmuring, "Why won't you? Why won't you?"[32] And this some three or four floors above Eleanor Roosevelt. That was the morning I saw the nuns, in their long black habits, dancing in the snow, a black circle in the blue-white morning of Washington Square.

MAY 12, 1985  "Oh—you're the great intellectual and arbiter, Diana Trilling," said [cartoonist] Bill Hamilton, coming up with his chum. "Yes, indeed," said our Di, "that is who I am. You are absolutely right." Diana: "My whole life has been based on logic and reason—none of that mysticism, not for me. Even when I was a little girl. I remember my brother saying: 'Oh that's Diana—reasoning it all out!' " She will be eighty in July. She is absolutely sure of her moral position in all matters and she is clear-eyed about who are Amenables and who are not. Nothing mystical—that is our Di.[33]

Conversation with Claudette (age eighty-three or -four) on the blower (her vitality, great good humor—a radiance), after which I know that "keeping busy" is the clue—until one is so eroded by time that only the shell is left. Claudette told me: "Oh—I have such a good time. This play [Aren't We All, by Frederick Lonsdale] is so easy and such fun!" She has a round, full voice, constantly colored by some bright source of inner laughter.

MAY 17, 1985  The School of American Ballet board met—eight members plus Lincoln. Four, including Nancy Lassalle, voted that he should be hospitalized and four against. Lincoln had the deciding vote: He voted against. What a farce!

MAY 18, 1985  In the [Plaza's] Oak Room, on the leather banquette, Goddard said to me: "You know, I'm not that way, but I understand." But I knew that he had "roamed" with [conductor] Lehman Engel. Lehman had told me certain

---

31. "TK" is editorial parlance for "to come." Talmey did not in fact die until March 4, 1986.
32. "Yul crept up behind me on Touche's terrace, high up over Washington Square, in the early morning, skimmed-milk winter light whispering, 'I'll throw you off if you don't. . . .' I didn't and neither did he." Journal, October 8, 1985.
33. "At Oxford, Diana kept saying that 'It has been decided that we are amenable.' Gray and I now call them The Amenables." Journal, November 26, 1964.

dimensional facts. I also knew that (this was rumored) he visited the Hotel Elysée.[34] . . . But what difference does any of that make now? All of that passion and frustration and planning . . . What difference if he had an affair with Felicia or let Lehman go down on him? The fact of his being a good friend, a sharp, witty tongue, an omnivorous reader, a shark of an executive business-man, a passionate admirer of quality and of glamour and of fame, a frustrated composer and novelist . . . and this only a makeshift catalogue—all of that is of importance. The good he did, the pleasure he gave, that is what matters—and—oh—how little time that will survive—only as long as memory. His grand-children will hear of him, a legend, and so memory will transform him, and who can tell what, or whether, he—or I, having no posterity—will be in a little while hence.

MAY 23, 1985 Last night, as Richard and I sat at the Brooks Atkinson Theatre, formerly the Mansfield (which had been the center of my life so long ago, and where I nightly stood in the wings [during *Behind Red Lights*], prompt book in hand, stage right, signaling curtain up, curtain down, dim this, douse that, jok-ing with the electrician—but all the while hungering to go to England where Richard was already), Richard said: "Well, we made it into our seventies!" Then the play [*Aren't We All*] began, and we were charmed, and here was Claudette on a free ride and Rex [Harrison], with a sly, eighteenth-century sort of humor, very Du Maurier seeming. We had first watched and laughed at Rex in 1937, in a theater in Piccadilly Circus, where he was playing *French Without Tears*. Knox Laing was his stage manager (I got over that). And Lynn [Redgrave now] reminding of Penelope. . . . And—as always—my whole past with me, and all I have loved, always there, while the "present" goes on happening.

My birthday celebration, not yet ended, rampaged, and so engulfed that at last the floral tributes almost undid the joys. What got me through, when the joy suddenly ran out like sawdust from a punctured play-pretty doll, was Katherine Mansfield saying: "The only thing you can give someone you love, when in a state, is your calm." But underneath I sank deep into the slough.

What is the worst that's happened to me? Not being able to do all sorts of lit-tle things for myself, not even being able to go about by myself, needing help in so many little ways, which cannot help but exhaust and so irritate. I try to cope, but I am not successful. I am also piggishly sloppy. I am a great trouble, but I have too much joy in life and too deep a sense of obligation to life and those who, at least temporarily, depend on me, to depart while the going is still good.

This is the best time. Silent, alone in my bed, a hum outside, the world not yet obliterating this wholeness, not even Mozart on the wireless—no wireless, nothing save the scratching of this pen as I talk to myself.

---

34. A hotel in midtown Manhattan that was hospitable to homosexuals.

The most touching present was from Mina: the copy of *Elegies* that Alexis [Léger] gave her when they were so deeply in love, with his inscription, their "secret" names, snapshots of Alexis and cats and Mina, all at Ashfield. Mina with her passions and her terrors and thick love for Lincoln, who now punishes her by telling her that he will never speak to her again. "Yes," she says, "the board has voted confidence in him, but he is crazy. . . . I try to take it, but it does hurt!" She is so loyal to those she loves.

MAY 26, 1985    I suddenly realized—I must be retarded—that so many of that little band had come to horrible ends: Ela murdered or accidentally a suicide—possibly pleased to sink into oblivion; Alice found frightened to death on her bathroom floor; Rut dead of a heart attack while *Marat-Sade* began, her life snuffed because she was thought to be part of the action of the play, while Ellen Stewart vainly called for help; Touche in his own blood on the loo in Vermont, Harry [Martin] inexplicably burning the bedclothes; Hellmut [Roder] and Fritz [Mosell] sordidly;[35] Laci a suicide; Bravig [Imbs] in an overturned Jeep on some road in France; Valeska [Imbs] in obscurity in New Mexico; Maggie Dunham [of polio] on a ship and buried at sea; Lili Darvas living through bad days cooking into better days and then dying of cancer; Max Reinhardt really euthanized by Ela.

JUNE 6, 1985    I would rather have made Kurt Schwitters's collages than written anything I have ever published. We ate up the morning with looking at "him" [in a retrospective at MoMA]. The works are the closest representations of my life. Here is a formula for my life, these fabulously arranged bits and pieces—detritus. He has made a work of art—a *Merzweld* order—of my chaos.[36]

I am held by the richness of [writer] Bobbie Ann Mason's observation of the inner poverty of her people. They have "things," but they have "nothing" save their material world. Carson, Truman, Eudora's people have glory in their past, hope in their pasts and futures. Bobbie Ann and Jay McInerney have no glory. They have Vietnam and Nixon in their pasts and the Reagan world in their present. So, they have nothing—no trembling—although they have touching observation—but not the deeps of Chekhov, or even the deep light and dark in Carson, Truman, and Eudora. These children of the television screen are less by magic endowed than those children of the "shadow." The young writers write about emotions, but they are never emotional in their writing. They're visual, screen trained to see, not to feel. They are part of the destruction of reality begun by the camera.

35. Roder died of meningitis in 1959, by which time the couple had separated. The editor doesn't know how Mosell died.
36. *Merz* is the name Schwitters (1887–1948) gave to his Dada-inspired collages of pocket trash—cards, ticket stubs, gum wrappers, etc.

Tina Brown said at a meeting that she wanted to make *Vanity Fair* "high-class trash," and that she can, and in doing that *VF* has the possibility of success.

Elsa Treves [di Figlia] is dead. She died (a month ago) of old age, in the bed in the room in the palazzo in which she was born. She had been in the hospital, came home, went to bed, called that sharp-nosed, villainous butler for champagne, and while sipping her wine she died. I know of no death more appropriate. She was a short, stubby, round-headed woman, a series of vigorous curves. She spoke all of her languages swiftly, with almost a liquid castanet rhythm. When I stood in her Art Nouveauish bedroom, peering at the painting-packed walls, and asked whether that one was Henry James, she said: "Oh, no, Mr. Lerman. He is not your Henry James—oh—those novels. I don't like them. I can't stand them—except that one about that foolish American girl who went out into the night air in Rome and died of it—so foolish! But . . ." and here her round, light eyes sparkled, "Do you know his letters and his notebooks?" Then she quoted from the notebooks extravagantly.

The last time she gave me tea, we sat munching small, delicious Venetian cakes—sugary, dense, dry—the breeze drifting in from the lagoons, drifting through those rooms congealed in time, the oval dark green and silver-white cave where Canova's *Castor and Pollux*, huge and white, wait while the painted history of their most glorious moment rests (can so crowded a painting so pulsing with pomp and praise and enthusiasm rest?) on an easel: The Austrian emperor and his entire court transfixed as they view with awe, in that very hidden chamber, Canova's masterwork.[37] That day in July, she sat pouring out tea, and suddenly I realized that she was speaking not really to me, but to Thomas Jefferson. Her mind had slipped, and we were in some pocket of history which she fancied and which I adored.

I remember Mrs. Murray Crane, for whom I became Walter Berry.[38] For ancient Mr. [Mark Anthony De Wolfe] Howe in Louisberg Square in Beacon Hill, I became Henry James. And with Eva Gauthier,[39] for one moving moment, I became, in that little room jammed with papers in the Woodward Hotel—Debussy, the Debussy she had known and loved when she was very young and very beautiful, before she journeyed in the "exotic" Far East and returned from Java mounted in jade.

---

37. "The palazzo [Treves dei Bonfili] is unique in Venice because the Treves family came out of the Venetian ghetto in the very early nineteenth century and, in 1820–22, completely redid this fourteenth-century structure." *Letter to RH, July 9, 1979.* The baronessa told Leo the Canova sculpture was Castor and Pollux. Guidebooks say Hector and Ajax.
38. Walter Berry (d. 1927), American expatriate, was best known as the close friend and travel companion of Edith Wharton.
39. Eva Gauthier (1885–1958), a Canadian-born mezzo-soprano, became the leading teacher of the French art-song repertoire in New York.

JUNE 8, 1985  Yesterday Marlene rang, at last, but I was not at Condé Nast. She called and talked a long time to Stephen, who was thrilled. He said she was clear, but toward the end a little muddled, obviously lonely, and said she'd rung us many times, but always the wrong number, someone gabbing Spanish. Then she mimicked (a trick she always had) the Spanish. "The phone is the only extravagance I have left," she told Puss about three years ago.

Diana Trilling talked on the blower about how squeamish the young are today, and how vomiting was something "we all did—during Prohibition—all that bootleg liquor. We held one another's heads and were proud of throwing up." She is nine years older, but we have become the same generation. She is writing about vomiting in her day. "Such an adorable subject," she said, meaning it, with all the memories this "adorable" subject seems to have brought her. Obviously vomiting holds the glamour of her past in the twenties and early thirties. I will immerse myself in *The House of Mitford [Portrait of a Family]*— that's my glamour.

JUNE 9, 1985  I must boldly say that [Cousin] Martin died this morning. When I heard, I suddenly was suffused with the sharp, autumn fragrance of apples, those apples that lurked in the back-porch barrel. Apples store up in their cold, red-blush skins Augusts and Septembers, all the long winter. This was the fragrance of long ago, when we were all young in Lakewood, and we each went our own private ways, loving one another rambunctiously, raging and laughing.

At night, in Lakewood, Marty and I, in bed together, became one experiment—secret, apart from the others, exploring together future possibilities through pleasure and trepidation, which neither of us understood. We became adolescents together. Then we became young men. We were one, seemingly dissimilar but one, and some part of this oneness became the lost physical intimacy—no matter what other intimacies we each formed—of seventeen or eighteen years. We never questioned this. We did not even acknowledge it. We were this hidden secret. Our terrible grandpa stumbled on our secret when we lived with him and tried to separate us, but he never did—only life did that. However, the oneness survived—not the physical manifestation, but the more important loving, admiring regard, the understanding which needed no words.

Martin had an affair with a nurse when I lived in [the rooming house] on East Seventy-first Street. She shouted "Whoopee!" when she had an orgasm. We heard this through the heavy, locked door of the room, and we teased him. . . . I never thought that any of the cousinage would die. Now I am relieved that he did die; his last months were so terrible. Martin, my dear, darling, lovely, loving cousin . . . He will have a military funeral in the national cemetery near San Diego. For some reason this amuses me: One of us lowered with full military honors—guns cracking, flags waving, trumpets cutting the air. How very unexpected at the other end of the street.

NOTE: In June 1985 a civil suit for defamation brought against Condé Nast by the writer Renata Adler required that Leo give a deposition. During his many hours of testimony, Leo learned that private journals may be considered evidence. Although the lawsuit was settled without Leo surrendering his notebooks, the prospect had horrified him. The result in his daily writing was first silence and then circumspection. That year their European summer began with a visit to London.

JOURNAL · JUNE 30, 1985 · LONDON  I've only written scraps in my accounts book. I can't force-feed these pages. I'll make myself write in Venice. But I will be adamant in August. I cannot measure the [psychological] injury or its permanence. Sudden weeping—very like precipitous showers.

JULY 8, 1985  "No human can guarantee their future, but we will manage our past." Reading Natalia [Murray]'s book of letters, *Darlinghissima*.[40] Janet Flanner is writing about the two parts of Barbette's face, the upper Victorian, prettily feminine, the lower a dreadful gash, a horrific male brute.[41] I think of Little T's body: The lower half was male and violently tough; from the hips up he was hermaphroditic; the lower half hairy, the upper half smooth; his self-mesmerized, semi-dazed, almost wholly absorbed upper half, feminine wiles and looks, his lower half a truck driver.

JULY 9, 1985 · VENICE  Nico Passante [manager of the Gritti] asked that I please "let a photographer take your picture for a magazine that is doing a story on the Gritti." I did. The photographer, a genial, tall, cropped and curly-head, blue-eyed American, asked Joel [Kaye], Lloyd [Williams], and Puss to move away. So—instant scene, most unpleasant, observed by all. Later, explanation: "I was never chosen for any team, when sides were being picked. I was always left to the last . . . rejected. The feeling is even stronger than I knew." So, almost sixty years later, we continue to pay for the horrors of childhood.

Maebelle traumatics—possible pneumonia reported, but then nothing wrong except age. But this Maebelle performance definitely has put paid to any moving-to-London plans for her duration. We couldn't indulge ourselves in such selfishness. Here, then, is one of the problems—not the moving, but how to cope with what must be an increasing problem—Maebelle's aging.

JULY 13, 1985 · VENICE
TO MINA CURTISS · WESTON, CONNECTICUT
Plunging through the proof of Janet Flanner's and Natalia's love letters and life, I came upon this in the 1947 section: "Mina Curtiss . . . drove down from

---

40. Italian-born publishing executive Natalia Danesi Murray (1901–94) was the lover of *The New Yorker*'s Paris correspondent Janet Flanner for thirty-eight years.
41. The transvestite high-wire artist Barbette had been disfigured by a fall in 1929.

Mentone to Alessio and up to Cuneo: She has never been to Venice or Rome. I dined tonight with her and she is 'so in love with Italy' (her phrase!) that she lands in Naples on her next visit to Europe. She compared the French so unfavorably with the Italians in kindness and charm and good nature as to make it painful to hear for me: I was never sentimental about the French." But as the years accumulated dear Janet's despair over the French grew, as did her loathing of "modern" life, until she had (and I did not know this) a "little" nervous breakdown and was hospitalized in Paris a few days. So there you are (truthfully reported or not) in 1947, and here I am somewhat visible, locally, in 1985. If Janet lived now she would possibly be beyond despair.

So many Italians, English think Reagan marvelous. I now avoid arguments. I always did (political arguments), but seethe with anger. Here the Canal seethes with its own peculiar vivid life, such a mixture of antique commercial enterprise, contemporary sordidness, and sometimes unexpected hilarities, unwittingly contributed by American females with country-club assurance. A superb collector's example held forth yesterday to a gape-mouthed circle. She said, "And then we went to this castle and there were these curtains, hanging in the same place, in the very same place, since the twelfth century!" Her circle gasped with awe. First the curtains, then the windows invented because of the curtains? Another (they are inevitably Southern) asked, "How do you get around here?" Her vis-à-vis: "You take a Tintoretto." This is as good as the creature who rushed to the edge of the terrace, screeching: "Look! Look! A granola!" But Venice is impervious to all. At this moment, the waters, the palazzi are all milky opaline, glinting with midday sun.

Some nights ago, for *House & Garden* to photograph, I had the Palazzo Pisani Moretta ballroom candlelighted—nine tremendous, jungle-vine Venetian chandeliers, six sconces springing like crazed thoughts from a trompe l'oeil painting, and mirrored vast walls. Great, sheer white curtains streamed into this shimmering room, and for a transfixed moment I could hear the sound of that room, a reward for a week of *House & Garden*ing.

Life here, in Venice, is a mixture of Proust and E. F. Benson (the Lucia books), while the cinemas here, and in the Veneto, show more pornographic movies than I ever knew were made, and everywhere—from Evangeline Bruce's luncheons to dinner in English country houses to "cocktails" in palazzi here, what is most talked about is *Dynasty*!!!

Gray's mother went on a hunger strike. She said, "I will not eat until my son comes home." A nurse has been installed. We get encouraging reports via telephone. She eats—but she has had a "moderate" stroke.

**JOURNAL · JULY 14, 1985** Listening to Verdi's *Falstaff*. I think of [Perrier heir] Alain Coblence's uncle, with his ancient appearance, his sexual curiosity, and sexually nourished wit. He is one year younger than I am. I suddenly feel myself a part of the community of old men. I have never before felt this, but I like the feeling, despite a shadow fear for loved ones in my heart. *Falstaff* gives me hope and confidence. As does Maestro. I see Ela, on a deep-snow day, trying to give [him] her birthday silver tray, at Lake Mohonk. Wanda, blacker than black in a mountain of blinding snow, intercepting her. Her harsh Italian words falling like cudgels on Ela's shawled head and shoulders. Later, invisibly bleeding, Ela leaning against the kitchen sink drinking milk, her smile a blue wound in her gone-gaunt face, in which her sea-green eyes seemed scooped out, the look of Oedipus after he had been blinded.

JULY 15, 1985  The maid put one foot and her face in—to come upon me naked, but I remained unembarrassed, having, with a urinary affliction this year, lost that "sense," for which I am grateful. If only I had not had that sense throughout my blighted, wet-pants, wet-bed (until I was eight) childhood. If only my embarrassment had left me then, how much happier my young life would have been.

JULY 16, 1985  The secret of glamour is to give a sense of occasion. Legend helps, sometimes it is Presence, sometimes it is Beauty, but Beauty alone, unless fortified by Celebrity or Legend (e.g., The Jersey Lily) can give only a comparatively brief sense of occasion.

Some experiences are imagined and then lived so strongly that they become real, imagined into truthfulness, an intellectual thread in the fabric of one's life. I was sure that I saw Duse, but did I? Or was our house so full of talk about it that my experience was made real?

**DUSE**  *I believe that my father took me to see Eleonora Duse. I think I was about eight years old, and I did not understand one word of Italian. I do not think my father understood much Italian—maybe a few curse words, neighborhood words. He held my hand, and we both sat there, tears running down our faces. I don't know why he was crying, but I was crying because, in what I now know was Ibsen's* The Lady from the Sea, *I saw this woman, far off, remote in a haze of light, a pale wisp of woman—all love-brimming eyes, all-embracing— holding out her hungry arms to me and I thought: She is my grandmother. . . .*

*Poppa first gave me a hunger for a rich, glittering life, a life of glamour, a life born of and appropriate to golden-paved streets of the immigrant imagination. Momma was the ambitious one; Poppa, I believe was a private dreamer. I had thought that my mother was the principal family influence in my whole life, but I now realize that my father was the predominant force in shaping or pointing the way I would go. Even as he lay dying, four long cancerous years, he said to me, sitting by his bedside and reading the collected works of George Meredith (for I thought him the most difficult writer, and so I read Meredith scrupulously day after day during these awful times), he said, peering at me, "Baby, what's*

*doing outside?" I think that in those last years he continued to see me as that lit-*
*tle boy he took to movies, theaters, even burlesque shows.*[42] (1993)

JOURNAL • JULY 17, 1985 Randy [Michaelson] spoke volubly on the Viardots, Pasta, Malibran (his passion). He's read through the Pasta archive, in the house of her posterity, and says she never did sing a whole *Norma;* that she never could. She mimed Act I and sometimes only sang Act II. There is no resemblance between Pasta and Maria. He says that Malibran was the Janis Joplin of her day—wild, probably taking some sort of drugs, spoke (and wrote many letters to Pasta in) five languages, was prodigal with her talents. He went to visit one who may be Pauline Viardot's last living descendant—Alice?—on the Riviera, and taped his visit. Alice, very old, but fully assembled, told him that Pauline had a big, metallic voice, that she burned all of Turgenev's letters the night she learned that he was dead—so much more. Randy's point: When Manuel García [II, brother of Pauline Viardot] was born Haydn was still alive; when García died, Aaron Copland was already born! He poured this and so much more out as we walked a two-bridge walk. He should write a little book about continuity. He is a prodigious monster of musical and Venetian knowledge and has a certain wry humor about his riches.

JULY 18, 1985 Memory is a cat, playing with its own special mouse, then apparently losing all interest in its plaything (or victim) and becoming totally (can we trust that?) preoccupied in cleaning its most private parts. . . . As a cat concentrates on a moth high above it, finally luring that creature to its doom—but how?—somewhere a cat is playing with me.

JULY 25, 1985 Our apartment was a refuge; my scribblings were a refuge: These are now threatened. Only our love is a refuge—solid, built over the years—I was about to say like a bird's nest, but how fragile—yet withstanding violent storms.

JULY 27, 1985 Lunch with Mary [Martin], Hal Prince, Bubbles [Sills]. Mary: "I felt it wasn't fair." She gave a look as if she felt that she had betrayed her "gift," and obviously loved proving that she could play again. "Six thousand people!" she crowed. Mary has incredible verve, a husky, just-grew spirit, is the real level-eyed optimist who flew, at seventy-one, from box to balcony in the original, unpadded, Peter Foy [aerial] harnesses: "Oh!" she spreads her arms table-wide, "It's, it's flying!"—all soaring exultation and Peter Pan's cracked voice. When she laughs, she is completely laughter. Mary adores children. She has a deep sense of obligation.

---

42. Duse played in *The Lady from the Sea* at the Metropolitan Opera in November 1923. She died the next year. Leo would then have been nine and a half.

Hal is the eternal "Oh gosh" kid, with his open-faced honesty, his Peter Rabbit smile. Beverly and Hal are like two kids playing hooky from school. B: "Must we go to this dinner? Must we sit through the whole opera?" H: "Yes . . ." B: "But we're too old to have to do all that." She was, typically, carrying a paper bag with fabric in it to the dinner at the Barbaro. "I don't miss the audiences, or performing. I miss singing." Beverly's smile was the smile of Rembrandt's Saskia—life realized, wise, contemplative, all-womanliness (mother, artist, woman). Her speaking voice is slightly shocking: "I barely got out of high school!" Beverly booms, with that special singer's diction sometimes taking over from the natural Brooklynese.

Mary on Garbo: "Oh—so stingy, the stingiest woman in the world." When Mary and [her husband Richard] Halliday lived in River House, with Valentina below "Miss Brown" (as Garbo was called)—a ménage à trois: "We all gathered for drinks at Valentina's. I had this [exercise] machine I had bought at Hammacher Schlemmer." (She mixed up the syllables, dyslexia being the one audible sign of deterioration.) "It whirled you around and turned you upside down. Garbo wanted me to strap her in. I wasn't going to be responsible for killing Greta Garbo, but one day I finally gave in, and there she was, upside down in that wheel, and when she came off it, she looked at me and she said: 'You must be crazy!' " Mary rolls on in the most exhilarated way, using the full range of her huskiness, her breathlessness, her baritones, her shouty laugh, her delight in life—Venus Rising Perpetually from Public Applause.

AUGUST 3, 1985 · PARIS  We went to visit Colette's apartment, 9 rue Beaujolais, now lived in by [decorator] Jacques Granges, who is off in Tangiers. We looked out through the windows she had looked from. Maria, on the cover of an album of *Norma*, watched from a low table. The apartment stretched across the whole depth from the rue Beaujolais to the center [courtyard]. The bedroom is where I felt her most. The inner Palais Royal was a photograph as I sat looking out at it, the trees all so precise, light aslant on their tilting trunks. [Colette's] rooms now filled with greed-and-envy objects of furniture;[43] objects recalling Pavlik [Tchelitchew], Baudelaire, George Sand; a life of Marie Bashkirtseff[44] next to a book on Luchino Visconti; on the bedroom shelves Pléaide editions of Proust, Colette, et al.; a Burne-Jones study on one dining room wall; a Second Empire sculpture of a woman; the colors and designs of the draperies and carpets are related to those in Ingres pictures. I also felt Little T in her bedroom, as he was before the rot took over . . . and Marlene . . . and Cocteau (a superb Cocteau in the bathroom). I asked Puss what he had to say:

43. Coming upon an object that he coveted and could not have, Leo liked to mutter, "Greed and envy, greed and envy!"
44. Although a painter, the short-lived Marie Bashkirtseff (1860–84) is usually remembered for her lively, frank journal.

"It's a modest, middle-class apartment that's been taken over by a person who has very fashionable instincts. It has a kind of serenity about it, but that's the building itself." Yes, but remember her paperweights, her play pretties—some of which were the roots of today's decorating fashionabilities.

NOTE: On returning to America in August, Leo found a notice from the Social Security Administration stating that checks would no longer be delivered, because he was dead.

JOURNAL · AUGUST 17, 1985 · NEW YORK CITY As of Thursday last, I am one of three Jewish boys resurrected: Lazarus, Jesus, and Label. One morning, the phone rang, and a woman said to Puss: "This is Social Security. What are we going to do about Mr. Lerman?" Puss said: "Oh, yes, Mr. Lerman is very eager to have a few words with you." A horrified silence. Then: "But Mr. Lerman is deceased!" "Nevertheless, he wants to have a word with you." Then he gave the woman my office number. I heard Stephen say: "Oh . . . but he does want to talk with you. . . ." I picked up the phone, intending to sound as from the sepulcher, but a mighty roar came out—all my anger against the incompetence of computers in the "modern" life: "What are you going to do about this?" I bellowed. A stunned silence. Then she said: "Is . . . this . . . Leo . . . Lerman?" "Yes!" Silence. "There's some mistake." "Yes!" "We've been sending checks to 205 East Fifty-seventh Street, but there's no such address. There's a mistake in the computer. The computer figured you were dead." Only now do I wonder how the communication that told me I was dead came to 205 West Fifty-seventh Street. "What is the next step?" I asked. She promptly answered: "Resurrection." I was flabbergasted. "Is that the official designation?" "Yes," she said, still shaken, but more in control. "Come in as soon as you can with two pieces of evidence that you are you, and we will start the resurrection proceeding." Social Security is now God? Telling this to all who have phoned brings gaiety to nations. Also, I will now have two birthdays. Born dead, dead quite a few times—lost during operations, nearly drowned, smashed into oblivion [in a taxi] against Grand Central Station . . . and now officially dead by government computer and in a state of Resurrection. I conclude that I have had a charmed life.

I finished reading *The Vicar of Tours*, in which Balzac shows that evil is victorious over good, especially when good is innocent. That Balzac permitted the Abbé Troubert and Mlle Gamard to triumph over poor Vicar Birotteau, leaving Birotteau nothing save old age, infirmity, and poverty, is another evidence of Balzac's genius. His villains may kill one another off and even become, in a sense, respectable (i.e., Vautrin). A prodigious cynic deals, as all cynics must, in ironies. He is a great peak above most of the "eminences" of nineteenth-century literature, as Beethoven is above those of music. Balzac is vast, a worldly writer who gets in from the outside. Proust gets out from the inside.

AUGUST 23, 1985  The demolition men shout to one another as they turn at the theater [behind our building] and torch it into refuse to be carted away, any old garbage. I make these shoutings into some far-off bucolic sounds—in the Veneto, or in the Pyrenees—trying to make this all somehow bearable—this little holocaust of the past. When I told Richard, he said, "There goes my whole theatrical career!" I saw his mother and his sister, Nancy, and his aunt and cousins in their velvet evening capes, stunned at his one line, as he ran across that stage now being ravished: "Wait for me, you dirty bastards!"[45]

The death of a theater—a special desolation. The magic despoilers, men in layers of muddy colors, murky blues, mucky hard hats, and huge goggles—insect eyes. The roar and creak and whine of the future. Raw gaping wounds, blacker than crusted old blood, the whimperings and groanings, the wrenchings and sudden outbursts of innards—corroded, twisted. Doré saw this, as did Piranesi. The anguish of this theater, the melancholy, the hopelessness where once aspiration and hope were the center of being, where once an enclosed world had managed to be forever. Then the unexpected moments of beauty: One of the rat-men dangling a stiff rope or rod, with a little star of blue light at its gently swaying tip, softly touching his blue star to this grimy wall, that bleak girder—volcanic showers of sparkler fires, huge Fourth of July sparkler fires, then flickers, and the wall crumbles, the girder melts, a patch of the firehouse, unseen from these windows for fifty or sixty years, appears across Fifty-eighth Street. The rat-men clot in scheming knots, hack, pound, wrench. These blackened, grimed, blue hard-hatted creatures, these from-the-Earth's-interior creatures contrast with the Venetian sun- and waterborne workers who inherently assume, while building, while manipulating garbage scows, while in repose, classic poses, antique configurations. Death and destruction here, life-giving individualities there, a contrast as dramatic as that between the Forces of Evil and the Forces of Good in some Biblical representation.

Barbara Epstein, at lunch, told me that when she stepped out of her taxi, at Gore's in Ravello, there he was with a big mustache. "Tennessee left it to me," he said, "in his will."

SEPTEMBER 1, 1985 · PALM BEACH, FLORIDA  Tornado watches, sullen skies, windows full of torsioning, weaving, plunging . . . every variation of movement. Luncheon [at Si and Victoria Newhouse's] in an all white, blue, black, full-of-light house. All very laughing and blithe and civilized and happy-serious, a luncheon full of sudden understandings. Talk of Mishima. I told how silent he was, and neat, and how I took him to lunch at Sardi's because he

---

45. Richard had taken his first Broadway bow there, as a walk-on in *Searching for the Sun*, which ran for five performances in February 1936. Leo's debut had been a year earlier, at the Vanderbilt Theater, in the drama *Creeping Fire*. He played a corpse. It was his only Broadway acting role.

wanted to see a theater "place," and found Graham Greene (who could write Mishima's life) two tables removed and introduced them. Mishima met everything with identical probity, a solemn smile. Graham was large, somewhat explosive. Mishima liked to walk me home from places. Then he would come in and sit. I chatted endlessly, while he was monosyllabic—a small, finely formed, intensely still man. Or so I thought then.

SEPTEMBER 24, 1985 · NEW YORK CITY Wrote reviews of about five cookbooks today—slow, very slow, but somehow reassuring. I can sit for hours and I *can* pound it out. These months, ever since the hours of grilling in June, have been an impoverished writing time. Impossible to write down most of what I see and hear, the social behavior that nourishes me. So this long grind at the cookbooks makes me, at least, clamp myself to my typewriter.

I wanted to write about how Number One looked yesterday in the morning, as he was coming out of 350 [Madison, Condé Nast], but how can I do that now? I cannot write it until the gag [the lawsuit] is removed. I dare not write down my feelings about this horror.

OCTOBER 8, 1985 At the Met Museum, stores everywhere sell not only reproductions, but men's ties. "Next, shoes," said Puss. "I wouldn't be surprised," replied a girl, bitterly, from behind a counter. The Met has become great (in collections) and—an awful shock—a total monster, bloated with beauty and sick with commerce.

OCTOBER 10, 1985 Now Orson [Welles] is dead. All of that frustrated, thrown-away greatness, that genius, dead. I find myself standing almost fifty years ago on a fire escape pleading with him to take Joe Cotten back into his company, because that awful [playwright] Aurania Rouverol made me fire Joe from *Places, Please*. "No," she said, "no real charm, no real looks, no real talent, no future. You'll see!" I saw. I hope that the cunt saw.[46] Orson took him back [directly into *Julius Caesar*], and *Places, Please* flopped. But Joe never again talked to me. Even when I stumbled over him as he sat on the floor at Judy Garland's party in the Waldorf-Astoria after the opening in Manhattan of *A Star Is Born*.

This brings me to Irene [Sharaff] (who did costumes and scenery for *Star Is Born*) and Mai-mai, and so back to Yul. When I told Paula that Yul had died at four this morning she said: "He had everything and he did it all, and he was so generous with himself and he was such a loyal friend." Of Orson, who gave

---

46. "Orson on the evening I went to ask him to take Joe Cotten back—enormous, petulant, wild-humored, in constant hulking motion, and somehow *grand-seigneur* agreeable—in a vest (not a waistcoat), short sleeves, cigar in mouth." *Journal, February 20, 1971*. Leo had supervised casting and was stage-managing *Places, Please* in November 1937. Richard Hunter was his assistant.

Paula "Helen of Troy" in his never-equaled *Dr. Faustus* (one of the most flab-bergasting theatrical experiences I have ever had) and made her the scampering woman in *Horse Eats Hat*, Paula said: "Oh, darling, he'd grown so monstrous. He'd become unemployable."

OCTOBER 14, 1985   The [William] Buckleys gave a celebration of Estée Lauder at Mortimer's, and all the *gratin* was in gushing attendance. Estée (wasn't she Esther Rappaport of Middle Village in cousin Estelle's class at Newtown?[47]) in lipstick red—everything save stockings—the rig in which she is photographed on the dust jacket of "her" new book. This photograph was enlarged to poster dimensions, hung here and there in full blazing color. All of the ceilings were hidden beneath thickset Estée red balloons. Glenn [Birnbaum, Mortimer's owner] and Pat [Buckley] had planned rooms after Cecil's Ascot, but—no—Estée commanded her red, and Estée got it. There she stood, at the head of her receiving line, glowing, an affirmation of the positive. She actually deserves this canonization: She labored mightily for it. When she saw me being helped out of the car, she and two minions rushed out and propelled me in. She made me feel that she meant this. Quite an art, this hostessing as the guest of honor. Then Pat, one shoulder bare, took over and ensconced me in a chair. I received Mitzi [Newhouse], intact in quite a few of her emeralds, looking marvelous, and her mind sharp as her eyes. Then Donald, Sue, and Si [Newhouse]. ("Estée did everything—the jacket, size of the book, typeface—everything. Maybe I should hire her to see the books through at Random House.")

   If one doesn't go out into this world, they are much more "pleased" to see you when you do. You become an event. The party for Estée did not flow, it coagulated, confined to Mortimer's two rooms. Rivulets of guests trickled here, there, bogged down in clumps of "peers." Playing entomologist, we spotted the rare specimens. ("There's Malcolm Forbes," murmured Joel [Kaye] glimpsing the short, rare power bug.) A silted-up pond, which is becoming a quagmire, the vegetation, the mud, the dragonflies and other insect life, the inhabitants of the water, the cloud reflections, the bugs peering at themselves in the looking glasses.

   Estée transforms her bulk adroitly, a soft jacket falling just so around the ample hips and her neatness almost excessive. But the essential, determined Jewish mother is always there. "Take your present!" she screamed as we left. Her ambition, no matter how fulfilled, is not ever fulfilled. The round, blue eyes open wide, I think even in sleep. She does not, and she will not, miss a thing. It's easy to make fun of her. She is larger than life, like old movie stars, but she survives the jibes and the jokes because she has a kind of grit, as they

47. Four years ahead of Leo at Newtown High School, according to Lerman family legend, was an Esther Rabinowitz, who became Estée Lauder.

did. Estée is the ultimate immigrant triumph—more than Helena Rubinstein, because the princess was always a foreign Jewish woman. Elizabeth Arden was always a monster American. Fannie Farmer was home industry brought to high economic triumph—but Estée is first-generation American, as I am.[48] She says she came out of an already "emancipated" family. I came out of a family supreme in their ghetto and breaking out of it.

OCTOBER 31, 1985 Mina died at seven p.m., suddenly, laughing and joking. The previous night she tore the oxygen mask off and the tubes out and shouted, "God, let me die!" But today, Lynn [her secretary] was told that she was lively, good-humored, and had something to look forward to. Mina left her body to Yale. Yale demurred, not wanting a body that had been operated on, but finally Yale accepted Mina's body. George [her brother], seemingly choking, said his thank-you, and Lincoln, absolutely dry-eyed, said he thought it was good luck. George is rude; Lincoln is crazy. Puss said the most helpful words: "It's just silence. And I've come to love silence." The most astonishing thing Mina has ever done is to vanish. I have no one with whom to talk about her. I can see her, a body, in the mortuary at Yale, but that isn't reality. Real is Mina in her bed in that house in Weston.[49]

NOVEMBER 24, 1985 Jeanne Moreau, when she came to lunch at Mortimer's, [when] asked what Cocteau and Colette talked about said, "Oh—the laundry and the maid and eating . . . ordinary things. I was meeting so many famous people in those days. I don't remember it all." I see Jeanne as autumn—the tawny, overblown blossoms of autumn, going almost to seed, those great, multi-petaled, dark-brown centered, deep red sometimes seeping into the dark honey-colored petals. People as seasons—Puss is winter, the winter seen in late-seventeenth, eighteenth-century personification garden sculpture, carried on to Victorian Christmas cards. Jack Frost silver. "That's why I love to polish silver," he said yesterday. "It calms me."

I still cannot come to terms with Mina's death, with that shut door. In all the years Mina and I were close, we never were harsh with one another. I saw her terror, her anguish, and I knew her self-absorption (especially about Lincoln), but also I knew her deep generosity, her acute sense of obligation. "You know," she said frequently, "I'm no intellectual. I'm not one for ideas." Yet Henry Adams was her god and Proust was her passion, other people's lives and letters her delight, detective stories her easy relaxation. She loved works of decoration even more than works of pure art. She made beautiful houses and ran them

48. Florence Nightingale Graham was the owner of the Elizabeth Arden beauty-product brand. Fannie Farmer, a culinary writer with a cookery school, taught precision and standardization of recipes.
49. George Kirstein (1906–86), Mina Curtiss's other brother, published *The Nation*.

decisively. She roared with laughter, rage, and compassion. She gave more than she took. She believed in character and she worked hard on hers. The night before she died, she begged for death: I do not know if the minute when she died she wanted to die. She had learned, in her last, bedridden years, acceptance. I talk to myself. Who knew her "better" than I did these last years? So much more to talk about: her liberalism; how she loved to hear about worldly "doings"; her great love—Lincoln and how much grief he gave her, even when he sat talkless she waited for his Saturday visits during these recent years; the whole matter of her taking to her bed; her incessant reading and her fulfilled hunger to write. She knew her limitations. She had a sense of proportion (emotional proportion? I wonder . . . ) and a sense of appropriateness, this last was a second skin. She loved everything to do with gardens and gardening. She adored her cats ("Here's Ibsen," she would croon) and her dog. She loved Ashfield, but she gave it up. She was hurt by Smith [College]. She never forgot anyone who served her; even when she couldn't afford to spend, she did send money constantly, and the standbys, even those she hadn't seen in years, are in her will.

NOTE: Demolition and construction progressed on the choir-school building adjacent to the Osborne and their apartment grew intolerable. Leo and Gray took a room for a couple of weeks at the New York Hilton, looking out to the Hudson River.

After going to southern California for the holidays, they then checked into the Gramercy Park Hotel, downtown, an affordable but rather carelessly managed place. Finally, the two of them borrowed the Upper East Side apartment of a friend, the writer Joan Juliet Buck.

JOURNAL · DECEMBER 14, 1985 Brilliant morning, like the sound of a burnished golden bell. [Seen from the Hilton,] the river has the blue of seafaring eyes, of Irish eyes, but this is a sad river: It is deprived of a part of its birthright. Even before Henry Hudson, it bore canoes and rafts . . . but now almost nothing where once such a teeming traffic, such a hooting and roaring and whistling and honking, such a constant celebration (midnight sailings!). Then the river was Alive. Now it lives in some forlorn dream. . . . But what of the turbulence beneath?

DECEMBER 15, 1985 Reading Philip Larkin's "Aubade" I am reassured. On the thirty-nineth floor, I came to understand—no, to appreciate—Death, the promised peace of Death—no problems, a forever of no problems, of nothing. I am sad only for Puss—that breaks my heart, but for myself, I have become reconciled to Death. Indeed, I see Death as the answer. "Aubade" is a very, very great poem, the greatest of this poet.

DECEMBER 29, 1985 · LOS ANGELES Carol (Matthau) said, "Thank you for all these years of trying to make me a star!" That has been one of the major aspects of my life, trying to make everything and everyone glamorous, a star—even when I was a little boy "putting on plays"—that was star-making. All of the fantasy—all life long. Now I have my vision of the river—smooth, aquamarine, still, eternal, no traffic upon it.

JANUARY 28, 1986 • NEW YORK CITY  This ancient, wandering Jew and his Huguenot life-companion have at last come to an interim resting place. This room, Joan's workroom, is quiet, white, soothing, curiously removed, and I feel her loving presence—a balm. Music furls from the bedroom . . . rivulets of music . . . Beethoven . . . as healing as a wide vista of sky and ocean, after the turmoil these past weeks.

FEBRUARY 1, 1986  Hurd [Hatfield] took me to Yul's memorial. "We should be titled: The Had and The Hadn't, with you starring in your original role of The Had," I teased him. Dorian Gray is in his seventies. The memorial in the Shubert was drab.

As I am led about, I become alarmingly like my mother. My fur hat could have been hers. I lunge over as she did. I peer with large, harelike, wondering eyes through my specs the way she did. I wonder if I think, if I feel the way she did? She takes over, having, as she inevitably had, the last word. When I see what becomes of radiance, my heart breaks, and I am happy for those who died young.

FEBRUARY 8, 1986  I buy "things" and then investigate them, and so find myself out. I accept "experiences" and the process is identical. I fell in love with Puss the moment I saw him. I have spent my life in finding him and finding me out.

In the beginning, the warrings are taken as challenges or ignored, because the emotion—falling in love—overwhelms all other emotions, even portents. Love will, must, conquer all. But love does not. The most love can do is understand, and to understand is to compromise. There is no such state as A Perfect Marriage. The degree of perfection is the measure of the compromise. Lesson in old age: To love is sufficient unto itself—no need to have that love returned. Strange lesson to learn at this time.

NOTE: Leo and Gray went to Laguna Hills for the wedding of Melissa "Missy" Cockrell, Gray's cousin. From there they went to Los Angeles to supervise the photography of Herbert and Nora Kaye Ross's house, a feature that Leo would write for *House & Garden*.

JOURNAL • FEBRUARY 28, 1986 • LAGUNA, HILLS, CALIFORNIA  We heard that [poetry critic] David Kalstone has AIDS. I think of all his quarried learning—then of that ultimate apathy, emptiness, removal from life in life that

Gerry Stutz [president of Henri Bendel] has described: "They become totally removed. They are there, but only the remains are there. They seem to have left their bodies. . . ." She sees this when she sits with AIDS victims. Judy Peabody [socialite AIDS activist] got some fourteen women to sit with AIDS victims, to go to them and comfort them. I try to console myself with Ruth Gordon's dictum: "Never accept facts!" But that does not help me.

MARCH 3, 1986   The wedding of Missy [Cockrell] put me into such a rage. The minister was the direct cause of my fury. He made the ceremony into a travesty. He translated the Bible into some sort of sub-talk: The Marriage at Cana became the lowest happening. This young cretin told the well-wishers, "They put out some of the good stuff first. Then they got the cheaper stuff out. . . ." So he went on—debasing the miracle. "So, Jesus Christ said, 'Okay!' " Absolute assassination of language, violation of spirit. He told the couple that Jesus Christ was going to be in bed with them. This bespectacled young horror made a mockery of some of the most beautiful language we have.

MARCH 7, 1986 • LOS ANGELES   We have been busy getting the Ross project under way. Herbert is deeply worried about Nora. Yesterday afternoon, when he asked that she be sent a set of the pictures, Puss and I, without even telling one another, thought, "Does she know how long she has to live? Is that it?" Nora, in bed, looked wonderful, pleading a cold.[50]

MARCH 8, 1986   Edie Goetz has a Degas, one of the bronze ballerinas, the only one with the original tutu (only five were made and this is the only one that will come on the market). She bought it at the Edward G. Robinson auction, and originally it came from Marie Harriman's [Impressionist] gallery, and that means my seeing it in the rotogravure, when I was about fifteen, set me to climbing the stairs of that gallery, hoping to get a glimpse of it. I was too timid to go in because I thought that I had to pay. "Come on in. It doesn't cost anything," she said to me.

We saw Misha [Baryshnikov] and his little Choura.[51] She is very beautiful, at five, and is a water baby, splashing about for hours in it. She looks as if she would marry great wealth. Sitting in the white sofa, eating a big dish of ice cream, she said, peering about, "They must be rich. . . ." And Nora, overhearing, said, "Yes . . . we are."

MARCH 11, 1986   Somehow, in these eleven days we all seemed, although so much later in years, to be working away to future goals: Julie [Harris] on [her

50. Nora Kaye had been undergoing treatment for cancer.
51. In 1981 Baryshnikov had a daughter, Alexandra ("Choura"), with the actress Jessica Lange.

solo show] *Countess Tolstoy*; Carol [Channing] on [the play] *Legends*; Herbie and Nora on new movies, theater pieces, and acquiring for their house; Hurd [Hatfield] for movies and television. We all seemed at beginnings, and Alessandra [Ferri] was a symbol of a dazzling future[52]—even Choura, with her future in the twenty-first century, when I will no longer be here. A radiant eleven days.

Like Lucien de Rubempré [in Balzac's *Lost Illusions*], when Lousteau initiated him to the Panorama-Dramatique and the supper at Florine's, I too stood, unwittingly, at the parting of two ways when Lucien Vogel took me to *Vogue* in the autumn of 1941. "The one, represented by the circle at the Quatre Vents, honorable and sure; the other—that of journalism . . . a perilous path, among muddy ditches, where his conscience, inevitably, must be spattered with mire." Did my character impel me "to take the shortest, and to all appearances the more pleasant way, to snatch at the quick and decisive means," as I sat waiting in that Elsie de Wolfe decor, staring at those gold-starred pavements and heard those two words: "Divine" . . . "Debauchery"?

MARCH 15, 1986  I wrote Allene's obituary all yesterday morning. Today a little cold thing was published [in the *New York Times*]—not a word I had written—nothing.

APRIL 13, 1986 · NEW YORK CITY  Last night, at seven, in Saint Bart's [church], Arianna Stassinopoulos in the most elegant silhouette, a molded-to-her-body Galanos in white lace, a cascade of lace falling from a cap of large white flowers in her chignon, the lace falling over her long train, a little glinting here and there—all most Queen Alexandra (the shoulders), the bodice built on a basque—such pre-1914 intimations of royals, but not her behavior in the recessional, when she made dry kissing moves, at the chosen (such as Henry Kissinger), and her huge, dark eyes glowed with triumph.[53] The church jammed to the doors, all black-tie and *echt* hightums, last year's Oscar de la Rentas and this year's Galanos and Saint Laurent. Very Byzantium. Bay leaves (Victory!), wreathing the rows out into Park Avenue. The aisles—tall poles surmounted by flickering fairy lights and trays of gardenias. A video man done up in clericals was stashed in the altar or discreetly proceeding up and down the aisles by dim flashes of light. Librettos provided. The bridesmaids, including Barbara Walters and Selwa Roosevelt, were in periwinkle blue, very modest costumes (but Arianna's Galanos cost, I should think, about fifteen or twenty thousand). Glorious music, specially an interlude from *The Magic Flute* while

---

52. Alessandra Ferri (b. 1963) had joined American Ballet Theatre the year before. Herbert Ross would soon direct her and Baryshnikov in the film *Dancers* (1987).
53. The biographer, later political commentator, Arianna Stassinopoulos (b. 1950) was marrying the Texas oilman, later congressman, Michael Huffington (b. 1947). They would divorce in 1997.

the bride and the groom walked about the altar under massive crowns (Greek-Orthodox).

Matron of Honor—and Backer—[the socialite philanthropist] Ann Getty read, badly, from the Song of Solomon; the groom's best man read Shakespeare's 116th Sonnet; [Arianna's sister] Agape read from the Bible, very well. ("Don't put your sister on the stage, Mrs. Huffington," I hummed.) Arianna pecked at her groom's cheek or whispered to him during the long intervals while they stood before the altar. We sat in a nest of sharp tongues. Nan Kempner [socialite] murmured, "She's sold the hair rights." So it went, for over an hour and a half. I was reminded of the Countess Greffulhe's heavy, brocaded, beaded, and pavéed gown (similar in silhouette), which she wore to her daughter's wedding, outshining the bride. I looked about Saint Bart's, saw our New Society, some six hundred of it, and thought: For this Lily Bart killed herself [in *The House of Mirth*]? *Women's Wear Daily* called it the "Wedding of the Week."

APRIL 26, 1986  The sadness I felt when I saw the astronauts walking on the moon, planting our flag there. At that moment my childhood had ended. The little boy who stood in a window, in his grandfather's house, peering up at the moon, wonderment enveloping him like a protective cloak, vanished. So when, after an afternoon's intense, brief rain, a glory of light streamed from the west out over the Hudson and into the streets of Manhattan, and I wondered at this miracle, at what poet would perceive eternity there in that effulgence, I suddenly knew that no poet could ever again perceive eternity in any natural beauty known to us, known to Shakespeare or Euripides or Shelley or the young Auden. The bomb had ended our eternity. My sadness as I was being driven north on Madison Avenue was more devastating than that sorrow I had felt sitting in Mina's "den" in her Bethel house, in Connecticut, peering at the astronauts' triumph on the moon.

MAY 3, 1986  Dining last night at Dolly and Al Hirschfeld's, because Maria Riva is here staying in Marlene's apartment on Park Avenue. "It's like *Great Expectations* . . . the curtains in shreds, the big looking glass over the bed crashing down. . . . I pulled the bed away from the wall. No, it doesn't light up from underneath anymore. . . . Yes, the lipsticks are still there in the bathroom, but—oh—falling apart, falling apart. . . . She never lied, always believed everything. She always believed she was in love. . . . I never thought that she would choose this end to her life. She had a choice—to get into bed or to try to walk, to lead an active life. She chose getting into bed because then she didn't fall down drunk. When she is high she is brilliant, when she is not high she doesn't make sense." Maria looks marvelous—very kempt, classy, fined down, no trace of Marlene, not a trace, save, now and then, a mannerism, but—

surprise—her tone, inflection is very like Marti Stevens. Ironic.[54] Maria is enormously competent. She exudes competence the way some people exude moral authority or intellectuality or humanism. She is battling Simon & Schuster about "her" book [about her mother], since it is not her work, but a "cheap, sentimental" thing written by a couple. "You know, I found, at sixty-two I can write. I can really write."

At the Hirschfelds, we discovered that the basement floor of 1453 has now become an English food emporium. A woman from Northumberland bought 1453 and lives there, on the parlor floor, and rents out the top floors. How appropriate that 1453 has become an English food shop. I see Edith Evans crouching by our fireplace in what was, at that time, the downstairs dining room, stuffing herself with magulala (an all-purpose stew) made by our tyrannical cook Gladys. Edith was ravenous after appearing in *Daphne Laureola*, but she always tucked in. (Gladys left us for Josephine Baker, and we were thrilled.)

Monday, the Capezio Award to Antony [Tudor]. For some two hours, I forgot terrorism, nuclear warfare, and breakdown. I forgot the world of today. Age and time were annihilated. On a dais sat Antony (his face—the granite look, the straight line from nose to chin tip, the humorous light lurking in the depths of his unblinking eyes); to his right, Nora; to his left, Hugh [Laing]; and, variously, Donald Saddler, Alicia Markova, Agnes de Mille, Bill Schuman, Oliver Smith, Jerry Robbins, Misha, Natasha [Makarova], Paul Taylor, Martha Hill[55] (she and I sponsored Antony when he was becoming a citizen, but he didn't because he would not swear that he would bear arms) . . . and others.

Agnes spoke the longest and the most rewardingly about the early days with Marie Rambert.[56] Alicia thanked him for "a great job," meaning [the role of] Juliet. Hugh wept throughout. Nora looked very well-to-do. Paul [Taylor] told about being a bad student and how Martha Graham had kicked Antony hard in the shins because he had said that she was guilty of "choreographic compromise." Antony talked about how he loved toe shoes.

But none of this is as important as the pure love that was the atmosphere we breathed in that room. For almost two hours, this was the ballet world in all of its former glory—that tightly meshed world of magical, dedicated people, ultimately as ill-fated as butterflies, the living symbols of transience, these dancers

54. Soprano and actress Marti Stevens (1919–2002) and Marlene Dietrich were living together in London when Gray and Leo were there in 1964–65. To some at the time, Stevens appeared to become a facsimile of Dietrich.
55. The Russian dancer and actress Natalia Makarova (b. 1940) had been a principal dancer with American Ballet Theatre, but she performed with many companies. Paul Taylor (b. 1930), one of America's preeminent choreographers, founded his own company in 1954. Martha Hill (1901–95) was a dance teacher and the director of dance at Juilliard (1951–85).
56. Polish-born dancer Marie Rambert (1888–1982) founded the first British ballet company and nurtured Antony Tudor (as well as Frederick Ashton). Laing and Tudor met in her company, Ballet Rambert.

and even choreographers and historians. Memory opens cracks in time everywhere. Hugh kissed me, held me, and suddenly said, "But who are you?" I looked at him, at his thick white hair, his worn face, his ravaged looks, and said, "I'm Leo! Leo Lerman!" He grabbed me tighter, kissed me hard, and wept even more vigorously: "I've never seen you with a white beard! Never!" So that is how time was recaptured.

When I say, for those two hours we were all young, that is not the truth. We were old—and young. But I think that even though, years ago, we did not physically show age, we were even at that time young and old. Now we are old and young. That is the kernel of our special magic. We are not Peter Pan or Wendy. We thought that we were. Or perhaps if we were, most of us are no longer. We recognize and even hug our shadows tight to us, and our shadows are enveloping us. . . . Is that why I love to look down into the street (I first discovered this in Munich) watching the passersby going west in the early sunny morning, their shadows preceding them; going east, their shadows behind them?

MAY 20, 1986   In the thirties I went up to City College of New York, and I looked at it for several months, and I loathed it. What did I want? I wanted to have my own way, to read and read and write and write. So, I got into bed and refused to come out.

Our high school group was the most brilliant—no drudges—and our high school teachers marvelous. We inherited modernism. We lived in the throes of experiment—not so sexually. What did we know of Freud? Not one of us was psychoanalyzed. The homosexual element was apart from this group, not within. We lived for words, cherishing them as only first-generation children could.

JUNE 6, 1986   Marlene called: "But put on Leo Lerman. You aren't Leo Lerman. . . . You're a young man. He's old and sick. You're young and healthy. Put on Leo Lerman!" Then we were cut off.

JUNE 19, 1986   "You'll love them," Carl Van Vechten said to me. "Dorothy [Gish] is the witty sister; Lillian is the pretty sister." Then, one evening, I sat watching them, while we all sat eating our dinners, at various tables, in the Woman's Exchange on Madison Avenue, and I saw Lillian say something to Dorothy, and Dorothy threw back her head and shook with laughter, rippled with it, and she was beautiful. And Carlo was right: I loved them.

JUNE 21, 1986   Franco Rossellini visited this week. He came to talk about a worldwide commemoration of the death of Maria, ten years ago, on September 16, 1977.[57] But mostly we talked about the Maria each of us had known so

---

57. Producer Franco Rossellini (1935–92), nephew of the director Roberto Rossellini, had persuaded Callas to star in Pasolini's film *Medea* (1969).

intimately, the woman who was essentially a bourgeoise, inhabited by that dybbuk-genius. When the genius left her, when the dybbuk left her actually, she died. She had the grace not to survive her dybbuk too long. Was Marlene's dybbuk her beauty? She had assorted talents, but she did not have genius. Her talents having deserted her, or been eroded by her own arrogance and time. She gracelessly lingers on, outstaying the self, the public and sometimes private self she once was. Or is she, poor dear, lost in time? People lost in time: an idea new to me. . . . I know about reputations lost in time and then discovered—a good example is Lionel, now beginning to be rediscovered as one of our most potent, critical forces and shapers. "I hope that I can get my book out before Lionel's reputation goes into a decline again," Diana said last night. We assured her that his reputation wouldn't and that her book would.

JULY 5, 1986 Early on—even before *Twilight Men* (and its revelations about men in blue shirts and black knitted ties)—I knew Oscar Wilde.[58] In the early thirties, high school students were not permitted to "research" in the Forty-second Street library. I lied about my age. It became my haven, my home away from home; it gave me protection—and sexual wondering at the men I saw. Nothing ever came of any of that fantasy, but I spent my summers there with Elinor Wylie, vampires, English, American, French, and German murderers and their trials—and reading everything I could find about Oscar Wilde—the court records, everything. I could not understand how so brilliant, so successful a man, so full of humor and wit, could land himself into so horrible a place. Finally, I realized that a supreme arrogance had done him in, a disdain of the everyday, the commonplace. He had underestimated the masses. Art, he thought, made him sacrosanct, but *épater* [to shock] *le bourgeois*—that did him in. He could not resist showing off.

Nora about Jerry Robbins: "I just can't talk to him anymore. He's so self-absorbed. He really doesn't have anything to talk about. We have these long silences. He's so boring. We were once so very close . . . so close." They were engaged to be married, until he went before the McCarthy people and talked.[59] Then Nora, a week before the wedding, walked out. What time does to friendships, to love—to "close."

Herbert [Ross] believes in the ritual obligation of old, now worn-out friendships.

JULY 12, 1986 The only words I know in Polish translate into "Fuck yourself," which I learned as a child from Momma, when she was watching the family

58. André Tellier's *Twilight Men* (1931), a novel about New York's homosexual world in the twenties, was well known to gay men of Leo's generation.
59. In 1953, Robbins testified before the House Un-American Activities Committee, naming others with Communist connections.

newsstand, and I thought they meant "Thank you!" That is all I know of that aspect of the family history.

Not a day passes without moments of wondering is this it, now, stepping carefully down a step, tottering across this room, trying to see—just trying to see. . . . What an agony light, which I love, has become. How I long for sunless days. How I fear cold. How heat now does me in. How my physical world has changed. But I devise little ruses to cope. I wet my pants and make believe that this has not happened. I hate smelling of urine: a telltale old man smell. I make believe that I am as fragrant as anyone in his fragrant prime. In short, I go on—trying to make more than the best of it all. I know that I am helped by a now long life lived, mostly, in fantasy, a life lived so unrealistically that it has taken almost everyone in. But the life has all been extra, all borrowed time, all never to be, and holding it up today, this man, these eyes are not the ones who lived that life.

JULY 13, 1986  Bleak, sunless morning, quiet but for the usual skin of city-summer hum: air conditioners. Far easier to accustom the ear to the furl, even tumult, of an onrushing stream, like the one that ran almost under Jo Washburn's shack, where we spent so much time in the thirties and during the early years of the Second World War. "Roll Out the Barrel" on that stony little beach at Westport, and how we polkaed and fell about almost destroyed by laughter . . . but at what? Those were dreadful times—yet we were so happy. I think that we were happy because we lived in an optimistic world, where the misery was not real to us. We heard, we even saw (in films), we were told, but we did not feel in our bones. Nothing actually happened to us. We were patriotic. We rallied and contributed and made our little efforts and were part of the bravado and the hope. We wanted the Nazis annihilated, but—still—we were all emotion and effort and having a wonderful time despite restrictions. This was a high time for us at home—almost fictional, more imagined than realized. We could not feel the agony in Europe. We were not part of it, only apart from it. We could feel for it, but not feel it. And we were in the center of a world of escape. Also, to be in the center of a world of escape, and the Europeans here had all escaped, was not conducive to agony, but to exhilaration.

Some mornings ago, I was telling David [Holland in the office] something, and suddenly lost all thought. I could not think of anything except to keep on talking about how I could not think of anything and to joke, in a vacant, bright electric-bulb vacancy, about senility. This slot-dropped-out feeling lasted a long time. David helped by smiling throughout. I smiled constantly, waiting for memory to return, and that butterfly finally fluttered into place again—as if it had never vanished.

JULY 18, 1986  Same hot July days, same Noël Coward voice on recordings— but that was 1943 and 1944, and that was in Ela's bedroom on East Seventy-third Street, above the carpenter shop and next to Fritz and Hellmut's queen-place (a leap from roof to roof), with Cesco on the other side in the basement of the house, and Rut and Elsa [Snapper] and Annettchen Kolb[60] in the next block west, and Ilse [Bois] still on Seventy-fifth Street, [Ilse's room] next to Lotte Lenya, and all of that world intact. Now this is 1986, and I sit here, four streets north, forty-three years away, at Joan [Buck]'s desk in our home away from home, and all of them—in that 1943 world—are gone, dead, or vanished. . . . The late-night secret Maestro visits, the intense consultations, the long, laughing hours, the rages, the loves and hates, the private passions, the unrequited pains, the intense pain, on a different scale, at what was happening in our world . . . all gone . . . all here in that reedy, misplaced, sentimental, somehow courageously sad Noël voice . . . following his "secret heart," "We must have music," "If love were all," "Don't let's be beastly to the Hun" (how Ela gurgled with laughter) . . . and in *Private Lives*, Noël and Gertie, very clipped, very bright young people, very protected and—oh—so brittlely aching . . . thin, high voices with a caress like a crease in it, sentimentality breaking through, while the fake moonlight never fades . . . never. ("Oh—darling, darling!" Ela would breathe, her green eyes brimming) . . . while the small, heart-cover, witty small talk washes up like seadrift—bits of colored glass, little exotic feathers, fluted shells—and the deep heart suddenly, convincingly, breaks through. That is the power; there is the truth—the sad-glad optimism. "I'll see you again, whenever spring breaks through again." And here I sit . . . the same July Friday afternoon heat, the same empty street feeling . . . everything, everything . . . except nothing left . . . voices on records, images on screens, and the past present in my heart . . . but even that past is changed . . . recaptured in the form of my present.

Sitting in the vast redbrick area outside the theaters in Purchase[61]—hearing echoes from the *Così Fan Tutte*, *The Robbers*, *A Midsummer Night's Dream*, the Haydn Quartet, the many public television screens with their sitcoms—sitting at a table in the restaurant "area" near a splendid buffet of sandwiches, cornucopias of fruit . . . watching the milling crowds of summer people in their summer de rigueurs and dishabilles . . . coagulations of people of all ages . . . constant movement, constant sound . . . having left the almost two-hour first act of *The Robbers* (the celebrated company from West Germany in a neo-Brechtian production notable for its absurdity and pig-headedness, its amazing body movements remotely rooted in Wigman and Kreutzberg,[62] kin to [current choreographer] Pina Bausch)—hating it, because I could see no

60. German Annette Kolb (1870–1967), biographer, memoirist, and novelist, was a wartime refugee in New York.
61. A state university campus thirty miles north of Manhattan, site of a summer theater festival.
62. German dancer and choreographer Mary Wigman (1886–1973) and her student Harald Kreutzberg (1902–68) were both exponents of spare Expressionism.

Schiller, no *Sturm und Drang.* (Amalia played by a boy; the brigand band more *Mahagonny* than eighteenth-century revolution.) I saw that this complex could become a concentration camp instantly. I can see New York "intellectuals" being bused in by the thousands to this awful place that [modernist architect] Edward Larrabee Barnes "designed." I saw a man intently counting out money, popping it into a bright scarlet bar. I [imagined I] saw Marguérite Moréno seated at her table, at the entrance of a Cocteau-imagined Hell,[63] and that gave me the clue: We had passed over, and this was our eternity, the afterlife of culture-vultures, destined forever to lurk in this Bartholomew's Fair of maltreated masterpieces, all of the goodies ersatz, all beauty debased, humiliated, mired . . . ceaseless *Kultur* . . . this was, indeed, HELL. So I got on the electrical-[chair] lift throne and descended majestically out into the night and was sped home through pelting bursts of rain that yielded not freshness, but steam, evaporating when it came to earth.

AUGUST 1, 1986 I have been reading again, after thirty-five years, *The Way We Live Now.* Trollope is not Dickens—no comedy (although Trollope seems to have heard of irony); no poetry of the commonplace—only the commonplace; no deeps and depths of London, only the surfaces, the necessary sets for his look at life. I do not hear, smell, see the city in Trollope. I do not think Trollope loves London the way Dickens does. Trollope is about, not from within. Trollope is chromolith; Dickens paints. There's Rembrandt in Dickens. I cannot think of a parallel life for Trollope.

At the Players [Club] last night, Helen Hayes said that John Barrymore was the best Hamlet she'd ever seen: "He didn't act the Prince. He was the Prince. I will never forget the look of sweetness that came over his face when he spoke to the Player King. John Gielgud—yes I liked him, but he was acting. . . . Barrymore was the Prince." About her dress: She wore a large, almost huge, oval opal of distinct colors, like marbleized paper, set in a sizable diamond-studded cross. "You see, when I wear this, I have to wear a simple dress. Lillian [Gish] gave it to me. Griffith gave it to her after she almost died on the ice floes in *Way Down East.* And Lillian said: 'You have it, Helen. He got the opal from Russia, and he had Tiffany set it, and you're Catholic. You have it!' It's the most extravagant thing I've ever had. But you have to wear it on a plain dress. I can only buy simple dresses now." The dress was quietly Elizabethan—the color of deep, almost Japanese-red-maple leaf. It suited her beautifully. I never thought Helen a beauty when she was younger—or witty. I never really liked her onstage—too goody-goody, almost "fake" goody-goody, I thought. She has become beautiful, very funny, and I dote on her.

I cried a lot at [Francis Ford Coppola's film] *Peggy Sue Got Married.* It sent me straight back into Momma's kitchen, on Seventy-fourth Street, long, long

---

63. Marguérite Moréno (d. 1948) was a star of the Comédie-Française.

ago on Thursday baking nights. Almost all night long Momma baked and I aided—mixing butter-yellow or honey-brown batters in huge, pale yellow crockery bowls, whirling the wooden spoon to bits from *Hänsel und Gretel*, cracking and shelling nuts, picking over dried fruits. And the fragrances: cinnamon, honey, raisins plumping in brandy, flour, hotting-up sugar (brown and white), chocolate in all stages. Momma, her arms in twenty-button gloves of flour, cheerfully bustling, kneading, calculating, slicing, pounding, rolling out, chopping. The baking sounds: sputterings, cracklings, steamings—and, always, the perfume of the cakes growing lustier and lustier. Then the bowls of icing and the rewards—licking the bowls clean! Then the cakes and cookies and rugelach and mandelbrot closed away in huge tins begged from fish and grocery stores, hidden away in secret places where we always found them . . . and so to bed, at dawn, and frequently no school. Baking was more important than school. What did we talk about all night long? We did not really talk. I mixed and cracked and chopped and sang, and Momma rolled out with her *volgar holz* [rolling pin] and punched and pounded and stirred and poured and tested. And we both tasted—oh—we tasted a lot. Those were the happiest times.

AUGUST 4, 1986  Last night, in the Tent Room of the Regency Hotel—Carol Channing and Charlie [Lowe]'s dinner—about twenty-four at brilliantly appointed tables—nosegays for the women, red-rose boutonnieres for the men, placecards (gone-past tickets to *Legends*, now in Boston).[64] Carol in last year's white longish Vionnet-influenced handkerchief hemline and Bea Lillie "Marvelous Party" ropes and ropes of pearls.

Carol's long toasts-to-each-of-us speech, during which she somehow managed to sweetness-and-light us all into fractured egos: She was so funny—specially about "My little costar Mary. . . ." Miss Martin grew smaller and smaller with each loving word . . . until she was so small that she almost disappeared into the mouse-box. "Oh—that lovely little Mary . . . my darling, darling, dear, sweet little, little costar. . . . She so did want to be with all of us here tonight . . . all of us loving friends . . . but she is surrounded at the Ritz in Boston by her darling children and grandchildren and even a darling little great-grandchild . . . so adorable . . . and she just—" At which point, Linda Janklow [chairman of the Lincoln Center Theater], in her raucous voice, shouted at Carol: "Did you invite her?" Carol, unperturbed, proceeded to sweetly demolish with knife-blade compliments, the rest of us—absolutely enchanting, delicious, and hilarious. . . . Carol on how Al [Hirschfeld]'s first, *Lend an Ear*, caricature of her [in 1948] set her makeup for life . . . How the "most wonderful agent in the world—he set everything I've ever done—Lee

64. Channing and Mary Martin had recently toured in the vehicle *Legends*, by James Kirkwood. Channing's husband, the producer Charles Lowe (1911–99), managed her career.

Stevens—didn't get me my contract until the 1,999th performance of *Hello, Dolly!* . . . How "I'm sure, Kitty, that darling Moss [Hart], who thought you were so beautiful, would think it—if he could see you now . . ." She never finished that one. "Darling Morty [Janklow] and Gray and Leo—they are my blood kin, because they were so wonderful to my darling Anita. She would call and tell me the filthiest gossip, and I would say, 'Oh—Anita—who ever told you that?' And she would say, 'Darling—Leo and Gray and Morty' and she loved you and I love you forever and ever. . . ."

SEPTEMBER 5, 1986  There is no bad taste—only taste and no taste.

# THE OTHER END OF THE STREET

JOURNAL • OCTOBER 12, 1986 Just some words—I am parched for words. Marlene's call last week: a long, sometimes incisive ramble—always very Marlene—the color edged in Berlin black—self-mockery. "I know that Maria loves me. She really loves me—but she hates me—maybe because, when she was little and fat, I was so be-oo-tee-ful . . ." syllabling "beautiful" into something that existed apart from herself and of which she was a worshipper. Then, "Why am I so burdened by memory? I remember everything—everything. . . ." Then, "Money—if you have money, that is everything—money. . . ."

NOVEMBER 16, 1986  One wet early November late morning, about 1934, I was out hunting jobs. Walking beside the Cort Theatre, on West Forty-eighth Street, I noticed a door slightly open. I instantly stole in, enticed by my passion to at least see, feel, be some little part of Broadway theater life. The theater was huge in its gloom, as mysterious as a Rembrandt etching. . . . Far off a single work light on a standing stem blazed onstage—a star in this satisfying night, which was fragrant with scenery paint, makeup paint, an effluvia of smell so potent that it rivals Proust's madeleine. In that circle, or nimbus, of light, I saw a figure—turbaned, a huge, V-shaped coat (broad dark fur on a brilliant, smoldering orange cloth that tapered to a tightness below the knees)—and this figure was so drawn to its own being that nothing could have distracted it. Her carriage—one gloved hand clutching coat, other on hip—was superb. As I watched, she walked some six paces upstage, made a half turn, stood a moment, obviously delivering some speech soundlessly, then moved downstage in a straight, sure line . . . stood a moment, head cocked, listening to some unheard speech, pivoted . . . moved precisely upstage again. She repeated this over and over again—aiming for some perfection known only to herself. I had recognized her immediately—Beulah Bondi, a veteran with theater in her veins rather than blood. And here she was in this wet, cold, awful November morning practicing more rigorously than any novice. Her sternly aquiline features, her huge painted eyes intent on one goal—some perfection, some miracle of timing, some miraculous effect which when the house was filled and the lights blazed would look effortless. I stood there marveling. This,

I knew, was the rigorous, quintessential essence of theater. I learned more, standing there, hardly daring to breathe, than in a year at the Feagin School.

NOVEMBER 24, 1986 · LONDON  Last night, Doris and Charles Saatchi gave a dinner for us at Caprice, inviting Min Hogg, John Mortimer, and the Steve Martins.[1] Victoria [Tennant] is more ravishing than her mother [the ballerina Baronova] when young, and much brighter, and Puss says that Victoria knows a lot and is politically aware. He took a violent distaste for our host, thinking him malevolent, evil, empty, utterly commercial, show-off, and know-nothing. The host said to Puss that he [Saatchi] was a vacuum cleaner, "sucking everything in." Pointing to his closely cropped, dark hair, Charles Saatchi said that in galleries he is never recognized by dealers: "They never think that I am anybody, and that helps." Puss's impression included that the host really knows no past. Doris does.

When I got them all to play that old game "Who Did I Want to Be and When?" the host said promptly, "Howard Hughes," which seemed to fill Doris with a cold horror. She said, "Catherine de Medici," and I said to her, "Endless ice cream." She said, "Those two Rubens panels." Min said, "Palladio—very young, before the whole career." John Mortimer: "Marco Polo." Steve Martin: "Picasso!" Victoria: "Mrs. Patrick Campbell." To which Steve Martin said, "Who's that?" and his wife explained with anecdotes, very well told with smiling, blond goodness, rather like a having-lived-in-the-world Desdemona.

Actually we had several casts for *Othello*, with Doris and Victoria alternating as Desdemona, Min as the lady-in-waiting, Mr. Saatchi and Mr. Martin alternating as Othello and Iago, Mr. Mortimer as the not-lover, Cassio . . . and the rest of us as everyone else, including a storm at sea. In *Othello* each character is a patsy.

NOVEMBER 30, 1986  This morning Pam [Harlech] rang to say that Cary Grant had dropped dead of a heart attack, somewhere in Ohio, where he was making "a personal appearance." Cary always had a brown-eyed kindness for me, an instinctive understanding of problems. I was always a little shocked by his four-letter words, studding the soft flow of his Anglo-American diction. Frequently, he seemed at odds with his life—as if he had had it all and what was the use of going on with the habitual—a kind of uncomplaining, organic discontent.

---

1. The comedian Steve Martin had recently married the actress Victoria Tennant. Charles Saatchi, the advertising-agency director and modern-art collector, was then married to art journalist and collector Doris Lockhart Saatchi. Min Hogg was the editor of Condé Nast's *World of Interiors* magazine. John Mortimer, a barrister, is best known as author of the *Rumpole of the Bailey* stories.

NOTE: Leo had a kidney stone attack that, for the second time in three years, put him into a London hospital.

JOURNAL · DECEMBER 7, 1986  I have been in Devonshire Hospital since Wednesday [December 2] and have suffered miracles, also great kindness from friends and strangers—the gaiety, amiability, and interest of the nurses here. The drama is: New York said my kidney wasn't worth worrying about—done for—kaput. London says: It's a good kidney—alive, salvageable! The horror is: Loss of faith in New York—except Bill Cahan, who has been marvelous.

[Actress] Pat Hodge said that she knows a woman who shared her gynecologist. That woman said that the gyno had also been Mrs. Simpson's, and that Mrs. Simpson's sexual power over the king [Edward VIII] had been her power to "make a matchstick feel like a cigar." With a band on it? Did Mrs. Simpson collect cigar bands? Line dishes with them?

DECEMBER 8, 1986  Listening to BBC classical today—nothing hackneyed, nothing packaged. At home everything is packaged, like the vegetables in our supermarkets, all fitting in-between commercials, "news," etc., all in "time-slots." This is quintessentially the American way of life.

This Reagan shame [the Iran-Contra affair]—I know of no term sufficiently obscene with which to pin down what has happened. The shame of our nation, in which almost all share, since the American people voted this emptiness to the top. This man was shallow, a second-rate actor, utterly dependent on superficial Irish charm—the kind the morning milkman or letter carrier or any man in the streets has. He was destined to be used by strong, self-seeking, unscrupulous men wanting power not for state, but for self. The man may be honest, but he is stupid, which in his position of highest power is criminal. He is also an actor, and so must, like a vampire, be nourished on adulation. That he has been, by a people besotted by screen images, a people so debauched by unreality, fed to them as reality, that his healthy, smiling, good-fellow self, the splendidly nourished vampire, flourished. He was always the man the people wanted to see. They did not specially want to hear him: They needed this smiling, honest-faced, bonhomie fellow—no matter what gaffes, what messes he made, no matter what irritations or excesses. Now that the vampire's nourishment is in decline, now that the actor's ego is less and less lovingly stroked, what happens? Does the actor become a costume? And is that costume, empty of its life, hung on a hook in some storeroom, waiting to become alive again when another "star" is born?

DECEMBER 10, 1986  To the Bethnal Green Museum [of Childhood] this morning, since I am told that I must exercise, and this museum is an enchantment. The dollhouses no longer harbor domestic tragedies. Some five years ago, all of the butlers were fallen into drunken stupors, the mistresses pitching downstairs, the maids tipsy-angled. Now they're stolid, proper, prim. This is the world of Ivy Compton-Burnett, with its malevolence suspected, but still unrevealed. The houses are superb, and today were decked for Christmas.

DECEMBER 21, 1986 • NEW YORK CITY I am crying because I *can* bear it. The women I have loved—Momma, Ela, Penelope, Nora—gave out a warmth, which immediately embraced and protected me. This is true of Puss and Richard, the only two men I have ever really, abidingly loved. Richard's "flame" is more temperate. Puss's is the most intense of anyone I have ever known, is of the greatest loves known, the love we find in the greatest of novels: Anna Karenina, Isolde . . . overwhelming, consuming all—the lover and the loved one. The final desolation comes with the realization that life is like fiction.

DECEMBER 25, 1986 Lincoln Kirstein's attack on Manet is really an attack on Mina.[2]

A respite for Nora—Herbert brought her home yesterday, and she instantly revived—looking at everything, loving all, and her doggies, loving her house. So revived is she that she was able to talk to us about an hour ago! This is, I am sure, a respite . . . but, at least, Nora and Herbert have this Christmas, so precious to them, together. Her voice was hers, but ragged with everything she has been through. Nora was loving, instantly caring.

DECEMBER 31, 1986 Herbert on the blower: "She has no pain. She's just very quiet. Every morning, I ask her how she is and she says, 'Fine . . .' It's her spirit." We all know the inevitable—even Nora knows, I suspect. So little time, so little time . . .

I must note the Van Gogh exhibit—his last year and a half. Can only madness and a technique so sound and a vision so steady, so inspired, make this glory? The great winds blow through these paintings and drawings. Genius is inadequate to explain it. Van Gogh is beyond genius. Even with my eyes dimmed, I saw this glory beyond our understanding—save by acceptance without questioning. These paintings, drawings, of these last months of Van Gogh's life are inexplicable facts like trees, clouds, flowers, butterflies, waterfalls, storms, God—not the God of the Bible, but the Universal Being—neither Vengeance nor Forgiveness—Being. This last year and a half of Van Gogh's is Being. We have had, in this dreadful year, several miracles: this vision of Van Gogh, my miracle in the Devonshire Hospital. And what is a miracle, but another name for faith and hope?

2. Interviewed in *The New Yorker*, Kirstein said Manet was "a simple bourgeois hedonist who thought painting was good food." Mina Curtiss had long planned to write a book on the artist.

JANUARY 1, 1987  Betty [Comden]'s annual party was a triumph of spirit. No longer in her big house, she gathered her chums into her small apartment, an eyrie. The annual event now a tribute to her spirit and her chums' love of her. Lennie [Bernstein] was there with a huge belly and Shirley [Bernstein] was unchanged—just more so.[3] Ruth Elizabeth Ford came up to me and poured out. She told me what I had meant to her all of these years and how sad she was that life had moved us in different directions. This was honest and generous and loving of her. I have always loved Ruth Elizabeth, but I haven't always liked her. In her "heyday" she trampled less-fortunates as she climbed, even clawed her way to some imagined top—a top that wasn't there. Now that she is in severe times, the true Ruth Elizabeth is visible. She was always a loving heart, but self-aggrandizement—yes—ambition, almost assassinated that loving heart. She became a taker rather than a giver. Many kissing chums— [actress] Marian Seldes: "I now live only a block away." That was her way of telling me that she has moved in with Garson Kanin [director and screenwriter], taking [the late] Ruth Gordon's place. Such a curious development. All the gritty-voiced "girls": Elaine Steinbeck [John's widow], Eileen Heckart [actress]. A thick soup of survivors and everyone chunked together. Said someone: "How would we know that we're still here, if we didn't come to Betty's on New Year's Day?"

JANUARY 4, 1987  With the help of Antony Tudor (who taught her how to use her neurosis and her humor) and Jerry Robbins (who discovered a useful monster in her [in *The Cage*]) Nora Kaye became America's, and then the world's, Greatest Dramatic Ballerina. But the straight-talking, never-phony Nora was always there. I recall standing in the stage-left wings of the old Metropolitan Opera house—a packed night. The ballet is Antony's *Pillar of Fire* [1942]. Onstage, Nora sits on the steps of her family house, twitching at the collar of her pale dress. The music swells; the golden scenic curtain unfurls; the stage light is shadowy-rosy where it spills into the orchestra. Nora is all brooding, all suffering. One arm rises, in an unforgettable gesture to her brooding, neurotic face. From backstage came the rhythmic, persistent pounding of someone using the rosin box, and from the great dramatic ballerina's mouth—while three thousand people swooned at her theatrical power—came: "If that fuckin' ballerina doesn't stop I'll break her ankles!" Out front, they never knew. We marveled at the artistry, the control, the fact of being Nora Kaye.

JANUARY 20, 1987  At least four calls yesterday from Marlene. These grew successively repetitious: about how overwhelmed she was at the tributes in the Council of Fashion Designers of America program: "That I am delighted is the

---

3. Shirley Bernstein (1923–98), sister of Leonard, was an agent and producer who had arranged Leo's appearance on *The $64,000 Question* in 1958.

understatement of the year!"[4] This went on in the early a.m., with side trips into Maria and her four sons. Gradually, as the day and evening extended itself, the content of Marlene's calls intensified about her four grandchildren and about how she didn't want anyone of her family to represent her at the [National Society of Film] Critics awards. This went on, with little variation, for a very long time. To divert her, I said: "Wasn't Kate Hepburn's poem a wonderful tribute?" And she said that Kate Hepburn was indeed wonderful, that Kate and she are in constant correspondence and telephone talk, that Kate was a "wonderful old man." Then she returned to her family and how she was responsible for Maria and had to send her money constantly, because "that's the way I brought her up" etc., etc. Finally I caused the connection to break and felt guilty, but I think that during the late day calls she had had too much to drink. While Marlene was asking for Misha Baryshnikov's telephone number, to thank him [for accepting her fashion award], he called to ask for hers— so finally they palavered. Marlene to me: "I'm in love! I'm in love! At my age to fall in love!" "What," I asked, "has age to do with it?"

FEBRUARY 4, 1987 When Diana Cooper was asked how she felt being ninety, she answered: "Posthumous."

FEBRUARY 7, 1987 At lunch at [fashion designer] Mary McFadden's hive of industry, high up in the [garment] market, chomping on jicama and talking kidneys to Mary, my throat suddenly clamped up, my eyes bulged, my voice departed, and with my voice, I, too, almost went—but somehow I survived—to hear the table at which I sat battle on about "whether you want to know if your passion was being unfaithful to you or would you prefer not to know?" [Humorist] Fran Lebowitz, who sat to my right, murmured, "Ye gods, I don't know anybody who has sex anymore. They don't seem to know what's going on in the world." Then she and I fell to talking about a *Vanity Fair* feature on AIDS, both of us feeling that it was exploitation rather than an attempt to help to educate. The others continued to rattle on about jealousy, sex, fidelity—all of that hollow, and now in the context of this plague "so old-fashioned," Fran said.

FEBRUARY 8, 1987 Diana Vreeland on the blower: "I think that we'll have a telephone relationship. I have three or four of those, and I find them most satisfactory."

Marlene: "I cut it all out of newspapers. I know it all. Don't think I don't know it all. I know what's going on all over the world. . . . I never slept with all those people they said I did. You can love somebody and not even touch them,

---

4. Dietrich received a lifetime achievement award from the organization. Leo and Katharine Hepburn both wrote tributes for the souvenir program. Baryshnikov accepted on behalf of Dietrich, who was then a recluse in Paris.

sleep with them. I love you. I never slept with you. I loved Hemingway. He loved me. We never slept with one another."

FEBRUARY 9, 1987  Gore on the blower from Rome: "We've been around the world . . . Morocco . . . highland, lowland . . . Bangkok . . . all the places where there was sex! sex! sex! And, alas, because of the plague, we've become voyeurs." When I reminded him of his afternoon in the St. Regis, years and years ago, with Noël and P [Graham Payn], he cried out, "How did you know about that?" Me: "You told me." G: "I never told you. I never told anyone!" Me: "You climbed five flights of stairs and told me." G: "Well . . . I probably did, because I knew that you would tell Troosey, and I wanted him to know." Gore, even now that Little T (Marge) has been dead these years, continues to want "Troosey to know." We never talk that he doesn't get Little T into the conversation and always on a note—a wild, exulting note—triumphant in his own survival! The jealousy festers.

*Prick Up Your Ears*—the film is brilliantly cast. I was not moved at Joe Orton's rise and bang up (unintended pun—rotten of me), but this is a wonderfully made film.[5] I sat thinking of T, and how his life was a *déchéance*, wondering if that self-destruction in Joe Orton and in Truman had been there even when each of them was in the womb, and how Nina [Capote] did herself in with drink and finally a last desperate self-annihilating act, and how T did himself in with annihilation (phony) and drink and drugs, as much self-annihilation as his mother's.

FEBRUARY 22, 1987  A "visit" to Memorial Hospital—a smooth-faced young woman, the technician, received us. She was wonderfully expert and indefatigably kind (I resented being immediately called "Leo"). She took four phials of blood, painlessly. Then she trundled me up to the X-ray place, Puss trotting along carrying all the clothes. As we went along the brightly lighted, *Kunst*-hung corridors, she, in her lilting, young, pleasing voice regaled us with her love of England. She said, in the same quiet, affectionate rhythm, "Oh, I can't wait to go to Whitby. They have the most wonderful Dracula towers there. . . . Bram Stoker . . ." "Yes," I said unthinkingly, "that's where he lived, and the graveyard where Mina walked in the beginning of the book . . . that's there. . . ." Suddenly, I thought: I shouldn't be telling her this—the four phials of my blood! She'll know that I know! We trundled on and up. When she deposited me, she said, "I'll need two more phials when you come on Tuesday." Then she went away. Puss and I were silent for a time. Then I said, "She looks awfully young to have been here seventeen years." Puss said, "They always look young, even when they are five hundred years old." What better

---

5. Joe Orton (1933–67), a British playwright of black comedies, was bludgeoned to death by his male lover.

place for a vampire than Memorial Hospital? Such a good gem of a plot for a Steve Martin movie.

Paloma [Picasso] is grave-seeming. Actually, not grave but composed. People who don't know her are surprised at how genuine she is. She breaks into a ravishing smile and frequently into deep chimes of laughter. She really has the grave look of her father's painting of the woman with what looks like pillows on her head, an earlyish painting, after the Cubist period—not abstract, not the Blue period. She has perfect composure, a loving heart, and a capacity for hard work. Paloma is a person of character, owing more to the northern Spanish genes of her father than to those of her French mother. She walks like a Spanish woman, in one piece. Her elegance is Spanish. Perhaps not as austere, but nonetheless, Spanish. She is Northern Latin, a combination of mountain snow and hot winter sun—irresistible. Her shadow was painted by de Chirico long before she was born.

Herbert says Nora, expected to die any minute early last week, was entirely herself, witty, loving, "adorable—and she looked so wonderful!" on Friday, when he took her to the hospital. The doctor said, "She has been living almost nine months longer than we expected." This is her love of life, her tremendous zest for living, her joy in living that keeps her going.

NOTE: Leo went into the hospital for lithotripsy, a procedure to pulverize kidney stones.

JOURNAL • FEBRUARY 25, 1987   Met at the hospital by Bobby the Vampire on arrival. This time, she covered her traces by hurting a bit when she took her rationed blood. We understand one another, playing our parts well in our intimate *comédie inhumaine* or, rather, *comédie rouge et noir*. I have been pricked, patted, punched, punctured, prodded, pounced on, paddled, pummeled—not yet pilfered. I have been medically made much of by brigades of doctors and platoons of nurses. When Dr. Freiman appeared, I told him, at last, about the shooting pains (mostly at night) in my right ankle, and this led to his finding an edema and that led to a scurry and flurry of doctors, and that led to a postponement of my kidney-stone operation, and here I am, with a needle in my left arm, hooked up to an antibiotic feeder, my right foot on pillows, and now all will be well-attended to and the operation some days off.

FEBRUARY 28, 1987   The edema almost completely healed. Puss, at last, off to the Osborne for necessary refurbishings. Puss is utterly dog-faithful and watchful. I am such a lucky man. This tiny room is embowered with floral tributes, fruit offerings, etc. I sent about ten of them to the AIDS patients.

These have been fraught political times. When The Emptiness at the Top [Reagan] testified that he "could not remember [events related to Iran-Contra]," I was immediately reminded of Johnny Gielgud, whispering to me, when we went back[stage] closing night of Edward Albee's *Tiny Alice*: "What was this all about? I never knew what this was all about." His Emptiness never knew.

MARCH 2, 1987 Nora died. "Such wonderful timing," said Deedee [Bail, Herbert's assistant], meaning that her death coincided with the Los Angeles opening of American Ballet Theatre's season. Yesterday, Herbert did some work. This is as Nora would want—life to go on.

I told Geraldine [Page] that for years I disliked Helen Hayes, while admitting that her [Queen] Victoria, Harriet Beecher Stowe, her drunk, even *Coquette* were good. The first time I really liked Helen Hayes, as a woman, was when Ela told me that she had come to her and said that she would pay for an around-the-world cruise, if Ela would take [Helen's husband, playwright] Charlie Macarthur, on it, in the hope that this would get Ela "out of his system." Ela roared with laughter when she told me this. She never wanted Charlie. He was so "hot" after her that he hid behind a snowbank, leapt out at Ela when she came down the steps to enter [Club] "21," threw her to the ground, breaking her leg, and shouted: "Now you'll have to be in one place. Now I'll know where you are all the time!" And she was—for weeks, in a plaster cast much autographed, including by Charlie, in a room supplied by Alice [Astor] in the Gladstone Hotel (owned by Alice's brother, Vincent), Ela having a glorious, laughter-filled time.

I was startled when Geraldine quietly asked, "Who was Eleonora von Mendelssohn?" "That's a very, very long story," I told her. "And I will tell you one day." The irony: how the most important person in so many lives can be no one in the life of someone who feels that she or he knows you very well. This is stated clumsily. It is the cause and heart of my book, the reason for my book: the sustaining of life and bringing to life of lost worlds.

NOTE: During Renata Adler's civil suit against Condé Nast that had so traumatized Leo in 1985, Jonathan Lieberson, a philosophy teacher and critic, son of Leo's friends Goddard and Brigitta, had given testimony for the plaintiff, which Leo thought unforgivable.

JOURNAL · MARCH 10, 1987 Jonathan Lieberson's proposal to Amy [Gross at *Vogue*] that he demolish Susan Sontag: She has never, he says, had a thought of her own. She has stolen every one of the ideas for which she has become famous (i.e., camp).[6] She is a plagiarizer. Jonathan is bad news. He is a hothouse traitor, a bone-deep malcontent, a Janus, a poor thing who has never been able to look in his glass, there to see himself as he is. He is a sick man, physically, and I believe bitterness is eating away his intelligence. He presents a question encompassed by the hackneyed designation "a born traitor." Can a

6. Sontag had published her influential essay "Notes on Camp" in 1964.

being be a traitor prenatally? Amy must not give up *Vogue* to the demolishing of Susan Sontag. If *Vogue* demolishes—Susan Sontag is not the monument, not the institution, not even the foible. She is not a crook, not a plagiarist.[7]

MARCH 15, 1987  I finished Marie Vassiltchikov's *Berlin Diaries 1940–45* this morning, having been obsessed with it.[8] I felt, finishing it, very much the way I remember feeling when I finished reading *Gone with the Wind*, but this is more personal, this tells what happened to everyone, and this is a natural masterpiece. Her record of the Berlin blitz ranks with Pepys's description of the Great Fire [of London]. I haven't felt so close to people in a book in years. I felt that I knew Vassiltchikov immediately.

At the very center of Marie Vassiltchikov's *Diaries* is Loremarie Schönburg. I never knew that she had been deeply involved in the July 20 plot to kill Hitler. When she came into my life, soon after the war, brought by Rut, I saw a faded prettiness. I saw an obsessed woman, a sort of tormented victim, married to Joel Carmichael, living over a shop on Madison Avenue. I liked her, and when Puss got to know her he liked her, but we never knew of her devastating past. She, I think, had a child or two with Joel, who was, I heard, a philanderer, and very attractive to women. I never could see why. Later, Loremarie vanished back to her Vienna, where she got involved in manure. I remember Rut returning from a visit and describing Loremarie and her "exquisite old mother, the princess" in their little palace, with its oval ballroom ("enchanting") in a big, wild park ("almost in ruins—they are so poor"). When we went to Vienna in 1955, we did not, although urged by Rut, go to see Loremarie. I was too shy. Now I find that she died in Vienna—in 1986.[9]

Herbert rang. His voice is thick, clogged, grief eating away at his innards, gorging on his hurt, his being. His voice separated . . . thick strands of wool . . . then, suddenly clear as it was before this horror consumed him, when he broke out of his grief to say how happy he is that I am all right . . . then the blackness consumed him again—and sobs—and he rang off. Will he ever become himself again?

MARCH 17, 1987  Thinking of Truman, Emma Bovary superimposed herself on his image. They are related, for T's and Emma's passion for "Society" was an affliction for both of them and did them both in.

7. In November 1986 *The New Yorker* had published Sontag's short story "The Way We Live Now." It portrays a brilliant, difficult man mortally ill, as told through various friends' gossip. At the time many believed that it portrayed Jonathan Lieberson.
8. A child of hard-pressed Russian nobility, Princess Marie Vassiltchikov (1917–78) worked at the foreign office in Berlin and Vienna through World War II.
9. Princess Eleanore-Marie "Loremarie" Schönburg-Hartenstein fled Germany after the failed assassination of Hitler, in which many among her family and friends colluded. In later years, she became an activist for the environmental movement, which probably accounts for the manure. Joel Carmichael (1915?–2006) was an editor and a historian of religion.

MARCH 22, 1987 I have always lived my life as a story, always lived in the reality of the fictional, the made-up. I don't even have a lifeline! Reaching my seventy-third year, I realize that the novel I have wished to write, I have written. My life is that novel. I have been writing it all of my life.

I held some of Mrs. Simpson's [the Duchess of Windsor's] jewels in my hands: good stones, well cut and made, but no fantasy, no beauty in the design. These are the very expensive baubles of an expensive, surprisingly constant, woman. Rich women in Grosse Point, Locust Valley, and Palm Beach could have had them. They do not compare to high Renaissance, eighteenth-century, or Second Empire jewels. A woman said to a man, as they peered at two feathers, one made of rubies, one of diamonds, each of small quill-pen dimensions: "I know what I could do with that on a simple dress." And that sums up Mrs. Simpson's rewards.

MARCH 23, 1987 This part of being old I hate: the machinery breaking down. Seeing almost everything in a Sara Moon haze, blasted by light.[10] I love light; I fear the dark. I'm apprehensive, terrified of falling as I pull or am pulled and pushed and tugged by genuinely loving or helpful hands upstairs, downstairs—sometimes not even able to raise myself off this bed. I hate all of this. But then, I am thankful. I must remember to be thankful: I can read even when the printed page separates into dim pointillism; I can eat, even though my teeth are mostly fake and in the morning the food makes little miseries; my mind remains sound, even when little hiatuses make patches of not knowing who . . . I could go on—but now I am, as I sit here, quietly waiting for the next assault. I am optimistic again.

APRIL 4, 1987 The Duchess of Windsor's common jewels brought $50 million, with some $40 million going to the Pasteur Institute. How fitting that the duchess's tight ass should bring this bounty to the "relief" of AIDS research.

APRIL 5, 1987 As I sat absorbed in Harvey Fierstein's [trilogy of plays] *Safe Sex*, I felt Puss and me to be Ancient Remains, surviving in a world taken over by Vandals, Visigoths, and Plague—the Four Horsemen of the Apocalypse triumphant. Harvey Fierstein is a mixture of Sarah Bernhardt, Laurette Taylor, and Jennie Moscowitz—that is Harvey Fierstein the actor. The playwright Harvey Fierstein is a female Tennessee Williams. Fierstein writes gorgeous arias, sans Tennessee's poetry, but nevertheless there is a bone-deep kinship. But most of all, Fierstein profits prodigiously from the "gains" of the modern theater (Ionesco, Beckett). He has absorbed them all and made them his own. They are his manure. Puss observed, "Isn't it astonishing? Not one four-letter

10. The kitsch photographs done by Sara Moon (b. 1940) often had a clear center but vanished into mist at the edges.

word in the entire evening. It can be done without." Note: Is AIDS our equivalent of the Deluge, destroying "good and evil alike"? See the Flood in Genesis.

APRIL 17, 1987 The desolation, the feeling of ghostliness, yesterday at noon in the lobby of the Algonquin, centered in a child-sized, seated, very somber, still, still figure—[William] Shawn of *The New Yorker*, formerly and forever. I went up to him and, as he stood up, such a wee, sober, slightly bewildered little person in his habitual solemnity and usual dark clothes, saying, "Oh, Mr. Lerman, so good to see you." I found myself patting him and saying, "Dear Mr. Shawn. I miss you." The hotel is more than usually musty: The glow is gone. Shawn, sitting there solitary, left behind in dustiness, was a symbol of what has happened to the Algonquin and to all of our electric-light past.

APRIL 20, 1987 Herbert, weeping bitterly, rang to tell us that Antony [Tudor] had just died. Antony has been in my thoughts constantly, but I believed in "forever." Perhaps now I no longer believe in forever. How Antony influenced our lives! What a wider vision he gave us. I have no tears about Antony, only wonderful memories. He takes a miraculous chunk of our world with him, but he leaves a world behind. How long will his world be perceptible? To have lived while he recalled this aspect of our world to us, that is part of the glory. The heritage is spread everywhere, even in movement that has never seen his movement.

A version from Isabel Brown:[11] Tudor and Hugh were in the kitchen, Hugh staying over because of early work at Grace [Costumes]. Hugh heard Antony call "Bugs!" (Antony's pet name for Hugh) and then some little sounds. Hugh rushed in. Antony was on his right side, dead. So almost sixty years of being together ended. So similar, the pattern—Antony and Hugh, Herbert and Nora—in each, Herbert, Hugh were Galateas.[12] . . . Not wholly true about Herbert, but both are lost and each will find himself through work. Hugh this morning weeping seemed so like Herbert weeping—no difference in tears or laughter. These three lives: Nora, Antony, Hugh, and their "ramifications": Herbert, Isaac [Stern],[13] Jerry [Robbins], Arthur [Laurents], Diana [Adams], etc. This is a fantastic book, but who could write it? It is so geometrical, basically, the design almost as clear as in a Renaissance masterpiece.

Remembered from dinner at Diana [Trilling]'s: Goronwy Rees, staying at Bowen's Court, was Elizabeth Bowen's lover, and then along came [novelist] Rosamond Lehmann ("The most beautiful woman in the world," said Diana),

11. Isabel Mirrow Brown (b. 1928) had danced with American Ballet Theatre (1946–53). Her husband Kelly and two of their children were also leading dancers in the company.
12. Galatea was the statue brought to life by Pygmalion's love.
13. Violinist Isaac Stern (1920–2001) had been married to Nora Kaye for five months in 1948.

and that very night he left Elizabeth's bed for Rosamond's—and that is how Elizabeth Bowen's [1938 novel] *The Death of the Heart* was born.[14]

APRIL 28, 1987  Last night went to the revivified [Club] "21." I had a revelation: "21" was Ralph Lauren's ancestor. It exploited, early on, the same American dream of an elegant, timeless, secure, rich, heavily furnished past, a WASP past for "upwardly mobile" ethnics. All of it, including Devoted Retainers seemingly centered on Serving You. Social structure, by the time of "21"'s opening had so broken down that in reinventing the "secure" domestic world of the 1880s, of the Astors, Vanderbilts, and Rockefellers, "21" also caught the progenitors themselves. They flocked to "21."[15]

MAY 9, 1987  Gayfryd Steinberg said to Iris Sawyer, "Some people called Cabot are coming to the PEN dinner at the [New York Public] Library. Who are the Cabots? I never heard of anyone called Cabot." Iris: "Every day *The House of Mirth* and *The Custom of the Country* become more pertinent. We haven't gone anywhere."[16]

Even Proust wouldn't have conceived the significance of Shirley Lord, Mrs. Rosenthal, buying Iris Sawyer's apartment through the real estate midwifery of Alice Mason, or the significance of Shirley marrying Rosenthal in John Kluge's apartment, the marriage having been "engineered" by Barbara Walters and Bubbles Sills, who are her "bridesmaids"!!![17] Meanwhile, Arianna [Huffington] "conquers" Washington with her Folger [Shakespeare Library] party—me oh my! Were the Astors and Vanderbilts any better on their climb?

MAY 19, 1987 · LAGUNA HILLS, CALIFORNIA  Puss is "cleaning" the terrace. Maebelle: "I thought I had everything so clean you wouldn't have to work!" No place will ever be tidy enough to please Puss. As he passes through Heaven's Gate, he will manage to give it a little burnish.

Maebelle mused on how "nice" and "quiet" and "gentle" Bill [Inge] was. I thought about how deeply troubled he was and how sad, how he sent for boys, paying them to fulfill his sexual fantasies, how he was restless and never could

14. Goronwy Rees (1909–79) was a Welsh journalist, academician, and memoirist. He confessed on his deathbed to also being a Soviet spy.
15. The "21" Club opened in 1922 as a speakeasy, at 21 West Fifty-second Street.
16. Gayfryd Steinberg was married to a soaring insurance company mogul of the eighties, Saul Steinberg. Iris Michaels Sawyer had been Leo's secretary at *Mademoiselle*. She subsequently became the longtime mistress of Thomas Kempner, chairman of Loeb Partners, the husband of prominent socialite Nan Kempner.
17. The monthly dinner parties of the hugely successful real-estate broker Alice Mason were then much publicized. Shirley Lord, beauty and fitness editor at *Vogue* and a novelist, had married A. M. "Abe" Rosenthal, a Pulitzer Prize–winning foreign correspondent and then executive editor at the *New York Times*. John Kluge was one of the richest men in America, largely from television production and syndication.

sit through a play or concert, how drink took over and "drying out" took over, and how, at last, it all sent him into his garage where carbon monoxide obliterated the horrors of his visibly triumphant life. Bill, despite a pixillated smile, was a sad man. Snatches of memory: He loved Rachmaninoff; he never had *histoires* like Tennessee, Little T, or Gore; he was always a yokel in Manhattan, a kind, Midwest-faced man with watery blue eyes, a mouth that tried hard to be a cupid's bow, a heart that was loyal and desperate for love, but distrusted it. His passion was the theater: His was a world of hungry little people, lonely people who let life pass them by . . . because they trusted false gods?

MAY 29, 1987   The "new" David Hockney: very civilian, gray buttoned-up suit, hair still dyed but not as blond, still trick [playful] shoes, and he's heavy, and, as always, loving. He came to [decorator] Rose Tarlow's marvelous house to see us, and he told us that Charles Ludlam was dead of AIDS—a devastating blow. This glorious actor and director—a total theatrical man, who made us laugh until we were delirious, and whose taste was almost always impeccable. I cannot go on now, but he was a loving, devoted friend. This is a disaster for all of us.[18]

MAY 30, 1987   David Hockney in his studio—definitely toned down and no Baron Ochs crew. His magical conception of *Tristan and Isolde*—the most revealing conception since Appia's.[19] David: "Space, painting, lighting doing it all, everything Wagner wanted"—thrusts into infinity. I had this feeling at Carnarvon Bay in 1937 (evening) and at Stonehenge at dawn in late December 1964. Hockney does it all with light, but not like Appia. I am worried about David. He is tense—a certain largesse of time is gone. In the studio light, a grayness underpainted his skin, the bone structure is more apparent. He hugged me more, as if he couldn't hug enough, an "in-case" hugging.

JUNE 9, 1987 · NEW YORK CITY   Antony Tudor Memorial at ten a.m. at Juilliard. Isabel Brown waited for us in the lobby. Greetings as we went below from women who seemed to know me. People pat me now with the pats given to older people and little children. Two different kinds of affection? Or reassurance? Or is it respect for innocence and worldliness returning to innocence? Or wanting to tap the strength, the magic?

Backstage: no light, but long-familiar shapes and voices and even glimpses of faces. The potency of this day began to fill (not the word), invigorate (no), enlarge (maybe) me. Donald Saddler, Nancy Zeckendorf [ballet patron] . . .

18. Leo had vastly enjoyed the melodramas and travesties of Charles Ludlam (1943–89), playwright, actor, and founder of the Ridiculous Theatrical Company, including Ludlam's impersonation of Maria Callas in *Galas* (1983).
19. The Swiss scenic designer Adolphe Appia (1862–1928) advocated nonrealistic, symbolic sets and lighting.

more and more arriving . . . Jerry Robbins, Misha . . . the sound of the house filling. I "cased" the stage, because of my infirmities. Everyone so solicitous. Isabel resembles Nora. She's now administrator of a ballet school: "I have over three hundred, mostly Koreans and Japanese, marvelous dancers . . . so few Jews . . . If a Cohen or a Stein calls up I'm tempted to let them in without even an audition!" Isabel's joke.

Then we went into the stage-left deep wing. As the mauve-pink stage light seeped from the stage, lighting our faces against the black of backstage, we peered out. The memorial began with the pas de deux from [Tudor's 1975] *The Leaves Are Fading*. In that fondant, satin light sat Agnes [de Mille] in her wheelchair, looking out at the stage ("Oh, darling," she whispered, "I can't feel anything on my right side. I'm paralyzed!" So I touched her on her left shoulder as I was placed directly behind her on a high steel stool.) Jerry Robbins leaned over her whispering, the light turning his white beard mauve, and Misha leaned over to kiss me, saying, "I love you." That was a surprise. Puss held me firmly from behind. On my head, my black "travel" hat, my white beard a dimness in the blackness. Donald Saddler was at my right, waiting to lead me on, and Herbert stood behind Puss—sobbing . . . and so many others, from my long-ago dance world. I could hear them breathing, anxiously waiting to go on. That is the best of the worlds—not book, art, music, theater—but dance—the most cohesive. This was a freeze-frame moment. The voices of the speakers oddly echoed through a backstage transmitter: Jerry's voice breaking with tears; Sallie [Wilson], who danced *Pillar of Fire*, weeping as she talked;[20] Agnes, trundling to the podium and very Pasionaria: "We must preserve Tudor's legacy! . . . I go to the ballet these days, and on the stage I do not see people!" Agnes is truth.

JUNE 14, 1987  Geraldine Page found dead in that Collier Brothers–Miss Havisham house on Twenty-second Street, alone when she died—that is the horror: this life of hard-won applause to end in solitary, perhaps choking silence. No standing ovations. I see her running down the steps of 1453, with Rosemary Harris and Ken Tynan. I see her when she was asked how she would play Gertrude [in *Hamlet*], beaming: "Fat! Fat! Fat!" I see her in beautifully cut black satin in *Separate Tables*—such a surprise. And in *Christmas Memory*. I see Geraldine darting hatred across the table at A Big Executive: "You fired my brother!"

She was the last of great leading ladies of that generation, but always, off stage, a bag lady. She exuded a kind of sunniness, a Midwest golden-grain aura. She made all of her inadequacies into elements of her art. She was always a little girl playing whatever part she lighted on. Here is where her special magic

---

20. The ballerina Sallie Wilson (b. 1932) had been considered a great dance actress, and she succeeded Nora Kaye in several of Tudor's ballets at American Ballet Theatre.

gave us back Laurette Taylor's: At some common or mutual point they met in innocence—wide, blue-eyed innocence. And Geraldine could make us laugh—howl—turning the howls into tears. She was utterly a woman—with all of her men. I remember, after an opening, I went back to congratulate her (she was one of the few I went back to see), and, not seeing Rip [Torn, her husband], made for her, only to be told in a fierce whisper: "If you don't pay attention to Rip, I won't talk to you anymore!"

And she wandered off sometimes. So full of dreams. So easy to make fun of—all of those calculated, scene-stealing mannerisms, tricks of voice, ungainliness, shifts in voice register, tongue and teeth clickings, ruminations that built conviction or pathos. All those awards. Born Kurzville, Missouri, married twice, two sons and a daughter.

JUNE 18, 1987  She had her standing ovation! Yesterday morning at the Neil Simon Theatre (once the Alvin where Ethel Merman was queen). Packed! Jammed! Standing in the aisles out onto the fire escapes, winding through the doors onto the street. Then, on the stage, in the *Blithe Spirit* set, almost obliterated by floral tributes, sat a large man. "Who is that?" That was Rip Torn! And colleagues and family, even her little grandchild. Rip rose. He walked to the mike. He said, "She would have loved this." The house rose to its feet. It roared for fifteen minutes! She had this standing ovation for two and one-half hours. No sadness. Tears, yes. And laughter, so much laughter. And love. Never for a moment was Geraldine absent. She was there, in that theater, where she last appeared, conjuring up the Dear Departed.[21] And she was still at it. I wonder if the cast feels her, even sees her there? I am sure that she is there, every performance. I know that I saw her in the large pink gingham that she wore the rainy spring night when she brought [novelist] Nelson Algren to a party at our house, and she told us how to play the game of the garden-in-the-bottle. Your garden told your character. Her garden was, I think, roses, roses all the way, forever blooming roses.

JULY 11, 1987  Almost a week of intermittent Ollie [North] watching. He gives us a new verb: to ollie, olliefate, olliefation.[22] Who is on trial is the president. As I watch, "history" images flash: great courts in Elizabethan England, the court and Jeanne d'Arc, the Inquisition . . . but these are reflex images. Colonel North is a fantastic actor delivering a fantastic script—arousing sympathy for this man who was doing his job, and doing that by his grandstanding, his self-righteousness, his self-publicizing of his patriotism, his

21. As Madame Arcati, the role she had been playing in *Blithe Spirit*.
22. Colonel Oliver North (b. 1943) had assisted members of the Reagan administration in their effort to fund insurgents in Nicaragua through sale of arms to Iran. Leo had been watching his testimony in congressional hearings.

mightier-than-the-law as protector and defender of the American way of life. He is wonderfully well spoken, brilliantly self-directed (as a great actor is directed by a great director), superbly costumed for this superstar role of the all-American-boy hero who is being made a patsy (and so, in this "morality play" symbolizes the freedoms of the free American people), who is the protector of these American principles and these pure people, including the basic American tenet: If you can get away with it, fine, but if you can't, you are a "dead duck"—not forever. Lawlessness as righteousness as patriotism.

JULY 19, 1987  Maria's *Carmen*—so right there in 1964. The first time I asked her to do it, she said, "Don't you think I'm too elegant for *Carmen?*" The second time, we were walking from the Ambassador, on one of the snow-dark winter nights that seem late even in early evening. She lifted her tapering, black skirt and said, "Look at these legs! Look at these legs! Are they legs for Carmen?" And here is her unique *Carmen*, one of the most extraordinary (recalling Supervia and Ponselle). Dark, lyrical, sensual, and so French—that acid twang—so French. Oh—foolish, foolish, driven Maria, who knew who she was and who wanted to be someone else.

Yesterday to lunch, Victoria [Tennant] (so cool looking, such a mixture of highly bred English and Russian and something of Ruth Stephan) and Steve [Martin] full of amazement at how *Roxanne* is being exalted to a work of art: "I never thought it was that much," he said. "Now they tell me I'm an artist!" He is such a quiet man, a face on which to paint.

I read some Elizabeth Bishop poems. I heard her voice: a quiet, correct voice, ladylike, with a smile in it, level as a meadow is level when there is no wind, not a breeze, nothing, but a summer-green meadow and summer-blue, high, early-morning sky. And, as I read, I saw typewritten on a single, crowded sheet of paper "I feel that I owe you a letter. . . ." Where, dear Elizabeth, is that letter? Somewhere. Somewhere in the tangled past of these deeply lived-in rooms where, mostly, I do not feel that I have lived very much at all.

JULY 31, 1987  Maria [Riva] about Marlene today: "She's so strong—all her brains are so strong. She'll outlive all of us. I know now what makes alcoholics live long. If they don't eat, they live forever. Her grocery bills are $500 a week, but she doesn't eat. She gives it all away to the concierge. She hates me because she gave me those pictures. The Daumier was so corrupted that Christie's [auction house] wouldn't touch it, and the Corot wasn't right. She thinks I'm a billionaire and I don't send her any money. . . ." Then Maria told me about [producer and writer Steven] Bach and how he bought some of Marlene's dresses and said that he would auction them in London, and anything over the price he paid, he would give her. Christie's wanted to put them in a movie-star auction, but she wanted them to be in a stage-star auction. She wanted to be with Ellen Terry. So the dresses weren't auctioned.

NOTE: On August 1, 1987, Leo and Gray went to Geneva, Switzerland, to visit Denyse Harari. From there they went to the Hotel Gritti in Venice, where they stayed for a month, and then finished their holiday in London. Leo would not again return to Europe. His physical troubles made international travel an ordeal and Venice had become unnavigable for him.

JOURNAL · AUGUST 9, 1987 · VENICE  [In Geneva,] Mme Caillot told us, after much prodding:[23] "I don't want to say anything against your President's wife . . . but—oh—she is an awful woman—so cold, so empty. I was with her three days and part of each night . . . really her hostess, representing the state. She hardly said a word to me—Rude! Unfeeling! We drove in the car and she was furious that she couldn't call California from the car. She was trying always to get 'George.' When she couldn't get George she was furious.[24] Wherever we went she was given bouquets, and sometimes she threw one to me. 'This is for you,' she would exclaim, not even looking, just throwing, like I was her maid. 'This awful country!' she said over and over again in front of me. When we went where she was to make a speech, it was so cold I offered her my sable coat, my mother had given it to me. Oh, no—she made a rotten face at it. All she was interested in was showing her red dress or red suit. She never looked at any of the speeches. 'What am I supposed to do here?' she would ask in her awful angry voice." Then Mme Caillot remembered the fuss Mrs. Reagan had made at the royal wedding [of Prince Charles and Diana], when Mrs. Reagan discovered that all of the heads of state were to be picked up by a bus. "The King of Norway was delighted. He had never been in a bus before, but Mrs. Reagan—she made such a fuss. To her, this was an insult!"

[Historian] Peter Lauritzen told us, on the plane from Lugano to Venice, all about Evelyn Lambert's great triumph. In June, the [English] queen mother came to Asolo and stayed at the [Villa] Cipriani: "The only person I want to meet," she said, "is the American woman who has a villa near here," she told everyone. So Evelyn had a great luncheon for her, and the queen mother rushed out into the garden and ate Evelyn's usual menu, and had the most marvelous time. Then Evelyn's ice-cream cart came up, and the queen mother had an ice-cream cone, as did her attending male, a cousin. "Why," she asked him, "is mine melting faster than yours?" "Because, ma'am, you've been hopping around so much!" She loved every moment. When the two went to the Valmaranas' [Palladian villa], she bounded up the tremendous pile of steps and stood there laughing while her followers came plodding and panting up. The contrast between the queen mother and Mrs. Reagan is the contrast between the true democratic spirit (queen mother) and the parvenu carpetbagger (Mrs. Reagan).

23. Madame Claude Caillot was married to the head of Morgan Guaranty Bank in Switzerland. He had previously been Swiss ambassador to London and Washington.
24. Presumably Vice President George H. W. Bush.

As we came across the lagoon, Venice restored my faith, my belief in solace. And here in the Gritti—with five men to raise me up [from the water taxi] and the genuine welcoming from everyone, perhaps even some strength is returning to my limbs. Yesterday morning, when Puss was not able to get me off the toilet, I was somewhat surprised to find that, because he was "ashamed," he would not for a long time call for someone to help. I gave up that shame a long time ago. I try to face each assault of age with dignity. I thank the Life Force every moment for having given me so good a nature.

AUGUST 10, 1987  We did not know on that Sunday night, in mid-November 1966, that this was our last party in our house on upper Lexington Avenue, and that by early July we would no longer live in that house, the last wholly occupied-by-one-family house on Lexington. "1453—Fall of Constantinople: All Culture Goes to the West," I would say, quoting Miss Josephine Farrell of P.S. 69, my childhood school, not realizing how apt a quotation this was until we two had moved west on Fifty-seventh Street, leaving in me a hunger for that house which has never been assuaged. Sometimes we pass it. It stands there, stark, bitter, hungering.

But all of this was months away, years away, that night of the last party, the house bursting with light, the lamp, whose summer-pavilion shade was inlaid with a splendor of improbable roses, stood luminous in the Red Room, the dragonfly lamp glowed greenly, goldenly, iridescently, in a corner of the back parlor, and poinsettias and poppies ran a crimson riot on Tiffany-glass-shaded lamps in other corners. A house furnished magically with accumulations that became in some nineteen years so accustomed to this place that they seemed to confirm its past and assure its future. What could menace this exuberance, this abundance, this living place where so very much had happened, was happening? We did not know that our world, our Manhattan, was fading as surely as my grandfather's had vanished, as surely as my father's had faded. We recognized that Manhattan was, is, always had been a flux, but what had that actually to do with us, with the impregnable brilliance assembled on all four floors of that house? On that November night in 1966, we were all, well, almost all of us, intact, safe in that shining moment. Nora and Sono showing Rudi *Petrouchka* up in my bedroom, while Cathleen Nesbitt snoozed on my bed . . . Marlene emptying ashtrays . . . Diana Trilling pouring out tea to Kerensky . . . but no—all this becomes confusing. There had been so many parties, so many little dinners, so many heart-to-hearts, so many tears and so much—oh, so much—light. So many women sitting by the telephone waiting and longing . . .

I could begin with another night, this one January 8, 1953, in Venice, a chill, black night. Gray and I are at the Fenice, having come from Rome, where a splotchy poster announced that Maria Meneghini Callas was to sing *Traviata*, the one-hundred-year gala anniversary, "original sets" etc., etc. At the Fenice, liveried footmen parting the curtains, and the sparkle, the gleam of the jewels, the satins rippling from the audience onto the party-thronged stage, where a woman in white flounces, seated downstage-left, tossed white camellias to a frenzy of waltz-mad guests. At that moment, as the tawny, almost tarnished, amber-gold poured out into the rapt house, as she sat there almost indifferently, I learned a harsh truth: The death of a huge, visibly healthy person from a broken heart (call it lung sickness, call it anything medical—but she did, does, perish eternally of the most complete loss of faith) was infinitely more upsetting than the death of a little, frail mist of a creature, expiring before her life begins. I could begin there—with what became years of friendship, of mutual admiration, of trust and love and eventually sadness. I could begin there on that dark Venetian night in the golden hollow of the Fenice.

I could begin with the evening of my birth, on a hot, gleaming, May Saturday in 1914, with Rita Glasberg, my mother's oldest and most long-lived friend, moving briskly from her parents' house on East 107th Street, in Harlem, the brownstone adjoining my grandfather Goldwasser's house, in whose parlor window, the Battenberg lace curtains hunched behind him, she could plainly see my father, a usually quiet, sober man, stark naked, his arms triumphantly flailing about above his head, shouting: 'I have a son!' " And, of course, he did—upstairs, in the second-floor back bedroom, where Momma lay inert and I was being pummeled. Rita joyed in telling this story. "Oh," she flowed, "for two and one-half hours that doctor worked over that poor, dead, little monster baby." Here Aunt Ida would flatly intone: "Monster—worse—he was awful—hands and feet like a duck and a hole in his head you could put a fist into." "Yes," said Momma, "but look at him now—everything fine. Just a little mark in the middle of his forehead, and when he's an older man no one will notice—no one." But the effect on me, of hearing that I was born dead, that I was doubtlessly the first baby to emerge screeching, wailing after hours of death—the effect of this has set me apart, made me feel singular all my long life. Everything, all of my days, has been triumphantly extra.

AUGUST 13, 1987 Grandpa's "house" was not exactly a house: It was a tenement, in which we all lived, as if it were Our House. Momma and Poppa, and, later, little Jerry, my brother, and I occupied what had been Grandma's parlor, complete with its green velvet suite of Queen Anne revival side chairs and sofa, now disarrayed by a huge, baroquely knobbed brass bed and Momma's upright piano, upon which music rack "Smile the While I Kiss You Sad Adieu," and "A Pretty Girl Is Like a Melody" mingled with "Over the Waves," and Beethoven's "Für Elise." It was Momma who massacred the classics, and Uncle Irving and Aunt Minnie the favorite songs of those post–kaiser's war days. We had come home to Grandpa's [on 106th Street] to live after Grandma had died in a flat in the remote Bronx, where we had lived a free-from-Grandpa life some three years.[25]

So we occupied Grandma's erstwhile parlor, looking out on the wide expanse of 106th Street, where huge horses pulled and clattered all day long and the street vendors called their individual wares among itinerant street singers, brass bands and hurdy-gurdy grinders, carousel and hokey-pokey wagons, strange wizened men in gaudy scarves prodding wizened monkeys into chatter or flashy, mean-eyed parrots into proffering fortunes. Once I even saw a huge, sad, chained bear lumbering along that street. And so many donkeys and ponies with enterprising men who took your picture for a pittance. Then there were the religious processions, the street suddenly thronged with dancing, jammed with long-coated, flat-hatted, chanting, pale-faced, men, with ritual curls dangling, beards flourishing, or men bearing Torahs to the synagogue on 103rd Street in throbbing, stately funeral procession.

AUGUST 15, 1987  The piano that Grandpa bought for his golden-haired, blue-eyed, amply fleshed daughter, my mother, survived vociferously until my brother and I [literally] demolished it sometime in the early fifties in the house on Lexington Avenue. When Momma was a little girl, that piano dominated a room in a flat that the Goldwassers occupied on Second Avenue in the nineties, in a row of buildings owned by Grandpa and his brother, Uncle Maxl. It was this piano, an upright with STRAND calligraphically lettered in gold above its at-the-ready, knicked, ivory-coated teeth, that my future mother attacked, doubt-less with flourishing vigor identical to that I later heard. She was a whiz at "The Maiden's Prayer" and a cross-handed tempest when stirring up "Waves of the Danube." That attracted the attention of "the upstairs neighbor" who had "a musical daughter" named Alma. Alas, Alma who "sang" did not have a piano. Matter of fact, Alma and her mother had hardly anything except Alma's "extraordinary" voice and chutzpah, which was in these circumstances neces-sary. So, Grandpa suggested that Alma vocalize to little Ida's pianistics, and, somehow, Alma's mother "managed." Alma trilled away, and Alma and her mother survived from day to day, until the day they and their very few posses-sions vanished. . . . At this point in the tale, my mother always announced, giv-ing Significant Looks, "She did not pay the rent. Not one single red cent!" The implications were obvious: Grandpa had had a "soft spot" for Alma's mother.

Some years later, Momma noticed that a new, much touted voice was to make its debut at the Metropolitan Opera—some girl named Alma Gluck. There was a photograph—a dark-haired girl with a big, almost disfigured nose. "This is our Alma!" Momma screamed. So the night of the debut some Gold-

25. In 1919 Yetta Goldwasser had suffered a fatal heart attack during a visit to the Lermans' apartment on the Boston Post Road in the Bronx.

wassers went off to the upper region of the sacrosanct Metropolitan. "Yes," they assured one another. "Alma!" Proud of their former "fly-by-night" tenant, rejoicing in Momma's agile hands, which had helped her along, they marched around to the stage entrance and stood waiting. Finally, out came the new star. "Oh—how we cheered: Alma! Alma! But that Alma never gave us a tumble!" Momma always vengefully told, "Never even gave us a look! Maybe," said Momma, always one for paying back, "she couldn't see us because of that huge nose. It was enormous. I always wondered, when she was really famous, why she didn't do something about it." I heard this saga many times and somehow distilled from it a golden glory, a glitter that made me look, with speculative, hopeful eyes at pictures in the Sunday rotogravure pages . . . those dazzling prima donna smiles behind barricades of prima donna roses—a magic which enthralled me. I believed—and did not quite believe—Momma's history of Alma Gluck.[26]

Many years later, reading the novel *East Side, West Side* [1947], by her daughter Marcia Davenport, suddenly, a page after I had read it, I realized that I had just had what was surely a confirmation of Momma's story, for in that novel Marcia Davenport's heroine was being conveyed across town in a taxi cab driven by Jacob Goldwasser, my grandfather, or rather the name of the man who had been her grandmother's and her now world-famous mother's benefactor.[27] That week, I sat chattering with a woman who said to me, "Oh— Marcia—Marcia Davenport will be here in a moment!" I was thrilled. In she came. I poured out Momma's saga. She turned her back. Thereafter, whenever she saw me—at the Berliners, at the Gunthers—she looked at me bleakly and never said one single word to me.

AUGUST 20, 1987  The brownstone house in which I was born on East 107th Street broke up when Uncle Harry [Goldwasser], married to Aunt Ida, who already had added to the family Rosalie, became so infuriated with Grandpa and his ghetto demands that he exploded. After scalding cannonades of curses, howls of rage, red-eyed taunts, Uncle Harry and Grandpa lapsed into a seven-year silence. Grandpa was notorious for his boiling, protracted silences, and Uncle Harry gathered his little family and moved them off to some more verdant Manhattan on the Upper West Side, not far from the Hudson—or the North, as we came to know it—River, where his brothers, his sister, his mother secretly visited him. Oh—there were many secrets in that family—almost all of

---

26. What Leo's mother probably screamed was "This is our Reba!" Soprano Alma Gluck was born Reba Fiersohn in 1884, about five years after Leo's mother, and came to America from Romania as a girl, but she did not take the name Alma Gluck until 1909.

27. The character in Davenport's novel was actually named Louis Goldwasser. Interestingly, however, the female protagonist asks him to take her on a slow, reminiscing drive up Orchard Street, on Manhattan's Jewish Lower East Side.

them kept from Grandpa, who was so sure of his power, or seemed to be, that he was oblivious to what went on so persistently behind his back.

Uncle Harry gone, Grandpa was on the move [to 106th Street], and this is when, much to his surprise, Momma and Poppa told him they were also moving [to the Bronx]. Years later, I heard that he had screamed: "Go! Go! Take your little bastard and go. Don't come near me. I curse you! I curse you!" Then he retreated into his usual silence, for his daughter, his possession, had now twice betrayed him, first by marrying a man unworthy, whose people despised his people, he thought, and now by leaving her father for some place where doubtlessly she would not keep a kosher house, would eat *trayf,* and certainly would be of no use to her father, to whom after all she "owed everything."

AUGUST 25, 1987    The secret life of children—in prehistoric caves under dining room and drawing room tables, in lavatories when old enough to "go" alone, in bed after "lights out," at times when by some strange juxtaposition of comings and goings the house is empty save for children, in basements so dark that to venture down into them unaccompanied by some other children bent on some sort of secret would be horror. Some of us, very little boys, were very curious about one another. Were we all the same in those parts which grown-ups seemed to consider shameful? We wanted to compare. Playing doctor, but not interested in playing with girls. So we compared, and one thing led to another, and some of us went right on that way for the rest our lives, while most of us did not.

When I was about fourteen, I came upon a pile of books hidden beneath a nightdress in a drawer of my mother's bureau (the one with the time-spotted oval looking glass held in place by a brace of muscular, flower-topped fairy figures). I did not understand much of what those books contained—so much Latin—but Krafft-Ebing's *Psychopathia Sexualis* described in detail sufficient to my understanding to leave me feeling that I had a high fever. The shock of recognition disturbed me less than it exhilarated me. I no longer felt alone, although I continued to feel singular.

One day, I heard Momma say to Aunt Rose on the telephone: "Listen, Rose, don't tell me I should make my Leo go out and play ball like the other boys. Leo doesn't like to play ball. He reads. He writes. He makes shows with the other kids. . . . He likes making believe. He's a born *macher.* . . . So he doesn't play ball. Playing ball isn't everything. . . . Listen, Rose, my Leo won't get married. He will never get married. . . . So, what do you care, Rose . . . and he's a mother's boy . . . I'm his mother."

Momma was not modernistic. She was Momma—a law unto herself and to anyone else who didn't watch out. Momma was law; Grandpa was terror. But a Presence in the Sky, a Presence I knew had a huge white beard and fierce, flaming eyes and bore aloft a flaming sword, was greater than Momma or Grandpa or Aunt Minnie. Did I think he lived in the *shul*? I begged him to bring back our dog when I heard that something awful had happened to that large, placid, trusting beast. I prayed to him, begging Him to save the life of an ailing kitten, kneeling in the embrasure of one of the deep-set windows of our bedroom, promising to do anything He wanted of me, even to be good. . . . I was suddenly wrenched up off my knees and slapped hard by Aunt Minnie, enraged, almost incoherent. "Not God for that! You don't ask God for that! Don't be a little fool! What do you wanna be, a sissy?" She slapped me again. I did not know at that time what a sissy was, but I knew that I would never again let anyone see what I was really feeling. I knew that Grandma was up there watching over me, as she always had, as she always would.

AUGUST 26, 1987  As years went on, I increasingly sat pumping away at the Pianola (piano rolls with transcriptions of *Carmen* and so forth). I was being the Great Pianists—Paderewski, Leschetizky, Hofmann. Or I sat, clamped by my ears to disks through which I heard, from far-off, fabled Chicago, voices Singing Opera, waiting patiently for [the baritone's] spreading, twilight voice, so different from the bird-noted women, the sob-caught-in-the-throat men. So, I fell in love with opera, as I had fallen in love with anything that moved me onstage or on a flickering screen. My secret life was so active that I scarcely had strength left for the everyday business of living. I went to school sometimes. I had the best excuse, the always-present fear so strong in Momma and Poppa that something could happen to me, because: "You know, he's not like other kids. He's not so strong. He had—well, he wasn't born so good." I stayed at home, endlessly reading—Muzzie's *History of the United States, Little Women, A Child's Garden of Verses*—believing every exotic word I read. All of the books came to me from Poppa and Uncle Charlie, who at this time painted the walls of schoolrooms and seemed to have no scruples in heisting a book, a package of paper, a bundle of pencils.[28]

SEPTEMBER 5, 1987  The pear-shaped, excessively restless man in a black suit and off-white shirt, who sits momentarily against the wall on the [Gritti] bar terrace, then wanders in, wanders out, and who only stopped to admire Martha (Paloma Picasso's bulldog) drinking water, is Giorgio Bassani! I had had a feeling, a premonition, but we never could have recognized this wonderful writer whom we so much admire and who came to lunch with us in the dining room of the Plaza over twenty years ago—his mother sitting at a nearby table, watching (we didn't know until later). Now he acts as if he has had a stroke, or has been impaired by time. At the table next to his—inevitably—the Vendramina sits, also impaired, leaning her somewhat girlish, but always Roman-senator head on one hand. What a juxtaposition: *The Garden of the Finzi-Continis* and

---

28. GF: "*A Child's Garden of Verses* was among Leo's favorite books. It would make him cry every time he read it—at the loss of innocence."

a woman who was one of the staunch Fascists, now both old and worn, both bewildered by time. I talked to him and patted his hand, and he said he would talk to me, but I will not go down today—Regatta Day.[29]

OCTOBER 4, 1987 · NEW YORK CITY  First glimpse of choirboy life in the choir building: Several dimly seen Sunday-suited boys flitting about, obviously rushing not to be late. I am a born voyeur, which in the most positive sense means: I love life.

OCTOBER 19, 1987  Puss, suddenly stricken by a massive blood clot, was saved from annihilation and is now "safely" home, after nine days in Doctors' Hospital, in a room notable for splendid views over the East River and the mayor's house. Under the punctilious care of young Dr. Anthony Cahan [Bill Cahan's son], Puss is delicately with us. With us!

OCTOBER 29, 1987  Dreadful weeks—eating up all possibility, save that of pulling Puss through these frequently horrible times. Now, perhaps, we are emerging from the most awful time. I am not sure. The only help I could be was to be calm, calm at all times.

NOVEMBER 4, 1987  In the evening, Richard rang and said, "Leo, please don't call every day. Howard says that, because when I was living there [at the Osborne] you told him not to call so much." I was astonished at this. And my astonishment was secure, because of the irrelevance of what I had heard to any of our current problems—some of them involved with mortality, all of them exhausting. I was bitterly disappointed in Richard. That is an exaggeration: I was sad, sad at how removed from the seriousness of living he (and they) are. I know that this is some part of a fight they have with one another. So we now have—what?—a hiatus in a fifty-five-year-long friendship? All so unnecessary— so silly and so upsetting. That last word is inadequate. There is no depth of feeling in that which I have just written because what has happened is such a trivialization of our deep devotion to one another during all of these fraught years. I can't take any of Richard's behavior last night seriously nor even believe that this silliness will cause any real break.

NOVEMBER 22, 1987  A Dr. Lewis diagnosed my tremendous bouts of hacking coughs. My left vocal cord is paralyzed. The goiter presses against that cord. The right cord is healthy and has taken over. I am grateful that some parts of the machine come in twos. I must carefully sip all liquids, and I must erase intensity from my speech. I chaired Spelvin [*Playbill* luncheon for the cast of

---

29. Novelist Giorgio Bassani (1916–2000) wrote *The Garden of the Finzi-Continis*, telling the story of the Jews of Ferrara and their exportation during World War II.

*Cabaret*] after Dr. Lewis's advice, spoke in my "new" angelic voice. [Soprano] Regina Resnik and Joel Grey, who have known me for years and did not know of the paralyzed cord, said: "My, your voice sounds so good—so different—so wonderful—and projects marvelously."

Momma may yet "have the last word." This is one of the many "illnesses" she had—and the one she feared the most.

NOTE: The doctors warned Leo that his fragility and complex health concerns could complicate surgery, and he chose not to pursue aggressive thyroid treatment. Gray's mother, Maebelle, came for the holidays and stayed six weeks.

JOURNAL · JANUARY 1, 1988  The long, dark year 1987 is ended, a black corridor in which were wonderfully lighted spaces—the Venetian month, the London two weeks—rather like those brilliant Mediterranean open spaces between the many tunnels as the train comes from Milan to Nice, or the motor carries us from Venice to Nice. But that was so many years past. . . . Nevertheless, we are still here. We have each of us been "saved."

Now we plunge into 1988. I count my blessings: Puss and Richard, [me] still able to get about, more than enough money comes in, loved ones, this remarkable apartment, possibilities. But 1987 was mostly a bad, black year, in which I wrote one "good" bit [for *Vogue*][30] and read some "good" books and loved and was loved. I will not count the bitter losses.

And soon Puss will be up and about, when he comes to "rescue" me, with a green glass of cool water at five a.m. He promised "a breakfast full of surprises." Surprises—I love them, but not shocks. At this time, a rapture of quiet, which I would not revel in if I did not know that down the little passage, Puss is sleeping, I hope, dreaming of doggies. 1888—A remarkable year, all those eights, but 1988 . . . Nine is a lucky number.

JANUARY 16, 1988  Nora's memorial [on January 4]—Perfectly balanced in structure and emotion. Now, in a pocket of Gray's overcoat, a handful of paper rose petals, gathered from the floor of the City Center stage, flung there during the Isadora corybantics Freddie Ashton devised for Lynn Seymour.[31] I never thought to see Jerry Robbins cry—he did—as did [director] Mike Nichols, each while talking to the thousands gathered in this theater, where Nora created *The Cage*, where she danced Antony's works, to celebrate her.

Margot [Fonteyn], now pale-haired but somewhere in that face, in that body, Princess Aurora lurking visibly, racing—soundlessly—not touching any concrete surface, fleeting down an incline into the festival hall of her Queen-

---

30. His review of Simon Callow's book *Becoming an Actor*.
31. At the Nora Kaye memorial, the British Royal Ballet dancer Lynn Seymour (b. 1939) had danced *Five Waltzes in the Manner of Isadora Duncan*.

Mother and King-Father, a creature, all youth, all spirit, all pale pink, earthborn, but not earthbound. "No individuals on stage today . . ." That was the pith of her talk [afterward at Herbert's reception]. As it was Agnes's at Antony Tudor's memorial.

JANUARY 24, 1988   Yesterday, to the "Fashion and Surrealism" exhibit, brilliantly installed [at the Fashion Institute of Technology]. Charles James's "lobster dress," Capucci's black "gown"—triumphs of dressmaking. Yves Saint Laurent's fish-scale sheath, edged in a fringe of waterdrop glass beads—a triumph of workmanship. The set table of [surrealistically] food-hatted heads . . . the brick suits and dress against bricks—miraculous. Such detail, such finish.

Then home, and Maebelle said, "There isn't much laughter in this house." What in these awful six weeks was there to laugh about?

I read two scenes in *The Tempest* and a clutch of metaphysics, and my heart leapt up with joy. My only garden is the carpet by my bed, but now I have a vast, flowing paradise each morning when I read *The Tempest*: all nature, a splendor, the flowering world after a great rain, sun-shattered, prismed, then furies of clouds, then sun-shattered again. What a feast. What a reassurance. The Psalms beat me down; *The Tempest* lifts me up, exalts me.

FEBRUARY 21, 1988   Yesterday, Maria Riva rang. She said that Marlene was pickled in scotch. Since Marlene never went out and no germs got at her, she would live forever. She then told me a little saga of degradation. I think that Truman could possibly have thought of it for "Answered Prayers." Sometime last year Marlene received a letter from a man in the San Fernando Valley. He told her how much he adored her, etc. When she saw, from his letterhead, that he was a doctor, she rang him. This began endless telephone exchanges, during which he became more and more enslaved. Finally, having been told so many pitiful tales: how her family never came near her; how she was penniless; how she had no one; how she had nothing to eat, etc., etc., he said that he was coming to Paris to "rescue" her. This she could not permit. So she told him that at last her family had rallied and that they were all going, for the holidays, to a castle in Wales (she was being very creative), and that he would not be able to "contact" her for some weeks. Weeks later, she rang him. His voice was different—tortured. What was wrong, she wanted to know? He told her that he was trying to get her out of his life, that he was going to a doctor, to get her out of his life. What kind of a doctor, she wanted to know. A psychiatrist, he told her. How much did he pay the doctor? Ninety dollars each visit, five visits a week. "Why don't you give me the money?" she asked. "I'll sing to you five times a week." He sent her a $5,000 check. She cashed it, Maria said. "Now she is singing to him five times a week." This is so awful, so degrading. What does she sing? "See What the Boys in the Back Room Will Have"? Maria went on: "She sings to him, and you should excuse me, but I have to put it blankly—he jerks off." This, then, is what "the most be-oo-tee-fool girl in the world" has come to? "Now, she's got a letter from some boy in Paris who says he's wild about her, and that he speaks perfect English and French. She called him and got his mother, who was overcome with delight, and so now she (Marlene) wants the boy to come to live with her. 'He can take care of me. . . . He can help me. . . .' Yes—he can rip her off. Who knows what he is. . . . If she was some little woman in Oshkosh I could have her committed. . . ." This is age in all of its horror.

MARCH 12, 1988  Reading the [Gerald Clarke] "life" of Truman: I did not know what a monster T became during the last years when I saw him so little, then not at all—a little, maniacal Mafia chief with an entourage (wrong word) of hit men—sometimes this verges on the farcical—and a little coterie of sleazy "chums." But all of this bother about a "legend" when all that really matters are a handful of stories and *In Cold Blood*. His "life" now overshadows his work— perhaps it always did. "A Miserable Person" I would title any life I wrote of him.

APRIL 22, 1988  On Monday evening: *Gaîté Parisienne* onstage even more disgusting than the audience in their hightums.[32] We enjoyed watching women in Lacroix being jammed by their escorts, into seats—very like women with fat feet trying to jam them into too-small shoes. That was the only joy in this miserable evening. The onstage outrage had no reference to *Gaîté Parisienne* and all to do with Lacroix.

MAY 1, 1988  Anniversary day. I made a tribute: thirty-eight hits and one to grow on.[33] Each hit—ecstasy and anguish; each hit—at times almost intolerable, and somewhere the ecstasy and the anguish are one. We spent the whole day hanging pictures.

MAY 11, 1988  Richard to have an operation—sudden and inexplicable. But Richard's cheerful and not too wan, stuck with needles, etc., like a ham to be festively baked. We were in and out of the hospital almost until midnight. Puss exhausted. I much delighted with the mica glitterings in the pavement on First Avenue. I have always been enraptured by this fool's gold in Manhattan pavements.

---

32. Couturier Christian Lacroix (b. 1951) had designed the costumes for an American Ballet Theatre revival of Massine's 1938 ballet.
33. An anniversary and birthday ritual: a playful punch on the shoulder for each year passed, plus one.

MAY 12, 1988  Now Hugh [Laing] has followed Nora and Antony, and all in a year. This trio is gone, while Herbert sports with the Princess [Radziwill], living on a yacht, her houses, plane trips. The grief is not that he is taken with a woman, but that she is *this* woman.

MAY 15, 1988  Finished reading *Much Ado*. The dazzlement of it! Again and again: How did he do it? Did the brilliance flow, a constant, almost blinding stream of light, a coruscation never seen before or since? This is the seed of Restoration comedy—the ceaseless flow of wit, genuine badinage, the dazzling complexities of language, the faceted puns. . . . How many in Shakespeare's audience blazed with this wit? How many actually talked this glorious way? I sit on the edge of my bed enraptured.

Then I finished the "Research" chapter of *The Magic Mountain*. Coming upon the prophetic "cinema" section. Mann foresaw the debasement of culture, the giving up of art and style and finesse to the yahoos.

JUNE 1, 1988  Great tide of rumors [about *Vogue*]—involving Grace [Mirabella], Amy [Gross], Alex, even [*New York* magazine's] Ed Kosner (reported in line to replace Alex!). Grace could have until next spring. How to rescue her?

JUNE 8, 1988  Grace Mirabella called. Liz Smith had on her television show the "news": Grace to leave *Vogue*, Anna [Wintour] to take over in September. Grace: "Say I've been thinking of leaving for a long time."

NOTE: In June, Gray and Leo went to the S. I. Newhouses' home in Palm Beach, then to Laguna Hills for a visit with Maebelle, and finished in Los Angeles, seeing friends and scouting potential locations for *House & Garden* photo shoots.

JOURNAL · JUNE 26, 1988 · LAGUNA HILLS, CALIFORNIA  I miss my early morning transfusions of Shakespeare. The Old Testament does not nourish me at this time—too much beholding to On High—glorious language, but at too high a price? I cannot find the necessary fear in me. I need the radiance Shakespeare found—the terrible black radiance, the pure joyful radiance—not the almost unrelieved demand to fear of the Old Testament.

JULY 1, 1988 · LOS ANGELES  To [architect] Richard Meier's eyrie—Japanese gone Richard Meier. There Kate [Meier], lovely children, and Richard live as if never a violent divorce. Richard outdoor-cooking several fish. Kate baking a crumble. Two perfect children helping, showing Gray their secret walk and most beloved flower—a sunset-flamboyant secret calla lily. All Los Angeles, to the Pacific, lost in the mist—a giant buzzard questing overhead, high in a skim-milk sky. A perfect evening.

JULY 4, 1988  To Dagny Corcoran.[34] That was horrible. Dickens could have written this evening; Hogarth definitely would have painted it. Dogs everywhere, under the table, underfoot, leaning through windows, baying in the distance. Twenty-two people. I never met most of them. More din than a popular yuppie Manhattan restaurant. The dining room was done up in a Beverly Hills mural of banana-leaf paper. I liked this—could be a treehouse, a folly—but, oh, the blackness of that room. A huge, oblong, gleaming black-glass table, on which black plates and black napkins and silver cutting implements—a brace of flickering candles, an enfilade of American flags (a Fourth of July touch!) in wine bottles. Din and darkness. Poor David Hockney to my left, affably: "I turned my hearing aid off. Perhaps I can hear better." [Actress] Coral Browne to my right, talked with the whites of her eyes across the blackness, or directly into my ear. Gray and Vincent Price occasionally surfaced for a moment. The food was uneatable. It went mostly to the dog rabble, standing under the table—and some of the pack stank. The dessert was a large strawberry-shortcake map of the U.S.A. "I don't know why," [the baker] said, "but Florida always drops off." I ate absolutely nothing. Save for Coral recounting in detail, I heard nothing. A positive hell. We fell into our beds.

JULY 5, 1988  Up and down [the canyon road], very Corniche, sometimes scary, to David Hockney's. This eyrie set in huge trees, and these house [enameled-steel mobiles] an aquatic tribe of sea creatures all painted by David in his joyous colors: children's paint-box sky blue, the yellow of yellows, the most orange, the primary green, and here and there lavenders, mauves. "I don't understand why artists want to lock themselves in buildings, when they can live on the ground floor with a garden," David said of artists who work and live in breweries and sweatshops. The studio rife with recent paintings—all joyous—foods, fruits, a Mexican inn. Color! Color! Color! David the most vibrant (a quiet blaze, a fire of giving, of humanity, of life) dispensing a real English tea—cucumber sandwiches, pound cake sliced thin, Marks & Spencer tea in a lavender-blue, gold-flecked tea service—all improvised, a henchman pouring. The glorious glitter and shimmer of sunlight and leaves—gold and green—in the slanting, near-ceiling windows—a glory of flashing light and color.

David reading in his Yorkshire voice—beautiful. He spoke of how "impoverished" Jasper Johns's work is, of how architects know not how to ornament and how architecture should be taken away from the architects, how humanity is gone and art must be organic. David is a teacher, a great talker, and a master reader.

AUGUST 5, 1988 · NEW YORK CITY  In each being there are occasional unshed tears and fountains of unsprung laughter.

---

34. Dagny Janss Corcoran, an art collector and patron, became a dealer in art catalogs.

AUGUST 12, 1988 I am fighting some sort of nadir of my spirits. I am trying to rise. Such awful times. All that I built at *Vogue* dismantled—vanished. Trumpery Time.

Herbert [Ross, directing] rang from *Steel Magnolias:* "What should I call the sale? I'm auctioning everything. . . ." Me: "The Nora Kaye Ross and Herbert Ross Collection!" H: "Oh—good." Me: "Are you married to her? [Lee Radziwill] ?" H: "No—but I think pretty soon . . ." A pause . . . "You know, I think Lee was disappointed not to be editor of *House & Garden*." Me: "Was she asked?" H: "No—she feels she's not being used to her full potential at Armani. . . ." As I said, Trumpery Time, time of the carpetbaggers again—the Slatterys take over Tara.

Autobiography is as much telling oneself about oneself as it is telling the "world." I think of the lost skies of my long-ago youth, those flaming, early-evening western skies we saw across the emptiness of sulfur-bright fields in what is now slummy Jackson Heights. Then the great—poplars?—lining the new-laid streets roared like the sea in the wind-turmoiled night. I can smell the green sharpness. I can hear restless birds. I can hear the distant desolation of a trundling train and the nearby clip-clop-clop and gentle clang of the early, early milk cart. He was very sexy, that ruddy, big-beaked, prune-eyed, Irish-faced milkman, his bottles clinking against our back door sill. I thought about him a lot—a lot—as I plunged myself into ecstasy in the skim-milk everyday dawning.

AUGUST 23, 1988 When Jack Houseman rang several days ago, he calmly told me that he had cancer, that this was (his words) "the Big C," that his legs were paralyzed. His voice was smaller, but it had lost none of its decisiveness or inherent irony, humor. He had been in the hospital three weeks, had had an operation. He was planning to read *The Decline and Fall* and Dr. Johnson. Then I spoke to Joan, and her voice was the same, a bubble of ironic laughter. "I'm all right . . . all better," she said, "at least now . . . I've got to go back in six months. . . ." The courage! No hysteria . . .[35] Paula Laurence said: "So many people owe their lives to him. He set them on the way." Last night, there he was in Woody's film [*Another Woman*] looking, as Puss said, one hundred years old. He has always been a loving friend.

AUGUST 27, 1988 To Stella [Reichman]'s nest—all red and patterned and leoparded (fake) and kitsch and window treatments and a touch of pale Fortuny and fantasy and jokiness and made for sex and food and fat and life and so pink with living and so *echt* Viennese, so Stella—massive ego but self-comedic.[36] She: "We had eighteen servants, four cars, a Rolls-Royce uphol-

35. Joan Houseman had cancer of the throat. She lived until 2001.
36. Stella Jolles Reichman (d. 1997) was an Austrian-born painter. GF: "Her father had been the petit-point king of Vienna before fleeing Hitler."

stered in petit point." Evening's high point: Stella and Donald Saddler dancing in that small, stuffed "living" room (a Bambi Vienna). Donald dances as high-spiritedly as ever. A good, happy, laughing evening.

Mitzi Newhouse is one of the twenty-five richest women in the world—$8 billion. Her mother, Mrs. Epstein, forbid her to "see" that no-good young man. Mitzi: "But he has a Cadillac!" Mrs. Epstein: "Borrowed!"

AUGUST 29, 1988  Herbert rang yesterday to say he was marrying the princess [Radziwill], would we come on the twenty-third to their "reception" [in New York]. We will be in Los Angeles. Herbert said, "You don't approve?" I said, "No." But we were amiable. I quoted Márquez about time bringing changes, etc.

SEPTEMBER 3, 1988  Reading Cocteau's diary—"Every singularity suppressed is a mistake: the first hole in a fine fabric. The hole quickly grows bigger. So big that it takes up all the space and the fabric vanishes." Despite his constant yammering about how the world doesn't appreciate his true self, Cocteau frequently makes passionate, penetrating, dismaying sense and, of course, he astonishes with his acute atmospheres, his portraits.

Yesterday at lunch—intimations of mortality—a sudden lifting up inside of me—almost ousting all my life—the horrible iron ceiling not descending to crush out life, but—oh—so unexpectedly—ascending. Then a flood of heat where the ascending iron ceiling almost did me in. I was as suddenly free of the horror—vacant. The restaurant, Jim McMullen's, returned—the shattering sunlight. This was a minute—perhaps less—of terror. Puss, observing me, burst into tears. For a time, five minutes or more, I felt removed. I saw the life around me. I saw it, noted it in its details, but I was not part of that life. I was alive. I was emptied out, but alive.

NOTE: Leo and Gray spent two weeks in September in Laguna Hills and Los Angeles.

JOURNAL • SEPTEMBER 13, 1988 • LOS ANGELES  To Malibu and the Housemans. "House" looked better. His skin actually looked healthy. This benign face looked as if all save sweetness had emptied out. All the hauteur fined away—the loving smile—all goodness and interest in that face. He said he'd been reading Michelet's *French Revolution*—and then his mischievous look: "He says it was the clergy!" Only one mention of his state: "This is such a relief from twenty-four hours of pain." He is interested in news, gossip, books—but, oh, we could see Houseman slowly separating. Joan is superb. She now looks like a Russian figure of stature. When we went away, I suddenly burst into tears. I thought of Mina constantly, and how her face had grown so ugly. Houseman's face is now full of a beauty.

OCTOBER 19, 1988 • NEW YORK CITY  The upset at hearing Jack Houseman's nurse, on the blower, "We're losing him. . . . He's gone. . . ." Meaning that his telephone connection was breaking down, not that he, on his deathbed, was forever gone. What is keeping him alive is his book [*Unfinished Business*] coming out. He is living paralyzed from the neck down—by sheer will. The astonishing surge of spirit, which gives him the strength to read programs [for radio]. So long as he works, he will—until his machine gives up—live. Astonishing.

NOVEMBER 9, 1988  Jack Houseman gone [on October 31]. Joan said: "I'll have to find something to do now. . . ."

DECEMBER 28, 1988  I reread my *Little Women* chapter in the early morning of this "holiday," always finding the freshness of that intact, laundered, steadfast, loving world, that lost American world, vivid, Even the sentimental parts—the parts like the anecdotal paintings of its day—are alive.[37] Then I read along in John Cheever's letters and was split over "boy meets boy" parts.

Puss said, "I never remember having to do so much for a party—ever." But we are now older. I dodder. Puss finds difficulty remembering. We are not what we were; we are not even what we will be. Latest bulletin: "I spilled half a bag of sugar into the cutlery drawer!" Puss in anger. Then he stumbled over a chair. "It happened again! I went into the kitchen and it was full of smoke! The potato dish boiled over! There was no reason for that to happen. I'll cut my throat!" Puss really distraught. I can do nothing save try to soothe, but soothing is less and less effective. Now the downstairs bell . . . This will be the last "big" party. We're no longer up to giving even a party for twenty-six.

JANUARY 8, 1989  Maebelle goes home tomorrow. She clings to vitality, to life ("I don't want to leave it," she murmured almost to herself yesterday), makes a symbolic tragic figure. She tries to help, but of course she can't. She is courageous, valiant, loving—but, oh, how the self-centered Maebelle takes over at times—the all-for-me girl she once was, the never-resisted Southern-belle—and poor Puss—almost impossible for him to bear. This has been, however, the best of the visits, and for that we are grateful.

JANUARY 29, 1989  [Novelist] Sybille Bedford's memoir, of her earlier days, came, in bound proof. One of her superscriptions or epigraphs is: "The way things looked before later events made them look different. And this is as much a part of history as the way things actually were" [Robert Kee]. That is why I do not go back to old scribblings. That is why I start over and over again.

FEBRUARY 2, 1989  At the *Gone with the Wind* fiftieth-anniversary celebration in Radio City Music Hall, a very preponderantly young audience—wildly

---

37. Leo reread the first chapter of *Little Women* annually at Christmastime.

enthusiastic, joining in on the popular "lines," almost giving standing ovations on "entrances," i.e., Vivien Leigh, Clark Gable, who is so undated (compared to Malkovich, to the latter's disadvantage). But we have become a cynical people. They laughed (good-humoredly) at Melanie's "goodness." "How could she be such a fool?"—that was their sentiment. They laughed at "manners." But this *GWTW* is a cherished icon, studded with icons (very popular Butterfly McQueen). I cried at the unrolling cast of characters because of what happened to so many of them—poor Ona [Munson], a suicide (that dripping faucet in the black-walled apartment, and Genia [Berman] with his nose running[38]); Vivien Leigh clutching my hand in a windswept October night, in Eaton Square; Leslie Howard shot down during the war—never found; even Butterfly trying to get a job and then working in Macy's, etc., now seventy-eight. When she appeared on the Music Hall stage—so small, her voice so hers, reciting her little homage song and verse—everyone stood and cheered. The young, despite cynicism, adore it. "Gorgeous!" That was the word.

FEBRUARY 15, 1989 Herbert said we must not tell that Margot is in Texas—cancer, "very bad." She wants no one to know. Again, I do not understand the necessity of this cruelty. Margot who gave the world so much pure beauty, so much ecstasy, such perfection . . . No final reward, since we must go off? No glorious exit? So much grace to come to such pain, such degradation?

MARCH 5, 1989 I must go into dinner in five minutes. I fell in the slough when Gray said, "This could be such a nice room. . . ." I have failed to make this "niceness" all of these long, loving years. The love undiminished, not even tarnished—but still—"nice room." Everyone who comes here loves this study, but . . .

Well, I do bills. I do my job. I do not write my book. In the street, below, the law rushes east, clucking—more chick-in-a-snit than relief-for-some-need. In this room—my room?—the radio soars Mozart. I poultice my gloom with those words. Now Beethoven's *Spring Sonata*—sweet, flowing, pellucid sound. Hoping that despair falls away like some worn veil, I will go to eat the good food which Puss has prepared so patiently.

APRIL 1, 1989 · LOS ANGELES *Vanity Fair* party at the Museum of Contemporary Art—I arrive upon a series of open lifts and then via a rattletrap wheelchair, like a secondhand Carabosse[39] whose mouse-footmen have gone off on

---

38. GF: "Genia Berman, her husband, was obsessed with Ona. Everything he did was for her. Ona told Leo shortly before she killed herself that she couldn't stand it any longer, he was so tiresome. After her suicide, Genia asked Leo to come and sit by the bedside, through the night, before he sent her to the undertaker." Their walls were painted black to flatter Berman's paintings.
39. The evil fairy in *The Sleeping Beauty*.

a cheese hunt. The shock: almost two hundred "guests" and hostesses in black and pearls. Gloom! A set piece for a first-act finale, in which the begetters have "dared" to "try something new." Perhaps the murder onstage of virtue, honor, morality, reality. Jean Howard [Hollywood hostess and photographer] was a loving exception—white and a touch of scarlet. Joan Juliet Buck in vivid green. Masses of "starlets"—even those thought of as stars are starlets. I do not mean the "serious" would-be "great ladies" of the screen (Streep, Anjelica Huston, et al.), but I do mean the tough fondants now adored by the public. Joan said, "I don't know how she's done it, but Tina [Brown] has made the Hollywood 'stars' try to live up to her magazine." [Art historian] John Richardson's excessively nervous, meandering, longish, sometimes offensive (to women) talk. However, this evening was an event and there was a sense of occasion, a sense almost lost in Manhattan. *Vanity Fair* was the star of what, to many who were not present, was a star-studded evening. This "affair" was so typically the contents of *Vanity Fair*—a mix of sleaze, bumpkin, "serious," sham, emptiness—all bound together by a high-gloss surface. This was the place to be last night.

APRIL 18, 1989 · NEW YORK CITY   When the airplane attendant turned Gray's chair, the back to me, I was suddenly in a panic. I had a revelation. I always thought that I gave "strength" to Gray. Now I abruptly realized that he gives as much strength to me as I do to him. I found that by tapping the underside of his seat with my shoe we were "in touch," since he waved his hand and passed me sucking candies to avert ear troubles.

In the seat facing Gray sat a woman in a bad Ungaro—black, asymmetrical rounded neck—unbelievably plain. Her nose job was a disfigurement— pinched, puckered, disproportionately small. She had the eyes of *Children of the Damned*. She read a paperback titled *How to Make ESP Work for You*, and she occasionally, with a little jab and a flourish, made markings with a huge, primary yellow–colored, bulbous plastic pencil. Sometimes she peered into outer space, seeking to commune with Visitors from Another Planet. When we had gone a good distance, she said to Gray, "I don't want to intrude on your privacy, but I must ask you a question: Is He (She referred to me in uppercase) your brother?" Gray looked at her soberly and quietly answered, "No-ooo." Almost a thousand miles later, she said to Gray, "Please pardon me, but I must know. Is He your father?" Gray looked reflectively. "No-ooo." Much later, after all of [the movie] *Working Girl*, as we began to descend, and Gray was passing candies to me, she burst out: "I've never seen such love!" Here she sobbed— tears and mascara rivulets. "Such love!!! I don't love anybody! Nobody loves me!" She was in an agony of grief as we landed, crying out about our love for one another and her loveless life. "I don't want to know your names! But I had to tell you! Such devotion, such consideration!" While I was being a man in extremes of senility, she left the plane sobbing.

MAY 16, 1989  I cannot make myself feel old, except in unexpected, sudden glimpses.

MAY 26, 1989  Today I saw a parallel: Maria & Onassis; Cleopatra of the Arts & Caesar of Commerce. I saw them in a sort of Inigo Jones mythological-historical spectacle, a Renaissance ceiling painting, a gorgeous masque. *The Conquest of Art by Commerce*—all in a Venetian, storm-tossed sunset splendor. I see Maria in full stage triumph—more Norma than Medea, more Amina than Violetta. Cascades of flowers, cataclysms of acclaim, the whole world enraptured, exulted by her art. I see Onassis—yachts, oil tankers, governments opening secret doors—money! money! money! His power drawing her power—a collision inevitable and neither triumphant. (Note: Commerce is an inadequate word.)

MAY 29, 1989  The ocean of my seventy-fifth [birthday] is now an eddy—the successive tumult now a sustained, sustaining loving sound. This morning I, who almost never feel guilt (or perhaps I do and, as with so much in my life, I do not recognize that for what that is) felt a twinge (I think the Gods tweaked) and said to Puss, "I feel well—and guilty that I feel so incredibly young!" "Good!" said Puss. "I don't feel young, so you have to feel young for both of us."

JUNE 14, 1989  Final result of the French Revolution: Marielle [Hucliez, design journalist] from Paris: "I went to the town hall yesterday. There was a big feast for the Revolution—its descendants. We had to wear badges, my sister and I, saying 'Victims of the Terror,' and there was a man who came up to us whose badge read 'Danton Descendant'!" Marielle's mother wore a red string around her neck!

JULY 3, 1989  I haven't written about Brigitta and her son Jonathan's death. His memorial in the Trustees' Room at the Forty-second Street Library was laid-on by the *New York Review of Books*. [Its editor] Bob Silvers's finale—a wrapping-up, but heartfelt, mind-felt. Brooke Astor gushing about Jonathan's lunch, pre-Christmas, when he came to her, gave her the greatest "gift" anyone had ever given her. ("Gifts are from God," said Mary Jane [Poole, editor in chief] years ago to the *House & Garden* staff, "presents are from people.") "The greatest two hours of my life." I wonder what Vincent gave her, other than the millions, which she has given away wonderfully, expertly. Lizzie Hardwick tried hard not to make a "true" assessment. Torsten [Wiesel, a neuroscientist], Jean Stein's chum, came closest to the truth about how not-too-easy was Jonathan, and how AIDS (covered up by the family) did him in. And Avedon, wild-faced, but intimate—at least he was personal. All about that stately room were women who did adore Jonathan—and others. They didn't get a chance to make this a "living" memorial. I love Brigitta, and I was devoted to Goddard, who (even though he also was fugitive) was more the man talked about at Jonathan's memorial than was Jonathan, without those talking knowing it. Jonathan could not reconcile his standards. After he testified against me [in the Adler lawsuit], I despised him, I having been so "helping" of him. But this is still too painful.

We supped with Brigitta and Paul [Wolfe] twice after the memorial.[40] She is haunted by Jonathan's last days. "Everybody should die at home," she says. The irony is that after years of alienation, Jonathan came home to his mother to die, and she then had him—after all the "bad" years. Some think he came home as a vengeance. I can't think that, no matter how shabby I think him. Brigitta is comforted by Jonathan's coming home, by how he gave himself to her during these last months. But she is haunted.

JULY 4, 1989 Francine [Gray] asked us to tea at the Coz Club to meet Svetlana [Makurenkova], who is tallish, slim, like one of those summer days— quiet, light, gleaming—but a passionate stirring underneath.[41] In profile, she was chinless, plain. Full face, Vivien Leigh transfigured her—that beauty appearing, disappearing. When I was little, and had to feign afternoon naps, I was transported by the fluctuating light and dark as the green-white blind billowed into and out of the window frame. So, Svetlana's Vivien Leigh beauty fluctuated in the plainness of her pale face. Large, researching eyes. And her "talk"!—about Donne, the metaphysical poets, the late plays of Shakespeare. "You do not understand. Here in the West, you make him into one person. We see him as many people, many people all working, writing, making these plays." She went on—not theory, but fact to her and, seemingly, her Soviet colleagues. She told the tale of the Englishman who, in the University of Padua, late sixteenth century, sat between Rosencrantz and Guildenstern. This is part of the evidence she gives for Shakespeare being many people. She told of discovering a first edition of Donne in the Lenin Library, brought to Russia, she believes, by one of the "great end-of-the-nineteenth-century collectors." I suggested that perhaps the Donne was brought back in the seventeenth century by one of the embassies to England. She was interested, but I do not think that she agreed—nor to the notion that the Donne came with a seventeenth-century English visitor. She talked about Arthur Miller and Inge [Morath, a photographer, his wife] and Genet and an early-twentieth-century Dutch writer of epic plays. She has Danish, Dutch, German, Russian—of course, French, English. Most of her research was done surreptitiously, because metaphysics was against the Soviet policy until *glasnost.* Manhattan made her cry. I think she

---

40. The harpsichordist Paul Wolfe (b. 1929) would marry Brigitta Lieberson in 1991.
41. Svetlana Makurenkova (b. 1958?) was a Russian professor of English literature in Moscow.

thinks this island is "against God," against nature. She is an astonishment, incredible. I wished that we could have spent a weekend with her. I hogged her. No regrets. When we were going away, she shook my hand and curtsied. Her speech, at first, was formal—almost proclamatory, almost handout, but then she flowered. In talking about Russia today, she said that it is being corrupted by all sorts of "foreign" influences.

JULY 30, 1989  Discovery—took seventy-five years—yesterday, in the early morning—that I have unwittingly worked at being the still center of the whirlpool.

SEPTEMBER 4, 1989 • PALM BEACH, FLORIDA  Sitting on the bed edge since eight, in semidarkness, curtains letting in a sliver of silvery light—insufficient to read by—can't turn on bedside lamp—not enough strength in hand and would probably tumble. I find all of this ironic, but not without giving me the possibility to scribble, in the almost dark.[42]

I want to write about Luise Rainer's visit on Wednesday night last. She came, small face wrecked by age, but smile and eyes as beautiful as when she had that famous Oscar-winning telephone agony with "Flo."[43] And we were given that agony, but "real life"—overwhelming. We had it intermittently for almost four hours: agony over [her husband] Robert [Knittel]'s death (We suspect bungled operations, etc.)—tumults, tornadoes of agony . . . interludes of almost pastoral, long reminiscence about what a good husband Robert had been, how he had devoted his life to her, how he had never let her know anything about money—interludes of concern for us: Gray didn't draw anymore? What did I really do?—interludes about what should she do with her life, about how wonderful Francesca (her daughter) is to her . . . then she began to curve into passion—how awful Los Angeles is, "They only talk about money—only money! I couldn't live there. . . . I can't live in New York"—the filth, the expense, the ugliness . . . so to conjectures about London, "the only place I could live" . . . then the currents of rage against the Swiss, "They are taking everything!" The voice and body patterns at our kitchen table were as they had been long ago in those prize-winning screen performances—identical—but this all too real, too searing, too no-exit—that tremendous crescendo rising to an enormous full-throated, sostenuto—no, a curve, a deep organ sound, almost a contralto shriek, sinking to a pianissimo so soft, almost soundless—the ghost of agony, of terror, of anger. . . .

OCTOBER 8, 1989 • NEW YORK CITY  When we asked Steve Martin about *The Merchant of Venice* (Dustin Hoffman in London), he said, genuinely amazed,

---

42. They were visiting Si and Victoria Newhouse in Florida over the Labor Day weekend.
43. He is recalling Rainer's best-known screen scene, in *The Great Ziegfeld* (1936).

"That play is a mess! What a mess!" He went on to explain that he knew nothing about Shakespeare, having almost none in school and having seen almost no Shakespeare. Steve is utterly, honestly disingenuous: "I have no way to judge . . . but that play . . . all those girls and the things in the boxes and the fun and that anti-Semitic other plot. . . ."

DECEMBER 31, 1989 · LAGUNA HILLS, CALIFORNIA   At Maebelle's—I thought to consider the approach of this next decade, a decade so different in our lives. It is the first decade that we contemplate with some foretaste of a more possible—no, more probable—mortality (mine, Richard's, even Puss's)—than any preceding decade.[44] I am seventy-five and a half, Richard seventy-seven and a half, Puss is eight years younger than I am. I now more fully, moment by moment, understand Rebecca's horrible, inconsolable weeping. Over the blower, three thousand miles away, I could hear this storm of raging grief at having to "go," from one of the great minds of our day. I understand Madame Du Barry's weeping, but that I always understood, thinking her of no splendid, or even special, intellect. She wept at the injustice of her fate, at giving up her life for—what?—perhaps even wept at her own arrogance. For her stupidity in returning to France, for her paltry reasons, was arrogance. But Rebecca—I was plunged into dark confusion. Now I understand that anguish.

So, here is 1990—Gay Nineties in the twentieth-century sense, not the nineteenth? Also, this will be the decade when the world divides between East and West. And we will probably eventually find Russia more East than West. We are no longer the "rulers" of the world.

So what other melancholy maunderings? I see no changes—emotional—in our life. The downs and ups will continue. We will, each of us, try to survive these. Physically, I can only look to deteriorate more and more, and I can hope to be able to cope and be coped with. What a future for Puss. If only he could take the little mishaps and the major awfulnesses more calmly—if only . . . I can only wish on whatever star—wish this for him. Now, about my book: I can only try. If it happens, it will happen. I have not given up the refuge of that dream.

Now I will, for these few moments, enjoy this oasis of sunlighted quiet, reading Proust's letters, finding assurance in them. If he could, despite his "predicament," so can I. I do not have his great genius, but I have my own little genius—very small, but some sliver of genius—and I have eaten copiously at his table. Alas, I must earn for all of us, and, alas, I don't have time—much of it—left, having spent so much of it already. But he didn't think that he had much, so perhaps our time ration is now equal?

44. Richard's lover Howard Rothschild had died suddenly of heart failure, aged eighty-one, during a visit to London that October.

JANUARY 2, 1990 New Year's Eve revelation, as we watched a televised Jule Styne tribute:[45] I missed my true vocation—a producer-director of top Broadway, specially "musicals." I realized, about fifty-five years too late, that this is when I "feel" most alive, during a wonderful musical—*Follies, Show Boat,* operettas of course, Gilbert & Sullivan, *Pal Joey.* . . . That is the world I wanted, but I went the other way. This began with Aunt Minnie and Uncle Irving and [Irving Berlin's] *Music Box Revue.* (Minnie and Irving playing four-handed on Momma's upright piano.) I hear the waltzes from *Madame Sherry* on a picnic when we lived in the Boston Post Road. I see the dancer leaping out of the music box, all brown and gold, on that music front. . . . I see a show-girl, very Poiret-Erté: She carries a staff and is bouffant at the hips and tapered at the ankles, her hair piled high (spit curls?), blue-purple and black—that was "Tell Me Pretty Gypsy." I hear the excitement in Uncle Irving's and Aunt Minnie's voices when they "told" about what they had seen and heard. This was the first glamour in my life—probably before Poppa took me to the moving pictures—*The Three Musketeers, The Thief of Baghdad, Madame Sans-Gêne, Madame DuBarry.* (I became a royalist instantly at five or six. The aristocrats were so beautiful. They wore beautiful clothes. The others who were "after them" so ugly, so dirty. I hated "the people." I loved the "shiny ones.")

JANUARY 3, 1990 Puss off to an unknown doctor after a terrifying, sleepless night upright in his bed, that being his only position in which breathing was less painful. So, plans for Los Angeles canceled.

Meanwhile, I immerse in Proust's letters, volume two [1904–9]. What an abundance in both Virginia Woolf's and Proust's letters—life furling on every page. (Extra in Proust's: Robert de Montesquiou's letters. How patient he is with Proust, how affectionate under his careful cover of detachment, how jocular—each in his own way. . . . What a flirtation.)

I long to write about this volume of letters, so exhaustively edited by Philip Kolb.[46] Having found Proust through Hester Sporer, when I was about sixteen or seventeen, in the Scott Moncrieff translation, helped me to realize and accept what I was, and so I became what I am. How amazingly ripe I was for that society transplanted by Hitler to Manhattan. Question: Would this life have happened this way sans Hitler?

JANUARY 5, 1990 Now the day here grows longer, as I sit listening to Puss breathing on the sofa, hoping that his epic attack of asthma is diminishing: He

---

45. Jule Styne (1905–94) was a composer of popular songs whose Broadway scores included *Gypsy* and *Bells Are Ringing.*
46. Philip Kolb (1907–92) wrote many books on Proust and edited several volumes of his letters.

is asleep, his breathing, at this moment, no longer is a much-traveled coach rumbling over much-traveled cobbles. . . . My heart stops when, as in this moment, I do not hear him breathe. . . . I trust. . . . Now I resume. . . .

In Proust's letters, the Louisa de Mornand "relationship"—this could have been "consummated." Ela told me that Noël slept with her out of "curiosity and affection."[47] That Proust was "taken" with "girls" like Mlle de Faure does not make him bisexual. I have loved—really still love Ela, Penelope . . . but I have never slept with them or with any woman. I love women, and some women I adore, but I have not even remotely wanted to sleep with any one of them. A few adolescent skirmishes, and I knew. I never had doubts about "the other thing." Not even when I was four years old, when I was first fiddled with by the boys next door—Louis and his brother Izzy. Because of their mother I found out about babies. Sitting under the dining-room table, in Grandpa's house, when I was about five and a half, for we had already returned to live with him after Grandma died, I heard Momma say to Aunt Minnie, "So, when's she expecting?" Aunt Minnie: "From the look of her—did you see that belly?—any minute!" Next morning, Aunt Minnie said to me, "There's a new baby. . . . Did you hear the stork bringing it?" "No," I said, trying to think where the stork fitted, my face clearly showing puzzlement. . . . "Well, where do you think the baby came from?" she asked. "Her belly!" I said. I was instantly slapped hard. And only years later, when I was in my forties, did I actually find out from where babies came. Sono drew me a diagram. But it was Marlene who showed me female anatomy, when she discovered that I did not know a thing about women below the neckline. That was when she had the intense affair with Yul?[48] Still later, when she was playing at the Lunt-Fontanne [theater], and I was in her dressing room before curtain while she was making up (a triangle over the nose, rubber bands around her hairline), she suddenly stood up, dropped her makeup robe, stood superbly naked, and said, as she peered ruthlessly into a full-length, lightbulb bordered looking glass: "The body of a girl of seventeen from the neck down, but the face . . ." Then she laughed, bittersweet humor—barroom interwined with a flight of small sweet bird notes—and fell to make her face steadfastly young—or at least youthful. Only when she minced onto the stage did she become once again the "fabulous" beauty so beloved by the world for so many years.

JANUARY 6, 1990 Another relentlessly peerless sun-daft day. A small flare-up at lunch, a firecracker whose short, sharp explosion can set a house afire, but

47. "It was in Ela's room that Garbo came one late night and, picking up Noël's photograph, asked, 'But why you?' as Ela lay back against her pillows, giggling." *Journal, October 16, 1984.*
48. GF: "Leo sat beside Marlene's bath, she having asked him in to demonstrate the female anatomy. She showed him her breasts, and said she was proud of her pink, delicate, and not-too-large nipples."

this one only singed. The wound is already aggravated by years of basic truths. Question: Better to hear these awful truths or let them lurk (festering?) beneath the salve of charm, goodwill, loving care, and kindness, which makes living possible? And will the "truths" always, inevitably explode, devastating the "good" living—at least for a time? Possibly these explosions nourish love as much as love nourishes love?

I write, actually write, whole paragraphs in my head, correcting the punctuation, changing words, reconstructing. . . . Maebelle reconstructs the past even as I try to reconstruct my past—both of us reinventing, I am sure, as we go along.

"It's so annoying to think so many things and to feel that the mind in which they're stirring will soon perish sans anyone knowing them. It's true that there's nothing very precious about them and that others will express them better."

—Proust to Mme Straus from Versailles, October 17, 1908

JANUARY 7, 1990 I am almost at the end of Proust's *Letters*, volume two, and these have opened a door into a room in which I peer, baffled. Having always thought Proust "m.g." or "so" (his designations), must I now consider the possibility of his being bisexual? I believe Proust basically m.g. but willing to experience anything and then use the experience in his work. I would like to write a probing of Proust's sexuality. I am sure such studies exist, but I would like to write my own. Proust is sexually curious, in all senses of that word. He always wants to note his curiosity.

JANUARY 8, 1990 I have been "taken to task." Deserved? Not in the balance of these years, but—yes—deserved because I have been graceless. The sudden outpouring had its direct cause in an observation, made at supper last night: "I feel that we're a very cold group." I hadn't made much of an effort. I will not make excuses to me. I should have made a characterization—blooming with cordiality, seasoned with small talk, all nods and becks and smiles. I should have thawed the Ice Age in me. I did not try hard enough. I was not the generous person that I thought I was being. I wanted so much to go to the wedding [of Anita's niece, Mary Anita Loos]. All of the "old" Hollywood gathered, my only chance to see the old stars, the survivors of that "golden" time—from everywhere—a mingling of Hollywood and Los Angeles "society" . . . Well— couldn't be helped. After this morning's reproach I am trying to chatter. I feel what is most required is to make a pleasant, very amiable noise.

All week at Maebelle's because of Gray's violent sickness [asthma]. I have not been out of my nightshirt and dressing gown since the evening of our arrival. I have not been out of this flat, but I have had a boggling education on Middle America via the television and "convenience foods." Well, Proust and Philip Kolb have saved me—also the PBS station and forays to the only "good music" station in Los Angeles.

FEBRUARY 22, 1990 · NEW YORK CITY  I fell two nights past. In the night, when I move, I feel that fall, but now, crouching over this desk, no discomfort. "He falls like a cat," Alex Liberman said. "I never saw anything like it." This morning Puss said, "I haven't dropped him [Leo] from the Empire State Building, yet."

MARCH 13, 1990  Last night *Otello*—[conductor Carlos] Kleiber plunged us into the fierce drama instantly, and no nuance was denied its full measure. Not since Maestro have I heard anything like it. Despite [Placido] Domingo's worn patches, the central three tangled miraculously into a black-blood snarl. Superb! The Friday night audience so solid a world; almost no outbursts during the action, but, oh, the thunder at each of the three acts' ends, specially for the "star" Kleiber! How many years since we have actually had a great (this debased word) conductor? He is, of course, physically a beauty—great height, never-ending arms, and huge, flapping hands. This is, physically, his most emotional, most frenzied performance.

MAY 1, 1990  Puss laughed a lot when I told him that I didn't dress [when visiting Maebelle] because I didn't want to wear out my clothes. "Like someone in Molière," he said. This is anniversary day—our forty-third year.

MAY 25, 1990  Robin Williams is shooting a movie in Grand Central Station about the homeless while being picketed by the Grand Central resident homeless. As prop men were carrying in cardboard boxes, in which the actor-homeless were to live, they were shouted at by a Grand Central resident: "We don't live in boxes! This isn't the Port Authority!"

A ghost moment last night, when I dimly discerned my nearest and dearest, in serried ranks, standing silently in Mary Cantwell's kitchen, to surprise me—with the most enchanting [birthday] party.[49]

JUNE 1, 1990  Not being able to write—sitting, staring at a page, which, empty, stares back, is an insomnia—an identical disability to achieve oblivion in dreams. I cannot see what I am scribbling. This light does not light, it obliterates. I am empty. I try to see loved creatures, "things" in this bedroom, but light obliterates almost all. I am as lost in light as anyone in a jungle is lost in a Hell of Green. This would be a Hell of Light, if I gave in to it. The room's inside light is diffused from the lamp; the outside light pours through three and a half windows. It is, through one of the windows, reflected from the Saint. Thomas Choir School. I am scrawling this because I have nothing else to

49. The editor and writer Mary Cantwell (1930–2000) worked at *Mademoiselle* (1953–76) before going to the *New York Times*.

scrawl. I cannot even see this scrawl. I will read *The Five of Hearts* [on Henry Adams] if light permits.

JUNE 4, 1990   Walking in the World Trade Center, Stephen didn't believe what I told him about the harbor when I was a small boy—the coffee, tea, and chocolate warehouses, the seamen in the streets. "I really felt old," I told Puss later. The scintillations of the river, the harbor, in my memory—only what I walked through *had* been there. It seemed so insubstantial in all this false grandeur, not even as substantial as the fantasy we know as theater lobbies or in Cecil B. DeMille's biblical movies (*Intolerance*). All served up by a shop selling "history" and another selling "occasions."

DECEMBER 2, 1990   If only I could see more clearly. If only these scrims, veils, clouds . . . these opaquities [*sic*] would vanish—just long enough for a rampaging scribble. I want to write a big set piece about the *Vogue* AIDS gala ["Seventh on Sale"], an event which apotheosized this Manhattan world—the *Vogue* cum social cum fashion cum entertainment cum art-and-performance cum political and commercial worlds. There in the Twenty-sixth Street Armory, where the 1913 show broke the mold, on Thursday evening last, [party decorator] Robert Isabell created a vast, shimmering, white tent, tables elevated on stands, lighted by candles suspended in glass from above, embosked in a forest of green-leafed trees—only clichés come—a white, gold, and green beauty—miraculous springtime now. Manhattan had never seen a party of such inconceivable beauty and splendor. When the tent flew upward, the entire vastness was flooded with blue light, and a great sigh filled the enormous room, while all around this great, central dining space women in grotesquely jeweled scraps of sumptuous fabrics snatched bargains from the booths. Carolyn [Roehm, fashion designer] in her totally inappropriate get-up, an eight-year-old-girl's *broderie anglaise* smidgen of a frock, epitomized the "Dance of Death" aspect of the "gala." The invitation's "come in festive dress"!!! Oh, the horror perpetrated to "do good." This side of [designer] "leftovers." I must really write this 1990 "Masque of the Red Death," this Carnival of Greed, which will "help" AIDS. Raffle prizes. Designers getting rid of inventory, samples, and models never cut past this first number. A woman who screamed: "Look! Look! A Geoffrey Beene for $120!" Me: "Did you try it on?" She: "Who needs to try it on for $120?" I sat between Paloma Picasso and [*Vogue*'s Paris liaison] Susan Train. Talked with Paloma about how she is her husband's greatest theater production. She agreed. Being with Paloma made the evening A Good Thing for me. This glittering celebration of materialism to ameliorate, even help prevent, the most devastating of plagues.

DECEMBER 24, 1990   Jerry brought a photograph of Poppa. A shock—Poppa in his twenties, perhaps in 1906, the year before he married Momma. I had never seen this photograph. I had never seen this boy—so full of dreams, so beautifully dressed, so serious, so sensual. This boy I never knew became the sleepy man I knew. The boy is irreconcilable with the man. There is no visible connection. What happened? Puss said promptly: "Your mother!" I could talk to that boy; I never talked to my father.

I just spoke to Bill Maxwell and told him about Poppa's photograph. He came directly to the heart: "Would you have fallen in love with him, Leo?" Bill asked. "Yes," I said. "I don't understand many people," Bill said, "but I understand you."

DECEMBER 28, 1990   Timing is all: Every day I think of the perfect exit. I have come to dread day: Night is beneficent; day brings turmoil, tension, tribulations. The little bodily pains of night are, thus far, bearable; the mental anguishes of day are unbearable. Latter obviously an exaggeration: Here I am. I read, with delight, V. Woolf's earliest diary. Nowhere have I so lived that late Victorian upper-middle-class domestic life, its to-and-froing, its daily aliveness.

DECEMBER 31, 1990   I sit on the side of my bed scribbling the year away, wondering whether anyone would read *A Lexicon of My Life*—an autobiography in lexicon form. I could handle that—two bits of it are already mostly written—Truman and Marlene. I mean all of the "important" people of my life. I could tuck everyone and everything in. I am best at short forms.

Passing our old house, Puss saw a big, lighted Christmas tree in the left window of the long parlor. This so pleased me, made me feel better about my beloved 1453. Someone cherishes it.

JANUARY 1, 1991   I have less hope this New Year's morning than I have ever had. Little brightness ahead—but perhaps some light at the end of the tunnel, if this is, indeed, a tunnel, and not a permanent night.

JANUARY 15, 1991   Awesome doldrum—a state of apprehension—a feeling that something beyond imagination pends. There are demonstrations, candlelight processions, great crowds shouting protests in Columbus Circle [against war in the Persian Gulf], in Midtown, at the U.N., below Washington Square. All over the city, massed cops silent, on the ready. Rumors. Bomb scares. Schoolchildren told not to drink the water in their schools—it's been poisoned. Traffic halted, and—always—New Yorkers rushing out of cars and buses—to hasten on foot . . . to annihilation? That is the question.

JANUARY 17, 1991   At 9:15 our time—when Puss was talking to Maebelle, she said: "Who are all those people here? That little boy brought them. I must go home. But I am home." This desolation . . . a confirmation. She is now elsewhere in her head. Her dream world is now part of her "normal world."[50]

JANUARY 27, 1991 The Gutfreund-Mossbacher party, as told to me by Anna Wintour with an air of "Well, that's the way of the world." For their birthdays, for these two, the Gutfreund and Mossbacher "ladies," the Hard Rock Café was taken. Robert Isabell makeover, victuals brought in—Le Cirque?—and the theme: a prize for the shortest skirt. "Guess who won?" Anna asked. "I did! I had a Versace I could lower or raise!" This as war was officially declared. That "world" is obsolete—the Gutfreund and Mossbacher and Anna Wintour world—but does not know that it is obsolete.

FEBRUARY 18, 1991 Catherine [Dreyfus Soguel] rang from Paris: Denyse [her mother] is dead—last night. "She wanted to go, I think. Her mind wandered sometimes, and that bothered her." Richard [Dreyfus, her first husband] was in Paris and they had a long talk in the afternoon. I think that she always loved him. I knew that she always loved me. I am consoled knowing that Denyse has been spared the degradations of old age, the loss of control over one's physical and mental being, the horror of increasing isolation—I could go on, but why unpack this bag? Denyse was the first to bring the highborn Jewish Egypt and the Egyptian-French culture to me. What an elegant woman . . . She was the best-dressed bluestocking . . . so strong-minded . . . a loving heart, but only given away—perhaps foolishly? . . . (I see her somewhat mournful face lightened into cascades of laughter. I could always make her laugh.) . . . her enchanting flat overlooking Place Vendôme. . . . How can I ever go back to Paris? I never realized how death limits geography.

If I could talk my book to someone. The entries in the lexicon are so firm, but if I don't talk them soon, they will go.

JULY 13, 1991 Perched on the slope-side of my bed where I have perched for some two weeks, because of a fungus irritation (so appropriate a word in every sense of its meaning). Then that "attack"—*panic*—not being able to breathe, intimations of mortality. Denis [the hired caregiver] sat up the night through. . . . I now sleep by "nightlight"—the greenery-yallery shaded lamp. Too much to scribble and not enough. I must dictate my book—the lexicon form—before others write from research what I know from experience.

NOTE: Leo did begin dictating his book—not so much a "lexicon" as loosely associated memories of family and friends. (Many of those reminiscences have appeared italicized in this book.) Leo's journal then dwindled to brief reminders and impressions. His still worsening eyesight was making private writing more difficult.

50. Gray was in California, caring for his mother, who died the following day.

JOURNAL • JANUARY 24, 1992   Odd tryout—I am attempting to write in light that makes this page almost invisible. If I can do this, I will try to write my cookbook reviews next week—the new plan—not monthly, as proposed, but every other month. I must break this hiatus. I will break it. I have malingered. In this way I can, I hope, get back to my book. I must also conquer my fear of falling. Only one case of fraught nerves to a home. I will to [*Harlot's Ghost* by] Mailer now.

NOTE: Marlene Dietrich died on May 6, 1992. In July, *Vogue* published a reminiscence by Leo, paired with photographs of her by Alex Liberman. It concludes with the following:

**MARLENE**   *One evening we went to a party together. And she was done up with perfect simplicity. She always let her body speak for itself. There wasn't a woman in the room—and the room was filled with all sorts of beautiful women wonderfully dressed—who looked better than Marlene. And little Hope Hampton,[51] a flurry of feathers, diamonds, crystal drop-beads, came up to her and peered at her and said, looking up at her face, "Who did it?" And Marlene said, "God." (VOGUE, JULY 1992)*

NOTE: On November 9, 1992, the Fashion Group International presented a specially created variety show, "The Fashion Follies," in Broadway's St. James Theatre, honoring Leo for his lifelong contributions to "fashion, theater, and all the arts."

NEW YORK CITY • NOVEMBER 16, 1993
**TO JANET LERMAN GRAFF** • CHICAGO, ILLINOIS

On November 28, 1952, I was walking in the golden pre-snowfall light of a Copenhagen afternoon, when I looked up suddenly and saw, hanging on a peg in front of an antiques shop, these summer-sky blue beads. I instantly knew that I should buy them for the "new" baby [Jerry's daughter]. I took them home to Lexington Avenue months later, and I put them in the bottom of a Chinese box. Occasionally I would open the box and look at them, thinking, "These should go to Janet," and revisiting that beautiful Copenhagen early afternoon. They were too full of Copenhagen to send, but now they are so full of love, sentiment, and memory that you must have them. They are, in substance, not valuable, but in love and sentiment they are boundlessly rich.

NOTE: Leo continued going to his Condé Nast office on weekday afternoons, finally taken in a wheelchair.

Friends surprised him with a large party for his eightieth birthday, on May 23, 1994. It would be Leo's last birthday. He died on August 23, from complications of the goiter, a swollen thyroid, that he had long endured.

He inserted the following on a loose sheet at the end of his last notebook:

51. Hope Hampton (1897?–1982) had been a leading lady in the silents, before becoming a socialite and New York opening-night fixture.

JOURNAL · DECEMBER 4, 1993 Each of us is an archaeologist. From the day we are born, we are engaged in Personal Archaeology, and we are born again and again, many times in a lifetime. We are constantly excavating the mansions of our dreams, the imagined palaces of our minds, the monuments dedicated to forever passions, to eternal loves as ephemeral as the towering cities in which they so impermanently stood—all now staunchly substantial, each solid stone, each love-laved face, in the moonlight of memory—

All the preceding must be redone: Too fancy.

# INDEX

Note: Leo Lerman's name is abbreviated as LL in the index.

# ILLUSTRATION CREDITS

Courtesy Betsy Talbot Blackwell Papers, American Heritage Center, University of Wyoming: page 6, above left.

Horst © Condé Nast Publications Inc.: page 6, above right.

Walter Sanders/Time & Life Pictures/ Getty Images: page 6, below.

WWD/Fairchild Archive: page 7, above right; page 14, below.

Copyright © 1981 Ted Leyson: page 7, below.

AP Images: page 8, above; page 9, below; page 12, above right and below right.

Jerome Robbins Dance Division, The New York Public Library for the Performing Arts, Astor, Lenox and Tilden Foundations: page 8, below; page 9, above.

© Sam Siegel: page 10, above.

© Louis Peres: page 10, below.

Copyright © 1973 V. Sladon: page 11.

Mark Gerson: page 12, above left.

Courtesy of Jane Imbs Trimble: page 13, above left and right.

Durlacher Bros. Records, 1919–1973, Research Library, The Getty Research Institute: page 13, below left.

© Estate of George Platt Lynes, courtesy of the Frances Lehman Loeb Art Center, Vassar College, gift of Agnes Rindge Claflin: page 13, below right.

Whitestone Photo: page 15, above left.

Bill Cunningham/The New York Times: page 15, above right.

© Bonnie Cashin Estate: page 16.

All illustrations not otherwise credited are from private collections.

A NOTE ON THE TYPE

*The text of this book was set in Electra, a typeface designed by
W. A. Dwiggins (1880–1956). This face cannot be classified as either
modern or old style. It is not based on any historical model, nor does
it echo any particular period or style. It avoids the extreme contrasts
between thick and thin elements that mark most modern faces, and it
attempts to give a feeling of fluidity, power, and speed.*

COMPOSED BY
*North Market Street Graphics, Lancaster, Pennsylvania*

PRINTED AND BOUND BY
*Berryville Graphics, Berryville, Virginia*

DESIGNED BY
*Iris Weinstein*